# BTEC NATIONAL

# *IT Practitioners*

## Software Development

BTEC NATIONAL

# IT Practitioners

## Software Development

Jenny Lawson

Alan Jarvis

K. Mary Reid

Neela Soomary

Peter Blundell

**www.heinemann.co.uk**

✓ Free online support
✓ Useful weblinks
✓ 24 hour online ordering

**01865 888058**

Heinemann Educational Publishers
Halley Court, Jordan Hill, Oxford OX2 8EJ
Part of Harcourt Education

Heinemann is the registered trademark of
Harcourt Education Limited

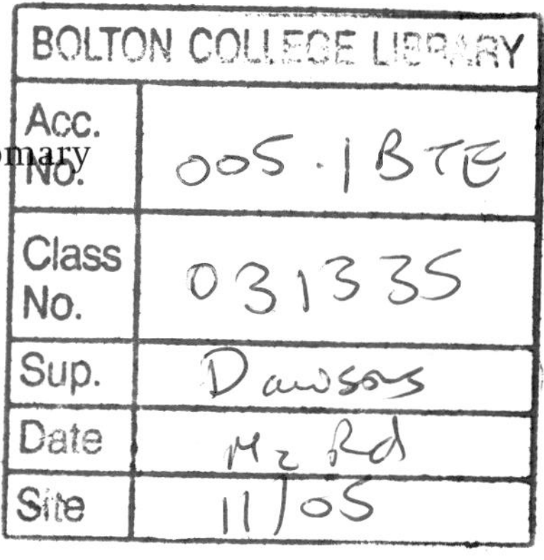




First published 2004

08 07 06 05 04
10 9 8 7 6 5 4 3 2 1

British Library Cataloguing in Publication Data is available
from the British Library on request.

ISBN 0 435 45667 9





Designed by Kamae Design
Typeset by TA Tek-Art, Croydon, Surrey

Original illustrations © Harcourt Education Limited, 2003

Cover design by Tony Richardson at Wooden Ark Ltd

Printed in the UK by Scotprint

Cover photo: © Getty

**Websites**
Please note that the examples of websites suggested in this book were up to date at the time of writing. It is essential for tutors to preview each site before using it to ensure that the URL is still accurate and the content is appropriate. We suggest that tutors bookmark useful sites and consider enabling students to access them through the school or college intranet.

**Acknowledgements**
Every effort has been made to contact copyright holders of material reproduced in this book. Any omissions will be rectified in subsequent printings if notice is given to the publishers.

Tel: 01865 888058 www.heinemann.co.uk

# Contents

# INTRODUCTION

The BTEC National for IT Practitioners is a collection of three related qualifications:

- BTEC National for IT Practitioners (General)
- BTEC National for IT Practitioners (ICT Systems Support)
- BTEC National for IT Practitioners (Software Development)

Within each of the three qualifications you can study for the Award, Certificate or Diploma. If you are studying for the Award you will need to complete 6 units, for the Certificate you will need to complete 12 units and for the Diploma 18 units.

This book provides you with sufficient material to complete the Award and the Certificate. It also provides you with most of the units needed for the Diploma.

# Units in this book

This book covers all the units for the BTEC National for IT Practitioners (Software Development) as shown in this table:

<table>
<tr><th></th><th>General</th><th>ICT Systems Support</th><th>Software Development</th></tr>
<tr><td>Compulsory core</td><td colspan="3">Unit 1: Language and Communications<br>Unit 2: Computer Systems<br>Unit 3: Business Information Systems<br>Unit 4: Introduction to Software Development<br>Unit 5: Communications Technology<br>Unit 6: Systems Analysis and Design</td></tr>
<tr><td rowspan="4">Compulsory specialist units (Bank A*)</td><td>Unit 9: Business IT Project</td><td>Unit 7: End User Support</td><td>Unit 8: Programming Concepts and Practice</td></tr>
<tr><td>Unit 10: Applications Software Development</td><td>Unit 21: Networking Project</td><td>Unit 10: Applications Software Development</td></tr>
<tr><td>Unit 13: Database Management Systems</td><td>Unit 24: Network Design and Administration</td><td>Unit 29: Software Development Project</td></tr>
<tr><td>Unit 18: Business Calculations</td><td>Unit 25: Data Communications and Networks</td><td>Unit 32: Visual Programming</td></tr>
<tr><td rowspan="2">Optional specialist units (Bank B*)</td><td>Unit 7: End User Support</td><td>Unit 10: Applications Software Development</td><td>Unit 12: Human Computer Interface</td></tr>
<tr><td>Unit 12: Human Computer Interface</td><td>Unit 12: Human Computer Interface</td><td>Unit 31: Web Development</td></tr>
</table>

* Edexcel refers to the specialist lists as Bank A (compulsory) and Bank B (optional)

The accompanying Tutor Resource File provides additional material for all these units.

# Units not in this book

There are some more optional specialist units in Bank B that are not included in this series. You may enter for a unit from the Bank B lists shown below, in place of any of the optional units that appear in this book.

| | General | ICT Systems Support | **Software Development** |
|---|---|---|---|
| **Extra optional specialist units (Bank B)** *Not covered in this book* | Unit 11: Website Management | Unit 11: Website Management | Unit 11: Website Management |
| | Unit 14: E-Commerce | Unit 15: System Justification | Unit 14: E-Commerce |
| | Unit 15: System Justification | Unit 22: Network Operating Systems | Unit 15: System Justification |
| | Unit 16: Expert Systems | Unit 23: Computer Hardware | Unit 16: Expert Systems |
| | Unit 17: Management Information Systems | Unit 26: PC Specification and Maintenance | Unit 27: Operating Systems |
| | Unit 19: Multimedia Technology | Unit 27: Operating Systems | Unit 30: Computational Methods |
| | Unit 20: Software Applications | Unit 28: Wide Area Networks | Unit 33: Control Technology |
| | Unit 25: Data Communications and Networks | | |

## Assessment

You will find assessment guidance for each unit in the Tutor Resource File.

Part of your assessment will be through an **Integrated Vocational Assignment** (IVA) and this will be set and assessed by Edexcel.

LVA assessed units (General):

| **Award** | **Certificate** | **Diploma** |
|---|---|---|
| Unit 8: Programming Concepts and Practice | Unit 8: Programming Concepts and Practice | Unit 8: Programming Concepts and Practice |
| | Unit 29: Software Development Project | Unit 29: Software Development Project |

All other units are assessed internally. By completing the assessment activities within this book, you will cover all of the assessment guidance required by BTEC for your internally assessed units.

# Acknowledgements

We would like to thank Matt Jackman at Heinemann for his enthusiasm for this project and his endless encouragement, and Gillian Burrell and Roger Parker for their painstaking work in the production process of this book. We are also very grateful for the help and support given to the author team by their respective partners.

Jenny Lawson

October 2003

Screen shots reprinted by permission from Microsoft Corporation and Borland (UK) Limited

The authors and publisher would like to thank the following for permission to reproduce photographs:

Alamy – pages 192, 333, 335
Corbis – pages 6, 169
Datadesk – page 332
Getty/Photodisc – page 122
Getty/Stone – pages 164, 336
Pete Morris – pages 340, 367
Photodisc – page 292.

# UNIT 1: LANGUAGE AND COMMUNICATIONS

The aim of Unit 1 is to develop learners' communication skills. The unit covers written, oral, aural, research and presentation skills. There are opportunities to demonstrate Key Skills in communication, information technology, improving own learning and performance, problem solving and working with others.

## Learning objectives

- To use communication skills effectively in a variety of contexts
- To produce written and graphical material to meet a range of end-user needs
- To select written research material to meet specified task requirements, to summarise the contents and to take notes effectively
- To produce relevant research data, using a variety of techniques

# 1.1 Communication skills

Communication is possible using a variety of media. The two most obvious forms are verbal and written communication.

- **Verbal communication** involves hearing a message – might be a one-to-one conversation (either face to face or using the telephone) or one to many as in a presentation to an audience (this could be live or via a television transmission).
- **Written communication** involves reading a message – could be on paper (a report, handout, leaflet or book) or displayed (on an OHP, a whiteboard or a blackboard).

### What does it mean?

OHP stands for overhead projector.

Communication is also possible without speech to listen to, or text to read. Disapproval can be expressed by a shake of the head, and approval by clapping hands, so **body language** is a powerful way of communicating. **Demonstration** also works well; a cookery demonstration, whether live or on a video, can show an audience exactly what to expect, e.g. how to test that a cake is cooked, in a way that a cookery book cannot.

To meet the needs of the receiver of information, it is often sensible to combine media. A presenter may talk, show slides and include a demonstration during the presentation. In this way, the same information can be shown in different ways, and thus appeal to the variety of learning styles of the audience.

### Check your understanding 1.1

1. List three different situations where you have been the receiver of communication. Note the form of communication used (verbal, written, etc.) and your relationship with the information provider.
2. List three situations where you have been the provider of communication. Note the form of communication used (verbal, written, etc.) and your relationship with the information receiver.
3. Make notes on how your communications could have been improved by using different or additional ways of communicating.
4. How does the relationship between information provider and information receiver affect the communication?
5. Compare your findings with others in your group.

### Further research 1.1

1. In pairs, list techniques that you notice your tutors use to create interest in a class situation.
2. As a larger group, discuss the component parts of a presentation. How can you put them together to create an interesting experience for an audience?

# Generating audience interest

You need to be able to use and evaluate a range of techniques to generate audience interest. The following case studies illustrate different contexts with different demands on the presenter and his or her audience.

## Case study: Image makers

Janette is an image consultant who specialises in helping people with their presentation techniques. Bill and George are two of her clients.

- Ben is retiring after 25 years of service with one company. His friend and colleague, Bill, is asked to make a short presentation at the farewell party to be held in the office reception area on Ben's final day. Ten people are expected to attend the party, and all are close friends of Ben. Bill has just a few things to say, 'We are sad to see you leave, Ben. We wish you well in your retirement. We have a small gift for you. We hope you like it. Perhaps you'd like to say a few words?'
- Margaret and Tom are to be married and George will give the father-of-the-bride speech at the wedding reception. He is happy for his daughter, but is nervous about the speech. The guests will include many of Tom's friends and family, none of whom George has met. In total, there will be 80 guests and, to be heard, George will need to speak into a microphone.

  There are lots of books written on how to give a good speech at such an occasion. George does some research and notes that he will be expected to thank several people, to say something amusing about his daughter and son-in-law, to wish them well and, finally, to propose a toast to them both. George is nervous already, and, on the day, may be even more nervous, so he plans to make notes and to practise his speech beforehand. This is partly to try out different things he might say, but also to check how long his speech will take. He wants to keep it to 10 minutes at most.

1. Think of a situation where you might need to make an informal presentation to someone. Write down what you might have to say. Keep it brief.
2. Check on the Internet for sources of books or articles that offer advice in preparing speeches. Make a list of these sources; you may need them later.

Notice the difference between Janette's two clients.

- Bill needs very little time to prepare for this presentation, and it should take only a few minutes to deliver his message. His audience is Ben, so Bill can talk to him on a one-to-one basis, although the others present will be listening. Bill's speech will be so short, he could probably remember his message without writing anything down. Bill's method of communication is verbal, but he will be using body language (smiling and nodding to show affection for his friend) and he will probably lead the applause after Ben's short acceptance speech.
- George is involved in a much more stressful situation. He will want the occasion to be a success for his daughter and her new husband, and not to let her down. He has a larger audience, and will need to keep their interest during his speech. He will have to read their body language to see how well his speech is being received, and overcome any nerves at the same time.

## Case study: Kari aboard Aristotle

Kari is an experienced sailor and she is soon to sail aboard a chartered boat called Aristotle in a regatta. For the first time, Kari will be skipper, and part of her duties will be to make sure all of her crew are aware of safety procedures while at sea.

Kari has been briefed by other skippers many times, so she thinks she knows what needs to be said: the importance of turning the gas off each time after using the cooker, the location of fire extinguishers, what to do if anyone falls overboard and how to avoid falling overboard in the first place. She is keen to make sure she presents the information in a way that will result in her crew feeling confident about what to do in the event of a disaster, but not too frightened to actually set sail.

Kari decides to write herself a checklist so that she does not miss anything out. She takes the crew through the boat, demonstrates how to turn the gas on and off, and points out the position of the fire extinguishers. Everyone takes a life jacket and adjusts it for size. Kari then takes the crew on deck to show them where to clip on, and what equipment is available if anyone does fall overboard. Some of the crew ask questions and Kari answers them as best she can.

1 You are to act as a guide for a group of six guests who are visiting your college. Before the 30-minute tour starts, you have to spend a few minutes telling them what to do if the fire alarm goes off. Write a checklist for yourself about what things you would need to mention.
2 Write another list of what things you might show them at your college, and the route you might take.

This second case study involves interaction between the presenter Kari and the audience. In the first case study, it does not really matter if the audiences of Bill and George ignore the message being given, so long as they do not interrupt the presenter in any way. Kari, however, needs to make sure her crew learn from what she says and understand what she shows them. She therefore asks them questions to check they have understood her message. This initial briefing will allow the crew to decide how much they trust Kari as their skipper. A relationship between Kari and her crew will begin at this point. During the sail, Kari will watch her crew to make sure they follow her guidance, and will correct them if they forget the safety procedures.

## Case study: Tanya and Tinselware

Tanya works as a demonstrator for a Christmas goods company called Tinselware. She takes bookings for parties and sells Christmas cards, decorations and other festive items suitable for Christmas gifts. Tanya relies on earning commission on her sales, so it is important for her to book as many parties as possible during September, October and November each year, and then to maximise sales at every party. Tanya has been selling Tinselware for four years and has developed a presentation style that works for her. Everyone enjoys themselves and she has many repeat bookings for parties. She arrives at her hostess's house about an hour before the party is due to start and puts up some decorations. As people start to arrive, Tanya serves a range of Christmas foods and party drinks to establish a Christmassy mood, even in

September. As soon as everyone has arrived, she starts her 45-minute presentation by introducing herself formally and giving each person a copy of the Tinselware brochure. During her presentation, Tanya hands round samples of her products so that everyone can have a close look at them. Tanya does not have notes to work from; she has learnt her presentation so well that she can do it from memory.

1 Compare this case study with the previous two, in terms of the audience size and the level of interaction involved.
2 What method of communication is used in each case?

Notice that Tanya is selling herself as presenter as well as her range of Tinselware products, so she needs to present a positive image and establish an atmosphere that will encourage people to book her parties and to buy from her. Her personality is important; if the guests don't like her, they are unlikely to book another party and may decide not to buy from her. While Kari might prefer her crew to like her, the important thing is that they respect her and her judgement, and will accept her commands as skipper. Kari therefore has to establish her own credibility to the crew.

### Case study: Steve the paramedic

Steve used to be a paramedic but now works as a freelance trainer delivering First Aid courses for a training school based in Southampton. The school plans and promotes a number of one-day First Aid courses; they take the bookings and cope with all the paperwork. For each course, Steve arrives at 9.00 am and then works his way through the syllabus. There is a mid-morning break for coffee, a lunch break and then another break for tea in the afternoon. There are usually 12 delegates on each course, most of whom do not know each other, and it is Steve's responsibility to ensure they learn enough during the day to gain a pass. At the end of the day, Steve completes the certificates for those who have passed.

1 Why should there be a break mid morning as well as mid afternoon?
2 How could Steve encourage his audience to get to know each other?
3 Steve needs to create an atmosphere that allows people to learn and to discuss topics which some of them might find distressing. In discussing accidents, he may raise topics which remind his delegates of painful memories, e.g. a close friend dying owing to lack of First Aid help. Steve needs to be sensitive to these feelings and yet he has to cover the syllabus if everyone is to pass. How can he achieve this balance?

## Visual aids

A visual aid is something used in a presentation to convey a message through sight rather than sound. Text that is presented on an OHP is a visual aid, but many visual aids have no textual content. The most important visual aid is you, the presenter. First impressions are very important, so take care to make a good impression.

- Be tidy, smart and have neat hair.
- Hold yourself well, i.e. do not slouch.
- Look confident, and have a smile on your face.

Your audience is then more likely to take notice of what you say.

**Check your understanding 1.2**

Each of the case studies above uses non-textual visual aids at some point of the presentation. As a class, discuss what these might be.

## Slide shows

A slide show is a type of visual aid and, as it can display text messages, it can be used to reinforce what you have to say in your presentation. The slides might be presented as OHP slides, or as a computer slide show. If using OHP slides, the presenter places each one in position, talks through the points and then manually removes the slide before replacing it with the next. Apart from automating the movement from one slide to the next, computer slide shows offer extra options, like **animation**, which can help to keep an audience's attention.

It is not essential for the slide show to contain anything apart from the bare bones of the presentation. Its purpose is more to hold attention than to impart information. If a presenter were simply to stand and talk for an hour, most audiences would lose interest. Having slides to change at regular intervals gives the audience something fresh to look at while they are listening to the talk. Each slide should relate to a particular point that is to be discussed.

One interesting way to maintain an audience's interest is to include cartoons that sum up the situation under discussion. This adds humour to what might be a dull or depressing topic.

Figure 1.1 A presenter may flash up a picture of a panda during a talk on IT, and then continue as if nothing had happened. This will make the audience sit up and take notice

Some presenters even reserve one slide that is totally out of context (as in Figure 1.1), just to wake up their audience should it seem necessary. Having shown it, and had the desired effect, the presenter reverts to the planned sequence of slides.

### Further research 1.2

Find out what presentation software is available on your computer system. Experiment with it to find out what facilities it offers.

- Discover what different styles of slides can be produced using wizards.
- Find out how easy it is to reorder the slides within a presentation.
- What options do you have to create notes to accompany your talk?
- What print formats are available: handouts, notes, overviews?

## Video conferencing

Most presentations take place with everyone (the presenter and the audience) under one roof. However, this is not always possible. One solution is to film the presenter, and then the audience watch the film at a later date. This provides no opportunity for interaction; the audience cannot ask questions and the presenter cannot check that the audience has understood the message. Video conferencing offers an opportunity for a presentation to take place in front of an audience with interaction as it mirrors more closely a live presentation. At the location of a presentation, there are video cameras and microphones to record what is being said; there are also screens and loudspeakers so that what is happening elsewhere can be seen and heard.

### Case study: Fast Forward Movers

Glenys Brooks is a choreographer, and masterminded the Fast Forward Movers organisation. She designs dance routines to match the latest songs as soon as they are released. Her team of instructors are situated throughout the UK and run dance classes in local sports centres. Part of the attraction of these classes (and part of their advertising image) is that the music is as up to date as it can be. Each week, Glenys listens to the latest releases, and for at least one of them she devises a routine to be used in the dance classes. Regular video conferences between Glenys and her dance instructors are used to keep the instructors fully up to date. The instructors practise the dances until they know the steps off by heart. Because there is interaction, they can make suggestions to improve the routine, and because Glenys can see her instructors, she can check they have followed her moves.

1. If there was no option to use video conferencing, how else could Glenys train her dance instructors?
2. Find other examples where video conferencing is used by an expert to train or guide others through complex procedures.

### Overhead projectors (OHPs)

An OHP can be used to show a sequence of slides, manually moving from one slide to the next. However, it also offers other opportunities to generate interest for an audience. For example, a presentation might involve a brainstorming activity to try to solve a particular problem. Prior to the invention of OHPs, presenters used flipcharts as a way of recording the outcomes of such an activity. Writing the information straight on to a blank OHT makes it easily visible to the whole audience, yet small enough to be photocopied and kept as a permanent record.

**What does it mean?**

OHT means overhead transparency.

OHTs also offer a way of presenting information to an audience one bit at a time. One snippet of information can be revealed and time allowed for the concept to sink in before revealing the next snippet. You might even create OHTs in 'layers', so that a sequence of actions can be seen in slow motion.

Yet another option is to present the audience with a question or problem on an OHT, and then challenge them to offer an answer or solution. The content of the OHT, i.e. the question or problem, remains in view, whereas, if spoken, it might need to be repeated several times, possibly interrupting the audience's flow of thought.

### Questioning the audience

For some presenters, there is no need to question the audience. The success (or otherwise) of the presentation is made clear by the reaction of the audience. For George at his daughter's wedding reception, if he tells a joke which is not appreciated he will hear silence; if he makes a joke which everyone finds funny, he will hear laughter. For other presenters, questioning the audience is an important part of the presentation.

Kari will ask her crew whether their life jackets fit properly. If they answer yes, she has succeeded in fitting them with a life jacket. If they say no, she has more to do to adjust the sizing. Kari asks everyone in her crew because it is important that everyone has a life jacket that fits.

Steve will ask more open questions to find out how much his audience know, 'What is the difference between a break and a fracture?'. The 12 people in his audience can offer almost as many different answers, and then Steve can correct all their misconceptions. During the discussion, different types of break/fracture will be mentioned and some of his audience may become more comfortable about discussing a sensitive topic. Steve asks everyone about the break/fracture distinction because to ask just one person would not show the breadth of misconception about these terms; this also provides Steve with an opportunity to encourage everyone to participate.

Tanya's questions might be geared to 'closing' a sale; 'Which of those do you prefer?' implies that the guest will buy one of two products, and a decision is only needed as to which of the two. In this way, Tanya can steer her guests towards accepting that they will buy something. Similarly, Tanya could ask, 'When you have a party next year, would you prefer it to be closer to Christmas?' or 'I am happy to do parties any night of the week. Which night is best for you?' Both are very positive ways of suggesting that a booking is inevitable; the guest just needs to decide on a day or date.

### Presenter and audience participation

Most presenters are confident (like the professionals, Tanya and Steve) or inexperienced but keen (like Kari); others may be reluctant or nervous (like George) but will rise to the challenge. Members of an audience, on the other hand, are unlikely to be so confident that they would want to be put under pressure to perform in front of the rest of the audience. If it is necessary to have audience participation, then the selection of the persons who are to participate should be done with sensitivity. Rather than directing a single question to individual people in the audience, the presenter can ask a less threatening question to the whole audience: 'How many of you have had to pull over when you have heard an ambulance behind your car? Hands up.'

If audience participation is an essential part of a presentation, then you must first create a safe environment for individuals before asking people to risk embarrassment in front of others. While some people may be willing or even keen to volunteer, for others, having to participate would make them nervous and prevent them from taking part in a relaxed and natural way. It must be made clear that their efforts will not be ridiculed, and that while they may make a mistake, taking part will provide a positive learning experience.

**Case study: Steve the paramedic**

When Steve demonstrates CPR (cardio pulmonary resuscitation) on his doll Betsy, each person then has to show they can do it too. Audience participation is therefore compulsory, but Steve will have encouraged those who are more outgoing to have the confidence to volunteer. Steve will ask, 'Who wants to go first?' Once one person has demonstrated CPR, and Steve has given excellent encouraging feedback on what they have done, others will soon feel safe enough to volunteer too.

1 List some situations in which you would not be happy to contribute to a discussion.
2 Think of ways in which the presenter could make you more willing to participate.
3 Share your ideas with others in your group.

## Delivery techniques and interview skills

You need to be able to use and evaluate delivery techniques and interview skills. Watching others and evaluating how they perform will allow you to learn what works, and what does not work. Then, when it is your turn to make a presentation or conduct an interview you will know what techniques to use and should have the necessary skills to apply them.

### Planning the presentation

There is no substitute for preparation. The very best presenters may look as if they are ad-libbing and that they have not prepared, but actually they are relying on years of experience and lots of behind-the-scenes preparation.

Before any presentation, you must decide on or find out the following parameters:

- **Who** is your audience? How many will there be? Do they all know each other? Do you know any of them?

- **What** is the presentation about? What is your message? Does it involve dissemination of information, training and/or testing?
- **Why** are you making this presentation? What will you be trying to achieve? What is your contribution to the presentation? What are your credentials?
- **When** will it be? How long will be allocated for your presentation? How much time do you have to prepare your material?
- **Where** will the presentation take place? Will you be travelling far to the venue? Will this affect what visual aids you can use?

## Delivery styles

The delivery style will depend very much on your audience, what you are trying to achieve and how much time you have.

- You may be informal or formal.
- Your pace may be leisurely or brisk.
- You may need to entertain your audience, or instruct and test them.

**Further research 1.3**

Spend ten minutes brainstorming in a group of five or six. Make a list of different delivery styles, and situations in which they might be appropriate.

A **didactic style**, in which instruction is given (perhaps dictatorially), can be suitable and is sometimes essential if time is restricted and it is vital that the audience follows the procedure. For a didactic style to be effective, the audience needs to respect the presenter and to accept his/her authority.

- Kari could adopt a didactic style. She needs to stress the importance of the safety procedures and to win the confidence of her crew.
- If Tanya adopts a didactic style it might alienate the guests and have an adverse effect on further bookings and/or sales.

An **interactive style** is more time-consuming, and requires greater skill on the part of the presenter. He or she has to 'work the audience' so that they are willing to participate in the presentation.

- Steve could be didactic and just present the facts of First Aid as a recognised expert. However, it might be a very dry and dull experience for his audience. By using an interactive style, he can draw on the experiences of his audience, clear up any misconceptions they might have, and create a 'safe' environment where they can be tested on their new skills.
- Glenys uses an interactive style. It is essential for her to check that her instructors have learned the dance routines properly.

### Verbal communication

People communicate verbally (talk to each other) all the time. They greet each other, exchange news and express views. The teacher talks to the class; the shopper talks to the market stall holder; the radio and television broadcast all day and all night to viewers, some of whom have the option to communicate back. Talking during a presentation is not the same as everyday chatter. A few well chosen words can be far more informative.

### Check your understanding 1.3

For each case study above, how much time will be needed to convey the message? Approximately how many words might this allow the speaker?

### Further research 1.4

You are going to take part in a group interview. As part of an ice-breaker exercise, you are asked to talk for a maximum of two minutes about yourself. Work out how many words you might say in two minutes and then write that many words to describe yourself. Start your talk with the words 'Hello, my name is ... and I am from ...'

- With three or four others, read out your presentation.
- While the others are giving their presentations, make notes about their delivery. What was good about it? What could have been improved?
- When everyone has introduced themselves, compare notes and decide how you could each improve on what you said.

## Body language

What is said is secondary to any body language that is displayed by a presenter. An audience will recognise instantly whether a presenter is confident or nervous, and may judge accordingly whether they will co-operate. During a presentation, the presenter may show more body language, as he or she relaxes and gets into stride. The audience will also communicate via body language. As a presenter, it is important both to display the correct body language to win over the audience and to read the audience's body language to gain feedback.

### Check your understanding 1.4

1. Think about what messages a presenter might convey through body language alone. If the audience were to show the same body language, what feedback would it suggest? Share your ideas with others in your group. Decide what body language a presenter should use. Decide what body language a presenter would like to see in his or her audience.
2. With the sound turned down so you cannot hear what is being said, watch a video of someone being interviewed (e.g. recorded from a news programme). Make notes on the body language of both the interviewer and the interviewee. Watch the interview again with the sound turned up. Does the body language reinforce what was being said, or does it contradict it?
3. With reference to the case studies above, imagine that you are Janette and have been asked to recommend body language to be used by Bill and George. How would you advise each of them? What advice might you offer to Kari, Steve and Tanya?

A combination of body language from one person can give conflicting signals. A presenter may try to look relaxed and confident in the way he stands or talks, but an underlying nervousness may result in him fiddling with his tie, or touching his hair. In the same way that you might rehearse what you are going to say during a presentation, you should practise your body language so that you convey the message that you intend. This means you will need to overcome any nervousness, or at least look as if you have.

**Check your understanding 1.5**

You are going to have another go at the group interview (see Further research 1.4, page 11). Look again at your text and rehearse it, taking into account your body language. Watching yourself in a mirror can help. In a small group, repeat the ice-breaker exercise. As well as listening to others while they speak, notice their body language. When it is your turn, watch the body language of those listening to you. If possible, video the activity, so that you can study each others' body language. Notice in particular any mannerisms, like fidgeting, that you will need to overcome if you are to appear more confident during a presentation.

## Dealing with disturbances and distractions

As far as is possible, presenters should deal with disturbances before they become a problem, or in such a way as to turn them to their advantage.

- Before you begin your presentation, close the windows and/or doors to shut out external noises. On a hot day, this may mean the room becomes too hot, so arrange for fans during breaks when the external noise will not cause a problem.
- Make sure that arrangements have been made for any refreshments to be set up beforehand, or outside the meeting room. Find out what time your audience are due to arrive and make sure your presentation plan fits around the timing.
- Make sure all necessary equipment is in place beforehand, and that it works. A delay due to a faulty OHP bulb will not impress the audience.
- Ensure that everyone who is expected to attend is there before you start, and make sure that everyone present understands why they are there, and for how long.
- If your presentation is one of many taking place at the same time, within the same venue, it is quite easy for someone to be in the wrong room and not realise for about ten minutes. A sudden departure may give rise to humour in your presentation, but will certainly disrupt the other presenter who will be confronted with his or her late arrival.
- If you need to start and are aware that some people will arrive late, reorganise your presentation so that you do not miss out anything vital for them. When they do arrive, maybe flustered from a long and tiring journey, make them welcome rather than show irritation for the inevitable disruption they are causing. Confirm that you will go over anything they have missed, so they need not bother their neighbours to catch up.
- Check that everyone can hear you and, if appropriate, can hear each other.
- Ask the audience to turn off their mobile phones.

Some disturbances are unavoidable, and may even be welcome.

- Someone in the audience may raise his or her hand to ask a question, or simply call out a question. React by welcoming their input, 'Good point' or 'Yes, thanks for asking that question'. Then, either answer the question, or defer answering it until later and move swiftly on. If you do answer straightaway, make sure your answer is addressed not just to that person but to the whole room. If you are pulled into a one-to-one conversation with one of the audience, the rest may lose interest and even start chatting among themselves.
- Someone in the audience may need to leave the room. If it is clear that it is a temporary departure and he or she will be back shortly, ignore it. If this happens towards the end of a presentation and the person makes a show of packing bags, etc. it can signal a mass

exodus. Find out beforehand if anyone has to leave early. Make sure that he or she is seated near the back and ask him or her to slip out unobtrusively.

**Further research 1.5**

Make a list of the 'housekeeping' matters that you might need to deal with at the start of a whole-day presentation. What happens after the course finishes?

# Negotiating skills

Negotiation is something that you do all the time, probably without even realising it. You might be negotiating with one other person (e.g. a parent or teacher) or with a group of people (e.g. the whole family or some friends). It may involve deciding on a time to meet, which channel to watch on TV or where to go on a rainy day.

You need to be able to identify negotiating skills. Negotiation suggests that two parties have different objectives but need to come to some compromise. It can be confrontational, with both parties at loggerheads; or it can involve co-operation, with both sides trying to see the other's point of view and seeking some middle ground.

It is important that both parties are clear about their own objectives beforehand, and that they let the other party know what they are. This will allow both sides to note areas of agreement or common ground, and to identify where there may be difficulties or resistance. Sometimes, trying to explain your own objectives, or your objections to another's objectives, makes you realise that the underlying problem relates to something quite different. Be prepared for this, and try to remain open-minded during negotiations.

## Exchanging ideas

The first stage in any negotiation is to exchange ideas. You cannot reach agreement with someone unless both of you know what the other wants. It is important to stay calm and to try not to say things that will make the situation worse rather than better. Avoid exaggeration and using emotional terms like 'everyone', 'no one', 'always' and 'never'. Personalised comments will not help either, and you should try to avoid taking anything that is said too personally.

## Creating opportunities for others to speak

While you may think it is important for the other party to know what you want, negotiation is a two-way process. There will be no compromise if you do not create opportunities to hear what the other party has to offer. Asking questions like 'What is important to you?' will open up the discussion.

## Interpreting others' points of view

Sometimes, the most difficult part of negotiation is seeing things from both sides. If you cannot understand why the other party insists on a particular course of action, ask for an explanation. The more questions you ask, the more you will learn about the other person, and what is important to them. Through discussion, both sides learn more about each other and, eventually, will find a way to bridge any differences and reach an amicable solution.

### Listening and responding sensitively to others

Listening isn't just a case of not talking while the other person speaks. You must take in what is being said and any clues that body language might offer. It is also important to respond sensitively. If someone makes a threat or shouts at you, you could easily shout back and the argument could escalate. Instead, stay calm. Ask yourself why this person is so angry. Is there any way you can diffuse the situation? Similarly, if you find yourself becoming angry with the other party, keep calm. You could use body language to express your feelings, for example look disappointed, or shake your head. Then, try to explain how you feel, and what it is that makes you angry, without resorting to shouting. Counting to ten really can work.

The important thing to remember is that the aim of negotiation is to reach a decision by consensus. By the end of the negotiation, for it to have been successful, both sides must feel they have 'won': a win-win outcome. If either side feels they have given way or that the other is the 'winner', then the agreement may not last very long.

## The structure and sequence of presentations

As with any structure, for each presentation there should be a beginning, a middle and an end.

### The beginning

The beginning of a presentation may be your first opportunity to make a good impression on your audience. Introduce yourself and establish your credentials in the minds of your audience, but be brief.

Whet their appetites by setting the scene: Why are we here? What topics will be covered? State clearly the time frame so that the end of your presentation is in sight from the very start. You may also need to tell the audience about housekeeping arrangements, such as the location of toilets, the timing of lunch, etc. Check that everyone can hear you and is ready to pay full attention before you move on.

### The middle

The middle section is the body of your presentation. During the planning stage, separate your material into discrete topics and decide how you will present each topic. You should try to vary the presentation for your audience. For one topic, there might a short talk, followed by a film clip, and then discussion in small groups before pulling the ideas together as a whole group. There might then be a short break for coffee, before starting the next main topic.

Decide the running order for delivering your topics and plan an **itinerary**. Remember to allow time after each topic for feedback or some activity to break up your presentation. Check that there will be enough time to cover all the material.

? **What does it mean?**

An **itinerary** is a list of the topics with starting and ending times for each part of your presentation.

Rehearse your presentation to check that the timing will work and make adjustments, either to the material or to your itinerary (or both) so that it is feasible. During the presentation, note the times that you start each topic. (Make sure the room has a clock that you can glance at. If not, take your watch off, and place it beside you where you can see it easily without the audience noticing your referring to it.) If you have to repeat the presentation, or do one that is similar, you will then know how long each section actually took.

### The end

You should try to finish your presentation on a 'high'. You want the audience to leave with a sense of achievement and to feel that their time has been well spent. They are unlikely to remember everything that has been covered, so remind them by summarising the most important points.

Keep your final comments brief. Aware that the presentation is over, many will be eager to escape. Thank them for their attention and wish them a safe journey. Your body language should convey that they may leave.

**Check your understanding 1.6**

Think about the body language that you could use to draw attention to the fact that you are ready to start your presentation. Then think how you could signal the end of the presentation. Notice how other people start and finish their presentations.

## The importance of speaking clearly

It goes without saying that it is important for a presenter to speak clearly.

- Speak as you breathe out. This makes your voice sound natural and relaxed, and your words will flow evenly.
- Make your diction clear and pronounce the words correctly. Do not leave off the ends of words and do not trail off at the end of sentences.
- Vary the speed. When making a presentation, you need to speak more slowly than usual. If you talk faster, it can add excitement and enthusiasm, but if you talk too fast, you will lose your audience. So take more time with important points or pause for a few seconds.
- Vary the tone of your voice. For serious points, give more depth and gravity. Make your words lighter to encourage people or to show that you are amused.

### Overcoming nerves

Feeling nervous before giving a talk is natural. To lessen the effects of nerves, try some of these exercises (not in full view of your audience!).

- Breathe in deeply through the nose and then hold your breath for the count of ten. Breathe out slowly, through the mouth.
- Clench your fists and then slowly relax them. Repeat this several times.
- Open your eyes and mouth as wide as possible, really stretching. Repeat this exercise two or three times.
- Try to release any tension in your face, and smile.

## Breathing properly

Everyone knows how to breathe, but did you know that public speaking requires a different breathing technique? Practise these techniques to improve your speech.

- Breathe deep down in your chest. This makes better use of your diaphragm. Even if you are naturally quietly spoken, it increases the volume of your normal voice.
- Deep, slow breathing relaxes you. Increasing the flow of oxygen-rich blood allows you to talk more clearly and also increases the flow of blood to the brain. This makes you more alert and able to order your thoughts.

## Forgetting your words

Drying up in the middle of a presentation will increase your nervousness. Avoid this by having notes to refer to. You could use **cue cards** or notes written to accompany your OHTs (Figure 1.2). Both will give you confidence, and they can be used to remind you of any difficult technical information.

### What does it mean?

**Cue cards** are small cards, each one with two or three points/ideas written on it to help you to remember the key points.

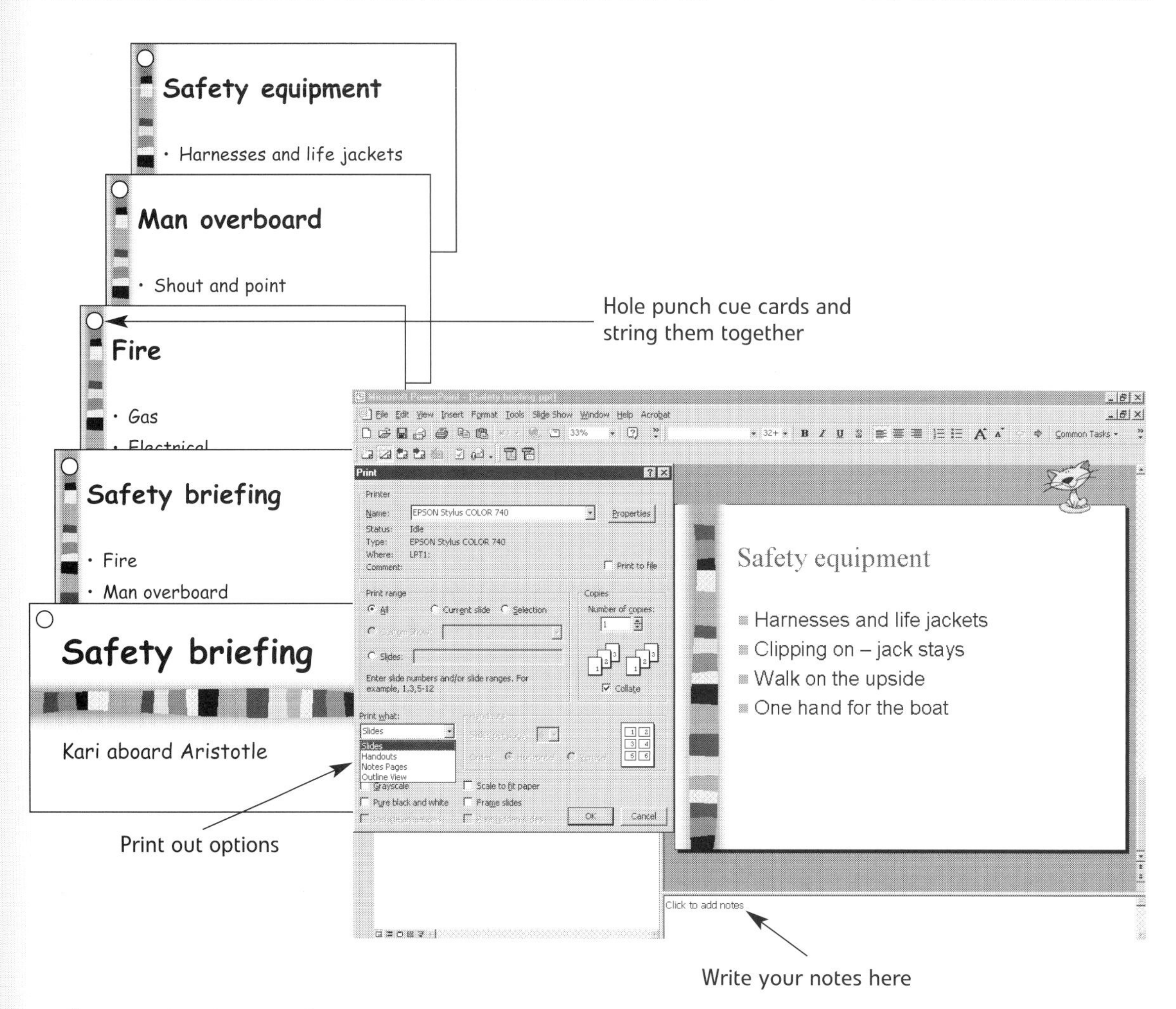


Figure 1.2 Sample cue cards

**Further research 1.6**

Find out how to produce notes to accompany your OHT slides.

**Assessment activity 1.1**

Your teacher will suggest various scenarios.

1 For each one, make notes on the delivery style that you think would be appropriate to suit each circumstance. Plan what you would say at each one.
2 On your own, or working with others, prepare materials for each presentation. Rehearse the presentations and draw up an itinerary.
3 As a group, take it in turns to deliver your presentations to each other. Those in the audience will evaluate the performance and give you feedback on your chosen delivery method and suitability.
4 Compare your actual timing to that planned in your itinerary. Note any improvements or modifications that you could make to your materials and/or your presentation technique.

# 1.2 Written and graphical material

We now concentrate on the skills needed to produce written and graphical material, such as handouts, memos, business letters and reports, minutes of meetings and specifications. You need to include both hand-written and word-processed work, but may also use software such as Microsoft® PowerPoint to produce presentation slides and the notes to go with them.

## Presenting information

You need to be able to select appropriate forms for presenting information.

- The **medium**: The information may be printed on paper, printed on OHTs or displayed on a screen. It very much depends on how you plan to pass the information on to others. Some information may be sent electronically, e.g. as an e-mail or as an attached file to an e-mail.
- The **format** or layout: This is normally determined by the type of information included. A brief internal note may be sent as a memo (or electronically as an e-mail). An official communication such as a job confirmation should be sent as a business letter.

When preparing any document, two parameters need to be established:

- What is its **purpose**? Is it to convey basic information? Is it to attract attention? Is it to impress the reader into doing something? Is it to request information?
- What is the intended **readership**? Who is going to receive this document? And who is going to need to read it?

Table 1.1 lists the forms of written material, their purposes and their intended readership.

| Form of written material | Purpose | Internal/ External | Readership |
|---|---|---|---|
| Handouts | To support a talk or presentation | Both | Those attending the talk |
| Memos | To record a decision or an appointment | Internal | Colleague(s) |
| Business letters | To communicate with a client or supplier | External | Client or supplier |
| Reports | To record the results of an activity | Internal | Management and others |
| Minutes of meetings | To record the discussions and decisions taken | Internal | Management and those who should attend |
| Specifications | To itemise details about a product or job | Both | Buyers of the product |

Table 1.1 Forms of written material, their purpose and intended readership

For each of these types of documents, there are conventions as to how they should be laid out. Figure 1.3 shows samples of these documents.

# The effect of new technology on standard conventions

You need to be able to explore the effect of new technology on standard conventions.

## Use of first names

It used to be the case that, as in the armed services, people would be referred to by their surname prefixed by their rank, e.g. Private Smith, Commander Bond. Today, especially when writing to someone, the title is often dropped and it is acceptable to use the first and second name, e.g. 'Jenny Smith', or if you are on more friendly terms, just the first name 'Jenny'.

If you address your letter to 'Mrs Smith' or to 'Jenny Smith' or to 'Jenny', implying you know her well enough, your letter should close with 'Yours sincerely'. If you do not know the name of the person you are writing to, you should consider telephoning to find out a name. If that fails, then you could write to 'Dear Sir or Madam' and sign the letter 'Yours faithfully'.

With the advent of e-mail communications, some of these conventions have completely disappeared. E-mails rarely start with 'Dear'; instead, they launch straight into the message, or offer a greeting such as 'Hi there'. The assumption is that, if you e-mail someone, you know them well enough to do so. The closing remarks can imply an even greater informality, 'Best wishes', 'Kind regards', 'Yours truly'.

**Fast Forward Movers**

**INDUCTION**

**Monday 3 February: 10 a.m. till 3 p.m.**

**Studio 2, FFM House, Woking, Surrey**

AIMS and OBJECTIVES

- To introduce prospective freelance dance instructors to FFM
- To establish choreography skills of new dance instructors

TOPICS TO BE COVERED

- The target market for FFM dance instructors
- How FFM choose the music to dance to
- How the dance routines are devised
- Video conferencing
- Contracts and payments
- Choreography test

**Fast Forward Movers**

PO Box 321 Knaphill Woking Surrey GU12 3XZ
01438 997111 • firstclass@btinternet.com

Terri Strutt
47 High Road
New Town
Surrey GU22 1DS

6 January 2003

Our ref: BS/06012003/JL

Dear Terri

**Freelance dance instructor vacancy**

Thank you for sending your CV and the completed application form. Your qualifications and experience match what we need at FFM, so we are interested in offering you work as a freelance dance instructor, subject to your passing our standard choreography test and attending our induction training session.

The next induction session will take place on Monday 3 February 2003 at our offices in Woking. I am enclosing a handout which explains what we plan to cover during the day. Please bring with you the clothes you would normally wear for a dance class. For the choreography test, please prepare a 4-minute routine for one of the dance numbers on the enclosed cassette. Note that you will be expected to teach this routine during the induction training session.

Do telephone me if you have any queries about the choreography test.

I look forward to meeting you on 3 February and to your joining the FFM team.

Yours sincerely

Glenys Brooks

Glenys Brooks
Director, Fast Forward Movers Ltd

Fast Forward Movers Ltd: Company No 1234567. VAT Reg. number: 123 4567 89

**Fast Forward Movers**

**MEMORANDUM**

| | |
|---|---|
| To: | Jenny, Les, Caroline, Andrew |
| From: | Glenys |
| Date: | 22 January 2003 |

I have arranged for the two new instructors to come into the office at 10 a.m. on Monday 3 February 2003 for their induction session.

I know Monday is our 'busy' day, but I'd be grateful if you could spare a few minutes to say hello to them both. Perhaps we could all have coffee together at 10.30?

**Fast Forward Movers**

**REPORT: Annual Conference plans**

PREPARED by: Caroline Clow
CIRCULATION to: All admin. staff, all senior dance instructors
DATE: Monday 3 March 2003

As requested at the senior dance instructors' meeting on Thursday 6 February 2003, I have started to plan for the Annual Conference.

DATES
As agreed, we expect to fly to the USA on Saturday 26 July, returning on Saturday 2 August. I have made initial enquiries regarding flight times and costs from usual UK airports to a number of destination airports in the USA. Appendix A shows all information obtained to date.
It may be more cost-effective for dance instructors in the Midlands to travel to Heathrow on the Friday. Additional hotel accommodation costs are included in Appendix A.

NUMBERS TRAVELLING
I have now contacted all dance instructors and expect 26 of the 28 currently working for FFM to attend, together with 17 partners and 11 children (4 under 12 years of age). There are 7 more instructors who may join FFM prior to the conference, and I will check with them whether they can attend and how many guests they expect to join them. Including office admin. staff, this means there will be a party of 70-80 this year. Appendix B lists those who are expected to attend the Conference.

STUDIO SPACE
I have completed the investigation on the availability of studio space in the USA and Appendix C lists all dance studios promoted by the dance studio website (www.dancestudio.com). Most states have dance studios for hire, but I have decided to concentrate on Florida since it should prove to be a popular venue for our dance instructors and their families.

HOTEL ACCOMMODATION IN THE USA
I will delay investigation into hotel accommodation until we have decided on a studio. I would expect this to be done in the next 4 weeks.

ITINERARY
I suggest we follow the same pattern as for previous conferences and book studio space on alternate days (Sunday, Tuesday, Thursday). This will allow time for sightseeing and relaxation. I recommend that we include one organised visit to Disneyworld (Monday). The full itinerary in shown in Appendix D.

Page 1 of 7 3 March 2003

**Fast Forward Movers**

**Minutes of the meeting of Senior Dance Instructors**

Held on Thursday 6 February 2003, FFM House, Woking, Surrey

| | |
|---|---|
| Attended by: | Glenys Brooks (chair)<br>Admin: Jenny P (secretary), Caroline C (events organiser),<br>SDIs: K Prentice, J Jay, Y Murphy, J Brown, F Newman |
| Apologies from: | Admin: Les L, Andrew L<br>SDIs: A Burford |

**Minutes of the last SDI meeting** held on Thursday 2 January were agreed and signed as a true record.
**Matters arising:** There were none.

**INDUCTION/NEW DIs**
Report from the chair: Glenys Brooks
GB reported that the induction session held on Monday 3 February 2003 was successful in that 4 additional DIs were to join FFM within the next three months: Terri Strutt, Amelia Payne, Georgina Webb and Hilary Hall.

The next induction session is scheduled for Wednesday 9 April 2003.

**VIDEO CONFERENCING**
Report from Kay Prentice (SDI)
The new video conferencing system seems to be proving successful despite a few last minute hitches. 6 DIs, all from the Midlands, took part in the first trial session on Sunday 19 January 2003. Initial reactions suggest that they were happy with the new arrangements, especially since it saved so much travelling time. Another session with the DIs in the West Country is planned for Sunday 23 February.

**FINANCE/STOCK**
Report from Andrew Little
In Andrew's absence, his report was read (attached). In summary:
- The new rates for instructors (DIs and SDIs) will come into effect as planned from Monday 3 March.
- Additional supplies of leotards with the FFM logo should be available within 14 days; apologies for delay from the supplier have been received.

**ANNUAL CONFERENCE**
Plans for this year's conference were discussed. It was agreed that CC would undertake an initial investigation into studios/travel to the USA: 1 week commencing Saturday 26 July. All DIs and their partners and children to be invited. CC to report findings to next meeting.

**AOB:** None
**DATE OF NEXT MEETING:** Thursday 6 March 2003

Figure 1.3 Examples of different types of documents: a handout, a memo, a business letter, a report and minutes of a meeting

### Further research 1.7

Smileys are combinations of text characters used to convey facial expressions or emotions. For example, if you key : (colon) and then - (a dash) and then ) (a closing bracket), a smiling face will appear.
Try to find some more combinations and make a list of them.

## Abbreviations

An abbreviation is a shortened form of a word (or phrase) that saves space while retaining meaning. Table 1.2 gives some examples, as well as some **contractions** and some **acronyms** that might be used in written material.

| Full form | Abbreviation | Contraction | Acronym |
|---|---|---|---|
| Doctor | | Dr | |
| *et cetera* | etc. | | |
| Mister | | Mr | |
| Mistress | | Mrs | |
| United Kingdom | | | UK |
| United States of America | | | USA |
| *id est* (that is) | i.e. | | |
| *exempli gratia* (for example) | e.g. | | |
| miles per hour | m.p.h. | | |
| first | 1st | | |
| second | 2nd | | |
| third | 3rd | | |
| *et alia* (among others) | | et al. | |
| Joe Bloggs | | J. Bloggs | |
| before Christ | | | BC |
| anno domini | | | AD |
| British Broadcasting Corporation | | BBC | |

Table 1.2 Abbreviations, contractions and acronyms

Notice that abbreviations have full points (full stops) to show where letters have been truncated.

?

### What does it mean?

**Contractions** (where the starting and ending letters are still present, and only letters in between are omitted) do not have full points.
**Acronyms** are created from the first letters of words, are written with capital letters and do not have full points.

With the introduction of text messaging on mobile phones, a whole new form of abbreviation has sprung up. Because on present mobile phone keypads, keying some characters requires as many as four presses, a shorthand has been developed which is proving very popular. Table 1.3 lists some examples.

| | |
|---|---|
| AFAIC | as far as I'm concerned |
| ASAP | as soon as possible |
| BFN | bye for now |
| CW2CU | can't wait to see you |
| FYI | for your information |
| HTH | hope this helps |
| KIT | keep in touch |
| PLS | please |

Table 1.3 Shorthand for use with mobile phone texting

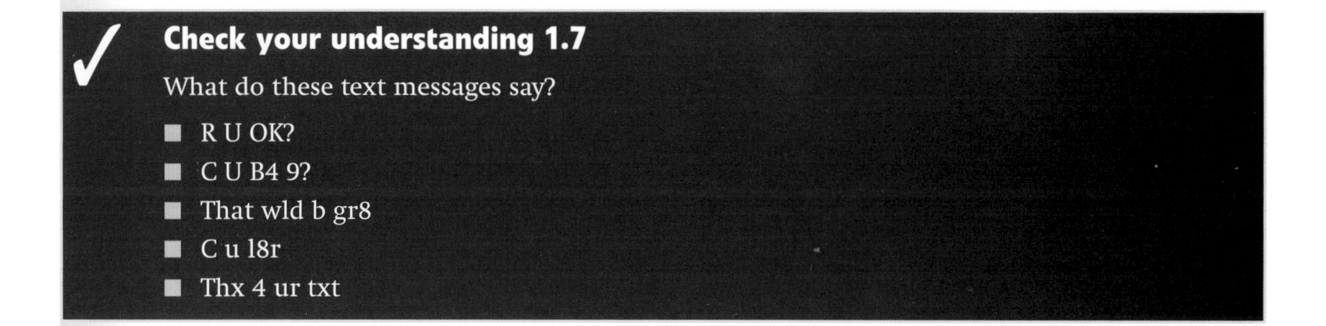

**Check your understanding 1.7**

What do these text messages say?

- R U OK?
- C U B4 9?
- That wld b gr8
- C u l8r
- Thx 4 ur txt

# Software applications

You need to use appropriate software applications to produce a range of documents. How can you decide which application is most appropriate to use for a given document?

## Word processors

Word processors allow you to enter text, amend the text, save it and print it out, on paper or directly on to an OHT. The text can be formatted so you can create a 'look' to suit you and your intended reader. You can use:

- different font styles (called **typefaces**), e.g. Arial, Times Roman
- different font sizes (called **point sizes**), e.g. 8 pt, 10 pt, 12 pt
- different text attributes, e.g. italic, bold, underlined, small caps
- different line spacing, e.g. single, 1.5, double.

You can also specify the paper size you want to use (such as A4, A3) and the orientation (portrait or landscape).

## Further research 1.8

1. Identify the following formatting features available in word-processing software: indentation, justification, tabulation.
2. If you had to prepare a presentation to explain how these features work to a small group of your friends, what delivery technique would you choose?
3. Prepare a presentation to explain one of the techniques. Limit yourself to 10 minutes.

## Desktop publishing

Desktop publishing (DTP) allows you to prepare documents ready for printing professionally. The emphasis in DTP is on page layout. It is assumed that your multi-page document is to have a consistent style throughout, based on a specific style template.

### What does it mean?

DTP stands for desktop publishing.

Although DTP software offers the usual word-processing features of entering and editing text, there are additional features that make it easy to create more complex document structures.

- Everything is in a *frame*, either a text frame or a graphics frame.
- The page layout allows multiple frames on any one page, e.g. two text columns with a graphics frame centred between them (Figure 1.4).
- Frames can be linked so that if you edit the text on one page any overflow runs automatically across to the linked text frame on the next page. It is also easy to flow text around graphics frames.

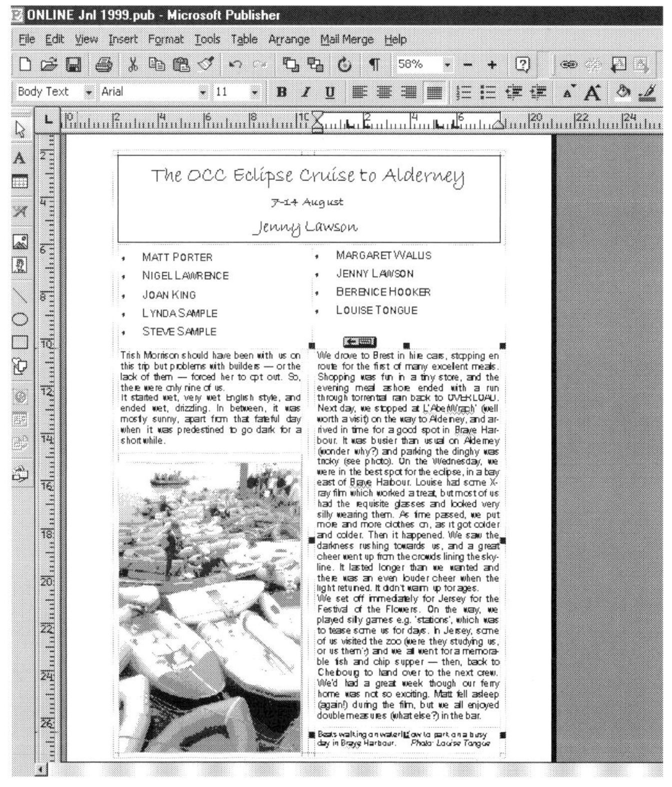

Figure 1.4 A sample DTP page

## Graphics

While word-processing packages offer limited graphics facilities, to produce a more professional looking diagram or illustration, better results can be achieved by using a graphics package.

### Further research 1.9

1 Find out what graphics facilities are available with your word-processing software. What extra facilities does your graphics software provide?
2 Illustrate the difference by producing two pieces of artwork: one that could be produced by either word-processing or graphics software and one that could be produced only using graphics software.
3 Incorporate samples of your graphics into a word-processed document and then into a DTP document to investigate the problems that might occur.

## E-mail

E-mails are used to communicate electronically and are best used for brief, informal messages. Although it is possible to write a long letter using e-mail, the formatting features are limited (or may not be acceptable to your recipient). If you want to communicate a more complex structure of information (such as a business letter, diagram or table), it would be better to use the most appropriate software, save it in a document and then send it as an attached file.

For example, you may need to prepare some material for a finance planning meeting. You could produce a budget using spreadsheet software, a map explaining how to reach the meeting using graphics software, and a covering letter including the agenda using word-processing software. All three can be saved separately and then attached to one e-mail, addressed to all those who are invited to attend the meeting.

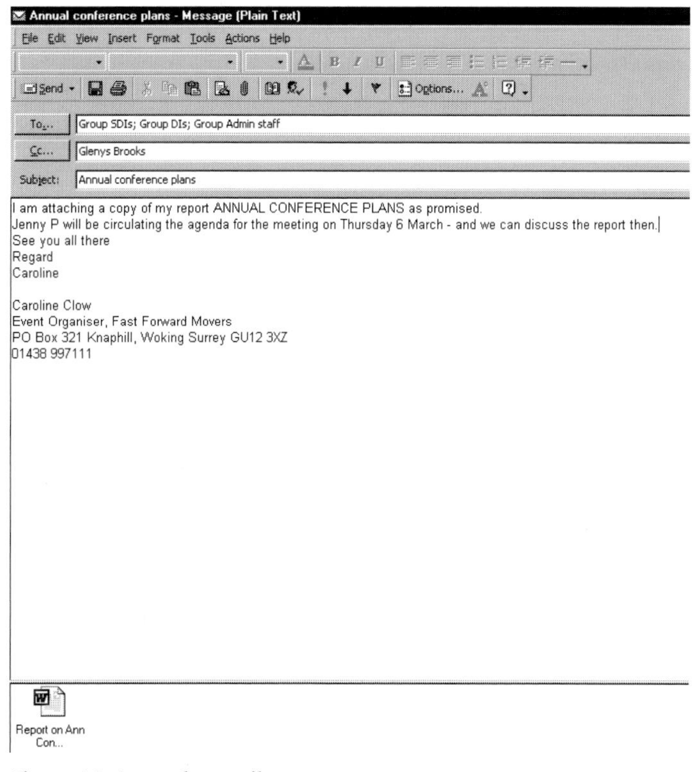


Figure 1.5 A sample e-mail

### Assessment activity 1.2

Referring to the presentations prepared for Assessment activity 1.1, review the software that you used to produce your notes and any other materials. Explain why you chose to use one type of software package rather than another.

# Writing style

You need to be able to select an appropriate writing style to suit the nature of the subject and the target audience or reader.

- The subject will determine what words (the **vocabulary**) you should use.
- The reader and your relationship with that reader will determine the **tone** that you should use.
- The **medium** you are going to use to present the material will also have an impact.

## Vocabulary

IT people are often accused of talking jargon, mainly by those who do not understand what they are talking about. In IT, and in lots of other technical subjects, there are specific terms that can be used to describe very succinctly what you are trying to say. To use other 'loose' terms in their place (trying to avoid jargon) can result in unclear communication. If there is one word which describes a piece of hardware, why use any other?

- Kari will use the correct terms for the parts of the boat (e.g. port, starboard, fore, aft, bow, stern, sheet, warp, spring), and give instructions using these terms. She needs to make sure the crew understand these terms; if they do not, problems could arise very quickly. She will reinforce the use of these terms during the sail, and part of the fun for novice sailors is to learn all these new terms.
- Steve needs to make sure that his audience learns about lots of different First Aid scenarios during the course. He may introduce the technical terms, but the important thing is for his audience to recognise situations and react accordingly, so he need not worry so much about teaching all the relevant terms. However, paramedics should know the correct terms, so that they can communicate effectively with the hospital staff when taking a casualty into the A&E department.

If the vocabulary you need to use is new to your audience, you need to explain each term the first time it arises. In this book, each time a new term is used, a definition is also given. In this way, the readers, i.e. the audience, learn the new terms and no longer see them as jargon. Instead, they learn to communicate on the same level as someone who is more expert on the subject.

### Check your understanding 1.8

Refer back to the formatting features presentation that you prepared (Further research 1.8 on page 22).

- Read through your notes and identify all the terms that you introduced to your audience.
- Did you explain each term?
- When others made their presentations to you, did you feel you were learning new terms?

You can increase your own vocabulary so that you can communicate more effectively with others. Your **active vocabulary** (the words and expressions that you use all the time and fully understand) can be increased by including words from your **passive vocabulary** (the words that you meet occasionally but are not sure what they mean and would not be confident enough to use them).

### Further research 1.10

While reading this book or a newspaper, or listening to the radio or watching television, notice ten words or phrases that you would not normally include in your own speech or writing. Look them up in a dictionary and think of ways of weaving them into your own conversation or writing.

## Tone

The tone that you use in your writing will depend very much on the circumstances, and your relationship with your readers.

### Check your understanding 1.9

1 In the case studies on pages 3–5, what tone should Bill, George, Kari, Steve and Tanya use?
2 Compare the words that you used in the group interview ice-breaker (Further research 1.4 on page 11) with those used for the scenarios in Assessment activity 1.1 (page 17). How did your tone vary? If you used the same tone throughout, think about how you could have varied it to better effect.

## Medium

Sometimes, words are written to be read by a reader, as is this book. Some are written to be read aloud to your audience, as with a speech. Some are written to be spoken during a dramatic performance. The medium affects the way words should be put together, and the effect they have.

### Further research 1.11

Try reading material in a different way to how it was intended to be received.

1 Read aloud from this textbook. How will you convey to your listener the use of bulleted lists?
2 Read the text of a speech. Does it convey the same passion as the oral presentation? Are the words alone enough?
3 Compare the written stage instruction for a play with its live performance. For example, you might obtain the scripts of comedy programmes (such as *Only Fools and Horses*) or watch a Shakespearian play having studied the text. How well do the written words convey the humour or drama? How much difference is due to the scenery, costumes and stage directions?

The words are important, but how they are presented can add to their value. The choice of words then has to match the medium.

# Writing accurately

You need to write accurately so that your audience is not misinformed. You must be sure of your facts and present them clearly with no grammatical errors or spelling errors.

## Clear meaning

The word 'clarity' is used to refer to how well you pronounce your spoken words. Can your audience hear every word? With written material, the reader can choose his or her own pace, so then clarity takes on a different meaning.

- Have you used the correct words?
- Have you spelt the words correctly?
- Have you put your words together with grammatical correctness?

If you know the subject you are writing about, you should know the correct terminology to use. If you are unsure, you will have to research the topic thoroughly so that you do become expert at it. Remember to avoid using jargon just for the sake of it; and when introducing new terms to your reader, define them so that the meaning is clear to them.

If you know what you want to write but are searching for the right word to use, you could use a **thesaurus** to look up alternative words with similar meanings. Given a choice, use a short word rather than a long one. You should also avoid **slang** and **idioms** such as 'a red herring', 'a wild goose chase', 'smell a rat'.

### What does it mean?

An **idiom** is a group of words whose overall meaning is different from what the individual words suggest.

## Grammatical correctness

You should have an instinctive feel for what is (and what is not) grammatically correct. There are some simple basic rules of **grammar** which will help you to build sentences that convey what you want to say without **ambiguity**.

### What does it mean?

**Grammar** is the set of rules that allow words to be put together into sentences correctly.

### What does it mean?

**Ambiguity** (noun) means a double meaning, i.e. an expression capable of more than one meaning.
**Ambiguous** (adjective) means obscure or with a double meaning.

Words can be separated into classes: nouns, pronouns, determiners, adjectives, verbs, adverbs, prepositions, conjunctions, exclamations, etc.

- **Nouns** name things (Jim, elephant, box).
- **Pronouns** are like nouns but replace them (he, it, them).

- **Determiners** come before nouns (or pronouns) to define them (*a* book; *an* apple; *the* page; *some* words; *this* pen; *that* pencil; *those* people). Notice that some determiners can be used without the noun, i.e. as pronouns (this, that, these, those).
- **Adjectives** are used to describe nouns (an *excellent* book; this *tall* building; the grass is *green).*
- **Verbs** are 'doing' words (the cat *sat* on the mat).
- **Adverbs** describe verbs and often, but not always, end in 'ly (I ran *quickly*, he ran *fast).* Adverbs can also be used to modify an adjective (Hugh was *incredibly* tall).
- **Prepositions** connect a noun (or pronoun) that follows it to some other part of a sentence (The cat sat *on* the mat).
- **Conjunctions** are joining words (and, but, that).
- **Exclamations** are outbursts and can be single words or a phrase (Ah! Oh no!).

Some words can be used in more than one class.

- Light my fire (light = verb).
- Put out the light! (light = noun).
- Light green is my favourite colour (light = adjective).

Words are put together to form phrases, clauses and sentences.

- A **phrase** is part of a sentence and does not contain a finite verb (The cat sat *on the mat*).
- A **clause** is part of a sentence and does contain a finite verb (This is the book *that I want you to read*).

There are different types of sentence; notice that each type can be positive or negative.

- **Declarative sentences** make a statement or an assertion. (My favourite colour is blue. John was running away. I cannot answer your question.) Notice that these sentences have a subject and this appears before the verb.
- **Imperative sentences** give an order, and can end with an exclamation mark. (Please help me. Don't forget to telephone your mother. Mind your head!) Notice that these sentences appear to have no subject; it is implied.
- **Interrogative sentences** ask a question and so end in a question mark. Some are simple yes/no **closed questions**. (Have you never been to France? Can Nigel ride a bike?) Notice that the subject appears after the verb. **Open questions** expect more than just a yes/no answer. (What is the time? Why can't you be more helpful?)
- **Exclamatory sentences** are used to show strong feelings. (No! Bother!)

All sentences start with a capital letter and end with either a full stop, an exclamation mark, a question mark or a colon. Every sentence should have a verb (an action word). Sentences can be simple, compound or complex.

- **Simple sentences** contain only one finite verb. (My favourite colour *is* blue. *Mind* your head! *Have* you never been to France?) Notice that the verb can be made from more than one word, and that an adverb can split the verbs.
- **Compound sentences** are simply two or more simple sentences joined with a conjunction. (I watched the film *and* I found it very interesting.)
- **Complex sentences** include a main clause and then one or more other clauses. (I started to read the book but, when I realised I had read it before, I stopped.) Notice how the commas help to break up a complex sentence. Notice also that, if you were to delete the text between the two commas, the sentence would still make sense.

**Check your understanding 1.10**

1 Write three simple sentences to show examples of nouns. Underline the noun in each sentence.
2 Think of three nouns that can also be used as verbs or adjectives. For each noun, write three sentences: one with the word used as a noun, one with it used as a verb, and another with it used as an adjective.
3 There are eight categories of pronoun: personal (e.g. 'I'), possessive (e.g. 'mine'), reflexive (e.g. 'myself'), demonstrative (e.g. 'this'), interrogative (e.g. 'which), relative (e.g. 'that'), distributive (e.g. 'all') and indefinite (e.g. 'any'). Check that you know what these terms mean, and list as many pronouns as you can within each category. Compare notes with others in your group to produce a complete list of pronouns.
4 Determiners can be split into articles (definite = the; indefinite = a/an), demonstratives (this, that, these, those), possessives (my, your, his, her, its, our, their), numbers (one, two, etc.) and indefinite determiners. Check that you know what these terms mean and list ten examples of the indefinite determiner.

### Avoid spelling errors

If you hand-write material, you have to be able to check your spelling manually. This means you need a good vocabulary and spelling ability. A dictionary will help you if you look up any words you are unsure of.

If you use a word processor to prepare your written material, you can use the automatic **spell-checker** to make sure there are no spelling errors. Unfortunately, spell-checkers are limited in their usefulness. If you mis-key a word, but inadvertently produce a word that is valid, the spell-checker will not flag this as an error, e.g. if you key 'worm' instead of 'worn' the spell-checker will not notice. If you miss the 'r' off 'your', this will pass unnoticed too. If you spell 'too' as 'to' or even 'two', the spell-checker will let it pass. Do use a spell-checker to spot the most glaring errors in your keying, but then proof-read your work carefully to find any other errors that are not trapped by the spell-checker.

## Organisation and presentation of material

You need to organise and present material to meet user needs, and to use appropriate conventional standards of written English.

### General organisation

If you organise material coherently, this will help your readers to follow your flow of thought and to understand your overall message. At the very beginning, there may be a title page indicating what is inside the document and telling the reader that you are the author. What next? That depends on the document and what you write.

If you are planning to present an argument, you might adopt a particular structure such as this:

- This document looks at the issue of ...
- Some would argue that ... and there is some evidence that ...
- Others disagree. They suggest that ...
- I believe that while ... it is obvious that ...
- So I would recommend ...

If you are telling a story or reporting on an event, it might make sense to present it in the order in which it happened, i.e. chronologically.

How you tackle the writing will be very much a personal preference; it will reflect how much of what you want to write is already in your head and how you see its structure. The mechanical part of writing can be done in many ways.

- *Top-down approach:* Start with the title of your piece. If you cannot think of a brilliant title, use a **working title** until something better occurs to you. Then decide on the main section titles, subheadings, sub-subheadings and so on, down to the lowest level. You could even draw the structure using a **mind map**. You now have a skeleton and can start to write.
- *Bottom-up approach:* Words will be grouped into sentences, and then sentences into paragraphs. Paragraphs will form subsections with headings and these will be grouped to form sections with their own heading. The sections will then form the total document, under one title. If you have certain facts to include, it might help just to write these facts and then try to group them into an overall structure. The final order can be decided once you have all the material to hand.
- *Starting at the beginning:* Some writers just start at what seems to be the beginning and write what they have to say. Having produced a first draft, they then review it and reorder their thoughts if necessary. Sometimes, what you write first actually makes a better conclusion for your piece. Often, reading through, or asking someone else to do it for you, makes you realise what you have not said, or how the sections could be better organised.

Some writers sit and think for ages and then burst into action, writing furiously until it is done. Others set themselves a target of so many words per day. The actual method used does not really matter; it is the end result that is important. Have you presented your thoughts, ideas and arguments in a way that helps your reader to follow and understand them?

What else might your document provide?

- If there are lots of sections and subsections, it will make sense to include a **contents list**.
- If your document includes many definitions or explanations of procedures, an **index** might help the readers to find what they need.
- If you have referred to other text, you must acknowledge them in the **bibliography**. The reader might also welcome a 'Further Reading' list.

## Organising material within documents

### Your personal CV

**What does it mean?**

CV stands for the Latin phrase *curriculum vitae.*

Your CV should summarise everything a potential employer needs to know about you. Often a job advert asks that you send a CV with your letter of application. This is then used to draw up a short list of applicants who will be called for interview. If you pass this stage of selection, you will be given the opportunity to impress the employer personally in an interview. Your CV therefore needs to advertise your plus points, and be presented in a way which takes the reader very little time to check that you have the desired credentials.

**Curriculum Vitae**

Janice Cloggs
37 Fancourt Road
Bisham Surrey GU1 5PQ

**Work experience**

August 2002 - present    Administrator at Bisham Library.

**Educational history**

Sept. 1997 – July 2002    Pennyhill Comprehensive School, Bisham

**Qualifications**

9 GCSEs including English and Maths. Grade A in Drama.

**Key skills**

Computer literate. Good communication skills.

**Hobbies**

Dance (tap, modern jazz), swimming, amateur dramatics and art.

**Interests**

I am keen on most sports and have a competitive nature. I like to keep fit. I enjoy meeting people and going to plays or visiting galleries.

Figure 1.6 A sample CV

## Letter of application

A letter of application is a formal letter sent by a job applicant to a prospective employer. It is usual for the employer to request that this letter be hand-written. This then provides an opportunity to check both the neatness of the applicant's writing and his or her ability to compose a letter. Figure 1.7 shows a sample advert and the letter of application. Notice that the letter obeys the standard conventions for business letters and is written in a formal way.

**VACANCY FOR OFFICE JUNIOR**

Fast Forward Movers train and co-ordinate the largest team of dance instructors in the UK, bringing fun dance classes to thousands of people all over the country.

FFM need a recent school leaver to join the administration team at the head office in Woking, Surrey. He or she will have at least 5 GCSEs at grade C or above, including English and Mathematics. Some work experience is useful, although full training will be given in telephone work and general office duties. Applicants who wish to take NVQ level qualifications will be encouraged to do so, and given time to attend college as necessary.

**Closing date: 31 March 2003.**
Interviews will take place on Friday 4 April 2003.
Interested applicants should send their CV with a covering letter to:
Jenny Perkins at FFM House, Woking, Surrey GU12 3XZ.

37 Fancourt Road
Bisham
Surrey GU1 5PQ
01483 567812

26 March 2003

Jenny Perkins
Fast Forward Movers
FFM House
Woking
Surrey GU12 3XZ

Dear Jenny Perkins

**Office junior vacancy advertised in the Bisham Echo 14 March 2003**

I am writing to apply for the post of office junior with FFM as advertised in the Bisham Echo last Friday.

I have been working at Bisham Library since I left school last July, and while I enjoy it, without further academic qualifications, I feel my chances of promotion here are limited.

Last year, I decided not to go on to college full-time because I wanted to take a job and become financially independent of my parents. However, I am now keen to combine work and study, and would like to enrol for an NVQ in Business Administration next September.

I would like the opportunity to work for a company like yours, who offer support in further training, and I would like to gain more experience in telephone work.

Yours sincerely

Janice Cloggs

Janice Cloggs

Figure 1.7 Advert and letter of application

## Further research 1.12

Scan the local papers for adverts for jobs that you might want to apply for. Select three different adverts and then compose a letter of application for each one. Hand-write your letters, together with envelopes.

# 1.3 Written research material

In preparing to give a presentation or write a document, you may need to conduct some research and to select material from a variety of sources. Being fully aware of current thinking on a topic allows you to write material that will be more interesting to your audience. It may also encourage you to consider the problems surrounding a topic, and to invent some new solutions to them.

## Research requirements

You need to select material to meet given research requirements. How will these research requirements be expressed? Having identified the general topic area, it is important to decide on the **scope** of the research. This limits the research, by deciding what is *not* to be covered. For example, in Further research 1.2 (page 7) you were asked to find out what presentation software is available on your computer system. This limited your research to presentation software (eliminating all other types of software) and to your computer (further limiting your research to the software available to you).

## The main points

You need to identify and summarise the main points in any article, report or other document you read as part of your research. This should be easy if the document is well structured; you need only refer to the contents lists or scan the main headings to find out what has been covered. Within the text, formatting may have been used to highlight important terms, so scanning through will allow you to see what terms are introduced.

If you are given text with none of these clues, you will need to read through and find the main points for yourself. As you read, make marks in the margin, highlight using a highlighter pen, or circle important text. When you have finished reading you can look back to see what seemed important and, from that, decide what the main points were.

## Making notes

You need to make notes that can be understood later when writing the target document.

- You may use a notebook, and jot down ideas as they occur to you.
- You may prefer to use Post-it® notes which you can then stick in a place to remind you.
- When writing a document, you might include notes to yourself within the text or as footnotes or endnotes. As you deal with each one you can delete it from the text.

The important thing is to decide on a method that suits you, and then use it to good effect.

| DO collect information and make accurate full notes | DON'T rely on your memory |
|---|---|
| DO note titles of books, articles, page references, etc. | DON'T forget to record important information |
| DO keep your notes in one folder | DON'T write notes on scraps of paper or backs of envelopes |
| DO finish one piece of work before going on to the next | DON'T leave notes half-finished |
| DO collect photos, etc. as you go along and store them carefully | DON'T leave things like artwork or other visual aids until the last minute |
| DO include a bibliography in alphabetical order | DON'T forget to list all sources of information |

Table 1.4 Do's and don'ts of note-taking

# Reading

You need to read with understanding and understand ways in which reading efficiency may be improved. What things will adversely affect your ability to read and understand a document?

- Material that is poorly presented may irritate a reader so that concentration is lost. This includes poor handwriting resulting in illegible words.
- Distractions such as background noise may interrupt your flow of thought. For some people, the opposite is true; silence prevents them from concentrating and they need music or some background noise.
- Mismatches between the writer and the reader in terms of vocabulary can prevent the reader understanding what the writer has to say. New terms need to be explained to avoid this problem.

Practice will teach you what conditions you need to be able to read efficiently and effectively. You then need to adopt these conditions whenever necessary.

## Speed reading

If you know what information you want from a document before you start reading it (e.g. if you only want an outline of the issue that the document discusses), then you can skim the document very quickly and extract only the essential facts. However, if you need to understand the real detail of the document, then you need to read it more slowly so that you fully understand it.

Most children learn to read either letter by letter or word by word. As you develop reading skills, you will probably fix your eyes on one block of words, then move your eyes to the next block of words, and so on; you are reading blocks of words at a time, not individual words one by one. Sometimes you may need to move back to a previous block if you are unsure about something.

Speed reading involves improving reading skills in three separate ways:

- *Increasing the number of words read in each block*. You need to make a conscious effort to expand the number of words that you read at a time. Practice will help you to read faster. You may also find that holding the text a little further from your eyes helps. The more words you can read in each block, the faster you will read.
- *Reducing the length of time that is spent reading each block*. The minimum length of time needed to read each block is probably only a quarter of a second. By pushing yourself to reduce the time you take, you will become better at picking up information quickly.
- *Reducing the number of times your eyes skip back to a previous sentence*. To achieve this, run a pointer along the line as you read. Your eyes will automatically follow the tip of your pointer, smoothing the flow of your reading. Your speed of reading then largely depends on the speed of the pointer.

It is possible to attend courses in speed reading, and to buy software that will give you practice.

**Further research 1.13**

Search the Internet for information on speed reading techniques. Make notes and write a document of no more than 1000 words on the topic.

# 1.4 Relevant research

When giving a presentation, it is important that you have the knowledge and expertise to pass on to your audience. To check that you can cover what is necessary, and to the required depth, you should carry out research into the subject, to support your own material and to expand on it.

- George has to write his 'father-of-the-bride' speech. His role is limited in that others will also make speeches at the reception (the best man and the groom); each of them have different responsibilities and different people to mention or thank. George can go to his local library or search on the Internet for advice in speech writing.
- For Kari, the topic is safety procedures aboard a yacht. She is limited to the bare essentials because time will prevent her going into detail. There are specialist books on the topic, which she will have obtained while attending shore-based sailing courses.
- For Tanya, her presentation revolves around her product range. She will be well versed in the range of products, their prices and so on. However, she will need to develop skills in handling objections and closing a sale. If she has no formal training in sales techniques, she would benefit from doing some research and practising these techniques.
- For Steve, his presentation is based on an examination syllabus for a First Aid qualification. He will rely heavily on his previous experience as a paramedic. However, he needs to prepare notes for his class. Steve may refer to his own notes obtained during his training, to guidance given by the First Aid examination board and to other textbooks or on-line sources of medical information.

# Research data

You need to identify and evaluate a range of research materials from different resources and sources. The most obvious source of information may be a library, or possibly the Internet. If you are looking for established facts and figures, such as unemployment rates, the government publishes these regularly. Printed copies of statistical information will be available at your local library, or you could search for these on-line. Data that has been collected by someone else is called **secondary data**; it is acceptable to use secondary data but you must acknowledge your sources.

If you want to collect data yourself (**primary data** research) you will need to decide on a method of data collection. One such method is to use a **questionnaire**. Using a questionnaire as a research tool is not as simple as it may sound. It is not just a case of listing a few questions, handing it around to your friends and asking them to fill it in and return it to you.

The questionnaire designer needs to know what problem is to be solved before any questions can be framed. Often the data has to be analysed according to the person who answers the questions (the respondent or interviewee) so some background information is needed, such as age range, salary range, occupation, etc. What answers might be expected can also affect how the question is to be asked. When generating a questionnaire, bear the following points in mind:

- Keep the questionnaire short and order the questions in the most logical sequence.
- Make the wording of instructions simple and keep the questions short.
- Use open/closed questions as appropriate, and check for vague or ambiguous questions.
- Remember to thank the respondent.

## Further research 1.14

Collect examples of questionnaires and, from them, identify the following features:

- instructions and 'thank yous'
- background data, so that the respondents can be categorised
- open questions (ones that allow more than a limited number of responses)
- closed questions (note what data they collect and think about how this data could be coded)
- unnecessary questions
- any restrictions on what data can be collected from respondents, how it should be held, and what it should be used for.

Share your findings with others in your group.

You will need to search, access and retrieve remote information from paper-based and electronic sources, and then to present this information in the appropriate format. The two main sources are the WWW and CD-ROMs.

## What does it mean?

WWW means the World Wide Web.
CD-ROM means compact-disc, read-only memory.

The WWW has been under development for many years. For more details on its history, you could search the Internet. It provides a rich, and almost free, source of information. The bad news is that there is very little control over what appears on the Internet, so you have to be aware of this, and any particular website may represent the provider's viewpoint rather than facts.

CD-ROMs are published in much the same way as books. Each CD-ROM can hold a lot of information and this may include video clips as well as figures and other diagrams. The costs involved in writing material and moving it through the production process so that it appears in the local computer store should reassure the purchaser of a CD-ROM that the content is worth accessing. The down side is that you have to buy the CD-ROM.

**Further research 1.15**

Starting at www.w3.org/History.html find out about how the WWW was developed.
Find out similar information on the history of CD-ROMs.

## Results

You need to evaluate the results of your research. This involves reflection on the research and asking yourself a number of questions.

- Did you discover the answer to the problem you were researching? Are there any points outstanding?
- Were your methods of research efficient and effective? Could you have tackled it any differently?
- If you were to undertake a similar research project, what would you do differently?

This period of reflection is important because it provides the opportunity for you to improve your techniques and to ensure greater success next time around.

**Assessment activity 1.3**

For a topic of your own choice, decide on the scope of your research and then select and use a range of written research materials from a range of sources to prepare a written document of no more than 2500 words.

# 1.5 Planning and time management

You need to plan work and use time effectively to ensure that completion deadlines are met.

- List what needs to be done.
- Estimate how much time each step might take (be pessimistic rather than optimistic).
- Work out a sequence of events. Take into account that some events will depend on earlier events having been completed successfully.
- Allow time for delays, e.g. a library being shut, a computer crashing, you being ill, etc.

- Use a spreadsheet to record your sequence of events. Input the time per step and make the spreadsheet work out a starting and finishing date for each step. Then see what will happen if you let a deadline slip; the end deadline will not be achievable unless you make up the time in some way.
- Record how much time each step actually takes. This will help you to revise the remainder of the plan, and to plan better in the future.

## Test your knowledge

1. List four different examples of communication.
2. List four different non-textual visual aids.
3. Explain how to make the best use of an OHP.
4. When planning a presentation, what should you take into account?
5. Explain what is meant by a delivery style.
6. Give three examples of how body language may reveal conflicting messages.
7. Suggest how a presenter can avoid distractions and disturbances, especially at the start and end of a presentation.
8. What are the main stages of a successful negotiation?
9. Explain the component parts or structure of a presentation and how you might decide on its sequence.
10. Suggest ways of overcoming nerves.
11. Distinguish between these documents: handout, memo, business letter, report, minutes.
12. Explain the differences between abbreviations, contractions and acronyms.
13. Explain these terms: typeface, point size, text attribute, paper size, orientation.
14. What is speed reading?
15. Contrast sources of research material with respect to their cost, availability and reliability.

# UNIT 2: COMPUTER SYSTEMS

This unit outlines the way in which a computer works, starting with simple logic and progressing to a simple model of a microprocessor. This is followed by an overview of computer hardware and peripherals to enable you to understand the way in which computer systems are constructed and how they work. The unit also covers the purpose of operating systems, some operating system processes and low-level programming. The unit is intended as an introduction to a broad range of important computing concepts, and presents opportunities to demonstrate Key Skills in application of number and communication.

## Learning objectives

- To describe the internal operations of a model microprocessor
- To demonstrate a thorough knowledge of modern computer systems' hardware
- To write simple-low level programs
- To install and use a modern operating system

# 2.1 Internal operations

Before you consider how a computer works, it is worthwhile knowing a bit about the history of how data – both numbers and text – have been written in the past.

### Case study: The written word

Before written words were invented, people drew pictures to record events. These ideograms developed into phonograms and, about 3000 BCE, the Sumerians conveyed ideas by creating wedge-shaped symbols called cuneiform. In 2100 BCE, cuneiform was developed by the Egyptians into hundreds of hieroglyphics. The Phoenicians then adapted this 'alphabet' and took it to Greece, where it was rationalised into a more manageable set of characters. From there, in northern Italy, the Etruscans adopted the Greek alphabet and, more recently, this was adapted by the Romans. The Latin alphabet contained 21 letters; the present 26 letter alphabet but without the letters J, U, W, Y and Z.

1. Search the Internet for information about the history of the alphabet. Why were the letters J, U, W, Y and Z added to the Latin alphabet?
2. Find out what alphabets are available on your word-processing system.

The fact that humans have five fingers (or four fingers and a thumb) on each hand has resulted in numbering systems that revolve around the number ten.

### Case study: Numbering systems

The Babylonians and the Egyptians used a single stroke to count things, e.g. a notch on a stick of wood or a mark scratched into a wall. A group of ten was given a separate symbol. In **tally charts**, we use a similar system, grouping each five strokes and cutting the fifth stroke across the first four strokes.

The Romans used a numbering system based on symbols rather than the Arabic digits 0–9 that are used today. The Roman digits are I (1), V (5), X (10), L (50), C (100), D (500) and M (1000). Notice that there is no symbol for zero. Numbers were then created by combining and repeating the seven basic letters I, V, X, L, C, D and M. For example, 3 = III, 7 = VII, 25 = XXV, 180 = CLXXX. Placing letters before, rather than after another letter subtracted the value. For example, 4 = IV, 9 = IX, 19 = IXX.

1. Find out what underscoring of Roman letters means.
2. Find some examples of Roman numbering still in use today.
3. Work out how to represent these years as Roman numbers: 1980, 1999, 2000, 2001, 2050. Where might you see these dates written as Roman numbers?
4. Convert 101 and 32 into Roman, and add them. Now convert 99 and 39 and add them. Notice that the Roman numbering system does not make addition an easy task.
5. Find out when a numbering system was invented that did include a digit for the concept of zero.
6. How does having a zero digit make sums easier to do?

Digits are grouped to represent numbers, e.g. 17 560. Characters are grouped to form text messages, e.g. Data.

- A number is made using the digits 0–9 and the position of each digit indicates its **place value**. Because there are ten digits, this system of data representation is called **denary**. Numbers can be positive or negative, and may be whole numbers (integers) or include decimal places, e.g. currency amounts include pounds and pence.
- Text data uses the 26 letters of the alphabet plus special characters like commas and full stops. Text could also include digits, as in an address or telephone number.

**Further research 2.1**

1 How many different numbers can be formed using the four digits 0, 1, 2 and 3? List them in ascending order.

2 How many different 'words' could be formed from the eight letters C, E, M, O, P, R, T and U? How many of these are real words?

# Data representation

You need to understand the basic concepts and principles involved in the representation of data within a computer system.

## Number system conversions

- Within a computer, the smallest unit of information, a **bit**, can be off or on, and this is used to represent the values 0 and 1. Because there are only two possible values, this system is called **binary**.

**What does it mean?**

A **bit** is short for ***bi**nary digi**t***.

- Groups of three bits can be used to represent the 8 digits from 0 to 7.
  000=0, 001=1, 010=2, 011=3, 100=4, 101=5, 110=6, 111=7
  This system is called **octal**.
  Notice that $2^3 = 8$; the power of 2 is the number of values that can be represented.
- Groups of four bits can be used to represent the numbers 0–15. The values for 10, 11, 12, 13, 14, and 15 are renamed as A, B, C, D, E and F to create the **hexadecimal** set of digits.
  0000=0, 0001=1, 0010=2, 0011=3, 0100=4, 0101=5, 0110=6, 0111=7
  1000=8, 1001=9, 1010=A, 1011=B, 1100=C, 1101=D, 1110=E, 1111=F

Table 2.1 shows these three number systems, together with their denary equivalents.

**What does it mean?**

**Hexadecimal** (or hex) is the number system based on 16 characters: the digits 0 to 9; and then 10, 11, 12, 13, 14 and 15 renamed as A, B, C, D, E and F.

**What does it mean?**

**Denary** is the number system based on ten digits: 0, 1, 2, ..., 9.

| Denary | Binary | Octal | Hex |
|---|---|---|---|
| 0 | 0 | 0 | 0 |
| 1 | 1 | 1 | 1 |
| 2 | 10 | 2 | 2 |
| 3 | 11 | 3 | 3 |
| 4 | 100 | 4 | 4 |
| 5 | 101 | 5 | 5 |
| 6 | 110 | 6 | 6 |
| 7 | 111 | 7 | 7 |
| 8 | 1000 | 10 | 8 |
| 9 | 1001 | 11 | 9 |
| 10 | 1010 | 12 | A |
| 11 | 1011 | 13 | B |
| 12 | 1100 | 14 | C |
| 13 | 1101 | 15 | D |
| 14 | 1110 | 16 | E |
| 15 | 1111 | 17 | F |
| 16 | 10000 | 20 | 10 |
| 17 | 10001 | 21 | 11 |
| 18 | 10010 | 22 | 12 |

Table 2.1 Binary, octal and hexadecimal number systems

Table 2.2 shows how to convert from one number system to another. Converting between binary, octal and hexadecimal involves grouping and regrouping the binary digits, and is straightforward. Converting to and from denary is not so straightforward.

Converting from denary involves dividing by the base of the other system (2, 8 or 16) and noting remainders. Converting back into denary involves using **place value**.

**What does it mean?**

In any number, the value of a digit depends on its position within that number and this is called its **place value**.

In modern numbering systems, each digit is placed in a column, and each column has a value, which increases as you work from right to left.

- In the denary system (**base** 10), the columns represent powers of 10: thousands, hundreds, tens, units, and after the decimal point tenths, hundredths, thousandths and so on.
- In binary (base 2), the columns represent powers of 2.
- In octal (base 8), the columns represent powers of 8.
- In hex (base 16), the columns represent powers of 16.

**What does it mean?**

The **base** is the number of digits available within a numbering system. Base 2 (binary) uses 0 and 1. Base 8 (octal) uses 0–7. Base 16 (hex) uses 0, 1, 2, ..., 9, A, B, ..., E.

| | To... | | | |
|---|---|---|---|---|
| **From...** | **Binary** | **Octal** | **Denary** | **Hex** |
| **Binary** | | Group the bits into 3s.<br>Convert each group of 3 bits into an octal digit.<br>101001010111<br>= 101 001 010 111 = 5127 | Use place value to convert each on bit into a power of 2.<br>Add the powers. | Group the bits into 4s and convert each group of 4 bits into a hex digit.<br>101001010111<br>= 1010 0101 0111<br>= A57 |
| **Octal** | Expand each octal digit into 3 binary digits.<br>5127 = 101 001 010 111 | | Use place value to convert each on bit into a power of 8.<br>Add the powers. | Expand each octal digit into 3 binary digits and then regroup into groups of 4 bits.<br>Convert each group of 4 bits into a hex digit. |
| **Denary** | Keep dividing by 2, noting remainders:<br>2)2647<br>2)1323 R 1<br>2)661 R 1<br>2)330 R 1<br>2)165 R 0<br>2)82 R 1<br>2)41 R 0<br>2)20 R 1<br>2)10 R 0<br>2)5 R 0<br>2)2 R 1<br>2)1 R 0<br>0 R 1<br>101001010111 | Keep dividing by 8, noting remainders:*<br>8)2647<br>8)330 R 7<br>8)41 R 2<br>8)5 R 1<br>0 R 5<br>5127 | | Keep dividing by 16, noting remainders:*<br>16)2647<br>16)165 R 7<br>16)10 R 5<br>0 R 10 = A<br>A57 |
| **Hex** | Expand each hex digit into 4 binary digits.<br>A57 = 1010 0101 01111 | Expand each hex digit into 4 binary digits and then regroup into groups of 3 bits. Convert each group of 3 bits into an octal digit. | Use place value to convert each on bit into a power of 16.<br>Add the powers. | |

* You might prefer to divide by 2 and to convert from denary into binary first. It is then easy to group the bits and convert into octal or hex.

Table 2.2 Converting from one number system to another $A57_{16} = 5127_8 = 101001010111_2 = 2647_{10}$

## Assessment activity 2.1

1 Convert these denary numbers to binary:
- 5
- 23
- 39
- 42

2 Convert these denary numbers to octal:
- 39
- 42
- 69
- 74

3 Convert these denary numbers to hex:
- 69
- 74
- 95
- 133

4 Convert the binary numbers from question 1 into octal and then into hex.

5 Convert the octal numbers from question 2 into binary and then into hex.

6 Convert the hex numbers from question 3 into binary and then into octal.

## Doing arithmetic

Doing arithmetic in binary is much easier than in denary. There are only three number bonds to remember:

- 0 + 0 = 0
- 0 + 1 = 1 + 0 = 1
- 1 + 1 = 0 carry 1

Compare the addition tables shown in Table 2.3. Notice that, when adding, as soon as you run out of digits, you 'carry 1'. In binary, the 1 that is carried is worth 2; in octal, it is worth 8 and, in denary, it is worth 10.

**Binary addition**

| ADD | 0 | 1 |
|---|---|---|
| 0 | 0 | 1 |
| 1 | 1 | 10* |

* 10 means 0 carry 1

**Octal addition**

| ADD | 0 | 1 | 2 | 3 | 4 | 5 | 6 | 7 |
|---|---|---|---|---|---|---|---|---|
| 0 | 0 | 1 | 2 | 3 | 4 | 5 | 6 | 7 |
| 1 | 1 | 2 | 3 | 4 | 5 | 6 | 7 | 10 |
| 2 | 2 | 3 | 4 | 5 | 6 | 7 | 10 | 11 |
| 3 | 3 | 4 | 5 | 6 | 7 | 10 | 11 | 12 |
| 4 | 4 | 5 | 6 | 7 | 10 | 11 | 12 | 13 |
| 5 | 5 | 6 | 7 | 10 | 11 | 12 | 13 | 14 |
| 6 | 6 | 7 | 10 | 11 | 12 | 13 | 14 | 15 |
| 7 | 7 | 10 | 11 | 12 | 13 | 14 | 15 | 16 |

**Denary addition**

| ADD | 0 | 1 | 2 | 3 | 4 | 5 | 6 | 7 | 8 | 9 |
|---|---|---|---|---|---|---|---|---|---|---|
| 0 | 0 | 1 | 2 | 3 | 4 | 5 | 6 | 7 | 8 | 9 |
| 1 | 1 | 2 | 3 | 4 | 5 | 6 | 7 | 8 | 9 | 10 |
| 2 | 2 | 3 | 4 | 5 | 6 | 7 | 8 | 9 | 10 | 11 |
| 3 | 3 | 4 | 5 | 6 | 7 | 8 | 9 | 10 | 11 | 12 |
| 4 | 4 | 5 | 6 | 7 | 8 | 9 | 10 | 11 | 12 | 13 |
| 5 | 5 | 6 | 7 | 8 | 9 | 10 | 11 | 12 | 13 | 14 |
| 6 | 6 | 7 | 8 | 9 | 10 | 11 | 12 | 13 | 14 | 15 |
| 7 | 7 | 8 | 9 | 10 | 11 | 12 | 13 | 14 | 15 | 16 |
| 8 | 8 | 9 | 10 | 11 | 12 | 13 | 14 | 15 | 16 | 17 |
| 9 | 9 | 10 | 11 | 12 | 13 | 14 | 15 | 16 | 17 | 18 |

Table 2.3 Binary, octal and denary addition

✓

### Check your understanding 2.1

1 Do these sums in binary:
- 1101 + 10
- 001 + 11
- 111 + 111
- 110 + 11

2 Copy and complete Table 2.3 to show octal addition.

3 Do these sums in octal:
- 32 + 15
- 45 + 41
- 27 + 61
- 54 + 36

4 Convert all the numbers in questions 1 and 2 into denary, and check your answers are correct.

In theory, there is no limit to the size of numbers that can be used in calculations. Apart from zero, we have an infinite number of whole numbers (and an equally large number of negative numbers) to play with. As well as this, between every pair of consecutive whole numbers there is an infinite number of fractional values; a half, a quarter, two-thirds, etc. On a computer, there is a limit to how many numbers can be represented using a given number of bits.

### Further research 2.2

1 What is the largest number that can be represented:
- using 4 bits?
- using 6 bits?

2 If 10 bits are allocated to represent whole numbers, what range of numbers could be represented? (Hint: Start with 00...00 representing 0 and work out what 11...11 represents.)

Because there is a limit to the range of numbers that can be stored in binary, when you add two numbers (or do a multiplication) even if both numbers are within range, it is possible for the result of the addition or multiplication to be too large to be stored. This is called **overflow**.

## Floating point numbers

At first glance, it seems that the range of numbers that can be represented depends entirely on how many columns of digits you allow. On your electronic calculator, or on your mobile phone calculator, the display may be limited to 8 or 9 characters. You may enter the decimal point so that it appears anywhere within the string of digits. What happens when you try to add a larger number (e.g. 1234 567.8) to a small number (e.g. 12.345 678)? How could you even enter very small and very large numbers (e.g. 0.000 987 765 543 321 or 1234 456 567 789) which need more digits than your display allows?

One solution is to use **standard form**. This cuts down the number of digits required, but it compromises on accuracy. In standard form, 0.000 987 765 543 321 is written as $9.88 \times 10^{-4}$ and 1234 456 567 789 is written as $1.23 \times 10^{12}$. Notice that the first digit is the most significant digit, and then the decimal point is written. The other digits at the tail end of each number are simply ignored so this introduces a level of inaccuracy. In the two examples above, the numbers are written with just 2 decimal places so the accuracy is 'to 3 significant figures'.

### What does it mean?

In standard form, a number is written as a **mantissa** (between 1 and 10, but not equal to 10) multiplied by 10 (the **base**) and raised to a power (called the **exponent**).

In a computer, a similar system called **floating point** exists. Instead of using a single string of bits to represent a number, two strings are used. One represents the mantissa; the other the exponent. The mantissa is assumed to commence with the (binary) point, so it takes a fractional value (anything between 0 and 1, but never equal to 1). In binary, the base is 2, so the exponent gives a power of 2. Table 2.4 shows some examples of standard form and floating point numbers.

| Number (decimal) | Standard form | Binary equivalent | Floating point | | Decimal equivalent |
|---|---|---|---|---|---|
| | | | mantissa | exponent | |
| 0 | $0 \times 10^0$ | 0 | 000 000 | 0000 | $0 \times 2^0$ |
| 1 | $1.0 \times 10^0$ | 1 | 100 000 | 0001 | $0.5 \times 2^1$ |
| 2 | $2.0 \times 10^0$ | 10 | 100 000 | 0010 | $0.5 \times 2^2$ |
| 10 | $1.0 \times 10^1$ | 1 010 | 101 000 | 0100 | $0.625 \times 2^4$ |
| 16 | $1.6 \times 10^1$ | 10 000 | 100 000 | 0101 | $0.5 \times 2^5$ |
| 32 | $3.2 \times 10^1$ | 100 000 | 100 000 | 0110 | $0.5 \times 2^6$ |
| 40 | $4.0 \times 10^1$ | 101 000 | 101 000 | 0110 | $0.625 \times 2^6$ |
| 100 | $1.0 \times 10^2$ | 1 100 100 | 110 010 | 1000 | $0.78125 \times 2^8$ |
| 128 | | | | | |
| 200 | | | | | |
| 5000 | | | | | |
| 5 000 000 | | | | | |

Table 2.4 Examples of standard form and floating point numbers

### Check your understanding 2.2

1 Copy and complete Table 2.4.
2 Splitting 10 bits into two parts increases the range, but reduces the accuracy. What is the largest positive whole number that can be held in floating point using a 6:4 split?
3 Experiment with other splits: 7:3, 5:5, 4:6. Which gives the greatest range?
4 Identify a whole number that is too large to be represented using a 6:4 floating format.
5 Identify a fraction that is too small to be represented using a 6:4 floating format.
6 Suggest some values within the range that can be represented using a 6:4 floating format, but not with 100 per cent accuracy.

### Assessment activity 2.2

1 Demonstrate your ability to add numbers held in at least two different formats, including floating point.
   - Decide on the number of bits you will work with, and on at least two different representations, one of which must be floating point.
   - For each representation, choose two numbers in denary that can be represented, and convert them to binary.
   - Add the two numbers (using binary addition) and then convert your result back to denary.
   - Check your working and then annotate it so it is clear how you achieved your results.

2 Repeat question 1 to show you can calculate the difference between two numbers held in different formats, including floating point. (You can use the same two denary numbers throughout if you wish, but make sure they demonstrate your skill in adding/subtracting in binary.)

3 Repeat question 1 for multiplication and division.
   Be careful about your choice of numbers. Make sure that your answers can also be represented.

## ASCII

### What does it mean?

ASCII stands for American Standard Code for Information Interchange.

ASCII is the recognised standard for representing characters such as the letters of the alphabet and other characters that you see on a keyboard. Groups of 8 bits form a **byte**. With 8 bits, you can represent 256 ($2^8$) values, enough for all the characters in the alphabet and many others besides.

ASCII uses 7 of the 8 bits for its code. The 8th bit is called a **parity** bit; this is used for checking that the code has not been corrupted during storage on, or transfer from, a peripheral device (e.g. a CD-reader) to the computer.

Table 2.5 lists the ASCII code groupings. Notice that hex is a convenient way of writing the code for an ASCII character. It also highlights the way the representations are separated into groups of 32, with the two alphabets starting at 41 (hex) and 61 (hex).

### Check your understanding 2.3

Using Table 2.5, write a message of at most 25 characters in ASCII using the hex code. Swap it with a partner and then (without referring back to the table) try to decode the message. Remember that a space is a character too.

## Bit masks

Although data (numeric or text) may be conveniently stored in one or more bytes, sometimes a single byte may be used to store eight different items of information, each one called a **flag**.

| ASCII codes | Hex values | Character | Comment |
|---|---|---|---|
| 0–31 | 0–1F | Control characters | These codes originally controlled the physical movement of printers, e.g. 'carriage return' |
| 32–64 | 20–40 | Printable characters, e.g. space, !, ", #, ... | These codes are mostly available using the shift key on the keyboard |
| 65–90 | 41–5A | The upper case alphabet, A–Z | The capital letters of the alphabet are all achieved using the shift key or with CAPS LOCK turned on |
| 91–96 | 5B–60 | A few more printable characters | These codes just fill the gap between the two alphabet sets which start at 41(hex) and 61(hex) |
| 97–122 | 61–7A | The lower case alphabet, a–z | The lower case letters are achieved by pressing the letter keys (with CAPS LOCK off) |
| 123–127 | 7B–7F | A few more characters, plus 'delete' | The code 7F (111 1111) represents 'delete' |

Table 2.5 ASCII codes

## Case study: Flags

Flags are used for the synchronisation of communication between a computer and its peripherals, e.g. a printer. A flag is a single bit register or store location, which may be set (on, with value 1) or cleared (off, with value 0).

Because the speed at which a computer works is much quicker than any printer, output for a printer is sent to a **buffer** by the computer, and the data waits there until the printer is ready to print it. One flag is used by the computer to signal that the buffer is full and ready to be printed. The printer notes this, resets the flag, and starts clearing the buffer, i.e. printing the data. Once the printer has cleared the contents of the buffer, the printer sets a different flag, so that the computer knows the buffer is now empty and that it can start to refill it. As soon as the status of any flag is noted, it is reset to zero.

1 Find out what a **DIP switch** is, and examples of where it is used.
2 Think of other examples where individual bits, or groups of bits, are used to hold separate data items.

Controlling individual bits within a byte to set flags on, to reset them, or to test their status, is done using **bit masks**.

## What does it mean?

A **bit mask** is a pattern of 0s and 1s that can be used to isolate the setting of individual bits within another pattern of bits.

### Graphic bitmaps

A black and white VDU screen may have a resolution of 720 **pixels** by 350 rows, a total of 252 000 items of data (either 0 for white or 1 for black) and each data item could be stored in a single bit.

> **What does it mean?**
>
> A **pixel** is the smallest level of control of a graphic image. The picture is broken into rows and each row into separate pixels, each one resulting in a dot (or square) of colour.

For a colour screen, each pixel needs more storage space, depending on the number of colours required. If each pixel has one byte allocated this allows 256 different ($2^8$) colours, but it requires eight times as much storage space.

**Assessment activity 2.3**

1. List the various ways a string of 8 bits might be used to represent data.
2. For each representation, explain the role played by each format and the basic concepts and principles involved.
3. Explain how errors might occur in data representation and how these errors might be identified and possibly corrected.

# Logic and fetch–execute cycle

You need to be able to describe the internal operations of a microprocessor. This will involve delving briefly into an area of mathematics, but first, you need to learn a bit about electronics.

Digital electronics involves **two-state switching circuits** that are designed to operate on voltage pulses in one of two levels: high or low, referred to as logic levels 1 and 0, respectively. These circuits are usually **integrated circuits (ICs)** ranging in complexity from simple logic gates to microprocessors. The actual voltage levels used differ between CMOS and TTL logic families.

> **What does it mean?**
>
> A **two-state switching circuit** is one that can carry one of two values (on or off) according to voltages running through the circuit, each value being transmitted as a pulse.
> An **integrated circuit** combines many logic gates on an individual chip.

- **CMOS devices** operate off supplies ranging from 3 to 15 volts (V), and the logic levels are relative to the supply voltage. A 'high' is anything greater than two-thirds of the positive supply rail and a low is anything less than one-third of the supply. Any voltage between these two states is known as an 'intermediate' state.
- For **TTL devices**, anything below 0.8V is low, anything above 2V is high, and anything else is 'intermediate'.

> **What does it mean?**
>
> **TTL** stands for transistor–transistor logic.
> **CMOS** stands for complementary metal-oxide semiconductor.

## Logic and logic gates

Logic is a part of mathematics that concentrates on there being only two possibilities, true or false, and then proves things 'logically' to be true or false, by the application of some strict rules of combining facts (or assumptions).

One mathematician, George Boole, developed an algebra (**Boolean algebra**) in which propositions (i.e. statements which we might assume to be true) are denoted by symbols (A, B, C, etc.) and can be acted on by symbols that correspond to the 'laws of logic'. Boole's basic concepts include being able to combine propositions as we do in any normal argument:

- If A or B is true, then ...
- If A and B are true, then ...
- If A is not true, then ...

**Venn diagrams** show this in a very simple way. A rectangle is used to denote the whole universe (or whatever it is we are interested in). Circles are then used to denote sets of things within our universe. Things that are true are written inside a circle; those that are false lie outside the circle, but within the rectangle. There is no other option, you cannot sit on the fence, i.e. be on the line of the circle. Figure 2.1 shows how the universe can therefore be divided into two parts; true and false (inside and outside circle).

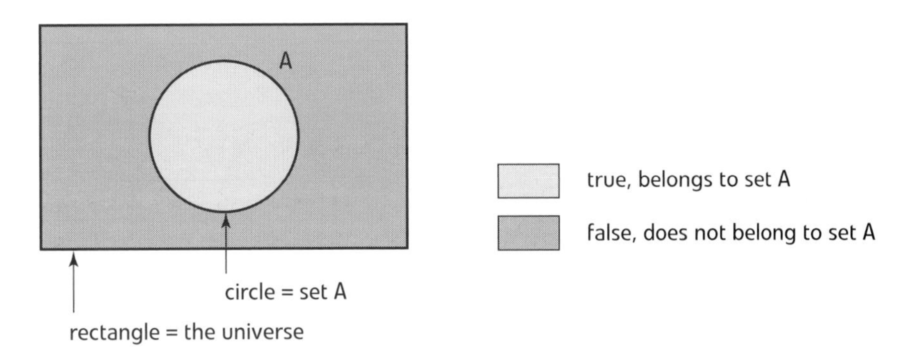


Figure 2.1 A Venn diagram showing how the universe can be divided into two parts

Figure 2.2 shows that, if another set is introduced, the two sets A and B may or may not overlap. Also, B could be entirely inside A, or vice versa.

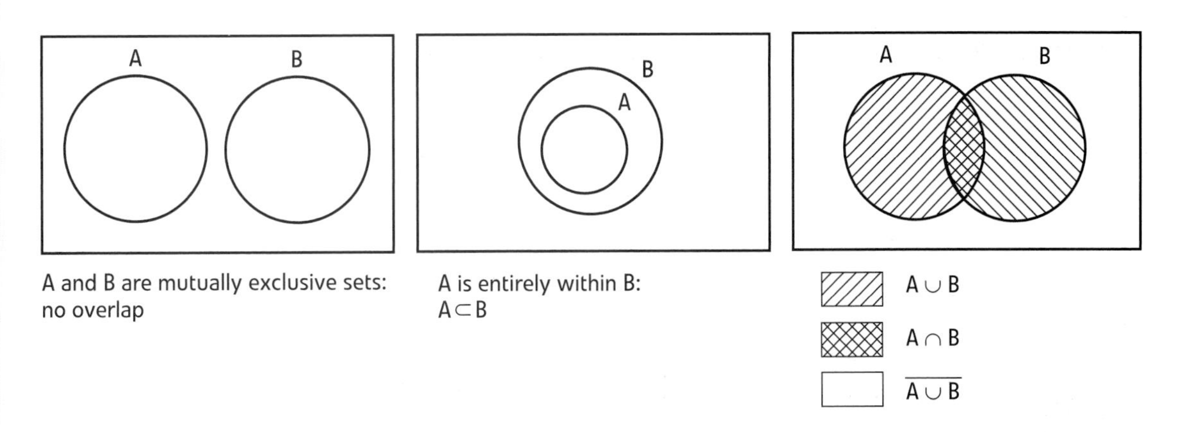


Figure 2.2 Venn diagrams showing mutual exclusivity, intersection, union and subset

- Sets that do not overlap are called **mutually exclusive**.
- Sets which lie entirely within another set are called **subsets** (written as $A \subset B$ for 'A is contained within B', i.e. A is a subset of B).
- The area where any overlap does occur is called the **intersection** of the two sets (written as $A \cap B$ and thought of as 'A and B').
- The combined area of the two circles for A and B, including the overlap, is called the **union** of A and B (written as $A \cup B$ and thought of a 'A or B or both').

Intersection and union are logical operators similar to operators like addition, subtraction, multiplication and division. Addition and subtraction are used on numbers to produce more numbers. Logical operators, though, are used with sets like A and B, to produce more sets: $A \cup B$ and $A \cap B$.

Introducing a third set, C, complicates the Venn diagram further, but the intersection of the three sets, in pairs or altogether, can be clearly seen. This method then falls down if you introduce a fourth set. Figure 2.3 shows how the 'universe' of the numbers 1–20 can be categorised into different types of number; prime (A), even (B) and square (C).

A = {2, 3, 5, 7, 11, 13, 17, 19}
B = {2, 4, 6, 8, 10, 12, 14, 16, 18, 20}
C = {1, 4, 9, 16}

Checking where a number lies within the Venn diagram will determine what kind of number it is.

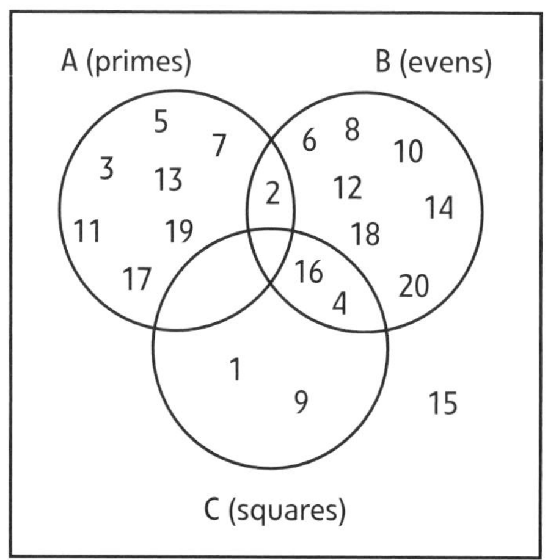


Figure 2.3 Venn diagram for universe of numbers 1–20

## Check your understanding 2.4

1. In small groups, brainstorm to create a list of names of 12 people all belonging to one 'universe' such as the world of politics, the world of music, or the world of your college.
2. For your list of 12 people, decide on at most three categories, and then produce a Venn diagram to show who belongs to which category. For the world of politics, your categories could be 'in the cabinet', 'female' and 'Labour'.

For individuals to appear in a particular section of your Venn diagram in Check your understanding 4, they had to pass the test of belonging to the category within which the section lies.

- To appear in the area $A \cup B$, either A or B or both are true for that individual.

- Looking more closely, to appear in A, A must be true; and to appear in B, B must be true.
- So, to appear in the area A ∩ B, A must be true as well as B for the individual.

You could think of this process as a series of barriers or gates, which, at each stage, separate individuals into two types: those who can pass through and those who cannot, i.e. those who are within a circle and those who are outside it.

**Logic gates** are the building blocks of computers. These simple transistorised electronic devices respond to electrical signals that pass through them. The input electrical signals may be high voltage (representing logic 1 or 'true') or low voltage (representing logic 0 or 'false'). The output signal is also high or low (logic 1 or logic 0, true or false) and will depend on the type of gate and the input signals received.

- An **AND gate** accepts two signals and only outputs a high/true/logic 1 signal when both inputs are high/true/logic 1.
- An **OR gate** accepts two signals and outputs a high/true/logic 1 signal if *one* or *both* of the two inputs is high/true/logic 1. An OR gate will *only* output a low/false/logic 0 signal if both inputs are low/false/logic 0.
- A **NOT gate** accepts a single input signal and *inverts* it: a high/true/logic 1 is turned into a low/false/logic 0, and a low/false/logic 0 is turned into a high/true/logic 1.

For two inputs A and B, each having two possible values, T (true) or F (false), there are four possible combinations (FF, FT, TF, TT). The output for each of these four inputs can be illustrated using a **truth table**. Table 2.6 shows the truth tables for AND, OR and NOT. Notice the order of the inputs: F before T.

| Input A | Input B | Output A AND B |
|---|---|---|
| F | F | F |
| F | T | F |
| T | F | F |
| T | T | T |

| Input A | Input B | Output A OR B |
|---|---|---|
| F | F | F |
| F | T | T |
| T | F | T |
| T | T | T |

| Input A | Output NOT A |
|---|---|
| F | T |
| T | F |

Table 2.6 Truth tables for AND, OR and NOT

NAND ('not AND') and NOR ('not OR') are two more logic gates, derived from AND, OR and NOT.

**What does it mean?**

NAND means NOT(A AND B). NOR means NOT(A OR B)

Using truth tables, it is possible to map the outcome for any two inputs through a circuit, i.e. a series of logic gates. Table 2.7 shows the outcome for NOT(A and B), simply by extending the AND table.

| A | B | A AND B | NAND (A,B) |
|---|---|---|---|
| F | F | F | T |
| F | T | F | T |
| T | F | F | T |
| T | T | T | F |

Table 2.7 NAND truth table

### Check your understanding 2.5

1 Write a truth table for NOR by extending the OR table.

2 Here are two more logical operators:

- EOR = Exclusive OR = (A OR B) AND NOT (A AND B) = (A OR B) AND (A NAND B)
- ENOR = Exclusive NOR = NOT (A EOR B)

Write truth tables for these two logic operators. Be careful that the order of F and T as inputs matches the tables.

So far we have been considering only two inputs. In a computer, a string of these pairs of inputs (eight in total) form input bytes, and the output is also a byte. Notice also two important facts:

- Combining a logic 0/false input with any other input through an AND gate gives a logic 0/false output; i.e. if you want to, for any input, you can guarantee a logic 0 output.
- Combining a logic 1/true input with any other input through an OR gate will give a logic 1/true output; i.e. if you want to, you can guarantee a logic 1 output.

These two facts allow us to set up bit masks to control the setting of individual bits within an 8-bit string, i.e. turn them on (logic 1/true) or off (logic 0/false). Suppose bits 4 and 5 of a byte are used to determine the setting of a feature: BB BB XX BB. The other 6 bits in this byte, shown as B, convey other information and their settings must be preserved. Notice that:

(BB BB XX BB) AND (00 00 11 00) = 00 00 XX 00

00 00 11 00 is called the **mask**. ANDing the mask with the original data isolates bits 4 and 5.

### Check your understanding 2.6

1 A floating point number is held in 8 bits, with 4 bits each for the mantissa and exponent.

- What mask will isolate the bits that represent the mantissa?
- What mask will isolate the bits that represent the exponent?

2 A computer instruction in machine code comprises an opcode and an address. Suppose that the 8-bit instruction is split 3:5.

- What mask will isolate the opcode?
- What mask will isolate the address part of the instruction?

### What does it mean?

**Opcode** is short for operation code. For each instruction in a language's instruction set, a unique numerical opcode is assigned. Programmers of assembly language use **mnemonics** for these opcodes.

In constructing circuits using AND/OR/NOT/NAND/NOR/EOR/ENOR logic gates, special symbols are used to denote each type of gate (Figure 2.4). Note that there are two standards for these symbols: the British standard 3939 and the American MIL/ANSI.

Notice that, in both systems, a small circle is used to denote NOT. The British system then uses a square with a label to distinguish between AND and OR, while the American system has three distinctive shapes for NOT, AND and OR.

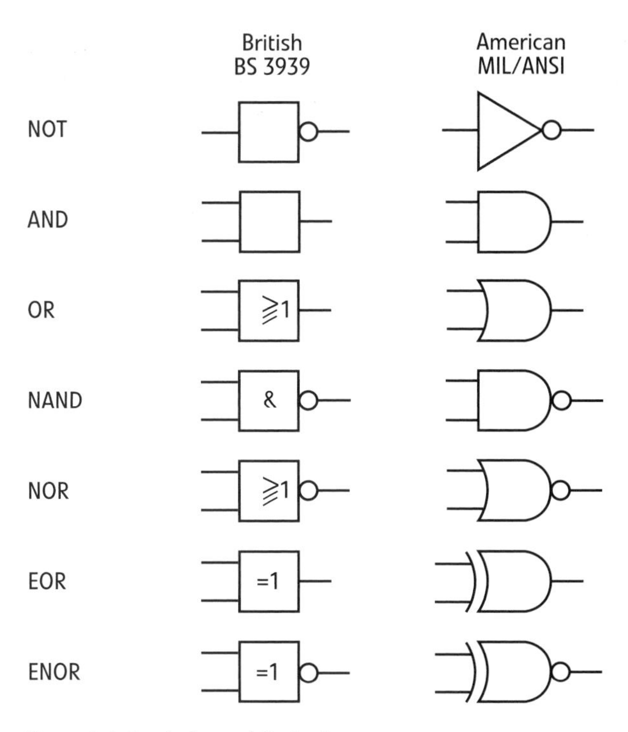


Figure 2.4 Symbols used for logic gates

## Case study: Generating logic 1 or logic 0

The first and simplest use of the AND/OR/NOT gates is to generate logic 1 or logic 0. Figure 2.5a shows how connecting appropriate input(s) to the positive supply rail or to the zero volt rail results in logic 1. Figure 2.5b shows how logic 0 can be obtained.

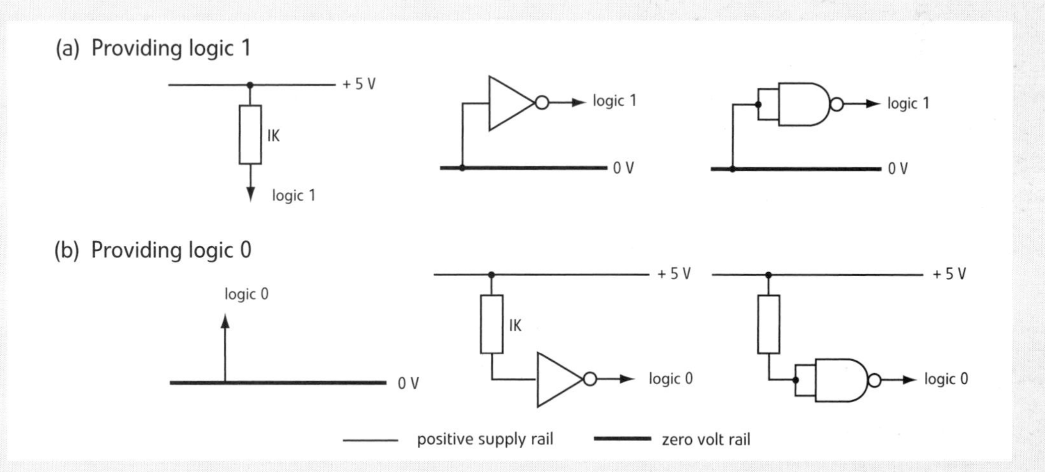


Figure 2.5 Using positive supply rail or zero volt rail to generate (a) logic 1 and (b) logic 0

Notes: As shown in the first diagram of part (a), a logic 1 should be obtained by the use of a pull-up resistor (1 kΩ to 10 kΩ) so that the current supplied to the gate is limited; this also protects against unpredictable rises in the supply voltage. The alternative arrangements of providing logic 1 have the advantage of shorting the input to the ground in the case of failure.

1 Copy each of the truth tables for AND, OR and NOT, writing 1 for true and 0 for false, to check that the input does produce the output.
2 Produce truth tables for each of the circuits involving gates shown in Figure 2.5 to confirm their outputs.

## Simple arrays of logic gates

One of the wonders of computer design is that, using just these two gates (NAND and NOT), and applying some of Boole's logic, all kinds of arithmetic can be done and the high-speed processing of data that we now take for granted can be achieved.

### Further research 2.3

1 Copy each of the circuits shown in Figure 2.6 and label the type of gates being used.

2 For each circuit, create a truth table to find out which gate the given combination of NAND and NOR gates replaces.

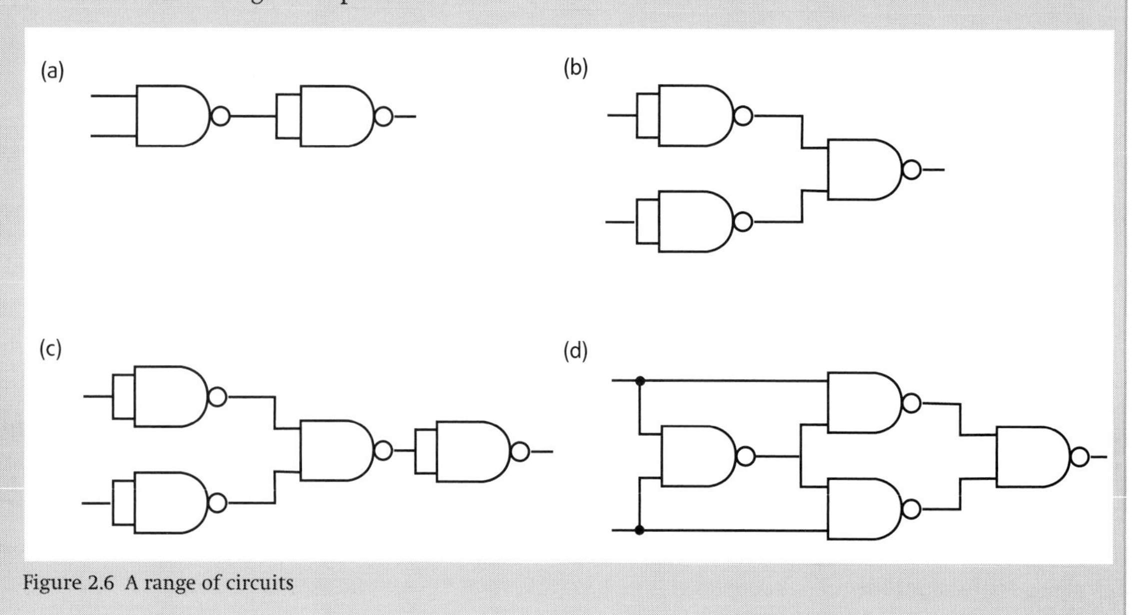


Figure 2.6 A range of circuits

We will now see how, by linking a few logic gates together, it is possible to carry out addition in binary. Table 2.8 shows the outputs needed when adding two single bits:

0 + 0 = 0

0 + 1 = 1 + 0 = 1

1 + 1 = 0 carry 1

| Input A | Input B | Output A AND B | Output A EOR B |
|---|---|---|---|
| 0 | 0 | 0 | 0 |
| 0 | 1 | 0 | 1 |
| 1 | 0 | 0 | 1 |
| 1 | 1 | 1 | 0 |

Table 2.8 Truth table for adding two single bits

Notice that putting both inputs through an EOR gate will give the 'units' column; putting the same two inputs through an AND gate will give the carry value. This circuit is called a **half adder** (Figure 2.7a).

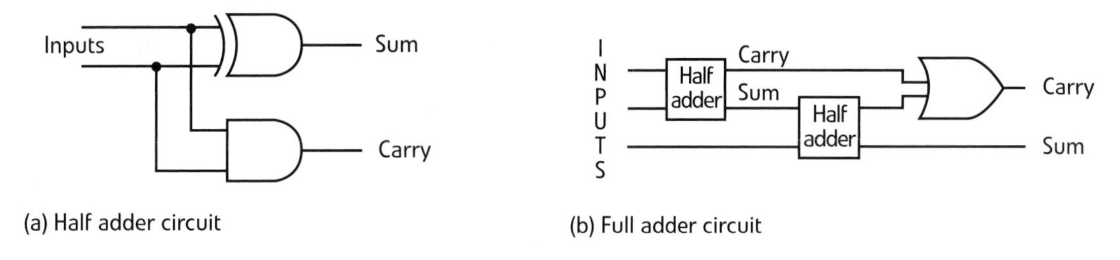


Figure 2.7 Half adder circuit and full adder circuit

If you were to use just NAND gates, this half adder would require two NAND gates for the AND gate, and a further four NAND gates for the EOR gate. However, having established the practicality of creating circuits with just the one gate, we tend to draw circuit diagrams using as few gates as possible. The **full adder** circuit takes the carry bit and includes it in the next stage of adding (in the same way as you would when moving to the next column to your left). So, there are actually three inputs, as shown in Figure 2.7b. Note that this circuit is built from half adder circuits plus an OR gate.

## Further research 2.4

Produce a truth table for the full adder circuit to confirm that it does produce the desired output.

In combining logic gates, the output has depended only on the inputs. If, instead, the output from a gate is fed back into the circuit, it is called a **sequential logic circuit**. The basic sequential logic circuit element is called a **bistable** (also called a **flip-flop** and referred to as a **latch**). It has two inputs (set and reset) and two outputs (Q and $\overline{Q}$).

There are two designs for a bistable, as shown in Figure 2.8: one based on the NAND gate and set/reset with logic 0; and the other with NOR gates and set/reset with logic 1. Both have the same effect; to set Q on/off according to the input being set/reset; and $\overline{Q}$ has the opposite value to Q.

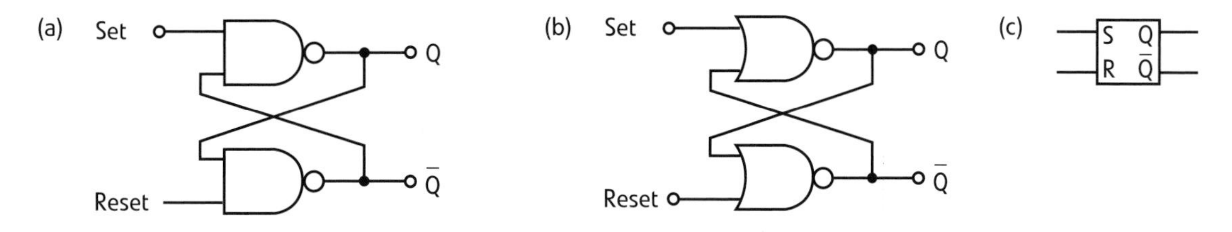


Figure 2.8 Flip-flop circuitry: (a) NAND gate bistable; (b) NOR gate bistable; (c) symbol to the set/reset (SR) bistable

## Further research 2.5

In pairs, produce the truth tables for both of the set/reset bistable circuits, one each. Check each other's table.

Flip-flops 'remember' their previous states, and so they are used in **registers**, such as **counters**.

**What does it mean?**

A **register** is a location where data or control information is stored, and on which limited arithmetic and logical operations can be carried out.
A **counter** is a memory location for data that needs to increase or decrease by 1, i.e. to count.

## Fetch–execute cycle

The computer may appear to be an amazingly clever machine, capable of almost anything. However, this apparent cleverness is due to one basic ability: to carry out instructions. The fact that computers do this tirelessly and continuously (except when they crash) is what makes them so invaluable.

The way it works is incredibly simple. Once the computer starts, all it does is 'do as it is told'. It has, in its memory, lots of instructions, and it carries them out one by one, in much the same way as you might follow a recipe in a cookery book. It keeps track of which instruction it is on now and, unless told otherwise, will do the next (sequential) instruction as soon as one has been completed. It only deviates from this simple sequence if told to 'branch'; i.e. go to a different instruction from the one that it would normally follow. Figure 2.9 shows how this 'program' works: the fetch–execute cycle, sometimes called the fetch–decode–execute cycle.

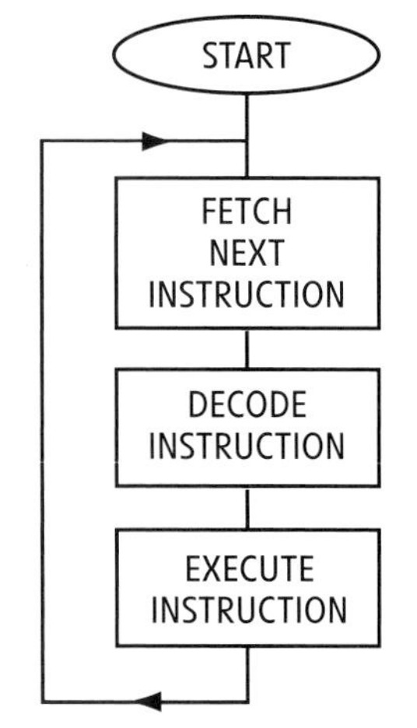

Figure 2.9 The fetch–execute cycle

The first and last boxes are self explanatory. The second box says: decode instruction. So, what kind of instructions can the computer understand? The simplest type of instructions are single-address instructions, and the minimum number of these that need to be offered is ten, as listed in Table 2.9.

| Instruction | Opcode | Operand | Execution |
|---|---|---|---|
| INPUT | 0 | To data address | 3, 8 |
| OUTPUT | 1 | From data address | 3, 9 |
| LOAD (to accumulator) | 2 | From data address | 3,5, b |
| STORE (to memory) | 3 | To data address | 3, 4 |
| ADD (to accumulator) | 4 | From data address | 3, 5, b, +a |
| SUB (from accumulator) | 5 | From data address | 3, 5, b, –a |
| GOTO instruction address | 6 | Instruction address | c |
| BRZA (branch on zero accumulator) | 7 | Instruction address | 6 = a 7TC/F |
| BRLA (branch on accumulator < 0) | 8 | Instruction address | 6 < a 7TC/F |
| STOP | 9 | | |

Table 2.9 Minimal instruction set

Most **instruction sets** offer more than single-address instructions, including the logical instructions (AND and OR) but, for the purposes of this explanation of the fetch–execute cycle, we will restrict ourselves to this minimal instruction set.

### What does it mean?

An **instruction set** is the complete list of instructions that a particular processor can perform. The instruction set, together with the rules of **syntax** (grammar), form a **programming language.**

### Further research 2.6

1 Find some examples of instruction sets for low-level languages.
2 Find out what is meant by 'single-address' instruction. Find an example of a two-address instruction. Can you think of any need for a three-address instruction?
3 Find out what shift instructions do. Why might they be needed?
4 Find out what INC and DEC might be used for.
5 Investigate other instruction types such as PUSH and POP.
6 Find out what instructions might be needed to offer the facility to include subroutines in a program.

The two right-hand columns of Table 2.9 explain what the instruction involves and how it is achieved. The 'execution cycle' column, in particular, shows the route the data will take, and links in with Figure 2.11. First though, to see how the simple fetch–execute cycle fits into the greater scheme of things within a microprocessor, we need to look at the essential parts of a microprocessor (Figure 2.10).

- **Input**: receives data from the outside world.
- **Store:** retains the data, but is lost when the processor is switched off.
- **Backing store:** retains the data, even when the processor is switched off.
- **Central processing unit (CPU):** comprising the **arithmetic and logic unit** (ALU) and **control unit.**
- **Output:** sends data back to the outside world.

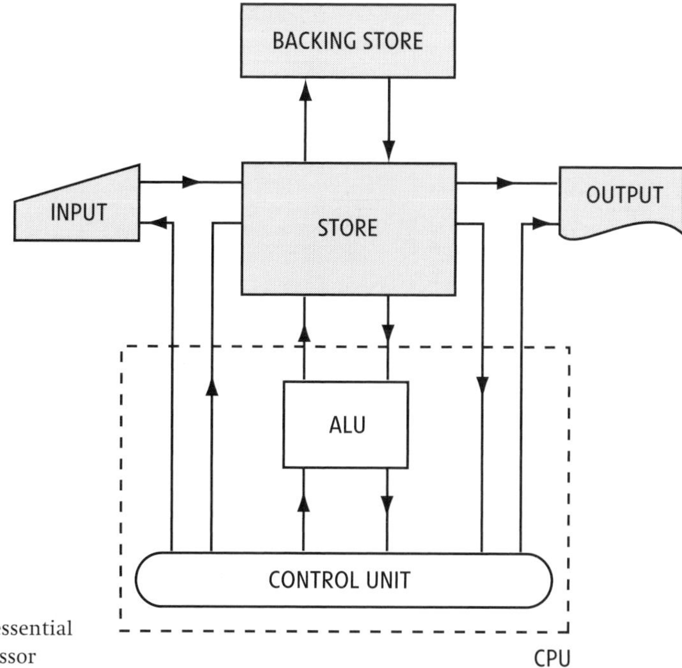


Figure 2.10 The five essential parts of a microprocessor

Figure 2.11 shows these components (excluding the backing store) in more detail, and how these components are linked by **buses**.

## What does it mean?

A **bus** is a pathway within a microprocessor, shared by signals travelling between the various parts of the microprocessor. A simple bus may comprise eight wires each carrying 1s or 0s. More advanced buses, such as the **USB (universal serial bus)**, allow data to be transferred more quickly, e.g. 12 Mbps (12 million bits per second).

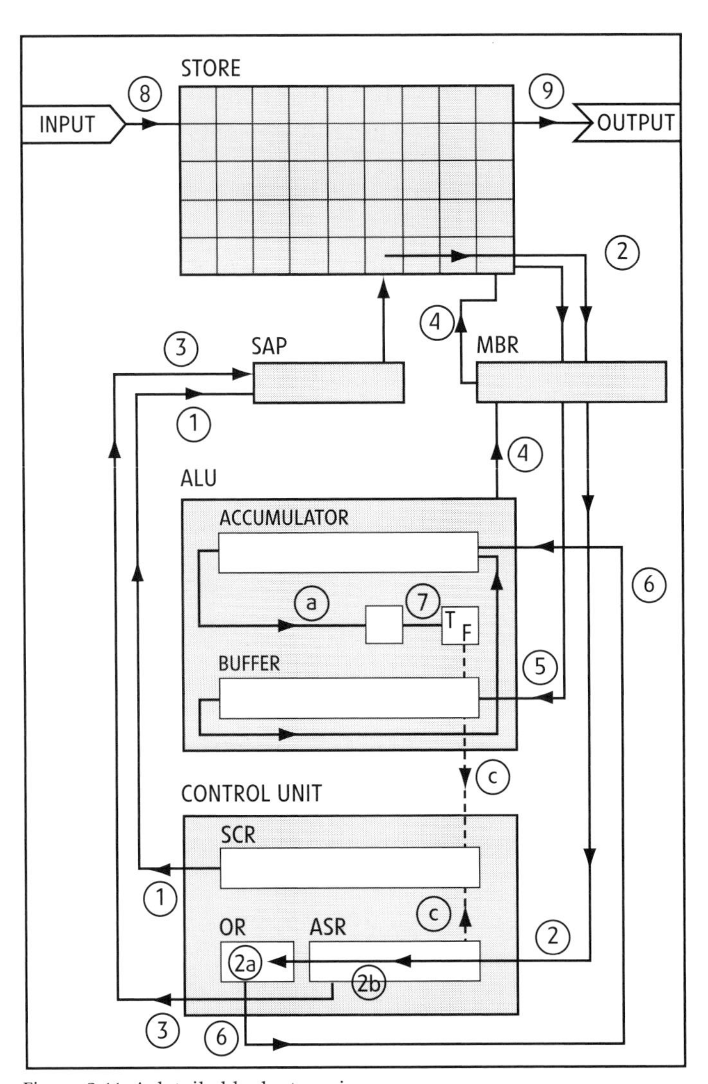

Figure 2.11 A detailed look at a microprocessor

Notice that the CPU contains some registers. All of these have a role to play in the fetch–execute cycle.

- The **IR (instruction register)** or **CIR (current instruction register)** splits into the **OR (operand register)** and **ASR (address storage register)**. The OR holds the operand part of the instruction to be executed, i.e. the part that determines what action is to be taken. The ASR holds the remainder of the instruction to be executed, i.e. the address of the data that is needed for the instruction to be executed. If the operand is a branching code, then the ASR will hold the address of the instruction that the program must execute next.

- The **accumulator** (AC) is the one register where arithmetic takes place. It may be cleared or complemented, and its contents may be rotated left or right.
- The **buffer** is an additional register within the ALU, needed for certain instructions.
- The **SCR (sequence control register)** or **PC (program counter)** holds the address of the next instruction to be obeyed in main memory. It is a counter and can be incremented by 1. Alternatively, if branching is needed, its contents may be overwritten with the address of the next instruction to be executed.
- The **SAP (storage address pointer)** or **MAR (memory address register)** holds an address of a memory location, i.e. points to the location from where the next transfer of data will happen, or where the next data transfer will go to, in memory.
- The **MBR (memory buffer register)** is used for all transfers between the central processor registers and the memory store. It holds the data or instruction that is to be transferred to or from main memory.

**Check your understanding 2.7**

1 Find out what is meant by the contents of the AC being 'complemented'.
2 Think of situations where it might be useful to rotate the contents of a register.

The fetch–execute cycle uses the above registers as follows.

- The contents of the SCR are copied to the SAP, moving along bus line 1.
- The instruction pointed to by the SAP is transferred to the control unit via the MBR, moving along bus line 2.
- The SCR is updated by 1 so that it points to the next instruction that will need to be fetched (counter c).

This completes the 'fetch' part of the fetch–decode–execute cycle. The instruction is safely stored in the CIR in the control unit, ready to be executed.

- The opcode in the CIR is separated from the operand and placed in the OR (bus line 2a). It now needs to be validated. Is it one of the opcodes recognised by the computer? If it is not, there is an error to be flagged. The computer cannot make further progress. If it is a recognised code, a series of transfers will take place, according to the type of instruction, and determined by a table of values within the computer (fetched and executed in much the same way) as shown in Table 2.9 on page 56.
- If the instruction is an unconditional branching instruction, the address in the operand, i.e. in the ASR, is copied to the SCR (bus line e), overwriting its previously updated value. This will result in a change in the sequence of instructions followed, as required.
- If the branch is conditional, it will depend on a test as to whether the SCR is overwritten.

The routes that data takes are given in Table 2.9.

**Check your understanding 2.8**

What size bus (i.e. how many bits) would be needed to access a store of memory 1 Mb in size?

### Clock and control signals

We now have a vision of pulses of 0s and 1s travelling along buses and the net result is a program executed. This activity needs more than just a plan, i.e. a list of instructions to be followed. The **timing** is important. The microprocessor needs a conductor, i.e. something to make sure everything keeps to time. The control unit acts as a conductor in a microprocessor. It sends timing pulses to synchronise activity. It also sends coded messages to the peripherals (for input and output) along the **control bus**. Just like the data bus, a control bus links these devices to the control unit and allows communication between it and them.

**Further research 2.7**

1 Find out at what speeds various devices work.
2 Find out what control signals might pass between the control unit and a printer.

**Assessment activity 2.4**

1 Describe, with the aid of diagrams, the hardware (including logic gates, registers, buses, CU, ALU and memory) and its function within a model microprocessor.
2 Describe the function of the fetch–decode–execute cycle and its relationship to the workings of a microprocessor, making detailed reference to the role played by hardware and software in this relationship

# 2.2 Computer systems hardware

In this section, you will learn how to select, design and build a computer system to meet a user's needs. You will also learn about the safety issues involved, gain an understanding of disk tools that you might use to maintain software and hardware, and learn to locate and repair faults.

## Computer selection and design

To select and design a computer you will need to analyse user needs and select hardware matched to a machine specification. The equipment will fall into the following broad categories:

- **input devices** such as a keyboard, a mouse, scanners or digital cameras
- **storage devices** including all input/output devices such as disc drives (hard disc drives, floppy disk drives, CD drives) and any other devices that may be used for long-term storage: e.g. Zip drives
- **output devices** such as screens (including touch screens), printers (inkjet, laser, black and white or colour)
- **processor**, which may contain other items of equipment such as hard disc, floppy disk drives, etc.
- **communications devices** such as modems.

Nowadays, computers may be supplied with preloaded software, and it may be advantageous for the buyer to opt for this, rather than buy the software separately and load everything from scratch. However, a user may need software over and above that offered, so you may need to select additional software, or choose an upgrade option.

## Further research 2.8

1. For your own PC, or another of your choosing, list the hardware with full technical details.
2. For each item of hardware, list its main functions and what purpose it serves as part of your system.
3. List the six most used software items on your system. For each one, identify which items of hardware are essential for its operation.
4. Identify any items of hardware that are surplus to your requirements. Explain why.
5. Identify any additional hardware or upgrades that might prove useful, with reasons.
6. Research costings of additional/replacement hardware and make a case for its purchase.

Table 2.10 gives a checklist of software that might be needed and the features that may influence a buying decision. Table 2.11 gives a similar checklist for equipment.

| Application | Purpose |
|---|---|
| Word processing | To input text via a keyboard or a stored text file. To process text by adding new text and deleting text. To format text. To produce documents. |
| Graphics | To capture screen images or generate new images. To process images by enlargement, rotation, cropping, etc. To produce graphics. |
| DTP | To combine material from text and graphics within a page layout. To produce documents. |
| Presentation | To input text and graphic images onto slide formats. To control movement from one slide to the next and navigation within the presentation sequence. To generate notes to accompany a presentation. To produce a slideshow. |
| Spreadsheet | To input text labels and numeric data. To generate formulae based on data within cells. To create charts from numerical data. To produce statistical information. |
| Database | To input text and numbers and graphics into a structure. To amend the data within the structure. To interrogate (search) the data and produce new information. To sort the data and present it in a given order. To produce answers to queries. |
| Communication | To transfer data from one computer to another, e.g. via e-mail. To code the outgoing data ready for transmission, and decode incoming data. |

Table 2.10 A software checklist

| Generic type | Particular type | Special features |
|---|---|---|
| INPUT | Keyboard | QWERTY keyboard is standard, but some applications may require a concept keyboard. |
| | Mouse | Mouse design can be very simple: left and right buttons. They may include a central roller button. They may use infra-red rather than a cable connection. |
| | Scanner | Scanners may be single purpose or incorporate other features such as 'straight to fax'. |
| | Digital camera | As with 'manual' cameras, there is a wide range to choose from. Resolution from 2.0 MP upwards; optical zoom (2×, 3×, etc.); digital zoom (3.2×, 3.6×, 6×); varying sizes of LCD to view the pictures (1.8″ LCD, 2.5″ LCD) and other features, e.g. fast autofocus. Also the option for a video camera, e.g. with Bluetooth technology. |
| | Joystick | May only be needed for certain applications, e.g. games. |
| PROCESSOR | Microprocessor | The choice lies in the chip (Intel Pentium, Intel Celeron, etc.), the processor speed (1.8GHz, 2.0GHz, 2.2GHz, etc.) with possibly extra enhancements (e.g. Intel Speedstep Technology). |
| STORAGE | Hard disc drive | SCSI-based hard drives may give a better performance, but E-IDE drives provide a more cost-effective solution. |
| | Floppy disk drives | May not be needed, apart from linking to data held on older systems. |
| | CD/DVD drive | As technology progresses, it is sensible to buy the best, so DVD may be preferred to CD. At least one DVD/CD drive should be recordable. |
| OUTPUT | Screen/monitor | LCD screens save space on a desktop, use less power, and look good, but CRT monitors provide the best resolution. Sizes range from 15″ upwards. |
| | Printer | Printers are available for black and white printing, or colour prining. The printing may be by laser or ink jet. |
| EXTRAS | Modem | Modems can be in-built or separate from the processor, but linked via a cable. |

Table 2.11 A hardware checklist

?

### What does it mean?

MP = Mega pixels, E-IDE = enhanced intelligent drive electronics, SCSI = small-computer system interface, LCD = liquid crystal display, CRT = cathode ray tube

**Assessment activity 2.5**

1 Karen is a keen amateur photographer. She has a PC but it is now four years old, and she is thinking about replacing it with a modern PC (one that will allow her to process her photos). She expects to buy a digital camera, plus whatever equipment she needs to go with it. She used her old PC for writing letters and keeping track of her finances, and she has a database of all her photos. She would like to transfer this data to the new PC.
   - How would you advise Karen?
   - Write a shopping list for her, with price estimates, giving her some choice in case your total package costs more than she is willing to spend in one go.

2 Neil is the editor of a technical journal which is printed four times each year. Papers are submitted to him for inclusion in the journal by specialists from all over the world. Each paper is about 20 A4 pages in length and can include as many as six photos or illustrations. Each issue of the journal comprises approximately 12 papers. Neil photocopies the papers and arranges for them to be vetted by a team of reviewers. The papers that are successful (about 60%) are then edited, ready for publication. At present, most papers arrive as hard copy, but some come with an accompanying floppy disk file. The artwork all arrives as hard copy and Neil sends them straight on to his typesetter to process and include in the printed journal. A few contributors, and most of his reviewers, do have e-mail facilities, so Neil would like to encourage them to send (and accept receipt of) papers as attached files. He would also like to get the papers ready for printing before sending them to the printer. In addition, he would like to send the papers to a website.
   - Recommend a suitable hardware configuration for Neil, listing all hardware and software requirements.
   - Make recommendations for software that his reviewers might need to have installed.
   - Suggest what instructions Neil might give to prospective contributors, so that the entire process can be electronic.
   - Suggest how Neil might take more control over the preparation of the papers, supplying his typesetter with material that is ready to go to print and/or be placed on the Internet.

# PC build

You need to be able to build and configure a PC to specification using appropriate safety and ESD precautions as appropriate.

**What does it mean?**

ESD stands for European Safety Directive. These are issued by the European Parliament and are adopted by the member countries of the EU.

**Further research 2.9**

1 Search the Internet for information on relevant European Safety Directives. Make notes on your findings.

2 Compare your findings with others and, between you, prepare a list of 'rules' for the safe construction of PCs.

Your teacher will present you with the various components needed to build a PC, and it will be your task to put them together and make sure they work together.

- If the system is brand new, there should be instructions supplied by the vendor. Read these carefully, and make sure you have received everything, especially everything that you have paid for.
- Clear a space, ready for the assembled PC. Computers work better if they are in a dust-free environment. Wipe down the surface it will rest on, and make sure there is nothing above it that might fall on it. Other aspects of the environment are also important for the prospective user, such as lighting, flooring and seating. These aspects are covered in Unit 12.
- Ensure your hands are clean and dry. Wet hands are not a good idea when working with electrical equipment. Make sure long hair is tied back, neck ties do not hang free, and no jewellery is likely to catch in the equipment. If your eyesight requires you to wear glasses for close work, put them on.
- Make sure no equipment is plugged into a mains socket. As a safety precaution, you should not connect (or disconnect) equipment while there is a power supply connection to the computer, even if the power socket is switched off.
- Make sure that, when it is connected, you will have sufficient sockets within easy reach to be able to supply to all devices that need them. You will not want to move the PC after everything has been connected.
- Start with the most important item, the processor. Place it approximately where it needs to go, but turn the back towards you. At the back, the processor has several **ports** into which you will need to attach the cables for each peripheral. These ports are often colour coded and the cable connector may have the same colour so that it is very easy to match them up. Ports may also have a picture showing what kind of peripheral is expected to be attached. A similar picture may be embossed on the cable connector too, again making it easy to make a match. If you have been supplied with connection instructions, read them.

Figure 2.12 shows the back of a PC with the cables for a screen and keyboard attached. Notice that the processor needs a power supply (1); the screen power (2) needs to be attached to the auxiliary power supply port on the processor (3) as well as by connecting cable (4). The keyboard takes its supply from the processor so only has a connecting cable (5).

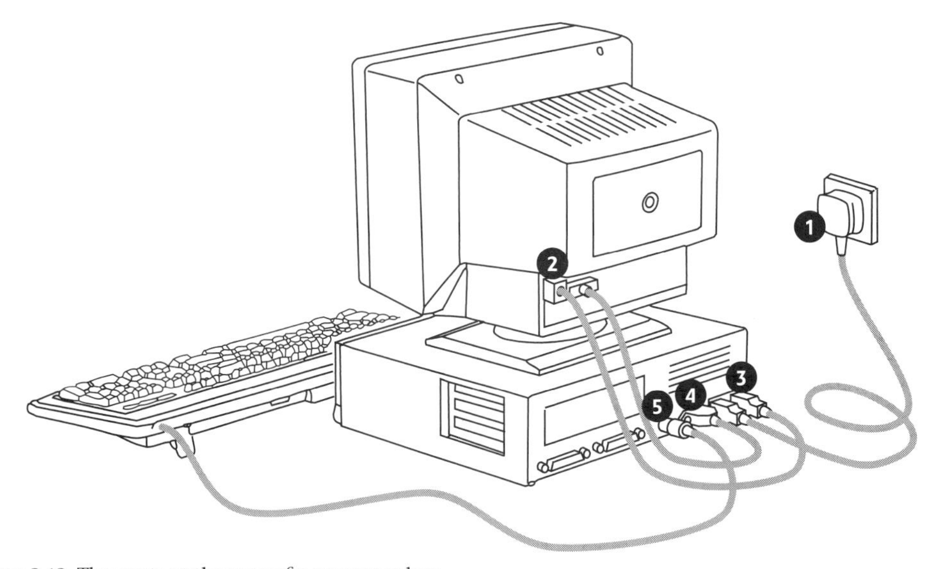


Figure 2.12 The ports at the rear of a processor box

- For each peripheral that needs to be attached, identify which ones have their own power supply, and make sure you have the appropriate cable for it. Attach this cable but do not plug it into the mains. Then, again for each peripheral, check that you have the correct cable to connect it to the PC. Do not connect anything; just check so that you are sure you have everything you need, and no extra cables, or peripherals without cables.
- Look once more at the back of the processor so you are familiar with all the ports. Look in particular at the **serial** and **parallel** ports. They are quite different so you should be able to distinguish them from each other and all the other ports. Figure 2.13 shows what the serial and parallel ports look like, what their connectors look like and how to connect them.

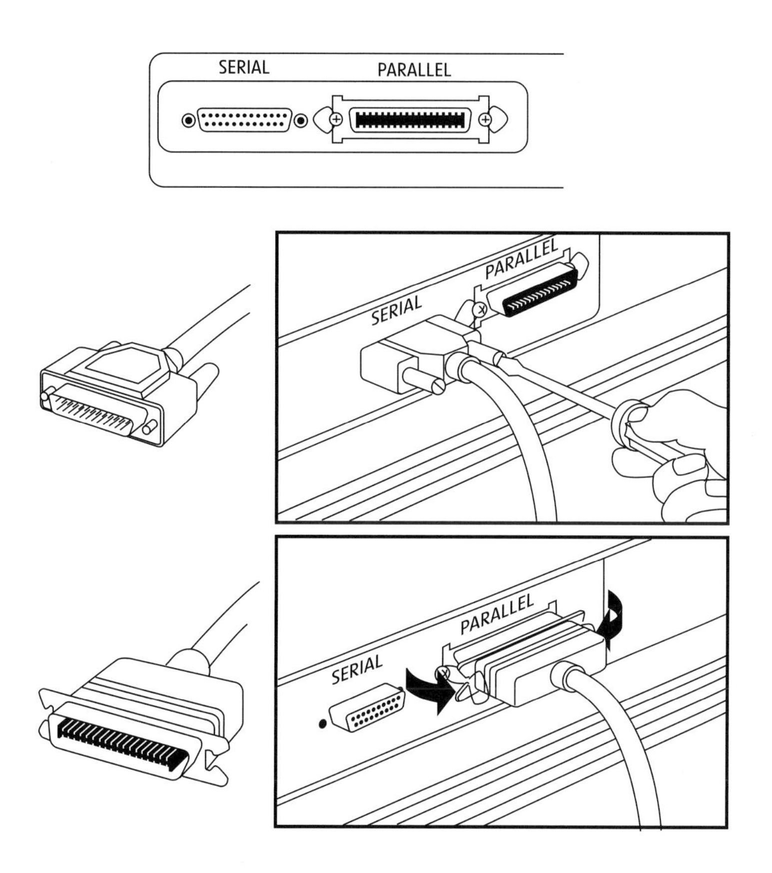


Figure 2.13 Serial and parallel ports

- Printers can be connected either by a serial port or by a parallel port. One other option is via a **USB (universal serial bus)** port. Many other peripherals may also be connected via the USB port, e.g. scanners, infrared mice, etc. Figure 2.14 shows the USB port being used for a scanner and for a printer.
- Notice also the ports used for the keyboard, mouse (if not via the USB port), any microphone and/or speaker system, and modem. Figure 2.15 shows examples of how these might look.
- When you think you have identified all the ports you are going to need, turn the processor around to face the right way for later use. Starting with the largest and/or heaviest items, place each peripheral in its correct position and attach it to the port at the back of the processor. Press the connectors in firmly, holding the front side of the processor to give some stability. Some connectors will need to be screwed into place; do not tighten them too much.

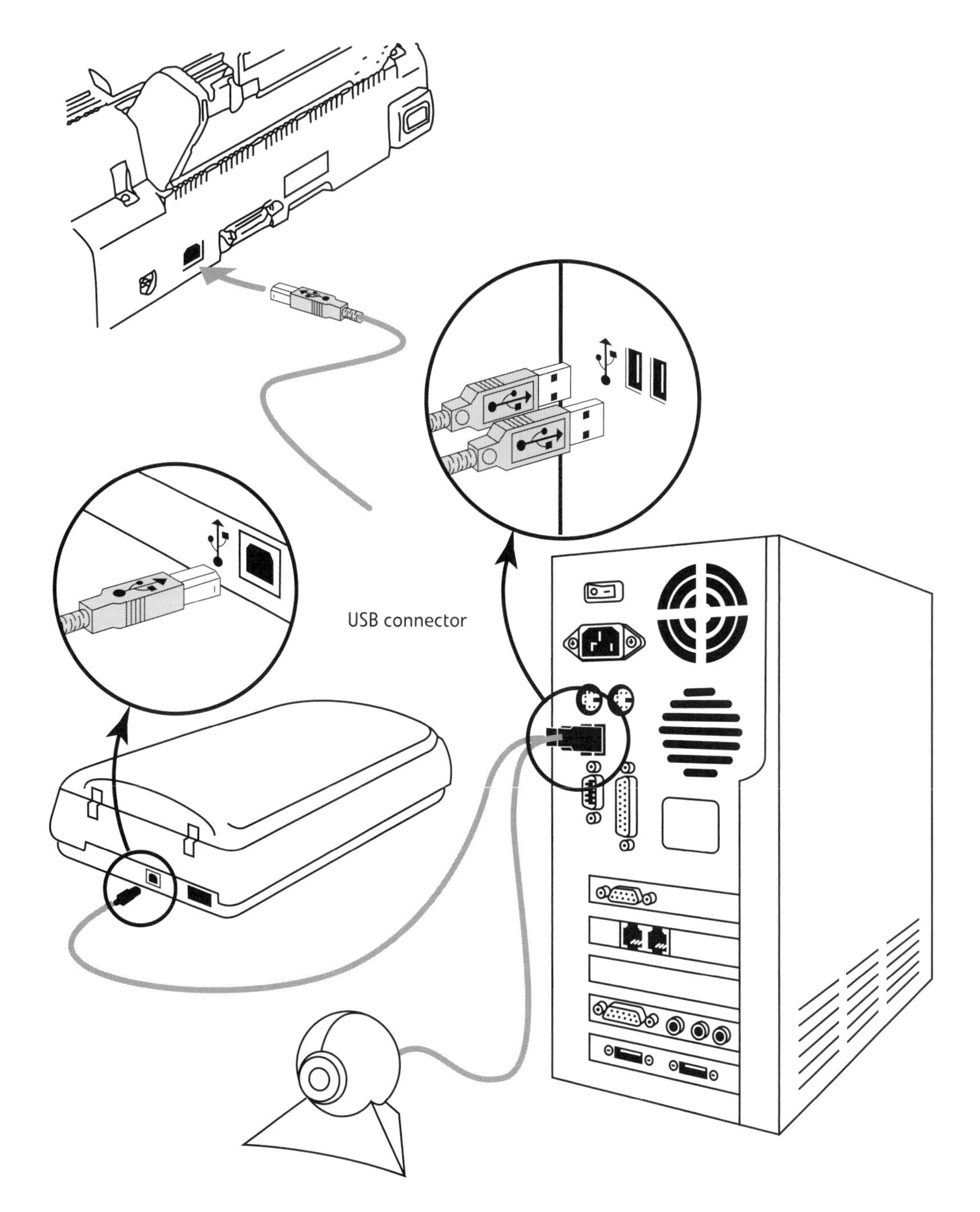


Figure 2.14 USB port usage

- Continue to attach one peripheral at a time, without any power being connected. Try to ensure that the cables are as tangle-free as you can make them. When all peripherals have been attached, check once more that you have no cables left over.
- Now plug the peripherals and processor to a power supply, one at a time, the processor last. If any are already switched on, turn them off before connecting the power supply to the next peripheral.
- When all are connected to the power supply, turn on the processor and the screen. Wait until any preloaded software has 'settled' and then turn the remaining peripherals on, one at a time.
- If everything works, fine. If not you will have to locate and fix the fault.

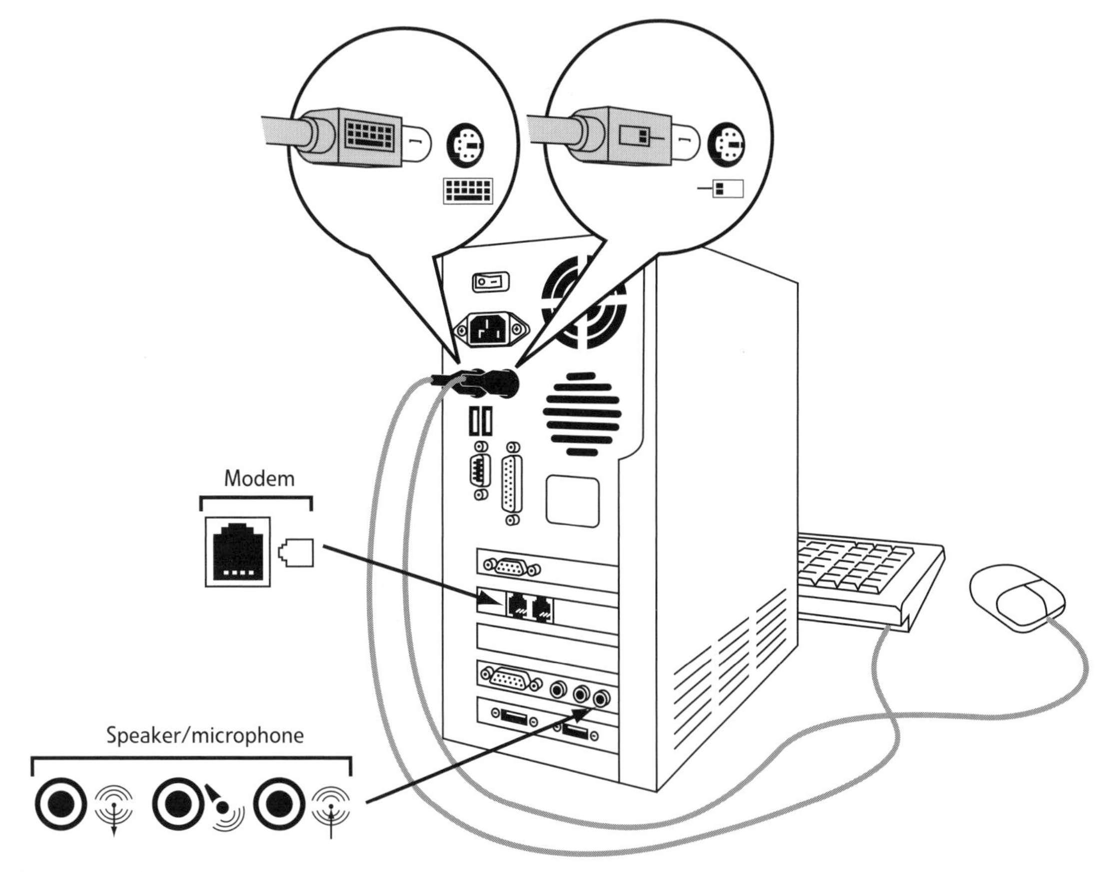


Figure 2.15 Other ports

## Check your understanding 2.9

Figure 2.16 shows the cables used to connect lots of peripherals to a PC.

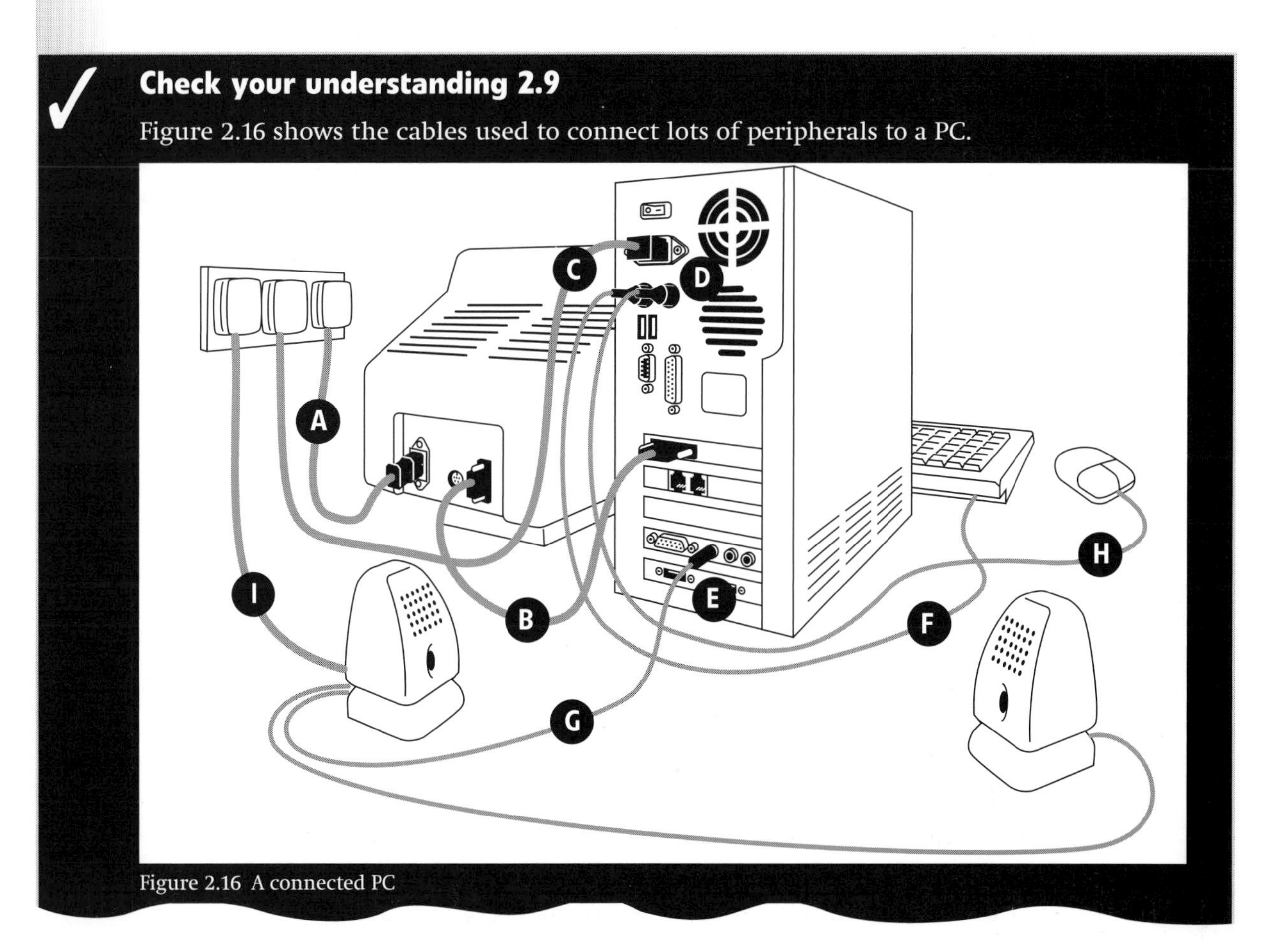


Figure 2.16 A connected PC

1 In a table, list all the hardware that is connected to the PC in Figure 2.16.
2 In the next column, identify each cable used with each peripheral. For those that have power cables as well as connecting cables, use two rows of the table.
3 Reorder the rows of your table to show the order in which you would connect the system.
4 Copy the layout of the rear of a PC and label each port with the numbers 1, 2, 3 to show the order in which you would connect these peripherals.

# Maintenance

You need to be able to maintain software and hardware using appropriate methods.

**Further research 2.10**

1 Find out what disk tools you have on your PC system.
2 Make a list of things you think need to be done to maintain your software.
3 Make a list of things you think need to be done to maintain your hardware.

## Maintenance of hardware

A PC will run better (is less likely to break down) if it is kept in clean and dry conditions. The most likely cause of failure is overheating of the fan within the processor box, caused by a build up of dust on the fan blades. Internal cleaning of the processor box needs to be done with the power disconnected (not just turned off) and is beyond the scope of this course.

However, there is still much to do to maintain good working conditions for your PC.

- Regular cleaning of the surfaces around a PC will reduce the amount of dust that collects.
- Use of anti-static wipes for screens can reduce the amount of dust attracted to the screen.
- 'Air duster' products can be used to blow dust and debris from inaccessible areas of electronic equipment.
- Special brushes can be used to clean keyboards and the rollers on a mouse.
- Special discs can be used to clean floppy disc drive heads. Similar ones are available for cleaning DVD lenses. It is also possible to clean and restore CDs.
- Products are available to clean the print heads on inkjet printers.

**Further research 2.11**

1 Find out about the cleaning products that are available for your PC.
2 List the ones you think should be used regularly.
3 Decide how regularly the PC should be cleaned, and therefore how long each item would last before new supplies would need to be bought.
4 Calculate the annual cost of keeping your PC clean.

## Maintenance of memory and storage

Memory requires no physical maintenance as such. If you have sufficient memory to handle all your applications, you should experience no deterioration in the speed at which processing happens. To gain maximum performance of a PC, it is advisable to limit the number of programs running at any one time. Each application that you are using, together with any documents that are open, will take up memory space. If the space needed for this exceeds what is immediately available in memory, the PC will use disc storage space to save your work, and swap files in and out. This swapping process takes time and, if you are working with lots of applications open and very large files, e.g. including lots of graphics, you may notice the PC slowing down. In addition, at start-up, several programs will be activated, such as virus protection software, and these run in the background while you are processing documents, etc. This makes sense for virus protection software, but there may be other programs which, when installed, include themselves in the start-up process, and some of these may not be essential for you.

You will have set up a directory system with separate folders for different areas of your work or home life. The number of files on your PC will increase daily until, eventually, you could run out of storage space on your hard disc drive. Therefore, you must maintain these directories by deleting files that are no longer used, thus freeing up space. This is especially important in communications software. You may receive many e-mails each day. They sit in your in-box waiting for you to read them and action them. Once actioned, you should file them if you expect you may need to refer to them again, or bin them. Binning e-mails will keep your in-box under control, but the bin is just another area in the memory of your PC, and this also needs to be emptied regularly.

You may also have many temporary files on your PC without even realising it. Internet Explorer is the biggest creator of temporary files, but Word also generates them. While you are working on a document, Word sets up a temporary file, and saves your work to this file at regular intervals. If your machine crashes, Word will attempt to recover your work by offering you the temporary file. It may be more up to date than the version you last saved. For various reasons, these temporary files are not deleted, and they take up valuable storage space on your PC. Your software should include a program that will allow you to clean off these unwanted files, plus any created by other applications such as Internet Explorer.

**Further research 2.12**

1 Find out how to discover which applications start up automatically when you switch on your PC.
- Decide if any of them need not run in the background, and prevent them from doing so.
- Write notes that would explain to someone else how to keep the number of applications running to the minimum.

2 Find out how to empty the 'deleted items' folder or 'recycle bin' within your communications software.

3 Find out how to remove temporary files using a disk tool.

## Maintenance of software

Most software can be maintained by accessing the software provider's website on the Internet. For some software products, you may need to register with the software provider, but for most products you can simply access information on the Internet and receive free downloads of updated software when necessary.

The Windows® operating system can be kept up to date by regularly accessing the 'Windows Update' option, checking what upgrades are available and downloading the ones that are needed. If you have installed virus protection software, you will most probably have subscribed to a virus protection service. The service provider will send messages direct to your PC to advise you of the latest virus threat and to offer an update on the virus protection software. You can accept their offer or postpone it, and then follow the on-screen instructions to complete the updating process.

Other software providers, such as Adobe®, will e-mail you with details of upgrades. Most of these have to be paid for, but at least you are aware of improvements in the software and can file these e-mails in case you want to upgrade at a later date.

**Further research 2.13**

1 Find out how to update your Windows® software.
2 For each piece of software on your PC, note the web address of the supplier. Visit the site and check for updates.

# Troubleshooting

You need to be able to locate and repair faults using appropriate fault-finding techniques. Often something goes wrong and you witness it happening so you know the cause, such as a cup of coffee spilled over the keyboard. There may be other evidence that explains why the PC is not working, such as when all the lights go out so you know there is a complete power failure. Sometimes the software will display a message that explains why the peripheral is not working as you want it to.

- With a printer, it may be because it has run out of paper, or an ink cartridge is empty.
- With a modem, the e-mailing software may share the same line as the incoming fax, so when you try to check your e-mail, the software tells you it cannot dial out through the modem, simply because a fax is being received.
- A disk drive door may be open, or you may have removed the disk that it was using.

Sometimes the PC is fine when you switch off, but when you switch back on the next day, something does not work as it should. It is frustrating when equipment does not work. It is quite usual for things to go wrong when a deadline is looming. Working out what is wrong when you are under pressure is more difficult, so it is important to try to remain calm.

To work out what is causing a problem, you need to think through how things work when they are working. You can then try to eliminate obvious things that can go wrong, one by one.

- Apart from those with remote controls, all peripherals have a cable that connects to the processor.
- Almost all peripherals also have a separate power lead.
- Most peripherals have a light that lights up when power is connected and turned on.

So, what can go wrong?

- The connecting cable may become disconnected, at one or both ends.

- The power supply may fail, e.g. due to a blown fuse.
- The power may be turned off at the socket.
- The peripheral may be turned off.

Remember that you should not fiddle with cables while the PC is turned on. However, you can look for signs that things have been turned off or disconnected. Start at the power supply socket and check your way back to the peripheral. Then check from the peripheral to the processor. Be systematic.

It helps to make a list of what you know to be OK, and what you will need to check when you close down the system and turn off the power supply. If, eventually, you decide you cannot trace the fault, you may need to report to someone else. It will save them time if they know what checks you have already carried out.

If you notice that a cable has become disconnected, or if you think this may be a problem, turn off the system and disconnect the power. Check all connections before powering up again. You may want to do this close-down and re-powering check anyway, just to eliminate this source of fault. If you are sure that everything is powered up and properly connected, how you proceed will depend on the nature of the fault and the peripheral.

Each peripheral will have been supplied with a manual, and this usually has a section headed 'troubleshooting'. Refer to the manual to see whether your problem is listed. If it is, follow the guidance given. It will be important to do things in exactly the correct order. Make a list so you can tick things off as you do them.

Having explored all these options, if your peripheral is still not working, what next?

You will need to determine the precise location of the fault. For example, if your scanner is not working, how could you tell if the fault is with the scanner, the lead connecting it to the USB port, or the USB port itself? One way is to replace each part, systematically, with a matching component that you know to be working. If the replacement component does not work on your system, then the fault lies elsewhere.

- If your component works when connected to another PC, you know this component is OK.
- If it doesn't work on another system, you've found the location of at least one fault.

If you have still not traced and fixed the fault, talk to those around you and ask for advice. It is quite possible that someone else has had a similar problem and can suggest a way of tracing your fault. If you keep a log of faults reported, and any success stories, everyone can refer to this when confronted with a problem. Help may also be available on-line. You could key make/model/problem into a search engine to see what sites are listed. One would probably be the website for the manufacturer of the peripheral.

In any event, visit the website of the manufacturer and add it to your favourites, even if you are none too pleased with their hardware at this precise moment. You may refer to their **FAQs** (**frequently asked questions**) and/or their search engine may allow you to type in a question. The website may also give you a telephone number to call. Make a note of the model number and serial numbers that you may need to quote.

If you decide that the peripheral itself is not working, you will need to have it fixed by someone with the appropriate technical expertise and/or replace it.

**Check your understanding 2.10**

1 Draw a flowchart to show what steps you would take to find a fault on your PC.
2 Compare your flowchart with others.
3 Amend your flowchart to include ideas gained from others.
4 Use your flowchart when next fault-finding, and amend it again if necessary.

**Assessment activity 2.6**

Your teacher will supply you with a selection of equipment from which you will need to select components to build a PC to meet a technical specification.

1 Identify which items you will use and which you will reject. Give reasons.
2 Using appropriate safety measures, build the PC to meet the technical specification.
3 Check that the PC works correctly and, if it does not, identify the fault and fix it appropriately.

# 2.3 Low-level programs

To tell the computer what to do, instructions are written using a programming language. One way of classifying programming languages is to divide them into two types: high-level and low-level.

- For a **high-level programming language**, the **source code** is very similar to English statements. You may solve a simple problem by writing very few of these instructions. However, for it to be carried out by the computer, your source code has to be translated (called **compilation** or **interpretation** depending on the high-level language) and, for each high-level instruction, this will result in many machine code instructions as the **object code**. The ratio between object code (what the computer acts on) and source code (what you write) is high.

**What does it mean?**

**Source code** is what you write by way of a program. The source code is then translated into **object code**, which the computer can execute.

- With a **low-level language**, the source code is the same as, or very similar to, the instructions that can be carried out by the control unit. So, for low-level languages, the ratio between object code and source code is low (close to 1). This makes it more difficult for you to write programs to solve even the simplest problem as there are many more instructions to be written. It is also more difficult for others to read the program, should they need to amend it in any way.

**Further research 2.14**

1 List some high-level languages.
2 Find out what instructions one of the high-level languages offers.
3 Find out the difference between compilation and interpretation.
4 List some low-level languages.
5 Find out the instruction set for one of the low-level languages.

# Machine and assembly language programming

You need to be able to design simple machine and/or assembly language programs.

- **Machine code** is the binary code that the computer acts on. Because it is in binary, i.e. lots of 0s and 1s, it is more difficult to read and write this code.
- **Assembly language** is similar to machine code in that a single assembly language instruction may be translated into a single machine code instruction. However, to make it more user-friendly, the opcodes are given **mnemonics**, and **symbolic addressing** is available. The code that you write, with its mnemonics and labels, still needs to be translated into machine code, and this process is called assembly (hence the name: assembly language programs).

**What does it mean?**

A **mnemonic** is something that acts as a reminder. The word comes from Mnemosyne (the Greek goddess of memory, mother of the Muses).
With **symbolic addressing**, labels are used for the addresses within the memory of instructions and data, rather than their binary equivalents.

## Programming constructs: sequence, selection and iteration

Your machine code and/or assembly level programs need to use data transfer, arithmetic and jump and branch instructions. This combination of instructions will be sufficient to demonstrate your ability to program at this level, because, between them, they cover all possible programming constructs, and give you enough 'power' to actually solve some simple problems.

In every computer program, at whatever level you decide to write your code, there will always be programming constructs (as shown in the list below) which determine the order in which the program instructions are carried out.

- **Sequencing:** Instructions are carried out, one after the other, as listed. This will apply to the data transfer instructions and the arithmetic instructions that you need to write.
- **Selection (branching):** Depending on some condition, control may pass to a different part of the program. (These will be your branch instructions.)
- **Iteration (looping):** Depending on a counter, a sequence of instructions will be repeated a given number of times. (These will be your jump instructions.)

## Flowcharts

Figure 2.17 illustrates the three programming constructs for a very simple program: to add a pair of numbers together and to print their sum, for three pairs of numbers.

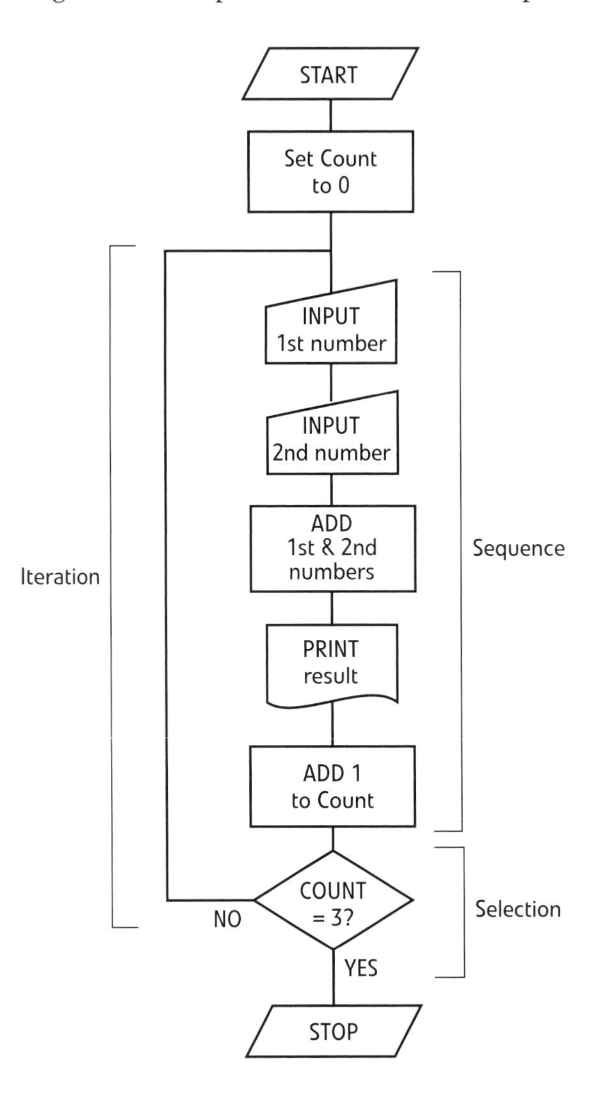


Figure 2.17 Flowchart to show program constructs: sequence, selection and iteration

Notice that the flowchart has five different shapes of box:

- lozenge (for START and STOP)
- rectangle (for arithmetic instructions like ADD)
- keyboard shape (for INPUT instructions)
- torn-off-paper shape (for PRINTed output)
- diamond (for a decision).

All of the boxes are linked by lines, which show the flow of control through the program. Most boxes have one line in and one line out, but decision boxes have more than one line out. In Figure 2.17, there are two, labelled YES and NO, as responses to the question written in the diamond. Some boxes can have more than one line in. In Figure 2.17, the INPUT box at the start of the loop has two routes into it: one from the START sequence, and the other during the iteration.

## Check your understanding 2.11

One of the skills you will need to develop and practise when writing programs is that of **dry running**. This involves following the flowchart, or code, obeying the instructions and writing what happens, line by line in a table. Table 2.12 shows how this might be done for Figure 2.17. Notice that the column headings show what data needs to be input, stored and output during the running of the program.

| BOX details | Count | Input 1 | Input 2 | ACC | TRUE/FALSE | PRINT |
|---|---|---|---|---|---|---|
| Set COUNT to 0 | 0 | | | | | |
| INPUT 1st number | | 3 | | | | |
| INPUT 2nd number | | | 7 | | | |
| ADD | | | | 10 | | |
| PRINT | | | | | | 10 |
| ADD 1 to COUNT | 1 | | | | | |
| Count = 3? | | | | | FALSE | |
| INPUT 1st number | | 2 | | | | |
| INPUT 2nd number | | | 4 | | | |
| ADD | | | | 6 | | |
| PRINT | | | | | | 6 |
| ADD 1 to COUNT | 2 | | | | | |
| Count = 3? | | | | | FALSE | |
| | | | | | | |
| | | | | | | |
| | | | | | | |

Table 2.12 Dry running for flowchart in Figure 2.17

1. Using test data of 3, 7, 2, 4, 5, 1, copy and complete Table 2.12 to **trace** through the flowchart.
2. If this flowchart were to be altered to process 30 pairs of numbers, how might you amend the trace table so that it can be fitted on a single page?

## What does it mean?

A **trace** is a step-by-step check of what a program does. It involves recording the changes in stored values and noting outputs in a trace table.

Table 2.13 shows how we can code the flowchart, based on the minimal assembly language instruction set introduced in Table 2.9 (page 56).

**Line numbering** has been included only so that we can refer to particular instructions. The introduction of line numbers in some languages was a welcome advance for most programmers.

Putting a hash (#) symbol before a value (lines 1, 10 and 12) shows that this is an actual number – called a **literal** – not the address of a storage location in which data can be found.

| Line number | Label | Instruction | Comment |
|---|---|---|---|
| 1 | | LDA #0 | Set COUNT to 0 |
| 2 | | STORE Counter | |
| 3 | A | INPUT Num1 | INPUT 1st number |
| 4 | | INPUT Num2 | INPUT 2nd number |
| 5 | | LOAD Num1 | ADD 1st number to 2nd number Addition is done within ACC and the sum is stored in Result |
| 6 | | ADD Num2 | |
| 7 | | STORE Result | |
| 8 | | OUTPUT Result | PRINT result |
| 9 | | LOAD Counter | ADD 1 to COUNT |
| 10 | | ADD #1 | |
| 11 | | STORE Counter | |
| 12 | | SUB #3 | COUNT = 3? |
| 13 | | BRLA A | Line 13 takes control back to the start of the loop for the NO option on the flowchart |
| 14 | | STOP | |

**Symbolic addressing** allows us to label locations in memory for the storage of data: Counter (lines 2, 9 and 11), Num1 (lines 3 and 5), Num2 (lines 4 and 6), Result (lines 7 and 8). The programmer of machine code programs has to decide exactly where to store these values within memory – say just after the program code. This is difficult to gauge until you have written the whole program!

Symbolic addressing allows us to label line 3 at the start of the loop as 'A'. Taking into account the memory location where this program actually starts and how much space each of instructions 1 and 2 takes, the assembly process can replace the label in line 13 with the actual address to which the program may need to jump. Working in machine code, the programmer would have to decide all label values. If extra instructions are inserted during program modification, this can upset all subsequent branch instructions! Symbolic addressing is therefore very useful.

Table 2.13 Coding the flowchart

Notice that the code takes 14 lines although there were only nine boxes on the flowchart, including START, which has no parallel instruction.

## Registers and two- and three-address instructions

There is a trade-off between the size of the instruction set and the number of lines of code that you need to write to solve a problem. Very limited instruction sets are easy to learn, they require very little decoding by the processor, but result in long programs. As assembly languages were developed, more and more instruction types were introduced to allow programers to achieve more and yet keep program length to a minimum. One easy way to reduce the number of instructions is to use **registers**.

### What does it mean?

A **register** is a data store on which limited arithmetic can be performed (add 1, subtract 1), plus the logic functions, rotations and shifts. It behaves like a secondary accumulator. A PC may have a number of registers for use in low-level programming.

- Setting a value in a memory location requires two instructions: one to load the value into the accumulator and another to store it in the memory location. This can be reduced to a single location if a register is used as a counter.
- The three instructions (lines 9–11 on Table 2.13) can be reduced to a single instruction. This is because, to support use of a counter, there will be instructions to increment (add 1 to) and decrement (subtract 1 from) the register.

The three instructions (lines 5–7 on Table 2.13) can also be replaced by fewer instructions, if only a more complicated type of instruction is allowed.

- A two-address instruction such as ADD Num1, Num2 (take Num1 into the accumulator, add the value in Num2 and store the result in location Num2) is useful, although it would overwrite the value in Num2.
- Another possibility is a three-address instruction, e.g. ADD Num1, Num2, Result (take the value in Num1, add the value in Num2 and store the sum in Result).

For the processor to decode and execute these more complicated instructions, the table referred to during this stage of the fetch–execute cycle needs to list all the buses along which the values must travel. It would increase the time taken to execute the instruction, which will mean cleverer timing on the part of the control unit. It will also mean that this particular style of instruction will take up more space (if the same area of memory is to be addressable) and thus complicate the process of keeping track of where each instruction starts and ends.

The development of assembly languages has overcome these problems and the net result is a more flexible instruction set at the disposal of the programmer.

### Check your understanding 2.12

1. Using an assembly language of your choice, identify the different types of instructions at your disposal.
2. Using the flowchart in Figure 2.17, write the assembly code.
3. Assemble your code, and annotate it to show how it links to the flowchart. (You could number the flowchart boxes.)
4. Decide on some test data and then test your program by dry running, and/or by running a trace automatically on your computer. Document your testing.

## Using data transfer, arithmetic, jump and branching instructions

- **Data transfer instructions**: Because all arithmetic takes place in the accumulator, instructions are needed to move data from the memory to the accumulator, and from the accumulator to the memory. To do any arithmetic, you will have to use instructions to load to the accumulator and store from it.
- **Arithmetic instructions**: These allow calculations to take place on whatever number is stored in the accumulator. For your program, check which arithmetic instructions, such as ADD, SUB, MULT and DIV, are available in the assembly language. (If MULT and DIV are not available, trying to divide or multiply using assembly code would involve repeated addition/subtraction while keeping a count of how many times you have added/subtracted and worrying about remainders for division.)
- **Jump instructions**: These cause the order of processing to jump out of the sequence in which the instructions are stored, and so must specify the location of the next instruction to be executed. These are examples of selection or looping constructs. Any program that involves repetition, i.e. looping, must include at least one jump instruction.
- **Branch instructions**: These allow the order of processing to alter, but only if a certain condition is met. Programs that involve looping until a value is met, or until something special happens, will require a decision to be taken, and hence a test for a condition together with a jump dependent on the result.

There are additional instructions that will be available to you, and there is no reason why you should not use these as well as those listed above:

- operations on the register (shifting bits left or right, rotating bits to the right or left)
- operations involving setting and clearing switches
- operations involving stacks and other data structures.

The greater the range of instructions that you can use, the more complex problem you can solve, using the least number of instruction lines for your program.

### Further research 2.15

In an 8-bit byte, the last bit (bit 7) can be used as a **parity** bit. With even parity, the number of bits set on is even; with odd parity the number of bits set off is odd. Assume a system is working with even parity.

1. How could the computer determine the total number of bits set on within bits 0–6?
2. If this was an odd number, how could bit 7 be set on?
3. If the number of bits on within bits 0–6 is already even, how could bit 7 be set off?
4. How could bit 7 be tested to check whether it was on or off, and hence whether the parity bit is correct?

### Assessment activity 2.7

Decide on a simple problem to solve; one that will allow you to demonstrate your use of data transfer, arithmetic, jump and branch instructions.

- Draw a flowchart, using 'English' to explain the steps in your solution.
- Decide on test data to prove that your program works.

- Dry run your flowchart to check that it does what you planned and to establish what output your code should produce.
- Write the code for your program, assemble it and test run it.
- Check the accuracy of your own work and eliminate obvious errors.
- Document your solution.

# 2.4 Operating systems

## Operating system functions

You need to be able to describe the functions of an operating system within a modern computer environment. This section gives an overview of the functions of an operating system, identifies the extra functionality needed for networked or mainframe computers over a single-user PC operating system, and looks at how to install operating systems.

**Further research 2.16**

Find out what operating system is installed on your PC.

### Overview of functions

Software may be thought of as layers as shown in Figure 2.18.

- At the very heart of the PC is the actual hardware (layer 1). All other layers act as an interface between the two layers each side of them.
- Layer 2 is software that drives the hardware, saving and retrieving data on disk drives, etc.
- Layer 3 is called the **kernel**. It controls the applications in layer 4 and makes sure there are no conflicts between the applications, e.g. in their requests for data from a disk or sending data to a printer.
- Layer 4 comprises the applications software. The ones you want to use are loaded into memory and run by the operating system.
- Layer 5 is the user interface, sometimes called the **HCI (human computer interface)**, what you see when you look at the screen, and how things that you key are dealt with. The HCI is an important topic, and is covered in Unit 12.

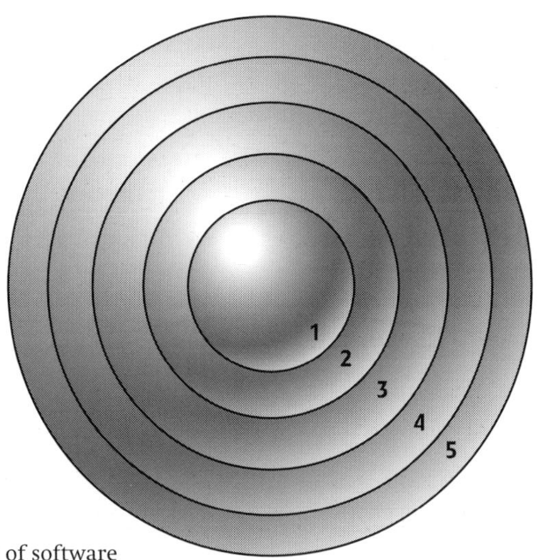


Figure 2.18 The layers of software

## Comparison between functions of different types of operating system

The essential functions of every operating system, regardless of the configuration of hardware (stand-alone versus networked, PC versus mainframe) are shown in Table 2.14.

| | |
|---|---|
| **Start-up** | Checking that all peripherals are working and properly connected |
| **Security** | Logging on procedures, controlling user access, checking passwords |
| **Communication** | Receiving commands from the user (e.g. from the keyboard) and displaying messages to the user (e.g. on the screen) such as the date and time |
| **Control of peripherals** | Sending data to the printer and communicating with the printer so that all data is printed, even though the printer and computer processor work at different speeds |
| **Control of memory** | Keeping track of what is held on disk by updating the disk directory |
| **Error control** | Checking data on entry and displaying messages if anything is wrong, e.g. a letter keyed into a numeric field |

Table 2.14 Essential tasks of any operating system

Table 2.15 considers this in more detail for a **stand-alone single-user PC**; there is (usually) just the one machine and one user, so the operating system, while clever, can be quite simple. The operating system may also offer the facility to allow extra users to have their own desktop settings. However, this works in much the same way as if the PC were a networked PC (see later).

| Feature | What the operating system does | Examples |
|---|---|---|
| **User interface** | Controls what the user sees<br>Accepts input from the user, interprets the command and then takes appropriate action | Opening and closing windows<br>Loading application software |
| **Multi-tasking** | Copes with the user running more than one application at the same time | When using facilities like a clipboard, if the user closes an application having left a large amount of data on the clipboard, the operating system will remind the user, in case this data needs to be used in another application |
| **Data movements to and from disks, and all other peripherals** | Accepts requests for data from applications, and sends messages on-screen to the user | Giving error message if the disk drive door is open, or the printer has run out of paper |
| **Peripheral management** | **Spools** output to a printer<br>Uses temporary disc files to save the data that is building up from each application, and deletes these files once the data has been sent to the printer | If data is sent to the printer from one application when the printer is already busy printing data from another application, the operating system keeps these two streams of data separate so that whichever application first started to send data to the printer has all of its data printed out before any other application's data is actually passed to the printer |

Table 2.15 Features of a PC operating system

For **networked** PCs, there is an added complication: the operating system needs to keep track of all users and their files, and to share the processor time between them in some fair way.

- All users need to be given log-in codes and ID numbers, which have to be checked every time they log in.
- The time that users spend logged on, which files they access and the processing time that they use are also recorded.
- Processor time is shared between users, giving each user a time slice of processor time. There are a variety of methods that can be used to **time share**. **Polling** involves checking with each user in turn to see whether anything needs processing. Having had a time slice, users then have to wait for their turn to come round again. Other timesharing methods can give certain users priority over others so that their work is acted on more quickly.
- Programs use processor time, and they may need to retrieve information from a storage device or send data to a printer. While this input/output is going on the program cannot continue with processing. The operating system notes when a program needs to communicate with a peripheral, cuts short that user's time slice, and moves on to the next user. In this way, maximum use is made of processor time.
- The **spooling** process is similar to that on a single-user PC when the user sends data to the printer from more than one application. On a network, several users could be sending data, each from more than one application, all at the same time, so the operating system needs to spool data for each user separately.

On a **mainframe computer**, time might also need to be shared between several programs running at once (multi-tasking). The **scheduling** of these jobs is also determined by the operating system.

### Assessment activity 2.8

Describe the functions of an operating system within a modern computer system.

# Operating system installation

You need to be able to install an operating system. This could be any one of the following 'standards':

- Windows® (modern versions)
- Linux
- AppleMac OS.

### Further research 2.17

1 Use the Internet to research the three types of operating system (above).
2 Make notes on the similarities and differences between them.

Most PCs are delivered with preloaded software. This includes the operating system (e.g. Windows® XP) and a 'bundle' of software. You should also receive one or more CDs, which hold a copy of the operating system, so you can reinstall it if there is a problem.

The process is made as easy as possible for the user. Simply follow the instructions given, insert the CDs in the correct order and respond to prompts on the screen.

## Check your understanding 2.13

1 Obtain a copy of the installation instructions for two different operating systems. Compare them, looking for similarities and differences between them.
2 Make notes, and compare your findings with others in your group.

# Computer operations

You need to use various computer operations on a proprietary operating system, such as those listed above (Windows®, Linux and/or AppleMac OS). If you are working on a Windows® system, much of the information that the operating system uses can be accessed through the **control panel** (Figure 2.19).

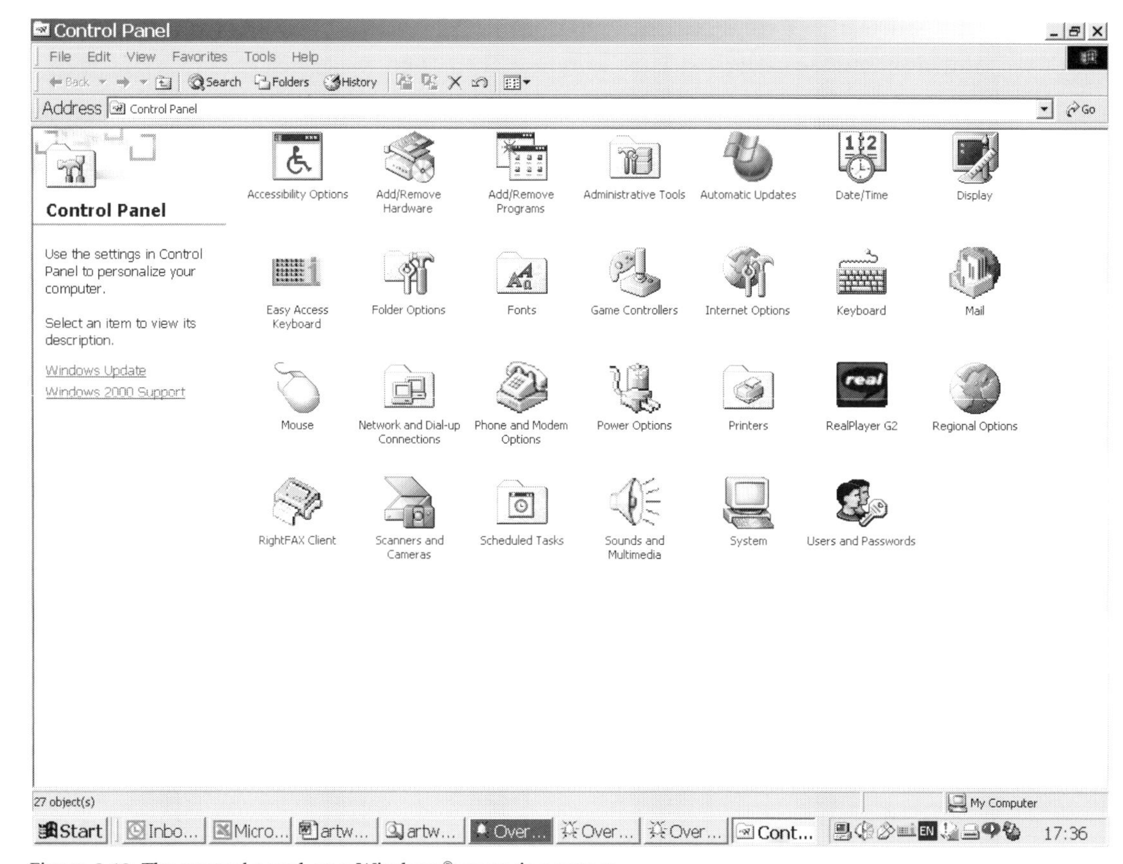


Figure 2.19 The control panel on a Windows® operating system

## Further research 2.18

1 Log on to a PC and explore the system's settings.
2 For six system settings, make a more detailed study, making notes as necessary.
3 Present your findings to others in your group.

### Generation of environment and systems for a computer user

When an operating system is first installed, a number of settings are preset at **default values**, and one of these is the **configuration**. The system assumes a standard keyboard, standard mouse, etc. so if a user connects a special mouse or a higher resolution screen, telling the operating system is called **configuring**. Nowadays, with plug and play peripherals, when the PC is switched on, the operating system spots these extra/replacement peripherals and automatically sets up the drivers that are needed to run them.

Other default values relate to how the interface between the computer and the user will operate, such as the background colour on the screen or security options such as passwords.

All operating systems allow the user to customise settings, i.e. to set up new default settings that are to apply every time the system is powered up. These can include the following:

- set up security **passwords**
- include **anti-virus checks**
- change the screen prompts or **desktop appearance**
- decide mouse settings (speed, **pointer style**, etc.)
- set up directory structures (**folders**)
- provide **icons** or **menus** to start software or to open specific files
- select appropriate **drivers** for printers and other devices
- organise **backing up** of data.

### Further research 2.19

1. Change your password. Choose a password that will be difficult for anyone else to guess.
2. Find out what anti-virus software is installed on your system. Check whether any updates are available on-line, and update the system if necessary. Scan the contents of a floppy disk for viruses. Write notes on how best to avoid introducing viruses onto a PC system.
3. Experiment with changing the appearance of your desktop: rearrange the icons, alter the background colour, introduce tiling, etc. Decide on a style that suits you and save this as a default setting.
4. Change the mouse settings so that the right and left buttons are interchanged. Use the mouse like this, and then change the settings to back to how they were. Find out what 'pointer style' is being used. Does your system allow you to change this setting?
5. Check that you know how to set up a new folder, how to rename a folder and how to move files from one folder to another. Check that you know how to copy files to and from one folder onto a floppy disk or a CD-ROM. Check that you know how to attach files to an e-mail.
6. Amend the start-up to include one extra software application. Turn off the PC and restart to check it works. Make notes on what you did. Then change it back to how it was before.
7. Check that you know how to set up the driver for a replacement printer. Check that you know how to install a new peripheral, e.g. a scanner or digital camera.
8. Investigate what backing-up facilities are available on your PC. Write notes on what files should be backed up and how frequently.

### Assessment activity 2.9

1. Install and configure an operating system and software to meet a client specification.
2. Evaluate the work done in building and configuring a computer system to a given specification, including how well the finished system met the specification, what went well, what went less well in the work, and what improvements could be made to the resulting system.

## Test your knowledge

1. Explain how data is represented within a computer, giving examples.
2. Explain these terms: overflow, parity, mantissa, exponent, pixel, flip-flop.
3. Describe three logic operations and explain what effect they have.
4. Explain how bit masks might be used.
5. Explain these terms: register, counter, bus, buffer, ALU.
6. The SCR (or PC) receives information from two different sources. Explain what these are and the circumstances under which each might happen.
7. What is the purpose of clock and control signals?
8. What safety precautions should be taken when building a PC?
9. Explain these terms: port, USB, parallel, serial.
10. List three tasks to maintain the environment for a PC.
11. List three tasks to maintain memory and storage within a PC.
12. How can software be kept up-to-date?
13. Give three key tips for finding a fault within a PC system.
14. What are the differences between the translation processes: compilation, interpretation and assembly?
15. Distinguish between high- and low-level language instruction sets.
16. Explain these terms: mnemonic, symbolic addressing, opcode, operand, dry running, trace table, literal.
17. List three programming constructs.
18. Explain these terms: kernel, HCI, multi-tasking, spooling, time share, time slice, polling, scheduling.
19. Explain the purpose of the control panel in a Windows® environment.
20. Explain these terms: configuration, default value, driver, folder, password, back-up.

# UNIT 3: BUSINESS INFORMATION SYSTEMS

Information technology (IT) is central to the workings of the modern organisation. In this unit, the structure of organisations and how information flows around them is explained. The methods that organisations use to handle and process data are also investigated. In addition, the legal responsibilities relating to the use of information technology in the workplace, such as health and safety, are described.

## Learning objectives

- To examine why organisations need information and how different organisations use information
- To investigate the functional areas within organisations and how information flows between them
- To examine how data is handled and processed within organisations and the role of a range of common business applications
- To understand the physical and operational requirements of a business system

# 3.1 Information in organisations

This unit is about organisations and how they use information. So, what is an organisation? If you ask a range of people what an organisation is, you are likely to be given a variety of answers as the term covers a wide spectrum from small clubs or societies through to huge multinational companies. In this unit we are concerned with business organisations.

**Check your understanding 3.1**

1 In small groups, list ten examples of organisations. Try to define the term 'organisation', and identify examples that support your definition.
2 As a class, pool your findings, and try to refine your definitions.

## Characteristics of organisations

All organisations have some things in common; they need two main resources:

- physical resources such as money, materials and equipment
- human resources.

They also have a **purpose** or aim (sometimes called a **mission statement**). For many, their primary aim is to make money, but an organisation such as a college would describe educating people as its main aim while a charity's main aim might be to help a particular disadvantaged group of people.

**Check your understanding 3.2**

Does your school or college have a 'mission statement'? If it does, find out what it is.

To achieve their aims, organisations need information:

- A college needs to know how many students are enrolled on each course.
- A supermarket needs to know the quantity of each item of stock it has on its shelves.
- A bank needs to know how much money each one of its customers has in accounts.
- A charity needs to know the names and addresses of each of its regular donors.

In many ways, information is the 'life blood' of an organisation. The most efficient way to hold, update, search for and communicate information is by the use of IT. That is why almost all business organisations make extensive use of IT.

While there are many different types of organisations, they do have a number of things in common. All organisations exist to achieve something and they need information to support them. Before we look at how IT is used in organisations we need to learn more about the different types of organisations and how they are structured.

# Types of organisations

There are a number of different ways in which we can classify organisations. One of the most basic is to divide them into public and private.

- **Public sector organisations** are controlled by the government and their costs are met by public funds (collected through taxes). They include schools, colleges, police, local councils and the armed services.
- **Private sector organisations** are controlled by individuals rather than the government.

Private organisations can be further subdivided based on the legal responsibilities of the people who run the company, although some business organisations, such as charities and trade unions, do not fall into these categories:

- **sole traders** (businesses run by one person who may or may not employ anyone else)
- **partnerships** (small businesses that are owned and controlled by a number of partners)
- **private limited companies** (businesses owned by shareholders; a group of people who have invested money to finance the business)
- **public limited companies** (as above but the shares in the companies can be traded on the Stock Market).

It is also possible to divide organisations into functional groups.

- **Industrial** organisations are those that make things.
- **Extraction** organisations are involved in extracting raw materials from the earth and include coal and ore mining, crude oil extraction, farming and fishing.
- **Manufacturing** organisations take raw materials and manufacture finished goods such as aeroplanes or shirts. These can be further subdivided into component manufacturers (e.g. electronic components and car tyres) and assembly of finished goods (e.g. televisions and cars).
- **Commercial** organisations sell things. They can also be subdivided into retail and wholesale organisations and service industries. **Retail and wholesale organisations** distribute and sell finished goods, either to the end customers (retail) or to retail organisations (wholesale). The most obvious examples are shops and supermarkets. **Service industries** sell some kind of service. Examples include banks, travel agents, insurance companies and hotels.

## Check your understanding 3.3

1. Take the list of ten organisations you created earlier and divide them into public and private sector.
2. Take the private organisations in your list and subdivide them into the relevant categories.
3. Make a list of companies that fit into each of the functional groups described above.

# Organisational structures

All but the very smallest of organisations need some kind of structure. Tasks and duties need to be divided between the employees, and workers need to be managed. Managers are concerned with making decisions and directing the staff below them based on those decisions. Most organisations have several levels of management, but not all managers do the same job. Typically management levels can be divided into strategic (at the top), tactical (middle managers) and operational (the lowest level of management).

- At the **strategic level**, managers are largely concerned with long-term organisational planning. Decisions tend to be unstructured and are made infrequently. However, the decisions made at this level are likely to have a large impact on the organisation as a whole and cannot be reversed easily. An example of a decision taken at the strategic level might be the choice of a new market to move into.
- At the **tactical level**, managers are largely concerned with medium-term planning. They monitor the performance of the organisation, control budgets, allocate resources and set policies. Decisions taken at this level are used to set medium-term goals that form stages leading to the accomplishment of the organisation's strategic objectives. An example of a decision taken at the tactical level might be setting a department budget.
- At the **operational level**, managers deal with short-term planning and the day-to-day control of the organisation's activities. The decisions taken at this level direct the organisation's efforts towards meeting the medium-term goals, abiding by the budgets, policies and procedures and have little impact on the organisation as a whole. An example of a decision taken at the organisational level might be the setting of daily or weekly production schedules.

The structure of an organisation is usually shown on an **organisation chart** that defines the division of work and the responsibilities of each manager. The purpose of an organisation chart is to illustrate the following:

- levels of management
- lines of communication
- spans of control
- levels of responsibility
- accountability
- promotion/career paths
- chains of command.

There are two basic types of organisational structure, **flat** and **hierarchical**. The difference between them is the number of levels of management between the most senior manager in the company (given a variety of names such as Managing Director, Chief Executive Officer, etc.) and the lowest level in the company.

A **flat structure** (Figure 3.1) has only a few levels in the organisation. Except for the smallest organisations, very few have an entirely flat structure with only one level of management. In some cases an organisation that wishes to avoid a cumbersome hierarchy will attempt to keep the number of management levels to a minimum. A flatter structure can encourage 'team spirit' through the avoidance of 'them' and 'us' feelings. It also, theoretically, improves communication because there are fewer layers of management for information to pass through from the top of the organisation to the bottom.

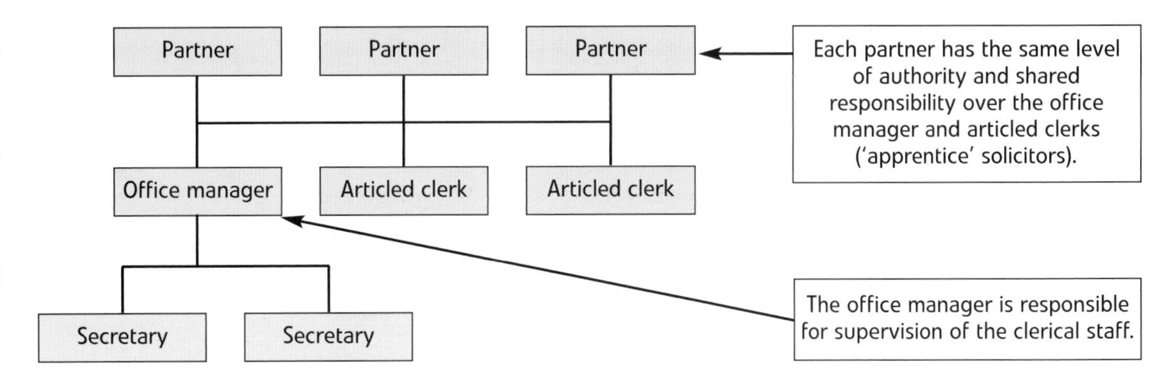


Figure 3.1 An organisation chart of a relatively flat structure, e.g. a firm of solicitors

In contrast, a **hierarchical (tall) structure** (Figure 3.2) has many layers of management and the organisation chart can resemble a pyramid. This type of structure is typical of large organisations. In general, the more layers in an organisation, the more difficult it is for information to flow from top to bottom and vice versa.

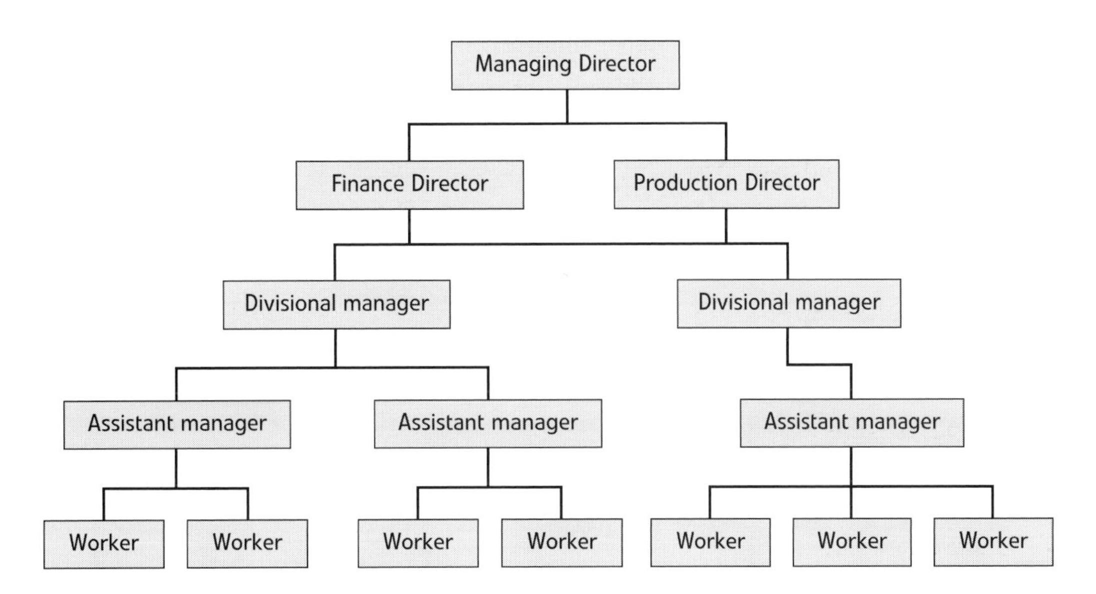


Figure 3.2 An organisation chart of a hierarchical structure

A **matrix structure** is sometimes found in large organisations that have several different divisions. As shown in Figure 3.3, groups of employees are organised into product teams (e.g. in an electronics company this might be televisions, computers and mobile phones, etc.) as well as by function (e.g. development, sales, production, etc.). In a matrix structure, a particular group of workers, e.g. television production, will be accountable to both the television division manager and the production manager. Each member of the organisation (below managerial level) is accountable to two or more managers. Marketing, sales and other functional managers will have a global responsibility for their functions within the organisation, while divisional managers have responsibility for these functions on a divisional basis.

The main problem with matrix structures is that they are complex; some people find it confusing to have more than one manager.

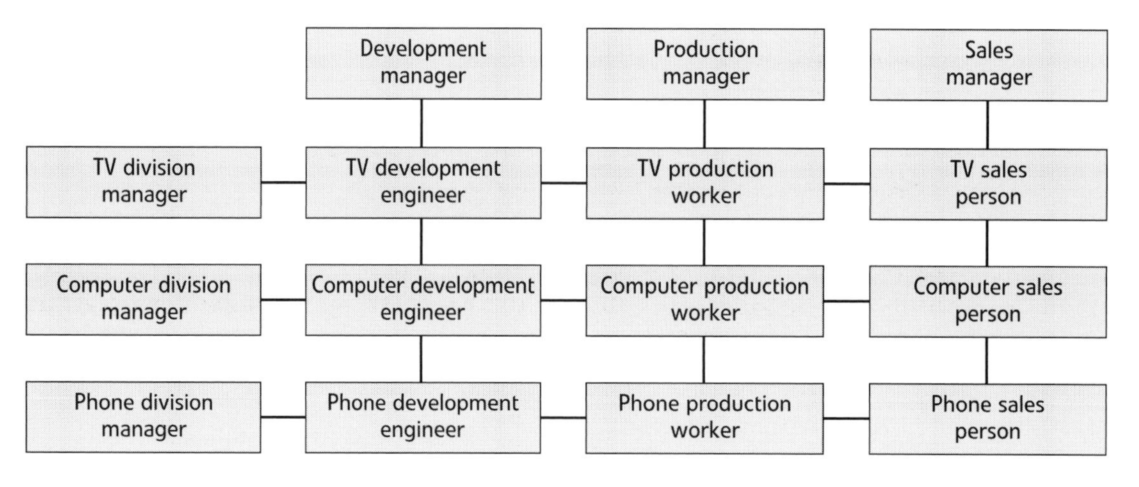


Figure 3.3 An organisation chart for a matrix structure

## Case study: Domestic Repair Ltd

Domestic Repair Ltd is a small company, employing 58 people, which operates in North London. Domestic Repair fix domestic appliances such as washing machines, dishwashers and cookers. They have a team of service engineers who visit people in their homes to repair their appliances. They are a limited company in the commercial service industry sector. Their head office and eastern area office is in Enfield; they also have a branch in Hendon, which covers the west side of North London. Domestic Repair's organisation chart is show in Figure 3.4.

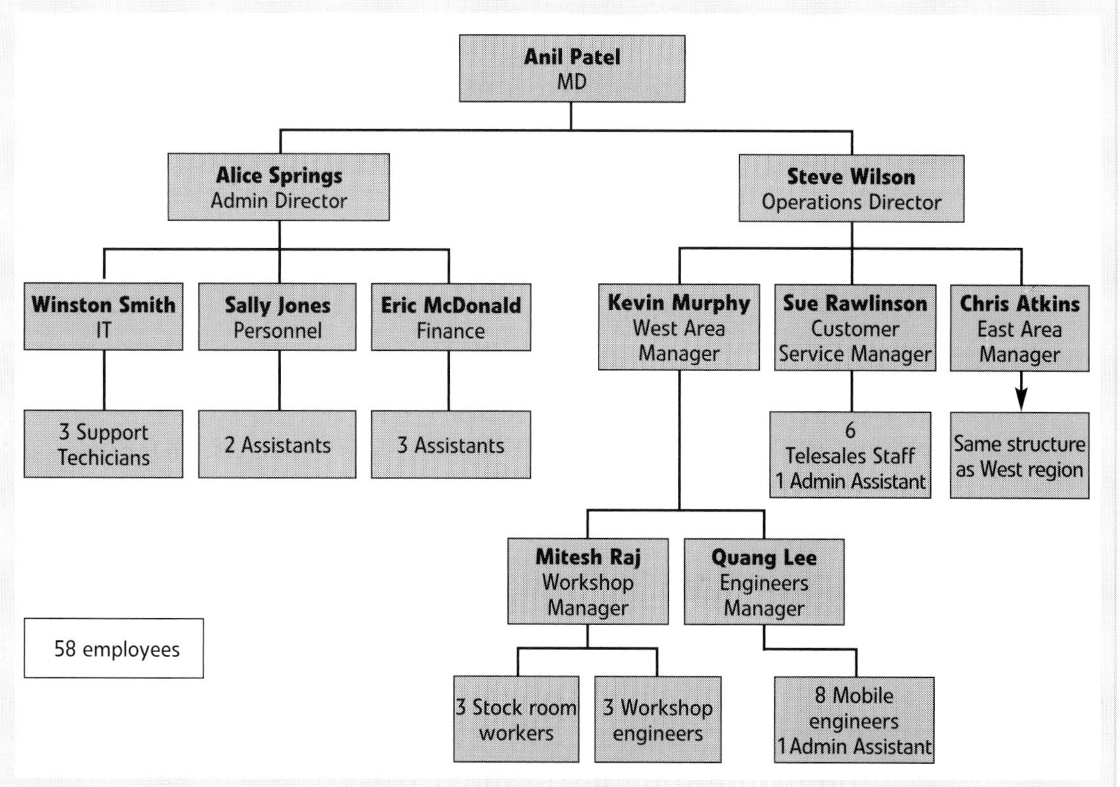


Figure 3.4 The Domestic Repair organisation chart

1 What type of structure does Domestic Repair have?
2 Collect information on the structure of your college or a company you have worked in. Find out who reports to whom.

**Assessment activity 3.1**

1 Using the information you collected above, draw an organisation chart, either for a company where you have worked or for the college you study at. How many levels are there between the most senior and most junior people?
2 Compare the chart you have produced with that of other people in your class. Try to find good examples of flat and hierarchical structures.
3 Identify two charts that illustrate the difference between hierarchical and flat structures.
4 Write a brief report explaining the differences between the types of organisational structures and illustrate it with the organisation charts you have found.

# Types of information

One thing that managers at all levels have in common is the need for information. Without information, it is difficult to make good decisions. There are a number ways in which information can be classified. First, it can be classified by type.

- **Verbal:** Spoken information is very important and can take various forms, such as face-to-face or telephone conversations. It should be borne in mind that this type of informal information is prone to misinterpretation. (See also *Verbal communication*, page 10.)
- **Documentary:** This type of written information includes letters, order forms, invoices, memos, etc. Documentary information is more formal than spoken information and can form a legally binding contract. (See also *Written and graphical material*, page 17.)
- **Electronic:** With increasing use of IT, this form of information is becoming more important. It includes e-mails, on-line information and other electronic transfers (such as credit card transactions). (See also *E-mail*, page 23.)

Information can also be classified by its source.

- **Internal information** comes from and is used within the organisation. For example, a sales person may pass the details of an order to the production department.
- **External information** comes from or goes to other organisations or individuals outside the organisation. A customer placing an order is an example of a piece of external information.

We can further subdivide this information into what the information is about.

- Almost all organisations need information about their **customers**: their names, addresses and contact details. In addition, **sales information** about what their customers have ordered is important.
- Organisations also need similar information about their **suppliers**, and the **purchases** made from the suppliers.
- For planning purposes, **market information** is important. How large is the market for the product(s) the company sells? Is it growing or shrinking?
- The day-to-day running of a company needs **operational information**, such as how many orders are outstanding, how many products are in stock, how many hours overtime were worked last week.
- **Design information** relates to a company's products. This can range from industrial equipment (e.g. a paint spraying robot machine) to customer products (e.g. a washing machine) to intangible products (e.g. a financial product such as an investment plan).

All of these products have a design that belongs to the company and needs to be recorded and protected. Product designs can be protected by **patents**, while designs of items such as logos can be protected by **copyright**.

- **HR** (human resources) information relates to the company's employees. This includes their personal details, their salary, work records (days sick, promotions, etc.), membership of pensions schemes and so on. It may also include information on the skills they have, training they have received, and plans for future training and development.

**Check your understanding 3.4**

Make a list of the sort of information that would fall into each of the above categories for a Further Education college. You might think that, as a college is not a commercial organisation, customer and sales information might not be relevant. But colleges do sell something (courses) and they do have customers (students).

# Flow of communication

Another characteristic of information in an organisation is the need for it to flow from one department to another (Figure 3.5). When a sales person takes an order from a customer, he or she needs to pass that order to the production department so that the goods can be made. This is an example of **sideways communication**, with information flowing across the structure of the organisation from one department to another.

As well as this type of information flow, information also needs to flow up and down the organisational structure. A sales person, as well as passing details of the order to the production department, will need to pass the details up to his or her manager so that the manager can compare the sales person's performance against sales targets.

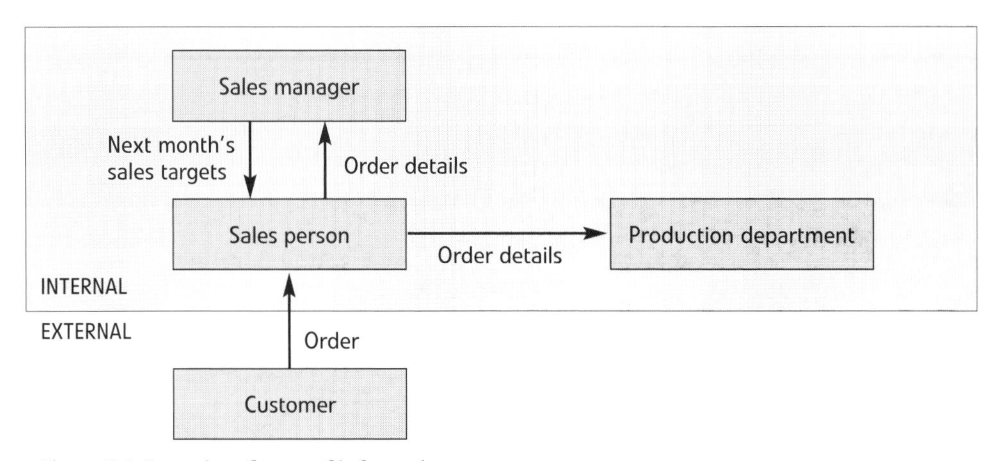


Figure 3.5 Examples of types of information

# The role of information

As stated earlier, managers can be broadly divided into three levels: strategic, tactical and operational. What should also be clear is that the type of information needed to make decisions at each level is different.

At the **strategic level**, managers need information about long-term trends. They do not need detailed short-term information (such as how many sales were made last week); instead they need long-term summarised information (e.g. the trend in sales over the last five years). They may also need external information, for example about how the entire market for the products the organisation makes has changed over the years or about how the financial situation is changing (e.g. interest or loan rates). Managers progressively lower down the organisation require information that is more detailed and relates to a shorter time period.

Managers also need information for **operational control**, i.e. the day-to-day management of people and processes. For example, they need to ensure their staff are at work and working the correct number of hours. Therefore, many organisations require their workers to complete a weekly timesheet to list the days and hours they have worked. Another example would be a job sheet, completed by a garage mechanic. For each car the mechanic works on, he or she completes a job sheet listing what work was done, what spare parts were used and how long it took. This information is used by the workshop manager, not only to keep track of what each mechanic has been doing during the day, but also so the customer can be charged correctly for the work done on the car.

## Case study: Domestic Repair Ltd

Mitesh Raj is the workshop manager for the West London area. Machines (and machine parts) are brought into the workshop when they cannot be mended in the customers' houses. He also manages the stock room where spare parts are kept for use both in the workshop and by the mobile engineers. Mitesh is an operational level manager making day-to-day decisions about what the workshop engineers and stock room workers should be doing. To make decisions he needs information:

- How many machines are awaiting repair?
- What spare parts need reordering?
- How much overtime was worked last week by staff?

Higher up the organisation Kevin Murphy is the manager for the West London area. He manages the overall performance of the whole area. He is involved in target setting and monitoring the performance of the area. The decisions he needs to make are at a tactical level, and cover a longer time period, so he needs a different sort of information:

- What money is available and how is it being spent (budgeting)?
- What are the performance figures, such as the average time to repair a machine (used for target setting and monitoring)?
- What is the area income and profit?

Anil Patel is the Managing Director of the company. Together with the other directors, he makes strategic decisions about the long-term future of the company. For example, he might consider whether to expand the company south of the River Thames by opening a branch there. He also sets targets for Kevin to achieve.

1. What sort of information would Anil need in order to make his decision about expanding the company?
2. What methods could Mitesh use to gather the information he needs?

# 3.2 Functional areas

The concept that most organisations have some kind of structure, which divides them into different departments that carry out different functions, has already been introduced. This section looks in more detail at the different departments that can be found in most organisations, the tasks they carry out and how information flows between them.

## Departments and their functions

The departments that exist in a particular organisation will, to some extent, depend on what the organisation does. Retail or service organisations, for example, will not have a production department (only a manufacturing organisation would have a production department). Also it is worth bearing in mind that some organisations use different names for departments for example, accounting and finance are different names for the same function, as are personnel and human resources.

- The **sales department** is responsible for selling the product. It involves creating and managing a sales force to contact potential customers, perform follow-up work with customers and handle complaints. The sales department takes orders, processes them, negotiates contracts and deals with customer relationships (discounts, problems, new products, etc.). The higher the value of the product being sold, the more sophisticated the sales function needs to be. In a department store, salespeople are often little more than shop assistants; however, in a company that makes passenger aeroplanes, the sales team selling a multi-million pound fleet of aircraft to an airline include senior members of the company and the negotiations may go on for months.
- The **accounts** or **finance department** monitors all aspects of the company's money including incoming and outgoing payments. The finance department is responsible for paying the company's suppliers, employees (payroll), bank and stockholders. It will obtain bank references, set customer credit limits and deal with bad debtors. It may also obtain finance (loans etc.) to support the development of the company.
- The **production** or **manufacturing department** is responsible for manufacturing the goods that are sold. Where high-value products are manufactured, they may be made to order. Lower value, high-volume goods are manufactured in large batches and these go into stock. The departmental managers are responsible for scheduling the manufacture of goods, either to meet specific orders or to ensure sufficient goods are in stock to meet the anticipated demand.
- The **operations department** delivers the service the organisation provides.
- The **warehouse department** stocks goods to be sold and materials for making products. It is responsible for receiving delivered goods, storing them in the warehouse and collecting them to send them to manufacturing or dispatch. It is important that accurate and up-to-date records of exactly what is in stock are kept. The warehouse department will reorder items if the number in stock falls below a pre-set level (the **reorder level**).
- The **dispatch department** (sometimes part of warehousing) is responsible for packaging and sending goods to customers. Some organisations have their own transport fleet to deliver goods but, in many cases, this is contracted out to specialist delivery companies such as FedEx or DHL.

- The **purchasing department** is responsible for buying all the raw materials, components and other goods that the company requires. This department selects the most suitable supplier, ensuring price competitiveness, and negotiates contracts with suppliers, including prices, discounts, delivery times, etc.
- The **HR (human resources)** and/or **personnel department** is responsible for hiring, training, and retaining the employees required to run the company. It is also responsible for staff welfare, contracts, pay, medicals, appraisals, maintaining employees records, maintaining information on job applicants, maintaining information on employee benefits and compensation and discipline.
- The **marketing department** is responsible for identifying potential customers and understanding market demand through the use of market surveys and other activities. It is also responsible for promoting and advertising the company's products. The marketing department often works closely with sales, and with **R&D** deciding on what new products or features customers will want.

### What does it mean?

R&D stands for research and development.

- The **R&D department** designs and develops new products, working closely with the marketing department and also with the manufacturing department, who make the products that the R&D department develops.
- The **IT department** is responsible for the provision of suitable hardware and software to the organisation. It decides the selection and purchase of hardware and the provision of user support services. It will investigate suitable software, and purchase existing software packages or, if none are suitable, then it will oversee the development of bespoke software.

### Case study: Domestic Repair Ltd

Domestic Repair Ltd has an operations department that is responsible for the service engineers who visit people's homes to repair their appliances. The operations department manager is responsible for scheduling the work that is done, and managing the workshop and the stock room where parts are stored.

1. Refer back to Domestic Repair's organisation chart in Figure 3.4. What other departments is Domestic Repair divided into?
2. What sort of functions do those departments carry out?

### Check your understanding 3.5

Earlier it was explained that organisations can be split into commercial and industrial. What departments might an industrial organisation have that a commercial organisation does not have and vice versa?

### Assessment activity 3.2

Write a report describing the various departments than can be found in a typical organisation. Illustrate your report with examples from an actual organisation.

### External organisations

As well as communications between the internal departments within an organisation, there must also be communication with external organisations and individuals. Table 3.1 lists the main external organisations with which communication needs to take place.

| **Organisation** | **Purpose** |
|---|---|
| Customers | Organisations need customers to buy the products or services offered. Without customers, the organisation would not exist. |
| Suppliers | Almost all organisations need to purchase raw materials, components, equipment or goods. They also need services, e.g. employment agencies, lawyers and accountants. |
| Bank | All organisations need banking services. In addition to bank accounts, many companies require loans to fund expansion. |
| Government | The government sets taxes, which must be paid. These include income tax and National Insurance contributions, which must be paid on employees' wages. Most organisations are also registered for VAT (value added tax), a tax paid on purchases, and charged on sales of most items. Payment of taxes is normally the responsibility of the finance department. The government also makes various regulations and laws, which affect companies. These range from product safety laws, with which an organisation must ensure its products comply, to employee legislation, which governs things like the number of hours an employee can be asked to work each week. |

Table 3.1 External organisations and their functions

## Division of organisations

As organisations grow and employ more people, so it becomes necessary to divide the organisation into manageable groups. A manager can only effectively manage a small number of people, which limits the size of teams. The accommodation available within a building or on each floor of a building naturally limits the number of people who can work together.

The division of an organisation can be done in a number of ways.

- The division may be by function into **departments**, as already discussed.
- Because their customers span a wide area, many organisations may be spread over a wide geographical area and this leads to a natural division into **regional groupings**.
- Organisations, such as banks, that need to maintain face-to-face contact with the customer base have a large number of **branches**. These are grouped into areas and are almost complete companies in themselves.
- Many large organisations are also divided by product or **product group**. Different skills may be needed to buy materials and/or to sell the product and it can therefore make sense to split the organisation this way.

Many large organisations have developed from **mergers** and **acquisitions**. When these occur, there is a period of consolidation but, even when this is complete, many organisations still have some kind of division based on location, product or some other differentiation. Some functions, such as finance or personnel for example, are often completely merged; others may remain separate.

### Case study: Ford Motor Company

Ford Motor Company is one of the largest organisations in the world. It has manufacturing sites all around the world and has been making cars in the UK since 1911. Currently, Ford assembles cars and vans and manufactures engines in its UK factories. In the 1980s, Ford purchased the famous UK luxury car manufacturer, Jaguar. The reason for this acquisition was that Ford wanted to increase its market share at the luxury end of the market. The Ford name was associated with small and medium sized family cars rather than luxury cars, so the acquisition was a way to purchase a 'name' and market image. The two organisations are closely linked. The Jaguar X-type car, for example, is built at the former Ford factory at Halewood in Liverpool and Ford engineers work closely with Jaguar engineers to introduce new technology into their vehicles. However, for marketing reasons, the customer-facing side of the organisations are kept completely separate. So, for example, Ford and Jaguar have separate dealers and advertising, and marketing is done separately so as to maintain the Jaguar image.

1 Using the departments listed earlier, identify which ones you think Ford and Jaguar could share and those that need to be kept separate.
2 Mergers and acquisitions occur all the time. Can you think of any well-known companies that have recently gone through these processes?

# Information flow

Understanding the way information flows between the departments of an organisation and to and from external organisations is fundamental to understanding how organisations operate. For an organisation to operate, information must flow both internally between departments and to and from external bodies.

With **internal information**, we can divide the flows into how information moves between the people identified in the organisation charts (Figures 3.1–3.3): upward, downward or across.

- **Upward** flows originate at the lower levels of the organisation (e.g. the 'workers') and pass up to the higher levels (the 'management').
- **Downward** flows are the reverse, with information originating at the management level and flowing to the lower levels. An example might be instructions from a manager on how a worker should prioritise the various tasks to be completed.
- Flows **across** the organisation stay at the same level but pass between staff, for example, in different departments.

There are many situations when it is important to have a clear understanding about exactly how information flows inside and outside the organisation to achieve a particular task. One occasion is when an organisation wishes to replace an existing (perhaps manual) system with a computerised one. **Information flow diagrams** model the information flows that are needed to achieve a certain task, show what people or departments the information flows to and from, and the nature of that information.

Many organisations have procedure manuals used for training new staff and to ensure that existing staff know the correct procedures. These procedure manuals clearly explain the information flows involved in each procedure.

In organisations such as banks, which deal with important financial transactions, knowing exactly the correct process for dealing with the flow of information is clearly very important. Organisations dealing with financial transactions usually keep detailed records of the information flows involved in each transaction; this is known as an **audit trail**.

Since most organisations are involved with buying and/or selling goods or services, placing and receiving an order are two important events which trigger a number of information flows between internal departments and external organisations. These flows are mostly in the form of named documents (such as **invoices**), which may be sent manually or electronically. The basic information flows for placing an order with a supplier is shown in Figure 3.6.

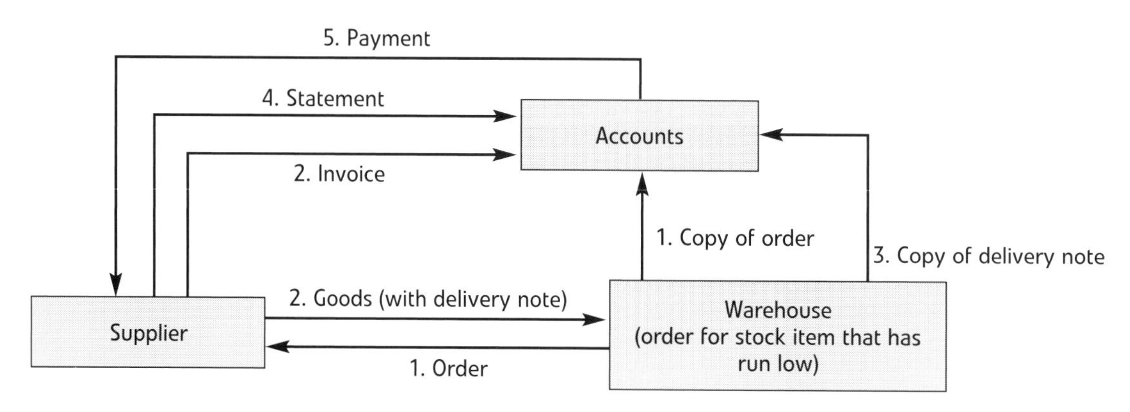


Figure 3.6 Information flow diagram for placing an order

## Case study: Domestic Repair Ltd

Domestic Repair Ltd is in business to provide a service to customers, therefore the information flows involved in requesting a repair are key to the way the organisation runs. Customers contact the company by telephone and their call is received by the centralised customer service department. The telesales person records details of the customer and the problem, and then schedules an engineer to visit the customer. When the engineer visits the customer, he or she repairs the appliance and gives the customer a bill which is paid there and then by cash or cheque. At the end of the day the engineer returns all the money he or she has collected, along with copies of the bills issued to the finance department. These information flows are shown in Figure 3.7.

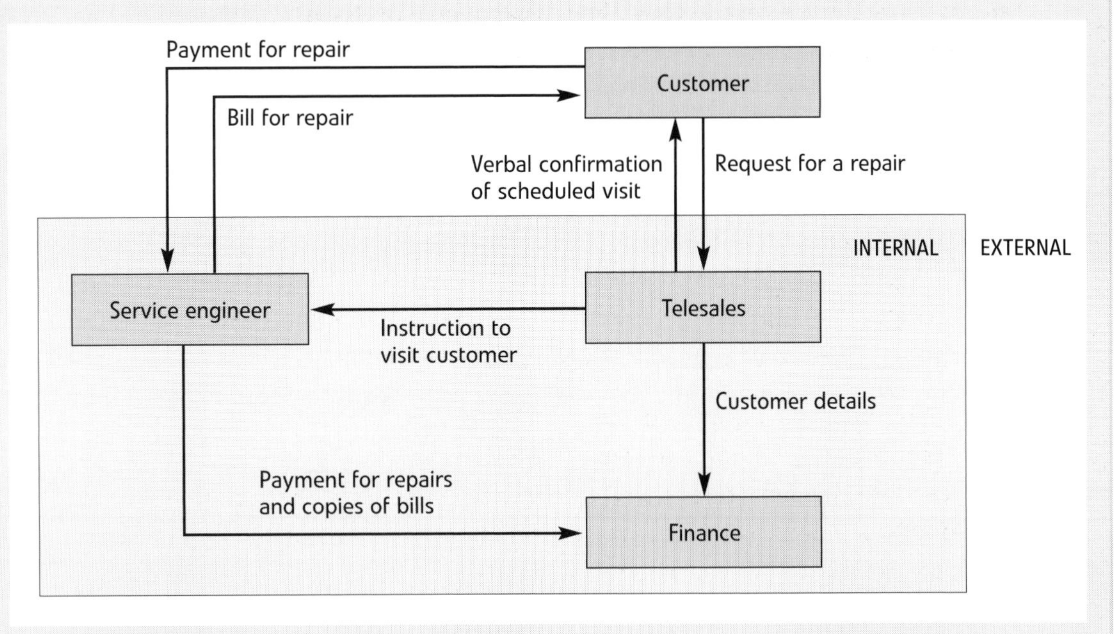


Figure 3.7 Information flows for repairing an appliance

1 Draw the information flow for ordering more spare parts for the stock room.
2 In a Further Education college, the process of enrolling a new student on a course is the closest parallel process to dealing with an order. Newly enrolled students must first be interviewed and accepted on the course by the course manager. Once accepted, they must then register on the course and pay their fees. They are then issued with a student ID card. Draw a diagram of the information flows involved with enrolling a student on a course at a Further Education college.

# ICT support of information flows

Traditionally, organisational information flows – both internal and external – were achieved by paper documents. Today, increasingly, this information flows electronically with the use of ICT.

- **E-mail** has become an essential business tool. For internal information flows it has begun to replace the memo as a way of disseminating information to individuals or groups of individuals within the company. Externally the letter is still used for formal communications but the e-mail is often preferred to a telephone call, for example to arrange a meeting, because e-mail does not require both parties to be available to communicate at the same time.
- **Electronic data interchange (EDI)** is extensively used by large organisations to place orders with their suppliers.

?

### What does it mean?

**Electronic data interchange** (EDI) is a computerised method for connecting customers and suppliers. It allows organisations that purchase large quantities of goods (e.g. a supermarket chain) to place orders with their suppliers (e.g. food manufacturers) electronically without the creation of the traditional paperwork (order forms, invoices, etc.), thereby improving efficiency by reducing the amount of administration required.

- Meetings have always been a vital part of business communication (both internal and external), especially for more senior staff. However, where meetings involve bringing together parties from different locations (perhaps even different countries), they can be costly and time-consuming. Tele- and video-conferencing offer an alternative. **Tele conferencing** brings the parties in the meeting together over the telephone, allowing a multi-way conversation to take place. **Video conferencing** adds a video link, so the parties can see each other and perhaps view diagrams, photographs, drawings, etc.
- The **World Wide Web (WWW)** has had a tremendous impact on business communications. All large companies, and many small companies, have their own website advertising their products and services. In addition, an increasing number of companies, as well as using their website for marketing purposes, have ventured into e-commerce, selling their products direct to their customers via their website. Using WWW technology to provide an internal-only source of information has also become very popular. **Intranets** have begun to replace the company noticeboard as a source of a wide range of internal information such as company policies, health and safety information, latest news and product information.
- **Electronic funds transfer at point of sale (EFTPOS)** is used by all supermarkets and most smaller shops too. Customers who pay using debit cards have their card 'swiped' in a card reader. The transaction is authorised and the money transferred from the customer's account to the shop's account electronically using data communications links. A similar system allows customers to pay using credit cards.
- **Portable devices** such as laptops and **PDAs (personal digital assistants)** are used for communication, for example, by travelling sales people who can send details of an order placed by a customer they have just visited as soon as they leave the customer, rather than having to wait until they return to their office. Portable devices are also commonly used for stock checks in large warehouses or supermarkets.
- More traditional electronic methods of communication such as **fax** and **telex** are still used but are increasingly being replaced by the methods listed above.

### Case study: Domestic Repair Ltd

Domestic Repair Ltd use a computer system to schedule the service engineers' jobs. Each engineer has a portable terminal in his van, which is connected to the head office computer via a mobile telephone data link. As the engineer completes one job, the details of the next job (customer name, address, nature of the problem) are displayed on the portable terminal.

Currently, when the stock room runs low on spares they send a fax to the supplier to order more. What more efficient method could they use?

### Assessment activity 3.3

1. Write a report explaining the main information flows that take place in a typical organisation.
2. What activities trigger the flow of this information? For example, what causes an invoice to be issued?
3. Give examples of information flows that support operational and strategic decision making and explain how ICT can be used to support these information flows and decisions.

# 3.3 Data handling and processing

Information is very important to organisations. Handling information and processing it, i.e. **data processing**, is a vital task. If information is lost or processed incorrectly, the organisation will suffer, perhaps seriously. The terms data and information are sometimes used interchangeably but they have different meanings:

- **Data** is the raw figures and facts.
- **Information** is data made useful, so it tells you something you need to know.

For example, data might be a complete list of all the orders placed last month. Information, derived from that data, could be a list of those orders that are outstanding, or the value of orders placed for each product, sorted from highest to lowest. While data processing is the name that has been traditionally given to handling, storing and processing organisational information, it is often replaced these days by the term IT (information technology) or more recently, by **ICT (information and communications technology)**.

## Data controls

It is essential that data be input accurately and kept up to date and that, during its processing, the accuracy and validity – i.e. the integrity – of that data is maintained. During the input of data to a computer system, humans can easily make errors, so controls need to be put in place in an attempt to prevent these errors.

### Further research 3.1

Think about the assignments you write for your college work.

1 What sort of mistakes are made in those assignments?
2 Why do these mistakes happen?
3 What could you do to try to prevent the different types of errors that occur?

**Data validation** involves checking that the data input is valid. An example might be a date of birth. A number of different checks can be done to ensure a valid date is entered.

- The date itself can be checked to ensure it is an actual date with a valid number of days and months, i.e. an **existence check**.
- A **range check** can be applied; a date of birth for a living individual must fall between the current date and a date 130 years (or so!) earlier. If a college course accepts people who are over 17 and under 21 on 1 September 2003, then each student's date of birth must be after 1/9/1986 and before 2/9/1982.
- A **length check** can be applied, i.e. checking the size of an input value. Data items such as account numbers are usually a certain number of characters. If more or less are input then an error must have been made.
- A **type check** can be applied. Some input values may only contain certain types of characters. People's names cannot contain numbers, while their ages cannot contain letters (i.e. alphabetic characters).

- A **format mask** can be applied where data must be in a certain format. National Insurance numbers for example contain two alphabetic characters followed by six numbers and a single alphabetic character (e.g. WZ209041A).

**Check your understanding 3.6**

For each of these types of data, list the sort of check that could be made.

1. A car registration number.
2. A house address (break it down into different parts).
3. A student ID number.
4. The price of an item in a shop.

For numeric data used to identify a client or product, a commonly used data validation method is the use of **check digits**. This validation method involves appending an additional digit to the number that is calculated from the original number. When the number is input the software can recalculate the check digit and, if it turns out to be different from the one input, then an error must have been made.

**Further research 3.2**

An example of a check digit can be found in the ISBN number that every book has. You can easily calculate and check ISBN check digits yourself.

An ISBN number is a nine-digit number with a tenth check digit appended at the end. The ISBN number for this book is: 043545669-6, where 6 is the check digit.

The check digit is calculated as follows: each digit in the ISBN number is multiplied by its digit position, starting with the least significant (right-hand) digit:

| | 0 | 4 | 3 | 5 | 4 | 5 | 6 | 6 | 9 |
|---|---|---|---|---|---|---|---|---|---|
| multiplied by | 10 | 9 | 8 | 7 | 6 | 5 | 4 | 3 | 2 |
| giving | 0 | 36 | 24 | 35 | 24 | 25 | 24 | 18 | 18 |

These values are then added together, in this case giving 204. That number is then divided by 11 and the remainder, 6, becomes the check digit.

Work out whether these two ISBN numbers are valid:

- 043545469-3
- 075065230-7

Check digits are powerful validation tools because they can detect common errors in entering numbers (such as transposition) as well as pressing incorrect keys. For example, suppose an operator entered an ISBN into a system but transposed the first two digits so it was entered as 3040394536. The system would calculate the check digit as 3, which is different from the check digit entered (6) so an error would be identified.

## Data verification

One method of verifying large volumes of numerical data is **cross casting**. This involves adding up tables of data by both row and column and checking that the two totals are the same. This is best explained with an example. Table 3.2 shows three months of sales figures from the three regions of a company.

| | Jan | Feb | March |
|---|---|---|---|
| Northern region | £3500 | £4255 | £3962 |
| Eastern region | £4985 | £4575 | £5025 |
| Western region | £2195 | £2225 | £2075 |
| Monthly totals | £10 680 | £11 055 | £11 062 |

Table 3.2 Quarterly sales figures

If the sales data were input into a computer application the software could calculate regional totals, by adding up the values across the rows. These totals for each region could then be added up and compared with the overall total calculated from the monthly totals entered by the operator. If the two overall totals were different then an input error must have been made.

## Check your understanding 3.7

Table 3.3 shows Westgate College enrolment data that have been input into a computer system. To verify the data has been input correctly, the software performs a cross casting check by adding up the total of the columns for each course and then adding all the totals for the courses to give an overall total. It then compares this total with the one shown in the table.

| No of students enrolled on each course | | | | |
|---|---|---|---|---|
| Week | ICT | Business studies | Leisure and tourism | Total |
| 1 | 35 | 22 | 18 | 75 |
| 2 | 38 | 20 | 26 | 85 |
| 3 | 24 | 25 | 28 | 77 |
| 4 | 20 | 22 | 21 | 63 |
| | | | Total: | 300 |

Table 3.3 Westgate College enrolment data

Try this cross casting check yourself. Has the data been entered correctly?

Another method of verification that is sometimes used when a large amount of data has to be input accurately is **batch control**. With a batch control, the data to be input (normally from some kind of form) is split up into batches of perhaps 20 or 30 forms. For each batch, a batch control slip is completed, an example of which is shown in Figure 3.8.

**Batch Control Slip**

| | |
|---|---|
| Batch No: | |
| Date: | |
| Number in batch: | |
| Total order value: | |
| Total of account numbers: | |

Figure 3.8 Batch control slip

The operator manually calculates one or more totals from the batch of forms to be input. For example, if the batch comprises order forms, a grand total order value could be calculated. In some cases, a meaningless total such as the total of all the account numbers is calculated. These are known as **hash totals** or nonsense totals. These totals are then entered on the batch control slip. The data from the batch of forms is input into the computer and, at the end of the batch, the values from the batch control slip are also entered. The computer software recalculates the totals that were included on the batch control slip and compares the two sets of totals. If they are not the same, then an input error (or an error in the manual calculations) has been made; there will be an investigation and the batch may need to be re-input.

In many data handling applications, the input data comes from a document or form that has been completed by someone else, e.g. an order form or tax return form. The design of that form can help ensure the accuracy of the data that is input. One technique that is commonly used is **turnaround documents**, computer printed documents that have some input data already printed on them (Figure 3.9).

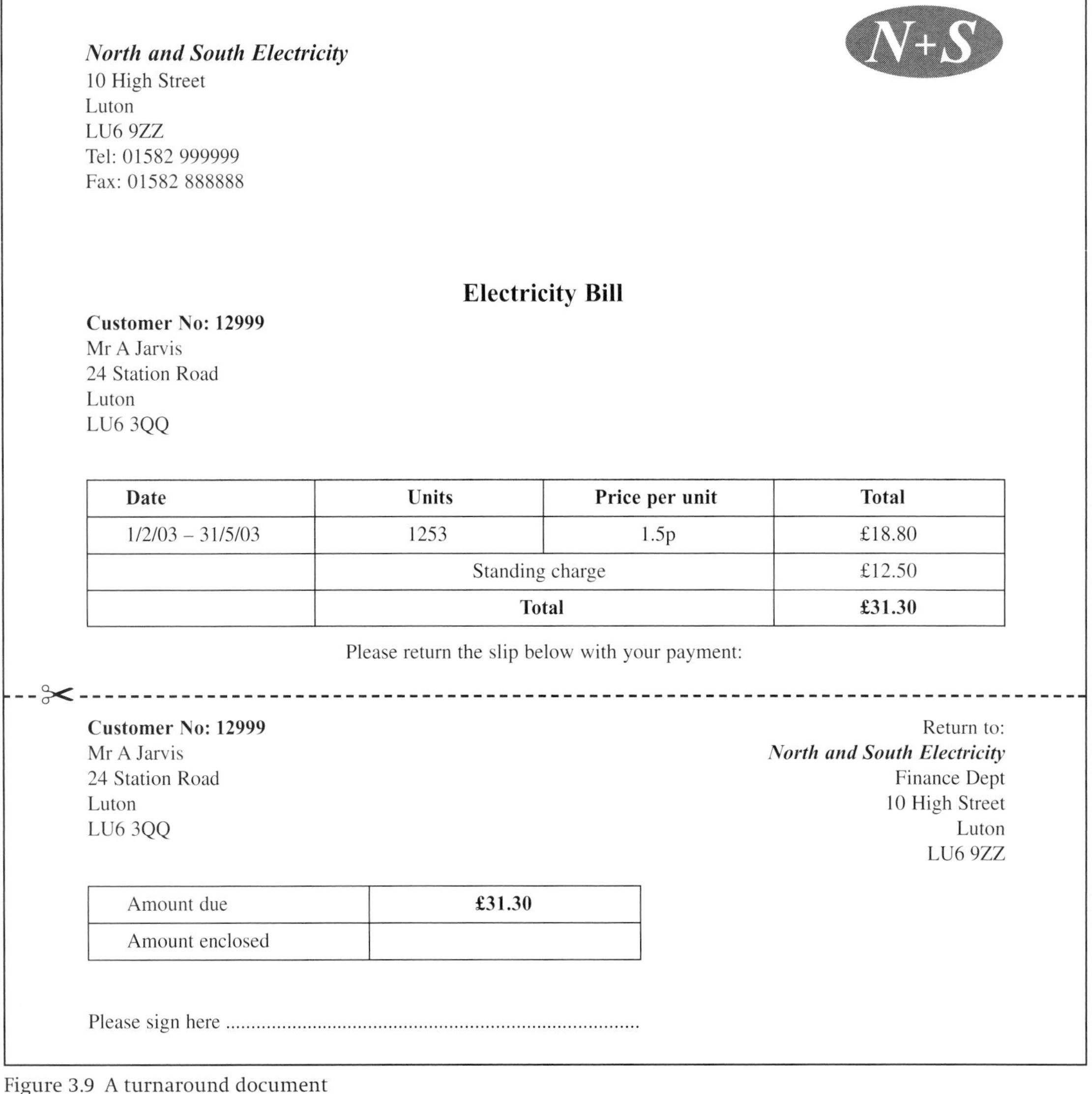

*North and South Electricity*
10 High Street
Luton
LU6 9ZZ
Tel: 01582 999999
Fax: 01582 888888

N+S

**Electricity Bill**

**Customer No: 12999**
Mr A Jarvis
24 Station Road
Luton
LU6 3QQ

| Date | Units | Price per unit | Total |
|---|---|---|---|
| 1/2/03 – 31/5/03 | 1253 | 1.5p | £18.80 |
| | Standing charge | | £12.50 |
| | **Total** | | **£31.30** |

Please return the slip below with your payment:

**Customer No: 12999**
Mr A Jarvis
24 Station Road
Luton
LU6 3QQ

Return to:
*North and South Electricity*
Finance Dept
10 High Street
Luton
LU6 9ZZ

| Amount due | **£31.30** |
|---|---|
| Amount enclosed | |

Please sign here ..............................................................................

Figure 3.9 A turnaround document

Turnaround documents reduce the amount of information the customer has to complete on the form, thereby reducing the likelihood of errors being introduced.

**Further research 3.3**

1 Find examples of turnaround documents. Junk mail advertising a product or service is often a good place to start looking.
2 Find a form, perhaps one you have completed recently such as a college enrolment form or a driving licence application, and list what type of data controls and validation you could use on the form.

# Data processing methods

Data processing systems can be broadly categorised as follows.

- **Transaction processing (TP)** involves validating and recording business transactions, such as sales made, or orders placed. TP systems need to record all information relevant to the transaction and may also need to communicate with other systems. For example, a TP system used to record sales made in a shop would need to record details of the sale (item sold, price, date, salesperson, etc.). If the customer paid by credit or debit card, the system would need to validate the card by communicating with the bank's computer (itself a TP system) and pass details of the sale to it. The system would also need to update the stock control system.
- **Information storage and retrieval** involves the storage of business information in a computer database. Businesses need to store a large amount of information such as customer details, stock levels, sales records, financial information and so on. The databases must keep this information safe and provide a way for it to be retrieved. Business managers often need to refer to this data to help them to make decisions.
  TP and information storage and retrieval systems usually work together, with TP systems providing much of the input data for the storage and retrieval system.
- **Batch processing** is used where large amounts of data need to be processed but human interaction is not required. Typical examples include payroll and utility (e.g. telephone, electricity or gas) bill production. In these situations, the input data (such as hours worked or amount of electricity or gas used) is collected and prepared before the processing begins. Once the input data is ready the processing starts, without human interaction, and typically produces printed output, such as wage slips or telephone bills.
- **Real time** is one of those terms that can have several meanings, depending on the context of its use. In this context, real-time processing is the opposite of batch processing. Real-time processing involves an almost immediate response to user input, unlike batch processing. (The term real time is also used to describe systems used to control industrial processes such as robot machines.)
- **Timesharing** is a term that was widely used in the early days of computing, but is less popular today. It refers to the use of a large central computer (a **mainframe computer**) to which a number of remotely located users are attached. These users access the machine via a **dumb terminal** (a VDU monitor and a keyboard). As the mainframe has only one processor and many users (unlike a PC which has one processor and one user) time available to carry out processing tasks is shared between the many users; hence the term timesharing. As mainframe computers have very powerful processors, many hundreds of users could be supported on a single mainframe, although only text-based applications, not modern windows-type applications, are suitable for this kind of system.

There are two basic possibilities for the geographical location of an organisation's business systems.

- **Centralised systems** use a single computer, called a mainframe, to which all users throughout the organisation are connected. These are often known as timesharing systems, and may be used by large companies such as banks and utilities, although they are less popular than they once were.
- **Distributed systems** use personal computers connected together in a network.

The type of data processing employed will, to a certain extent, depend on the size and structure of an organisation. In a small company with just a few employees, it may be the case that the cost and set-up time involved in a computerised data processing system cannot be justified and traditional paper-based methods may be adequate. However, as the volume of transactions increases, computerised techniques will become cost-effective and a point will be reached where it would be impractical to process the data manually.

As well as the size of the organisation and the volume of transactions, the structure of the organisation can also influence the data processing methods employed. In an organisation with a flat structure, efficient information flow many be achieved by manual methods (e.g. internal post). However, in organisations with many levels in their structure (i.e. hierarchical rather than flat) data will be required to flow up and down through these many levels, and to achieve efficient movement of this information, electronic methods, such as e-mail, may be required.

**Check your understanding 3.8**

A large organisation might use most, or all, of these different methods of data processing in the various departments they have. Can you list the departments that might typically use these different methods?

# Data handling applications

There are very many different data handling (or processing) applications. This section looks at the most common and widely used applications.

## Accounts

The accounts system is designed to track an organisation's flow of funds coming in and going out of the firm. The accounts system can be subdivided into accounts receivable and accounts payable. The **accounts receivable** (also known as **sales ledger**) system tracks all the monies that are owed by the customers to the organisation. It is designed to record all customer transactions, such as when an invoice or a credit note is issued, and also when a payment is received from a customer. The department that controls this system is the sales department. When a customer makes a payment, the payment is matched to an invoice and the computer is programmed to note the invoice as paid. A copy of the entries made in the sales ledger may be sent to the customer to allow the customer to reconcile this information against his/her account (and as a reminder of what is due for payment). This is called a **statement** (Figure 3.10).

**Educational Supplies Ltd**
13 High Road
Hornsey
London
N11 5EJ

Tel: 0208 555555
Fax: 0208 222222
e-mail: edusupplies@blotmail.com

***Customer:***

Westgate College
High Street
Westgate WG1 4RP

***Date: 1/3/03***

**Statement No: 123526**

| Invoice Number | Date | Amount | Due? |
|---|---|---|---|
| 115629 | 9/12/02 | £156.29 | Overdue |
| 116724 | 3/1/03 | £576.54 | Overdue |
| 116429 | 9/2/03 | £225.25 | Due |
| 118563 | 12/2/03 | £856.25 | Due |

Terms: Strictly 30 days
Please make cheque payable to Educational Supplies Ltd

Figure 3.10 An example statement

The **accounts payable** (also known as **purchase ledger**) system holds similar data to the accounts receivable system; the system tracks all monies that the organisation owes to other organisations, for example when the organisation orders goods/materials from suppliers. The department that controls this system is the purchasing department.

Accounts payable and receivable are part of the **nominal ledger** (Figure 3.11) or general ledger. This system controls all the organisation's transactions, for example, how much is owed to and by the organisation. Table 3.4 summarises the three applications for accounting: sales, purchase and nominal ledgers.

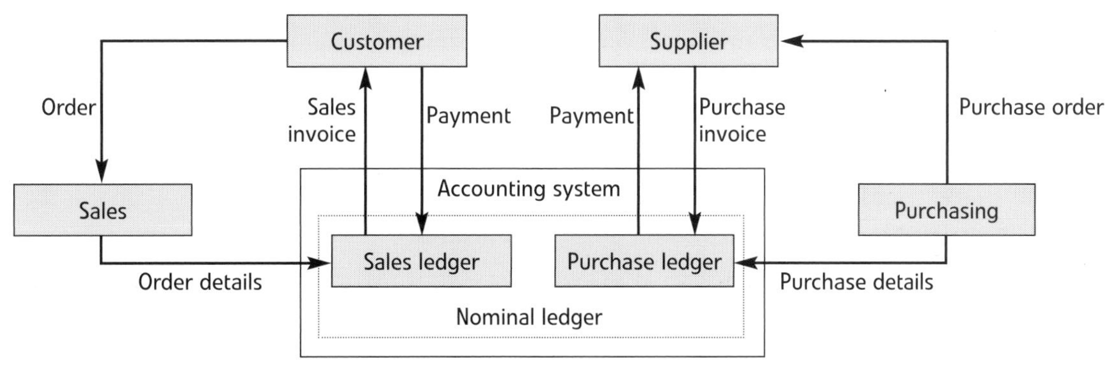


Figure 3.11 The nominal ledger

| **Application** | **What it produces (outputs)** |
|---|---|
| Sales ledger | Invoices for customers, sales journals, cash receipts lists, analysis of sales by customer, sales area and product |
| Purchase ledger | Purchase journals, cheques and remittance advices, analysis of purchases by suppliers |
| Nominal ledger | Trial balance, financial reports |

Table 3.4 Computer applications for accounting

**Check your understanding 3.9**

For each arrow shown in Figure 3.11, list the type of data that would need to be included.

## Payroll

The first commercial computer in the world (the 1951 British Leo 1) was designed to calculate employee wages, and payroll processing is now almost universally done by computer. Payroll is a relatively simple application. However, there are a number of calculations that need to be done, and the need for speed, accuracy and security is obvious. With hourly paid workers, the number of hours worked per week or month needs to be multiplied by the employee's rate of pay. Any overtime hours need to be calculated and added on. Deductions for National Insurance and income tax must be calculated along with any other deductions (pension contributions, etc.). Money must then be transferred electronically by EFT (electronic funds transfer) from the company's bank account into each employee's account, and transfers also need to be made to the Inland Revenue and the destination accounts for other deductions. Payroll is normally processed using the batch method described on page 105.

**Further research 3.4**

1 Find out more about the historic Leo 1 computer. Check the Leo website at www.leo.computer.org.uk.
2 Find out how companies are encouraged to use computers for tasks like paying taxes.

## Sales order processing

Sales order processing systems are used to record customer orders. They are particularly important for organisations that sell their goods over the telephone or via the Internet. These systems provide sales people with product information, including pricing and availability. They also record customer details and can interface with debit or credit card payment systems to charge the customer. Having recorded details of the sale, the sales system passes on financial information to the accounting system and also to the warehouse or dispatch system so the goods can be dispatched to the customer. In organisations that sell goods, the sales system is central to the running of the organisation.

## Invoicing

Invoicing is part of the accounting system and includes both sales invoicing and purchase invoicing. When a business's customers purchase goods, a **sales invoice** is sent from the business (the seller) to request payment from the buyer. Records need to be kept of these invoices (and the sales they relate to) and, at the end of each month, a statement listing any unpaid invoices may be sent to a customer. If invoices are unpaid after a certain length of time (normally 30 days) then a reminder may be sent. When payments are received they need to be recorded against the correct invoice.

When an organisation purchases goods or services, the supplier sends an invoice. For the supplier, this is a sales invoice, but, for the organisation buying the goods or services, it is called a **purchase invoice**. These purchase invoices need to be recorded and checked against actual goods received, before payment is sanctioned. Payments then need to be sent, in line with payment terms agreed between the seller and the buyer.

## Purchase ordering and stock control

Organisations that manufacture or sell goods need a **purchase ordering** system. Closely related to the stock control system, this system records details of goods ordered from suppliers. In many cases, orders are transmitted electronically to suppliers using EDI (electronic data interchange). The system also interfaces with the accounts system, passing financial information about purchases made.

Most industrial organisations and commercial organisations that sell goods keep some kind of stock. This can be stock of parts from which products can be manufactured and/or stock of finished goods. In either case, having the correct amount of stock is important for the efficient and cost-effective running of the company. If too much stock is held, money and space are wasted; if too little, customers will not be able to purchase the items they want and may take their business to competitors.

**Stock control** software relies on being able to identify every type of item that is stocked. This is often done with barcodes that can be read with a light pen. These barcodes uniquely identify each type of item by a product or item code. When stock comes into the warehouse (delivered from manufacturing or suppliers), warehouse workers must identify the type of stock (using the barcode) and the quantity, and enter these details into the system. The system can then tell them where within the warehouse the item should be placed. When items are ordered from the warehouse, either because they have been sold or because they are required by manufacturing, the system can subtract the number of items removed from the total in stock. When the number of each item in stock drops below a predetermined level (the **reorder level**), the stock control system will issue a request for more to be ordered from the supplier (this may involve direct links to manufacturing and/or purchasing systems).

## Bookings

Airline seat booking was another of the first commercial computer applications to appear, pioneered in the 1960s in the USA. Airline seats were traditionally booked at travel agents but, nowadays, on-line booking using the Internet is increasingly popular. Today, booking systems are used in other areas as well as airline seat booking. These include holidays, trains, boats and ferries, theatres, hotels and car hire. Booking systems involve checking the availability of the seat (or show or car) on the particular date and to the required destination. Customer requirements may also be recorded, such as an aisle or window seat, type of food required and so on. Customer details and payment will need to be recorded, and for payment the system needs to interface with credit or debit card transaction systems. Web-based booking systems are typically 'ticket-less' with no traditional ticket issued; instead, a booking reference is provided. Many booking systems also sell 'added value' services; for example, flight booking systems also interface with car hire and hotel booking systems. Customer contact details are often used for marketing services.

## Case study: EuroDisney Paris

EuroDisney Paris is the largest theme park in Europe. The giant complex on the outskirts of Paris has seven hotels. Bookings for all the hotels are handled by a single computer system called the Hotel Information System (HIS). All bookings are made centrally. In the hotels themselves, the system is used by three main groups of users.

On the front desk, staff welcome the hotel's guests and use the system to check details and allocate rooms quickly and efficiently. During their stay, the system records purchases in the hotel restaurants and any other facilities that guests use. When guests check out, the system provides a fully itemised bill, checks payment details and accepts payment if required. (Some guests pre-pay their visit but may still have to pay for extras.) The system also provides front desk staff with accurate data about how many rooms are occupied, how many are free and how many are in need of maintenance.

The system provides housekeeping staff with data about which rooms need cleaning and which need a change of linen because the guests have completed their stay. It also provides maintenance teams with details of rooms where repairs are required.

The hotel management use the system for planning and budgeting. They can forecast likely room requirements based on current bookings and past trends. They need this information to plan the purchase of items such as food and drink for the restaurant and to schedule staff so the correct number are on duty at any one time.

1 Why is it important to provide guests with a fully itemised bill?
2 What other use might the hotel management make of the information forecasting likely room occupancy levels?

### Personnel

Keeping records on company employees is a relatively straightforward application, although the need for security is clear. Information that needs to be recorded includes contact details, pay and benefits, training courses attended and health records.

## Assessment activity 3.4

1 Write a report explaining how the choice of data handling and processing methods is affected by the size and structure of the organisation.
2 Using example data handling activities, describe how data is processed, including the method of processing. Describe how these activities are used within an organisation.

## Case study: Domestic Repair Ltd

Domestic Repair Ltd have a sophisticated computer system used to record customer details and to schedule the engineers' visits. Part of the system involves recording details of the repair, including how long it took, what parts were used and how much was charged. Initially, this information is recorded manually by the engineer at the customer's house. On completion of the repair, the engineer completes a bill (Figure 3.12) on a two-part document. Whatever the engineer writes on the customer's top copy is copied on to the second copy using carbonless copy paper.

**Domestic Repair Ltd**

13 High Street
Enfield
London
EN9 1ZZ

Tel: 0208 888 8888
Fax: 0208 888 8889
e-mail: domestic-repair@topmail.com

**DRL**
**We fix it fast**

Date:
Customer:
Address

Post code:
Job number:
Machine:

| **Description of fault:** | | | |
|---|---|---|---|
| **Parts:** | | | |
| **Part no:** | **Description** | | **Price** |
| | | | |
| | | | |
| | | | |
| | | | |
| No of hours with customer: | | @ £25.50 per hour: | |
| | | VAT @ 17.5% | |
| | | **Total** | |

Paid with thanks, signed ............................................................

All workmanship and parts are guaranteed for 12 months.
VAT No 10222222

Figure 3.12 Customer bill

The engineer collects payment from the customer in the form of cash or a cheque. At the end of the day, when the engineer returns to the office, the administration assistant prints a batch control slip (Figure 3.13) that lists all the repairs the engineer has done that day. (This information comes from the scheduling system.) The engineer completes the amount charged for each repair and then totals up the amount of money collected. This provides the cross check with the amounts listed on each bill.

The engineer then hands the money, the batch control slip and the bills to the administration assistant. The administration assistant checks the amount of money and then enters the total money collected from the batch control slip into the system, together with the amount charged for each repair. If the total calculated by the system is the same as the manually calculated total from the batch control slip, the batch is accepted; otherwise, it is rejected and must be checked.

The cash and cheques are passed to the finance department who bank the money. The data recorded about each repair is used by the finance department to calculate income and profit. This is an example of information flowing sideways across the organisation from operations to sales. Managers receive various reports compiled from the data including overall and per

**Domestic Repair Ltd**

**Batch control slip**

Engineer: Clive Wilson

Date: 17th Feb 2003

Batch Number: 13721

| Job No | Postcode | Labour charge | Parts charge | Total inc. VAT |
|---|---|---|---|---|
| 12530 | EN6 1FF | | | |
| 12672 | NW6 3PP | | | |
| 12685 | NW8 2RB | | | |
| 12688 | N22 3RZ | | | |
| 12725 | N14 3RZ | | | |
| | | | | |
| | | | | |
| | | | | |
| | Totals | | | |

Check your addition – if there is an error the slip will be returned to **you**!

Figure 3.13 Batch control slip for customer bills

engineer average repair times. This information is flowing up the organisation, from the engineers to their managers.

1 When inputting the data from the customer bills what other data validation checks can be used?
2 What might the managers use the engineer average repair times data for?

## Assessment activity 3.5

1 Write a report explaining why information is important to an organisation in meeting its business objectives. Give examples of why information needs to flow upwards, downwards and sideways within the organisation.
2 Select a suitable data handling activity and design the document from which the data will be input. Design a batch control document that can be used with this data handling activity. Describe what other data controls could be used to ensure the accuracy of the data. Explain how the documents could be used and the stages required in their input and validation. Explain how document design can aid accuracy of data input.

# System life cycle

It is important to understand how data processing systems are developed. The system life cycle is a model that can be used to explain the stages in system development.

Many large, and some medium size, organisations have software developed especially for them. This way they can ensure the software exactly matches their requirements. This software is developed either by the company's in-house IT department or by a **software house**. A software house tends to be used either because an organisation's own IT department does not have the capability to develop software or because the software house has some specialist expertise that the in-house IT department lacks.

**What does it mean?**

A **software house** is a company that develops software for other organisations.

Like most large and complex tasks, system development is broken down into stages. It usually involves the automation of an existing procedure, and so, to explain what is required, the people within the organisation that are currently involved in using this existing procedure need to work with the people who are developing the software. A six-stage model of the development life cycle (Figure 3.14) is explained below.

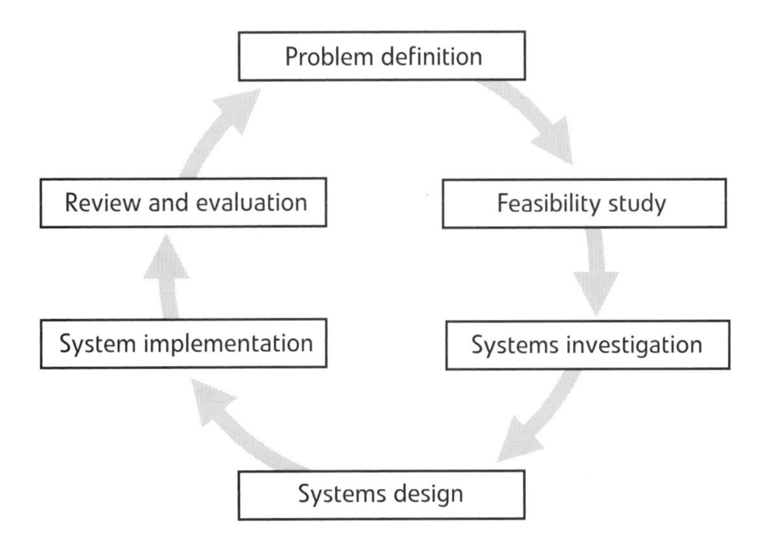


Figure 3.14 The system life cycle

- The **problem definition** stage involves an investigation of the existing procedures by working closely with the users in the organisation so as to identify the actual organisational requirements.
- A **feasibility study** involves a brief review of the existing system and identifying possible alternative solutions, costs and benefits. Before an organisation embarks on a costly project involving the development of a new information system, it is important to identify whether the system can be developed in such a way that the benefits outweigh the costs.

- The **systems investigation** stage requires that all parties concerned agree with the feasibility report. A detailed analysis of all aspects of the existing system is then needed. This involves identifying the tasks being carried out, how they are being carried out, the number of times these tasks are carried out, the staff involved in carrying out the tasks, what is lacking in the system, the types of faults that occur and how the current system could be improved. The result of this stage is a document, called the **system specification**, which describes in detail what the new system will do.

During these first three stages, the organisation must work closely with whoever is developing the software to ensure that the software developers fully understand what is required.

- The **systems design stage** is a technical phase. Using the information identified in the previous stages, a detailed design of the new system is developed, including its inputs, outputs, and all processing required. The document produced at this stage, called the **system design**, describes how the system will achieve what the system specification describes.
- At the **system implementation** stage, the programmers write the programs for the new systems, using the design created at the previous stage. The programs, once written, are tested to ensure they conform to the system specification. When they have been written and tested, the new system is then introduced to its users.
- Once the new system has settled down and been in use for some time, it will be **reviewed** to consider whether it has met the aims that were initially identified. It is very likely that further improvements or corrections will need to be made to the new system, at which point the development process returns again to the first, problem definition, stage. Hence the use of the term 'system life cycle'.

The software development process is important to the development of the organisation in a number of ways.

- Analysing business processes should lead to a better understanding of the processes within the organisation and may lead to opportunities to improve the processes rather than just create exact computerised copies of the manual processes.
- Having computerised one part of the business process, the organisation should now be in a better position to computerise and integrate other parts of the process.
- Computing skills within the organisation will have increased.

For these reasons, the term **spiral** is often used in preference to cycle, since this term captures the cyclical nature of software development but also adds the dimension of progression and improvement (Figure 3.15).

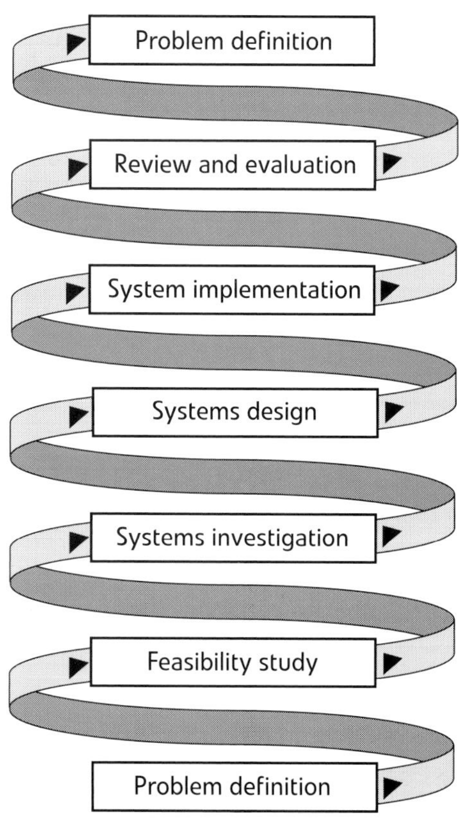


Figure 3.15 System development spiral

**Assessment activity 3.6**

1 Describe the purpose of the systems life cycle and the stages within it.
2 What is the importance of the process to the organisation?

# 3.4 Business systems

This section concentrates on three more aspects of an organisation:

- physical elements, i.e. assets
- operational requirements
- e-commerce.

## Physical elements

Organisations have many **assets**, i.e. buildings, equipment (industrial and business machines including computers), vehicles, data and people. All of these assets are valuable and need protecting, both physically and by an insurance policy to guard against damage, loss or theft.

Organisations are usually measured by the profit they make, the **bottom line**. Achieving profit is not simply a matter of buying for less than you sell. An organisation needs customers and attracting customers costs money. Many companies, particularly commercial organisations, strive to develop a **brand image** for their products. Well-known examples include McDonald's, Sony, Adidas and Coca Cola. These companies have a clearly defined **company image** and this can include a company logo, corporate colour scheme and a corporate philosophy. This image is carefully developed and protected by **copyright**.

All companies also need to insure themselves against lawsuits from employees, customers and visitors who may injure themselves visiting company premises or using a company's products.

There are, therefore, a number of essential issues that all organisations need to address, not least because they relate to their legal responsibilities:

- health and safety
- data protection
- security of assets such as copyright.

Failure to comply with the legal requirements related to these issues can result in the organisation facing heavy fines or, in extreme cases, in senior managers being sent to prison. As well as the necessity to operate within the law, organisations need to ensure that the data on which the successful running of the company relies is safe and secure from loss or theft.

**Check your understanding 3.10**

Make a list of all the things that a company needs to protect.

# Operational requirements

## Health and safety

Organisations have a duty of care to their employees, to ensure their workplace is both safe and reasonably comfortable. This impacts on the standard of the office environment, which should have the following:

- adequate ventilation
- sufficient good light
- a comfortable temperature.

It also affects computer users and the equipment provided in the following ways:

- Monitors should be adjustable and fitted with filter screens if glare is a problem.
- Chairs should be adjustable so employees can sit comfortably at the keyboard and monitor.
- Regular breaks from using the computer should be encouraged.
- Desks and floors should be free from trailing cables.
- The computer users themselves must not tamper with any electrical equipment or consume food or drink while working at the computer, in case of spillages.

**Check your understanding 3.11**

Make a poster for your computer rooms outlining the rules for safe use of computers.

## Privacy and confidentiality

Privacy is the right of an individual to have control over his or her personal information, and to determine what information about the person is communicated to others. **Confidentiality**, on the other hand, is an organisation's right, for example whether to communicate commercial data held on the computer such as sales data and financial figures.

Databases can contain huge amounts of personal data about a person's life, financial transactions, medical record, criminal record and other information. Such data needs to be protected as it could easily be accessed via a computer system by anyone within or outside the organisation. There is a growing fear that information stored on computer databases about individuals can be misused, in particular that information about the individual can be transferred to unauthorised third parties quickly and at a low cost.

The current UK legislation covering data held about living individuals is the **Data Protection Act** (DPA) 1998. This Act is an attempt to protect information about individuals. Under the DPA, organisations wishing to store personal information on a computer system must register with the Data Protection Registrar. They must indicate the type of data they are storing, and how they intend to use it. Any individual has the right to request details of any personal information held about them. (The data subject must pay a small fee to access the information.) Organisations that store personal data must abide by certain rules:

- They must protect the data from unauthorised access.
- They must not hold personal data for a purpose other than the specific purpose or purposes intended.
- They must not pass on the data to other organisations without the individual's consent.

- The data they hold must be accurate and up to date, and must not be held for longer than necessary.

**Further research 3.5**

1. Only brief details of the Data Protection Act are given here. Find out more by going to the data protection website www.dataprotection.gov.uk.
2. Many famous people have problems with intrusions into their privacy. The Press Complaints Commission is an organisation they can complain to if they think the Press has been intruding too much into their lives. Read about the privacy rules that newspapers are supposed to follow and the complaints that have been made on the Press Complaints Commission's website at www.ppc.org.uk.

The **Computer Misuse Act** 1990 (fraud and computer misuse) was introduced to address the increased threat of **hacking** in to computer systems and trying to gain unauthorised access to data.

**What does it mean?**

**Hacking** means gaining unauthorised access, usually through communication links.

Prior to this Act there was minimal protection and difficulties in prosecuting, because theft of data by hacking was not considered to be deprivation to the owner. New technologies generally introduce opportunities for new crimes, new things to steal and new ways to hurt others. The act makes certain actions an offence:

- attempting to gain unauthorised access to a computer system
- gaining unauthorised access with the intention of committing another offence (e.g. obtaining money by deception)
- making unauthorised modifications to programs or data; this covers introducing a virus to a computer system.

**Assessment activity 3.7**

The Director of a small company is concerned about its responsibilities with regard to its physical and operational requirements. Write a report for the Director covering issues such as health and safety, data protection, copyright and computer misuse.

# E-commerce

The Internet is a global network which is increasingly being used by businesses for the following:

- marketing their company's brands and products
- selling their products
- setting up relatively low-cost links with customers, suppliers and distributors.

Many businesses, including supermarkets, travel agents, wine merchants, book sellers and car sellers now sell their products through e-commerce websites. With a computer, Internet connection and web browser, a consumer can visit these virtual stores and view, select and pay for goods which can often be delivered within 24–48 hours. E-commerce is fundamentally changing the way businesses of all sizes operate, affecting their internal operations and their relationships with suppliers and customers. E-commerce can improve the efficiency of all stages of the business process, from design and manufacture to retailing and distribution.

## Case study: Low-cost airlines

An example of the tremendous improvement in efficiency that can be achieved by using e-commerce can be found in the airline industry where traditional carriers such as British Airways have been facing a significant challenge from low-cost airlines such as easyJet. Using traditional telesales to sell airline seats requires a large number of telesales operators (typically 50–100 people at peak times). To sell the same volume of seats on an e-commerce website requires only 2 or 3 technical support personnel, representing an enormous saving in employee costs. In addition, the use of a ticket-less system, whereby travellers are issued with a booking reference number rather than a traditional ticket, has simplified the booking process, making further efficiency improvements.

1 What are the disadvantages of Internet booking systems?
2 What other types of commercial organisations have taken advantage of the Internet to sell their goods or services?

Another efficiency improvement that can be made with e-commerce is that of **fluid pricing**. E-commerce booking systems commonly do not have fixed 'brochure' prices. Instead, prices are varied depending on demand. For example, with an airline seat booking, when seats for a flight first go on sale, they are available at the lowest price. As the plane fills up the price of the remaining seats rises. Seats on flights at popular times (weekends, school holidays, etc.) are also more expensive. Fluid pricing gives organisations the opportunity to maximise the seat occupancy on flights and also to maximise income. There is also considerable opportunity for marketing promotions. Token collecting offers in conjunction with newspapers are often used to boost seat occupancy, especially on flights at less popular times (e.g. midweek).

The typical features of an e-commerce system are outlined below.

- A **catalogue** presents the company's goods and services. This often includes a search facility so customers can search for items that match their requirements.
- Websites selling simple products such as books or groceries have a virtual **shopping basket** (Figure 3.16), into which goods can be placed (and removed).
- Seat booking sites have a **configurator** (Figure 3.17) where different options can be selected (e.g. the morning or afternoon flight) and the price including taxes, etc. is shown.
- The **check out** is where the customer needs to pay for the selected products using a debit or credit card. To protect sensitive financial information (e.g. debit card numbers), this part of the website typically uses a **secure web server** that **encrypts** data sent to and from the customer's computer
- The purchaser is normally provided with an e-mail confirmation of purchase.

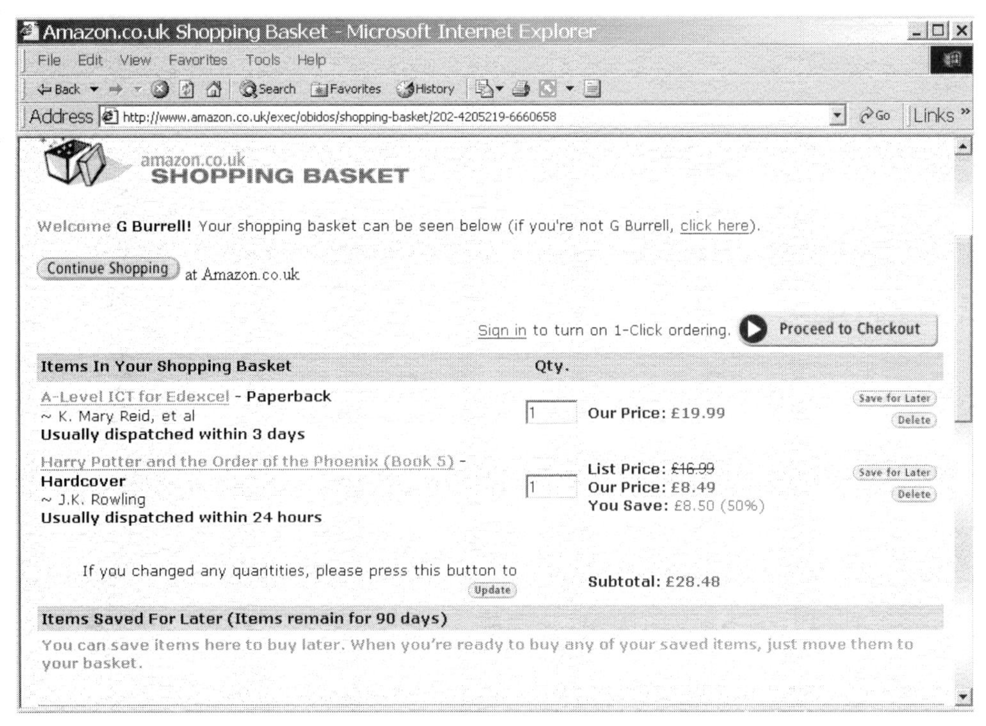


Figure 3.16 Amazon shopping basket



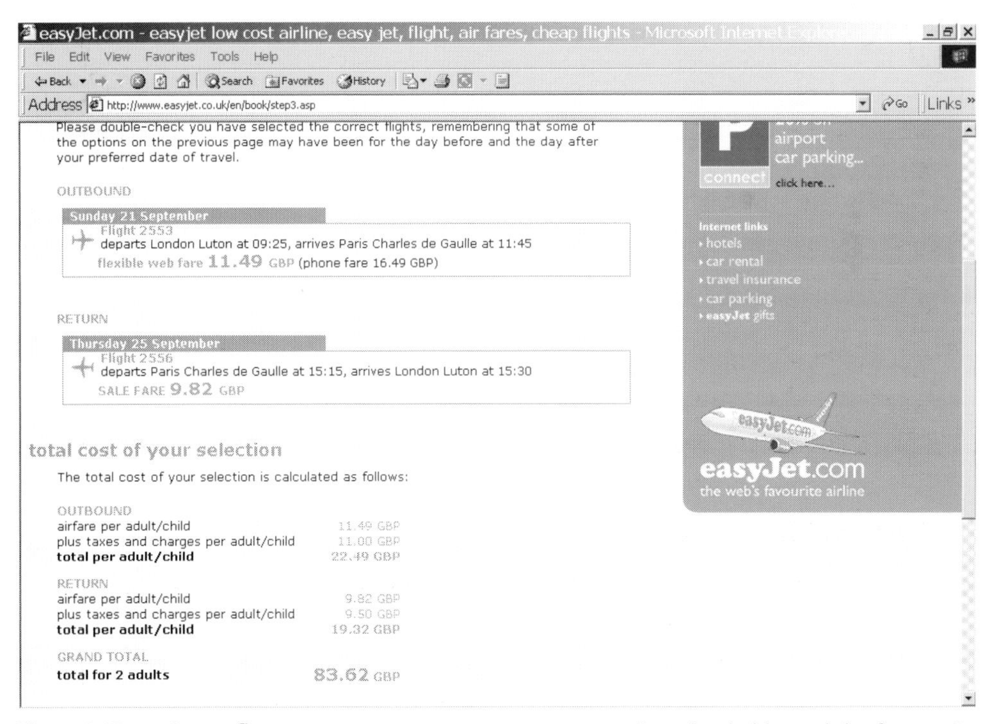


Figure 3.17 easyJet configurator



## What does it mean?

Data that is **encrypted** is encoded so that it cannot be read, except by the intended recipient. This protects sensitive data from unauthorised access or interception.

## Test your knowledge

1 What is the difference between public and private sector organisations?
2 What is the difference between an industrial organisation and a commercial organisation?
3 What sort of information do senior managers require?
4 Explain the difference between flat and hierarchical organisation structures.
5 Explain the difference between data and information.
6 Give some examples of information in document form.
7 How does a batch control slip work?
8 What is the difference between batch and real-time processing?
9 What is the purpose of a statement?
10 What does payroll processing involve?
11 In a stock control system, what is the reorder level?
12 What does the personnel department do? Give some examples of the information it might use.
13 What is the difference between a sales invoice and a purchase invoice?
14 List the steps in the system development life cycle.
15 What does the production department do?
16 What is a turnaround document? Why is it used?
17 What does EFTPOS stand for? Describe what it involves.
18 What is the purpose of a feasibility study?
19 What is the purpose of copyright law?
20 List the main requirements of the Data Protection Act.

# UNIT 4 INTRODUCTION TO SOFTWARE DEVELOPMENT

Mention the term 'software development' and most people probably think it involves writing computer programs. It does, but it also involves a number of other important activities.

This unit looks at all of the phases of software development: analysis and design, programming, testing and documentation. It is worth bearing in mind that, although most of the programs you develop will be created by you alone and used by you, in reality, most commercial programs are written by a team of developers and used by other (often non-IT professional) users. For these reasons, and because of the limitations of space and time, the processes described here are somewhat simplified compared with what happens in the 'real world'.

## Learning objectives

- To apply analysis and design techniques to the software development process
- To develop basic high-level code using an appropriate programming language
- To produce documentation
- To use testing methods

# 4.1 Analysis and design techniques

This section looks at some simple analysis and design techniques. The purpose of these techniques is to take the programmer from the client's written description of what they want to a design from which the program(s) can be written. Most of the techniques used in this process involve creating a simplified model of the system (often using diagrams) and then progressively adding more detail to the model until it represents quite closely how the actual programming code will be written. As with most complex problems, a sensible technique for dealing with the complexity of a computer program is to break down what is required into manageable chunks. Then each chunk can be analysed individually.

The case study below is an example where software is developed to meet a company's individual needs by a team of programmers who work for that company. This is common practice in large organisations but not all software is written this way. Most of the software you have probably used (Microsoft® Office for example) is not written for the individual needs of one particular company. Instead it is written by a company that specialises in writing software and is designed to meet a wide range of users' needs. These general-purpose programs are sold to anyone who wants to buy them.

### Case study: Fast Cash Bank

Like all banks, Fast Cash relies heavily on computers to process the large number of transactions that take place every day in their customers' bank accounts (salaries paid in, withdrawals of cash, payments by credit or debit card, etc.). It also uses computers to provide a wide range of facilities and services to customers.

Fast Cash Bank relies heavily on computers

Fast Cash offers a foreign exchange service. This means that customers can exchange their money for foreign currency, such as euros or US dollars. Each currency has a different exchange rate. For example, at one time the exchange rate for British pounds to euros was about 1.6, so for £10 you could get 16 euros. However, exchange rates change over time. Fast Cash wants to provide its cashiers with a simple currency converter program that will calculate the correct amount of foreign currency that they should give to a customer.

1 Start thinking about the program you plan to write for your portfolio.
2 Identify a suitable third party and write a report about what they require.

# Analysis

The first step in analysis is to obtain a statement of the user's requirement, i.e. what they want the program to do. This may sound like a simple task, but, for a number of reasons, it is often a difficult task.

- The user may not clearly understand what is required, or might not be able to give sufficient detail.
- The users' requirements may be stated in terms which relate to their businesses. Users in the banking world will tend to state their requirements in banking and financial terms, but the programmer is an expert in programming, not banking.
- The user may not understand what is (and is not) possible when writing the software.

The user's requirement may therefore need to be the subject of some discussion and negotiation between the user and the programmer. There are a number of key questions that need to be asked:

- *What are the aims of the system?* One of the first things that needs to be decided is: what are the primary purposes or aims of the system that you are planning to develop? This will probably be in terms of the problem that it is intended to solve or the opportunity it will take advantage of. It is important to clarify this at the start, because sometimes during the process of developing the software people can lose track of the original reason for which the software was required.
- *How does the current system work?* In many cases, the software to be developed will replace an existing system. It may be a manual system (i.e. using people rather than computers) or it may be an old computer system which has outlived its usefulness. In either case, it is important that the current system is thoroughly understood so that the new software can preserve its essential elements and its good features and avoid the problems that it now suffers from.
- *What other systems does it need to interface with?* No system works in isolation. All systems take input from the user or another computer system, and also produce some kind of output. Part of understanding the system to be developed involves defining these inputs and outputs.
- *What is the scope of the system and what are its boundaries?* What will the system do, and what won't it do? This may sound like an obvious question, but it is an important one. Also, it is important to decide what is to be included and what is to be left out. Computers are very powerful machines and there are many facilities you could include in the software you are developing if you had endless time and money. In some cases, you may want to decide on the most important features (referring back to the aims of the system) and to develop the first version of the software with those features, putting the remaining features on the 'wish list' for future versions.

## Case study: Fast Cash Bank

The basic user requirement for the foreign currency converter at Fast Cash Bank is as follows:

- The foreign currency converter will allow cashiers to enter an amount of money in Sterling (British pounds), select from a list of currencies to convert to, and then display the amount of foreign currency that should be exchanged for the Sterling. The program should also display the conversion rate that has been used.
- The program should subtract a commission of 5 per cent from the Sterling amount before the conversion is done; the amount of commission should also be displayed.
- The program should deal with any incorrect entries by displaying an appropriate error message and allowing the user to re-enter the value.

During the investigation phase at Fast Cash Bank the following information is discovered:

- *What are the aims of the system?* Fast Cash want to provide cashiers with a quick and easy-to-use method to calculate foreign currency transactions. It also wants to reduce the number of errors made.
- *How does the current system work?* The cashiers look up the exchange rates for a certain currency in printed tables and then work out the correct amount of currency using a calculator.
- *With what other systems does it need to interface?* The program will need to download the current exchange rates each day, perhaps from the Internet. (For the sake of simplicity, the program we write will use fixed currency rates.)
- *What is the scope of the system and what are its boundaries?* In the first version of the program it will provide only the functionality described above. It should not, for example, print a receipt or keep a record of the transaction, although these functions may be added at a later date.

1. What are the aims for *your* proposed program?
2. How does the current system it is intended to replace work?

## Assessment activity 4.1

Write the user requirement for your proposed program, making sure you include a description of the data to be input, output and stored.

The end result of the investigation stage should be a document that draws together all the information collected and puts the case for developing the software. It should also describe the costs involved. Before the project can go ahead, this document will be presented to the manager in the company who is responsible for authorising the expenditure. The decision on whether to proceed will most probably be a commercial, rather than a technical, one. In other words, the manager will need to decide whether the cost can be justified and what the return on the investment will be.

To keep things simple, we will write a program that can deal with just three currencies, US dollars, euros and Japanese yen. The user will enter 1 for yen, 2 for dollar and 3 for euro. In reality a much wider range of currencies would need to be dealt with. The program should continue to run until the user indicates that it should end.

# Design

Having completed the investigation stage and received the go-ahead from management, the next step is to produce a design. There are a number of things that need to be designed and planned. What is done at the system design stage involves taking what has already been decided in the investigation stage and adding more detail about the internal workings of the software.

Programs take some kind of data as input, perform some kind of processing on that data (perhaps a calculation) and produce some kind of output. At the design stage, we need to add more detail about what data is to be input, how it will be stored and processed, what will be output and how it will look to the user.

## Inputs and outputs

Making a list of the data to be input and output will provide a starting point for defining the variables that will be required, as each item of data that is to be input and output from the program will require a **variable** to store it. For each variable, we need to decide on a name and a data type. This information can be summarised in a data table (see Table 4.1). The program may also require **constants**. These, like variables, are places in which you can store values; however, while the values in variables can be changed while the program is running, constants do not change.

| Attribute | Description | Example |
|---|---|---|
| Name | Given by the programmer, variables should be given a name that indicates their purpose. For example, x is a valid variable name, but it does not mean anything. For a variable that holds the balance of a bank account 'acc_balance' is a more helpful name. | First_name |
| Data type | This indicates the type of data that the variable will hold. The most common data types are *integer* (for holding whole numbers), *real* (for holding numbers with a fractional part) and *string* (for holding text). | String |
| Value | This is the data that the variable holds. It will change (vary) depending on what the user enters (inputs) and what processing takes place. | 'Alan' |

Table 4.1 Characteristics of variables

## Case study: Fast Cash Bank

By examining the user requirement for the program the following variables can be inserted in the data table:

| Input/Output | Variable name | Datatype |
|---|---|---|
| Amount of money in Sterling (input) | sterling | Real |
| Amount of commission (output) | comm_amount | Real |
| Choice of currency to convert to (input) | currency | Integer |
| US dollar conversion rate (input) | dollar_rate | Real |
| Euro conversion rate (input) | euro_rate | Real |
| Yen conversion rate (input) | yen_rate | Real |
| Amount of foreign money (output) | result | Real |
| Exit indicator (input) | exit | String |

Table 4.2 Data table for Fast Cash Bank

In addition, we know that a commission of 5 per cent needs to be subtracted from the amount of foreign money. The commission rate should therefore be stored in a constant:

| Use for | Constant name | Value |
|---|---|---|
| Commission rate | Com_rate | 0.05 |

**Create a data table for your proposed program.**

Although using the inputs and output is a good place to start creating the data table, it may not identify *all* the required variables, some additional ones may come from the design of the processing.

### Processing

With the inputs and outputs identified, the processing requirements can be designed. Again, our source of information for these designs must be the investigation we did earlier. We should have discovered how the current system works, and what calculations or other manipulations are done. We now have to decide how our program will carry out these calculations, and what types of processing (sequence, selection and iteration – see Unit 2, page 73) are required. There are a number of different techniques used for designing the processing that a program must do. We shall look at **flowcharting**, one of the many techniques which utilises diagrams, and **pseudo code**.

### ? What does it mean?

A **flowchart** is a diagram that shows the steps which must be taken to carry out a task, the sequence they occur in and how they are linked.

**Pseudo code** is a kind of 'half way house' between the actual programming code and normal spoken English. There are no precise rules to writing pseudo code but it is used to work out the sort of program code needed without having to worry about the exact instructions. Pseudo code is best used at the later stages of program design. It is a much more detailed technique than flowcharting and is much closer to the code that will eventually be written.

**Flowcharts** can be used to design all sorts of processes, not just programming ones. Flowcharts use a variety of symbols, linked by arrows to indicate the type of step involved at each stage. Flowcharting is a good technique to use in the early stages of program design because it is useful for producing a generalised design without too much detail.

- They start with a circle containing the word Start with a single arrow leaving the circle, and end with a circle containing the word Stop, with a single arrow entering.
- Processing steps (a sequence building block), such as doing a calculation, are contained in a rectangle with a brief description of the step inside the rectangle (see Figure 4.1). The rectangle has one arrow entering (from the previous step) and one leaving (to the next step).

Calculate foreign currency amount

Figure 4.1 Flow chart processing step

- Steps that involve some input are shown in a skewed rectangle, also with a brief description of the step written in the box, and with one arrow entering and one leaving (see Figure 4.2).

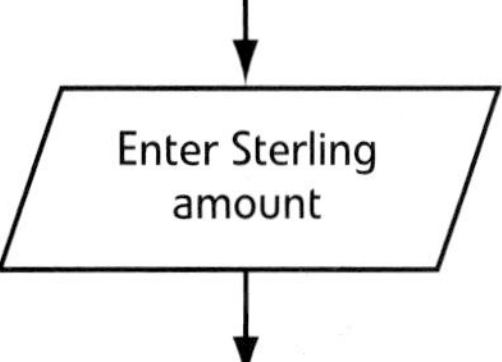


Figure 4.2 Flow chart input box

- Output steps are shown as a box which is meant to look like a torn-off piece of paper, as shown in Figure 4.3.

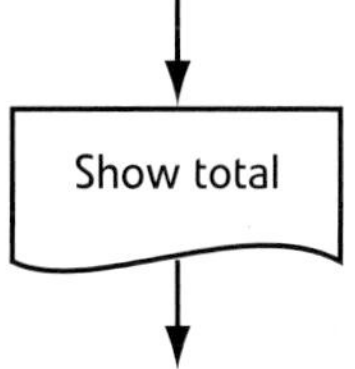


Figure 4.3 Flow chart output box

- Where a choice or decision needs to be made (a selection building block) a diamond shape is used, containing a question that describes the choice. While one arrow enters the diamond shape, two leave it. One shows the route taken if the answer to the question is yes, the other if it is no (see Figure 4.4).

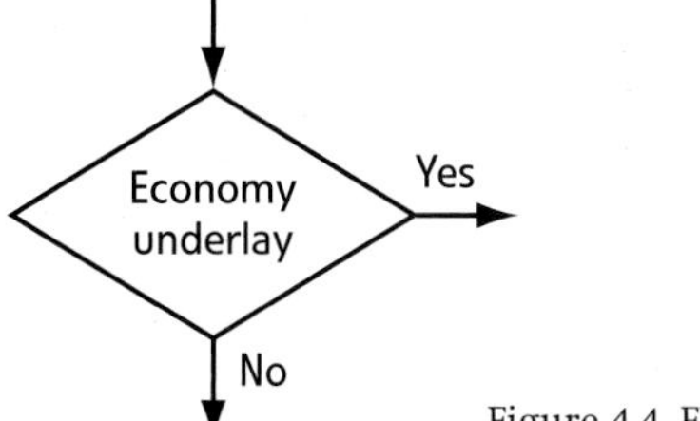


Figure 4.4 Flow chart decision box

Flowcharts are a good introduction to program design methods. However, they are not good for complex problems as the flowcharts themselves can become complex and difficult to follow.

## Case study: Fast Cash Bank

The flowchart for the Fast Cash Bank currency converter is shown below.

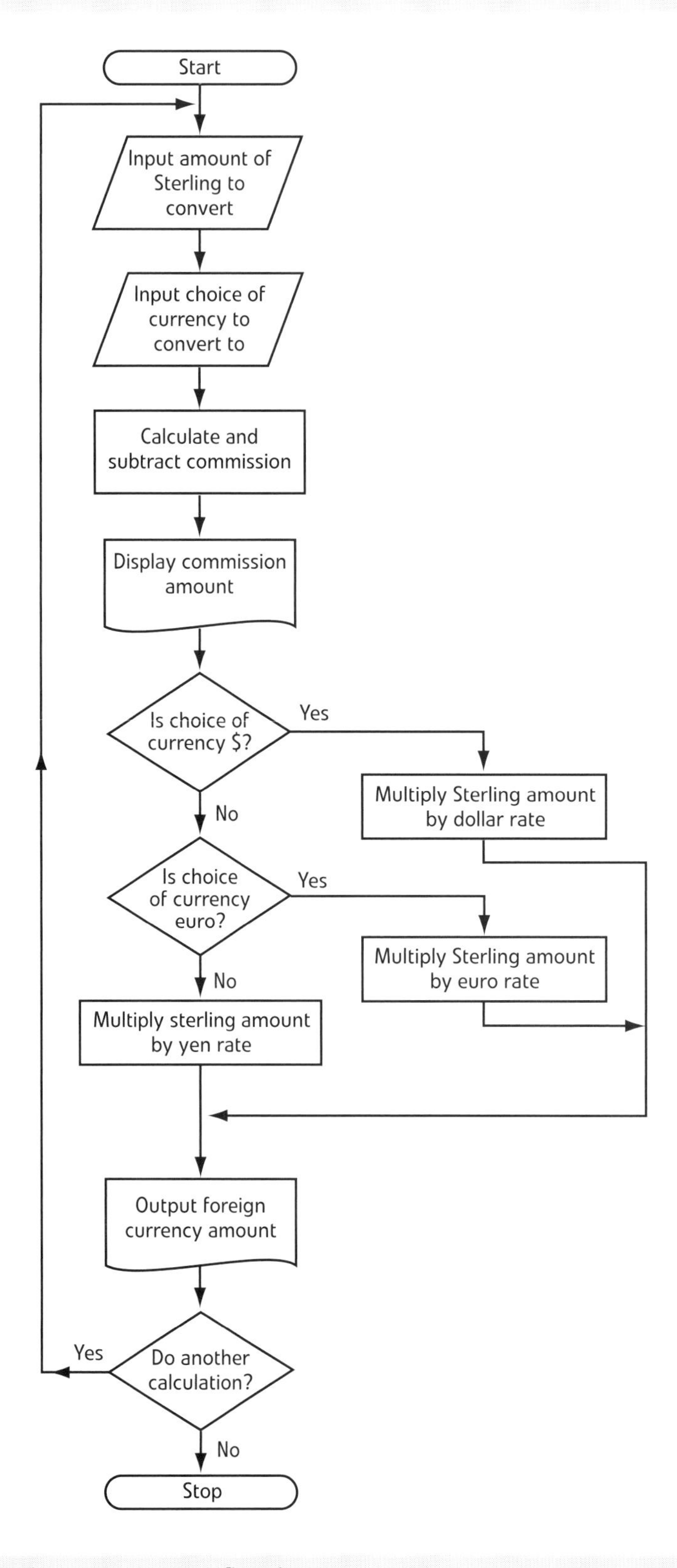


Figure 4.5 Fast Cash Bank currency converter flow chart

**Draw a flowchart for your proposed program.**

**Pseudo code** is normally written only for the more complex parts of the program, such as where complex calculations or data manipulation need to be done.

### Case study: Fast Cash Bank

The calculation of the commission required is the most complex calculation done in this program, so it makes sense to write pseudo code for it. The calculation involves calculating 5 per cent (stored in the constant com_rate) of the Sterling amount (store in the variable Sterling) and storing that in the comm_amount variable. The commission amount is then subtracted from the Sterling amount.

We can write this calculation as:

```
comm_amount = Sterling * 5%
Sterling = Sterling - comm_amount
```

This pseudo code, as you will see when we come to write the program, is very similar to the actual code.

**Write the pseudo code for the most complex part of your proposed program.**

The design process described in this section involves taking the understanding of the system that the investigation stage provided and developing that understanding using pseudocode, a flowchart and data table. The end result is a design from which the programming code can be written.

The system design is normally produced as a document which describes the design of the system and includes all the diagrams which have been produced. This document is important because the designer of the system may not be the person who is going to write the programs. The person, or team of people, who write the programs need this design document as their 'guide book' to produce the programs.

### Assessment activity 4.2

Produce a complete design document for the program you propose to write. Include the data table, flowchart and pseudocode you have previously created. Identify where the different programming methods of sequence, selection and iteration are used (the flow chart can be used as a guide).

# 4.2 Programming language

A **program** is a set of instructions that tells the computer what to do. Whatever function you want your computer to perform, all you have to do is to write the program.

The microprocessor or chip at the heart of a computer can only understand instructions in the form of binary codes (made up of ones and zeros), but as binary codes are very difficult for humans to understand, all modern programming is done using symbolic languages with English-like statements. These are then converted into the binary codes that the computer understands using a piece of software called a **compiler**.

There is a wide range of programming languages available. Among the more widely used commercial languages are Visual Basic (produced by Microsoft) and C++.

- **Visual Basic** includes tools for creating Windows® forms, text boxes, buttons, etc. and is often used when developing Windows® programs.
- **Pascal** is easy to use and understand, and so it is popular for teaching programming. You can compile and run all the examples using a commercial compiler such as the Borland Turbo Pascal, or you can use the free Pascal compiler available at www.freepascal.org.

## Programming language environments

In the past, programming was done in a text-based environment (like the DOS operating system). An editor was used to type the program code; this was then saved in a text file and compiled with a separate compiler. Most modern programming languages come packaged as a complete programming environment, with a windows-type visual interface. Known as **IDEs (integrated programming environments)**, they include an editor so you can type the code of the program, and a compiler, along with all the usual features of a visual environment such as pull-down menus, help menus, etc. In many cases, the editor is context sensitive; in other words, it identifies some errors in the code as you type them and also prompts for valid options as you type commands. IDEs also include facilities to debug the program, i.e. to identify and remove logic errors from the code. All the examples in this Unit are written using the Borland Turbo Pascal IDE. Although this is a DOS program, it has a Windows-like IDE, as shown is Figure 4.6.

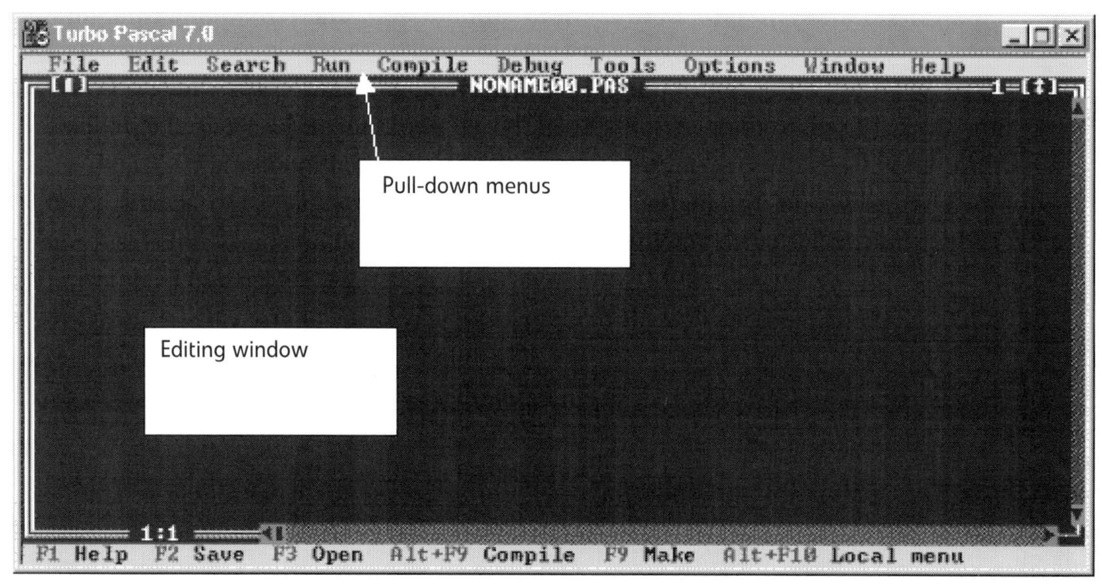


Figure 4.6 The Borland Turbo Pascal IDE

## Good programming practice

Programs are usually complex and often contain many hundreds if not thousands of lines of code. It is important that certain rules of good practice are followed when the programs are written to make sure that they are as easy to understand as possible.

- **Descriptive identifiers:** It is important to choose variable and constant names that give some idea as to what is stored in the variable.
- **Indentation:** By indenting sections of code, such as the code within a loop or an if statement, the code becomes easier to read.
- **Comments:** Adding descriptive text to a program is also an important aid to understanding the program. These so-called comments are ignored by the compiler, but are very helpful to human readers. In Pascal, program text that is a comment must be enclosed with curly brackets. An example of a well commented program is shown in Figure 4.7.

```
program simcalc(input, output);
{Written by AEJ Jan 2003}
uses crt;
var
    num1 : real;
    num2 : real;
    answer : real;          <---- Meaningful variable names
    opcode : string;
    reply : string;
begin
    ClrScr;
    writeln ('Calculator Program');
    repeat                  <---- Indented sections
        {Input numbers}
        writeln ('Enter first number');
        readln (num1);
        writeln ('Enter second number');
        readln (num2);
        {Select operation}  <---- Comments
        writeln ('Enter + for add or – for subtract');
        readln (opcode);
        {Do calculation depending on operation entered}
        if opcode = '+' then answer := num1 + num2;
        if opcode = '–' then answer := num1 – num2;
        {Display result}
        writeln ('Answer is ',answer:4:2);
        writeln ('Type X to exit, or any other key to continue.');
        readln (reply);
      {Keep going until user enters X}
    until (reply = 'X');
end.
```

Figure 4.7 A program conforming to good programming practice

What sort of instructions can you put in a program? Most programs have instructions that do one of three basic things:

- **input**, taking some data from the user (or from a disk file)
- **output**, displaying some data to the user (or writing it to a disk file)
- **processing**, modifying data in some way.

Programming tradition dictates that the first program you write in any language is the 'Hello world' program. This program simply displays the message 'Hello world' and requires only output instructions. The program is shown in Figure 4.8.

Note that each statement ends with a semi-colon (;), except the last one, **end**, which finishes with a full stop. You must follow these **syntax rules** carefully, otherwise the program will not compile successfully.

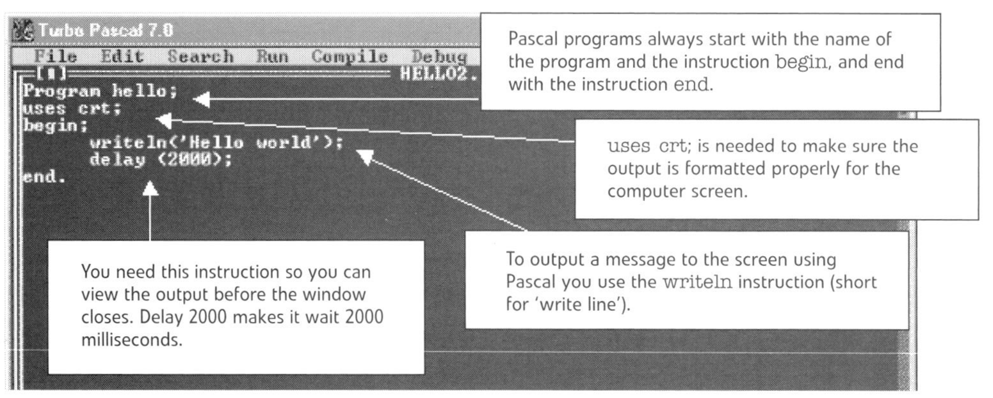


Figure 4.8 The Pascal 'Hello World' program

## What does it mean?

All programming languages have rules about how the instructions can be written – these are known as **syntax rules**. If you break the syntax rules the program will not compile.

Borland Turbo Pascal provides a Windows-like interface. When you start the program, you have a blank screen where you type, and edit your program, as shown earlier in Figure 4.6. You can use the pull-down edit menu to copy and paste sections of code, if required.

Having typed the program into the editor and checked it carefully, the next step is to compile it. The compiler checks that the syntax of the program you have typed in is correct (that you have included a semi-colon at the end of each line, for example) and, if the syntax is correct, it converts the program into binary codes that the computer can understand. In Turbo Pascal you choose Compile, from the Compile menu. If the program compiles successfully, you will see a message like the one in Figure 4.9.

```
Turbo Pascal 7.0
 File  Edit  Search  Run  Compile  Debug  Tools  Options  Window  Help
                          HELLO2.PAS
Program hello;
uses crt;
begin;
     writeln('Hello world');
     delay (2000);
end.
                    Compiling
     Main file: HELLO2.PAS
     Done.

     Destination: Memory     Line number:     0
     Free memory:   293K     Total lines:     6

          Compile successful: Press any key
          1:1
 F1 Help | Compile source file
```

Figure 4.9 Compiling a program in Turbo Pascal

Before you run the program, it is wise to save it. If you are using Borland Turbo Pascal, choose the Save option under the File menu. Type the name of the program and click OK. Remember that in DOS programs, file names are limited to eight characters, with no spaces.

You can then run your program, by choosing Run from the Run menu to see whether it works properly. It is important to understand that the compiler only checks that you have typed each instruction correctly. It does not check whether they are the correct instructions and in the correct order. Just because a program compiles successfully does not mean it will work the way you want it to! When you run the 'Hello world' program, it should produce output similar to that shown in Figure 4.10.

```
Turbo Pascal 7.0
Turbo Pascal  Version 7.0  Copyright (c) 1983,92 Borland International
Hello world
```

Figure 4.10 The 'Hello world' program working

## Check your understanding 4.1

Write a program that will display the message 'Good Morning'.

The 'Hello world' program is very simple and only shows how a program can produce output. A program that adds two numbers together will provide us with a slightly more complex program, one which demonstrates input and processing as well as output. This program needs to accept two numbers from the user (input), add them together (processing) and display the result (output).

Before you can use a variable you must declare it at the beginning of the program in a special area that starts with the instruction *var*. The calculator program is shown in Figure 4.11, and Figure 4.12 shows the screen display when this program is run. The user keyed in the numbers 5 and 3 and the program calculated the answer as 8.

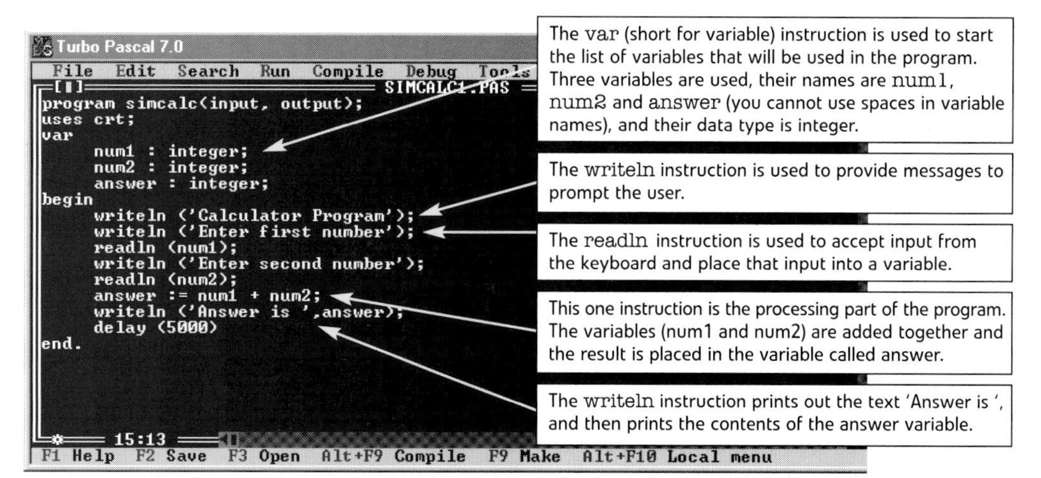

Turbo Pascal 7.0
File Edit Search Run Compile Debug Tools
SIMCALC1.PAS
program simcalc(input, output);
uses crt;
var
num1 : integer;
num2 : integer;
answer : integer;
begin
writeln ('Calculator Program');
writeln ('Enter first number');
readln (num1);
writeln ('Enter second number');
readln (num2);
answer := num1 + num2;
writeln ('Answer is ',answer);
delay (5000)
end.
15:13
F1 Help F2 Save F3 Open Alt+F9 Compile F9 Make Alt+F10 Local menu
The var (short for variable) instruction is used to start the list of variables that will be used in the program. Three variables are used, their names are num1, num2 and answer (you cannot use spaces in variable names), and their data type is integer.
The writeln instruction is used to provide messages to prompt the user.
The readln instruction is used to accept input from the keyboard and place that input into a variable.
This one instruction is the processing part of the program. The variables (num1 and num2) are added together and the result is placed in the variable called answer.
The writeln instruction prints out the text 'Answer is ', and then prints the contents of the answer variable.


Figure 4.11 The calculator program code

```
Turbo Pascal 7.0
Turbo Pascal Version 7.0 Copyright (c) 1983,92 Borland International
Calculator Program
Enter first number
5
Enter second number
3
Answer is 8
```

Figure 4.12 The calculator program running

## Check your understanding 4.2

1 Write a program that adds three numbers together.
2 Write another program that calculates the differences between two numbers.

The simple calculator program demonstrates some important programming concepts, but it is still rather limited in what it can do – it can only add two numbers. How could we introduce the ability to do subtraction as well as addition in the same program? To do this the program needs to be able to make a choice (between adding and subtracting). It needs to know what the user wants to do and then carry out the appropriate action. For this, Pascal (and most other programming languages) provides an **if** instruction.

Figure 4.13 shows the calculator program rewritten using the if instruction to allow either addition or subtraction.

```
Turbo Pascal 7.0
File Edit Search Run Compile Debug Tools Options Window Help
SIMCALC1.PAS
program simcalc(input, output);
uses crt;
var
    num1 : integer;
    num2 : integer;
    answer : integer;
    opcode : string;
begin
    writeln ('Calculator Program');
    writeln ('Enter first number');
    readln (num1);
    writeln ('Enter second number');
    readln (num2);
    writeln ('Enter + for add or - for subtract');
    readln (opcode);
    if opcode = '+' then answer := num1 + num2;
    if opcode = '-' then answer := num1 - num2;
    writeln ('Answer is ',answer);
    delay (5000)
end.
20:1
F1 Help F2 Save F3 Open Alt+F9 Compile F9 Make Alt+F10 Local menu
```

Another variable is needed to store the type of operation that is required, either add or subtract (entered as + or –). This is stored in a variable called opcode, and its data type is string (text).

These lines first ask the user to indicate whether to add or subtract (by entering either + or –). Whatever the user types is stored in the opcode variable. The contents of the opcode variable is then tested using an if instruction and the chosen calculation is carried out.

Figure 4.13 Modified calculator program

**Check your understanding 4.3**

Modify your program to do multiplication and division as well as addition and subtraction.

The calculator program has one major limitation. It only adds or subtracts one pair of numbers; then it stops. To do any more calculations, you would need to run the program again. It would be better if the program were to go on running until the user indicates that it should stop. To repeat code in a program, a **loop** is needed. Loops make part of a program repeat until some condition is met. In the modified version of the calculator program shown below, the loop continues until the user enters the character X:

```
    program simcalc;
    uses crt;
    var
    num1 : integer;
    num2 : integer;
    answer : integer;
    opcode : string;
    reply : string;
begin
    writeln ('Enter first number');
    repeat
      writeln ('Calculator Program');
      readln (num1);
      writeln ('Enter second number');
      readln (num2);
      writeln ('Enter + for add or - for subtract');
      readln (opcode);
      if opcode = '+' then answer :=num1 + num2;
      if opcode = '-' then answer :=num1 - num2;
      writeln ('Answer is ',answer);
      writeln (Type X to exit, or any other key to continue.');
      readln (reply);
    until (reply = 'X');
end.
```

Because the condition that ends the loop, until (reply = 'X'), is tested at the end of the loop this is known as a **post-conditioned loop**. In a **pre-conditioned loop** the test is at the beginning of the loop. A **fixed iteration** loop repeats a certain number of times.

With this simple calculator program, the three basic programming constructs have been introduced.

- **Sequence:** program instructions are followed one after another.
- **Selection:** there is a choice to be made, as with the if instruction.
- **Iteration:** instructions are repeated, in a loop.

**Check your understanding 4.4**

Compare this with the use of these constructs in low-level programming languages (page 73).

# Data representation

So far we have met variable data types for whole numbers (integer), numbers with fractional parts (real) and for text (the string data type). Another data type, called **Boolean**, can only take the values 'true' or 'false'. Boolean variables are generally used to store the results of logical tests, and because they can be tested easily they can make complex expressions more readable. A simple example program using Boolean variables is shown in Figure 4.14.

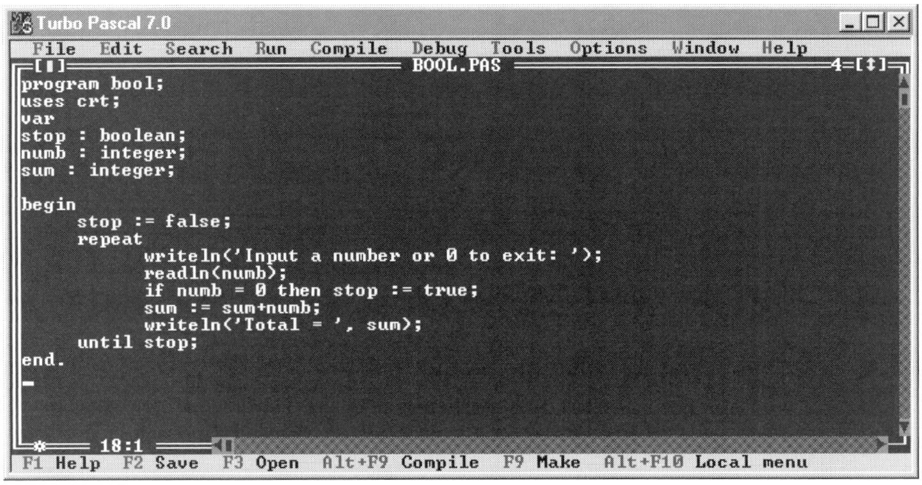

```
Turbo Pascal 7.0
File  Edit  Search  Run  Compile  Debug  Tools  Options  Window  Help
BOOL.PAS
program bool;
uses crt;
var
stop : boolean;
numb : integer;
sum : integer;

begin
      stop := false;
      repeat
            writeln('Input a number or 0 to exit: ');
            readln(numb);
            if numb = 0 then stop := true;
            sum := sum+numb;
            writeln('Total = ', sum);
      until stop;
end.

18:1
F1 Help  F2 Save  F3 Open  Alt+F9 Compile  F9 Make  Alt+F10 Local menu
```

Figure 4.14 Using Boolean variables

## Check your understanding 4.5

What variable names and datatypes would you use to store these values?

- A person's name, e.g. John
- The number of students in a class
- The average height of the students in a class
- An indicator showing whether someone is a student

# Program development

Having spent a considerable amount of time on the design, in theory at least, the program writing should be fairly straightforward. The more detailed the design is, the easier the programming should be. However, nothing in life is simple and, typically, inadequacies and omissions in the design will be revealed at this stage or when the program is tested. The more complex the system, the more likely this is to be the case.

We will follow the program writing process using the case study. We will write a simplified version of the program and then add some additional features, although an experienced programmer would probably write the complete version from the start.

The first step is to create the variables and constants, using the data table from the design stage. Creation of constants is done in a similar way to the variables, at the top of the program, in a section marked *const*.

The constant used to store the commission rate (5 per cent) is created using the following code:

```
Const
   Com_rate = 0.05;
```

The code used to create the variables is:

```
var
   sterling : real;
   currency_type : integer;
   dollar_rate : real;
   yen_rate : real;
   euro_rate : real;
   result : real;
   exit : string;
```

Having written the code for the constants and variables, you should then refer to the design documents such as the flowchart and pseudocode and use these as your guide for creating the main code of the program.

The first part of the flowchart we need to consider is the arrow that comes from the decision box labelled 'Do another calculation?' (see Figure 4.5). This is the start of the loop that makes the program repeat until the user decides he/she has finished doing calculations. At the start of the loop we only need one instruction:

```
repeat
```

Following the start of the loop is an input box which contains the text 'Input amount of Sterling to convert'. The code for this is fairly simple:

```
writeln ('Enter sterling');
readln (sterling);
```

The program must then calculate and subtract the amount of commission and display the result. The code for the calculation is written using the pseudo code created at the design stage:

```
comm_amount := sterling * comm_rate;
sterling := sterling - comm_amount;
writeln ('Amount of commission is ',comm_amount:0:2);
```

Note that, because the variable comm_amount is of data type real, it should be formatted when output. The :0:2 after the result variable in the writeln instruction formats the output of the value stored in result; the 0 displays the next character position after text and the 2 displays two decimal places.

The next flowchart box, which is labelled 'Input choice of currency to convert to', is coded in a similar way, although we need to prompt the user with a list of valid currencies:

```
writeln ('Enter 1 for Yen');
writeln ('Enter 2 for Dollar');
writeln ('Enter 3 for Euro');
readln (currency_type);
```

Once the amount of Sterling and the required foreign currency are known, the next step in the flowchart is a series of decision boxes that choose which currency conversion to do. This is coded using three if instructions:

```
if currency_type = 1 then result := yen_rate * sterling;
if currency_type = 2 then result := dollar_rate * sterling;
if currency_type = 3 then result := euro_rate * sterling;
```

This is followed by an output step, which displays the foreign currency amount. This can be coded using a single instruction:

```
writeln ('Foreign currency amount is ',result:0:2);
```

The final step in the flowchart involves choosing whether to continue the program or not. This is the ending point of the loop, and as this is a post-conditional loop we need to add an 'until' conditional statement:

```
writeln ('Type X to exit.');
readln (exit);
until (exit = 'X');
```

The complete code for the program is shown below:

```
program currency;
uses crt;
const
    comm_rate = 0.05;
var
    sterling : real;
    comm_amount : real;
    dollar_rate : real;
    euro_rate : real;
    yen_rate : real;
    result : real;
    exit : string
    currency_type : real;
begin
    dollar_rate := 1.6;
    euro_rate := 1.8;
    yen_rate := 5.0;
    writeln ('Fast Cash - Currency Calc');
      repeat
            writeln ('Enter sterling');
            readln (sterling);
            comm_amount := sterling - comm_amount;
            writeln ('Amount of commission is ',comm_amount:0:2);
            writeln ('Enter 1 for Yen');
            writeln ('Enter 2 for Dollar');
            writeln ('Enter 3 for Euro');
            readln (currency_type);
            If currency_type = 1 then result := yen_rate * sterling;
            If currency_type = 2 then result := dollar_rate * sterling;
            If currency_type = 3 then result := euro_rate * sterling;
            writeln ('Result is ',result:0:2);
            writeln (Type X to exit.');
            readln (exit);
      until (exit = 'X');
end.
```

**Assessment activity 4.3**

Using the design you created earlier, write the program keeping to the good programming guidelines described on page 131. Keep screen shots of writing, editing and compiling the program using the IDE.

## Loops

So far we have only see one type of loop, a do ... until loop. This sort of loop continues until the condition specified in the 'until' part of the loop is met. This is called a post-conditional loop because the exit condition is tested at the end of the loop. The 'while' loop is similar to the do ... until loop but the exit condition is tested at the beginning of the loop (a pre-conditional loop). A simple example is shown in Figure 4.15.

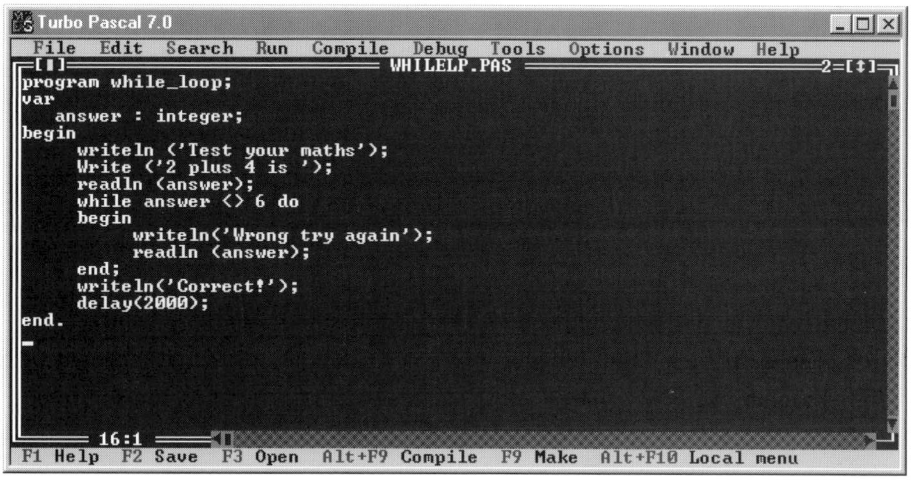

```
Turbo Pascal 7.0
File  Edit  Search  Run  Compile  Debug  Tools  Options  Window  Help
WHILELP.PAS
program while_loop;
var
   answer : integer;
begin
      writeln ('Test your maths');
      Write ('2 plus 4 is ');
      readln (answer);
      while answer <> 6 do
      begin
           writeln('Wrong try again');
           readln (answer);
      end;
      writeln('Correct!');
      delay(2000);
end.
16:1
F1 Help  F2 Save  F3 Open  Alt+F9 Compile  F9 Make  Alt+F10 Local menu
```

Figure 4.15 An example of a 'while' loop

A third type of loop is called a 'for' loop. This **fixed iteration loop** executes a certain number of times.

```
For loop_counter := start_value to end_value do
    begin
       {Code}
    end;
```

Here loop_counter is a variable, and start_value and end_value are either constants or variables. At the start of the loop, loop_counter is set to the value of start_value; each time around the loop, loop_counter is incremented (1 is added to it) until it reaches end_value, at which point the looping stops. A simple example program using a 'for' loop is shown in Figure 4.16

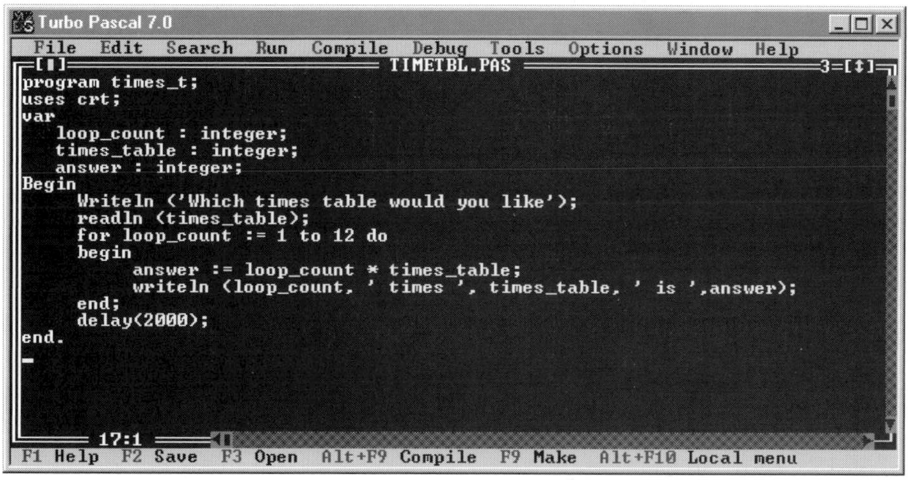

```
Turbo Pascal 7.0
File  Edit  Search  Run  Compile  Debug  Tools  Options  Window  Help
TIMETBL.PAS
program times_t;
uses crt;
var
   loop_count : integer;
   times_table : integer;
   answer : integer;
Begin
      Writeln ('Which times table would you like');
      readln (times_table);
      for loop_count := 1 to 12 do
      begin
           answer := loop_count * times_table;
           writeln (loop_count, ' times ', times_table, ' is ',answer);
      end;
      delay(2000);
end.
17:1
F1 Help  F2 Save  F3 Open  Alt+F9 Compile  F9 Make  Alt+F10 Local menu
```

Figure 4.16 The 'for' loop

## Modules

When developing a simple program it is fine to write it from start to finish as one linear program. However, with more complex programs, this approach would produce a very long program that is difficult to read and understand. It would also involve a great deal of duplicated code, as most programs need to do the same thing on many different occasions, such as validating user input. To avoid these problems all but the simplest of programs are split into different modules.

### What does it mean?

A **module** is a program within a program that carries out some clearly defined purpose. Modules are sometimes called **subroutines, procedures** or **functions**.

Programming languages come with a wide range of built-in modules (often called functions) which carry out tasks like mathematical calculations and string manipulation. An example of a built-in function in Turbo Pascal is the length function which returns the length of a string of text. Functions usually need to be passed some value, known as a **parameter** (which in the case of the length function is the string of text). The function will then return another value (the length of the string of text). The simple program shown in Figure 4.17 demonstrates the use of the length function.

```
Turbo Pascal 7.0
 File  Edit  Search  Run  Compile  Debug  Tools  Options  Window  Help
                              LENGTH.PAS
program simcalc(input, output);
uses crt;
var
   word_in : string;
   length_of_word : integer;
begin
     writeln ('Enter a word');
     readln (word_in);
     length_of_word := length(word_in);
     writeln ('This word is ',length_of_word,' characters long');
     delay(2000);
end.

       1:1
 F1 Help  F2 Save  F3 Open  Alt+F9 Compile  F9 Make  Alt+F10 Local menu
```

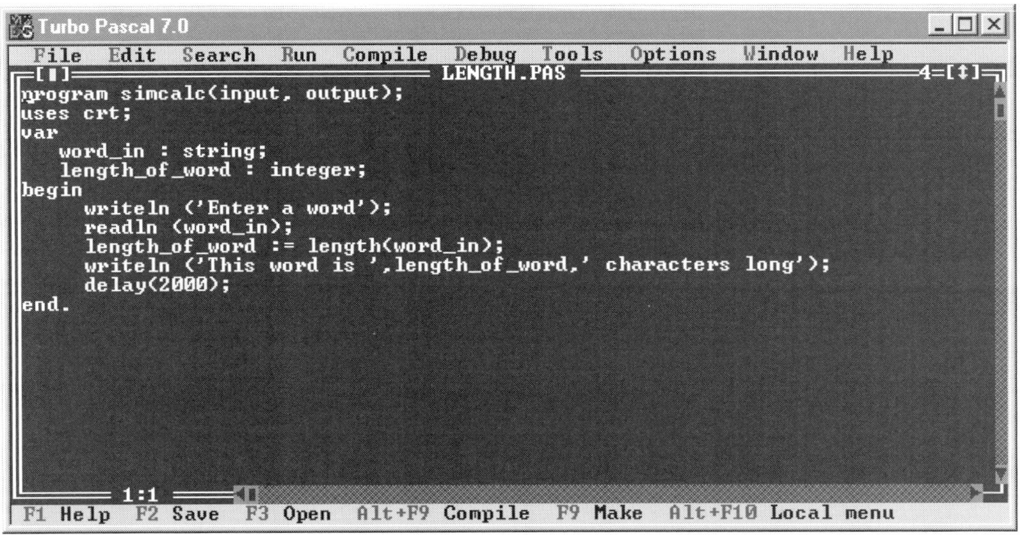

Figure 4.17 The length function

Writing your own functions is a little more involved. You will first make design decisions: what the function will do, what parameters it should be passed and what values it will return. In terms of designing the input, output and processing that the function will do, the design techniques discussed earlier (data tables, flowcharts, pseudo code) can be used.

User-written functions (as opposed to built-in ones) are declared at the top of the program, after the variable definitions, so a program with one procedure would have a structure like this:

```
Program progname;
uses crt;
const
    {constant declarations}
var
    {variable declarations}
    function function_name(parameter_name; parameter_type):return_type)
var
    {function variable declarations}
begin
    {function code}
    function_name := return_value
end;
begin
    {main program code}
end.
```

Note that, as well as giving the function a name, you must list the parameters that are passed to the function, and their data types and the data type of the value that is returned by the function.

Although the Fast Cash currency converter program we have written appears to work, there is one problem with it. If, when using the program, the user enters a text character rather than a number, either for the Sterling amount to be converted or the type of currency, the program will crash with an 'Invalid numeric format' error.

One way around this problem is to place the user's input into a string variable and then use the **Val** procedure to convert it to a number.

### What does it mean?

**Val** is a built-in procedure which has three parameters; a text string, a real or integer variable into which the text string is converted, and an error flag. The error flag is set to 0 if the conversion was successful, and 1 if it was not.

The most likely reason for a conversion not being successful is that the text string did not contain a number. Therefore, we can detect whether the user has made a mistake by inputting a text character rather than a number by testing the error flag. If the user does enter a text character then an error message needs to be displayed and another opportunity given to enter a number.

If a loop is used with an exit condition that the error code must be 0, then the program will not continue until a number is entered. A flowchart for the required code is shown in Figure 4.18.

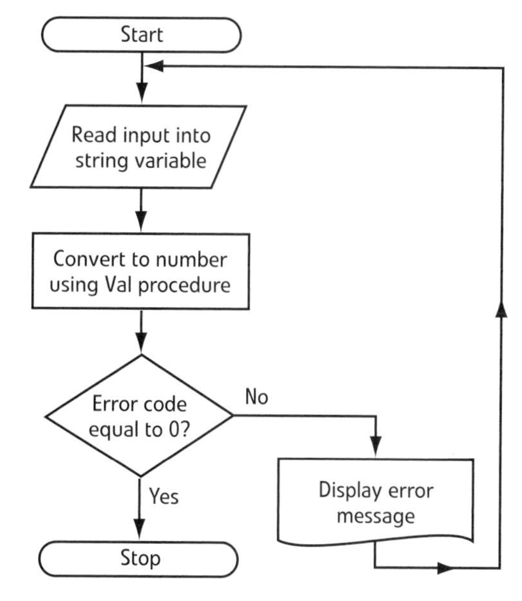


Figure 4.18 Flow chart for the number validation procedure

We could, of course, add the code to do this checking each time a numeric input was made, but that would mean writing the same code twice, and in a much larger program there may be lots of numeric inputs, not just two. A function is a much neater way of dealing with this situation. There is, however, one minor problem: the Sterling amount is input into a variable with a real data type whereas the choice of currency is input into a variable with an integer data type. It would be difficult to write a function that dealt with both data types, so for the purpose of demonstrating how to write a function we will change the data type of the currency_type variable to real (as you can input an integer value into a variable with a real data type but not vice versa).

The code for the function can now be written using the flowchart in Figure 4.18 as a guide:

```
function getnum : real;
var
    inputstr : string;
    inputnum : real;
    error : integer;
begin
    repeat
      readln (inputstr);
      val (inputstr, inputnum, error);
      if error > 0 then writeln ('You must enter a number, try again');
    until error = 0;
    getnum := inputnum;
end;
```

The main program also needs modifying. Instead of using readln to input the Sterling amount and the choice of currency, the function is called. The code for the complete program is shown below. Note that the data type of the currency_type variable has been changed to real.

```
program currency;
uses crt;
const
    comm_rate = 0.05;
var
    sterling : real;
    comm_amount : real;
    dollar_rate : real;
    euro_rate : real;
    yen_rate : real;
    result : real;
    exit : string;
    currency_type : real;
function getnum : real;
var
    inputstr : string;
    inputnum : real;
    error : integer;
begin
    repeat
      readln (inputstr);
      val (inputstr, inputnum, error);
```

```
      if error > 0 then writeln ('You must enter a number, try again');
    until error = 0;
    getnum := inputnum;
end;
begin
    dollar_rate := 1.6;
    euro_rate := 1.8;
    yen_rate := 5.0;
    writeln ('Fast Cash - Currency Calc');
      repeat
            writeln ('Enter sterling');
            sterling := getnum;
            comm_amount := sterling * comm_rate;
            sterling := sterling - comm_amount;
            writeln ('Enter 1 for Yen');
            writeln ('Enter 2 for Dollar');
            writeln ('Enter 3 for Euro');
            currency_type := getnum;
            If currency_type = 1 then result := Yen_rate * sterling;
            If currency_type = 2 then result := Dollar_rate * sterling;
            If currency_type = 3 then result := Euro_rate * sterling;
            writeln ('Result is ',result:0:2);
            writeln (Type X to exit.');
            readln (exit);
      until (exit = 'X');
end.
```

If the user makes a mistake entering either the Sterling amount or the currency type, this new version of the program will display an error message and allow the user to re-enter the value. The program will not go any further until a numeric entry has been made (see Figure 4.19).

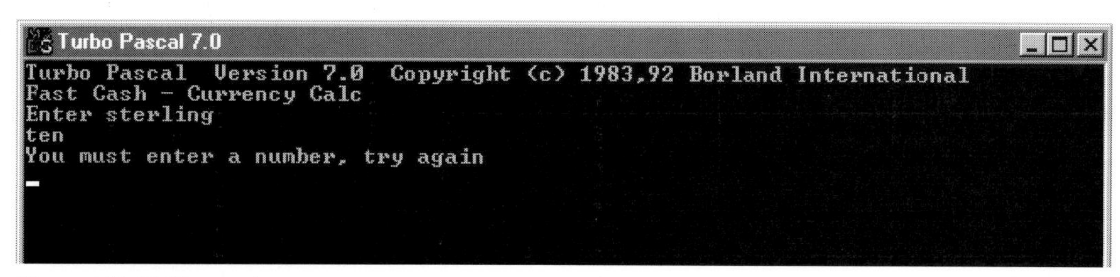


Figure 4.19 Making an incorrect entry

Further improvements could be made to the currency calculator:

- Additional currencies could be converted.
- The user input for the type of currency could be validated. Currently there is nothing to stop an invalid entry being made.
- When exiting the program only an upper-case X will be accepted; it might be easier if a lower case x was also acceptable.
- There are no limits on the amount of currency that can be input for conversion.

### Check your understanding 4.6

Add any procedures to the program you have written. If your program accepts numeric input you may be able to use the one written here.

**Assessment activity 4.4**

You need to consider how your program could be improved and expanded. In terms of improvements you should be able to add user input validation facilities like those described above. You should also enhance the program's user interface by adding to or improving the messages that are output on the screen.

### Scope of variables

Notice that in the modified currency calculator with the user-written function the program has two sets of variables – the variables declared at the beginning of the program and the variables declared within the function. This raises an important question: are *both* sets of variables available to be used throughout the program? The answer is that the variables declared within the function are *not* available within the main program. These are **private** variables, which exist only in the function itself. However, the variables declared at the beginning of the program are available for use in the function as well as the main program; these are **public** variables (no matter how many functions you have they can all use the same variables if they are declared here). The use of public variables within functions is not considered to be good programming practice, unless absolutely necessary. This is because the programmer may forget what the variable is being used for and accidentally misuse it (by changing a value that should not be changed) in one or more of the functions.

# 4.3 Documentation

Simply handing over a completed program on a disk is not sufficient. People need to know how to install the program, how to use it and how to deal with problems that might arise. The completed program must therefore be supported by documentation. Two types of documentation need to be produced:

- **User documentation** explains to the program's users how they should use the program.
- **Program or technical documentation** describes the internal working of the software.

The contents of these two types of documentation are rather different.

## Presentation of documentation

Although the term documentation tends to suggest a printed book of some kind, it is increasingly popular to do away with the expense of producing user documentation in the form of a book. Instead on-line help is provided. The Windows® operating system provides a way of producing help files in a standard format, with search and index facilities already built-in. It is beyond the scope of this unit to explain how the Windows® help system can be used to provide on-line user documentation. However, you should be aware that this common way for user documentation to be provided has a number of benefits: as well as being cheaper than manuals, it is also easier to update and offers more powerful search facilities.

Documentation produced in paper format should contain as many illustrations as possible. A word processing program such as Microsoft® Word 2000, which has built-in diagram drawing tools, is probably sufficient for producing the material (the Word 2000 drawing tools include 'autoshapes' for all the flowcharting symbols, making drawing flowcharts simple).

Documentation should be written to certain professional standards, to ensure it is consistent in appearance, structure and quality and is therefore easy to read and understand. Typically these standards should include:

- use of a 'house style' to govern the formatting of the titles, headings and subheadings in the document
- use of document structure including page numbering, section numbering and headers and footers
- inclusion of a table of contents, index and glossary
- use of spelling checker, grammar checker and proof reading to ensure the text is error free and as understandable as possible.

Much of the material, especially for the technical documentation, will come from documents that have already been created, for example the user requirement and the system design. If the documentation standards are applied from the beginning of the software development process, then time will be saved when you need to complete the documentation process at the end of the project.

# User documentation

User documentation is written for the program's users, and is sometimes called the **user manual** or **user guide**. There are two main approaches when writing user documentation:

- **Reference guide**: Each function and feature is described, normally in some logical order.
- **Tutorial:** This teaches the user how to use the program in a step-by-step fashion.

Some user manuals combine both approaches. However, whichever approach is taken, user documentation must be written in a way that the target audience can understand. Therefore, technical jargon needs to be avoided and the manual must be relevant to the way the program will be used in the work place, i.e. using realistic examples. Annotated screen dumps need to be used rather than long explanations; these are much easier for the users to follow. Users can compare what they see on the computer when running the program with the screen dump in the manual.

The user documentation needs to contain the following information:

- There should be details of how to start the program (e.g. how to find the program icon on the desktop or under the Start menu).
- There should be comprehensive instructions for using each of the program's features such as buttons, text boxes, list boxes, menus and shortcut keys.

- There should be explanations of any error messages that the program displays, including an explanation of what to do to correct the problem and how to avoid the error in future.
- There should be details of what to do if something goes wrong or the program crashes, such as who to contact.
- It should be stated how to exit the program.
- It is useful to include a section of frequently asked questions (FAQ), although you may need to use some imagination to decide what questions users may ask. Showing the program to a group of people who are unfamiliar with it and seeing what questions they ask may prove helpful.

**Assessment activity 4.5**

Write user documentation for the program you have written.

## Program documentation

Program documentation is written for support staff and programmers. Throughout the life of a program, changes or improvements may need to be made, and it may be the case that, despite careful testing, some errors surface only after many years of use. The programmers who originally wrote the software will probably have moved on to new projects or perhaps different companies. Technical documentation is therefore needed so that the people who need to modify or correct the program can understand how it works.

The technical documentation for each procedure in the program should include:

- details of the operating system and version the program will work with
- a listing of the program code
- a print of the form, including the object names
- the design specification
- details of testing carried out, and any modifications made as a result of testing.
- disk space and any other hardware requirements
- how to install the software.

When improvements and/or corrections are made to the program, details of these changes should be included in the technical documentation.

**Assessment activity 4.6**

Write technical documentation for the program you have written.

# 4.4 Testing methods

Testing is a vital part of software development. The users of the software would not be very impressed if the program produced the wrong answers; nor would they be happy if the program kept crashing while they were using it. Testing is the process of checking that all the functions of the program work as they should and give the correct results.

As well as checking that the program works correctly when used correctly, the software developer also needs to check that the program is **robust** and can withstand being used incorrectly without crashing. The reason why this is important is because the users of the program are unlikely to be computer experts; they may misunderstand how the program is supposed to be used. They may also make mistakes when using the program, such as pressing keys or clicking buttons in error or making inappropriate entries in a text box.

Making sure that a program works properly may sound like a simple task, but software testing, except for the very simplest of programs, is a complex and involved task which requires planning.

Testing can be done using one of two basic methods:

- With **black-box testing**, the tester only knows what the software is supposed to do (from the specification), not how it does it. The workings of the code are not considered.
- With **white-box testing**, the tester examines the code to look for clues that will help in the testing. For example an examination of the code may show that some inputs are more likely to cause failures that others.

## Black-box testing

Before you can start testing a program, you need to know what the program is supposed to do. This information must be taken from the original specification as supplied in the analysis and design stage. The next step is the selection of test cases. These are specific inputs that you will try and the procedures you will follow when you test the software. The selection of test cases is probably the most important task that a software tester does. Improper selection may result in testing too much or too little or testing the wrong things. To overcome this, **equivalence partitioning** is used to select a set of test cases.

?

### What does it mean?

**Equivalence partitioning** is the process of reducing the infinite number of test cases into a much smaller, but effective set. An equivalence partition is a group of test cases that test the same thing.

- The **test-to-pass** approach involves checking the standard facilities the program has, without trying to break it. You choose simple and straightforward test cases rather than ones which will push the program to its limits.
- With the **test-to-fail** approach you 'throw the book' at the software, trying the most extreme values and erroneous inputs. Test-to-fail is sometimes called **error-forcing**.

If you want to find bugs then you should test-to-fail. However, with software testing you usually start with test-to-pass. When you are satisfied the basic facilities work fine under normal circumstances then it is time to start testing-to-fail.

### Check your understanding 4.7

You have been set the task of testing the Windows® Calculator. To test every possible combination of input numbers and operators (add, subtract, multiply, etc.) would take a very long time indeed. However, you might reasonably expect that if you tested 1+1 and 1+2 then 1+3 and 1+4 would also work. These test cases are in the same equivalence partition. But what about 1+9999999... (with 32 9s it's the largest number you can type in)? 1+4 looks like standard addition but 1+999999... is testing the software to the limit (or boundary to give it its proper name) which is where bugs are often found, and is therefore in a different equivalence partition to standard sums like 1+4. Make a list of all the Windows® Calculator functions you would need to test.

## Data testing

Equivalence partitioning your test cases should be done using three key concepts:

- boundary conditions
- nulls
- bad data.

**Boundary condition** testing basically says 'if the software can operate properly on the edge of its capabilities, it will almost certainly work OK under normal conditions'. Selecting data at the boundary depends upon the application, but here are some examples:

- If a text field allows between 1 and 255 characters, 1 and 255 characters would be a good choice for a valid partition, while 0 and 256 would be suitable for the invalid partition.
- If a program reads data from a file on a floppy disk, try a file that is very small, perhaps one character; and one that is just on the limit of the capacity of the floppy disk.
- A program might allow an ID number to be entered which is in the range 00000 to 99999; use these as the valid partitions and one more and one less than the number of digits that is allowed as the invalid partitions.

**Nulls:** Well-behaved software should be able to cope with a situation where a text box for example is left blank, or contains zero. You should always create an equivalence partition that deals with empty, blank and zero conditions to check that the software copes with these situations.

### What does it mean?

A **null** value is an empty value, it doesn't contain a zero, or a space.

**Bad data:** This is really test-to-fail, i.e. entering rubbish data and seeing whether the program copes. Some might argue that if you prove the software works when it is used properly then there is no need to check whether it can deal with being misused. However, it is difficult to predict how the software will be used, and if things go wrong you will certainly be held responsible. There are no rules for thinking up garbage data, although you can start by entering the opposite of what is required, e.g. text instead of numbers.

Once the test data has been chosen, a test plan can be drawn up. A test plan is a table that lists the input data for each test case and the expected outputs. The test plan can then be used with the real program: the listed inputs are made and the actual outputs compared with the expected ones. Any difference between the expected outputs and the actual ones needs to be investigated because this indicates that the program is not working as it should.

### Case study: Fast Cash Bank

Here is an example of some test data for the currency calculator, divided into equivalence partition:

| **Test data for foreign currency amount** | | | | | |
|---|---|---|---|---|---|
| Equivalence partition: | | Boundary conditions | | | |
| Inputs: | | Outputs | | | |
| Sterling amount | Currency choice | Commission | | Foreign currency amount | |
| | | Expected | Actual | Expected | Actual |
| 1 | 1 | | | | |
| 1000 | 1 | | | | |
| 1 | 2 | | | | |
| 1000 | 2 | | | | |
| | | | | | |
| | | | | | |

Table 4.3 Test data for the currency calculator

**Complete this test plan, adding test data for the nulls and bad data groups.**

### Assessment activity 4.7

Create a test plan for the program you have written.

### White-box testing

White-box testing involves inspecting the code of the program in an attempt to identify errors. One example of a white-box testing technique is to use a **trace table**. The expected value of a variable, for example in a loop, can be listed in a trace table. The program can then be run and, using a debugging tool, the value in the variable can be viewed and compared with the expected value. Trace tables are explained in more detail in Unit 2.

## Testing tools

Most modern programming languages come built into an IDE, which includes debugging tools. These tools allow you to investigate the cause of **program bugs**.

### What does it mean?

Bugs are faults in a program that prevent it working correctly. With some bugs it can be very difficult to identify what the cause of the problem is.

Debugging tools allow you to stop the program in the middle of running and inspect the values contained in the program's variables. Consider the simple program shown in Figure 4.20. The purpose of this program is to print out the numbers 1 to 10, but when the program is run it displays the numbers 0 to 9.

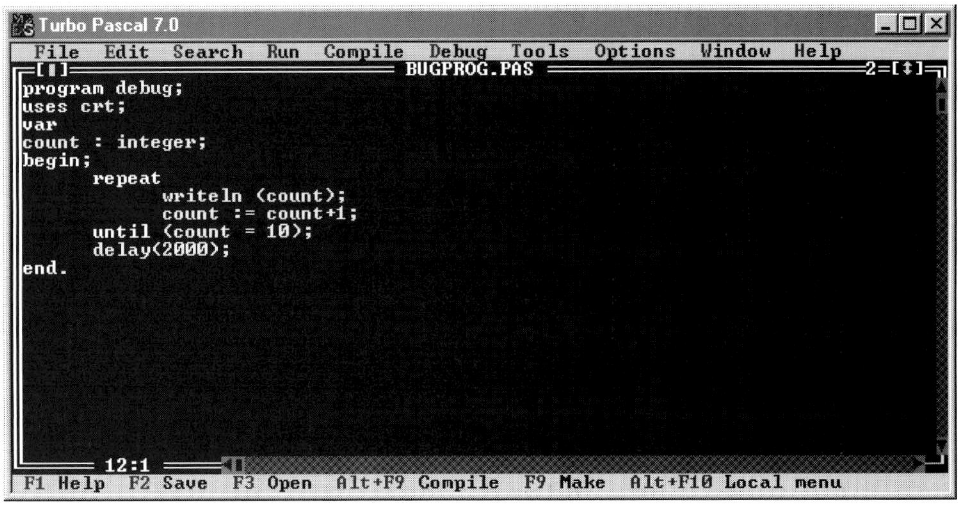

```
Turbo Pascal 7.0
 File  Edit  Search  Run  Compile  Debug  Tools  Options  Window  Help
[■]                          BUGPROG.PAS                           2=[↕]
program debug;
uses crt;
var
count : integer;
begin;
        repeat
                writeln (count);
                count := count+1;
        until (count = 10);
        delay(2000);
end.

          12:1
 F1 Help  F2 Save  F3 Open  Alt+F9 Compile  F9 Make  Alt+F10 Local menu
```

Figure 4.20 Example program

To find out why this happens, the first step is to create a trace table for the variable called 'count', and this is shown in Table 4.4.

| Times around the loop | Exit condition (count = 10) met? | Expected value of variable 'count' |
|---|---|---|
| 1 | No | 1 |
| 2 | No | 2 |
| 3 | No | 3 |
| 4 | No | 4 |
| 5 | No | 5 |
| 6 | No | 7 |
| 7 | No | 7 |
| 8 | No | 9 |
| 9 | No | 10 |
| 10 | Yes | |

Table 4.4 Trace table for the variable 'count'

The debug facilities in Turbo Pascal can then be used to step through the program, stopping at each line and viewing the value in the count variable.

## Further research 4.1

1 Turn on the Watch window, by going to the Debug menu and choosing the Watch option. This opens up a new green window at the bottom of the screen.

2 Tell the program which variable to watch, so go to the Debug window again and chose Add Watch. This displays the add expression dialogue box as shown in Figure 4.21.

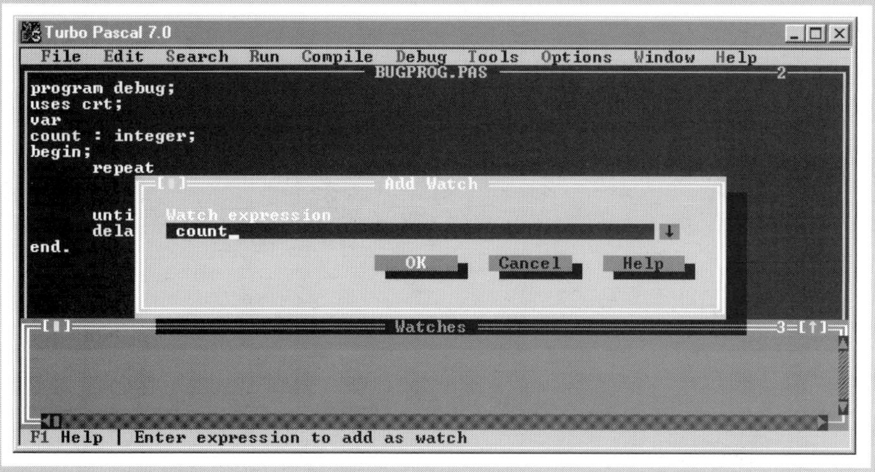

Figure 4.21 The add expression dialogue box

3 Type the name of the variable to be watched (count) and click OK. The Watch window will show the name of the variable, with 'unknown identifier' (because the program has not started yet) displayed after it.
4 Now stepping through the program one line at a time, the value in the count variable can be observed to see how it changes. Go to the Run menu and choose Step over, and the program will stop at the first instruction (begin). The value contained in the count variable will be displayed in the watch window (0).
5 Press the F8 key to step to the next instruction (writeln), and the screen will look like Figure 4.22.

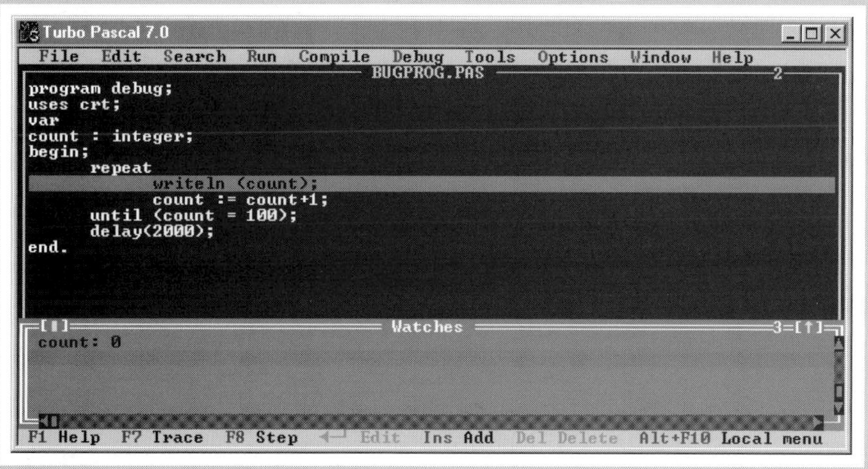

Figure 4.22 Using the Watch window

Note that count is still set to 0; that is why the program counts from 0 rather than 1, as shown in the trace table (Table 4.4).

6 Step through the program line by line (by pressing F8); each time the program goes around the loop, note the value in the count variable. You should notice that after the program has displayed 9, the value in count is incremented, so it becomes 10. The loop exit criteria is then met and the program exits without displaying the final value in the count variable.

By using the debug tools we have been able to identify that our trace table is in fact incorrect. The value of count is 0 when it is first displayed, and although it reaches 10, this occurs only *after* it has been displayed on the last time around the loop.

### Check your understanding 4.8

Correct this program so it does display the numbers 1 to 10 with one very simple change.

In a large and complex program, stepping through each line one at a time would be rather time-consuming. You can therefore add what are called **breakpoints**, which allow you to stop the program when a certain condition is met and then inspect the variables.

### Further research 4.2

Suppose the program we have just been looking at was intended to display the numbers 1 to 100 rather than 1 to 10, but we could not work out why it stopped at 99 rather than 100. Instead of stepping though all 99 iterations of the loop we could set a breakpoint when the value in the count variable reached 98.

1 Position the cursor at the place in the program where we want it to stop (on the writeln statement is a good place).
2 Go to the Debug menu and choose Add Breakpoint. Then a dialogue box, shown in Figure 4.23, is displayed.
3 In the Condition box type 'count = 98' and click OK. The line with the breakpoint is displayed in red.

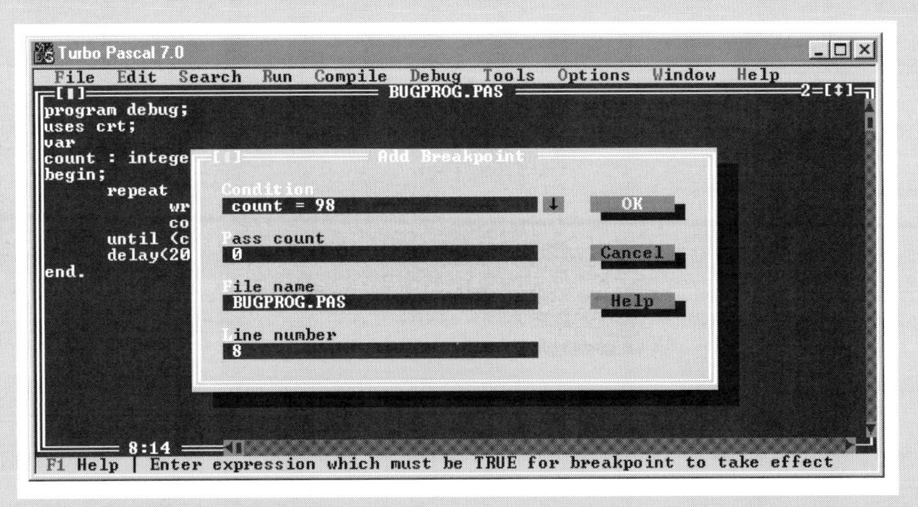


Figure 4.23 Adding a breakpoint

4 Making sure the Watch window is open first, run the program, using the Run option under the Run menu. There is no need to step through the program as it will automatically stop at the breakpoint. The message will then appear 'Conditional Breakpoint count = 98 in PROG.PAS line 7 is true' (the text PROG.PAS will depend on the name you saved your program as). See Figure 4.24.
5 Click the OK button on the message box and you can then step through the program (using the F8 key), observing the value in the count variable in the Watch window.

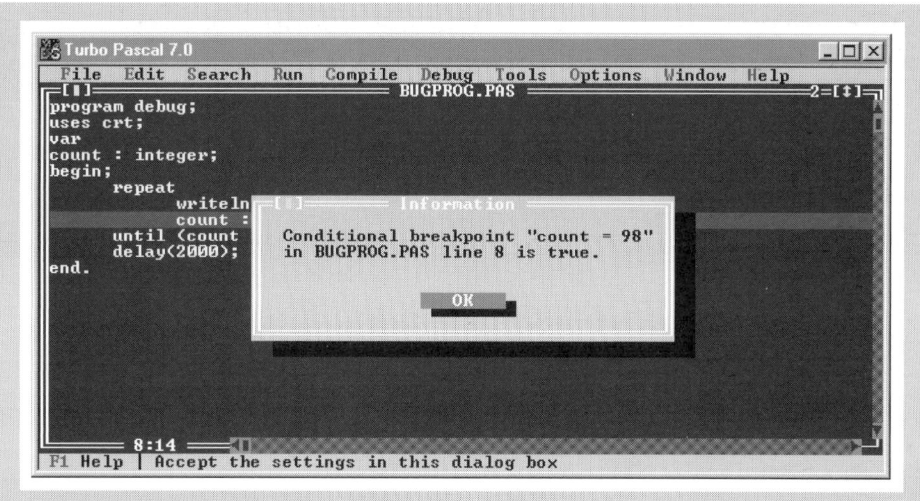


Figure 4.24 Program stopped at a breakpoint

Note that once you have fixed the problem you must clear the breakpoint, otherwise the program will always stop at this point. Go to the Debug menu and choose the **Breakpoints** option, then click the **Clear all** button on the dialogue that appears. Debug tools are very useful to the programmer as they allow you to look inside the program during execution.

## Assessment activity 4.8

Create a trace table for one of the loops in the program you have written. Test your trace table using the debug facilities in the IDE you are using. Take screen shots of the debug facilities in use as part of your evidence.

## Test your knowledge

1. Why is it often difficult to identify a user's requirements?
2. What is pseudo code use for?
3. When drawing a flowchart, what shape boxes do you use for (a) an input step, (b) an output step, and (c) a selection (decision) step?
4. What tools would normally be included in an IDE?
5. Why is it important to choose meaningful variable names?
6. What sort of data is held in a Boolean datatype?
7. What instruction is normally used to allow a program to make a choice between two or more possible courses of action?
8. What is the purpose of a compiler?
9. What is the difference between a post-conditional and a pre-conditional loop?
10. What instruction is normally used to set up a fixed iteration loop?
11. Why is it a good idea to break a program down into modules?
12. What is the difference between a public and a private variable?
13. What sort of information is contained in a user guide?
14. What sort of information is contained in the technical documentation for a program?
15. Testing is done to check the program works correctly and for what other reasons?
16. What is the difference between white- and black-box testing?
17. Explain the data testing terms: boundary conditions, nulls and bad data.
18. What is the purpose of a breakpoint?

# UNIT 5: COMMUNICATIONS TECHNOLOGY

What was originally known as information technology (IT) has now been renamed information and communications technology (ICT), such is the importance of communications in computer applications.

Early computers were stand-alone machines with their users, storage and processing facilities all located in one place. However, it was not long before the benefits of enabling computers to communicate over local and wide areas become evident. Early networks were mainly concerned with attaching remote users to large centralised mainframe computers but, as the technology developed, sophisticated applications for computer networks were made possible.

In the commercial world today, it is hard to imagine what life would be like without computer networks. A wide range of applications rely on communications technology such as:

- credit and debit card transactions in shops
- e-mail for commercial and personal communication
- cash machine withdrawals
- on-line shopping.

The technology that has been developed to support the explosion in computer communications is complex and sophisticated, and this unit is intended to develop a basic understanding of the hardware and software involved. In particular, it considers the development of computer networks, how reliable communications between systems can be achieved, and the importance of the Internet.

## Learning objectives

- To explore the main elements of data communication systems
- To describe the hardware and software used in data communications
- To investigate computer networks and their development
- To explain the importance of the Internet and the World Wide Web (WWW)

# 5.1 Data communication systems

The term 'data communications' can cover anything from a single **PC (personal computer)** sending some data to a local printer through to a vast world-wide communications system involving millions of computers such as the **Internet**. This section considers signal theory, methods of communication, the communication standards authorities and the transmission media. Unit 2 covers **data representation** in some detail.

## Signal theory

All data (documents, sound files, images, etc.) stored and used by computers is in digital format. That is, it is represented by binary numbers (ones and zeros).

- A single binary digit is called a **bit**.
- Characters can be represented as binary digits using the ASCII (American Standard Code for Information Interchange) coding scheme.
- ASCII represents every letter of the alphabet (upper and lower case), numbers and many other symbols using a combination of 7 bits. The letter 'A' for example is represented as 1000001, while 'B' is 1000010.
- An additional bit is used for error checking (called the **parity bit**) making 8 bits per character.
- Groups of 8 bits are called a **byte**.
- 1024 bytes make 1 kilobyte (Kb) and 1024 Kb make 1 megabyte (Mb).

For computers to communicate, there needs to be a way for them to transfer this binary data.

### Case study: A simple communication system

Two devices are attached by a copper cable. One device wants to send binary data (the transmitter) and the other device is ready to receive data (the receiver). How can the binary data be represented on the cable?
Digital data is signalled on the cable using a variation in electrical voltage. However, for the two devices to communicate, there must be a standard that both the sender and receiver adhere to (a simple **protocol**).

1 Apart from a variation in voltage, are there other ways digital data could be represented?
2 Find out what standards are available for data communication.

### ? What does it mean?

For computers to communicate, there needs to be a set of rules that they obey. These rules are called **protocols**. There are many different networking protocols in use, governing the wide range of technical details that have to be agreed before two or more computers can communicate.

Without standards, it would be impossible for computers of different makes and in different countries to communicate. Standards are normally set by some national or international organisation (see page 162). One of the most common is the **RS232C standard**.

### What does it mean?

The **RS232C standard** was created by an organisation called EIA (Electronics Industry Association) and defines how two computers (or communications devices such as **modems**) can be connected by a serial cable.

Using the RS232C standard, a 0 bit is represented by a positive voltage of 12 volts, and a 1 is represented by a negative voltage of 12 volts. Therefore, to send the character B from the sending device to the receiving device, the bit stream would be signalled on the cable as shown in Figure 5.1.

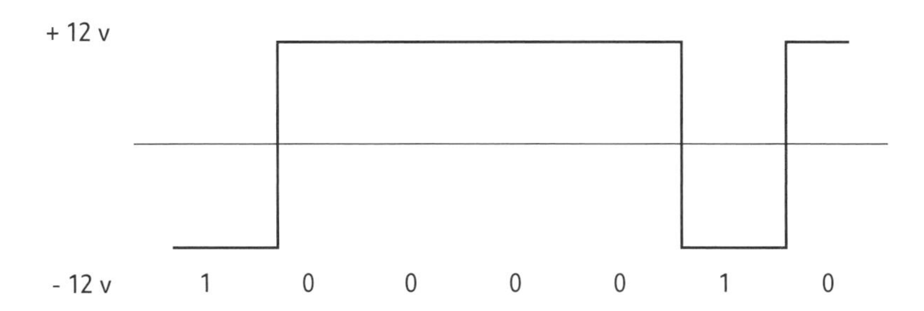


Figure 5.1 Signalling the character 'B'

An important question is 'For how long should the signal for each bit last?' This is important especially where there is a series of the same bit. For example, in the middle of the bit stream in Figure 5.1 there are four zeros. Unless the receiving end knows exactly how long each bit signal lasts, it would not be able to tell if this +12V signal represented three, four or five zeros. If the signal length was set to 1 second (i.e. the length of time the voltage level was held for each bit) then the letter B above would take 7 seconds to send (1 second for each bit). Clearly, to achieve faster data transfer (i.e. to send more bits in a shorter time), the duration for each bit needs to be shorter. The number of bits that can be sent in a second is called the **data rate**. The data rate described above is 1 bit per second (bps). Typically, data rates are much higher than this; for example, a signal duration of 1 ms (millisecond – one hundredth of a second) will give a data rate of 100 bps. The term **baud rate** is sometimes used to describe the data rate; 1 baud is 1 bps.

In network communications, the term **bandwidth** normally refers to the amount of data that can be sent across a communications medium (e.g. a cable) in a given time, and is often described in bits per second. However, somewhat confusingly, the term bandwidth also refers to the range of frequencies that a particular transmission medium can support.

The **transmission medium** is the physical method by which the communication link is established. Copper wires (or cables) are the traditional method of linking devices so they can communicate, but there are a number of other media in common use (see page 163):

- **Fibre optic** cable is used where high capacity and speed are required.
- **Wireless media** are also increasingly popular including infrared and radio.

**Check your understanding 5.1**

1 What is the difference between analogue and digital?

2 For you and a friend to talk to each other over the telephone, there needs to be a type of 'protocol' that you both stick to. What sort of things need to be agreed in this protocol? For example one of you needs to know the other's number, but which one? Who initiates the call?

## Synchronous and asynchronous transmission

The type of data transmission described so far is called **asynchronous transmission**. Characters are sent one at a time and the receiving end does not know when the next character will be sent until the arrival of the start bit. There is no timing information sent within the data. A single 7-bit ASCII character, along with its start, stop and parity bits, requires 10 bits. The asynchronous character representation is shown in Figure 5.2.

| Start bit | 7-bit ASCII character | Parity bit | Stop bit |
|---|---|---|---|

Figure 5.2 Asynchronous character representation

An important point with asynchronous transmission is the amount of overhead that is required to send data. Each 8-bit ASCII character (7 bits plus the parity bit) requires 2 extra bits (the start and stop bits) to be transmitted; this represents a 20 per cent overhead, i.e. an efficiency of 80 per cent. To improve the efficiency of the data communications system, we need to keep this overhead to a minimum, because any overhead is wasted data that lowers the effective data transmission rate.

Asynchronous data transmission is fine if the volume of data to be transferred is low. However, owing to the high overhead incurred, transferring large volumes of data asynchronously is very slow. Also, the lack of timing information sent with the data restricts asynchronous transmission to low data rates.

**Synchronous data transmission** is used to overcome these limitations. With synchronous transmission, rather than sending individual characters, a block of characters is sent. This is preceded by timing information, so the receiver can 'lock on' to the timing of the sender. The exact structure of the block of data sent when using synchronous data transmission is dependent on the protocol in use, but its general structure is described here.

When synchronous transmission is in use, data and control bits are put together in a structure called a **frame** or **packet**. At the start of the frame are a number of **synchronisation characters**. These contain the ASCII control character called SYN and are used by the receiving end to lock on to the timing of the sender. These are followed by the ASCII control character that indicates the start of the block of characters (STX – start of text). When a block of characters is sent, the length of the block is protocol dependent, but imagine a protocol where the block is up to 50 characters long. The end of the block of text is marked by a ETX (end of text) ASCII control character. This frame structure is shown in Figure 5.3.

| SYN | SYN | SYN | STX | Block of up to 50 characters | ETX |
|---|---|---|---|---|---|

Figure 5.3 Synchronous transmission frame

One of the major benefits of synchronous transmission is the improvement in efficiency over asynchronous transmission. For example, suppose there are 5 control characters, required to send 50 characters. To calculate the efficiency of the system, we use this formula:

efficiency = (useful data/total data) * 100%

So, in this example

efficiency = (50/55)*100% = 90.1%

Whereas, with asynchronous transmission, the efficiency is only

(8/10)*100% i.e. 80%

Clearly, the larger the block of data, the greater the efficiency will be. You may ask 'Why restrict the size of the block to 50 characters?' The reason is that the larger the block, the greater the likelihood of an error occurring during the transmission of that block. If an error does occur, all of that block of data must be retransmitted. If the block size is very large, then a lot of time may be wasted resending blocks and this would negate the potential improvement in efficiency by using a large block size. Therefore, there is trade-off to be made: if the block size is too small, the efficiency is reduced because of the large overhead; if the block size is too large, efficiency may also be reduced because errors may cause retransmissions.

### Check your understanding 5.2

Calculate the efficiency of these different block sizes:

- 5 control characters to 70 characters of useful data
- 8 control characters to 100 characters of data
- 10 control characters to 250 characters of data.

### Assessment activity 5.1

Write a report explaining basic signal theory and the difference between asynchronous and synchronous communication.

So far, we have considered a simple communications arrangement where a single sending device is directly connected to a single receiving device. What about when a very large amount of data has to be sent (greater than the block size in use)?

### Case study: Sending large amounts of data

Where a large amount of data has to be sent (greater than the block size in use), the data must be split into a number of packets. To allow the receiving end to reconstruct these packets into the original data, each packet has an ID number as part of the control information that is sent with the data. This ID number enables the receiving end to reassemble the data into its original format. As well as the packet ID, the packet will need to contain the full address of its destination.

In the simple example we have used so far where there is only one receiving station connected to the sender, the issue of addresses and routes has not occurred. However, in a more complex network, where there are multiple devices connected, packets must contain a destination address. Where several different routes exist between sender and receiver, it is possible that different packets arrive at different times and, hence, not in sequence. To recreate the original data in the correct sequence, the receiving end must therefore be able to re-sequence the packets.

1 Why might you need more than one route between two locations?
2 As well as knowing what sequence the packets belong in, what other information will the receiving end need to reconstruct the original message?

## Error correction and detection

It is important that the data received is exactly the same as the data sent, so error checking is an important aspect of data communication. When signalling data over electrical circuits, there are many sources of possible errors, such as electrical noise, timing errors, etc. Error in data transmission can cause all sorts of problems. Imagine withdrawing £50 from your bank's local cash machine and, due to a data transmission error, the cash machine telling the bank's central computer you had withdrawn £100!

**Parity** is a simple error checking method that can identify single bit errors. Parity can be set to either odd or even. In the case of even parity, an additional bit is set on or off to make the total number of binary ones even. With odd parity, a bit is set on or off to make the total number of binary ones odd. At the sending end, the parity bit is appended to the data. At the receiving end, the parity bit is checked; if it is found to be incorrect, the data is ignored and requested again.

### Check your understanding 5.3

1 What would the parity bit be for the bit patterns shown below, using odd or even parity?

| Character | ASCII 7-bit code | Even parity | Odd parity |
|---|---|---|---|
| E | 1000101 | | |
| h | 1101000 | | |
| 6 | 0110110 | | |
| m | 1101101 | | |

Table 5.1 Bit codes for four characters

2 Parity is not very effective at detecting errors. Consider this situation: The bit stream 1101100 is transmitted using even parity, so a 0 is used as the parity bit. But during transmission errors occur which change the first two bits so the data is received as 0001100. Calculate the parity bit for these 7 bits. Will the error be detected?

More sophisticated methods than just parity checks are commonly used. Packets may be lost or corrupted during transmission and the receiving end must be able to both detect and recover from this situation. To detect packets that are in error, the most widely used techniques are **check sums** and **CRC (cyclic redundancy checks)** – complex mathematical calculations that identify up to 99.99 per cent of errors.

**Further research 5.1**

Use the Internet to find out more about check sums and CRCs.

Once an error has been detected by the receiving end, action needs to be taken to resolve the situation. In the simplest arrangement, the sender waits after it has sent each packet, to receive an acknowledgement (sometimes called an ACK, after the ASCII control character) from the receiver that the packet was successfully received. If the receiving end detects an error in the packet, rather than sending back an ACK, it returns a NAK (negative acknowledgement). If the sender receives an ACK, it sends out the next packet; if it receives a NAK, it sends the same packet again. If it receives nothing, it waits a certain amount of time (called the **timeout**) and sends the same packet again, assuming the original one was lost. Waiting for an acknowledgement for each individual packet is rather time-consuming so most systems send several packets before expecting an acknowledgement. However, with this system, when an error is detected the receiving end must tell the sending end which packet (of the several it will have received) needs resending.

## Baud rates, bandwidth and compression

You have already seen that the bandwidth of a communications channel refers to the amount of data that can be sent in a given time. Different types of channel have different maximum data rates owing to their different electrical properties. Analogue channels such as telephone connections generally have the lowest bandwidth, with digital channels supporting much higher data rates. The actual data rate a channel can achieve will often be significantly lower than its maximum possible rate. This is due to errors that can be caused by **noise** or **crosstalk**.

**What does it mean?**

**Crosstalk** and **noise** are among the principal causes of error in data communication. Electrical noise comes from equipment like electric motors and switches. It can interfere with the signalling of binary data on the transmission media, causing it to become corrupted. Crosstalk can occur when cables are close to each other and the signal on one cable interferes with the signal on the other.

Some **channel types** such as fibre optic cables are not susceptible to electrical interference and so can achieve actual data rates very close to their theoretical maximum. Data transmission rate is normally measured in bits per second (bps) although sometimes the term **baud rate** is used.

**What does it mean?**

The term **'baud'** was originally a unit of telegraph signalling speed, set at one Morse code dot per second, and was named after the French telegraph engineer Baudot (1845–1903). Today is it taken to mean one character per second, but the term causes confusion because it ignores control bits. Bits per second (bps) is the preferred term.

**Compression** is a method widely used to increase the speed at which large files can be moved across slow communication links. Compression involves reducing the size of a file by coding it more efficiently using fewer bits. There are many different methods of compression in use, suited to particular applications. **Run length encoding** is an example of a compression method that takes strings (runs) of repeated characters and replaces them with a single character and a count. This method works well with graphics files. Compressed data must be decompressed at the receiving end before it can be used.

**Further research 5.2**

Use the Internet to find out more about compression techniques, particularly for graphics.

# Methods of communication

As well as being able to communicate with **LAN**s (local area networks) and **WAN**s (wide area networks), PCs also need to communicate with local devices, such as printers, digital cameras and scanners.

?

**What does it mean?**

A LAN is a network of computers within the same building or complex of buildings. A WAN is a network of computers that are spread across a wider geographical area. It may be within the same town, the same country or world-wide.

## Simplex and duplex

- On a **simplex** communication link, data is transferred in one direction only. TV is an example of this; the signal is broadcast from the TV transmitter to the TV set in your home.
- A **duplex** link is where there is simultaneous transmission in both directions. The telephone is an example of this.
- **Half-duplex** is where communication can take place in both directions, but only one at a time. An example of this would be the police 'walkie-talkie' type radio where only one person can talk at a time.

## Serial versus parallel communications

In the past, PCs have been provided with two basic types of port: serial and parallel.

- With serial transmission, each bit is transmitted down the cable one at a time.
- With parallel transmission, eight separate wires within the cable are used to transmit 8 bits (1 character) simultaneously, and additional wires within the cable carry control data.

Parallel connections are therefore much faster than serial (potentially eight times as fast). However, owing to minute differences in the properties of the individual wires, data travels at slightly different speeds down each wire and this limits the distance over which parallel transmission will work. Therefore, parallel links are only used at distances of up to a few metres. Parallel cables are also expensive (as they have more conductors than serial ones) and difficult to install, as they do not bend easily. Serial ports are used to connect devices like mice and external modems and conform to the RS232C standards (page 156). Parallel ports are used to connect printers.

The **universal serial bus (USB)** was developed as a standardised way of connecting all common serial devices to a single port. Up to 127 devices can be connected by daisy chaining or by use of a USB hub. USB was designed using the plug-in-and-play philosophy (i.e. no complex settings or drivers are needed) and it eliminates the need to add separate expansion cards inside the computer. USB is also a high-speed interface running at 12 Mbit/s.

**Firewire (IEEE1394)** is similar to USB in many ways but it is much faster, running at up to 400 Mbps. Firewire was developed by Apple Computer and is ideal for connecting devices such as digital cameras, digital video cameras and external hard discs which need to transfer large files.

### Wireless communications

All the peripheral communication methods described so far require cables. Running cables in an office environment is disruptive, expensive and not very flexible. Wireless transmission offers the promise of connections that do not require cables and are therefore flexible and easy to install. Two techniques that have been developed for PC peripheral connections (and also for connecting mobile devices such as **personal digital assistants (PDAs)**) are IrDa and Bluetooth.

- **IrDa:** Formed in 1993, the Infrared Data Association has been working to establish an open standard for short-range communication using infrared light. Communication using infrared is limited to line of sight and uses similar technology to television remote controls. Typical applications include synchronisation of PDAs with desktop machines and connecting a laptop computer to a mobile phone to establish a dial-up connection to the Internet. IrDa has never become very popular and has a reputation for being difficult to use.
- **Bluetooth:** Named after a tenth-century Danish king, Bluetooth is a specification for a low-cost radio data communication system design to link portable devices such as laptop computers, mobile phones and PDAs. First published in 1998, Bluetooth is restricted to a distance of only 10 metres and a speed of 1 Mbps; it is not intended to be a replacement for high-speed links like USB or Firewire. Instead, its main benefit is intended to be convenience. Bluetooth devices in the same personal area network (PAN) are designed to automatically recognise each other and synchronise their databases without any complex set-up.

## Communication standards authorities

When the first computer networks were developed in the 1970s, each computer manufacturer produced their own (incompatible) networking system. To develop common networking protocols and standards, independent, non-commercial organisations developed **open standards** (i.e. not tied to a particular manufacturer) to allow networks to connect and communicate freely. The main ones are described below.

- **CCITT** – Comité Consultatif Internationale de Télégraphie et Téléphonie. This organisation is part of the UN and is based in Switzerland. It makes recommendations on most aspects of telephone and computer networks. It is perhaps best known for the 'V' series of modem standards (see page 167).
- **ANSI** – American National Standards Institute. ANSI has created a range of standards in the computing field, particularly in programming languages and peripheral interconnection.
- **IEEE** – Institute of Electrical and Electronics Engineers. This is an American organisation that sets standards in the field of electrical and electronic engineering. It set many of the standards for LAN access methods; e.g. IEEE802.3 is the standard for CSMA/CD, and IEEE802.5 is the standard for token rings.
- **ISO** – International Standards Organisation. ISO sets standards on a wide range of topics, not just computing, and is best known in networking for the specification of the OSI 7-layer model (see page 175).

# Transmission media

So far, we have been mostly thinking of the connection between two devices in terms of a copper cable or wire. Today there are a range of other media available. There are three key differences between the different media:

- cost
- bandwidth
- ease of installation.

The different media are described below.

- **Unshielded twisted pair (UTP)** cable is widely used in LANs. It consists of pairs of insulated copper cable twisted together (the twisting reduces problems of crosstalk and noise). Various categories of UTP cable have been developed, with the main difference between them being the bandwidth available. Category 1 is normal telephone cable and is only suitable for low speeds. Currently Category 5 cable is the standard in network installations and has a bandwidth of up to 100 Mbit/s using the Ethernet LAN protocol (see page 174). UTP is cheap and easy to install.
- **Coaxial cable** is similar to the cable used for TV aerials. It has a central copper conductor, surrounded by a thick plastic sleeve, which is, in turn, surrounded by a braided metal shield and an outer plastic insulation. Coaxial cable is capable of higher data rates than UTP but is more expensive and not as easy to install (the cable does not bend easily and can be damaged by excessive bending). Coaxial cable was originally the method used to cable LANs but it is no longer widely used.
- Unlike UTP and coaxial cable, **fibre optic cable** does not use electrical currents to represent the data to be transmitted; instead, it uses light impulses. The cable is made of fine strands of glass, the light being internally reflected down the strands. Fibre optic cable requires an optical transmitter at the sending end, which converts the digital signals into light impulses, and a receiver at the other end, which converts the light impulses back into digital signals. Fibre optic cables can support very high data rates and have very low error rates, as the cable is not affected by electrical noise or crosstalk. However, they are expensive and need careful installation (bending them can break the glass strands). They are generally used for network backbones (e.g. interconnecting several smaller LANs, such as those on the separate floors of a large building).
- The traditional analogue **telephone** network was designed for voice transmissions but, because of its universal availability, it has been used for computer communications. Connections via the telephone network (sometimes called **dial-up connections**) require the use of a **modem** to convert the digital data to and from the analogue signals that the telephone network accepts (see page 167).
- The invention of **radio** for broadcasting goes back to the beginning of the twentieth century. Radio and TV are examples of simplex transmission, in that the information is sent in only one direction. Radio transmitters work by creating waves of electromagnetic energy, and information can be encoded in these waves using a technique called **modulation** (see page 167). Radio waves can vary in their **frequency**, which means that different information can be transmitted at the same time using different frequencies. For example, FM radio broadcasts are in the frequency range of about 88 to 108 MHz. Radio is not limited to simplex transmission. Mobile phones are an example of duplex radio devices; they use the 824 to 849 MHz frequency range. Network connections based on radio

waves have a number of potential advantages. Not having to install cables avoids the expense and disruption and provides considerable flexibility. Wireless LANs operate at around 2400 MHz.

### What does it mean?

Radio frequency is measured in **megahertz** (MHz). One megahertz is 1 million cycles per second.

- **Microwaves** are a form of super-high frequency radio waves that can be used to transmit digital data. However, microwaves have a maximum range of around 20–30 miles, so repeater stations are required for longer distances.
- Prior to the launch of the first communications **satellites** in the early 1960s, voice and data communications between continents could only be achieved by the use of undersea cables. Satellites provide a cost-effective alternative to undersea cables, with microwave radio used to transmit data to and from the satellite. Satellites also provide telephone connections in places that would otherwise be impossible to reach using traditional methods, such as ship-to-shore communications and links to remote locations. Satellites are not only used for communications links; other familiar applications include television broadcasting, weather forecasting and the global positioning system (GPS) navigation system.

Satellites provide a cost-effective alternative to undersea cables

### Further research 5.3

1 What different communications media does the network in your school or college use?
2 Draw a diagram showing what media is used, and where.
3 Why are different media used?

**Check your understanding 5.4**

This first section has introduced lots of terms that you need to learn.

1 Using a word-processor, list all the technical terms and acronyms in this chapter. (They are all highlighted in bold.)
2 Sort the list into alphabetical order and then, for each entry, write a definition, in your own words, explaining what the term means and what it relates to.
3 Use the book's index to locate the terms again and check that your definition is correct. Amend your list as necessary.

**Assessment activity 5.2**

1 List the different communication channels available and typical applications of each one.
2 Write a report explaining the differences between the communication channels listed above.
3 Explain the advantages and disadvantages of the different types of transmission methods and assess their suitability for the communication channels described above.

# 5.2 Hardware and software

The basic requirement for computer communication is that the computer has some kind of hardware interface to allow it to communicate over the chosen medium, and that it has software loaded to implement the protocol in use and to provide various network services.

## Communications software

### Purpose, types and functions of communications software

Communications software is required to carry out a wide range of complex tasks such as:

- organising streams of bits into packets
- adding control information to the data, such as source and destination addresses
- adding error checking data and checking them on receipt
- resending lost packets or packets that have errors
- breaking large amounts of data down into packets and reassembling them on receipt
- establishing connections with remote machines.

To simplify the development and maintenance of this software, it is commonly split into a number of layers (see page 176).

### Protocols

Protocols determine how a number of important tasks are performed, including flow control, error detection and compression. Error detection has already been discussed on page 159, and compression was discussed on page 161.

Situations can occur when the device at the receiving end of a connection is not ready to receive data; for example, the computer may be involved in other processing tasks. In these situations data could be lost unless the receiving end has some way of telling the sending device to wait. The part of the communications protocol that deals with this issue is called **flow control**. Different protocols use different methods of flow control. RS232 connections, for example, have dedicated pins in their connectors that electrically signal that the device is ready to receive data. Pin 4 is known as RTS (ready to send); when the sending device wants to send data, it raises the voltage on this pin. Pin 5 is known as CTS (clear to send); the voltage on this pin is raised by the receiving end when it is ready to receive data.

**Compression** is a method of representing data that can be used to reduce the transfer times across a network. There are many different methods of compression in use, all of which reduce the size of a file, so fewer bits need to be transported across the network. Compression is particularly important when transferring graphics, audio and video files as these tend to be very large. For example, bitmap graphics files can be stored in an uncompressed format such as BMP, or in a compressed format such as JPG, and typically JPG files are around 10 per cent of the size of BMP files.

Graphics files come in a variety of formats, most of which are named after the file extension that the file has. **BMP** files are uncompressed bitmap (BMP is short for bitmap) files created by programs such as Windows Paint. **JPG** is a shortened version of JPEG which stands for Joint Photographic Experts Group. This group of technical experts designed a graphics file format which included a compression system, specifically aimed at photographic bitmap images. Because of the significant reduction in file size JPG is almost universally used for photographic images embedded in Internet web pages, allowing the pages to load more quickly than if BMP files were used.

### Assessment activity 5.3

Write a report describing the main functions of a protocol. You may find it helpful to refer back to Check your understanding 5.1.

## Network applications

The popular network applications include e-mail, FTP (file transfer protocol) and bulletin boards.

**E-mail** has become one of the most widely used network applications. It is a convenient and flexible method of personal and business communication, which is much faster than traditional postal services. To use Internet e-mail the following are required:

- a computer with an Internet connection
- e-mail software such as Microsoft® Outlook
- subscription to an e-mail service.

An e-mail address (provided by the e-mail service) is in the format username@e-mailservice.com. E-mail services provided by companies such as Yahoo! and Microsoft® (who provide the Hotmail service) forward the users' outgoing e-mails using the e-mail address to decide how the e-mail should be routed. Incoming e-mails are stored until the user is online. (Routing of messages on the Internet is described in more detail on page 181.)

**FTP** (file transfer protocol) allows the transferring of files from one location to another. It is often referred to as **downloading** a file, and is popular for downloading music, graphics and programs. For example, the website www.download.com provides thousands of shareware and freeware programs for anyone to download and try.

**Bulletin boards** work like an electronic notice board. Organised around a particular subject, people can place comments or questions on the bulletin board and other users can reply. Used for all sort of subjects from fishing to racing cars to software problems, bulletin boards can be a very useful source of information.

**Further research 5.4**

1 List the different network applications you have used, either at home or in school or college. Include the software you use, the type of network (LAN or WAN), the type of connection used and the purpose of the application.

# Communication devices

## Analogue communication devices

Communication networks that use the traditional telephone network require a **modem** to interface between the computer and the telephone line. This is necessary because, traditionally, telephone networks have been designed to carry analogue signals (i.e. voice) rather than the digital data that computers use. Even though much of the telephone network today is digital, many home computer users still use modems, and the connection between most homes and the local telephone exchange is analogue. This situation is beginning to change with the increasing popularity of **broadband digital connections**.

**What does it mean?**

**Modem** stands for **mo**dulator **dem**odulator. The modem converts the signal from digital to analogue, and vice versa, by modulating (or altering) the carrier signal to represent the digital data.

Over the years, modems have developed and become more sophisticated, and the speed at which data can be transmitted has increased. A series of standards, known as the V series, developed by CCITT, have been used to ensure compatibility between different manufacturers. The key features of the V series specifications are show in Table 5.2.

| Standard | Date | Bits/second | Megabytes per hour |
|---|---|---|---|
| V.32 | 1984 | 9,600 | 4 |
| V.32bis | 1991 | 14,400 | 6 |
| V.34 | 1994 | 28,800 | 12 |
| V.34+ | 1996 | 33,600 | 14 |
| V.90 | 1998 | Up to 50,000 | Up to 22 |

Table 5.2 V standards for modems

To encode the digital data, a modem uses a carrier signal, as shown in Figure 5.4. The carrier signal is modulated by changing one of its physical characteristics.

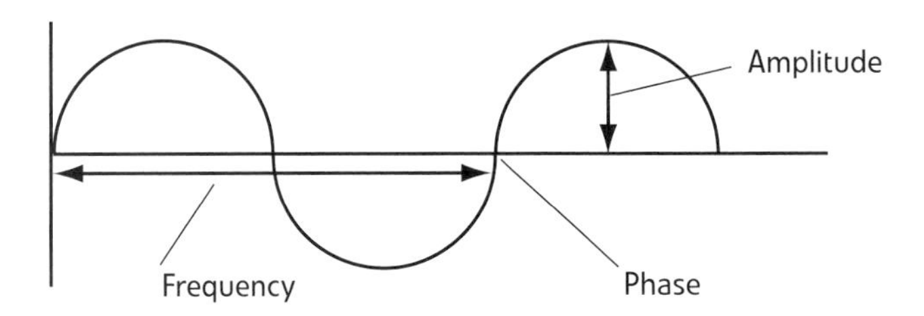


Figure 5.4 Carrier signal

The carrier signal has three basic physical properties:

- **frequency**: how long it takes to go through a complete cycle
- **amplitude**: how high the waveform rises and falls
- **phase**: where each cycle starts in relation to the previous one.

Using a change in frequency to signify the difference between the 1s and 0s in the binary data is known as **frequency shift keying (FSK)** (Figure 5.5).

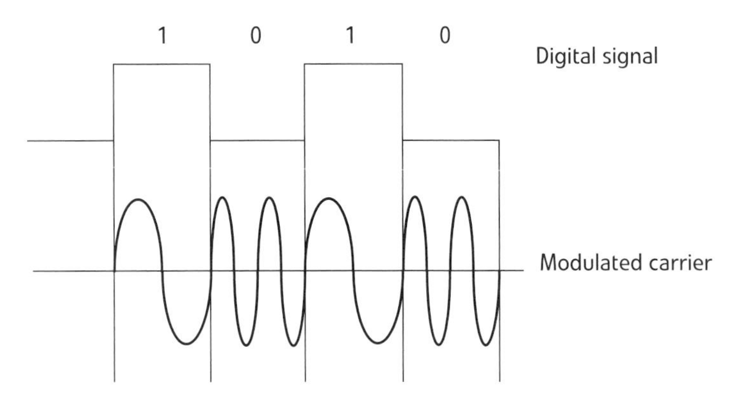


Figure 5.5 Frequency shift keying to represent a binary number

FSK only works well with low-speed modems, while changing the amplitude of the carrier signal does not work well because telephone lines can only accommodate a limited number of amplitude changes. Most modern modems use some kind of phase change to represent the binary data; the basic technique is called **phase shift keying (PSK)**, and a more advanced technique called **quadrature amplitude modulation (QAM)** involves changing both the phase and the amplitude of the carrier signal.

The current standard for modems is known as **V.90**. This standard was developed primarily for connecting home computers to the Internet (see page 181). With a V.90 connection the analogue to digital conversion is carried out only at the user's home computer; this allows data to be transmitted from the Internet to the user at a speed of 56 Kbps and hence complex web pages can be downloaded quickly. However, for communication from the home user to the Internet the lower speed of 33.6 Kbps is used.

## Other analogue communications devices

There are a number of general communications devices used with WAN networks:

- Mainframe systems support large numbers of terminal devices, from a couple of hundred to several thousand in a very large organisation. Such a large number of terminal devices place a very heavy load on the processor of the mainframe computer. A **front-end processor** is part of a mainframe system and deals with input from and output to the terminal network, thereby offloading the main processor.

- Early WANs were connected using the traditional telephone system and modems as described above. Where permanent connections were required, **leased lines** were used rather than dial-up connections. With a leased line, rather than having to dial a number, the connection is always available, but only to a fixed location. However, as both dial-up and leased line are analogue connections, they provide very limited bandwidth.
- A **multiplexor** allows multiple connections to share a single transmission channel (i.e. a single cable supports several connections). Normally, the transmission channel is a high-speed link while the individual connections are low-speed. Multiplexors share the channel either by allocating short periods of time to each connection in rotation (**time division multiplexing**) or by dividing the available bandwidth on the channel into multiple channels of a smaller bandwidth (**frequency division multiplexing**).
- A **concentrator** is a device that serves as a central connection point for several terminal devices. It is similar to a hub (see page 174).

## Client devices

Networks are generally made up of end-user devices that provide access to the network, known as client devices or **workstations**, and **servers** that provide the network services (file sharing, e-mail, etc.). Both client and server devices are basically computers, although client workstations can be normal desktop computers, portable laptop computers, PDAs (personal digital assistants) (Figure 5.6) or even mobile phones. Mobile workstations such as PDAs and mobile phones rely on the cellular radio network for connection (see page 172).

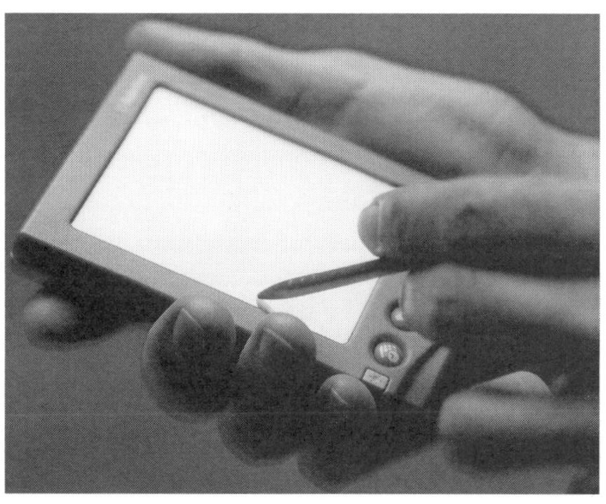

Figure 5.6 Personal digital assistant

### Check your understanding 5.5

This section has introduced yet more terms that you need to learn.

1 Update the list of terms you produced for Check your understanding 5.4.
2 For each new entry, write a definition, in your own words, explaining what the term means and what it relates to.
3 Use the book's index to locate the new terms within the text and check that your definition is correct. Amend your list as necessary.

### Assessment activity 5.4

Write a report that explains, for the benefit of someone who is new to IT:

- the purpose of a modem
- why it is needed
- how it works.

# 5.3 Computer networks

## Concept of networking

Computer networks can be classified into LANs and WANs. Networks can also be classified into private and public.

- **Private networks** are constructed and used exclusively by one organisation; most LANs are private.
- **Public networks** are open to the general public; the best-known example of a public network is the Internet.

Some networks are a combination of LANs and WANs. A large organisation such as a bank may have a LAN connecting its computers within each of its branches, and a WAN interconnecting the branches in each town with its centralised head office.

Just as LAN connection techniques have developed over the years, the same is true of WANs. WANs have been around longer than LANs. Early computer networks, built in the 1960s and 1970s, were designed to connect computer terminals to mainframe computers. Mainframe computers have all the processing and storage (memory, discs, etc.) located in a central computer room. Users of the mainframe have a terminal device (basically just a monitor and keyboard) which is linked by a serial connection to the mainframe; all the keyboard input is sent to the central mainframe processor and screen output is returned from the mainframe. Systems like this are less common today but are still found in large organisations like banks, telephone companies, utility companies (e.g. electricity suppliers) and supermarkets. Today, WANs are mainly used to interconnect an organisation's LANs (private LANs) or to provide the Internet connections.

### Network topologies

Another way in which networks can be classified is by their topology, i.e. the layout of the devices and the interconnections between them. It is important to understand the difference between logical and physical network topology (layout):

- The **logical topology** is used to explain the workings of the particular networking technology.
- The **physical topology** is used to describe the actual layout of the cabling used, and is not necessarily the same as the logical topology.

There are three main types of network topology, as described below.

- The **bus topology** (Figure 5.7) has a single cable to which all the devices are attached and share. This is the logical topology of the **Ethernet LAN system**, which is the most widely used office LAN.

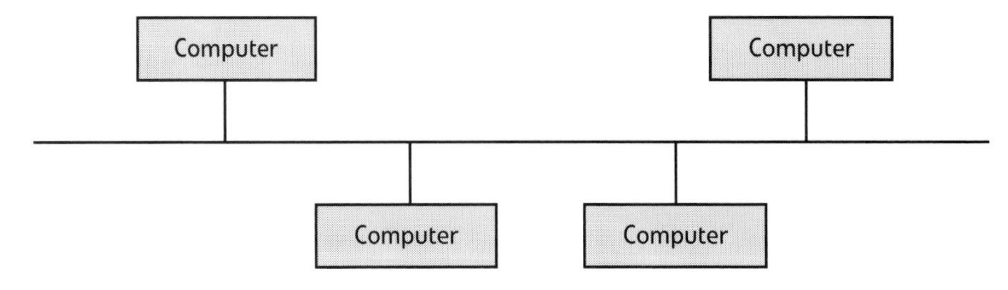


Figure 5.7 Bus topology

- With the **ring topology**, devices are attached to a loop of cable. Data flows around the ring in one direction. This type of logical topology was used with LAN implementations such as the **Cambridge ring** and the **IBM token ring**, but it is no longer widely used.
- In the **star topology** (Figure 5.8), devices are all connected to a central hub or concentrator. This is the most commonly used physical cabling topology today.

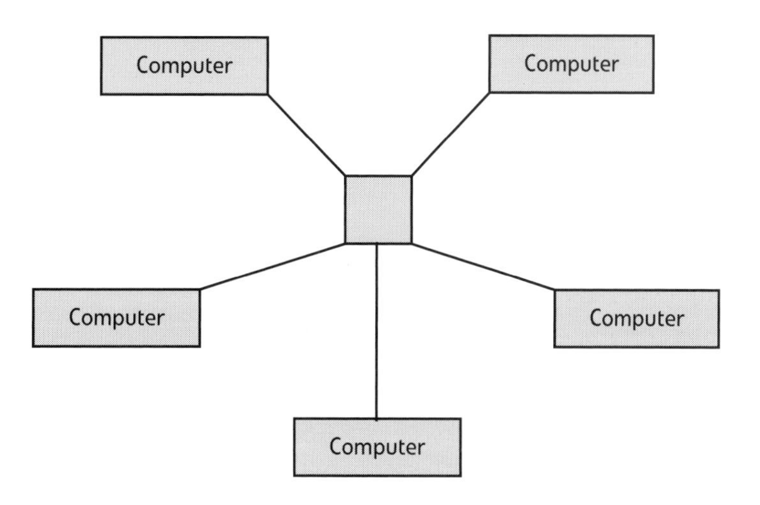


Figure 5.8 Star topology

During the 1980s, two different LAN access methods were developed. IBM produced the token ring while Digital, Intel and Xerox developed the Ethernet system. Both access methods were made into open (i.e. not tied to one or a group of manufacturers) international standards, Ethernet became IEEE802.3 and token ring became IEEE802.5. For various reasons, some commercial rather than technical, Ethernet came to dominate the LAN market and token ring is rarely found these days. Nevertheless it is worth explaining how token ring works, as well as Ethernet. Both techniques are designed to share a single transmission medium (a cable) and to share out the use of the medium evenly. You can find more detail about these techniques on page 173.

## Network services

Telephone companies, such as British Telecom, offer a range of services to both business and private users to allow them to connect their computers to either private or public WANs.

- **PSDN** (packet switched digital network) networks were first developed in the 1970s and are sometimes called X.25 (after the protocol used) or **value-added networks** (VANs). Like leased lines, a PSDN service is provided by a telephone company; unlike a leased line, the PSDN is not a point-to-point connection, but a network over which virtual circuits can be established. Data is sent as fixed length packets, to which a destination address is added. The address is used by the network to route the packet to its destination. PSDN is not particularly fast, with speeds up to 64 Kbps.
- **ISDN** (integrated services digital network) is a digital network, designed to transmit both voice and data.
- **ADSL** (asynchronous digital subscriber line) is a service provided by British Telecom, which allows a digital connection over a standard telephone line, normally at 512 Kbps which is

around 10 times faster that the fastest analogue modem. As well as providing a high-speed digital connection, it also allows simultaneous voice connection, so normal telephone use is not disrupted.

- **ATM** (asynchronous transfer mode) is a high-bandwidth packet-switched network technology aimed at business users. It allows simultaneous data, voice and video links to be established over the same communications link.

## Wireless networks

The **cellular mobile telephone** system offers a way for remote users to connect to the various networks, both public (e.g. the Internet) and private. In this way, a sales representative visiting customer locations around the country could connect to his or her company's network to input orders from a laptop computer.

The original cellular phone networks launched in the 1980s were analogue and each company developed a different and incompatible system. In the late 1980s a Europe-wide organisation was formed to develop a standardised digital mobile phone system that became known as **GSM** (**global system for mobile communication**) and spread across not only Europe but also the Americas, Asia, Africa and Australasia. GSM provides data communications at 9600 bps, which is not particularly fast. An upgrade to GSM, called **GPRS** (**general packet radio services**), provides a packet switched system that is better suited to data transmission than the point-to-point connections that GSM provides. When using applications such as web browsing, data tends to come in 'bursts', for example while downloading a web page, followed by a period of low data activity, perhaps while the user reads through the page. A continuous connection such as that provided by GSM is wasted on this type of application; however, packet switching is a much better solution and allows resources to be shared by multiple users. GPRS provides speeds of up to 384 Kbps, and is ideal for WAP, which is described below.

Currently under development are the so-called **third-generation (3G) cellular services**. 3G services will not start in Europe until 2004; using a system known as **UMTS** (**universal mobile telephone system**), it will provide packet switched data connections at up to 2 Mbps.

**WAP** (**wireless application protocol**) was designed with the aim of providing mobile telephone (and PDAs and other handheld devices) users with access to the Internet. WAP allows devices to access any WWW site that supports WAP. WAP defines a mark-up language, called **WML** (**wireless mark-up language**), which allows the creation of web pages and uses the **XML** (**extensible mark-up language**) standard already used by many websites.

### What does it mean?

XML is a specification for a more advanced version of HTML (hypertext mark-up language) which is used to format web pages.

WML is designed to optimise text delivery on limited-speed connections to small-screen devices. It also supports simple navigation without a keyboard. WAP was heavily promoted by service providers and phone manufacturers but, owing to problems with compatibility, and especially performance, WAP proved to be a big disappointment. GSM's transfer rate of 9600 bps proved too slow even for simple text applications.

# LAN components

A basic PC LAN (Figure 5.9) consists of a server computer and several workstation computers. Each computer must have a network card, sometimes called an **NIC (network interface card)**, and there must be some way of interconnecting the computers.

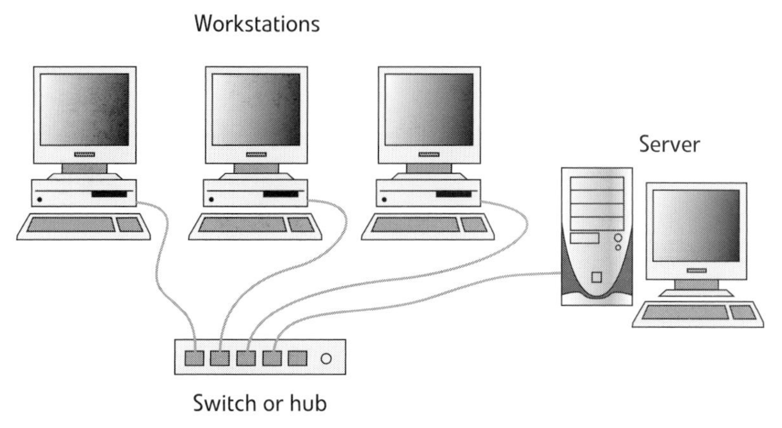


Figure 5.9 A simple LAN

A **server** is a computer that provides LAN services to all the workstation computers. There is not necessarily anything special about the hardware of a server computer; the services it provides to the LAN are software based.

In a PC, the NIC is an expansion card that slots into the **motherboard** (although in some cases the NIC may be built into the motherboard). A NIC is designed to work with a particular type of network and media. The most common type today is the Ethernet NIC, fitted with a RJ45 female socket for use with UTP cables. Fast Ethernet NICs (100 BaseT) can often work at either 10 Mbps or 100 Mbps and automatically select the correct speed.

With the original coaxial cable version of Ethernet, a **transceiver** was a device used to connect the NIC to the coaxial cable. Current versions of Ethernet have the transceiver built into the NIC.

## What does is mean?

The **motherboard** is the main circuit board of a computer. It has slots into which all the other boards fit and connectors for other devices (such as discs, keyboard, mouse, etc.).

**Token ring**, as the name suggests, uses a logical ring topology. A special packet of data known as the token passes around the ring at all times. Devices on the ring that do not want to transmit anything pass the token on to the next device around the ring. If the token reaches a device that does want to send data, that device marks the token as in use and attaches the data it wants to send, along with the destination address to the token. The token is then passed on to the next device in the ring. Each device then checks the destination address to see whether the data is for that device. If it is not, the data is just passed around until it reaches the device to which it was addressed. When the data reaches its destination, that device removes the data, marks the token as free again and passes it on to the next device in the ring. If a device that wants to send data receives the token and finds that it is in use, it knows it must wait until the next time the token comes around.

**Ethernet** uses a logical bus topology. Access to the cable is controlled using a technique called **CSMA/CD (carrier sense multiple access / collision detect)**, which works in the following way:

- When a device wants to send data, it first 'listens' to the cable to check whether it is free. If it hears traffic on the cable, it waits a random amount of time and tries again. If the cable is free, it transmits its data on the cable. Note that unlike token ring, data does not pass down the cable in a particular direction, instead data is transmitted in both directions from the sender.
- Once data has been transmitted, the sending device listens to the cable to check whether transmission is successful or if there is a collision. A collision occurs when two devices transmit their data at (or very close to) the same time. When a collision occurs, the data from both the sending devices is lost.
- If the sending device detects a collision, it waits for a random amount of time and goes through the whole process again.

This technique may sound as if it will cause a lot of collisions and retries but, as long as the cables are not too long and network traffic is not very heavy, it works well. It is also worth remembering that Ethernet runs at quite a high speed. The original Ethernet ran at 10 Mbps, the current Ethernet version, often called **100 BaseT**, or Fast Ethernet runs at 100 Mbps. Also available for very demanding applications is Gigabit Ethernet, which runs at 1 Gbps.

Ethernet's flexibility and relative simplicity to set up, combined with its attractive combination of speed, low cost and ease of installation and use, has made it by far the most popular LAN access technique. Indeed, it has become so popular that people often don't use terms such as 'Ethernet network card' any more, referring instead to just a 'network card'; the fact that they mean Ethernet is implied.

**FDDI (fibre distributed data interface)** was developed in the mid-1980s by ANSI as a high-performance LAN. It consists of a dual ring of fibre optic cables running at 100 Mbps using a token passing protocol. Although it has a dual ring, only one of the rings is used at a time for data transmission, the other providing a backup. It is used in applications that require high performance and high reliability. Since fibre optic cables allow a network to span greater distances than a typical LAN, it is used in applications such as a university campus-wide network.

### Assessment activity 5.5

1 Draw diagrams of the three main types of network topology and explain how data flows around each one.

2 Explain access methods used in Ethernet and token ring networks.

# Interconnection devices, media and protocols

## Devices

- **Hubs** are probably the most common piece of network hardware in Ethernet networks. They connect a number of computers (usually 8 or 16) together in a star topology. Computers are connected to the hub using UTP cables with RJ45 connectors at each end.

A hub simply takes the signal sent from each computer, amplifies it and transmits it to all the other computers attached to the hub. An RJ45 socket is used to connect the hub to another hub, thus providing a way to expand the number of computers on the network.

- **Switches** look very much like hubs and, on the surface, perform the same function, i.e. they connect a number of computers together in an Ethernet LAN. However, hubs are 'dumb' devices; they simply receive a message, amplify it and transmit it to all the other computers that are connected to the hub. Switches are 'intelligent'; they inspect the message sent from one computer, identify the computer to which it is being sent and transmit the message only to that computer, not all the others connected to the switch. The benefit of this is that network traffic is significantly reduced, which reduces the possibility of collisions occurring. Switches are slightly more expensive to buy than hubs but, because of their ability to improve the performance of the network, they are commonly used in preference to hubs.
- **Repeaters** are rather like two-port hubs. They have just two RJ45 sockets and are mainly used as a way of extending cable lengths. Ethernet has limits on the length of cables that can be used (about 100 metres) and repeaters can be used to increase this distance. However, even with repeaters, there is an absolute maximum of around 1000 metres. Like hubs, repeaters are 'dumb' devices; whatever signals they receive they simply amplify and send on.
- **Bridges** appear to work very much like repeaters, but just as switches are intelligent versions of hubs, bridges are intelligent versions of repeaters. Bridges are used to interconnect two separate LANs (perhaps on different floors of a building). They listen to the network traffic and learn which destination address is located on which LAN. Using this information they filter the messages they hear on each LAN and only pass across the messages that need to be transferred between the LANs.
- **Routers** carry out a similar task to bridges but they do it differently. Bridges operate at the OSI link layer (see page 176) while routers operate at the network layer. Routers inspect each packet, extract the destination address and use this to route the packet from one LAN to another. Routers pass information between each other and build their own routing tables that contain information about the best routes to various destinations through a complex network of many LANs.
- **Gateways** are devices that translate one type of network data to another. A gateway is used where you need to connect different types of networks together, such as an Ethernet LAN and a token ring LAN.
- **Concentrators** serve as a central connection point for several terminal devices and are similar to hubs.

**Assessment activity 5.6**

Make a list of the different network interconnection devices and briefly explain their purpose.

# Open System Interconnection (OSI) model

The techniques required to achieve data communications have been developed into an international standard known as ISO/OSI (International Standard Organisation / Open Systems Interconnect). The development of an international standard means that (in theory at least) computers and operating systems from different manufacturers can communicate. Because of the complexity of the software required, it is broken down into seven layers; hence the standard is sometimes called the OSI 7-layer model. The layers are shown in Figure 5.10.

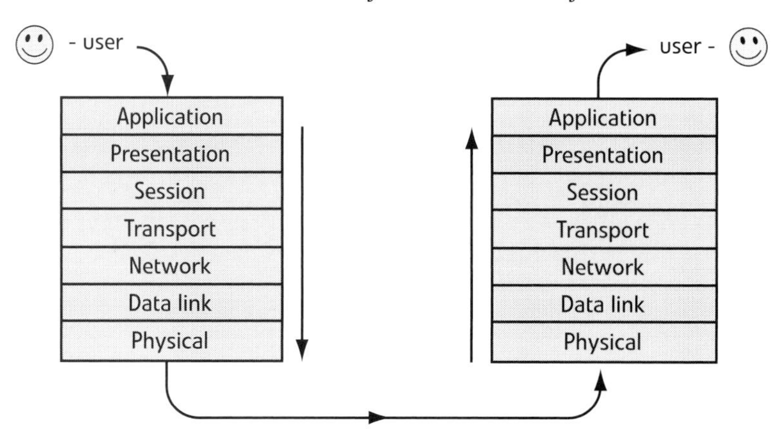


Figure 5.10 OSI 7-layer model

The purpose of each layer is as follows:

- **Physical layer**: This defines how signalling is done (i.e. electrical properties such as voltage levels), the physical connectors (plugs and sockets), the media used (type of cable) and the mode of communication (e.g. simplex or duplex).
- **Data link layer**: This is sometimes called just the link layer. This layer accepts the stream of bits from the physical layer and organises them into packets. It is also responsible for error checking. The data link layer at the sending end adds a source and destination address and a CRC field that is checked by the same layer at the receiving end. If the CRC is incorrect the receiving end requests a retransmission.
- **Network layer**: This deals with routing of packets (i.e. which way they should go to their destination). While the data link layer deals with physical hardware addresses, such as the unique MAC address that is given to every network interface card during manufacture, the network layer deals with logical addresses (such as Internet addresses) which are allocated by network managers. These allow the network layer to identify the network (for example a local or a remote network) for which a message is destined. This allows LANs and WANs to be connected together using devices called **routers**. These devices forward only messages with remote logical addresses on to the WAN while keeping local messages within the LAN. The network layer takes data link packets and adds addressing information, making them into frames.
- **Transport layer**: When large amounts of data need to be transmitted over a network, the transport layer is responsible for breaking the large file down into smaller packets. In a large WAN, different packets from the same file may not all take exactly the same route across the network, so the packets may not arrive in the same order at the destination. At the receiving end the transport layer reassembles the packets back into the correct order.
- **Session layer**: This defines how connections between applications (called sessions) are established across the network. It co-ordinates choice of protocols and establishes checkpoints for recovery, allowing data to be retransmitted if there is an error. An example of a session would be using an FTP program to download files from a remote system.
- **Presentation layer**: This deals with data formats, compression and security (e.g. encryption). This layer allows systems using different operating systems to communicate, for example, by converting between different character sets.

- **Application layer:** This provides a range of user applications such as FTP and e-mail. This is the layer that the user deals with; it hides the complexities of the layers beneath from the user.

The layer of the OSI model that each of the network devices operates at is shown in Table 5.3.

| Device | OSI layer |
|---|---|
| Hubs | 1 - physical |
| Repeaters | 1 - physical |
| Switches | 2 - data link |
| Bridges | 2 - data link |
| Routers | 3 - network |
| Gateways | 3 - network |

Table 5.3 Network devices and their relationship to the 7-layer model

### Assessment activity 5.7

Take the list of network interconnection devices that you made for Assessment activity 5.6 and explain the layer of the OSI model at which each device operates.

# Network software

To provide the network services and applications required, the servers and workstations in a LAN need to run a **network operating system**. The most widely used commercial network operating system is Microsoft® Windows® 2000, which was developed from the earlier Windows NT. This is available in two versions: Windows® 2000 server and Windows® 2000 workstation. Other network operating systems include Linux and Novell. The services provided by the server include the following.

- **User authentication:** It is important that the system is able to identify users, not only to prevent unauthorised users from gaining access to the network, but also to give individual users the correct **rights and permissions**. Users on a network are generally divided into groups to which permissions are allocated. For example a network may have a group for clerks and another for managers. The clerks may be given permission to read some files which contain financial information, but not to modify or delete those files. The manager's group, however, may be given permission to read *and* modify those files.

### ? What does it mean?

**Rights** are things that a user can do, such as close down the server or backup data on the server. **Permissions** are the ability to access certain network resources such as files or printers.

- **File sharing:** The ability to allow a group of users to share files is one of the most powerful network facilities. It enables users on the network to share important company-wide information such as price lists or customer orders. However, it needs careful control, using permissions to prevent information being deleted or misused.

- **Hardware sharing:** It is convenient to share some hardware facilities such as printers. Network operating systems provide for hardware sharing, and in the case of printers, allow jobs to be queued while waiting to print.
- **Network connection software:** A range of different software is available to allow the user to communicate over a network. The best known are Microsoft® Internet Explorer (a **web browser**) and Outlook (an **e-mail** program). **Hyperterminal** is a program included with the Windows operating systems which allows text-based access to remote computers using the Internet Telnet protocol. This allows bulletin board services (BBS) to be accessed. Telnet predates the World Wide Web. File transfer programs (FTP) such as Cute FTP and WS-FTP (both available as shareware) allow users to upload and download files over the Internet and are commonly used to upload web pages on to a web server.

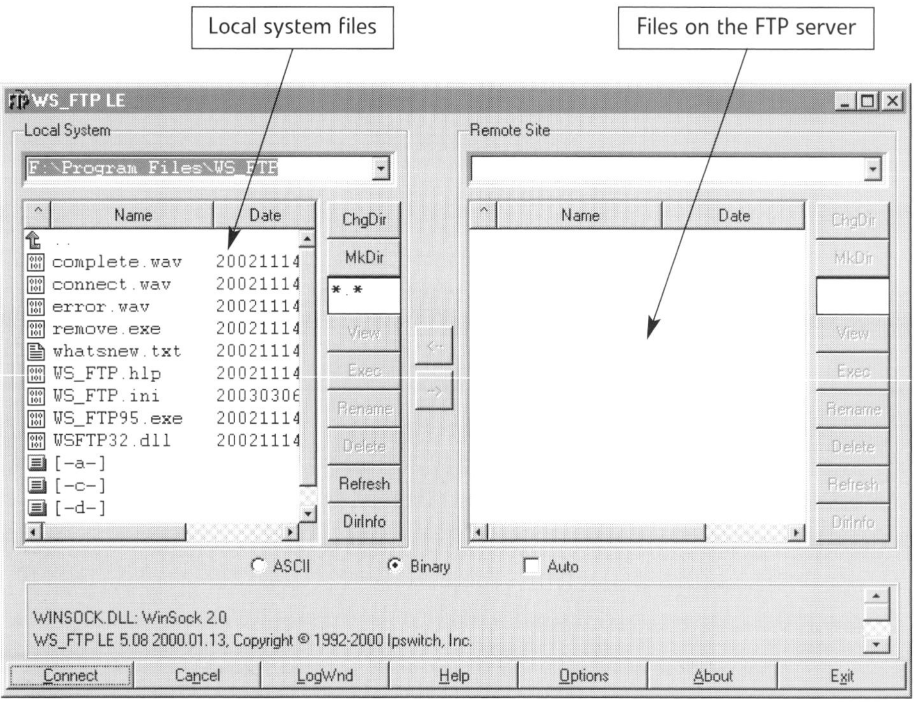


Figure 5.11 The WS-FTP program

# Network development

## Development life cycle

Installing a large LAN in a building or group of buildings or constructing anything other than the simplest of networks is a complex process that needs to be tackled in stages. Typically, there are four stages: establishing user requirements, checking feasibility, design, and implementation.

To establish user requirements – in other words, to understand what the user wants – the following questions need to be answered:

- How many connections are needed and what is the likely future expansion?
- What are the usage levels and performance requirements?

- What applications are required?
- What level of security is required?
- What external connections are needed (e.g. to the Internet or company WAN)?

To check the feasibility you need to know whether the user requirements can be met and how much this will cost. It is worth bearing in mind that the cost of installing the cable itself will in most cases be considerably greater than the cost of the network equipment (switches, routers, etc.).

A detailed design for the network, including locations for wall sockets, cable runs, equipment cabinets, etc., will have to be drawn up. This will also need to consider building regulations, fire safety and electrical requirements.

Installing the cabling in an office environment can cause a considerable amount of disruption, especially if the office is occupied at the time. Disruption may also affect any existing computer or network installation. As well as physically installing cabling and network equipment, it must be tested to ensure it is working properly.

## Operating requirements

Only in the smallest offices and networks does the UTP cabling lead directly back to a switch or hub. The most common arrangement is to install RJ45 sockets mounted on faceplates in the wall or floor (some offices have false floors with space beneath them for cabling, which makes installation easier). Owing to the cost and disruption of installing the cabling in the office environment, it is common practice to install sufficient sockets to meet the maximum likely need, rather than the current requirement. This is because adding sockets at a later date would be far more expensive. These RJ45 sockets are attached to computers, printers, etc. with UTP fly-leads which have RJ45 male plugs at each end.

Hubs or switches and other network equipment are normally located in a dedicated network room. In a large office with several floors, there would be a network room on each floor. The network equipment is usually installed in a rack mounting cabinet. The cables from all the office sockets are terminated in what is called a **patch panel**, which is basically just a row of RJ45 female sockets. A patch panel is used to connect the office sockets to the hubs or switches. Because not all the office sockets will be in use, the patch panel allows the active sockets to be attached to the hubs or switches. Sufficient switches or hubs to supply all the active sockets with connections are also rack mounted in the cabinet. The connection between the patch panels and the switches/hubs are made using UTP fly-leads. A diagram of this configuration is shown in Figure 5.12.

## Performance

The performance of a LAN network depends on a number of criteria. Clearly, the number of computers connected is a factor, but more important is the amount and type of data they need to exchange. In a database application, such as stock control or sales processing, relatively small amounts of data will be transferred between the user's computer and the server, but the transfers may be very frequent at busy times. In applications such as graphics or video editing, very large files may need to be transferred.

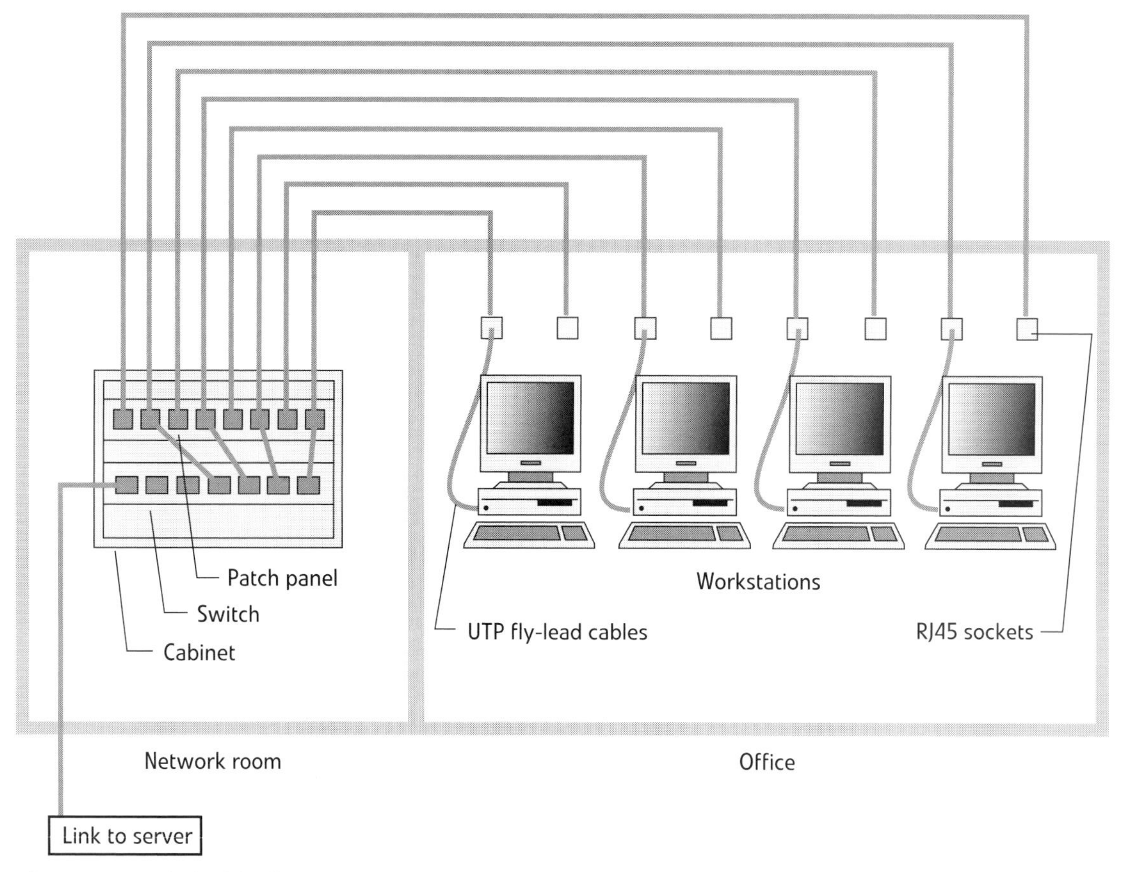


Figure 5.12 Typical wiring layout

One problem with an Ethernet-based LAN is that, as the network traffic rises, the number of collisions increases. Increased collisions result in more network traffic (because data must be retransmitted) and so a vicious circle can occur until the point is reached where every transmission ends in a collision and the network grinds to a halt. Over the years, since the original Ethernet system came into use, two improvements have helped to reduce the performance problem:

- An increase in speed from 10 Mbps to 100 Mbps means large files can be sent quickly, and this reduces the likelihood of a collision.
- The use of switches rather than hubs significantly reduces network traffic.

Another technique to reduce network traffic and therefore improve performance is the use of bridges or routers to divide the network into sections, perhaps one for each department in the company. Communication within a department stays within that department; only inter-departmental communication spreads across the whole LAN.

## Check your understanding 5.6

This third section has introduced yet more terms that you need to learn.

1. Update your list from Check your understanding 5.5, and for each new entry write a definition, in your own words, explaining what the term means and what it relates to.
2. Check that your definition is correct and amend your list as necessary.
3. Revise the entire list. Check that there are no terms that you are still unsure about.

**Assessment activity 5.8**

1 Investigate the network you have at school or college. You may need some help from your computer technicians.
2 Draw a diagram of the network showing as much detail as possible, including the type of interconnecting devices and cabling used.
3 Describe the role of each item in your network diagram.
4 For the interconnection devices (hubs, switches, routers, etc.) in your diagram, explain why these devices were chosen and any possible implications.

# 5.4 The Internet

The Internet has become the best known network. It spans the globe, connects millions of computers and is changing the way we do all sorts of things, from shopping to communicating with friends and family. The Internet provides a range of facilities such as e-mail, the World Wide Web and file transfer.

## Concepts of Internet communication

Most of us connect to the Internet by a modem, although broadband connections using a digital interface are becoming more popular. Whatever method is used, the connection is made to a company called an **ISP (Internet service provider)**. ISPs are connected to each other and large ISPs maintain 'backbone' connections using fibre optic cables for a whole country or region (Figure 5.13). These, in turn, are connected to ISPs in other countries. In this way, all the computers on the Internet are, indirectly, connected to each other. Connections within the Internet are made using the **TCP/IP protocol**.

**What does it mean?**

**TCP/IP** (transmission control protocol / Internet protocol) is actually a whole suite of protocols which control how computers communicate on the Internet (and many other networks including LANs).

Computers connected to the Internet can be divided into **clients** and **servers**. When you connect to the Internet and view various web pages, you are acting as a client. The web pages you are viewing are being sent to your client machine from computers which act as servers. For example, if you view the BBC's website at www.bbc.co.uk your computer connects to a computer (probably a group of computers) at the BBC where those pages are held. Your computer requests the particular page you wish to see on the BBC website and the BBC's computer sends the page. Like all networks, the Internet uses a variety of different protocols. The transfer of web pages is achieved using **HTTP (hypertext transfer protocol)**.

This raises an important question: 'How do you find the server on the Internet that has the web page you want?' If you know the **URL (uniform resource locator)** such as www.bbc.co.uk then you can just type that into your web browser. However, what

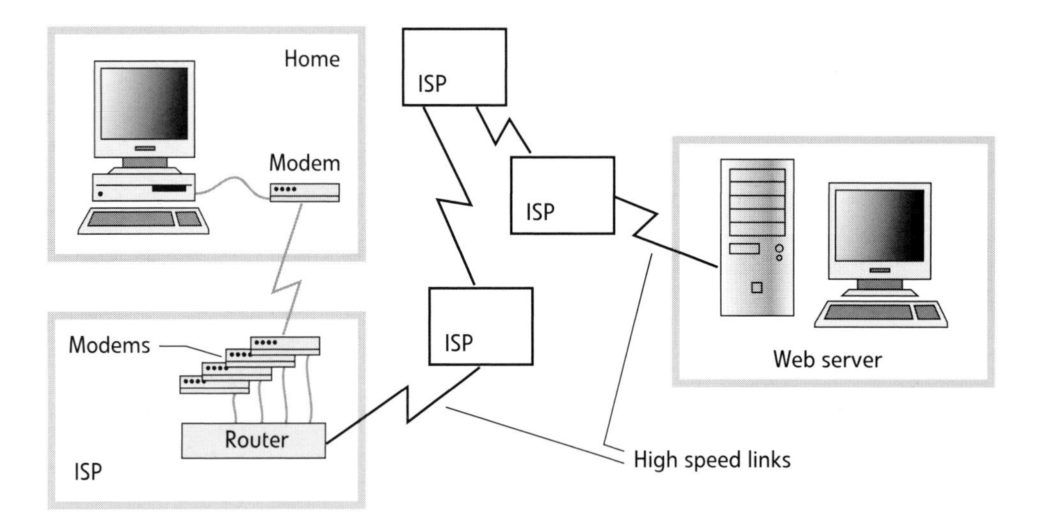


Figure 5.13 How Internet connections are made

happens 'behind the scenes' is a little more complex. Every computer (for both clients and servers) on the Internet is assigned a unique address called an **IP (Internet protocol) address**. IP addresses are 32-bit numbers that are normally shown as four numbers, each of which can be in the range 0 to 255. So a typical IP address would look like this: 255.255.10.12.

Servers have static IP addresses that do not change. Your client machine has an IP address that is allocated by your ISP every time you dial in, and therefore changes. If you know the IP address of a server on the Internet you can, in fact, access that machine using the IP address alone, instead of the URL. However, remembering IP numbers is not easy, so servers on the Internet also have the domain names such as www.bbc.co.uk. The translation between the domain name URL and the IP address is done by a number of special Internet servers called **domain name servers**. When a domain name is typed into a browser on a client machine, the browser contacts a domain name server, which returns the correct IP address for the domain name.

This works fine as long as the user knows the URL of the website. However, in many cases the user may want to find some information (e.g. cheap airline flights) without knowing the URL of any suitable websites. In these situations, **search websites** provide a method of finding the required information. Many of these sites exist; these three are among the best known:

- Yahoo!: www.yahoo.co.uk
- Google: www.google.co.uk
- Lycos: www.lycos.com

Many search websites have a server which runs in the UK as well as the USA and other countries. National sites are best if you are looking for services or information related to the country in which you live. For example, if you are looking for cheap flights from the UK to Europe, then it is best to search on www.google.co.uk. If you are looking for information on the conservation of wild animals, you may find more world-wide information if you search on www.google.com.

Also popular is the Ask Jeeves website (www.ask.co.uk). This website allows you to enter questions that you may have (such as 'where can I find the cheapest music CDs') and then it attempts to find websites which answer your question.

Sites such as Yahoo!, as well as providing search facilities, also include a wide range of other information services, such as financial information, news, weather, jobs and cars for sale. Like Google, Yahoo! has various national versions: www.yahoo.com is the US version, www.yahoo.co.uk is the UK version and www.yahoo.fr is the French version.

# System requirements

To connect to the Internet, there are a number of requirements. First and foremost, you need a computer, either a PC with the Windows® XP, ME, 98 or 95 operating system, or an Apple Macintosh. As well as installing the necessary network protocols such as TCP/IP on the computer, some application software is required. For viewing web pages, a web browser such as Microsoft® Internet Explorer is required. For sending and receiving non-web-based e-mail, an e-mail program such as Microsoft® Outlook is needed. To use FTP you must have an FTP program.

You must be registered with an ISP to connect to the Internet. Many ISPs offer free registration; others, in return for additional services, charge a monthly fee. Once you have registered with an ISP, they will provide you with a telephone number for your modem to dial, a username and password to access their computers. For a traditional dial-up connection, you need a modem, which is connected to your regular telephone line. The dial-up settings are made in the 'My Computer' window, using the Dial-up networking icon. A step-by-step wizard, called Make New Connection, is provided which takes you through the set-up procedure. Figure 5.14 shows typical connection properties.

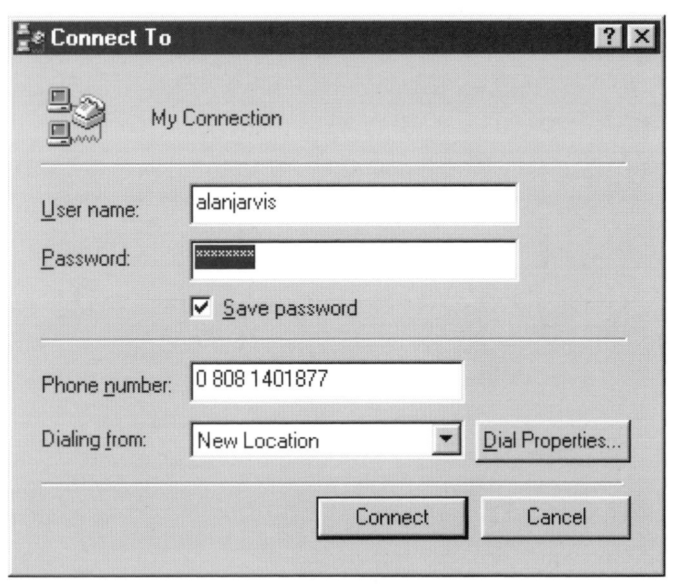


Figure 5.14 Dial-up connection properties

To set up Microsoft® Internet Explorer to use the dial-up connection, the *Internet Options* option is chosen from the Tools menu within the Explorer program, and the *Connections* tab is selected. The dial-up connection can then be selected from the list displayed (Figure 5.15).

Figure 5.15 Internet Explorer connection settings

If you purchase a broadband connection from your telephone or cable TV company, they normally provide you with an interface device, such as a cable modem, which is attached to the USB port on your computer. This type of Internet connection is permanent and no dialling is required.

## Check your understanding 5.7

If you have a friend or relative with a new computer (or an old computer they want to connect up), offer to help them set it up for use on the Internet. You will need to keep a record of everything you do to set up the computer. Using screen shots of the various settings you make is a good way to do this.

Alternatively, write a guide the new user could follow to connect a computer to the Internet.

To use FTP software, you must know the URL of an FTP server, and have a valid FTP username and password. Figure 5.16 shows typical settings for the WS-FTP program. Once you have successfully logged-on to an FTP server, you can transfer files to and from the server.

Session Properties
General | Startup | Advanced | Firewall
Profile Name: Ipswitch
Host Name/Address: 80.6.61.75
Host Type: Microsoft NT
User ID: myaccount
Password: ***********
Account:
Comment:
New
Delete
Anonymous
Save Pwd
OK | Cancel | Apply | Help

Figure 5.16 Log-in settings for WS-FTP

### What does it mean?

An **FTP server** is similar to a web server, but instead of using the HTTP protocol to serve web pages, it uses the FTP protocol to allow files to be uploaded and downloaded. Many ISPs provide you with web space on their web server. You can upload your own web pages using an FTP program to this web space, so the pages are available on the WWW.

### Check your understanding 5.8

Update your list of terms and definitions and make sure that you are happy with your understanding of all the terms introduced during this unit.

### Assessment activity 5.9

1 Write a report describing the difference between the Internet and the World Wide Web and explaining the range of services available on the Internet.

2 Draw a diagram of how a computer can connect to the Internet, including both the client and server. For each item in the diagram describe its function. List the software required and describe the function of each item of software.

3 Set up a computer so it can be used on the Internet to browse web pages and use FTP. You will need to keep evidence in the form of screen shots to show how you have done this.

### Test your knowledge

1 Explain the difference between analogue and digital signalling.

2 What is a modem?

3 Describe the main functions of a communications protocol.

4 Describe how the CSMA/CD LAN access method works.

5 Draw diagrams of three LAN topologies and explain the differences between them in the way data flows around the network.

6 Explain the OSI 7-layer model in relation to interconnection devices.

7 Identify and describe the functions of the minimum hardware and software elements which make up the Internet and the WWW.

8 Explain these terms: RS232, flow control, and compression.

# UNIT 6: SYSTEMS ANALYSIS AND DESIGN

Before a software system can be developed, the needs of the users must be understood and a design produced for the system which meets those needs. This unit looks at some techniques for gathering information about the users' requirements and for producing the design.

## Learning objectives

- To understand the principles of systems analysis and design and their importance for system development
- To investigate and analyse problems for clients and to document the results of the analysis
- To produce and document a design solution to the problem
- To produce a test plan for the completed design

# 6.1 Principles of systems analysis and design

Organisations such as banks, hospitals and supermarkets use computer systems as tools to help them to carry out their business. Their computer systems have to be developed, not by the users of the system, but by IT professionals. The computer system must meet the needs of the users, so the IT professionals have to understand those needs in detail. The process of analysing and understanding user needs is called **systems analysis**. There are two main difficulties systems analysis must overcome:

- The users of the system and the developers of the system are experts in two different areas. For example, in a bank, the users are experts in banking and finance; the system developers are experts in IT. However, the users need to be able to communicate in detail what the system needs to do, so the system developers need to become experts in the area of banking that the system will address.
- Computer systems need to model real-world situations, such as withdrawing money from a bank or buying goods at the supermarket. These real-world situations are highly complex with many interrelationships with other systems. Ways are needed, not only to understand this complexity, but also to describe (model) it in some formal way.

System analysis is of critical importance in the development of a complex computerised system. Errors at this stage may result in a system that, no matter how good the programming or the user interface is, fails to meet the primary goal of any computer system, i.e. to meet the needs of the user.

## The system development life cycle

Systems analysis is part of the system development life cycle (Figure 6.1). As the word cycle suggests, it has no clear start or finish but it is useful to think of the start of the cycle as being the point where dissatisfaction with the existing system (either computerised or manual) reaches such a level that a new system is considered. It may be that the existing system is unable to cope efficiently with an increasing volume of work, or it may be that other companies in the same business have introduced systems which give them a competitive advantage (e.g. an Internet shopping service) so a similar (or better) system is needed to regain the competitive edge. This is the point where system analysis begins; the existing system and its limitations are analysed, the needs of the users are identified and the way forward is investigated.

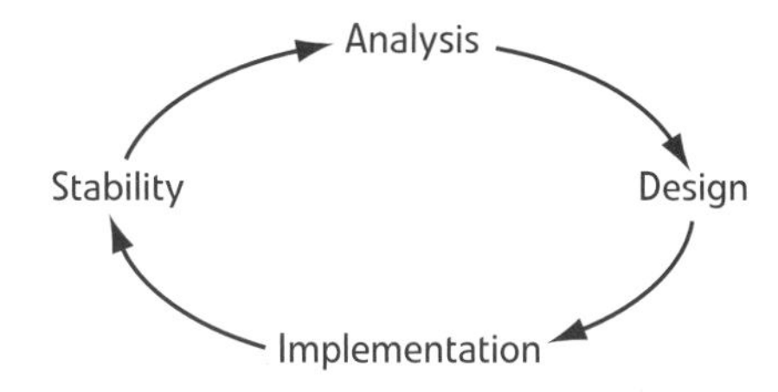


Figure 6.1 The software development life cycle

Once the analysis stage is completed, then it is time to start on the detailed design of the required system, followed by the development of the programs, testing and implementation. This unit concentrates only on the analysis stage. After the system has been implemented and initial teething problems have been ironed out, the system should enter a period of stability. However, there will come a time when, owing to further increases in work load, new developments or changes in the market, the system will no longer fully meet the needs of its users and the need to develop a new or modified system will arise. So, the whole process begins again. Hence, the use of the term cycle.

## The stages of systems development

The process of systems analysis can be broken down into a number of stages:

- initiation
- investigation
- analysis
- design
- implementation
- testing
- maintenance.

The **initiation** stage is an initial look at an existing system to see how it can be improved. The end result of this stage is a **feasibility study** report. If the feasibility report is accepted, then more detailed research is carried out.

**Investigation** is a fact-finding stage which involves defining the **scope** of the system, its boundaries and the users' requirements. The systems analyst investigates in detail how the current system works, including how data is put into the system (input), how it flows around the system and is processed and what types of output are produced. The system analyst also needs to identify the system boundaries and what its interfaces are with other systems.

At the **analysis** stage, the use of structured analysis tools involves using a number of techniques (often utilising diagrams) to model the flow of information and the interrelationships in the system.

At the **design** stage, the systems analyst takes the information that has been gathered and analysed in the two previous stages and produces a detailed technical design for the system, as a guide for the programmers who will implement the system. This design is often presented in a document called the **system specification**.

The remaining stages of implementation, testing and maintenance are beyond the scope of systems analysis, although a good understanding of the whole software development process is important to the systems analyst and details of this can be found in Unit 4.

The division of the software development process into these stages is sometimes called the **waterfall model**, because the stages cascade into each other with each stage feeding information into the next like water falling over the rocks of a waterfall. However, many software development projects do not proceed in such a smooth way. Also, as the customer is required to agree to the design at an early stage, it is difficult to respond to changing customer requirements. The waterfall model is therefore best suited to situations where the requirements are well understood.

**Evolutionary development** provides a more flexible approach. This is based on the idea of developing an initial implementation, demonstrating this to the users to gauge their response and refining the software product through many versions until a suitable system has been developed. Evolutionary development is also sometimes called **prototyping**. Evolutionary development is often more effective than the waterfall approach in producing systems which closely meet the needs of the users. However, there are some problems with this approach. For example, as it is not known at the outset exactly what will eventually be developed it can be very difficult to estimate how much the development will cost.

# Feasibility study

Let's go back to the very beginning, the feasibility study. A feasibility study answers a very important question: can the need for a new system be justified? In other words, is it technically feasible and economically desirable? The feasibility study begins with a preliminary investigation and this involves obtaining the following general information:

- details of the system currently being used, its benefits and limitations
- additional requirements of the new system.

From the information gathered during this preliminary investigation, a report is produced which includes the following information.

- **A statement of the purpose of the system**: This includes a brief description of what the current system does, and an indication of any new developments that are required in the new system.
- **A definition of system scope**: This section establishes the boundaries of the system analysis process and includes any constraints, such as cost of development. It includes all areas of the system that should be developed and identifies any other systems that might be affected by this development or that provide information for this system. It is important to remember that when a new system is being developed, it is almost certain to be affected by, and have an effect on, other systems that are used within an organisation. Often, when researching one system, faults can be identified with other systems. It is important to establish in this section the exact limits of the task.
- **A list of current deficiencies**: This section includes all the problems of the current system. However, it is also important to make a note of those parts of the system that are identified as working well, so they can be preserved in the new system.
- **A statement of user requirements**: Clearly, this section needs to be developed in close consultation with the users and there are various ways their requirements can be defined. One way is to ask users to compile a list of what they require from the new system. Another is for the systems analyst to interview users to identify what they think needs to be achieved by the new system. It is important for the users to prioritise the list of requirements, as not all may be achievable owing to constraints on time or money. Using the information provided by the users, the system analyst then identifies the outputs that are required from the system. That enables him/her to decide on the appropriate data inputs and data capture methods. Finally, once the inputs and outputs are identified, the general processing steps required are outlined.
- **Cost benefits or limitations of development**: Every software development project has a limit on the funds available to complete the project, and this budget is normally set by the

sponsors of the project. During the feasibility stage, the systems analyst may or may not know this financial limitation. The feasibility study will need to estimate the cost of completing the project, including the cost of hardware and software, manpower costs for developing new software and training costs, and so on. The new development will probably also have cost benefits. These might be tangible cost benefits such as reduced costs of processing or manpower, increased sales, etc., or they may be intangible benefits like improved customer service. The systems analyst may have to identify what cost benefits the project sponsors are expecting and to consider these carefully to see whether they are achievable.

- **Conclusions and recommendations:** This section of the report clearly lays out the best way forward for developing a new system. By comparing cost, benefits and limitations, the systems analyst makes recommendations that are achievable within an agreed time plan and budget. In some situations, there may be a number of ways that the problem can be approached. For example, it may be possible to buy 'off-the-shelf' software rather than developing a system from scratch. In these situations the analyst will have to identify the benefits and drawbacks of each possible approach, and then justify the selection of the recommended solution. Purchasing off-the-shelf software will normally be much cheaper and faster than developing it from scratch, but the end result may not match the users' needs as closely. If the analyst believes a sensible solution cannot be achieved, then the reasons why are identified in this section.

Finally, the management of the organisation makes its decision whether to go ahead with a fuller analysis of the system. If the analyst has recommended that there may not be a workable solution, they need to decide whether:

- to remove any constraints that may be causing the analyst to give this recommendation
- to seek other alternative solutions, and/or
- to stay with the current system.

The primary source of information for the feasibility study is the users of the current system, but an equally important source is the sponsors of the new system, i.e. the management or directors of the organisation who will pay for its development. While both groups will need to be satisfied with the eventual outcome (i.e. the new system), their requirements may be quite different.

## Case study: Read-a-Lot Books Ltd

Read-a-Lot Books Ltd (often called RAL Books) is a small company that sells fiction and non-fiction books. The books are written by freelance (self-employed) writers who are paid a royalty (a percentage of the sale price) for each copy of the book sold. Currently, the accounts department use a simple spreadsheet to work out how much royalty money to pay each writer, but, as the number of books the company sells has increased, this system is time-consuming to use.

RAL Books have asked Wendy Jones, a systems analyst, to produce a feasibility report for the development of their royalty payment system. Wendy has spoken to the Managing Director of the company, and some of the staff in the accounts department who use the current royalty system. Using the information she obtained, along with her experience of analysing and developing similar systems, Wendy has produced her report. The summary of her report is shown in Figure 6.2

## Feasibility Study – Read-a-Lot Books Ltd.

System: Royalty payment system
Analyst: Wendy Jones
Date: 24/11/2002

### Summary

**Purpose of the system**

- To record details of writer to whom royalties are due.
- To record, for each book, who royalties are due to and what percentage.
- To calculate royalties due.
- To produce royalty payment reports.
- To produce management reports.

**System scope**

- Needs to run on existing PC in accounts department.
- Approximate budget of £4,000 for purchase of software and development costs.
- Data for the system to be provided by sales recording system.
- System to provide data to the accounting system.

**Current deficiencies**

- Current system requires manual input of data and the process of producing the royalty payments takes too long.
- Mistakes are not easily identified.
- Royalty payments reports sent to writers do not provide sufficient detail.
- Details of payments made have to be manually entered into the accounting system.

**User requirements**

- Faster processing.
- Improved accuracy.
- Improved detail on reports.
- Automatic collection of sales data and output of accounting data.

**Cost benefits/limitations**

- The new system will reduce the need for overtime payments in the accounts department.

### Conclusions and recommendations

A new royalty payment system can be developed using the existing PC in the accounts department with the addition of a database package, which will allow the development of a customized application to meet the users' requirements. The development of the system should take approximately 6 weeks and be achieved within the budget.

Figure 6.2 Read-a-Lot feasibility study

**How would Wendy collect the information needed to complete the feasibility study?**

## Case study: Northtown Health Centre

Northtown Health Centre has three GPs (general practitioners), a practice nurse and a receptionist. Patients who want to see a GP or the nurse must make an appointment via the receptionist. Currently, the receptionist keeps track of appointments using a manual system, but a computerised system would be more efficient.

The three doctors at Northtown Health Centre have a receptionist who makes patient appointments for them. The patients ring up when they need to see a doctor and the receptionist uses a diary to find a suitable slot when the doctor is free. Twice a day (morning and afternoon surgery), the receptionist needs to copy the list of each patient due from the book on to an individual list for each doctor.

**What problems can you see in using a manual system like this?**

## Assessment activity 6.1

Produce a **problem definition** for the Northtown Health Centre manual system. A problem definition is a feasibility study without the last two sections (the cost–benefit analysis and the conclusions and recommendations). Work in groups to research how health centre appointment systems work. You can use your own experience of booking an appointment with the doctor. You could also take a trip to your local health centre or doctor and see what system they use. Remember that people who work in health centres are busy people but you may find a receptionist who is willing to spend a couple of minutes with you explaining how the system (manual or computerised) works. Alternatively, if you have a friend or a relative who works in a health centre, he or she may be able to provide you with some information. You should work in groups to collect this information.

Check that your feasibility study covers these points:

- a statement of the purpose of the system
- a definition of system scope
- a list of current deficiencies
- a statement of user requirements.

# System development methodology

It is possible to develop software using an informal design, which can be just a written description of the way the system will work supported by a few simple diagrams. As the program is written, the design is modified as required so the finished program may bear little resemblance to the original design. While such an approach may work reasonably well when developing a simple system, it is a recipe for disaster when developing a large and/or complex system. For this reason a number of different design methodologies have been developed. Among the best known of these structured methodologies are **SSADM** (**structured systems analysis and design method**) and **object-orientated design**. These methodologies provide a framework, or an agreed structure, in which the design of the system can be modelled. They are intended to improve the efficiency of the software development process and hence improve the quality of the resulting system. Also, as most software is developed by a team of people rather than one person, and over the lifetime of the software many people may be involved in its maintenance and modification, using a known methodology means all the people involved will understand the method used.

Methodologies embody the knowledge and wisdom gained by software developers through trial and error over a number of decades. For the inexperienced software developer, a methodology provides a tried and tested 'recipe' to follow. Most methodologies involve creating a simplified model of the way the system works, often using a diagrammatic technique. This simple model is then refined and more detail is progressively added using what is called **step-wise refinement**. The design methodology used here is based on SSADM.

?

### What does it mean?

**Step-wise refinement** is a technique for dealing with large and complex problems that involves starting with a very simple description or model of the system and then, step-by-step, refining (adding detail to) that model.

Different methodologies may be more suitable to a particular type of system. For example, the methodology used to design a system for a doctor's surgery would probably not be suitable for designing a missile control system. However, all methodologies have a number of basic features:

- They have some kind of notation (commonly diagrammatical) that records the design of the system. Rules exist which describe how the notation is used – what is allowed and what is not allowed.
- The rules of the methodology provide a clear and standardised way of describing the system.
- While the methodology has rules, they are not so rigid that they cannot accommodate most situations.

The tools and techniques of SSADM are described as you work through this unit. Most system design methodologies are quite complex, and even though a simplified version is described here, it will take some practice before you become proficient in the techniques.

The object-orientated design methodology has become increasingly popular over recent years.

While SSADM concentrates on identifying the operations or functions of the system, object-orientated design focuses on 'things'. An object-orientated system is made up of a number of independent objects which interact with each other to provide the functionality of the system. The objects within a system are often derived from the real-world objects in the system being modelled. For example, in a system which implements a company's personnel records an employee object would probably be required. The employee object would have various attributes such as name, address and date of birth, and various actions (called methods) such as join the company, leave the company, change details, etc. Object-orientated methods are often used to model complex systems, but are conceptually more difficult to grasp than SSADM.

# 6.2 Investigating and analysing problems

This section focuses on the investigation stage of the systems analysis process. This is when information about the existing system and what is required of the new system is gathered using a number of different techniques. This information must be analysed so we can draw conclusions from it, and also be properly documented so we can refer back to it during the later phases of the project.

## Using analytical techniques

There are a variety of techniques that can be used to gather and analyse information about the required system:

- **observation**, i.e. watching what is done
- **interviews/meetings** (possibly based on a questionnaire)
- **document analysis**, i.e. looking at input or output forms/reports, reading manuals or files
- **data analysis**, i.e. looking at what data is input into or output from the system
- **procedure analysis**, i.e. observing organisational procedures, reading about them in a procedure manual or identifying procedures from interviews
- **identification of need**, i.e. discovering the needs of all the users of the system
- **output analysis**, i.e. looking at the outputs of the current system.

One or more of these methods may be appropriate, and different methods are more suitable in different circumstances.

**Questionnaires** can be useful where you need to gather information from lots of people. However, the questionnaire will need careful wording to make sure the correct information is gathered. Also, people are notoriously bad at returning questionnaires.

An analyst has to work closely with the users of the existing system and needs to consider from whom to collect the information. In some circumstances, users may not be keen to see the system change and they may even be hostile to the idea, perhaps owing to fears about job losses. In these situations, an analyst has to use tact and diplomacy to be able to collect the information successfully.

For each technique, it is important to identify exactly what information is required. Questionnaires and recording documents can then be designed to control the amount and the quality of information gathered.

Table 6.1 summarises the advantages and disadvantages of the four main investigation methods.

| Method | Advantages | Disadvantages |
|---|---|---|
| Observation | The effect of office layout and conditions on the system can be assessed.<br>Work loads, methods of working, delays and bottlenecks can be identified. | Can be time-consuming and therefore costly.<br>Users may put on a performance while under observation.<br>Problems may not occur during observation. |
| Interview | A rapport can be developed between interviewer and interviewee.<br>You can adjust questions as the interview proceeds.<br>You can add more in-depth questions to find more information. | Can be time-consuming and therefore costly.<br>Poor interviewing can lead to misleading or insufficient information.<br>May not be feasible for a large organisation; you may not have time to meet all the people involved. |
| Document analysis | Good for obtaining factual information e.g. volume of sales, input and outputs of the system. | Not an option if input, output and information flow is not document based. |
| Questionnaire | Many people can be asked the same questions, so comparisons are easy (e.g. 58% of respondents said they were dissatisfied with the current system).<br>A cheaper option than interviewing large numbers of people.<br>Anonymity may encourage honest answers. | Questions need careful design e.g. using tick boxes, which are simple and easy to answer.<br>Need to avoid ambiguity. Questions may require interpretation.<br>Cannot guarantee 100% return rate. |

Table 6.1 Investigation methods

## Case study: Read-a-Lot Books royalty system

Wendy Jones, a systems analyst, has been asked to carry out the investigation stage of a systems analysis. She will need to collect the following information:

- ***The people involved:*** These include the Managing Director (MD) of RAL, who will be paying for the system development (the sponsor of the system); Steve, who works in accounts and currently does all the royalty calculations on a spreadsheet (the user of the system); and all the writers who receive their royalty cheques (the customers).
- ***Data capture methods:*** How does data get into the system? Does Steve type it into his spreadsheet himself or does the spreadsheet download it from some other database?
- ***Data types, sources and flows:*** Where does the information about how many copies of each book is sold come from? How does Steve know what percentage to pay each writer? Does all the data come from the same place or does it come from different sources?

- ***Decisions taken and types of processing:*** How does Steve's spreadsheet calculate how much to pay each writer? How often are the payments made?
- ***Storage methods:*** How does Steve store the data he uses? Is it all kept on the spreadsheet? Does he keep historic data? Does he keep paper copies?
- ***Documents used:*** Does Steve use any input documents (e.g. lists of books sold)? What output documents does his spreadsheet produce? Does he produce management reports for the MD to look at?
- ***Types of output:*** What are the outputs of the system? How is the money paid to the writers (e.g. by cheque or automatic payment via BACS)?
- ***Manual and automatic operations:*** What parts of the system are carried out manually? What parts are automatically carried out by Steve's spreadsheet?

**Wendy needs to gather information from the MD, Steve and the writers. What techniques do you think she should use?**

She may, of course, use more than one technique with each person.

### Assessment activity 6.2

1 Write a report explaining the stages of the systems development life cycle and describe the methods used in the system investigation stage.

2 Complete a detailed feasibility study for a suitable problem, either for a real-life business problem or a fictional case study. Make sure you cover all aspects of the report including the cost–benefit analysis. You also need to consider alternative solutions to the problem and justify your recommended approach.

# Analysis and documentation

Once all the information described in the investigation phase has been collected, the next step is to analyse it. The aim here is to take the unstructured data that has been collected and use a variety of tools to describe or model the system in a structured way. Several modelling and **structured analysis tools** are available:

- high-level data flow diagrams (DFDs)
- process specifications
- entity (or data) relationship diagrams (ERDs)
- low-level (detailed) data flow diagrams
- entity-attribute definitions
- data dictionary.

As well as these formal, structured tools, less formal diagrams can be helpful when communicating with users who may not understand the methodology in use. These 'rich picture' illustrations can be used in the initial stages of the design to clarify the workings of the existing system or the intended working of the new system with the users (see Figure 6.3).

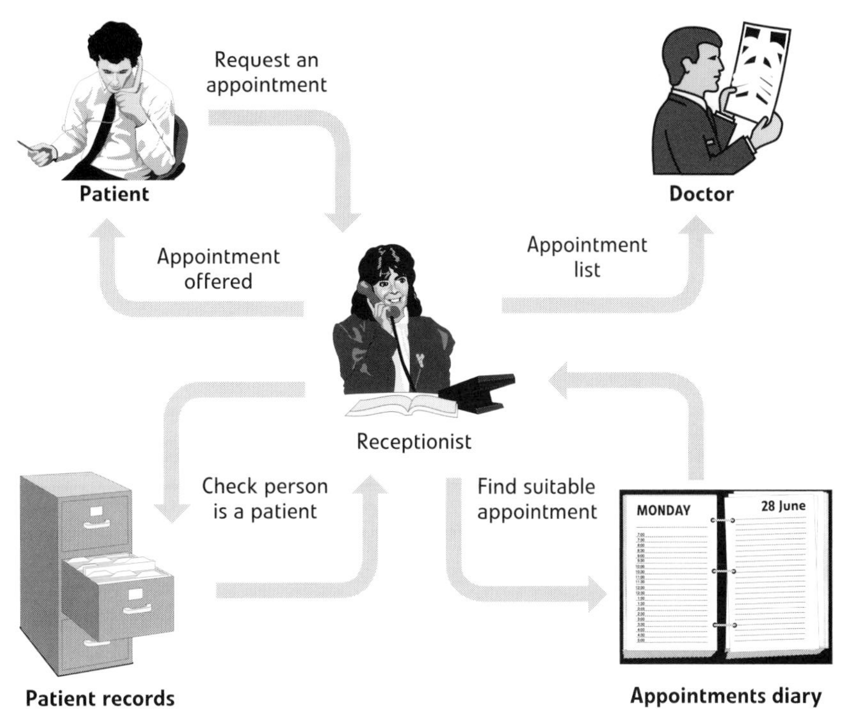


Figure 6.3 Rich picture illustration, making an appointment

> **Check your understanding 6.1**
> Draw a rich picture illustration for the RAL Books royalty system.

## Data flow diagrams (DFDs)

DFDs are, as the name suggests, a diagrammatical way of representing the flow of information in a system. It is normal to create a series of DFDs starting with a general overview of the information flow (high-level DFD) and then progressing to more detailed and complex diagrams (low-level DFDs). To draw DFDs correctly, you must follow certain rules about how the boxes, circles and arrows that make up the DFD are drawn.

A high-level DFD (sometimes called a **context diagram**) shows how the system interacts with the outside world. To construct a high-level DFD, you must undertake the following:

- Identify all the sources and recipients (inputs and outputs) of data that are external to the system. These are called the **external entities**, and may be people or they may be other systems.

For RAL Books there are four external entities:

1. The sales system
2. The writers
3. The accounting system
4. The Managing Director

- List the data that flows to and from these external entities.

For RAL Books there are six data flows:

1. Sales – number of books and games sold (input)
2. Sales – details of new games (input)
3. Writers – royalty payments (output)
4. Writers – details (input)
5. Accounting – payment details (output)
6. Managing Director – summary report (output)

- Take a piece of A4 paper and draw each of the external entity names in an ellipse around the outside of the paper, and in the centre of the page draw a single process box, with the name of the system in it. Write number 1 in the process box as its identifier. All process boxes are numbered so you can easily refer to them. Now add arrows to indicate the data flows that have been identified. With input data flows the arrow must point into the process box, output arrows must point to the external entity. Each arrow must be labelled with the data flow name. The complete high-level DFD for RAL Books is shown in Figure 6.4.

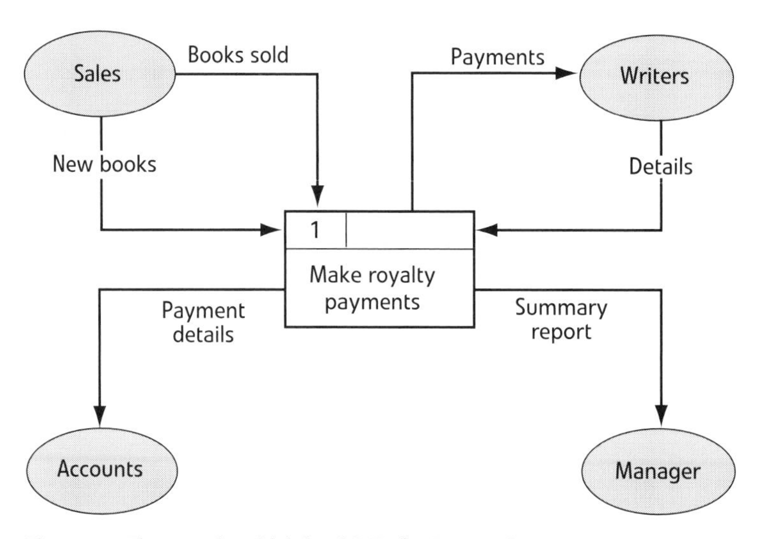


Figure 6.4 The complete high-level DFD for RAL Books

**Check your understanding 6.2**

Working in groups, identify the external entities and data flows for the Northtown Health Centre appointments system. Then draw the high-level DFD for the system.

The high-level DFD then needs to be broken down into more detail (decomposed) to produce a low-level DFD. To do this, the single process (make royalty payments) is divided into several, more detailed processes. Don't be tempted to divide the process into too many processes or the diagram will become too complicated. Your low-level DFD needs to fit onto a single sheet of A4 paper. You should have a single process dealing with each data flow attached to an external entity.

The single process in the high-level DFD of RAL Books can be broken into six processes in the low-level DFD:

1 *Calculate payments:* Take the data about the books sold and calculate how much to pay each writer.
2 *Make payments:* Take payment details data and print cheques for each writer.
3 *Update accounts:* Take payment details data and transfer that information to the accounting system.
4 *Create reports:* Take payment details and print a management summary report.
5 *Record new book:* Take details of a new book from the sales system and record them.
6 *Record writer details:* Take writer details and record them.

A new component is also introduced in the low-level DFD, the **data store**. This is where data is held or stored in the system, and represents real-world stores of data such as files, lists, tables, etc. It is important to remember when drawing DFDs that only a process can write or read data to or from a data store, and that each data store must be written to and read from at least once. A data store is drawn as an open-ended box, as in Figure 6.5.

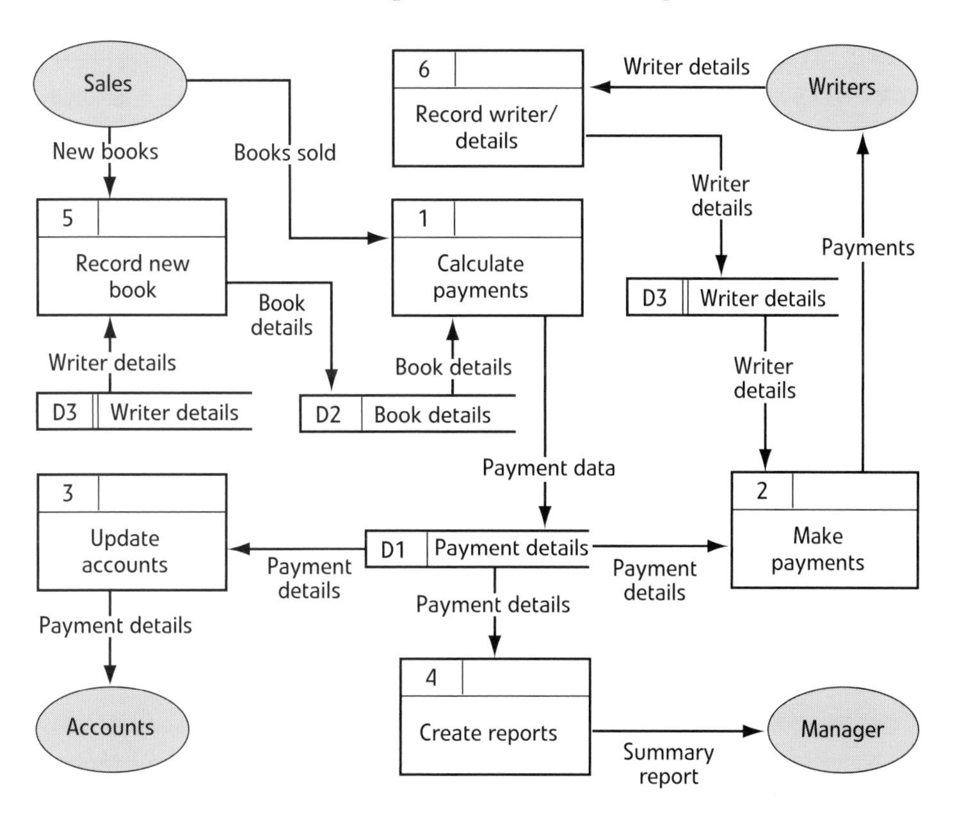


Figure 6.5 Completed low-level DFD for RAL Books

Notice that three data stores are added to the low-level DFD of RAL Books:

1 D1 Payment details holds data about how much to pay a particular writer for the sales of a particular book.
2 D2 Book details holds data about all the books the company sells (e.g. their name and who wrote them).
3 D3 Writer details holds data about the writers (e.g. their name and address).

D3 is shown twice to make the diagram easier to draw. Without it, a data flow arrow would have to cut across several other data flows, making the diagram messy and difficult to follow. Notice that duplicate data stores are shown by an additional bar inside the box containing the identifier.

### Further research 6.1

Are there any functions that are likely to be required which are omitted from the DFD shown in Figure 6.5?

It is important to remember that, when creating a low-level DFD, the same external entities and data flows in and out of the external entities appear as in the high-level DFD. If you realise you have missed out an external entity and/or data flow, you must go back and redraw your high-level DFD.

### Check your understanding 6.3

Working on your own, attempt to draw a low-level DFD for the Northtown Health Centre appointments system. You may find it helpful to practise drawing DFDs in small groups so you can discuss different ways of drawing the diagrams.

Creating DFDs can be quite difficult and requires practice. It may take several attempts to get the DFD right; and although there are rules about how to draw the DFD diagrams, there is not necessarily one right diagram for a particular system. Although we have only looked at two levels of DFDs, an analyst may go on decomposing the processes in the DFD to show even more detail.

## Entity-relationship diagrams (ERDs)

When an analyst has used the DFDs to identify the processes and data stores in the system, the entity-relationship (ERD) diagram can be produced (sometimes called a **data-relationship diagram**). These diagrams are used to model the relationships that exist between different entities in the system.

| Entity | Possible attributes |
|---|---|
| Customer | Name |
| | Address |
| | Credit limit |
| Product | Description |
| | Type |
| | Price |
| Book | Title |
| | Publisher |
| | Price |

Table 6.2 Examples of entities and attributes

### What does it mean?

**Entities** are real-world things (customers, products, books) that need to be represented in the system. Entities have **attributes**, which are elements that define a particular entity.

One (or more) of the attributes of a particular entity is normally defined as the **primary key** attribute. The primary key is used to uniquely identify a particular occurrence of an entity (see Figure 6.6). To guarantee uniqueness, numbers are normally used for primary key attributes. So, for example, on a database recording details of the entity 'student', the attribute 'student number' would be the primary key. The system would need to ensure that each student received a unique number.

Most systems have a number of entities within them, and entities often have relationships between them. For example, the entity 'customers' and the entity 'orders' are related, because every order a company receives comes from a customer. The relationship between two entities can normally be described by a verb. In this example, the verb is 'place', because customers place orders (see Figure 6.6).

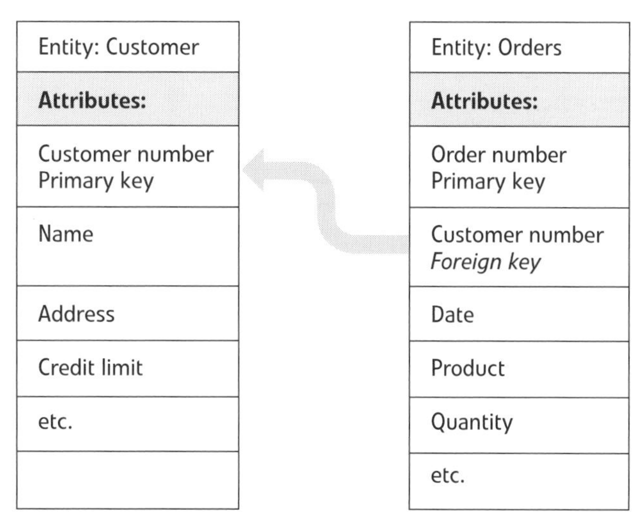


Figure 6.6 Primary keys and foreign keys

How do we know which orders were placed by a particular customer? One of the attributes of the entity 'customer' will be the customer number. This unique number identifies each customer and so is the primary key of that entity. When that customer places an order, an occurrence of the orders entity is created. So that it is possible to tell which customer placed the order, the customer number is inserted into that occurrence of the orders entity. This is known as a **foreign key** (foreign because the key value belongs to another entity). See Figure 6.6.

Each customer would have at least one and probably many more orders that were placed. So, for one customer, there would be many occurrences of the orders entity. This type of relationship is therefore called a **one-to-many relationship**. In an ERD, this is shown by a forked end to the line at the 'many' end that joins the two entities (see Figure 6.7). One-to-many relationships are the most common type of relationship between entities, but are not the only types.

Imagine a company that has a system to store data about its employees. The entity 'employee' would have attributes such as name, address, salary and the primary key would probably be employee number. The sales people who work for the company are provided with a company car. That gives us another entity, 'company car', which has attributes such as registration number, make, model, etc. There is a relationship between these two entities, which can be described by the verb 'uses' as a salesperson uses a company car. However, each salesperson is assigned only one company car at a time, so this isn't a one-to-many relationship; this is a **one-to-one relationship**. The ERD diagram for this type of relationship is shown in Figure 6.7.

This example also introduces another concept. A newly employed salesperson may not receive his/her company car until he/she has finished training, so the relationship between the two entities is optional. In other words, a salesperson does not have to have a related record in the

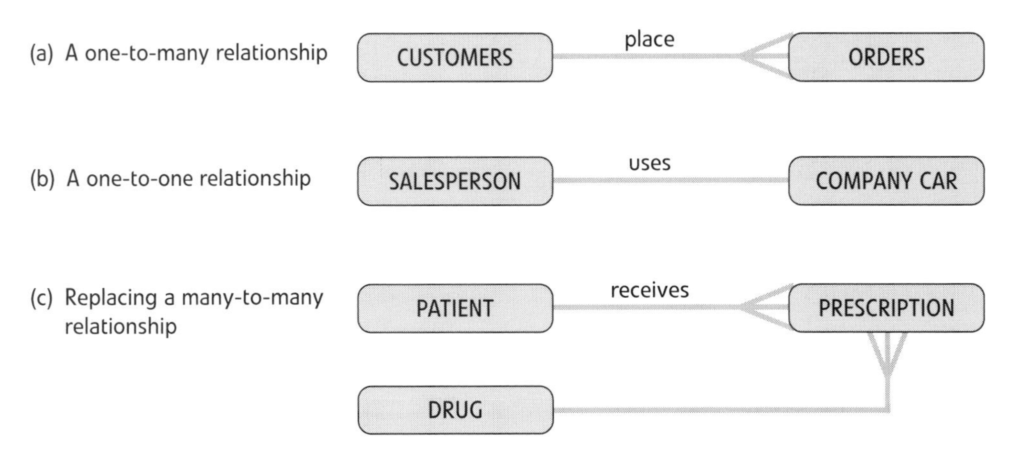


Figure 6.7 One-to-many and one-to-one relationships, and replacing a many-to-many relationship

company car entity. Likewise, when a salesperson leaves the company his/her car will remain unassigned to a salesperson until it is either sold or assigned to a new salesperson. Therefore the relationship is optional at both ends.

With the previous example of customers and orders, an order must be related to a customer (otherwise who could have placed the order?). This relationship is mandatory at the many end. Since a new customer could register their details with the company without placing an order, a customer does not have to have a related occurrence on the orders table (although most will) so it is optional at the one end.

There is a third type of relationship between entities. This is called a **many-to-many relationship**. Imagine that in the Northtown Health Centre, as well as looking into an appointments system, they are also investigating a system to keep track of which drugs have been prescribed to patients. Two of the entities that would be defined are 'patients' and 'drugs'. For each patient, at various times, the doctor may prescribe different drugs. This appears to be a one-to-many relationship as one patient can take (or be prescribed) many drugs. However, if we look at it from the point of view of the drug entity, then one drug can also be prescribed to many different patients. It is therefore a many-to-many relationship. These sorts of relationships would cause a problem in the system. Remember that with a one-to-many relationship the way we identify, on the many side, which particular occurrence it is linked to is by inserting the foreign key from the one side of the relationship. However if the entity could be linked to many different occurrences, which foreign key would we insert?

The problem with many-to-many relationships is that, for a given occurrence in one entity it is not possible to tell to which occurrence in the related table it is related. For this reason, many-to-many relationships have to be re-thought to identify a link entity which contains the foreign keys from both the two original entities. Thus the two original entities both have one-to-many relationships with the link entity. In this example, we might call the link entity 'prescription'. This is shown in Figure 6.7.

## Check your understanding 6.4

In the example above, each prescription can only contain one drug. How could you modify this design so that a prescription could have as many drugs as desired? (Hint: you need another entity.)

## Case study: Read-a-Lot Books

The entities we can define for RAL Books are as follows:

- books
- writers
- payments.

A simple ERD can be created showing the relationship between these entities:

Figure 6.8 ERD diagram for RAL Books

This diagram shows a one-to-many relationship between writers and books, i.e. each book is written by one writer, but writers can write many books.

1 What type of relationship exists between writers and payments?
2 RAL Books has three entities: books, payments and writers. What attributes might these entities have? What could be the primary key for these entities? What foreign keys would you need to include in the entities?

## Check your understanding 6.5

Suppose some books were written by more than one writer. What kind of relationship would that create between books and writers? Can you work out what you need to do and redraw the ERD? You might find it helpful to complete this activity is small groups.

Once DFDs and ERDs have been created, this information about the data in the system can be summarised using a **data dictionary**. This lists the entities in a system, the name and description of each attribute and the relationships between entities.

Many CASE (**computer-aided software engineering**) tools create data dictionaries for the analyst or programmer automatically. However, you can create simple data dictionaries yourself. The data dictionary for the payment details file from RAL Books is shown in Table 6.3.

| **Entity name: payment details** | | | |
|---|---|---|---|
| **Relationships:** | | | |
| **Related to:** | **Type** | **Which end?** | |
| Writers | One-to-many | many | |
| **Attributes:** | | | |
| **Name** | **Key type** | **Format** | **Length** |
| Payment number | Primary | Numeric | 6 |
| Date | – | Date | |
| Writer number | Foreign | Numeric | 6 |
| Total amount | – | Currency | 5 |
| Payment flag | – | Boolean | |

Table 6.3 Data dictionary for RAL Books

**Check your understanding 6.6**

1 Complete the data dictionary entries for all the entities in RAL Books.
2 Create ERD diagrams and a data dictionary for all the entities you identified for the Northtown Health Centre.

## Process models

Having identified the processes needed within the system using the DFDs, it is time to create a process specification for each process. This describes in more detail exactly what each process does. A variety of different methods can be used to create process specifications:

- structured English
- structure chart
- decision table.

Typically, you would choose one of these techniques to describe a particular process, rather than using all three.

- **Structure charts** are good for providing a general outline of the processing involved, but often do not relate well to the actual code that is eventually written.
- **Structured English**, on the other hand, is much more detailed (sometimes too detailed for this stage) and is closely related to actual programming code.
- **Decision tables** are useful where there are a lot of different options to choose from and you want to identify what happens in each circumstance.

You should remember that process modelling is the final stage in the 'top-down' approach to system design. We started with the very generalised high-level DFD, which was then broken down into a low-level, more detailed DFD which identified individual processes. We now need to create a design for these individual processes. The actual programming code that will eventually be written is quite complex but we can broadly divide the code that will be written into three basic functions or building blocks:

- **Sequence** is where the instructions in a program are followed one after another in sequence.
- **Selection** is where a choice is made as to which set of instructions to carry out. The choice is made based on some criteria, such as an option that the user has selected.
- **Iteration** is where instructions are repeated either a certain number of times or until some criterion is met.

One of the main purposes of this process design stage is to identify where each of these functions will be used. We will look at the three process design techniques, starting with the most generalised first and the more detailed ones later.

### Structure charts

Structure charts are simple diagrams that identify which of the basic program functions are used and in what order. Creating a structure diagram involves taking each of the process boxes identified in the low-level DFD and then deciding what detailed processing steps are required. For each step, as you break the process down, you need to decide whether it is a sequence, selection or iteration type processing step.

A structure chart for the Calculate payments process for RAL Books is shown in Figure 6.9.

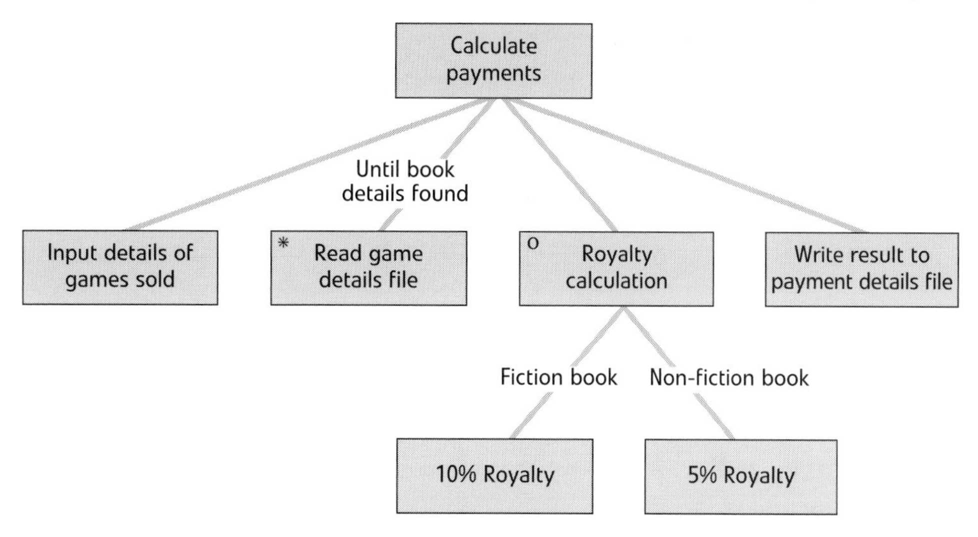


Figure 6.9 Structure chart for the calculate payments process

The name of the process, taken from the low-level DFD, is shown in a box at the top of the diagram. Underneath, the steps needed to complete this process are shown in boxes, in the order they will be completed, from left to right. Some of the steps are broken down further, with boxes beneath. Steps which are classified as sequence functions are shown in a plain box, those which are selection steps have a 'o' in the corner of the box, and those which are iteration steps have an asterisk '*' in the corner. With selection steps, the criterion on which the selection is based is written above the box. With iteration steps, the criterion that brings the repetition to an end is written above the box. Selection steps normally have additional boxes beneath them showing the different actions taken.

**Check your understanding 6.7**

Create a structure chart for one of the other processes.

## Structured English

Structured English is a 'half-way house' between actual program code and normal spoken English. It is used to describe the steps in a process without having to worry about the exact programming syntax. It is sometimes referred to as **pseudo-code**.

The Make payments process from RAL Books is shown below in structured English.

```
1   Open PAYMENT DETAILS file
2   Open WRITER DETAILS file
3   Repeat until end of WRITER DETAILS file
4       Read next WRITER DETAILS record
5       Select PAYMENT-DETAILS where WRITER-NUMBER = WRITER DETAILS.WRITER-
            NUMBER and PAYMENT-FLAG = unpaid
6       Repeat until end of selected PAYMENT-DETAILS
7           Cheque-total = Cheque-total + PAYMENT-AMOUNT
8           Set PAYMENT-FLAG to paid
9           Rewrite PAYMENT-DETAILS record
10      Loop
```

```
11  Print using cheque format WRITER-NAME, PAYMENT-TOTAL, DATE
12      Loop
13  Close WRITER DETAILS file
14  Close PAYMENT file
15  End
```

The example above shows use of the construct Repeat Until ... Loop to cause the process to loop through each author on the writer details file until the end of the file is reached (the construct Do While provides an alternative but similar method, e.g. Do While not end WRITER DETAILS).

Two other structured English constructs are often used to control loops:

- If ... Then ... Else is used where a choice needs to be made based on some condition. This construct takes the form:

  ```
  If (condition) Then (action)
  Else (alternative action)
  ```

- Select case ... End select is used instead of multiple If statements where there are many different choices to be made.

These looping constructs are used in conjunction with operators (see Table 6.4). The AND operator was used in line 5 of the example above:

```
5     Select PAYMENT-DETAILS where WRITER-NUMBER = WRITER DETAILS.WRITER-
          NUMBER and PAYMENT-FLAG = unpaid
```

Here, it is used to make sure that *only* those occurrences are selected from the payment details file which have the same writer number as the current occurrence of the writer file and their payment flag was set to unpaid; i.e. *both* conditions have to be true. Using OR instead would have meant that occurrences where selected when *either* condition was true.

| **Relational operators** | | **Logical operators** |
|---|---|---|
| Equals | = | AND |
| Less than | < | OR |
| Greater than | > | NOT |
| Less than or equal to | <= | |
| Greater than or equal to | >= | |
| Not equal to | <> | |

Table 6.4 Logical and relational operators

There are no exact rules on how to use structured English, but you need to use your experience of real programming languages and bear in mind that the result should avoid any ambiguity. Vague statements like 'Process PAYMENTS DETAILS file' should be avoided; instead, you should try to identify exactly what processing is required. As with the other techniques in this section, you need practice to become proficient.

**Check your understanding 6.8**

Choose one of the other processes defined in the DFD for RAL Books and create a process specification for it using structured English.

## Decision tables

Decision tables are useful where the processing step includes a range of true or false conditions. Depending on the combination of conditions, different actions need to be taken.

A decision table has two parts:

- The conditions are listed at the top of the table (you must list all possible combinations).
- The actions (i.e. what to do in each condition) are listed in the lower part of the table.

At RAL Books, rules as to how the royalties are calculated are based on the number of sales (sales above 1000 per month earn a higher percentage royalty) and whether the book is fiction or non-fiction (fiction books attract a high percentage royalty). Table 6.5 shows the decision table for all possible combinations.

| **Condition** | | | | |
|---|---|---|---|---|
| Fiction book? | Y | Y | N | N |
| Sales over 1000 per month | Y | N | Y | N |
| **Action** | | | | |
| 5% royalty | | | | ✔ |
| 7% royalty | | | ✔ | |
| 9% royalty | | ✔ | | |
| 10% royalty | ✔ | | | |

Table 6.5 Decision table

Some applications can be developed directly from decision tables using a program generator that allows entry of information in the form of decision tables.

Notice that decision tables provide an easy-to-read way of identifying the action to be taken in all the different combinations of conditions. It is certainly easier to write the structured English once you have the decision table to guide you. Also, you are less likely to omit possible combinations.

### Assessment activity 6.3

Northtown Health Centre has decided to set up a number of specialist clinics for particular groups of patients:

- Well woman's clinic – for women aged between 19 and 100
- Over-60s clinic – for men and women over 60
- Men's health clinic – for men aged between 19 and 100

Draw up a decision table to show whether a particular patient is eligible for each clinic.

To complete the investigation and analysis phase you need to draw all the information together in one document which adds a descriptive narrative to the diagrams.

### Assessment activity 6.4

Take the work you have already done on the Northtown Health Centre (including the DFDs, ERDs, data dictionary and process designs) and produce a complete investigation and analysis document for the system.

# 6.3 Producing a design solution

The next step of the analysis phase is for the analyst to produce a design. This phase draws together the information and analysis done and adds details about the inputs and outputs of the system. The following information is included in the system specification:

- process specification
- input specification
- output specification
- accuracy and validation controls.

In large and complex systems, an approach that is often taken initially is to produce an outline design, which explains only in broad terms how the system will work, perhaps breaking it down into distinct modules, each with its own function. Having completed the outline design, a detailed design is then produced for each of the modules.

## Process specification

The process specification will consist of the DFDs, structure charts, structured English and decision tables produced at the analysis stage.

## Input specification

An input specification includes the following descriptions:

- data sources
- methods of data capture
- data input forms or/and screen layouts
- verification methods applied during input
- validation methods applied after the data is entered.

The **data sources** identify the origin of each piece of information.

The **method of data capture** describes how the data gets into the system. For example, some data may be entered manually by the system's users; other information may be retrieved automatically from another computer system. Clearly, understanding where data comes from is important in deciding how it can be captured. There are many data capture methods, such as bar-codes, magnetic strips, etc. It is important that the best method is chosen to suit the system requirements, taking into account factors such as:

- accuracy of input
- reliability
- cost
- ease of use.

The **specification of input forms and screen layouts** only requires written information about what detail should be included in such documents or screens. The actual drawing of these forms or screens will be carried out during the design stage of the system development. However, the analyst may provide some guidance on how such forms and screens may look by including one or two examples. The specification of these screen layouts should include:

- the title of each screen to be used for entering data into the system
- a brief description of purpose
- a list of data items that will be collected using the screen or form
- any data items that are printed/displayed on the screen/report before or during use with details of where these data items are obtained from
- instructions to help the user
- error messages.

Ensuring the accuracy of data entered is very important. The analyst must include in the specification methods of checking that data has been entered correctly and that the data is reasonable. It is easy for an operator to misread information from a source document or to mis-key the data; steps must be taken to avoid these errors entering the system.

**Verification** is the method of checking that the data entered on to the system is the same as that on the original source. Methods used to check this include requesting the operator to enter important data twice and then checking to see whether both entries are the same. This method is usually needed for high volumes of numeric data that are very difficult to 'read'. Another method is to re-display entered information and request the operator to check it and confirm that it is correct.

**Validation** is the process of checking that data entered into a system is reasonable and in the correct form. A common example is dates. A date such as 34/4/2003 is clearly incorrect and a system should always check that dates are reasonable. Data items like account numbers or employee numbers are not so obvious when incorrect, although it may be possible to check them against a database of valid numbers. In these cases, there are a number of other types of validation checks that can be made. See section 3.3 in Unit 3 for details of:

- check digits
- type checks
- length checks
- range checks.

When designing an input form, as well as designing the layout of the form, the specification should also list the verification or validation methods used for each input field.

### Check your understanding 6.9

Using the low-level DFD you previously created, take all the inputs to the Northtown Health Centre system and create an input specification for them including this information:

- Where will the data come from?
- How will it be input into the system?
- What input screens may be needed? (You could use the form creation facilities in a program such as Microsoft® Access to create an example input screen.)
- What attributes may need verification or validation? (Use the data dictionary you created to identify the attributes that will be input.)

# Output specification

An output specification is a description of all the information that is produced by the system, such as:

- the data required for output
- screen display layouts
- printed report layouts.

For each screen or printed report it is necessary to provide the following information:

- *Type:* is it to be printed or screen displayed with or without an option to print the displayed data?
- *Purpose:* Who is it for? What is it to be used for?
- *Data required:* the attributes to be shown and any calculated data items to be displayed. Are processes such as sorting or grouping of data needed? If so, which attributes should be used for these processes?

An example output specification for a management report in the RAL Books royalty system is shown in Figure 6.11.

| **RAL Books – Output specification** | | |
|---|---|---|
| **Report R-1** | | |
| **Name:** | Monthly payment summary report | |
| **Type:** | Printed report | |
| **Purpose:** | Management report which lists each month's royalty payment and shows totals | |
| **Data required:** | **Source** | **Sort/Group** |
| **Book type** (e.g. Fiction or non fiction) | Book details file | This report is grouped by type |
| **Book name** | Book detail file | Sorted alphabetically |
| **Monthly sales** | This is taken from the payments file | |
| **Writer** | This is taken from the book detail file | |
| **Royalty amount** | Payments file | |
| **Total sales** | Calculated field showing total sales per book type | |
| **Total payments** | Calculated field showing total royalty payments per book type | |

Figure 6.11 Example output specification for management report

**Check your understanding 6.10**

When writers are sent a royalty cheque, they are also sent a summary report showing on which books the royalties are earned and the quantities sold. Create an output specification for this report.

# Documentation

Once the design is completed, it needs to be carefully documented; this documentation will be used by the programmers who implement the system. The designs for the input, output and processing required are all drawn together into the **system specification**. Many organisations that develop software have detailed written standards which describe exactly what should be included in this documentation and the methodologies and techniques that should be used. Producing documentation is not very exciting and there is a temptation to neglect this area. However, proper design documentation is vital, not just because it will be used to implement the system but also because in the future – when problems arise or modifications need to be made – this documentation will help the programmers who will deal with these problems or modifications to understand how the program was originally constructed.

As well as including the diagrams produced earlier, a written narrative needs to be included explaining the way the system will work. Typically your design specification will include:

- a table of contents, listing all the items it contains in a logical order
- a summary of the users' needs as identified in the investigation stage
- an overview of the whole system, how it is structured, and how different modules interface with each other
- input specifications, including form layouts, verification techniques used, etc.
- output specifications
- process specifications, including structure charts, structured English and decision tables
- test plans (see below).

It is important to remember that the design specification will probably need to be updated and corrected during the implementation phase. This is because, during the writing and testing, problems or errors will almost certainly be discovered in the design. Therefore you must decide on some method of updating the design specification, and keeping track of changes to it. You must at least make sure your original version is dated.

### Assessment activity 6.5

Produce an outline design for the Northtown Health Centre appointments system. Use the structured methodology described on page 196 correctly and use appropriate technical language clearly and correctly. Your analysis and design document should include detailed and coherent narratives to support the diagrams and other information.

# 6.4 Producing a test plan

Programs must be thoroughly tested before they can be used. Testing is the process of checking that all the functions of the program work as they should and that they give the correct results. The definition of terms like 'work as they should' and 'correct results' comes from the system specification that has just been completed. The input specification in that document describes what data is to be input into the program, and what should be rejected. The output specification describes what results should be produced. From these two sections of the specification, we should be able to design tests that will check if the program works as it should.

As well as checking that the program works correctly when used correctly, the software developer also needs to check that the program is robust and can withstand being used incorrectly without crashing. The reason why this is important is because the users of the program are unlikely to be computer experts.

The test plan we will produce at this stage will, of course, not be used until the program has been written and is ready for testing. Testing a program is often split into **data testing** and **event testing**. A plan needs to be created for both types of testing.

**What does it mean?**

**Data testing** involves checking that the program can deal correctly with the data that is input by the user and produces the correct output.

**Event testing** involves checking that all the different options such as buttons and menu options produce the expected results.

## Data testing

Creating a data testing plan involves the following steps:

- choosing input values
- manually working out what output the program should produce with these chosen inputs (the expected outputs)
- running the program using the input values
- comparing the expected outputs with the actual ones the program produces.

If there is a difference between the expected outputs and the actual outputs then the program has failed the test and will need to be modified so that the actual and expected values match. At this stage, only the first two steps can be completed.

The choice of input values is important. A range of values needs to be chosen in each of the following categories:

- **Normal** values are what would normally be expected as an input value.
- **Extreme** values are, in the case of a numeric input, unusually large or small values. In the case of a text value they might be a very large or a very small number of characters. For example, in a text box where someone's name is to be entered, two extreme values might be 'Ng' and 'Fotherington-Thomas'.
- **Abnormal** values are incorrect entries: for example 32/10/02 for a date, 205 for someone's age or a text value where a numeric one is expected.

For each input that the program can accept, values in each of these categories need to be created, along with the expected values. You may need to refer back to the input specifications to see what the expected outputs should be. You may also find you need to modify your input specifications so that they specify what should be done with extreme and abnormal values. Once you have completed these first two steps in the testing process your test plan needs to be kept safe ready to hand to the person who will test the program once it has been written.

# Event testing

Event testing involves identifying all of the actions that a user can carry out on each of the input forms that have been designed. For example, if the form has a number of buttons, then clicking each of the buttons should carry out some action. Your event testing plan should therefore list all the input forms in your program, all the actions the user can carry out on each form, and the expected results of each action. As with the data testing, the results of each action should be described in the design specification. Also you should leave space in the plan for the tester to comment on whether the completed program works as described in the plan.

Both the event test plan and the data test plan should become part of the design specification document.

### Assessment activity 6.6

Produce a data test plan and an event test plan for the inputs you identified in the Northtown Health Centre design document.

### Test your knowledge

1. List the topics that should be covered in a feasibility study.
2. Why is it important to define the scope of the system in the feasibility study?
3. List four techniques that a systems analyst can use to investigate a system.
4. For two investigative techniques, explain the advantages and disadvantages.
5. Name the three components of a high-level DFD.
6. In a supermarket stock control system, what might the external entities be?
7. In a low-level DFD, data stores can only be read from and written to by what?
8. In a hospital database system, each ward has several beds. What kind of relationship would exist between the entities WARDS and BEDS. Draw the ERD of the relationship.
9. Explain the meaning of the term 'foreign key'.
10. Explain what many-to-many relationships are and why they have to be removed.
11. What information is contained in a data dictionary?
12. What is a decision table and what is it used for?
13. A pharmacist prepares drugs from a doctor's prescription. The rules on whether the patient has to pay for the prescription are as follows:
    - People under the age of 17 and over the age of 60 do not have to pay.
    - Women who are pregnant also do not pay.
    - Everyone else must pay.

    Create a decision table describing the processing required to decide whether the patient has to pay.
14. Describe what the following structured English does:
    ```
    Enter monthly_sales
    If monthly_sales > 200 then discount = 10%
    If monthly_sales > 800 then discount = 25%
    Else discount = 0
    Endif
    ```
15. Describe the purpose of an input specification.

# UNIT 8: PROGRAMMING CONCEPTS AND PRACTICE

In this unit, you will learn to use a standard design methodology such as Jackson structured design. The aim of the unit is to enable you to make good use of an up-to-date programming environment. It will enable you to code, test and debug programs to given designs. When you have completed the unit, you will be able to solve realistic problems involving realistic data. This unit presents opportunities to demonstrate Key Skills in application of number, communication, information technology, improving own learning and performance, and working with others.

## Learning objectives

- To make correct use of recognised methodologies for design and documentation
- To use a programming environment and its related tools
- To implement a program making use of design concepts
- To test and document an application

# 8.1 Methodologies

This first section looks at the methodologies or formal ways of designing and developing a computer program through six important topics:

- Top-down design
- Modularisation
- Structure diagrams
- Data dictionary
- Alternative design approaches such as rapid application development (RAD), bottom-up design and data-driven design
- System requirements

## Top-down design

A top-down design for a computer system or program means that the designer breaks down the overall design from the top into smaller and smaller parts. These parts are called **modules**. First, the designer considers the major functions he or she wants the program to perform, and then breaks down the design into one module for each of these functions. A typical program might have one simple control module as shown in Figure 8.1. This would call one module that handled the input (from a screen or elsewhere), a second module that processed the data, and a third that handled the output to a screen, database, printer or elsewhere. As far as possible, these modules would be self-contained, each having its own sets of variables. Communication between modules would be preferably by passing information or **parameters** between them, rather than by updating **shared variables**.

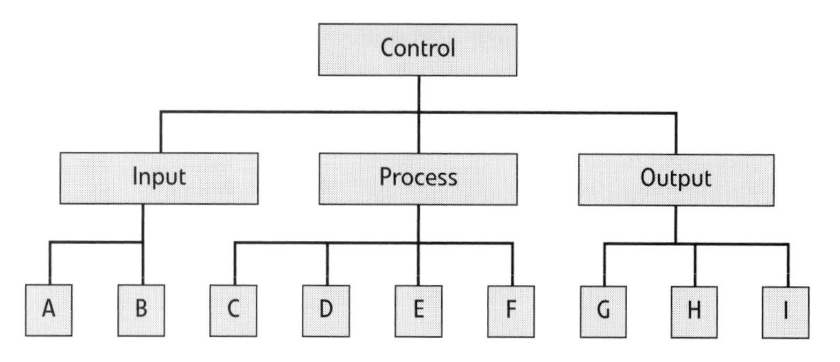


Figure 8.1 Tree structure of modules

**What does it mean?**

A **shared variable** is a variable which two or more modules use.

Each of these first-level modules would then be divided into lower-level modules. The designer would then continue breaking down each function into several modules, and adding more and more detail, until it is simple to convert all functions into code. This is called a **tree structure** or **structure diagram**, as it looks like an upside-down tree.

At the lower levels of the design tree, it is likely that **subroutines** or **functions** are called in several places in a program. These may be part of a standard environment library, e.g. for mathematical functions, date manipulation functions or field validation routines. Alternatively, they may have been written as standard or common routines for an installation or the developer may write them just for use in this one system or program.

**Check your understanding 8.1**

1 Draw a tree structure for a program to take the user's name as input and output the phrase 'Hello <*name*>'.
2 Draw a tree structure for a program to take a number between 1 and 9 as input and output the multiplication table for that number.
3 What are the similarities between the two tree structures?
4 What are the differences between the two tree structures?
5 What common functions could you use in both programs?

**Further research 8.1**

1 Find out what libraries of standard functions are available to you in your environment.
2 Who provided them?
3 Can you add your own library?
4 Can you add functions or subroutines that you write to one of the installation libraries?

# Modularisation

Modularisation is the name given to the breaking down of a computer design into smaller parts. The advantages of modularisation include documentation, design, testing, allocation to team members, re-use, speed of compilation and version control.

## Documentation

This applies to both the design and the program, so is more likely to be both accurate and kept up to date. Either the designer, the programmer or a technical author can produce the final version of the top-down documentation.

## Design

A top-down design can be meaningful to both the customer and the business systems analyst because many of the technical details of the design are in the lower levels of modules. They only need to understand *what* is to be done, not *how* it is done. The modular design is also meaningful even to a junior programmer because he or she only needs to understand how one module works at a time and what it does. The person need not be confused by the complexity of the whole program, or by technical complexities that he or she has not yet learned.

## Testing

With a modular design, testing can begin as soon as the first module is complete, rather than waiting until the whole program is written. The tester usually does this from the bottom up using a **test harness**. This simulates the parameters that are passed to the module. This means the tester can check the effect of the processing the module has done. As the tester completes more modules, they can be tested together in groups. Finally, the program as a whole can be tested. Where the tester has yet to complete some lower-level modules, or there are still errors in these modules, he or she can use the test harness to return the expected values to the calling routine.

## Allocation to team members

As the program is broken into many parts, it means two or more team members can share the work.

- This can enable them to finish the work more quickly, which may be especially important if there is an urgent need for the program.
- It facilitates the best use of specialist skills; for example, a database specialist could write only the database handling modules.
- It can facilitate training; a trainee or junior developer may write only the simpler modules or those modules that need only the skills learned so far.

## Re-use

With a top-down design, programs of the same type have very similar high-level structures. This means that this high-level code structure can be re-used in several different programs, even though the detailed code in the low-level modules may be very different. Alternatively, detailed pieces of code or subroutines, probably from a program library, can be re-used in several programs that have a very different high-level program structure or business functions.

## Speed of compilation

In many programming environments, the developer can compile each of the modules separately. The developer then links them together into a program to run the program in production, or just to test the program. If the developer makes a change to a module, then he or she only recompiles, or compiles again. That module then re-links, or links again, the changed module into the program, rather than recompiling the entire program. This is usually much faster.

## Version control

The developer will find it is easier to control different versions of the program because the changes being made typically apply only to one or a small number of modules of the program. The developer can therefore control more easily different versions for different users, or go back to an earlier version if the change is in error.

### Check your understanding 8.2

1 Find out what common subroutines already exist in your programming environment.
2 List those that would be of use in building a payroll system.
3 What additional common subroutines might you want for that payroll application?

# Structure diagrams

A structure diagram is a way of representing the steps in a computer system in a diagram. Each box shows a summary of the function that each module performs. Boxes at the same level of the diagram show control passed sequentially, while boxes at different levels show modules that are called. This simplified set of steps for getting up in the morning is expressed in the structure diagram shown in Figure 8.2.

1 Get up
   1.1 Alarm sounds
   1.2 Wake up
   1.3 Switch off alarm
   1.4 Get out of bed

2 Have breakfast
   2.1 Make toast
   2.2 Make tea
   2.3 Eat toast
   2.4 Drink tea

3 Get washed and dressed
   3.1 Have shower
   3.2 Clean teeth
   3.3 Get dressed

4 Leave house
   4.1 Shut door
   4.2 Walk to bus stop
   4.3 Catch bus

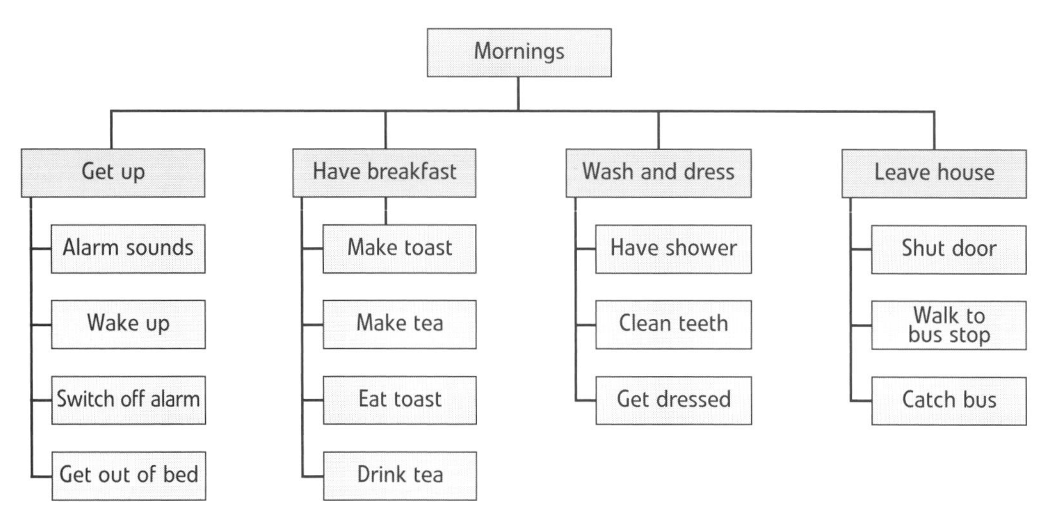


Figure 8.2 Structure diagram for getting up in the morning

## Check your understanding 8.3

1 Produce a structure diagram for a computer-based activity or process you are familiar with, such as reading and answering your e-mails, producing a written document or using a search engine.
   - Write this out also as a series of steps.
   - Which is easier to follow? Why?

2 Produce a structure diagram with several levels for a simple computer program. At what point, if at all, does it have any technology-specific parts?

# Data dictionary

While a structure chart records the functions of a program, the data dictionary records the data that a program uses. The data dictionary holds **metadata**, data about data or details of all of the data that your databases hold. It contains the dataname, what the data is in business terms, and technical information for the developers and maintainers. This includes data type, length and format. Most data dictionaries are integrated with the development environment. This means that they can identify where data is created, read, updated and deleted.

## Case study: Hobby Computing

Jane is the senior developer at Hobby Computing, a small software house specialising in producing PC-based software to help people to enjoy their hobbies. Their flagship product helps family historians to record data about their ancestors. This program also produces family tree diagrams and reports to the PC screen and printer. One source of data for the program is the census that takes place in most countries every ten years. Table 8.1 shows part of Hobby Computing's data dictionary, with part of the census record.

| Data name | Datatype | Length | Format | Description |
|---|---|---|---|---|
| Census_Year | Numeric | 4 | NNNN | The year that the census took place; e.g. 1901 |
| Census_Address | Character | 255 | Text | Where the person was living; street address followed by village, town and county |
| Census_Name | Character | 50 | Text | Forenames first then surnames |
| Census_Relationship | Alphabetic | 20 | Text | Relationship to the head of the household; common values are Head, Wife, Son, Daur, Mother, Lodger, Boarder, Inmate |
| Census_Marriage_Status | Alphabetic | 1 | Code | Whether the person is married; allowable values are S for single, M for married, W for widowed, D for divorced, blank for below marrying age |
| Census_Gender | Alphabetic | 1 | Code | Male or female; allowable values are M for male, F for female and blank if gender not stated |
| Census_Age | Numeric | 3 | NNN | Age in years |
| Census_Occupation | Character | 100 | Text | What the person does; e.g. 'Farmer employing 3 men' |
| Census_Birthplace | Character | 50 | Text | Where the person was born; town followed by county, possibly abbreviated, followed by country, if present; e.g. 'Aylesbury, Bucks' |
| Census_Disability | Character | 1 | Code | Whether the person suffered any major disability; e.g. codes are B for Blind, D for deaf |
| Census_Reference | Character | 100 | Text | Public Record Office Census reference; e.g. 'RG13/3454/6' |
| Census_Person_Record_Id | Numeric | 6 | NNNNNN | Record number of the person in the family tree to which this census record refers |

Table 8.1 Hobby Computing's data dictionary

1 Conduct a sample census on a few of your colleagues. Are the data types shown in Table 8.1 suitable for this?
2 Why do you think each of the three numeric fields are defined as numeric?
3 List the fields that should be mandatory or must be present, and those which should be optional or may be present.

Hobby Computing sells its products through a range of channels from the Internet to the specialised press and suppliers catering for a particular hobby. It has a good relationship with a loyal customer base, with a high percentage of the revenue coming from customers buying upgrades to the products.

Jane's small team of developers are expected to produce fixes for problems that customers report and to develop upgrades as well as new products.

1 Conduct a survey among your friends to find out how many hobby PC products they have. What do they like about each product? Why did they choose it?
2 Pick a hobby that could benefit from a PC-based product. Produce a list of requirements for a new product to support that hobby.

**Further research 8.2**

Look at a data dictionary that supports a database product, such as Oracle or SQL Server.

1 What other business information does it hold?
2 What other physical information does it hold?
3 Why and when would you want to use this information?

# Alternative design approaches

As well as the usual top-down modular approach to the design of a program or system, there are three other approaches that the developer can use for special needs: rapid application development (RAD), bottom-up design and data-driven design.

Sometimes, the business problem is not well defined or the customer is not used to specifying computing needs. Here, the **rapid application development** (RAD) approach of developing a **prototype** and repeatedly refining produces benefits. The developer starts with some idea of the problem and the solution design. Working with the customer, the developer produces a prototype to show to the customer. The customer then tries this out and gives the developer feedback on what is wrong and what features need adding or improving. They repeat this several times until the end of the initial **timebox** or fixed development period; the application as it then stands is put into production. Two or three or more phases follow this with appropriate timeboxes until the application no longer justifies further development.

## Case study: British Logistics

British Logistics (BL) is a large diversified international organisation. James Anderson joined the IT development team at BL straight after leaving university. He was competent at using a computer, but his degree was not in ICT and he had no IT qualifications.

He was offered the post of Trainee Developer because he had worked at another company in the logistics business during his holidays. He had worked in various departments, both in the main operations department, dealing with customers, and in the offices at their international headquarters. He was recognised by BL as a person who understood what the logistics business was all about and how different departments worked together. He had used various computer systems and also used his home PC extensively.

James was given a three-month training period during which he attended several training courses and had a more senior developer as a mentor. He was introduced to the various hardware and software systems that he was developing at BL. After two years at BL, he is now a highly valuable member of the IT development team. He spends as much time talking to his customers, solving their problems and producing documentation as he does developing and maintaining code. He enjoys the work, especially the problem solving.

BL had a system to manage the complex scheduling of its vehicles and staff to their workload to minimise costs and maximise flexibility. The main thing the customers did not like about the system was the user interface. The IT department tackled this as one of their first major RAD developments. The customers were really happy with the prototyping of the user interface. However, most of the development effort was required to improve the scheduling algorithms. As the new system had to replace completely the old scheduling system, the IT department could not put it into production until it had at least all the features of the old system. So, after several timeboxes with no implementation and wasting a lot of money, management stopped further development and threw out the new system.

1. Notice that James was offered the job because he knew about BL's business and had technical ability. What alternative route could an IT developer take to get this job? What qualifications might be needed?
2. Scan through some newspapers and cut out any adverts for developers. You might also search on the Internet for vacancies. Identify what skills are listed as basic requirements. What working conditions and pay are on offer?
3. What other reasons might there have been for the failure of the RAD development?
4. How would you have approached this project?
5. What sorts of system will benefit most from a RAD approach?

The **bottom-up design approach** is like an assembly process where the developer selects components already built and adds a control structure to link them together. The developer then adds or changes any of the low-level modules that do not quite do what is wanted, to make the program complete. The developer uses this methodology when building many similar programs for different customers. Only a limited amount of customising is needed to meet slightly changed needs. This is also a good approach to use in configuring application packages where, again, there are repeated similar business needs.

## Case study: Hobby Computing

Hobby Computing wants to produce a range of PC-based software for collectors. This would include collectors of DVDs, CDs, tapes, records, videos through to antique collectors, stamp collectors and number collectors such as train-spotters.

1 Would a bottom-up design be a good approach for this new range of software?
2 What would be the benefits and drawbacks to this type of design in this range?

In a **data-driven design**, the developer breaks down the design so that each module processes one of the main items of data rather than one business function. It therefore has a lot of similarities to top-down design. The **JSD methodology** is one example of data-driven design.

## What does it mean?

JSD stands for Jackson structured design.

The advantages and disadvantages of each approach compared with the top-down approach are shown in Table 8.2

| Approach | Advantages | Disadvantages |
|---|---|---|
| RAD | The user starts to derive benefits from the program most quickly. The delivery period is fixed, while the functionality delivered can vary. The continued investment in this system can be stopped at the end of any timebox. | It typically costs more to develop in the long term because of the need to throw away code that the developers have written. It costs more to maintain, because the design is less robust. It may never meet *all* the customers needs, because the design may be such that if you had known it had to do that, you would have done it a different way! |
| Bottom-up design | It delivers the program or system quickly once the initial investment has been made. There is little marginal cost. | A large up-front investment is necessary to produce all of the low-level components that could fit together. It needs to be part of an assembly line process to solve repeated similar problems. |
| Data-driven design | It shares most of the same modularisation benefits as top-down design. It is easier to use where the program functions align closely to the data structure, as in many data capture applications. | It does not embed the business process. It is difficult to use for many business- or function-driven applications. |

Table 8.2 Comparison of RAD, bottom-up and data-driven design approaches with the top-down approach

## Case study: Hobby Computing

Hobby Computing wants to produce a PC-based Family History program. The main business need is for the user to record and change information about family members in a simple way. This includes data such as dates of births, marriages and deaths, and husband–wife and parent–child relationships. The secondary need is to display and report on this information.

1 Why would the data-driven design approach be good for this application?
2 What would be the benefits and drawbacks of this type of design for this application?

## System requirements

The result of the design is a system requirements document, which can have four parts:

- The **data design** contains the detailed data content from the data dictionary. It also has an entity-relationship diagram (ERD), which shows the relationships between the data items.
- The **architectural design** shows how the main parts of the system link together.
- The **interface design** shows the human computer interface (HCI) – see Unit 12 – or how the users communicate with the system. This part of the document also shows the interfaces with other systems and between the main internal parts of the system.
- The **functional design** specifies the detail of how the system works. It shows how the design meets the 'what' requirements that have come from the analysis phase.

# 8.2 Programming environment

This section considers how to use a programming environment, its tools and its data, and is in two parts. The first part covers topics about the environment:

- User interface
- Design tools
- Input events
- Use of a variety of features and tools that are provided with the given software application used
- Components, their properties and methods
- Reserved words
- Control structures
- Functions and procedures

The remainder of the section covers data types:

- Character
- Numeric
- Boolean
- Date
- Time

### Check your understanding 8.4

Programming environments differ a great deal between languages and system environments.

1. List the main features of your programming environment.
2. What features do you think are missing from your programming environment that would make a useful enhancement?
3. What features can you not see a use for?
4. What features seem to duplicate other features?

### Further research 8.3

Research at least one other programming environment and produce a comparative chart between the programming environments.

# Tools of the programming environment

## User interface

For a system developer, the earliest user interfaces that are still in use are **line editors** (see Figure 8.3), where the programmer specifies the number of the line he or she wants to change, add or delete and the editor does that. These run either in batch mode, from a command line or from a full terminal screen. More modern versions, such as MS *Notepad*, are **screen editors** and allow you to work on a screen at a time. They provide no support for the application development process. For simple tasks, line or screen editors are adequate, but it is hard work to use these for a program or system of any complexity.

```
C:\WINDOWS\System32\edit.com
  File  Edit  Search  View  Options  Help
              C:\...\My Documents\Peter\BTEC\heinemannwebpage.txt
<!DOCTYPE HTML PUBLIC "-//W3C//DTD HTML 4.01 Transitional//EN">
<html>
<head>
<meta http-equiv="Content-Type" content="text/html; charset=null">
<meta http-equiv="Content-Type" content="text/html; charset=iso-8859-1">
<title>Heinemann - inspiring generations</title>
<!-- Inknowledge Code 14/01/2003 -->
<script>function process()
                                {
                        //dummy
                                }
          </script>
<!--<link rel="stylesheet" href="splash.css" type="text/css">-->
<meta name="keywords" content="Heinemann, Educational, Publishers, Books, Ginn
</head>

<body bgcolor="#ffffff" onClick="process(3);" onSubmit="process(21);" onUnload

F1=Help                                                  Line:1     Col:1
```

Figure 8.3 Traditional screen editor

Nowadays, line and screen editors have been replaced by the programmer's equivalent of a fully functional word processor. This supports multiple windows running different elements of the development environment and includes at least three features:

- a control window
- a listing of the program source
- debugging information from an executing copy of the program.

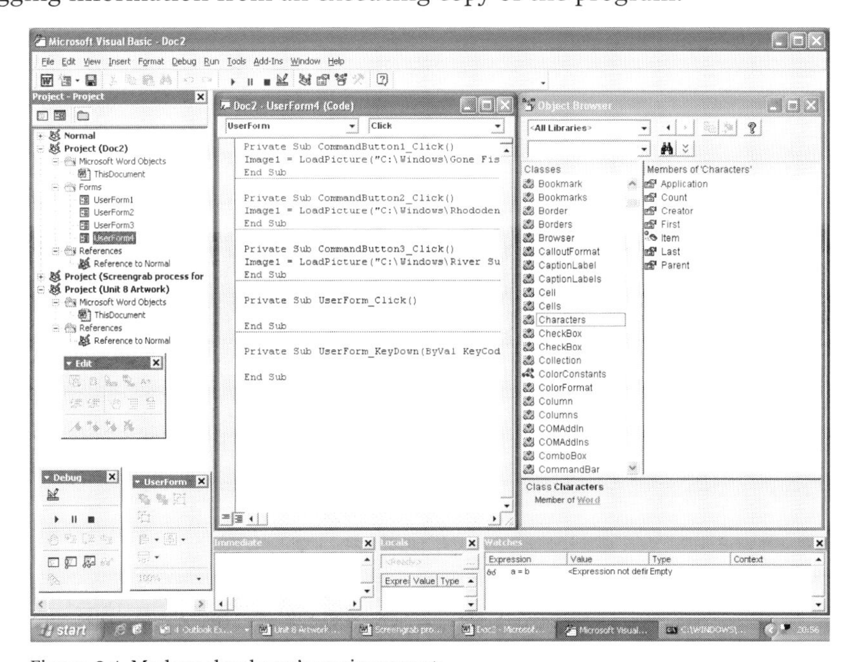


Figure 8.4 Modern developer's environment

For further information on the user interface for the program user see Unit 12.

## Design tools

Developers use design tools to help to convert the proposed solution to the business problem into the design of the computer system or program. They often enforce particular methodologies, so they have processes, terminology and document templates that are expected from that methodology. A design tool will have the following features:

- A **diagramming tool** helps the designer with both the creation and display of diagrams in a particular notation such as JSD.
- A **word processing engine** allows input and output of text along with the diagrams.
- A **knowledge engine** understands the rules of the design methodology and so can check whether the design is feasible. It is often able to convert diagrams into either 'English' written documentation or into pseudo-code ready for the developer to construct the actual code.
- A **data dictionary** is used to record information about metadata (see page 218).

Almost all tools provide support for **top-down development** to help the developer break each module down into a group of modules, each of which has a specific independent function. This is repeated recursively (over and over again) until every module cannot be broken down further in design; it is then coded.

Many tools also support JSD. This methodology views a system as one large program. It is data-driven design extended to include multitasking. It considers the IT inputs as sets of business transactions, restructuring the data streams to make this happen better, and is best suited for real-time transaction systems. This methodology involves designing the program around the data structures and the relationships between them. It has five steps:

1. Define the data structures.
   - Records: sequences of different data structures
   - Arrays: repetition of the same data structure
   - Variant records: alternatives between several different data structures
2. Find out the relationships between the data structures.
3. Work out the program structure. This can be instruction sequences, iteration or conditional statements.
4. Write down and number the main steps of the program, working out where they fit in the structure.
5. Form schematic logic.

## Input events

An input event is a user action that a program needs to process (see Figure 8.5).

- When you type a key on the keyboard, this is a **keyboard event**.
- When you move or click the mouse, this is a **mouse event**.
- In a process control application, a change of state or value of some sensor is a **sensor event**.

The operating system needs to associate mouse events with the window that the mouse is currently over. Mouse events can be further divided into mouse button events, mouse movement events and mouse enter/exit events; for example, if the mouse pointer enters a button region.

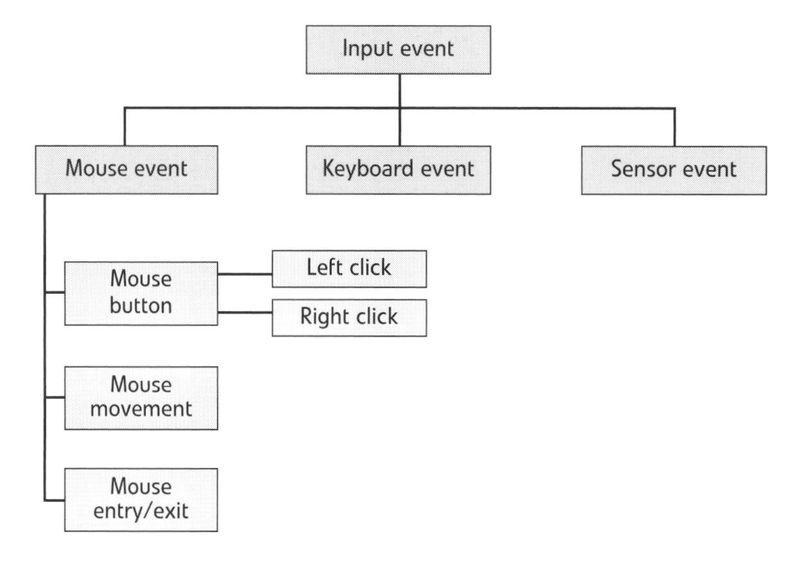


Figure 8.5 Input events

## Use of features

All computer systems have essentially three types of function: input, processing and output. Much effort can be saved if the features of the chosen programming language or application system can be exploited to simplify each of these types.

- *Input:* This could be an input event as described above. Here the application system may want to process the complete message or understand the complete mouse movement with the help of system features before taking appropriate action. Alternatively, the input could be characters read from a disk or tape or other peripheral device. Many programs will use the operating system and database features that combine all the characters into a block of data, split that block of data into logical records and then present only the fields wanted.
- *Processing:* The underlying hardware of almost all computer systems can perform only simple arithmetic, compare and branch to execute the next instruction at a different address. The features of various layers of the operating system, language compiler or interpreter, system component and environment raise this to let the programmer write the program code in a language much closer to how the problem is defined.
- *Output:* The application system will probably deliver a message, a complete record or a set of fields to the output process. The features of the operating system and the database are used to work out what to do with this group of data, assemble it into one or more physical blocks of data, and send it (one character at a time) to the requested output device in a format that the chosen device understands.

**Check your understanding 8.5**

1 Write a program that sends 'Hello World' to the user's screen or printer.
2 Which lines of your program relate to input, which were processing and which were output?

3 Change your program to have the user input a name (*name*) and then send 'Hello *name*' to the user's screen or printer.
4 Which lines of your program now relate to input, which were processing and which were output?
5 Which input, processing and output features did your program use?

### Further research 8.4

Find out, for each of the features you used, from manuals or from the Internet, what it did 'behind the scenes'.

## Components

### What does it mean?

A **component** is a hardware or software or design part of a computer system.

In an object-oriented system, a component has properties (things that the component *has*), and methods (things that a component *does*).

- A **method** is something that an object does or a predefined action on an object. For example, the method *Show* makes a hidden form visible.
- A **property** is something that an object has. Properties define the appearance or behaviour of an object. The properties of an object depend on what sort of object it is. For example, the properties of a command button include name, caption, height, width, background colour, location and font.

For more information, see Unit 32, page 309.

### Check your understanding 8.6

Hobby Computing's Family History program has a birth component. Some of the methods that this component has are to record a birth and output birth details. Some of the properties the birth component has are date of birth and mother's name.

1 Define other methods and properties for the birth component.
2 Define a set of methods and properties for the marriage and death components.

## Reserved words

Most computer languages have reserved words, i.e. names that have a special meaning to that language. For example, in most programming languages, the names DO, FOR, IF, THEN, ELSE, TIME, DATE are reserved words. This means that the programmer must not use any of these words to name a variable. Even if the language environment can tell by the context what they mean, it is not a good idea to use as a variable a name that has a special meaning to your language. Apart from possibly having an unexpected effect, this will only confuse anyone who maintains the program.

### Check your understanding 8.7

1 Explain what the programmer who wrote ADD ADD AND AND really meant.
2 Write an equivalent statement in your programming language. Run it on the computer and find out what it does. Is it what you expected?

## Control structures

In a traditional development environment, there are only five control structures:

1 The most common is a **command** or **sequential structure** where each statement executes in turn: DO this, DO that.
2 The **conditional** or **decision-making structure** is of the form
IF (this condition is true) THEN DO this
and optionally,
ELSE DO that.
3 The **repetitive structure** is of the form
DO this WHILE (this condition is true)
or
DO this UNTIL (this condition is true).
4 The **module structure** is DO (this procedure) and then return here on its completion.
5 The **branching** or **transfer of control structure** is DO or JUMP there.

Use of the branching structure is discouraged today; however, it is found a lot in some older programs and code written by non-professional programmers. Sometimes, the command and module structures are treated as a single control structure, giving the three main structures: sequence, condition, repetition.

## Functions and procedures

A program typically consists of functions and subroutines, which together are called procedures or modules. The main difference between them is that a **function** returns a value, while a **subroutine** does not return a value. For example, the mathematical function sin (X) returns a value. The procedure 'write to screen' is probably designed as a subroutine as it is unlikely to return a value.

### Check your understanding 8.8

1 Look at the design of any modular program. List the modules that you would implement as functions and those that would become subroutines.
2 Compare your answers with those of your colleagues. If you have different answers, why are they different?

A **macro** is where one complex language statement expands into a group of simpler language statements. This is similar in concept to a procedure, but is implemented differently. The programmer can call both a procedure and a macro many times with different parameters from different parts of the program. However, a procedure has its code stored only once. This procedure code is often stored away from the main body of the program. In contrast, a macro generates a different copy of its code each time the programmer calls it.

### Case study

In an assembly language, to add two numbers *a* and *b* together and store the result in a third variable *c* might be done through a macro ADD *a,b,c*. This generates the following code:

```
Load Register  a
Add Register   b
Store Register c
```

However, to find the square root of a variable *a* and store the result in variable *b*, which is a much more complex function, could be done by the code

```
Load Register  a
Call           Function_Square_Root
Store Register b
```

or even just

```
Call           Function_Square_Root(a,b)
```

1 Write code to add two numbers together and store the result as:
   a a function
   b a subroutine
   c a macro.
2 Which was quickest or shortest to write?
3 Which is the easiest to understand?

### Further research 8.5

1 List the various ways in which your language and development environment supports functions, subroutines and macros.
2 What are the differences in structure in your language?
3 When is it best to use each structure in your language?

# Data types

A data type specifies what sort of data a variable is expected to contain. There are many data types, the five most common being character (including alphabetic), numeric, Boolean (or binary), date and time.

## Character

The character data type is used to store letters A to Z, a to z, numbers that are not used for calculations, and words, text and codes. It includes special characters such as £$%&*()-. The developer uses this data type for general storage of information when it is not necessary to do calculations on the data. Examples are names, street addresses, telephone numbers, e-mail addresses, etc. The **alphabetic** data type is a subset of the character data type which allows only the letters A to Z, a to z and space.

### Numeric

The numeric data type is used to store numbers that are used for calculations. Internally, within the computer system, these may be held in a number of ways such as in binary, integers of various sizes and floating points of various sizes. These internal forms vary a lot between computer systems.

### Boolean

The Boolean or binary data type is used to indicate yes or no, or on or off, as in a switch. Internally, it is represented by the values 0 or 1.

### Date

A computer environment often allows dates to be input and output in several different ways. For example 21/11/2003 and 21-Nov-2003 clearly mean the same date. To an American, 11/21/2003 is also that same date. However, the computer system holds all of these as the same numerical value, usually in days since some internal origin date.

### Time

With time data there is often flexibility for input and output: for example, 1736 in 24-hour clock and 5:36 pm in American format. These are usually held in time units (often minutes, seconds or milliseconds) since midnight. Sometimes, the time data type includes the date as well, so that 1736 on 21/11/2003 is stored as one date/time field. Systems that allow this option have a system function that extracts just the date, or just the time, from the combined field.

Sometimes, the developer may want to hold data in a way that is not specifically catered for by the system being used. Here, you could have a **user-defined data type** with the properties that you need, such as a date or a time in a non-standard format.

### Check your understanding 8.9

1 Look at the properties box of a document in Word or another desktop program you know.
   - List the properties that you think are held as a character data type.
   - List your suggested data type for those that are not character, and your reasons.
2 For your computer environment, list the different numeric data types, such as integer and binary. When would you use each one?
3 For your computer environment, list the different date and time data types. How is each held internally? What system functions are available to help you to use dates and times?

### Case study: British Logistics

British Logistics personnel database contains 50,000 records, one record for each employee. Each record has many fields and these hold information such as staff number, current work address, current home address, current job title, work telephone number, home telephone number and mobile telephone number.

1 What other information might BL want to hold about their staff?
2 What are the data types for each field of this information?

**Further research 8.6**

Hobby Computing have asked you to develop some date manipulation modules for their Family History program. You decide that you need two user-defined types: history_date and history_time_interval. History_date will contain the date of an event in one of three ways:

- year, for example 1901
- month and year, for example July 1901
- date, for example 29 July 1901.

History_time_interval is the interval between two dates and might be described in days, weeks, months, years or combinations of these.

1 List which functions and data types are meaningful. For example, a time interval added to a date gives another date. A date minus a date gives a time interval.
2 List the functions that are not meaningful and give your reasons. For example, a date plus a date has no meaning.

# 8.3 Design concepts

This section shows how a developer implements a computer program, making use of design concepts. It covers these design concepts:

- Data structures
- Developing a design from a specification
- The importance of correct design methods
- Understanding the original problem and designing an appropriate solution to this problem
- Modularised code – procedures, functions and subroutines

## Data structures

Most computer programs are about taking in data in one form, doing some processing on it, usually storing the data and then outputting that data, possibly in a different format. Each piece of data in a program, known as a **variable**, has a unique data name, a data type and a length. The **data name** is needed so that the program knows which piece of data to operate on. The **data type** is needed so that the program knows what to do with it. The **data length** is needed so that the program knows how long that piece of data is. From the data type and length, the program knows three things:

- how much storage to keep for that variable
- what code it needs to generate to process that data
- what operations are valid for that data.

For example, it does not make computing sense to ask the computer to add the number 1 to the character string 'ABC'.

**Field**, **record** and **file** are business concepts that the developer can apply at the analysis and design stages and to a manual system. When the developer implements this in a relational database, a record is similar to a row, a field is like a column, and a table or database is like a file – Figure 8.6 (a) and (b).

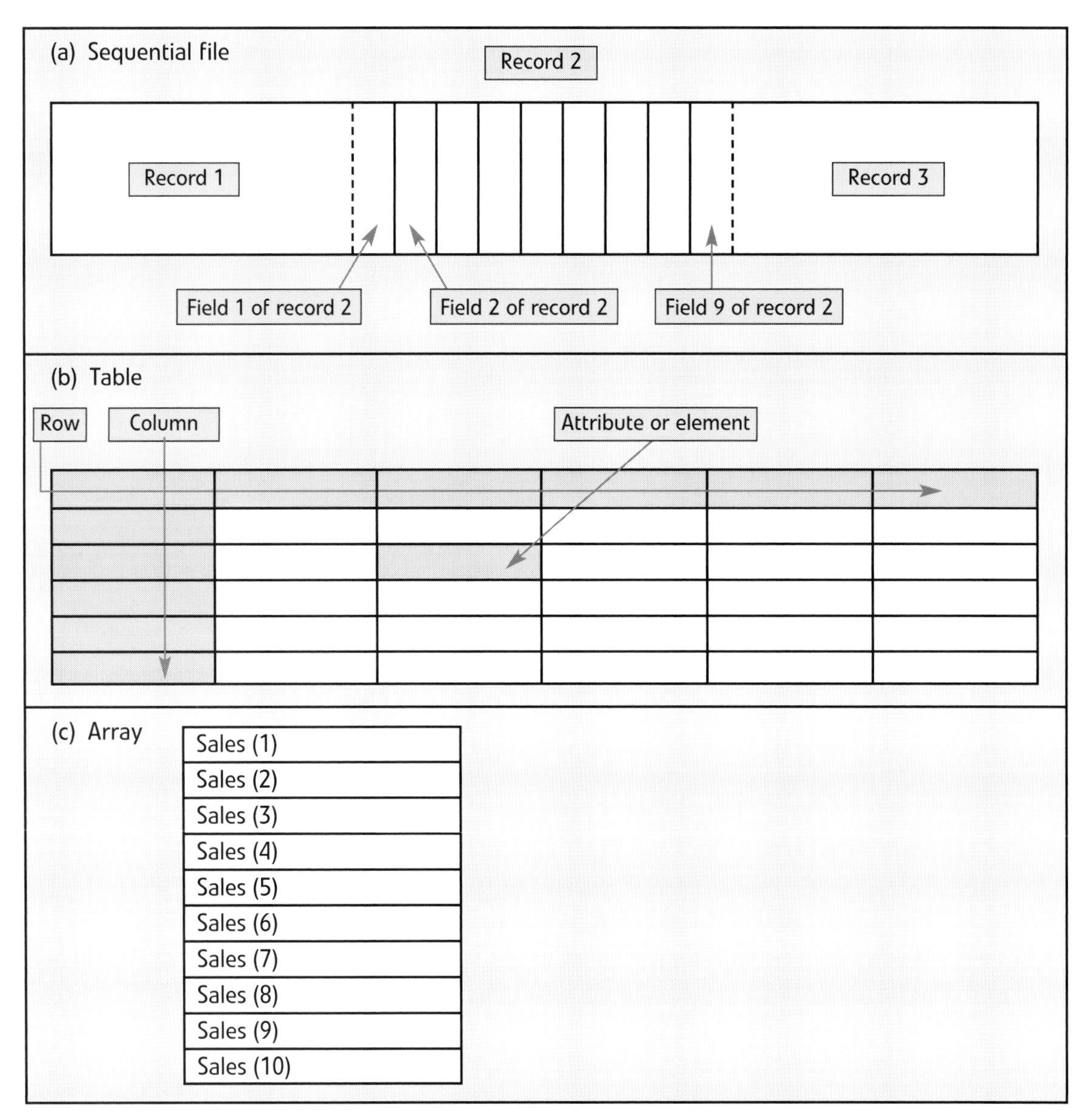


Figure 8.6 Diagram showing (a) field/record/file, (b) column/row/table, and (c) an array

While some programs operate only on single pieces of data, more complex programs work on repeated groupings of data. A **data structure** is how related pieces of information are organised. These structures can be files, lists, arrays, records, trees or tables.

- A **file** is a collection of data that has a filename that the computer operating system knows about.
- A **list** is a set of entries in a file or folder together with their properties.
- An **array** is a set of objects that are all the same size and data type. Each object in the array is called an **array element**. An array appears to be all stored together with no gaps. A one-dimensional array is called a **vector** and a two-dimensional array is called a **matrix**. For example, an airline passenger booking system would have a three-element array of total passengers booked by class. The first element is for first-class passengers, the second element is for business-class passengers, and the third element is for leisure-class passengers.

  An example of how a program might use an array is to hold 10 years of sales figures. Instead of defining 10 variables, Sales1, Sales2, ..., Sales10, the developer could define an array called SALES (see Figure 8.6 (c)). The sales for year 1 would be held in the element

SALES (1), for year 2 in SALES (2), and so on up to year 10 in SALES (10). The advantage of using an array is that the developer could use a DO loop to look at all of the elements of the array in turn. The developer could also use the array index (1 to 10) to access just one element rather than writing complex IF statements. Some languages such as Java start their array indices at zero and these are called **zero-based arrays**. If the sales years were 1995 to 2004, a few languages will even let the developer define a 10-element array as SALES(1995) through to SALES(2004).

- A **record** is a complete set of information about just one entry in a file or database.
- A **tree** is one of the ways in which an index determines where records or keys are stored in a database. The search routine repeatedly makes choices on which **branch** of two or more to follow until it finally reaches a **leaf** or record location (see Figure 8.7). The starting point of the tree is called the **root**. Although this structure is straightforward, the process can be expanded to cope with the largest commercial databases.

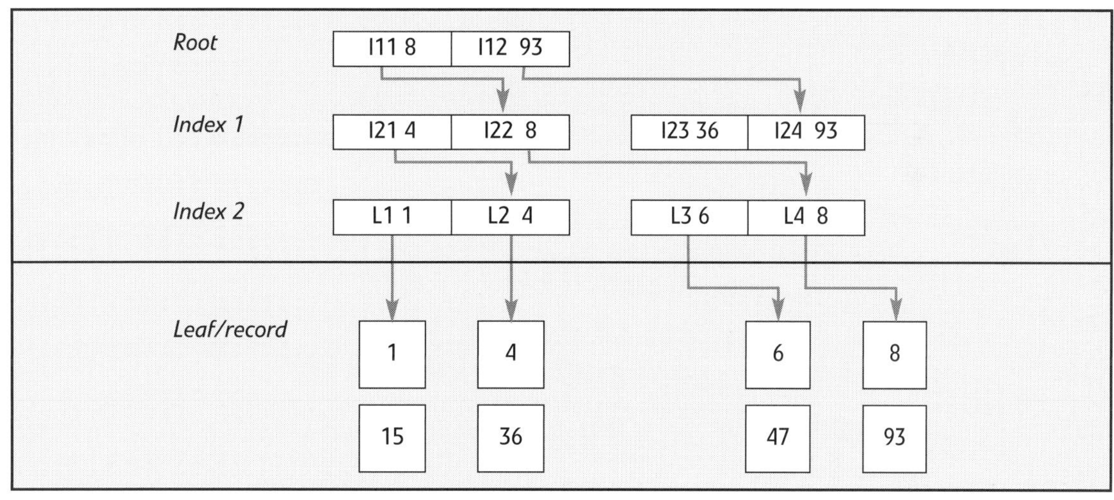


Figure 8.7 How to store numbers in a tree

- A **table** is a set of rows and columns containing a variable number of entries with all that is held about one thing or entity. This is a similar concept to a record, except that records are usually read sequentially while tables are usually indexed. Tables may also be relational, which means that the tables may be linked by **foreign keys**: by following links between the tables, a program can extract data from more than one table at a time.

## Case study: British Logistics

British Logistics' purchasing department buys goods and services for the company. It buys one item at a time from its many suppliers. Its purchase ordering system is built around three tables (see Figure 8.8). An orders table, with a key of order number, contains details of the goods or services ordered, together with the supplier key and a buyer key. A suppliers table gives details such as supplier company name, supplier address and trading details. A buyers table gives details about the buyer such as telephone number and department. The link between the orders table and the suppliers table is the supplier key, which appears in both tables. The link between the orders table and the buyers table is the buyer key.

1 List what other information BL might hold on its orders, suppliers and buyers tables.
2 What other tables would BL need in its purchase ordering system?
3 List examples of the content of the tables identified opposite.

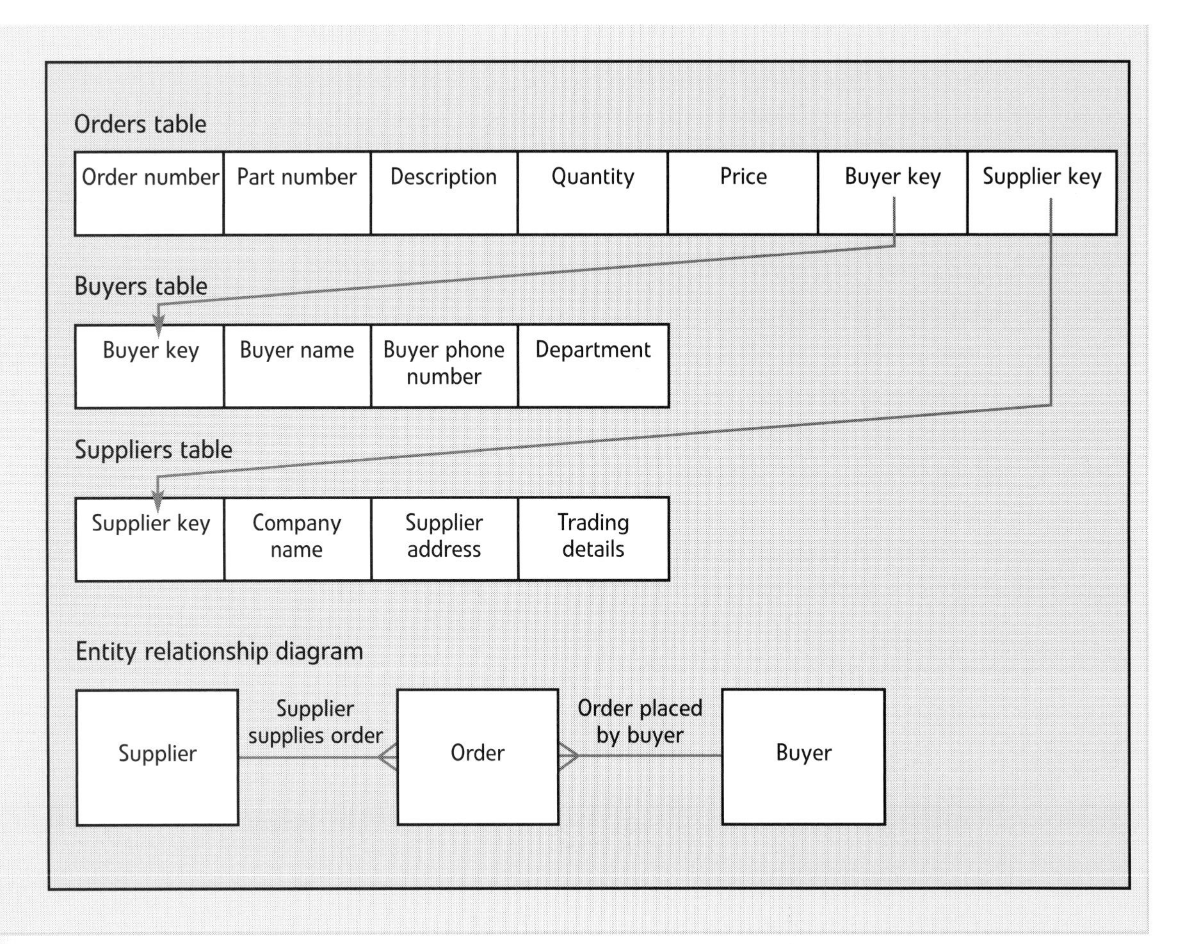


Figure 8.8 Entity relationship diagram of BL's ordering system

# Developing a design from a specification

The specification states in business terms *what* is expected from a computer system or program. However, it does not tell the developer *how* to proceed. What key skills does a computer system designer need to have?

- A good understanding of the business is needed so the developer understands what the specification means and how important each element of the specification is to the final delivered product.
- The developer needs the vision to turn the specification into something that can be built, by choosing the best option for the job in hand.
- Sufficient technical knowledge of the target computer system is needed to design a system that can be built easily in that environment.

There are three elements to developing a design from a specification:

- Use a design method.
- Understand the problem in business terms and use technical knowledge to turn that into the technical design for the computer system or program.
- Break the design into manageable chunks of code, programs or modules, each of which does only one thing or a group of related things.

# Importance of correct design methods

When correct design methods are used it is much more likely that the system will be a success. There are three aspects to this:

- The system will be in agreement with the specification; it can be shown how the system implements each part of the specification.
- The system will be built in the time required. The developer can accurately estimate the time to build a lot of little items, then add the estimate up, rather than using a rough estimate for the whole job.
- The system will be easy to maintain. A correctly designed system makes it more obvious where future changes will fit in. As a result, these changes will not make other unrelated parts of the program stop working.

# Understanding the problem and designing an appropriate solution

The design approach falls into three parts based on the following three skills:

- Understand – from the business user, the systems analyst or potential customer feedback – what is needed.
- Consider the different ways in which the system could be built and the functions of the various pieces of software.
- Perform the technical design of the system:
  - Work from the top down.
  - Group the similar pieces of functionality together.
  - Produce design specifications from which the developer can write code.
  - Ensure that the interfaces between each part of the system in both function and data terms are well-defined.

**Check your understanding 8.10**

Describe how would you expect a specification to look and who would you talk to about the specification if you were developing:

- a business system for a large organisation
- a PC-based desktop utility that you intend to market via the Internet
- some enhancements to an existing server-based system for a medium-sized organisation
- configuration of a package that your company bought from an applications vendor
- your idea for a great PC game that you hope will bring you fame and fortune.

# Modularised code: procedures, functions and subroutines

Different programming languages have different names for the chunks of code that you put together to make up a computer system. Code in a modularised computer system consists of up to four different sorts of code chunk. These are called, in increasing size: blocks of procedures or functions, subroutines or modules, programs, and systems.

- A **block** is the smallest group of code that has meaning. When a program calls a procedure, it does what it does and then returns to where it was called from. A function does the same, but also returns a value. Both may have parameters, or data that the block works with, passed to them.
- A **subroutine** or **module** consists of a group of one or more procedures, functions or statements that does a recognisable piece of processing. They may call other subroutines or modules to any depth and may also call themselves.
- A **program** is a standalone collection of code that performs a recognised independent part of a business function.
- A **system** is a collection of programs that computerise a complete business activity.

### Check your understanding 8.11

Find out whether your programming environment has all of the functions given above. List what your programming environment calls each of them.

### Further research 8.7

1 List the component parts of a PC-based function that you are familiar with, such as a desktop office suite or your favourite PC game.
2 This section uses terms from the ADA language. Research and list the full definitions of these terms in the ADA language.

### Assessment activity 8.1

Design and document, for an application of your choice, a system that reads input from and displays output to a screen and updates a database.

### Assessment activity 8.2

For the system that you designed in Assessment activity 8.1, or another appropriate system, document in a data dictionary all of the data items. This includes the properties of each item and shows where each is created, updated, displayed and deleted.

### Assessment activity 8.3

For the system that you designed in Assessment activity 8.1, or another appropriate system, design a user interface. This should take into account the skill level of the user and demonstrate your knowledge of the features of your user and your development environments.

# 8.4 Test and document

Once a developer has completed the design and programming of a computer system, the next stage is to test and document it before it is complete and ready for use. Testing is about making sure that the program does what the designer and the user expect it to do, checking that the program does not process data that is in error, and checking that the program does not crash, or fail, when something unexpected happens. This section covers the following testing activities:

- application of designed tests
- breakpoints
- step over and trace
- checking values of variables at runtime
- appropriate use of built-in functions for debugging and testing
- ensuring adequate testing is completed before the program becomes operational.

Documentation is about recording what your program does for later use by you, the program users and anyone who may need to change your program. It covers the following topics:

- test log documentation
- user documentation
- analysis, design and implementation documentation.

## Testing

### Application of designed tests

Testing is the process of making sure that a program does what it is supposed to do. In a complex IT environment, there can be five levels of testing:

- module testing
- unit or program testing
- system testing
- customer or user testing
- beta testing.

Module testing checks that a module, subroutine, subprogram or part of a program does what it should, according to the module specification. The programmer who writes a module usually produces his or her own module test data.

Unit or program testing checks that all the modules of a program fit together correctly. It confirms that the program functions in line with the program specification:

- All the input modules validate and pass data correctly to the processing modules.
- The processing modules perform their calculation functions according to the specification.

- The output modules write correctly to the screen, printer, database or other output device.

The team leader or programmer with overall responsibility for the program will usually write the unit test data.

System testing makes sure that a suite of programs, such as a payroll or accounting package, meets the computer design specification. It checks that the output from one program is acceptable input to the next program, and checks that databases are updated consistently. In a large IT organisation, there may be a testing quality group who write the system test data, or the systems analyst or programming team leader may write it.

Customer or user testing and beta testing are described on pages 240–1.

## Check your understanding 8.12

1 A module is expected to accept a date input, check it and then convert it into a standard date format. What date formats might this module accept? Write a specification for what date validation should be done. Produce a set of test data for this date conversion module, saying which dates the module should accept, which it should reject, and why.

2 Divide into groups of five. You are going to role-play the part of a program that adds a time period on to a date to produce another date.
- Person 1 is the user.
- Person 2 is the input module that takes the input of a date and a number representing a period and converts them both to integers for the use of the calculation module.
- Person 3 is the calculation module that adds the numbers together to give a third number that the output module uses.
- Person 4 is the output module that converts this one number to a date.
- Person 5 is the control module.

With the only communication between the team being the values in writing passed by the control module, simulate the user giving a date and a time period and receiving another date as a response.
Did you each choose the same base or origin date for your internal date store? Was the output date in the same format as the input date? What were the units of the input period: minutes, hours, days, months, or years?

## Further research 8.8

Examples of systems consistency testing are consistent screen colours, menu usage, use of function keys and mouse clicks.

1 Look at two pieces of desktop software from the same supplier, for example *Word* and *Excel*. How similar are the main menus?

2 Compare these with desktop software from a different supplier. How similar is this to the first pair?
3 How much easier is software to use when it is similar to something that you already know?

## Breakpoints

A breakpoint stops a program whenever a certain point is reached. The programmer can set conditions for the program to decide whether to stop. He or she can also set a breakpoint where an exception is raised.

### Check your understanding 8.13

For your preferred language and environment, find out what conditions you can set for a breakpoint. Give examples of why you might use each of these. Are there any more that you would wish to add?

## Step over and trace

- The **step over** command executes the current line of the program under test, without stopping in any functions or routines called within the line.
- To **trace** a program is to receive information about how a program is executing at run time. This information may include messages about which code has just been executed and the values of variables. The programmer can add a trace to an application while it is being developed, and use that trace both while testing and after the application is put into production. The programmer can use a trace both to display information when there is an error and to act as a performance monitor.

### Check your understanding 8.14

1 What step commands are available in your computer's testing or debugging environment? For each of these commands, when might you want to use them?
2 If you are testing a large distributed application with many users, how might a trace help you? Where might you use a trace command in that application?
3 In your environment, what capabilities does the trace command have to let you know what is going on?

## Checking values of variables at runtime

Almost all computer functions act on variables.

- Input is taken from a screen, file, mouse or instrumentation and sets input variables.
- Output functions expect values in output variables to be set correctly for the output device.
- Calculations take input variables and turn them into output variables.
- Program flow of control looks at variables to decide which line of code to execute next.

In all of these cases, if the program is not working correctly, then the developer needs to check that the variables needed by that part of the program are set as expected. An important part of the testing environment, therefore, is to display the values needed by that piece of program.

**Check your understanding 8.15**

1 Find out how your testing environment displays variables at a breakpoint.
2 How can you change a variable you find during a test that is in error?

## Appropriate use of built-in functions for debugging and testing

The programming environment, described on page 223, usually gives most of the debugging and testing functions that a developer needs to test a program. Sometimes, the developer needs even more testing features and will need to use built-in functions. This can be achieved in the following way:

1 Declare a global variable, test_mode, to control whether the program is in debug and test mode. Set this variable off initially.
2 Write whatever testing statements are needed in the program. They should be of this form:

   IF test_mode THEN DO... ... END; or IF NOT test_mode THEN DO... ... END

   They should not contain any transfer of control outside the DO statement. Typical testing statements would write to the screen, printer or log file, but they may include setting variables or arithmetic calculations.
3 Test the program, selectively switching into test mode when needed.
4 When debugging is nearly complete, run the final tests with test mode remaining off throughout.
5 Recompile the program with the testing statements converted to comments and rerun the final tests. Check that the results are still as expected.

## Ensuring adequate testing is completed before the program becomes operational

For **customer or user testing**, the IT department or the supplier hands over a system to the customer or user for controlled testing before it is used for real. It involves putting real data through the system and making sure that it is processed according to the rules of the business.

- For in-house-developed business software, it checks that the IT department have understood the company's business needs.
- For bought-in business software, it checks that the software has been set up correctly for use by this company and that the changes in business processes necessary to use the new software have happened.

Before using a new system, there is usually a period of **parallel running**, where both the old and new systems run together in parallel and the results are compared. The new system replaces the old system only when the results from the new are at least as good as the old. When a new system is put into production, this is called **cutover**.

For mass market PC software, **beta testing** is where the vendor has a controlled programme of customer testing in which users can download a new program and test it for errors before it is generally released to the market.

**Further research 8.9**

Go to a PC software vendor's website and subscribe to a beta test programme for PC software that you are familiar with.

1 What sort of tests are vendors looking for you to do?
2 How do vendors want you to let them know of any errors?

# Documentation

Documentation is writing down both *what* a module, program or an application does and *how* it does it. It is used by three groups of people:

- The author(s) use documentation to help them to build the programs and maintain and change them afterwards. They want to know how it works.
- The users use documentation to help them to use the program and to derive value from it. Typically, they do not care how a program works but want to know what it does.
- Other developers and technicians will want to know both what it does and how it does it. This is so that they can write programs that interface with it, so that they can configure the program to their environment, or so that they can troubleshoot any problems with the program on their own computers.

**Further research 8.10**

For these programs, identify what documentation would be needed and who would use it:

- Microsoft® *Office* (*Word*, *Excel*, *PowerPoint*, *Publisher* and other components)
- The payroll program suite for your establishment
- Your favourite PC game

## Production of test log documentation

An important task between program specification and code delivery is the production of a test plan of how to test the application or program. The major parts of this plan are sets of test cases that go through all major paths of the programs and many error conditions, and a set of expected outcomes for these test cases. Table 8.3 shows an example of part of a test plan for a date validation routine.

Once the programs are ready for testing, a log is made for each test run showing which test cases had the expected outcome and which did not. For unexpected outcomes, the tester raises an error log showing the test case, the expected outcome, what actually happened and any other relevant documentation (see Figure 8.9). It also shows the priority of the fault. This can vary from making the system unusable through to a nice-to-have improvement. The programmer uses this error log to investigate the fault. When the programmer has found and corrected code causing the fault, he or she passes this error log back to the tester who can then re-test the program.

| Test case | Input value | Expected result<br>V is Valid R is Reject |
|---|---|---|
| Start of year | 1/1/2000 | V |
| End of year | 31/12/2005 | V |
| Last day of month | 31/8/2007 | V |
| First day of month | 01/03/2004 | V |
| Last day of February | 28/2/2002 | V |
| Last day of Feb in leap year | 29/2/2008 | V |
| Day too small | 0/7/2009 | R |
| Day too large | 31/4/2002 | R |
| Month too small | 23/0/2008 | R |
| Month too large | 5/13/1996 | R |
| Year outside range (1000–2099) | 22/7/999 | R |
| Year outside range (1000–2099) | 14/6/3000 | R |
| Bad character in day | X/3/1998 | R |
| Bad character in month | 17/y/2010 | R |
| Bad character in year | 27/6/2z06 | R |
| Wrong format | 12042002 | R |
| Missing date | Blank | R |
| A final valid date | 15/6/2003 | V |

Table 8.3 Example of date test plan

| Error Testing Log | | |
|---|---|---|
| Project | Reference | Priority |
| Tester name | Date | Test case |
| Expected outcome | | |
| Actual result | | |
| Cause of problem | | |
| Developer name | | Date fixed |

Figure 8.9 An example of an error log

### Check your understanding 8.16

1 Produce a graph of errors found and still outstanding against a test run or date for a program you are testing. What does this tell you about how good your program is?
2 Now let someone else test your working program. What does their error graph look like?

If developers produce a new production version of a program, they may have changed only a small percentage of that program. They should still test that the unchanged part of the program works as expected. This is called **regression testing**.

### Further research 8.11

What facilities does your environment have to help regression testing? Write notes on how you would use these facilities.

## User documentation

The users want to know what a program does so they can use it effectively, but not how it does it. They also have different knowledge levels, ranging from complete novice to expert who needs to know exactly what each function does. To meet each of these needs, the developer produces some or all of the following documentation (shown here for a PC application). In a large team, either the systems analyst or a technical author produces this user documentation.

- **Getting started**

  Written in simple terms, this covers how to install the software (for a simple PC program); the main system functions; major inputs and major outputs. It is designed for the user who is eager to try out the new software, and it is probably supplied as a text or PDF document. It may also have an online element such as a product tour.

- **Tutorial**

  Written in slightly more complex terms, this takes the more methodical user through each of the main functions, again with their main inputs and outputs. It probably shows some of the more likely error conditions and how to recover from them. It is usually supplied as a text or PDF document.

- **Reference guide**

  This highly detailed document shows, for every function, what it does and the effect that it has on the rest of the software. It often has a technical rather than a user focus, probably listing functions in alphabetical or menu hierarchy order rather than as a user would view them. This is more likely to be a PDF document than a text document.

- **Online context-sensitive help**

  Delivered as part of the software package, this is aimed at providing brief, easy-to-use help when a user with some experience wants to know how to perform a function.

- **What's new?**

  This is aimed at experienced existing users of a program to support a new release. It gives details of new functions, additional features of existing functions, any changes to how existing functions work and, sometimes, considerations about how to implement the upgrade to the new release. It may be a text or PDF document, or it may be part of online help.

- **Knowledge base**

  This contains a list of known problems with the software together with any work-arounds. It often contains patches or upgrades that you can download to fix these problems. It may also contain various educational, reference and marketing information about the program and give opportunities to log any errors with the software. It is held on the developer's or vendor's website.

**Check your understanding 8.17**

List the different ways to call up online help in different systems. List the advantages and disadvantages of each.

## Analysis, design and implementation documentation

This documentation is for IT professionals. It is used both to develop the software and to communicate technical information about the software to other IT professionals afterwards.

For smaller, simpler systems, text documents, web pages and comments within the program code all hold IT documentation. With a large or complex system, the application development environment holds much of this information, generated as part of the development process.

- **Feasibility study**

  This describes the business requirements and proposed system in high-level terms, the expected benefits and costs of the system, the approximate timescale and the business case for the project. The sponsor or main beneficiary of the project signs this document off before detailed development begins.

- **Functional specification**

  This is the main analysis document. The systems analyst records the business requirements and specifies how the system meets these in terms of screens, inputs, processing, outputs and databases. It is usually technology-independent.

- **Design specification**

  This turns the business system functions specified in the functional specification into computer functions which the developers build into programs. It is specific to the technology chosen for implementation.

- **Application, program and module specifications**

  These are program design level specifications from which the programmer writes code. They are usually updated after coding to record the detailed program design.

### Data model

This chart records the business relationships between items of data. It may show, for example, that one customer may place many orders, but each order is only for one customer. This is the data equivalent of the functional specification.

### Database, table and record specifications

These show how the computer system physically holds what it calls each item of data. They are the data equivalent of the design and programming specifications.

### Implementation documentation

This is a project plan of the activities from the end of coding to a fully working live system. It includes the test plan, education and training activities, hardware and software purchase, installation and testing, parallel running and the cutover sequence.

### Post implementation audit

The final document is a review that is produced several months after full cutover. It documents the lessons learned from the project and compares the actual costs and benefits to those expected in the feasibility study.

## Further research 8.12

Each methodology or application development environment has different names for the above documents. Take the documents that yours produces and map them on to this IT documentation. Are there any overlaps? Are any missing?

## Assessment activity 8.4

1 Build the system that you designed in Assessment activity 8.1 or use another provided for this purpose.
2 Test the system using the techniques in section 8.4. Do this by producing a test plan, documenting the tests that you carry out, and exploiting the features of your development environment.
3 Produce a report on the development and testing process that you followed and how successful it was.

## Test your knowledge

1. What are the advantages of modularisation?
2. Draw a structure diagram of how to revise for an exam.
3. Write the data dictionary entries for an e-mail.
4. Draw a structure diagram and then write a program, to accept two numbers input from the user, add them together and return the result to the user.
5. Modify the program in Question 4 to multiply the two numbers instead.
6. Modify the program in Question 4 again to accept two numbers and select an add, subtract, multiply or divide function and then return the result to the user.
7. Add validation to the above program, so that a friendly error message is returned if, for example, there are alphabetic characters in the numbers or if the user attempts to divide by zero.
8. What are the differences between the structure diagram for the program in Question 7 and the structure diagram for the program in Question 4?
9. What are the various numeric data types?
10. What is a table, a row and a column?
11. What are the five main stages of testing?
12. What is customer or user testing?
13. What are the benefits of customer or user testing?
14. Who needs documentation and what do they need it for?
15. What IT documentation can be produced for a system?

# UNIT 10: APPLICATIONS SOFTWARE DEVELOPMENT

Most PCs include a wide range of applications available for effective data processing, such as databases, spreadsheets, word processors and presentation applications. To demonstrate your skills in applications software development, you are going to enhance an application using programming facilities to provide customised functions and adapt the user interface to provide a professional, easy-to-use application.

This unit concentrates on developing applications by writing macros within spreadsheet software, but similar development could be applied to word processing applications, database applications or presentations. Database programs like Microsoft® Access offer more sophisticated facilities than can be found in any spreadsheet programs. So, if you would like to demonstrate your programming skills for a 'heavier' database application, refer to Unit 13 (in the General book) for details of how this could be achieved using SQL.

## Learning objectives

- To use appropriate methods to plan and design a system
- To customise the way an application processes data
- To customise an application's user interface
- To use programming facilities to enhance an application

# 10.1 Planning and design

The familiar general-purpose applications such as word processing, spreadsheets and databases are often bundled together in a complete suite of applications such as Microsoft Office. These 'office' applications are designed to be 'jacks of all trades' with a wide range of in-built facilities. However, there are times when you may want to add to some of the facilities provided by these programs so that novice users can use them more easily:

- in word processing, automating a procedure such as a mail merge
- in a spreadsheet, automating some complex formulae and building a user interface
- in a database, providing forms and a menu system as a user interface.

Database applications tend to require lots of customisation and so the applications software provides a query language called SQL (covered in Unit 13 in the General book).

Each of the standard applications offers a common, built-in programming facility using macros, and this unit concentrates on how to use these in the following ways to demonstrate your programming skills:

- controlling what the user can and cannot do, to prevent a user from doing things with which they are unfamiliar
- making sure that users carry out actions in a certain order, e.g. completing data entry before printing the spreadsheet
- doing complex calculations
- making sure the user enters valid data, such as a date in a particular format
- providing the users with buttons to perform certain functions.

Each individual macro provides a single facility, such as a button to click which results in saving and printing a spreadsheet or document. Several macros can be combined to create a complete application.

The first step in creating any application-based program, as with creating any program, is to understand the user requirements. The stages in the development of a system (investigation, analysis and design) are described in detail in Unit 6 so they are not repeated again here.

**Check your understanding 10.1**

1 Refer to Unit 6 to refresh your memory of the stages of development for a system.
2 In a group of five or six, hold a brainstorming session to discuss options for enhancing applications software to meet user needs. The user may be an experienced user who is looking to save time or a novice user; the latter may provide more options to customise an application.
3 Draw up a short list of users and the user requirements for systems that you may decide to provide as a demonstration of your ability to develop applications software.

Once the user requirement has been investigated and understood, the next step is to design the way the application program will work. There are number of aspects of the system that you will need to design:

- the system plan, showing the objects in the system (such as forms), the links between them and how the user will progress through them while using the application
- the methods of input and output, including the user interface, and items such as customised reports
- the processing which will be carried out, including any calculations required.

# Creating a plan of the system

This stage involves creating an overall plan of how the system will work, including:

- the **objects** that are to be provided
- how the different objects in the system are linked together, e.g. on one form
- the logical progression through the system
- for larger, more complex system involving a number of different forms, how the user is to navigate around the system
- any procedures and functions.

?

**What does it mean?**

The **objects** in a system are the tables, forms and customised outputs.

## Case study: Cellphone World

Cellphone World sell a range of mobile phones to the public. They need a system to estimate customer phone bills, based on their expected duration of peak and off-peak calls per month. They decide to use a spreadsheet application, but need this to be customised so that it guides the shop assistant through the process of estimating a customer's monthly bill. The system should allow the shop assistant to choose different networks and to see the monthly bill for that network.

The solution to this user's needs involves the use of menus and buttons, and will need to incorporate validation to prevent the shop assistant entering invalid data.

This solution requires five separate steps (Figure 10.1):

- Display an opening screen.
- Show a form where the user can select which service company is to be used and enter the number of minutes of calls made.
- Display total estimated bill.
- Print a record of the calculation.
- Exit or do another calculation.

1 Check that you understand the plan for the Cellphone World system.
2 Working with others, sketch plans for systems that you might develop and discuss them.

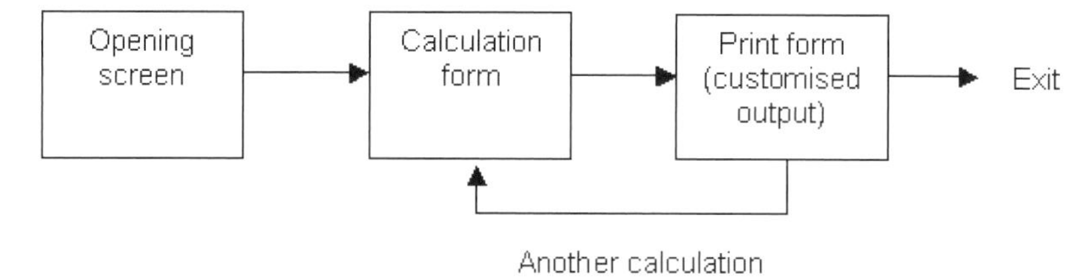


Figure 10.1 The steps involved in solving Cellphone World's problem

The plan is shown as a simple diagram as in Figure 10.1, with boxes representing the different objects and arrows showing how they are linked. This type of diagram is sometimes called a **state diagram** because it shows the different states that the application can be in. The procedures and functions required depend on the **controls** that are added to the forms to make the application work.

**What does it mean?**

A **control** may be a button or a field on a form or a field on a report.

# Designing system controls

For any system being designed, the investigation stage should provide a clear idea of what the user will need to input into the system and what outputs will be needed. For input, different system controls can be used depending on the type of input required (Figure 10.2):

- **Buttons** are used to indicate that some action should be carried out, such as a calculation to be done or results to be printed.
- **Text boxes** are used to allow the user to make text (or numeric) entries. They may also be used to display a text or numeric result.
- **Radio buttons** are used to allow the user to make a choice between a number of different options.
- **List boxes** (or combo boxes) allow the user to see a list of values, and the user can select an item from the list.
- **Text labels** are included to provide the user with information about what each particular control is to be used for.

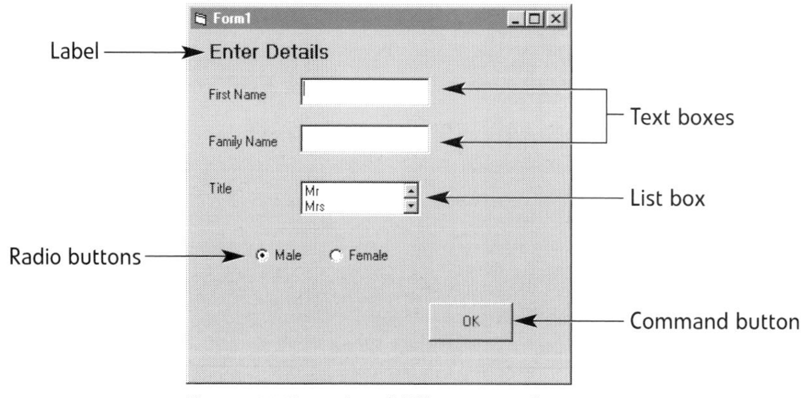


Figure 10.2 Examples of different controls

In designing the layout of these controls, you could use graphic software, but it is simpler to sketch it by hand on a piece of paper, and to refer to this when placing the controls on-screen.

The way that the input data should be processed also needs designing. There are number of different techniques available for designing data processing, some of which were covered in Units 4 and 6:

- dataflow diagrams
- structure diagrams
- flow charts
- pseudo code.

## Grouping controls logically

When designing the user interface, it is important to remember that the layout needs to be clear and logical for the user.

- Make sure that the layout is neat and consistent.
- Identify controls that are related to each other (e.g. title, first name and surname) and group these together, perhaps surrounding them by a box to focus the user's attention.
- Include labels to identify what the various controls are for. For many controls, you might have one label per control; where controls are related, a single label may serve the whole group, e.g. title/first name/surname may be given the label 'Customer name'.

## Headers and footers

Forms and reports used for printing also need careful consideration.

- Standard features like headers and footers should include information like titles and dates. Page numbers should be included for reports of more than one page, and headings may need to be repeated.
- When filtering and/or sorting data, it should be clear which field has been used for sorting purposes, e.g. in the column headings of a table or as part of the title of a screen.

## Commercial standards

When creating a system for a particular organisation, appropriate commercial standards will need to be met, such as:

- company colour schemes
- use of particular logos and the positioning of these.

### Further research 10.1

1. Identify five different organisations, who have a recognised company brand/image, such as a car manufacturer (e.g. Ford), a charity (e.g. The Prince's Trust), a sportswear company (e.g. Nike), a corporation (e.g. the BBC) and a service company (e.g. your local accountant or solicitor).
2. Working with others, collect material that shows the corporate image of each of these organisations. You could visit websites or collect hard copy examples such as brochures, business cards and business letters.
3. Identify how these organisations use graphics to convey a company image.

## Case study: Cellphone World

More detail can now be added to the plan shown in Figure 10.1. For each of the forms, a separate Microsoft® Excel worksheet is needed.

- To display the opening screen, a worksheet can be displayed with a title and a button attached to a macro which takes the user to the next sheet (Figure 10.3).

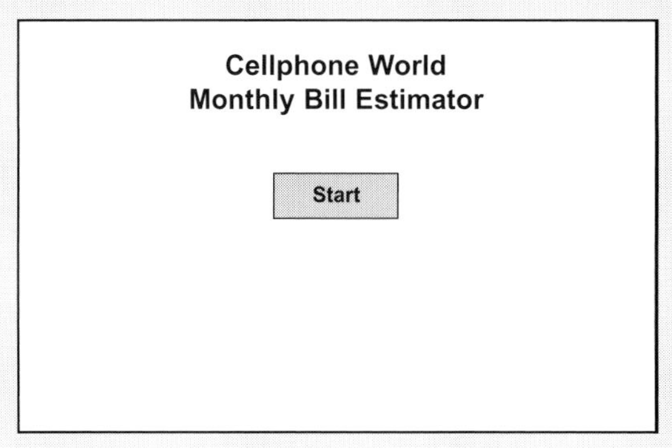


Figure 10.3 The opening screen

- For the next step, to select which service company is to be used, another worksheet is needed with buttons to allow the user to select the service company (Figure 10.4). These buttons need to be attached to macros that set the charges for the particular network chosen.

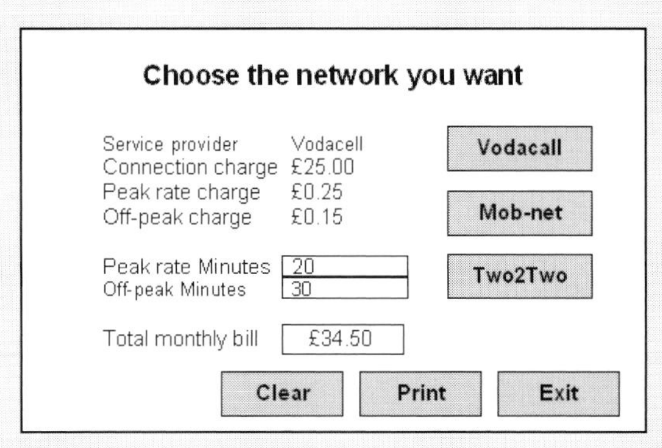


Figure 10.4 Calculation worksheet layout

- The same worksheet is used to enter the number of minutes at peak and cheap rates. It needs to display an input box to allow the user to enter the number of minutes of use at peak and then at cheap rates. Validation is needed to make sure the user enters only a numeric value (i.e. not text).
- Buttons will be needed on the calculation worksheet to allow the user to select the service provider and then display the total estimated bill.
- Printing a record of the calculation will involve transferring the data from the main worksheet on to a separate worksheet laid out for printing and **Exit options** must offer the user the choice of redoing the calculation, perhaps for a different service, or with different numbers of minutes usage, or to exit to the initial screen, ready to do a calculation for a different customer.

1 Check that you know how to place labels and text boxes on a worksheet.
2 Sketch a layout for the printing sheet.

Note that the Cellphone World case study presents the user with a series of screens in a predefined sequence; it produces results from calculations on values input by the sales assistant. To achieve this, the programming will involve setting up a number of worksheets (forms), adding controls (titles, boxes), incorporating validation of data that is input, writing macros to perform calculations and printing out the results. This is just one example of enhancing applications software to meet a user's needs. The next case study gives another example, involving interrogation of a table of data via the filter function.

## Case study: Car-Call

Car-Call are an agency who match up people who want to buy sports cars with dealers. They use a Microsoft® Excel spreadsheet (Figure 10.5) to store details of the cars that are for sale. They need to provide an easy way for their telesales people to find the car that matches the customer's requirements.

Microsoft Excel - Car_call.xls

Car-Call - Cars for sale

| Stock No. | Make | Model | Colour | Max Speed | Zero-60 | Price | Dealer | Phone No |
|---|---|---|---|---|---|---|---|---|
| 1 | BMW | M3 | Black | 162 | 5.7 | £28,995 | Gates | 0208 999 8888 |
| 2 | Ford | Focus RS | White | 138 | 6.3 | £19,499 | Arlington | 08870 160180 |
| 3 | Lotus | Elise | Green | 131 | 7.3 | £20,200 | Carings | 0800 751792 |
| 4 | Mazda | MX5 | Black | 115 | 10.1 | £9,995 | Carings | 0800 751792 |
| 5 | McLaren | F1 | Red | 231 | 3.2 | £599,995 | Gates | 0208 999 8888 |
| 6 | Porche | 911 Turbo | Red | 180 | 3.7 | £84,495 | Arlington | 08870 160180 |
| 7 | TVR | Griffin 500 | Green | 151 | 4.2 | £29,225 | Gates | 0208 999 8888 |
| 8 | Vauxhall | VX2200 | White | 143 | 8.2 | £16,825 | Arlington | 08870 160180 |
| 9 | MG | F | Green | 123 | 8.7 | £13,250 | Carings | 0800 751792 |
| 10 | Toyota | MR2 | White | 134 | 7.4 | £15,995 | Gates | 0208 999 8888 |
| 11 | BMW | M3 | Red | 162 | 5.7 | £25,499 | Arlington | 08870 160180 |
| 12 | Ford | Focus RS | Black | 138 | 6.3 | £17,995 | Carings | 0800 751792 |
| 13 | Ford | Puma | White | 112 | 9.5 | £8,975 | Gates | 0208 999 8888 |
| 14 | BMW | Z3 | Black | 115 | 7.8 | £14,395 | Gates | 0208 999 8888 |

Figure 10.5 The sports cars table

The telesales people would like buttons on the form to carry out certain functions:

- A button is needed to filter the display of cars so only those of a certain make are shown (e.g. Ford). This should be combined with a text box where they can type in the make they want, and another button to remove the filter, displaying all the records again.
- A button is needed to sort the list of cars displayed by price, showing the lowest priced car first.
- A button is needed to print out the current list of cars on a customised form.

Figure 10.6 shows a suggested design for the layout of these buttons and the text box needed to enter the make of car.

**Car-Call – Cars for Sale**

Enter make: [ ] Find | Show all | Print list | Sort by Price

| Stock No. | Make | Model | Colour | Max Speed | Zero-60 | Price | Dealer | Phone No |
|---|---|---|---|---|---|---|---|---|
| 1 | BMW | M3 | Black | 162 | 5.7 | £28,995 | Gates | 0208 999 8888 |
| 2 | Ford | Focus RS | White | 138 | 6.3 | £19,499 | Arlington | 08870 160180 |
| 3 | Lotus | Elise | Green | 131 | 7.3 | £20,200 | Carings | 0800 751792 |
| 4 | Mazda | MX5 | Black | 115 | 10.1 | £9,995 | Carings | 0800 751792 |
| 5 | McLaren | F1 | Red | 231 | 3.2 | £599,995 | Gates | 0208 999 8888 |
| 6 | Porche | 911 Turbo | Red | 180 | 3.7 | £84,495 | Arlington | 08870 160180 |

Figure 10.6 Design for spreadsheet controls

1 With others, discuss your short list of possible users, and consider what functions could be automated in a similar way.
2 Review your sketch plans for systems that you might develop and choose one to concentrate on. For this system, sketch a more detailed plan of the objects involved and how they might be linked. Identify buttons that you would need, and how the user would navigate through the system.

Having found out what a user needs in the way of buttons, you, as the designer, need to decide exactly what each button will do. For example, Car-Call will need the following four buttons:

- a 'Find' button to apply a filter to the data, using the value in the text box as a parameter for the Make field
- a 'Show all' button to remove the filter
- a 'Sort by price' button to sort the data in ascending order (lowest first) on the price field
- a 'Print list' button to copy the current list to a separate sheet, formatted with appropriate labels, as shown in Figure 10.7.

The first three buttons require functions (apply filter, remove filter, sort) which are all available using the auto-filter facility within Excel, but which will need to be automated using macros.

Car-Call – Cars for Sale
The following cars match your requirements:

| Stock No. | Make | Model | Colour | Max Speed | Zero-60 | Price | Dealer | Phone No |
|---|---|---|---|---|---|---|---|---|
| | | | | | | | | |
| | | | | | | | | |
| | | | | | | | | |

Thank you for using Car-Call!

Figure 10.7 Print sheet

## Check your understanding 10.2

1 Check how to apply a filter in Excel and how to remove it.
2 Check how to sort data in a spreadsheet.
3 Check how to copy cells from one worksheet to another, and then how to print.

## Start up

Consideration also needs to be given to how the application will appear to the user when it is first started and how access will be given to the various options and facilities within the application. To a certain extent, this will depend of the type of application. Some applications may follow a logical flow through a series of forms; others may present the user with a series of options at the outset, presented using a **switchboard** type form.

### What does it mean?

A **switchboard** is an opening screen from which all other screens/forms are accessed.

Special spreadsheet macros can be created which automatically run when the spreadsheet file is opened, so these can be used to set up toolbars or menus. This approach is explained in detail on page 395. When an Excel spreadsheet is opened, the first worksheet is always displayed, so if an opening menu is to be displayed as in the Cellphone World case study, then this menu needs to be placed on the first worksheet.

### Assessment activity 10.1

Create a plan and design for the application you will develop. Include a state diagram and sketches for the forms the application will use, and include details of how the application will start up.

# 10.2 Customising data processing

Having designed the application, the next step is to create it, using the design as a guide. This section looks at creating some simple applications that concentrate on automating the processing of data. Before beginning to write some spreadsheet applications, we must first look at some basic concepts of spreadsheets.

## Spreadsheets

A spreadsheet presents the user with a worksheet made up of rows and columns (Figure 10.8). **Columns** are named letters of the alphabet and **rows** are numbered. The box where a row and column meet is called a **cell** and the **cell reference** or address is made up of its column letter and row number.

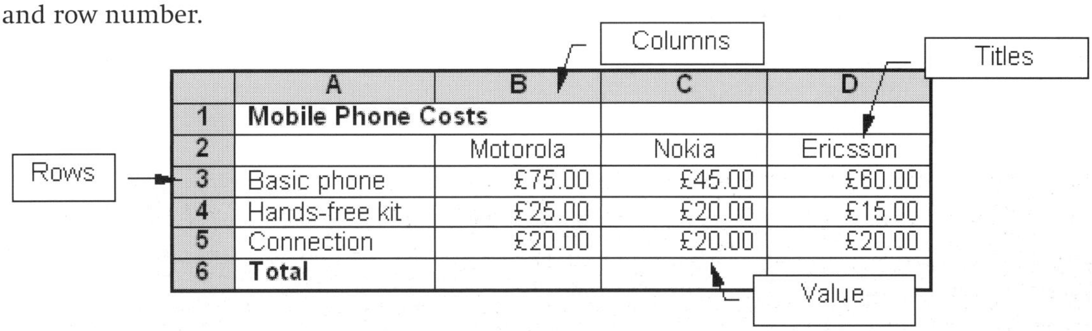

Columns

Titles

|   | A | B | C | D |
|---|---|---|---|---|
| 1 | **Mobile Phone Costs** | | | |
| 2 | | Motorola | Nokia | Ericsson |
| 3 | Basic phone | £75.00 | £45.00 | £60.00 |
| 4 | Hands-free kit | £25.00 | £20.00 | £15.00 |
| 5 | Connection | £20.00 | £20.00 | £20.00 |
| 6 | **Total** | | | |

Rows

Value

Figure 10.8 Spreadsheet basics: mobile phone costs

Each cell in a worksheet can be empty, or can contain one of three things:

1 **Text**: Sometimes called row or column titles or labels, these are used to help the spreadsheet user to understand what the numeric data in the spreadsheet shows and how to use the spreadsheet. In Figure 10.8, cell A1 contains a main title, cells A3, A4, A5, A6 contain row titles, and cells B2, C2 and D2 contain column titles.

2 **Numbers**: Sometimes called **values**, these can be formatted in a number of ways. For example, a number can be displayed in **currency format** (as shown columns B–D in Figure 10.8). Another example would be a **percentage format**. The value 0.12 formatted as percentage would be displayed as 12%.

3 **Formulas**: Formulas are the real power of a spreadsheet. They allow calculations not only of a fixed value but by reference to a cell address. For example =B2+B3 will add together the values found in cell addresses B2 and B3.

## Check your understanding 10.3

1 Columns are labelled A to Z. What happens after 26 columns, i.e. when there are no more letters of the alphabet left? What is the maximum number of rows and columns on the spreadsheet you are using?
2 Find out what other formats are available for numbers on your spreadsheet. Hint: You will probably find these listed in the help facility.
3 Cellphone World need simple spreadsheet as shown in Figure 10.8 to calculate the total cost of different types of mobile phone.
   a Enter the data shown in Figure 10.8 using your spreadsheet software.
   b To calculate the total cost of a Motorola phone, enter a formula into cell B6 to add together the contents of the cells, B3, B4 and B5. What formula did you put into cell B6?

B3+B4+B5 gives the correct result to question 3b (above), but an alternative spreadsheet facility, called a **function** could be used. The SUM function adds up all the values between two cells, so =SUM(B3:B5) has the same effect as =B3+B4+B5.

To total the costs of the other phones, another important spreadsheet facility is needed: copying formulas. Rather than entering another formula in C6 and yet another in D6, the existing formula could be copied and pasted.

## Check your understanding 10.4

The formula entered in cell B6 should be =SUM(B3:B5).

1 Copy this to cells C6 and D6.
2 Inspect the formula in C6 and check how it has changed. Copying across a column (from column B to column C) changes the columns in the cell addresses so, in cell C6, the formula should now read =SUM(C3:C5). When copied into D6 the formula should read =SUM(D3:D5).
3 Check that your spreadsheet totals match those in Figure 10.8.

The way the cell addresses change when the formula is copied is called relative referencing (or **relative addressing**), because the address changes relative to where it is copied. Note that if you copy a formula down the rows rather than across the columns then the row number will change rather than the column letter. There are circumstances when you will not want this to happen. For example, when calculating the VAT that is to be added to the total cost of the phone, this depends on a fixed rate (currently 17.5%).

| | A | B | C | D | E |
|---|---|---|---|---|---|
| 1 | **Mobile Phone Costs** | | | | |
| 2 | | Motorola | Nokia | Ericsson | VAT rate |
| 3 | Basic phone | £75.00 | £45.00 | £60.00 | 17.5% |
| 4 | Hands-free kit | £25:00 | £20:00 | £15:00 | |
| 5 | Connection | £20:00 | £20:00 | £20:00 | |
| 6 | **Total** | **£120:00** | **£85:00** | **£95:00** | |
| 7 | VAT | | | | |
| 8 | **Grand Total** | | | | |

Figure 10.9 VAT rate

The formula needed in B7 to calculate the VAT is =B6*E3 (the total cost for the Motorola phone multiplied by the VAT rate). However, if you copy this formula to C6, it would change (due to relative addressing) to =C6*F3. The C6 is fine, that is the total cost of the of the Nokia phone, but F3 does not contain the VAT rate. In this situation, where the VAT is stored in a fixed cell, you need to turn off the relative referencing effect on the E3 cell address. The $ sign can be used to turn off relative addressing, so that **absolute referencing** can be used instead.

**Check your understanding 10.5**

1 Enter the text shown in rows 7 and 8 and column E on Figure 10.9.
2 In B7 enter the formula =B6*$E$3.
3 Copy B7 across to C7 and D7.
4 Check the contents of C7 (should be =C6*$E$3) and D7 (D6*$E$3).

In some circumstances, when you copy a formula, you may want the column address to change (relative referencing), but the row address to be fixed (absolute referencing) or vice versa. In these cases the $ sign is placed in front of the part of the address (column letter or row number) that is to be fixed. So for example when the formula =B5+E$8 is copied, relative referencing will effect all parts of the formula except the row number 8, which is fixed by the $ preceding it. This is known as **mixed referencing.**

# Creating applications

The way an application is created depends very much on the program being used. This unit looks at creating applications in spreadsheets using Microsoft® Excel. If you decide to create an application in Word, Access or PowerPoint, you will need to check what options are open to you by way of programming tools.

One way of creating a customised application within Excel is to record macros, and then to refine and add to them by editing them like normal programs. Recording a macro involves switching on a facility called a **macro recorder**. Then you carry out the actions you want to record (e.g. select cells, choose menu options) and the macro recorder records whatever you do. Once you switch off the macro recorder, you can then replay your recorded actions whenever you want. You need to make sure that you understand the design of the macro and practise the actions you want to record before you actually record it. If you don't do this, you may well end up recording mistakes in your macro; this will mean you have to record it again or edit out the mistakes.

Having recorded a macro, you can then create a button or a shortcut key to make it easy for the spreadsheet user to run the macro. The case study below looks at a simplified version of the spreadsheet application designed earlier. Later, the complete application will be created, but first we need to understand the basics of recording and editing macros.

## Case study: Cellphone World

Cellphone World have created a spreadsheet to calculate customers' monthly bills on the different networks (Figure 10.10).

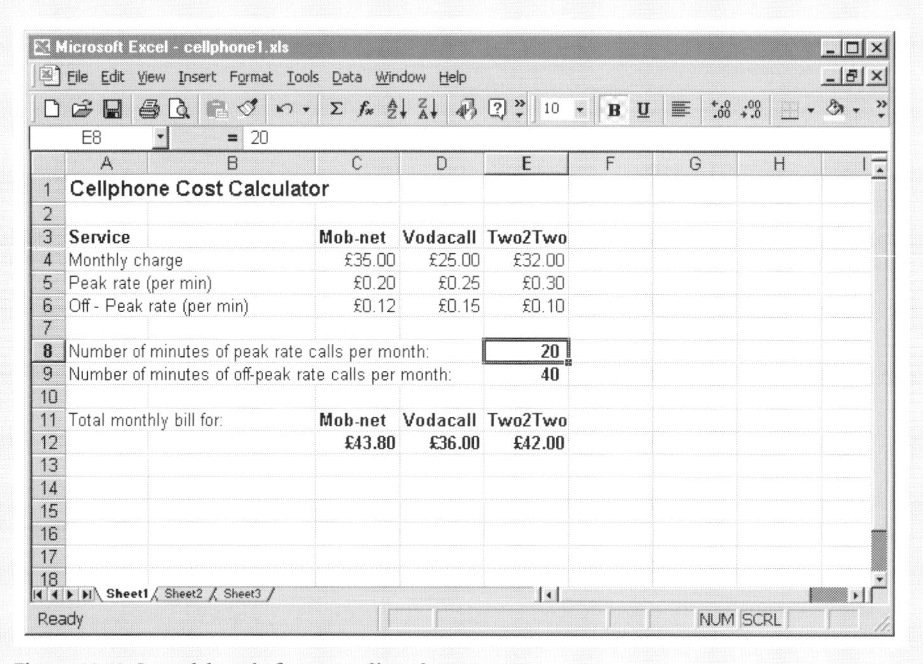


Figure 10.10 Spreadsheet before recording the macro

The user enters the estimated monthly minutes at both peak and off peak times and the spreadsheet shows what their monthly bill would be on each of the three networks. When a customer wants to see an estimate of their monthly bill, the sales assistant wants to be able to click a button to remove the previous customer's entries for the number of minutes they expect to use at peak and off peak rates. So a simple macro is needed to clear the spreadsheet of its previous entries.

1 Make sure your spreadsheet looks like Figure 10.10.
2 Prepare to record a macro:
   - Go to the Tools menu and select the Macro option.
   - A sub menu will pop out and you need to choose the Record New Macro option. You will see a dialogue box asking you for the name of the new macro.
   - Type the name clear_entries into the box.

3 From now on whatever you do will be recorded in the macro, so be careful to do only the things you want in it:
   - Click on Cell E8 (which contains the number of minutes of calls at peak rate) and press the delete key to remove the entry.
   - Click on cell E9 and press delete again to remove then entry in that cell.
   - Choose the Tools menu again, select the Macro option and from the sub-menu, choose Stop Recording (or click the stop recording button in the macro toolbar, which appears when you start recording a macro).

4 Test the macro by pretending to be a sales assistant at Cellphone World. A customer asks for an estimate of his/her bill, so enter the number of minutes they think they will use at peak time and the number at cheap rate. Then, another customer asks for an estimate. To clear the previous entries, use the macro.

At the moment, to run this macro you need to go the Tools menu, select the Macro option then the Macros sub-option, click on the macro name in the box that appears and then click the Run button. The macro should, if it has been recorded properly, remove the previous entries. At the moment, to run the macro takes more key strokes than deleting the entries yourself! To make the macro easy to run, a button to run the macro is needed or shortcut key must be set up (see page 271).

## Further research 10.2

Macro recording is available in most Microsoft® applications.

1 Check how macros can be recorded in Word and PowerPoint.

2 Find out how macros operate within Access.

Excel macros are written in a programming language called **Visual Basic for Applications (VBA)**, which is a version of Visual Basic, so as well as recording the macros, you can edit and add to the Visual Basic code yourself. The code for the macro is placed in a procedure, which starts with the word 'Sub' and the name of the procedure (Clear_entries) and an empty set of brackets (indicating that no parameters are passed to the procedure when it starts). The procedure ends with the 'End Sub' statement. Each macro you record is placed in a separate procedure (see Figure 10.12).

Having created the basic macros for an application, they now need to be made easy to run. There are two simple ways to do this:

- by adding a **button** (see page 273)
- by incorporating a **shortcut key** (see page 271)

A button requires a single click of the mouse, but while it is user friendly it does take up space on the screen. A shortcut key is particularly helpful when the spreadsheet operator may be already using the keyboard when they want to run the macro, as they could then run the macro directly from the keyboard rather than having to use the mouse. It requires the user to remember the shortcut key, but also frees up space on the screen.

## Check your understanding 10.6

1 Look at the code created by the macro recorder for the macro: Select the Tools menu, the Macro option and Macros sub-option and the Macros dialogue box (Figure 10.11) will appear:

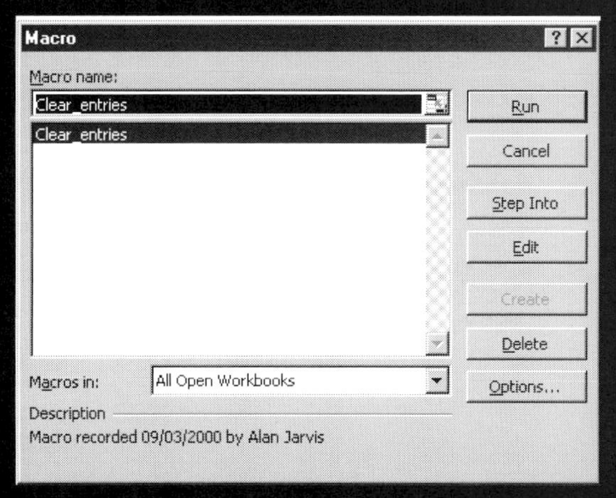


Figure 10.11 The Macros dialogue box

2 Click the macro name (Clear_entries). Then click the Edit button on the right. The Visual Basic editor program will start, in a separate window with the macro code shown on the right (Figure 10.12).

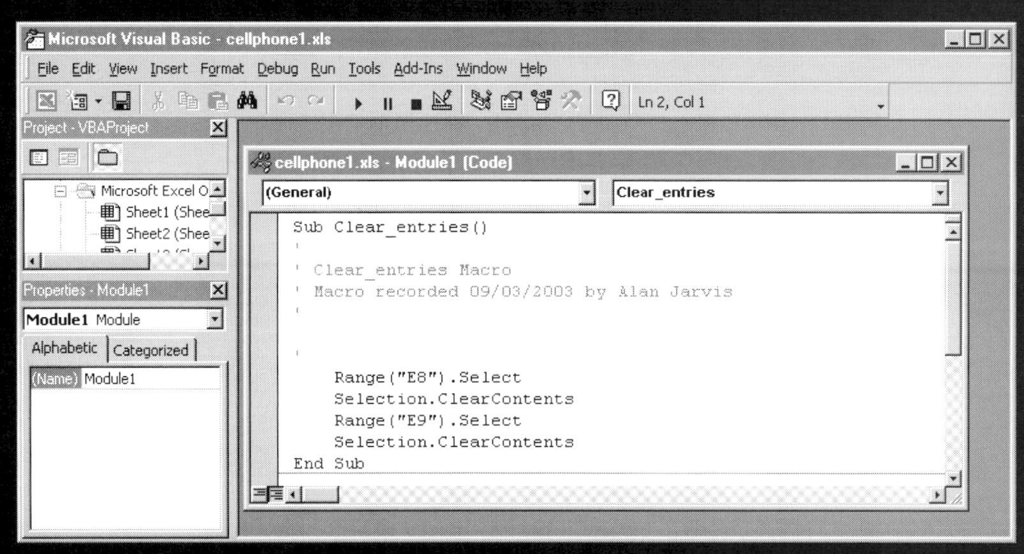


Figure 10.12 The editing window

3 Note the structure of this procedure.

4 Compare the coding used for a macro in Excel with one written in Access.

To create your application, you will need to set up tables and forms (in Access), or worksheets (in Excel), or screens (in PowerPoint), or documents and maybe other formats of material, or templates (in Word). You will need to customise reports and any other outputs that are to come from your system.

Once you have created your application, you will need to check your application against the design criteria:

- Does the application provide all the features required by the user?
- Do all your controls function as required? You will need to test every button and every short cut to make sure these work as expected.
- Does your application accept input as expected, and reject invalid data?
- Does your application produce the expected results?

**Check your understanding 10.7**

Refer back to your design documentation. Check that you have specified exactly what your user requires, so that, when the time comes to evaluate it, you have criteria against which to judge the success, or otherwise, of your finished product.

# Adding controls

Controls are used for input and output. For input, there are several options; **buttons**, **text boxes**, **radio buttons**, **list/combo boxes** or **text labels** (Figure 10.2). Similarly, for output there are a variety of controls.

**Further research 10.3**

1 Investigate the availability of controls in Microsoft Excel forms. Find out about at least four controls that have not been covered in this unit.
2 Investigate the output control options available in Microsoft® Access reports.

## Adding a button

To add a button to run a macro, the Forms toolbar must be shown on the screen. If the toolbar is not displayed, you can display it by choosing the Toolbars option from the View menu. Once the correct toolbar is displayed, follow these steps:

- Click on the Create button button.
- Move to the place on the spreadsheet where the button is required and drag out the button shape.
- Release the mouse and the button will have been created.
- A dialogue box will appear asking which macro the button is to run.
- Click on the clear_entries macro; then click OK.
- Change the name on the button by clicking inside it and removing the existing name (Button 1) and typing the name 'Clear Entries'.

Every time the button is clicked the macro will run.

**Check your understanding 10.8**

1 Set up a button as described above and compare it to the completed spreadsheet shown in Figure 10.13.
2 Test that the button works.

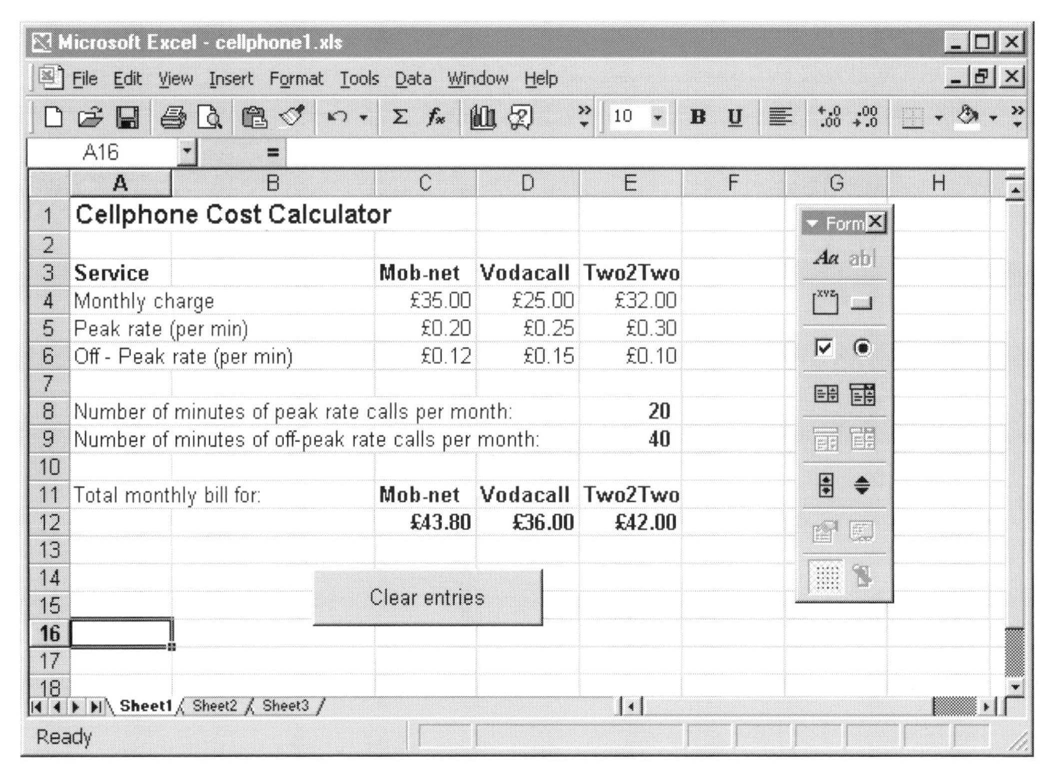


Figure 10.13 Spreadsheet with macro button

## Editing a macro

More sophisticated applications can be built by linking together several simple macros. The case study below demonstrates how this can be done.

## Case study: Cellphone World

Before clearing the entries, the sales assistant would like to save the spreadsheet and print out a copy for the customer. Creating a macro to save and print the spreadsheet is simple. Creating a macro to clear the entries is also straightforward. The next step is to link the two macros together so that having saved and printed the sheet, the entries are cleared.

1 Use the Record Macro option, and name the macro 'Save_and_print'.
  With the macro recorder running, click the Save button, click the Print button and then stop the macro recorder.
2 To link together macros, edit the macro code:
  - Go to the Tools menu and choose the Macro option.
  - Select Macros sub-option again, to display the Macros dialogue box.
  - Click on the second macro (Save_and _Print) then click the Edit button. This will open the Visual Basic editing window.
  - At the end of the Save_and_Print macro, add this instruction: Application.Run macro:="Clear_entries".
3 Compare your edited macro with that shown in Figure 10.14.
4 Test the edited macro by running the Save_and Print macro. Not only should it save and print the spreadsheet, it should also clear the peak and off-peak minutes from cells E8 and E9.

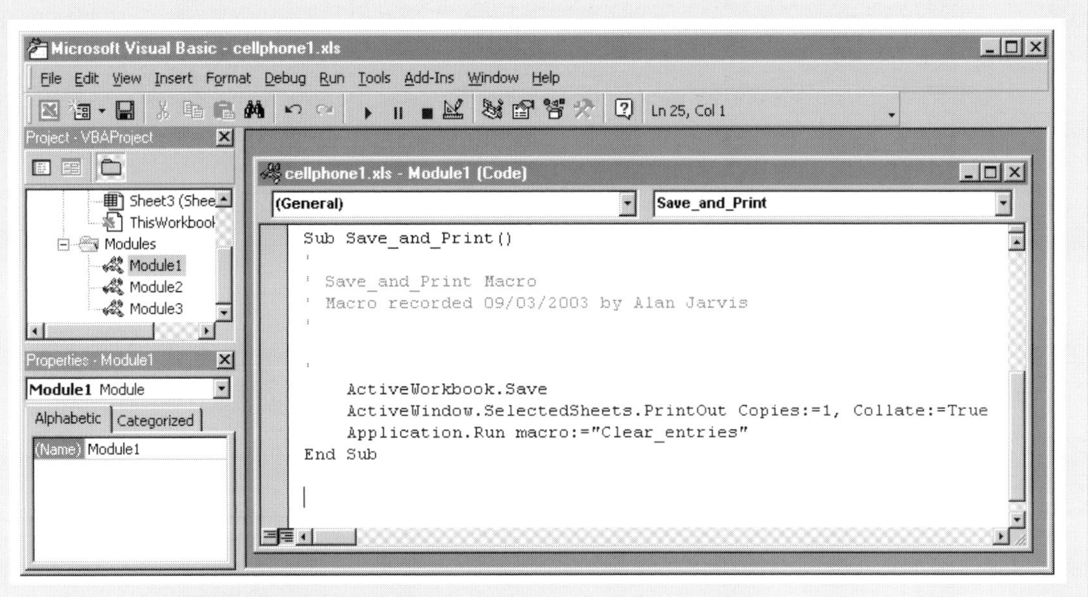


Figure 10.14 Save_and Print macro modified

## Using an autofilter

The next case study demonstrates how relevant data within a spreadsheet can be extracted.

### Case study: Car-Call

The spreadsheet Car-Call use to list the cars they have for sale is shown in Figure 10.15. They need an autofilter so that cars can be shown for one particular make.

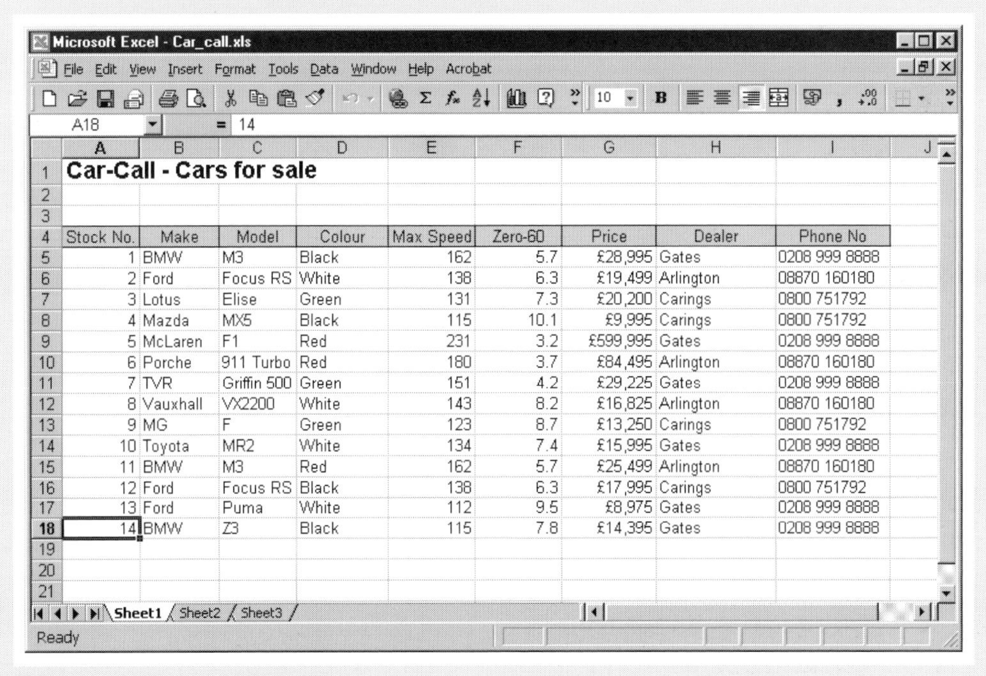

Car-Call - Cars for sale

| Stock No. | Make | Model | Colour | Max Speed | Zero-60 | Price | Dealer | Phone No |
|---|---|---|---|---|---|---|---|---|
| 1 | BMW | M3 | Black | 162 | 5.7 | £28,995 | Gates | 0208 999 8888 |
| 2 | Ford | Focus RS | White | 138 | 6.3 | £19,499 | Arlington | 08870 160180 |
| 3 | Lotus | Elise | Green | 131 | 7.3 | £20,200 | Carings | 0800 751792 |
| 4 | Mazda | MX5 | Black | 115 | 10.1 | £9,995 | Carings | 0800 751792 |
| 5 | McLaren | F1 | Red | 231 | 3.2 | £599,995 | Gates | 0208 999 8888 |
| 6 | Porche | 911 Turbo | Red | 180 | 3.7 | £84,495 | Arlington | 08870 160180 |
| 7 | TVR | Griffin 500 | Green | 151 | 4.2 | £29,225 | Gates | 0208 999 8888 |
| 8 | Vauxhall | VX2200 | White | 143 | 8.2 | £16,825 | Arlington | 08870 160180 |
| 9 | MG | F | Green | 123 | 8.7 | £13,250 | Carings | 0800 751792 |
| 10 | Toyota | MR2 | White | 134 | 7.4 | £15,995 | Gates | 0208 999 8888 |
| 11 | BMW | M3 | Red | 162 | 5.7 | £25,499 | Arlington | 08870 160180 |
| 12 | Ford | Focus RS | Black | 138 | 6.3 | £17,995 | Carings | 0800 751792 |
| 13 | Ford | Puma | White | 112 | 9.5 | £8,975 | Gates | 0208 999 8888 |
| 14 | BMW | Z3 | Black | 115 | 7.8 | £14,395 | Gates | 0208 999 8888 |

Figure 10.15 The Car-call spreadsheet

1 Apply an auto-filter to the table of cars for sale:
- Make sure the currently selected cell is within the list of cars (A4:I18).
- Select Filter, and then Auto-filter from the Data menu.

- Check that this has added drop down arrows to the field names at the top of the table of data.

2 Now create the macro for the Find button. This will allow the telesales people to enter the make of car, click a button and see a filtered list of cars with only those of the make they entered showing. Initially, record a simplified macro:

- Go to the Macro option in the Tools menu and select the Record Macro option from the fly out menu.
- Enter the macro name as find_make in the dialogue that appears, then click OK to start the macro recorder.
- Click on the drop-down arrow in the Make field name (B4) and choose (Custom...) from the list that appears. The dialogue shown in Figure 10.16 will then be seen.
- Enter the name Ford, and click OK. Only Ford cars will now be shown in the list. The word Ford is used as a **parameter** for the filter.
- Stop the macro recorder.

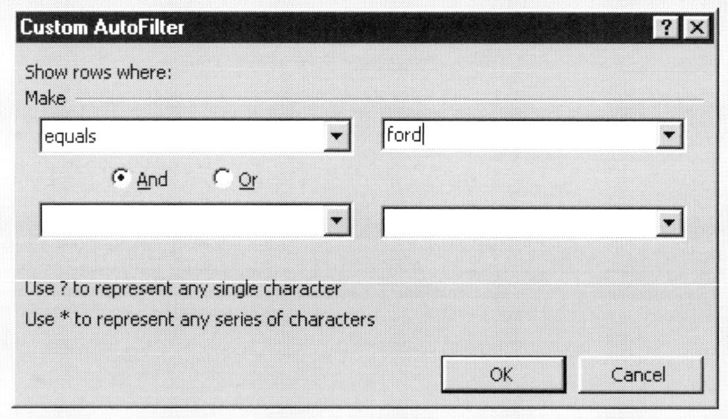


Figure 10.16 Custom Auto filter box

### What does it mean?

A **parameter** is a value that is input to a procedure or function that controls how the procedure or function works.

## Adding a text box

The macro as it is now will only show Ford cars, but suppose that the telesales people want to be able to list all cars of any given make of car. Adding a text box would allow the make of car to be entered and you would then need to modify the macro just recorded to use this input data. To add a text box, follow these steps:

- To display the Control toolbox toolbar, go to the View menu, select Toolbars, and the Control toolbox sub-option.
- Click the text box button and drag out a text box at the top of the sheet, as shown in Figure 10.17.

A text box gives the user freedom to enter whatever text he or she wishes. An alternative is to offer a limited list of options using either a combo box or radio buttons.

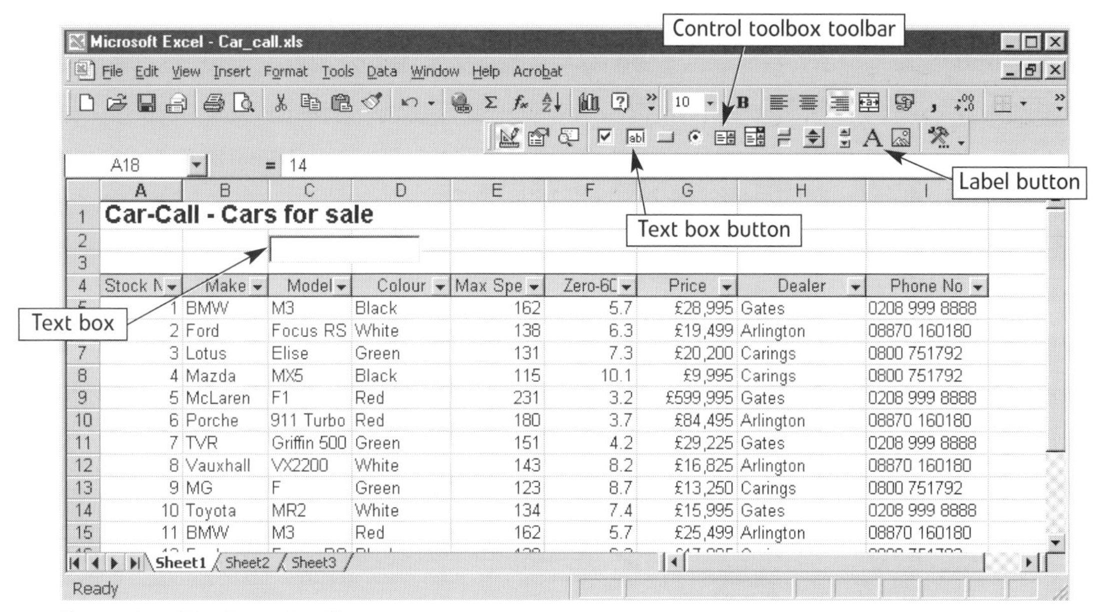


Figure 10.17 The Control toolbox

## Further research 10.4

1 Find out how to add radio buttons. Make notes so that you could explain it to someone else.
2 Find out how to create a combo box. Consider how a combo box might suit the needs of your user.

## Adding a label

Any text box should have a label so that the user knows what to put in the text box. You can use the Label button in the same was at the Text box button to create an area on the form where the label will appear. Modifying the text in the label is done through the label's properties. To do this, display the Properties window by clicking the Properties button in the Control toolbox (Figure 10.18).

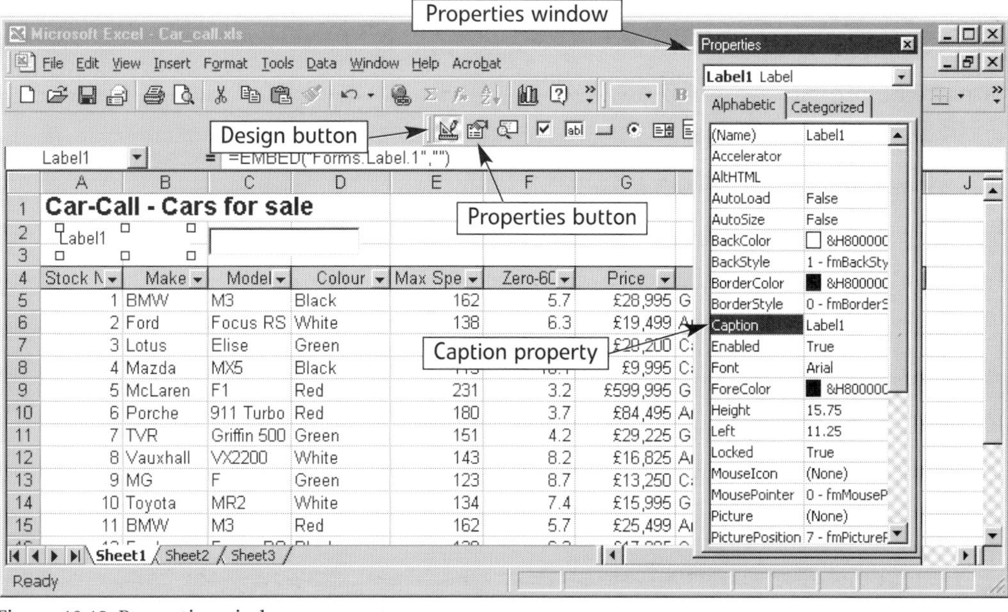


Figure 10.18 Properties window

The Caption property controls the text displayed in a label. Change its value from 'Label1' to 'Enter make'. Then to activate the controls so they can be used, click the design button to turn off design mode.

Having created a text box named Textbox1, the macro recorded earlier can be modified so it takes the car make from this text box, as follows:

- Go to the Tools menu, select Macro, and then the Macros sub-option.
- Click on the find_make macro, and click the Edit button. This will open the Visual Basic editing window, as shown in Figure 10.19.

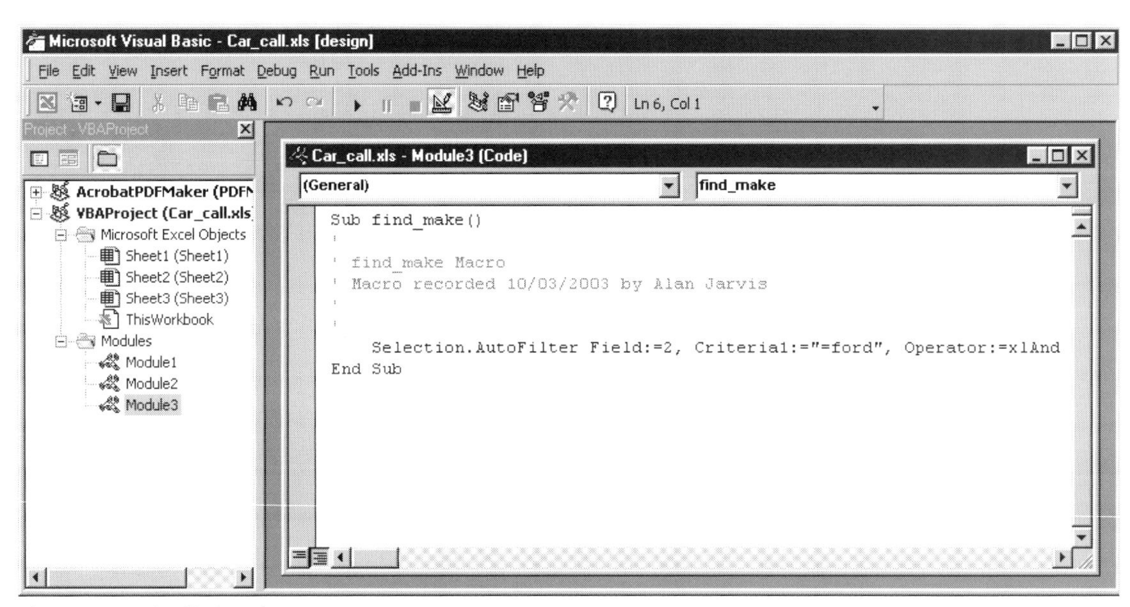


Figure 10.19 The find_make macro

- The parameter Criteria1:="=ford" must be replaced with the value in Textbox1. This is achieved by placing the value in Textbox1 into a variable (called make), adding an equals sign to it and then using it as the parameter for the autofilter. The modified code is shown in Figure 10.20.

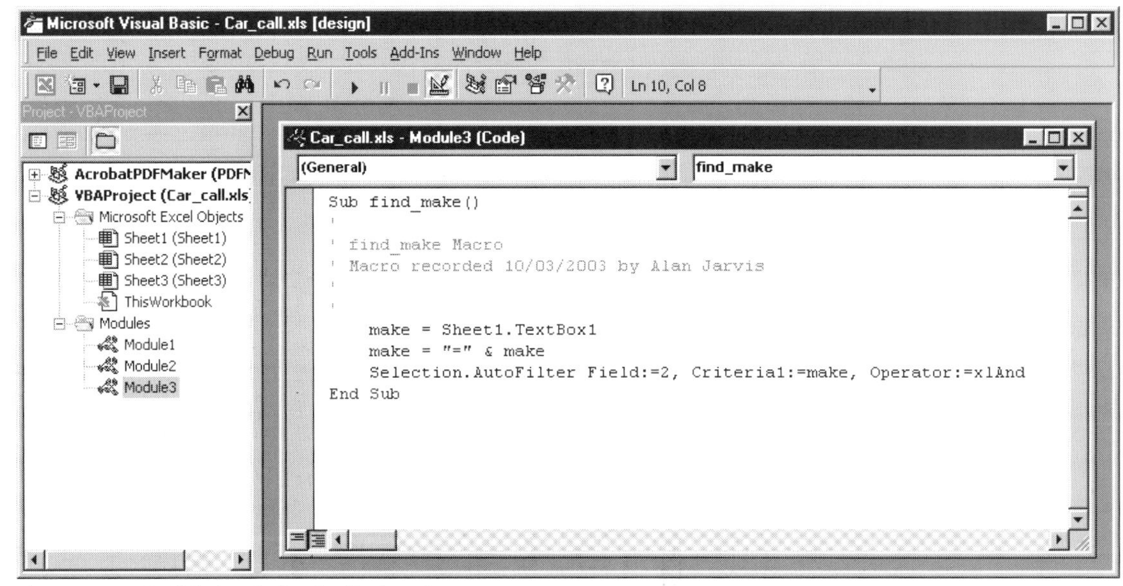


Figure 10.20 Modified code for the find_make macro

## What does it mean?

A **variable** is like a box allocated to store something in.

- Finally a button to run the macro is needed and then the edited macro can be tested. To add a macro button, display the Forms toolbar, go to the View menu, choose the Toolbar option and Forms sub-option. Click the **Button** button and drag out a button on the sheet. Select the find_make macro from the dialogue that appears and change the text on the button to read 'Find'.

If the name of a car make is now typed into the text box and the Find button is clicked, the list of cars will only display those made by the maker entered, as shown in Figure 10.21.

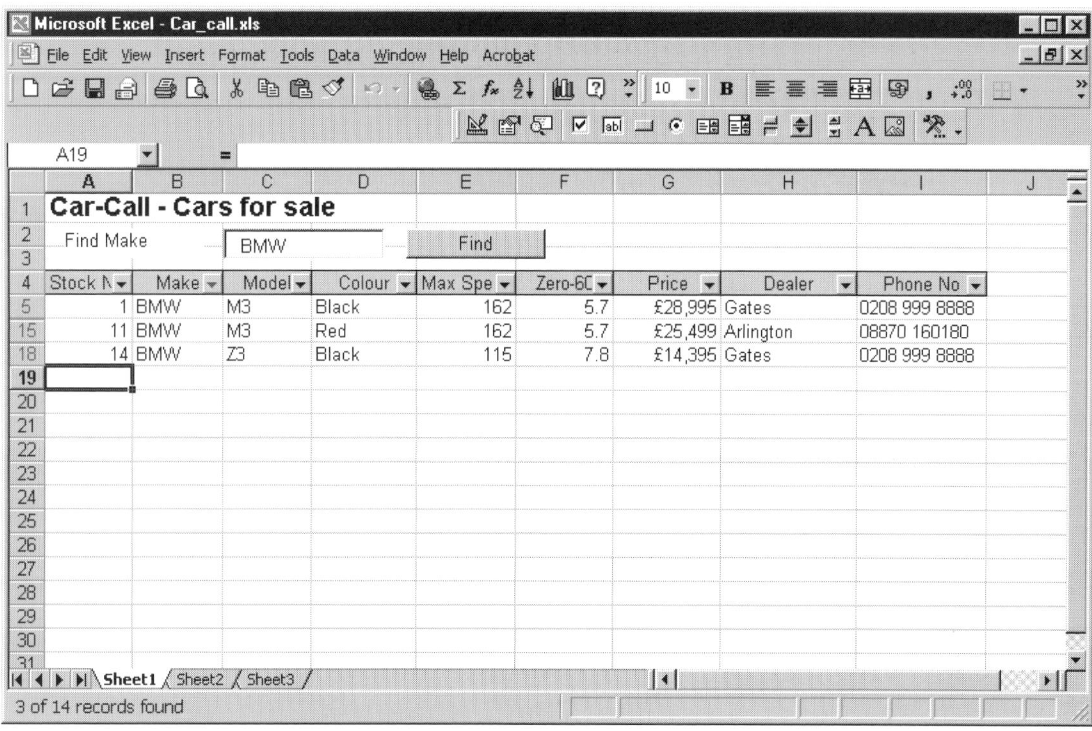


Figure 10.21 The Find button working

Entering text into the text box gives the user more flexibility in the output that can be expected. What would happen if the user entered text incorrectly, e.g. 'Frod' instead of 'Ford'? No matches would be found and the user would soon realise the mistake. You could include all the possible names within a combo box, so that this type of mistake could not happen.

## Check your understanding 10.9

1. Following the instructions given in the text above, create a text box and a label for it.
2. Modify the macro so that it uses the value entered in the text box.
3. Test the macro to make sure it works.

## Further research 10.5

Extend the application to confine the user's entries to selection of an item from a combo box list.

Three more buttons are needed for your spreadsheet application:

- the Show all button, needed to remove the filter and display the complete list of cars again.
- the Sort button
- the Print button.

For the Show all button, create the macro by recording; there is no need to edit the code.

- Turn on the macro recorder as before, calling this new macro show_all.
- Click on the drop down arrow above the make column (if the Find button has previously been used, it will be blue indicating that this column has a filter applied).
- Select (all) from the list.
- Stop the macro recorder.
- Create a button using the Forms toolbar (not the Control toolbar), and assign the show_all macro to it.

The macro for the Sort button is also simple to record:

- Turn on the macro recorder.
- Click in the price column (anywhere in the range G5:G18 will do).
- Select the Data menu and the Sort option. This will display the sort dialogue box, with the Price field selected.
- Click the OK button on the sort dialogue box and the list will be sorted by price.
- Stop the macro recorder.
- Create a button, attach the macro just recorded to the button and change its label to say 'Sort by price'.

Finally, to complete the spreadsheet application, you will need to add a print button.

## Numeric input

When an input is numeric, it is important that it is valid. Input of incorrect data could produce silly results. For example, if the user types 'thirty' instead of '30', the calculation will not work. So some validation is necessary: input from the user needs first to be accepted and then to be validated.

To investigate how to validate numeric entries, we will use the Cellphone World spreadsheet (Figure 10.13) and record and modify a macro to validate the number of minutes used at peak rate (cell E8).

To create a more complex macro, it makes sense first to record a simple version of it, and then to edit the Visual BASIC code to refine the macro. In this example, the end result of the macro will be to insert a number in cell E8, representing the number of peak rate minutes. To start with, record a macro that does just that, insert a number in cell E8:

- Make sure the cell pointer is not in E8.
- Start the macro recorder, calling the macro set_peak.
- Move to cell E8 and type in a value (any value will do).

- Stop the recorder.
- Click the Edit button on the Macro dialogue box to start the Visual Basic editor to inspect your macro (Figure 10.22).

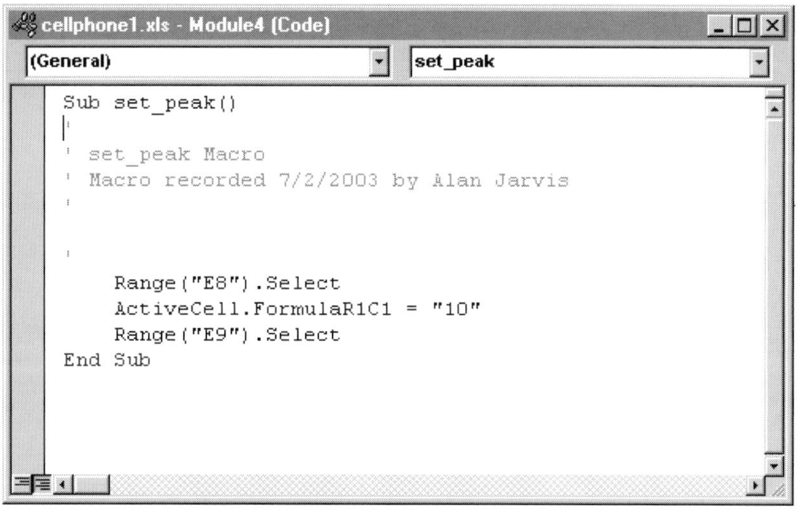

```
cellphone1.xls - Module4 (Code)
(General)                    set_peak

Sub set_peak()
'
' set_peak Macro
' Macro recorded 7/2/2003 by Alan Jarvis
'

'
    Range("E8").Select
    ActiveCell.FormulaR1C1 = "10"
    Range("E9").Select
End Sub
```

Figure 10.22 The set_peak macro

## Using variables

At the moment, this macro will always place a fixed value (in this case 20) in E8. The user needs to be able to specify this amount and, as this will vary depending on the customer, a variable is used to store the value.

The value stored in the variable will not be known until the macro is run, but the box (or variable) is given a name so that it can be referred to in the macro. The modified macro is shown in Figure 10.23. Notice that the name of the variable is peak_mins, and that an input box is used to collect the real value from the user. The contents of the variable are placed in the cell E8.

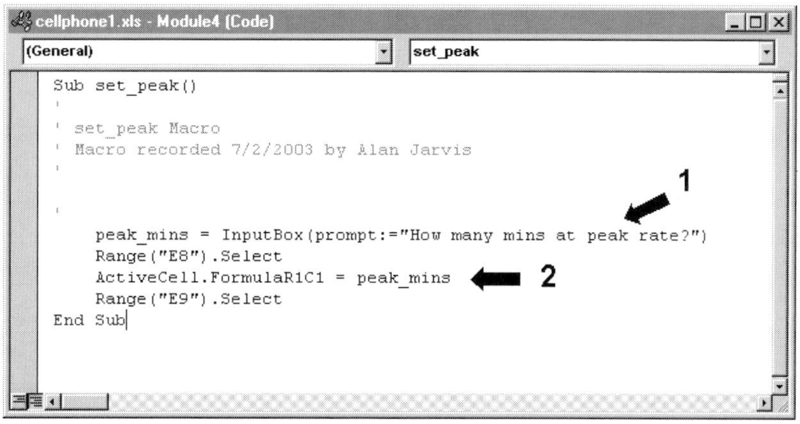

```
cellphone1.xls - Module4 (Code)
(General)                    set_peak

Sub set_peak()
'
' set_peak Macro
' Macro recorded 7/2/2003 by Alan Jarvis
'

'
    peak_mins = InputBox(prompt:="How many mins at peak rate?")   <- 1
    Range("E8").Select
    ActiveCell.FormulaR1C1 = peak_mins   <- 2
    Range("E9").Select
End Sub
```

Figure 10.23 The Modified set_peak macro.

*Notes:*

1 This new line of code uses a variable called peak_mins. The contents of this variable are collected from an input box that appears on the screen with the message (prompt) "How many minutes at peak rate?".

2 In this modified line, rather than having the 'ActiveCell' (E8 here) set to 10, which was the value that was typed in when the macro was recorded, it is set to whatever is contained in the variable peak_mins.

## Check your understanding 10.10

1 Create a macro off_peak to allow the user to enter the value for the off-peak minutes.
2 Run this macro, and check that it displays the input box and places whatever value you type into the box in cell E9.
3 Experiment with different values including a text entry instead of a numeric entry.

## Validating data

The macro set_peak now allows data to be entered and correctly placed in cell E8. However, it does not validate the entry, so if you leave the input box empty or type text into it, it still accepts this and is happy to put text in E8, although this prevents the formula that calculates the total bill from working correctly and it displays an error. Any entries that are non numeric therefore need to be rejected.

To do this, you not only need to check if the entry made is numeric, you also need to send the macro around in a **loop**.

### What does it mean?

A loop is a type of programming construct known as repetition in which one or more statements are repeated, either a fixed number of times or until some condition is met.

In this case, the loop will display the input box and check the entry to see if it is numeric. If the entry is not numeric, the loop will continue. The only way out of the loop will be if a numeric entry is made. To achieve this, a 'do until' loop is needed; it does the loop until a numeric entry is made. The code needs to be modified as shown in Figure 10.24.

cellphone1.xls - Module4 (Code)

(General) | set_peak

```
'
' set_peak Macro
' Macro recorded 7/2/2003 by Alan Jarvis
'

'
    peak_mins = InputBox(prompt:="How many mins at peak rate?")
    num_check = IsNumeric(peak_mins)         ← 1
    Do Until num_check = True         ← 2
        MsgBox ("Numbers only please!"), 0         ← 3
        peak_mins = InputBox(prompt:="How many mins at peak rate?")
        num_check = IsNumeric(peak_mins)
    Loop
    Range("E8").Select
    ActiveCell.FormulaR1C1 = peak_mins
    Range("E9").Select
End Sub
```

Figure 10.24 Testing for a numeric entry.

*Notes:*

1 This new line uses a new variable, num_check, which holds the result of testing peak_mins to see if it is numeric. This is done by a function called IsNumeric. If peak_mins is numeric it returns the value True, if is isn't it returns the value False.
2 This is the do until loop. Everything between the do until statement and the loop statement is repeated until num_check is true.
3 This statement displays a message box on the screen, showing the message in quotes. The 0 at the end indicates that the message box contains an OK button to remove it from the screen.

**Check your understanding 10.11**

1. Edit your macro to include the do until loop and check that it works. You should find that it will only accept a numeric value. Any other entry (including making no entry at all) results in the appearance of the message box demanding 'Numbers only please'.
2. Check what other looping instructions are available.

# Creating a shortcut

Designing a system includes trying to make the system as user friendly as possible for the user, as well as offering the quickest way of achieving what they want to do.

- Providing buttons attached to macros presents the user with a one-click option for tasks that you know he or she needs to do. The button should be labelled so that it is clear what effect clicking on the button will have.
- Toolbars also offer a swift route to particular features. The user clicks on an **icon** and any highlighted text or cells or records can be affected, e.g. emboldened, italicised, right aligned and so on.
- A shortcut is a combination of key depressions, usually involving the ctrl key and/or the alt key and/or the shift key together with a sequence of one or more of the standard QWERTY keys on a keyboard.

**What does it mean?**

An **icon** is a graphic image used to represent a particular feature, e.g. on a toolbar.

The term 'shortcut' is also used to describe the use of an icon within a toolbar to represent an application. These may be created by the user to speed up the process of opening applications, although usually this involves a double click on the mouse. The same technique is used when icons are used to represent documents or other files; a double click acts as a short cut to opening that file. Here we concentrate on shortcuts involving combinations of key depressions.

Before the mouse was invented, the main shortcut keys were the function keys on a standard keyboard. These can be programmed in much the same ways as macros can be assigned to shortcut keys. Software used to be supplied with a cardboard or plastic strip that could be placed above the function keys and this would explain exactly what each function key could do, if pressed on its own, or with the shift key or with the ctrl key and so on. Much emphasis was placed on keyboarding skills which was fine for clerical staff who were touch typists, but it did not really suit the newer breed of user. Enter the mouse and icons that could be clicked on and the complete **WIMP** environment.

**What does it mean?**

**WIMP** stands for windows, icon, menu, pointer.

Suddenly everyone was learning how to click, double click, drag and drop. However, history seems to have come full circle, recognising that many users can work more quickly without the mouse! All Microsoft applications offer an extensive list of shortcuts; they have always been there. There are predefined shortcut keys for just about everything that you might do frequently. To discover the full list of shortcuts in Word, for example, including any that you have set up, follow these steps:

- On the Tools menu, point to Macro, and then click Macros.
- In the Macros in box, click Word commands.
- In the Macro name box, click ListCommands.
- Click Run.
- In the List Commands dialogue box, click Current menu and keyboard settings.
- On the File menu, click Print.

Different procedures are necessary in other Microsoft applications.

### Further research 10.6

1 In a small group, brainstorm to create a list of shortcut keys that you already use.
2 Check the shortcut keys available in two or three Microsoft® applications, and decide to use a few of them in place of the mouse.

To use a shortcut key for a macro in Excel, follow these steps:

- On the Tools menu, select the Macro option Macros sub-option.
- Select the macro that you want to create a shortcut for.
- When the dialogue box appears, choose the Options button.
- In the box marked Shortcut key, type in the key to be used. It will always be used in conjunction with the CTRL key. For example if 'Z' is entered as the shortcut key, pressing CTRL+Z will run the macro.
- Click OK and close the Macro dialogue box.

### Check your understanding 10.12

1 Set up a shortcut key for a macro and test that it works. For example, for the Clear_entries macro, you could enter some values into the relevant cells, and then press the shortcut key combination that you chose and see what happens.
2 Check other Microsoft® applications for details of how shortcuts can be created, e.g. for opening applications.

### Assessment activity 10.2

Using the design that you created earlier, develop the application, using appropriate features. Include controls such as buttons and shortcuts as appropriate. Check your application against the design criteria.

# 10.3 Customising the user interface

This section looks at some more options for automating procedures, focusing particularly on the user interface, and considers customising toolbars and menus. So far, the macros created have been run using command buttons and shortcut keys. There are a number of other ways that macros can be run, allowing the user interface to be customised to suit different requirements. Two techniques are discussed:

- adding buttons to the toolbar
- creating menus.

# Adding buttons to a toolbar

Excel has a wide range of toolbars, all of which can be customised by adding and removing standard buttons. Custom buttons can also be added to toolbars to run macros. This example shows how this is done using the first version of the mobile phone call cost calculator created earlier (see Figure 10.13 on page 262).

Suppose that, instead of having a button on the spreadsheet to clear the entries, the user would prefer a button in the standard tool bar. To set this up, follow these steps:

- Go to the View menu and choose Toolbars.
- Choose Customise from the bottom of the sub-menu in the dialogue that appears, as shown in Figure 10.25.

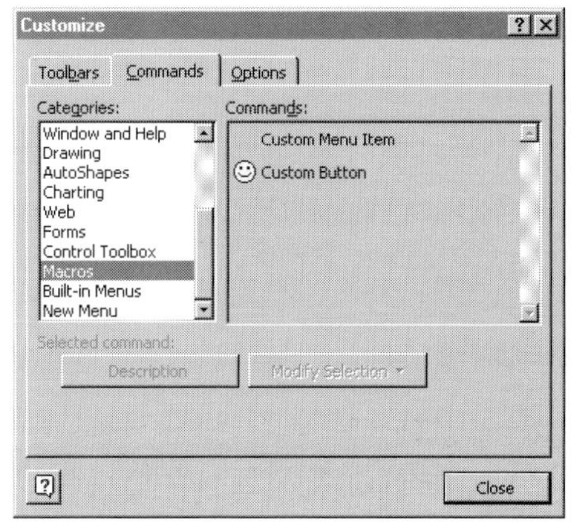


Figure 10.25 The Customise dialogue

- In the Categories list box, scroll down and select Macros.
- Click the custom button on the right side of the dialogue (the smiley face) and drag it into the desired place on the standard toolbar (see Figure 10.26).

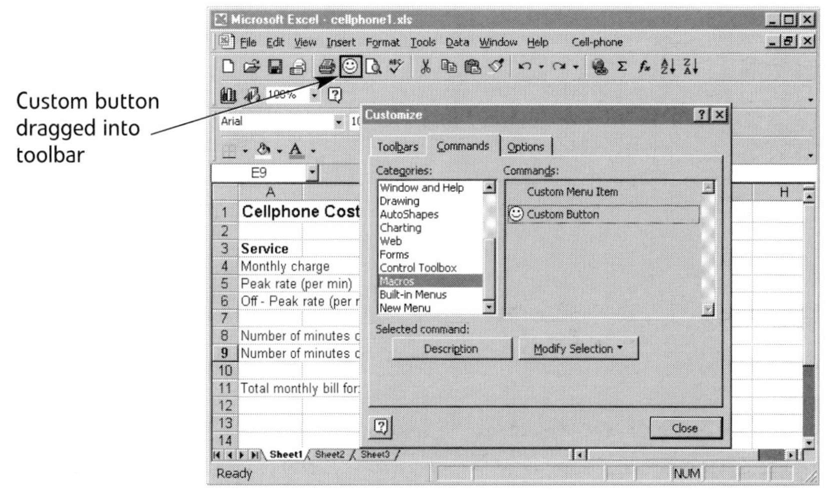


Figure 10.26 A customised button

## Customising a toolbar button

Once a button is in a toolbar, it can be customised and can be given a name, which will appear in the tool tip when the mouse is held over it. For our purposes, it also needs to have a macro assigned to it:

- Right-click on the button and the menu shown in Figure 10.27 will appear.
- Change the name to 'Clear Entries'.
- Click the Assign macro menu item at the bottom of the menu and select the clear_entries macro from the list that appears.

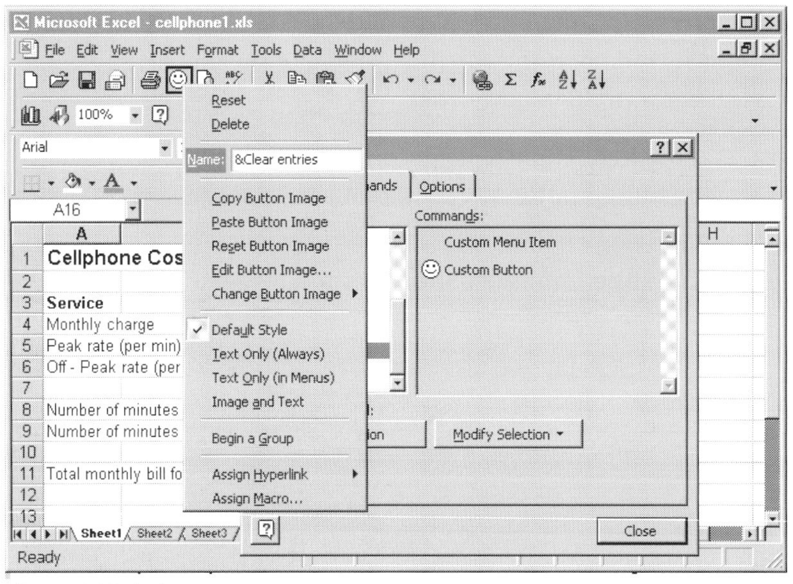


Figure 10.27 Assign macro

## Editing a button image

The button image can also be changed if the smiley face is not appropriate:

- Click on the Change Button Image menu item. A submenu appears with other button images that can be chosen. If none of the button images are suitable then the existing image can be edited.
- Choose the Edit Button Image option from the right click menu. The Button Editor dialogue will appear, as shown in Figure 10.28.
- By selecting the colour required in the Colours area and clicking on the cells in the Picture, the icon can be altered to achieve the required effect.
- Click OK to complete editing the picture and update the icon image in the toolbar.

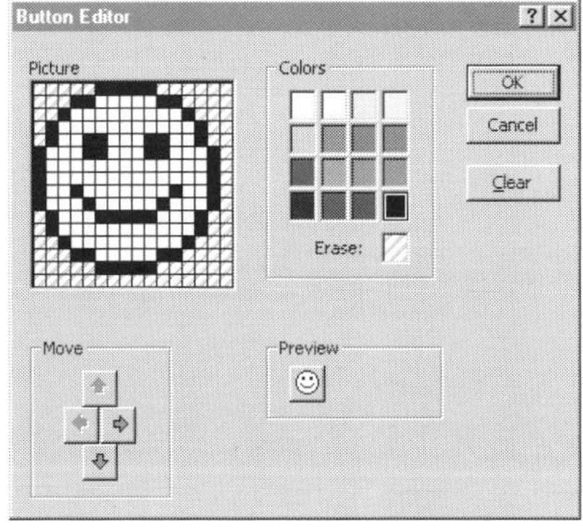


Figure 10.28 The Button Editor

## Creating a new toolbar

There is a problem with placing buttons like this in the standard toolbar. The button will now be there no matter what spreadsheet file you have open, yet the macro it is associated with only applies to the Cellphone spreadsheet. Running the macro in other spreadsheets may cause important data to be deleted. A better approach to attaching macros to toolbar buttons is to create a special toolbar for that particular spreadsheet. Remove the button from the standard toolbar, by returning to the Customise dialogue box (Commands tab) and dragging the button off the toolbar into the dialogue box. To create a special toolbar, follow these steps:

- From the Customise dialogue box, select the Toolbars tab.
- Click the New button.
- Give the new toolbar a name (e.g. custom1) and then click OK. A new, empty, toolbar will appear.
- Select the Commands tab on the Customise dialogue box, and then, as before, select macro from the list and drag the smiley face icon onto the new toolbar, see Figure 10.29.
- Use the icon's right click menu to change its name and to assign a macro as before.

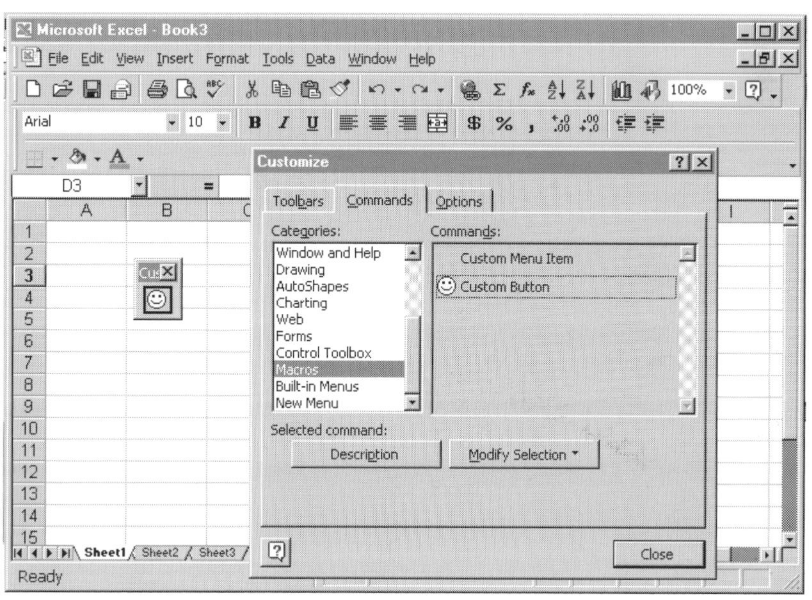

Figure 10.29 Placing an icon on a new toolbar

## Assigning a toolbar to a particular spreadsheet

This toolbar still suffers from the same problem as we had before, i.e. once you display a toolbar, it stays on the screen regardless of the spreadsheet file you have open. What is needed is some way of displaying this toolbar when this spreadsheet file is opened, and hiding it when it is closed. To do this, two special macros need to created:

- A macro called auto_open will run automatically when the spreadsheet file in which it is saved opens.
- A macro called auto_close will run when the spreadsheet file is closed.

Recording the auto_close macro is easy:

- Start the macro recorder as before, calling the new macro auto_close.
- Click the close button (with the 'x' in it ) on the new custom toolbar so it disappears, then stop the macro recorder.

Recording the auto_open macro is almost as simple:

- Run the recorder again, calling this macro auto_open.
- Go to the View menu, and choose Toolbars.
- Select the name of the custom toolbar from the sub-menu (custom1), so the toolbar reappears.
- Stop the recorder.

The new macros can be tested by closing the current file (the custom toolbar should disappear), then opening the file again (the toolbar should re-appear). The code for these two macros in the Visual Basic editor is shown in Figure 10.30.

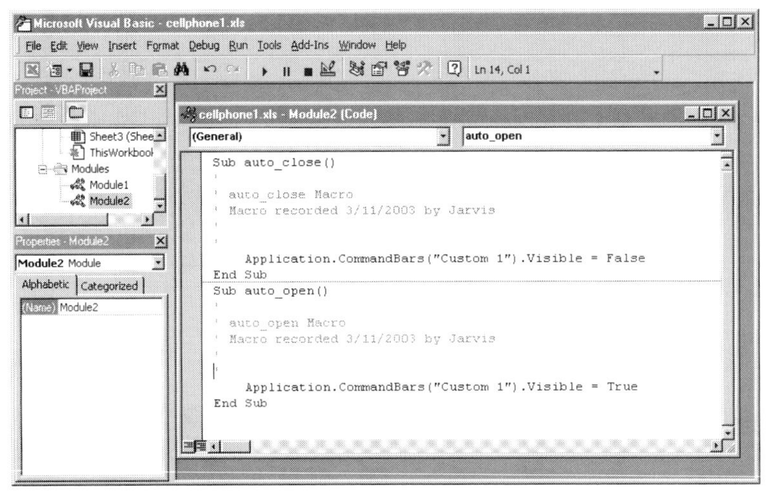


Figure 10.30 The code for the auto_open and auto_close

The auto_open and auto_close macros can be used for other things as well as displaying and hiding toolbars. Also, because as many buttons as needed can be added to a custom toolbar, it can contain buttons for a number of macros as well as standard spreadsheet functions.

## Check your understanding 10.13

1. Add a button to an existing tool bar, and then remove it.
2. Customise a toolbar button and then edit the image.
3. Set up a new toolbar, add some buttons to it and assign it to a particular spreadsheet file by setting up the two macros: auto_open and auto_close. Then, test your toolbar.

It is often a good idea to provide users with some form of help. This should provide instructions on how to use the application and how to deal with common problems. The simplest way to provide a help facility is to add a button (or a toolbar shortcut) which will take the user to another worksheet where help instructions are provided, using a text box. Alternatively, you can add pop-up **comments** to individual cells using the Comment option under the Insert menu.

# Creating menus

An alternative to using toolbar buttons to run the macros is to add a custom menu to the menu bar. To add a custom menu to the Cellphone cost calculator, follow these steps:

- Return to the Customise dialogue box, and select the Commands tab.
- In the Categories list, scroll to the bottom and select New Menu.

- Drag the word New menu from the Commands box on the right side of the dialogue box into the menu bar to the left of the Help menu.
- Right click on the New menu in the menu bar and fill in a name for the menu, Cellphone (Figure 10.31).

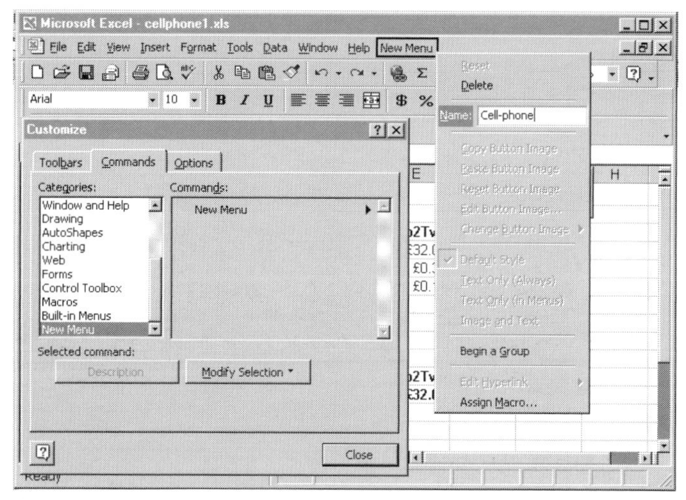


Figure 10.31 Adding a new menu

- Select Macros in the Categories list on the left side of the Customise dialogue box.
- Drag the words Custom Menu Item from the Commands box into the Cellphone menu in the menu bar, making sure it is dragged into the empty menu that pops down below the Cellphone menu name when the mouse is dragged over the Cellphone menu.
- Click on the Cellphone menu so it drops down showing the menu item and right click on that menu item to show the right click menu.
- Change the name of the menu item to Clear Entries.
- Use the Assign macro option to assign the clear_entries macro to this item.
- Close the Customise dialogue box.

A new Cellphone menu should now be displayed, with a single menu item, Clear entries. If this menu item is selected it will run the clear_entries macro (Figure 10.32).

Microsoft Excel - cellphone1.xls

File Edit View Insert Format Tools Data Window Help Cell-phone

Clear entries

F3

| | A | B | C | D | E | F | G | H |
|---|---|---|---|---|---|---|---|---|
| 1 | Cellphone Cost Calculator | | | | | | | |
| 2 | | | | | | | | |
| 3 | Service | | Mob-net | Vodacall | Two2Two | | | |
| 4 | Monthly charge | | £35.00 | £25.00 | £32.00 | | | |
| 5 | Peak rate (per min) | | £0.20 | £0.25 | £0.30 | | | |
| 6 | Off - Peak rate (per min) | | £0.12 | £0.15 | £0.10 | | | |
| 7 | | | | | | | | |

Figure 10.32 The Cellphone menu

However, a menu added in this way will suffer from the same problem as the first attempt to add a button to the toolbar, that is, it will always appear in the menu bar rather than just when the Cellphone spreadsheet is loaded. Just as it is possible to hide and display a toolbar button with auto_open and auto_close macros, so the menu bar can be modified. The changes needed to these two macros are shown in Figure 10.33.

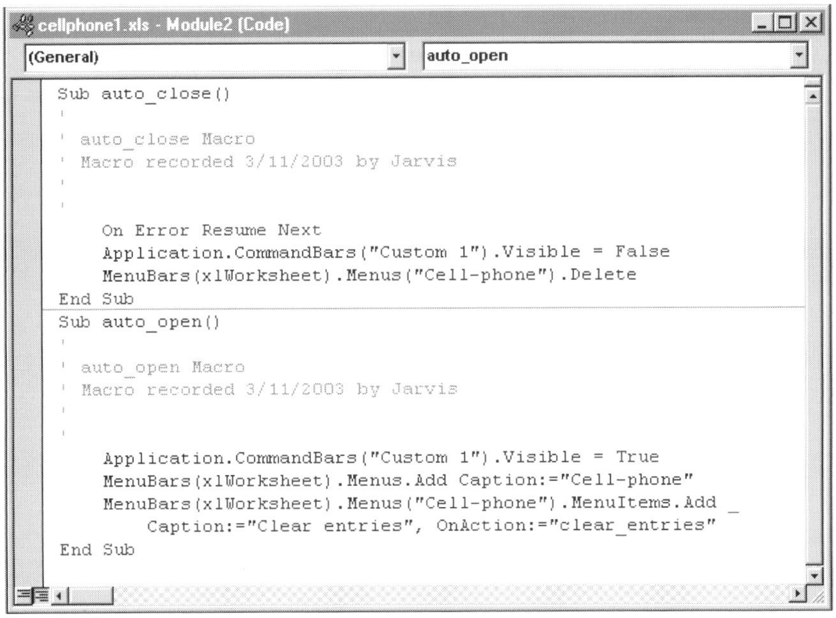

cellphone1.xls - Module2 (Code)

(General) | auto_open

```
Sub auto_close()
'
' auto_close Macro
' Macro recorded 3/11/2003 by Jarvis
'
'
    On Error Resume Next
    Application.CommandBars("Custom 1").Visible = False
    MenuBars(xlWorksheet).Menus("Cell-phone").Delete
End Sub
Sub auto_open()
'
' auto_open Macro
' Macro recorded 3/11/2003 by Jarvis
'
'
    Application.CommandBars("Custom 1").Visible = True
    MenuBars(xlWorksheet).Menus.Add Caption:="Cell-phone"
    MenuBars(xlWorksheet).Menus("Cell-phone").MenuItems.Add _
        Caption:="Clear entries", OnAction:="clear_entries"
End Sub
```

Figure 10.33 Creating and deleting the menu

**Assessment activity 10.3**

Customise the user interface of the application you have created by adding menus, toolbar buttons and dialogue boxes.

For the merit grade, you will need to add advanced features such as finding and printing specific records, printing customised reports, setting up and help file.

For the distinction grade, you will need to provide your application with a number of alternative ways of accessing the application's features which give it a professional appearance and make it easy to use.

# 10.4 Programming facilities

The subject of software development is covered in detail in Unit 4. You need to read that chapter before working through this section because concepts explained there are not repeated here. In this section, we look in more detail at some of the features of Visual Basic for Applications (VBA) programming language.

## Defining variables and constants

VBA allows the programmer to be lazy about defining variables. Explicit declaration of variables is not required; any variable can be used and it will automatically be defined and given a data type of **variant**.

**What does it mean?**

The variant datatype can hold any type of data.

There are rules for **variable names**:

- They must begin with a letter.
- They cannot contain a space, full stop, comma or dash.
- They must not exceed 255 characters.
- They must be unique within the procedure.

It is wise to give variables names that give some clue as to what they are used for, so, while x and variable1 are valid variable names, a name such as peak_mins is a better choice for a variable that holds the number of minutes of calls made at peak rate. Descriptive variable names make programs much easier to understand, particularly when problems occur with programs and you need to work out what is happening.

There are four basic data types:

- integer – for whole numbers
- single – for single precision floating point numbers
- double – for double precision floating point numbers (can contain more numbers both before and after the decimal point, and only really necessary for scientific calculations)
- string – for text.

Constants are similar to variables in that they reserve a memory area for a value, but, unlike variables, the values in constants cannot be changed (they are constant, hence the name). Declaring constant is done like this:

```
Const my_const = 3.14
```

where my_const is the name of the constant and 3.14 is the value assigned to it.

## Explicit declaration of variables

While not having to declare variables is convenient, it can lead to subtle errors in your code if you misspell a variable name. When VBA encounters a new name, it cannot determine whether the programmer actually meant to implicitly declare a new variable or it is just a misspelled existing variable name, so it creates a new variable with that name. To avoid the problem of misnaming variables, it can be stipulated that VBA always issues a warning whenever it encounters a name not declared explicitly as a variable:

- From the Tools menu, choose Options.
- Click the Editor tab and check the Require Variable Declaration option.

This automatically inserts the Option Explicit statement in any new modules, but not in modules already created; therefore, Option Explicit must be manually added to any existing modules within a project.

To explicitly declare a variable, the Dim instruction is used, so the instruction

```
Dim my_variable As Integer
```

will declare a variable with the name my_variable and a datatype of integer (whole numbers only).

## Scope of a variable

It is important when defining and using variables to understand the issue of the scope of variables. Variables defined in a procedure are local to that procedure, they have no meaning in other procedures, their scope is limited to the procedure they are defined in, and they are known as **local variables**. You can also define **global variables** whose scope extends across all the procedures in a module. Global variables are defined in the General Declarations section at the top of the module code window. This can be selected using the objects drop down box at the top of the code window, as shown in Figure 10.34.

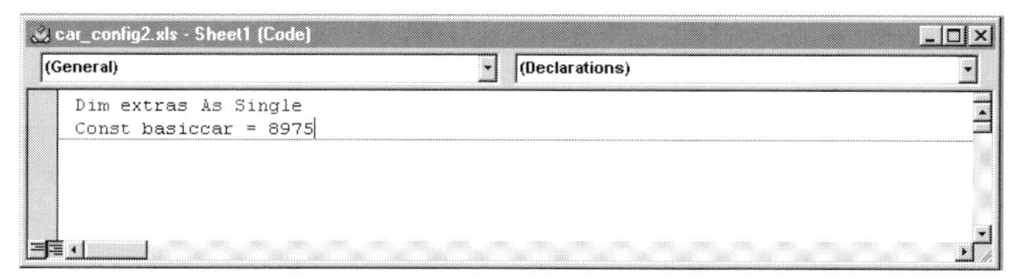

Figure 10.34 Declaring global variables

## Naming conventions

It is also important to choose descriptive variable names for objects such as command buttons, text boxes and list boxes. These are automatically given default names when you create them, for example, the first command button you create will be called CommandButton1. You should therefore rename these objects with descriptive names. However, to be able to tell which objects are command buttons, which are text boxes and so on, you should use a naming convention which adds a prefix to the name which identifies the type of object. So, a text box which holds the total of a calculation might be called Total, but to identify it as a text box the prefix txt is added so it is named txtTotal. The prefixes used for different objects are shown in Table 10.1.

| Object | Prefix |
|---|---|
| Text box | txt |
| Command button | cmd |
| List box | lst |
| Label | lbl |

Table 10.1 Object prefixes

# Creating procedures

VBA is an event-driven language, i.e. code procedures are run when certain events occur, such as an object is clicked or a mouse pointer is moved over an object. An example is given below to demonstrate how event procedures can be programmed, and also some of the points made earlier about variables. The spreadsheet shown in Figure 10.35 is used to calculate the cost of

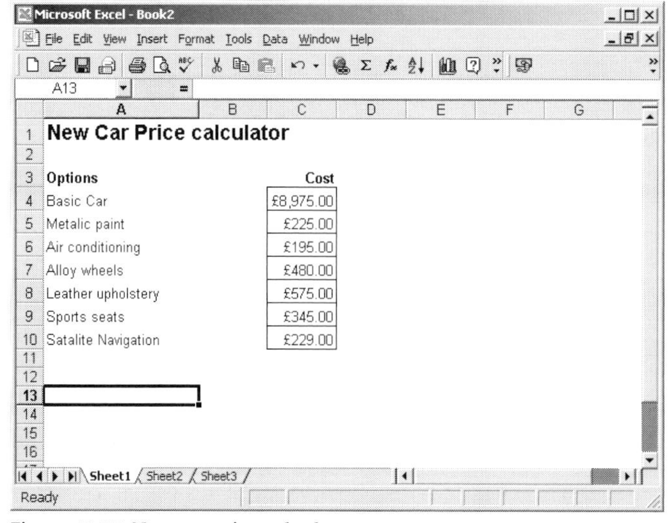

Figure 10.35 New car price calculator

a new car. Note that the gridlines can be turned off by clicking the Gridlines check box on the View tab of the Option dialogue on the Tools menu.

As well as the cost of the basic car, various extras can be chosen. To allow the customer to see how the cost of various extras affects the total cost, each item needs a **check box**:

- Clicking a check box puts a tick in the box, indicating the option has been chosen.
- Clicking the box again removes the tick.

## What does it mean?

**Check boxes** use a toggle; when you click them, if the tick is in the box it is removed; if it is not then it is added. A check box with the tick in it is known as checked, without the tick it is unchecked.

To add these types of controls, follow these steps:

- Display the Control toolbar (View menu, toolbars option).
- Add a check box for each option.
- Add a text box for the total, with a label so it is clear what it is for, as shown in Figure 10.36.
- Name each of these objects using the Properties window, as shown.

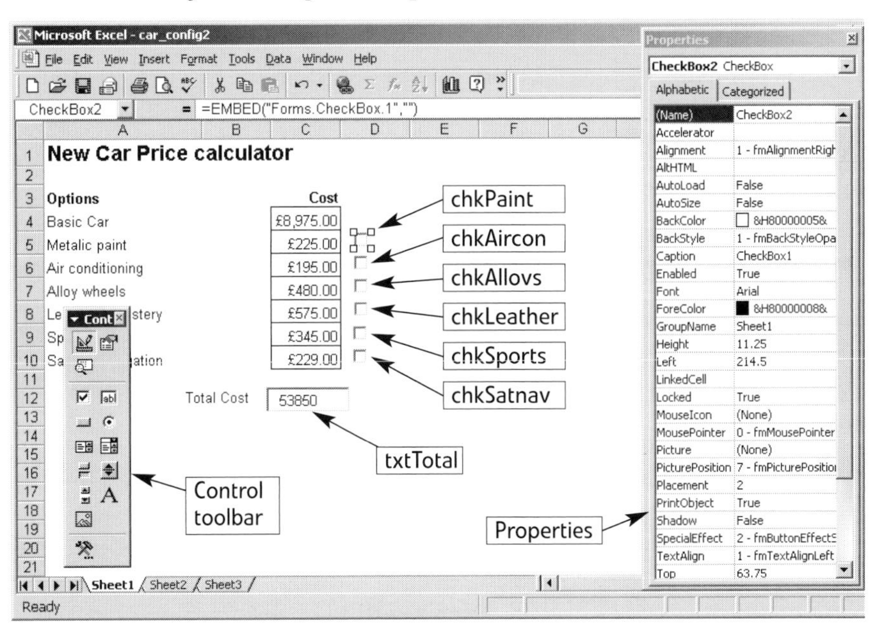

Figure 10.36 Object names

Event procedures are needed for each of the check boxes so when they are clicked they can test to see whether the tick has been added or removed from the box:

- If the box is checked then the cost of the corresponding extra is added to the total.
- If it is unchecked then the cost needs to be subtracted.

A variable is needed to hold the total cost of the options, and this variable needs to be available to all the different event procedures that are attached to each of the check boxes, therefore a global variable will be needed rather than a local one:

- Double-click the first of the check boxes (chkPaint) to open the Visual Basic code window. This will create an empty event procedure for the click event for this check box.

- To create the global variable, click on the object drop down box at the top of the code window and choose General from the top of the list.
- Use the Dim instruction to create a variable called extras, with a data type of single.

The cost of the basic car is also needed, which, as it does not change, can be held in a constant. The declarations for both the global variable and the constant are shown in Figure 10.37.

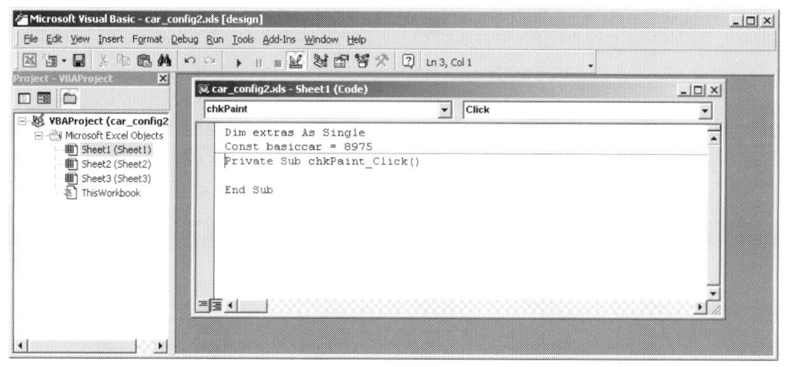

Figure 10.37 Creating a global variable

The code for the event procedure can now be written. As explained earlier, the procedure needs to test whether the check box is checked. Fortunately, this is easily done as the box has a value of true if it is checked and false if it is unchecked. Therefore, the state of the box can be tested with an if statement (objects which can only take the value of true or false are known as **Boolean**). However, before testing the state of the check box, the code needs to select the cell that contains the cost of the option, which for the first check box (for the cost of metallic paint) is C5. The code then needs to add the contents of C5 to the running total of extras if the box is checked, or subtract it if it is unchecked. Finally the cost of the extras needs to be added to the basic cost of the car and transferred into the total text box. The complete code is shown in Figure 10.38.

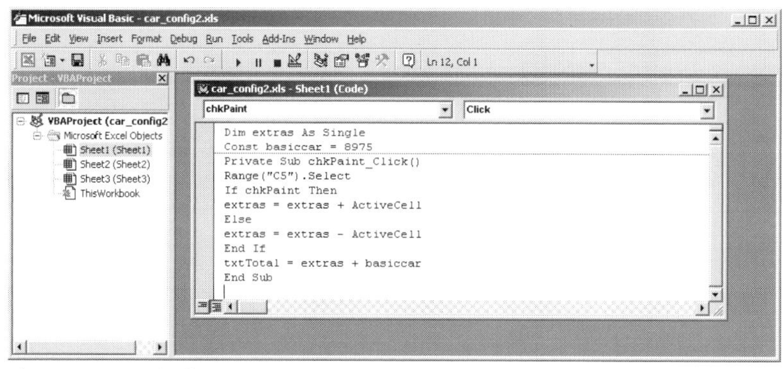

Figure 10.38 Code for the chkPaint procedure

Testing whether this works is straightforward:

- Return to the spreadsheet and click the check box next to the metallic paint option.
- The total cost in the total box will be shown as 9200 (basic cost of the car, £8975 plus the cost of the metallic paint option, £225).
- Click the check box again and the box becomes unchecked, so the total cost of the car becomes 8975.

The only problem is that the total cost of the car in the txtTotal box is not formatted as currency with a pound sign (£) and two digits after the decimal point. To correct this, modify the last line of the procedure so that it reads:

```
TxtTotal = format(extras +basiccar, "currency")
```

The event procedures for the other checkboxes are almost identical to the first one. All that needs to change is the cell that is selected in the first line and the name of the checkbox in the if instruction. It would be possible to simply copy and paste this procedure and make the changes for each of the checkboxes. However, repeating the same code time and time again is a sure sign that a function is needed.

# Creating functions

A function is a piece of code which carries out some clearly defined task. Excel and VBA have many built in functions which can carry out a variety of different tasks:

- carry out mathematical calculations such as averages
- convert dates into different formats
- do financial calculations such as calculate the interest payable on a loan.

As well as using the built-in functions, you can also write your own. The example used here tests the status of a checkbox in the car cost calculator program. Functions can be passed values from the procedure that calls them, and, in this case, the procedure needs to pass the function the check box that needs to be tested. The function itself will need a Boolean variable to hold the parameter that the calling procedure passes it. To create a function, follow these steps:

- Go to the Visual Basic window and from the menu bar choose Insert.
- Choose Procedure and you will see the Add Procedure dialogue box as shown in Figure 10.39.

Figure 10.39 The Add Procedure dialogue box

- Give the procedure a meaningful name, such as Test_checkbox, and set the Type to Function, then click OK. This will create an empty function in the code window. The empty set of brackets after the function name is where the variable must be declared that will hold the parameter that is passed to the function by the calling procedure. As already discussed, this must be a Boolean variable; therefore, this first line of the function must be modified so that it reads

  ```
  Public Function test_checkbox(checkbox_state as Boolean)
  ```

  where checkbox_state is the name of the variable used to hold the parameter passed to the function.

The rest of the code for the function can simply be cut from the original chkPaint procedure, leaving behind the first line of the this procedure (Range("C5").Select) as this line will be different for each checkbox click procedure, so it is not worth putting it in the function. The only modification needed to this piece of code is to change the if statement so it uses the checkbox_state variable. The complete code for the function is shown in Figure 10.40.

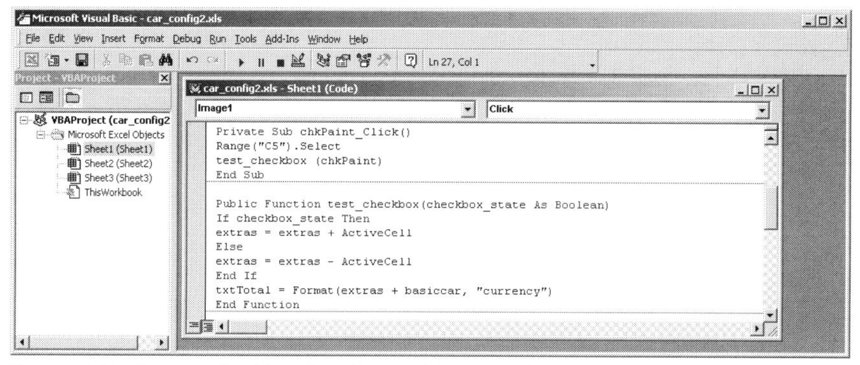

Figure 10.40 The test_checkbox function and the modified chkPaint procedure

The chkPaint procedure now needs to have the function call added to it, passing the function the check box as a parameter (see chkPaint_Click() code shown in Figure 10.40). The click event procedures for the other check boxes can now be created:

- Double-click on each check box in turn to create the empty event procedure.
- Copy and paste the procedure code from one of the other checkbox click event procedures.
- Change the cell that is selected to pick up the price of the particular option and change the name of the checkbox that is passed to the test_checkbox procedure.

The click event is not the only event that procedures can be written for. The next example demonstrates event procedures that respond to the **mousedown** and **mouseup events**; these occur when the user clicks and then releases the mouse button. This example adds a picture of the car to the car cost spreadsheet. When the user clicks the picture the image will change to a different picture of the car:

- First an image box must be added to the spreadsheet using the image box button on the Control toolbar.
- Then, using the picture property of the image box, select a suitable picture of a car (see Figure 10.41).

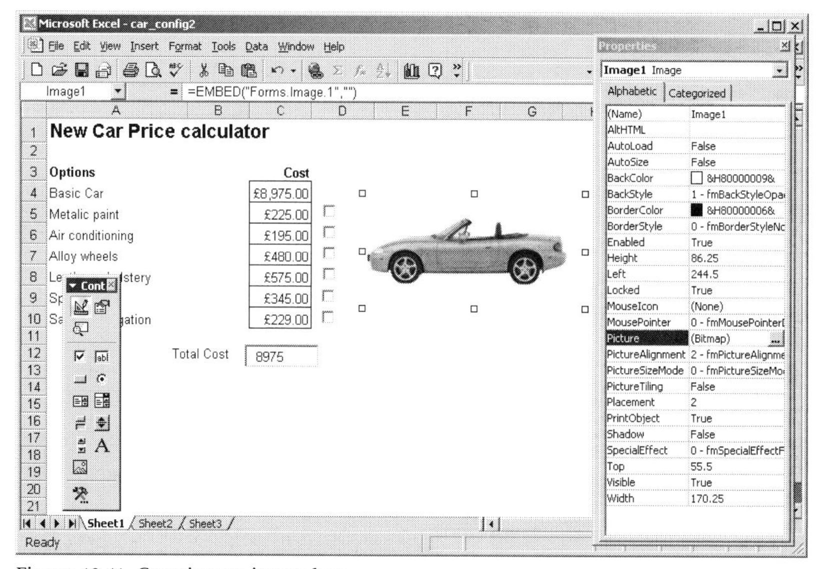

Figure 10.41 Creating an image box

- Double-click the image box, and by default a click event procedure is created.
- Use the Procedure drop-down box at the top of the code window to select the mousedown event, and an empty event procedure will be created for that event (the click event procedure can be deleted, although it will not cause any problems if it is not deleted).
- Enter the code to load a different picture into the image box, as shown in Figure 10.42.

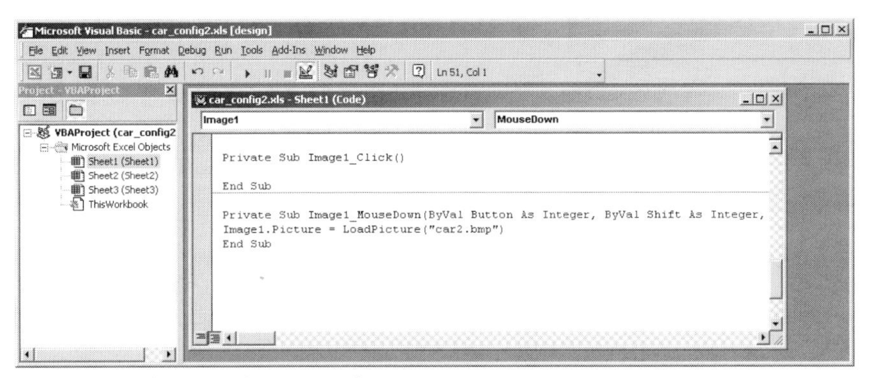


Figure 10.42 The Mousedown procedure

A mouseup procedure is also needed to revert to the original picture when the mouse is moved away form the image box:

- Select the mouseup name from the Procedure drop-down box.
- Enter the same code as in the mousedown procedure, but this time the image file name should be the original one.

**Assessment activity 10.4**

To obtain the merit grade your application will have to utilise some of the features of VBA such as defining local and global variables, reacting to various events and using functions.

For the distinction grade, you must use both a standard naming convention for objects and make appropriate use of functions to modularise your application.

# Debug facilities

Programs can become quite complex and difficult to follow, and when these programs do not work correctly, it can be very hard to work out why. To help you in these situations, Visual Basic has built-in facilities to help you to write correct programs in the first place. Other facilities are then available to identify the bugs in your programs. When writing a program, Visual Basic provides context sensitive help which provides a list of valid options when writing program instructions. An example is shown in Figure 10.43.

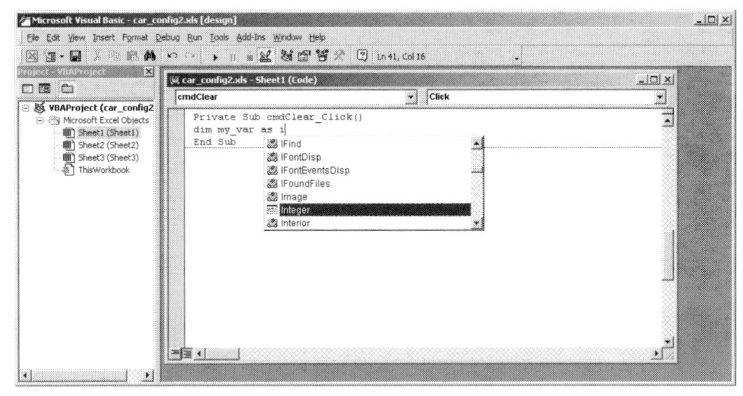


Figure 10.43 Context sensitive help

Visual Basic also checks the instructions as they are written and will display them in red if they are not valid, along with an error message, as shown in Figure 10.44.

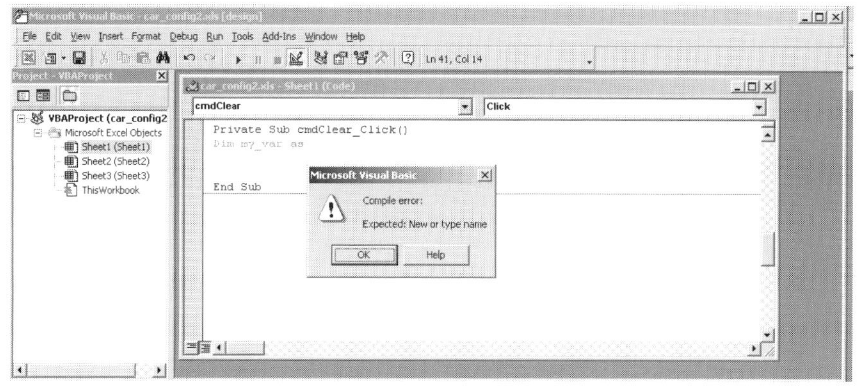


Figure 10.44 Invalid Instructions

However, even if your program statements are valid, when you run your program, it may either not work the way you want it to or it may fail unexpectedly. If the program fails unexpectedly (known as a **run-time error**), you will see a message such as that shown in Figure 10.45.

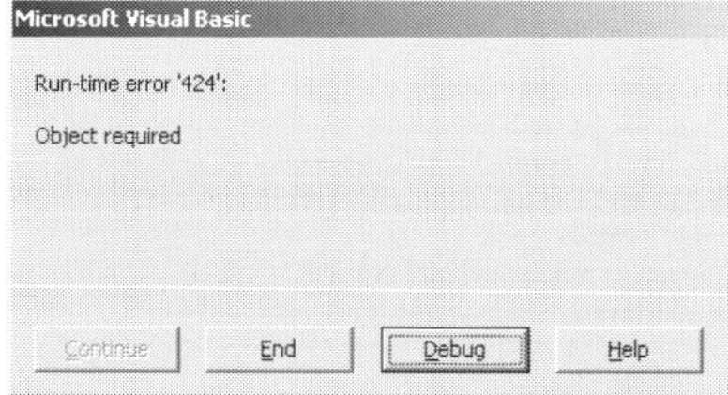


Figure 10.45 Run-time error dialogue box

If the Debug button is then clicked, the Visual Basic code window will open with the line that caused the failure highlighted, as shown in Figure 10.46.

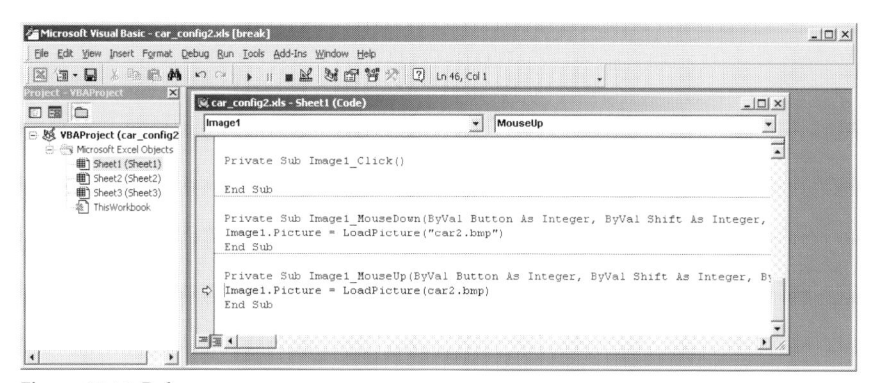


Figure 10.46 Debug screen

It may be that the program does not produce any run-time errors, but it still does not give the expected results. In these cases, it may be helpful to set what is called a **breakpoint**.

> **?**
> ### What does it mean?
> A **breakpoint** stops the program running at a chosen point so that the user can check the contents of each of the program variables.

The next example is from the car cost calculator:

The program is not working properly. It does not calculate the cost of the car correctly when the different options are added. A breakpoint is set at the point where the test_check box adds the cost of an option:

- Click at that point in the Visual Basic code window.
- From the Debug menu choose toggle breakpoint. This puts a maroon coloured bar though the code, indicating that a breakpoint has been set (Figure 10.47).

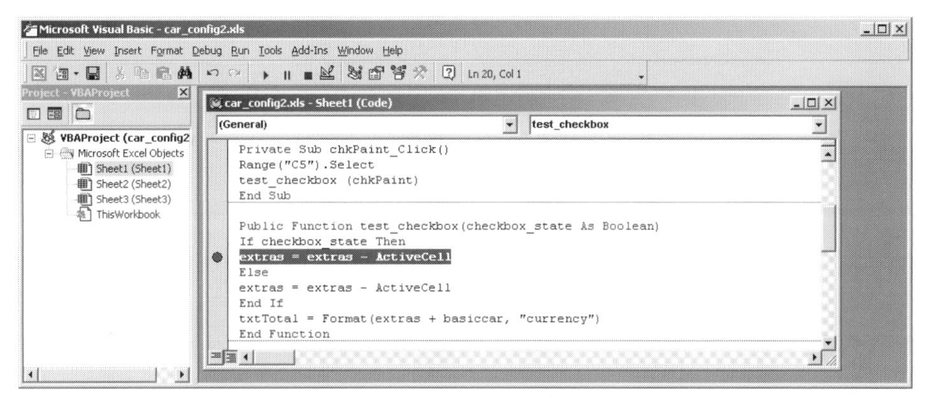


Figure 10.47 Adding a breakpoint

- Return to the spreadsheet and click one of the unchecked boxes. The code window will reappear with the breakpoint highlighted in yellow.
- Move the mouse pointer over any of the variable or object names, their value will be shown in a pop-up box (Figure 10.48).

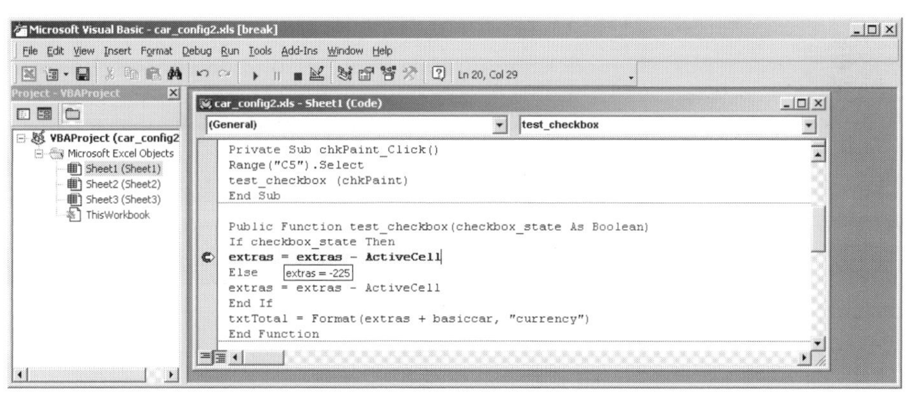


Figure 10.48 Viewing variable values

Being able to view the contents of the variables during the execution of the program can help to identify where things are going wrong. Once you have resolved the problems with the program, you can remove the breakpoint:

- Go to the Debug menu.
- Choose Remove all breakpoints.

## Assessment activity 10.5

Provide evidence that you have identified and corrected errors in your application. You can do this using the debug facilities explained in this section.

# Portability

Although it is not possible to create a stand-alone executable program with VBA, Excel VBA applications can be distributed to other users that have Excel installed, simply by giving them the .xls spreadsheet file that contains the application. To make applications easier to access, a shortcut to the spreadsheet file can be placed on the desktop and its icon can be changed so it looks like a stand-alone application rather than just an Excel spreadsheet. To create a shortcut, simply right click on the Excel file in Windows Explorer and choose Send to Desktop (Figure 10.49).

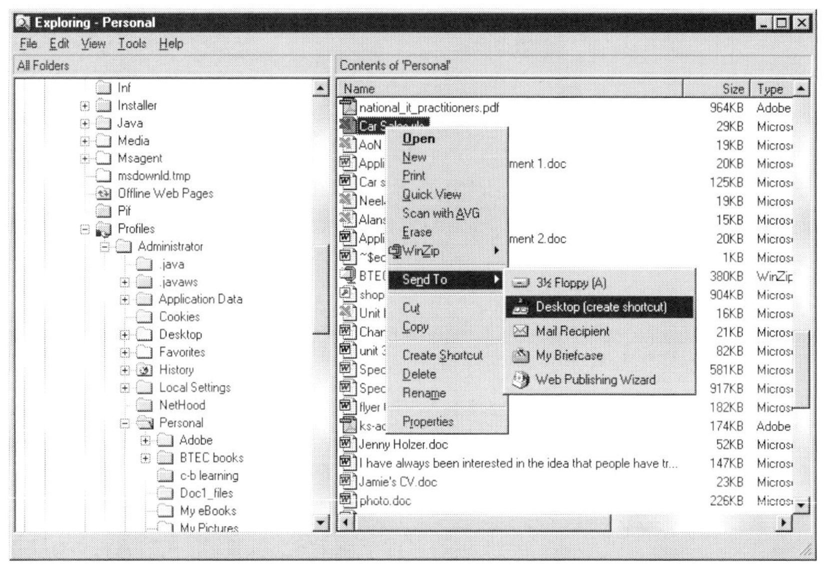


Figure 10.49 Creating a shortcut

You can change the icon for the shortcut displayed on your desktop by right clicking on it and choosing Properties. Then click the Change icon button and choose the icon you require (Figure 10.50).

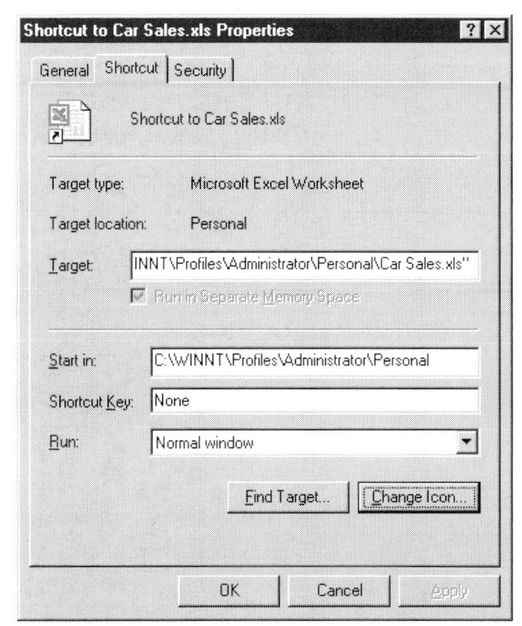


Figure 10.50 Properties dialogue for a desktop shortcut

Alternatively you could add a toolbar button to the standard Excel tool bar which runs a macro that opens the worksheet that contains your application. However, when you record the macro that opens your application you will need to use the *Store this macro in:* drop-down, and select the Personal Macro Workbook option. Macros stored in the Personal Macro Workbook are available to all Excel files, not just the one you save them in. Adding a button to the standard Excel toolbar in this way, users would be provided with an easy way to access the application from within Excel.

## Assessment activity 10.6

1 Provide a method of starting the application you have created, either from the desktop or from within Excel.
2 Provide evidence, including screen shots of how to run (execute) you application.
3 Create a document which shows how you developed your application starting with the plan you originally created, through the design stage to the final working application. You should include the diagrams you created during the planning and design stages, printouts of your worksheets and code modules and screen shots showing how the various features of your application, including shortcut keys and menu, work.

## Test your knowledge

1 List some of the techniques that can be used to design the data processing in an application.
2 What is the SUM function used for?
3 How can you make a formula use absolute addressing?
4 What is the simplest way to create a macro?
5 What are an object's properties used for?
6 What is a variable?
7 How can you test that user input is numeric?
8 What is a loop?
9 What name do you give to a macro you want to run when a spreadsheet opens?
10 What sort of data can be held in a variable with a data type of variant?
11 What is the difference between a local and a global variable? How do you create a global variable?
12 What is the meaning of the term Boolean?
13 How can you format a value as currency in VBA?
14 What is a function?
15 What is a breakpoint? What is it used for?

# UNIT 29: SOFTWARE DEVELOPMENT PROJECT

In this unit, you will plan and implement a software development project. It provides an opportunity for you to use some of the skills you have developed in the other units that you have studied. This unit is externally assessed through an IVA.

## Learning objectives

- To select, specify and plan an appropriate project
- To develop the project to the agreed specification and plan
- To implement the project
- To demonstrate and evaluate the project

# 29.1 Plan an appropriate project

You have to develop a piece of software to meet some realistic requirement. To do this, you will need to build on what you have learned in other units, particularly Units 5, 6 and 8. In addition, in Unit 3 you learned how organisations work and how they make use of computer software. You may be able to develop a piece of software to meet a business requirement. You could use the knowledge you gained in Unit 31 about website development to produce a web-based program.

It will be to your benefit to choose something you are interested in. At the same time, you need to make sure you choose something which you can achieve with the resources and the time that you have available.

Having decided on a project, you have to create a project plan which will identify the steps you need to go through to complete the project and set your timescales.

## Project selection

The first step is to decide on a suitable project. You must think of a project that involves software development and meets either a real computer user's need or a realistic imaginary need. This will involve you in some research and review of your areas of interest. You must make sure that whatever you decide to do, it meets the following requirements:

- *It must be within your own capabilities.* Be realistic about your own level of expertise, and try to choose a project that demonstrates your strengths, without revealing any weaknesses.
- *It must be possible within the resources you have available.* There are two main resources to consider: IT hardware/software and time. If the project you have in mind requires special software, you will have to check whether this can be made available in your school or college.
- *You must consider the constraints (limitations) that you have to work with.* Your teacher will almost certainly give you a deadline date by which the project must be completed; so, one constraint on your project will be that it must be completed by this date. Be realistic about the amount of time you are able to spend on this project and build in time for contingencies such as illness, lack of access to computers, etc. You will also have other work to do while working on the project so there will be a limited number of hours per week that you can dedicate to your project work. Most commercial projects are constrained by a budget, which limits the amount of money that can be spent on the project. In your case, the cost of completing the project will not be a financial one; instead, the cost will be in terms of your time and effort.
- *It must be interesting.* It makes sense to choose something that you are interested in. If you are interested in computer games, you might like to choose a project that involves creating a simple game. If you are interested in web development, you could consider developing an interactive website.

It is probably best to think of a number of ideas for a project, do some research into each idea to check whether it is feasible, and then make your final choice.

**Further research 29.1**

1. List your own strengths and weaknesses.
2. List the resources you have available.
3. List your own interests.

One technique that is very helpful in coming up with ideas is **brainstorming**. This is a method of free expression and can be great fun as well as very useful. Brainstorming is used when you have to create new ideas, and works best in groups. One person's idea may not be brilliant, and it may not be the answer to the problem, but it can trigger a better idea from someone else in the group. In this way, brainstorming stimulates the production of ideas.

Brainstorming can be a fun way of coming up with ideas

For any brainstorming session, you may be more successful if, before you start, you follow a few rules:

- Have a clear idea of your problem, e.g. 'To think of a suitable IT user or system problem'.
- Agree who is in your group and appoint someone as 'leader'. This person will make sure other rules are followed.
- Appoint someone else as 'scribe'. This person will write down ideas as they are suggested. A flip chart is excellent for this, but a large piece of paper will be fine.

The group size should be somewhere between four and eight. Fewer people means you may not be able to generate enough ideas. With more than eight people, it may become difficult for anyone to get a word in! When everyone is ready, remind yourself of the brainstorming 'goal posts':

- Each member is asked for an idea in turn.
- Each member can offer only one idea per turn; if they have no idea to offer they say 'pass'.
- All ideas are accepted, even if they seem really silly, and are written down. A flip chart is useful for this, because everyone can see it, and only one person has to take notes.
- While ideas are being generated, questions are only asked if an idea is not clear.
- No criticism, discussion, interruptions, comments or judgements are allowed during this early stage.
- Ideas are not evaluated during the brainstorming session at all, that is left until later.
- An informal atmosphere helps to create the right environment for new ideas.
- Exaggeration may be a useful tactic. It adds humour and can also provoke new ideas.

When no more new ideas can be thought of or time runs out, it is time to evaluate the ideas and pick out the best ones.

## Further research 29.2

1. Hold a brainstorming session to generate ideas for projects that you and the other students in your group could do.
2. From the list generated, identify several options that you can consider.
3. Make a list of possible projects.

The most successful projects tend to be based on a real-life need. So, take every opportunity to base your project on a real-life system problem, perhaps linked to your work experience or a work placement.

## Further research 29.3

Review your thoughts so far on a possible project. In groups compare your ideas, discussing their suitability and any problems that might arise.

### Assessment activity 29.1

Produce a basic project plan for your choice of project and write a brief report explaining how you identified this project as being suitable.

### Case study: Jessica and Winston

Jessica's little sister, Emma, has not long started school and she is learning to do addition and subtraction. Jessica decides to write a program using Visual Basic, which is an adding and subtracting game for her little sister to play.

Winston has developed a database which records students' assignment marks, and now he wants to add the facility for students to check their assignments on-line.

**What are the most important features of the programs Jessica and Winston are planning to develop?**

# Project specification

Once you have decided on the project, the next step is to identify and document the detailed requirements in a project specification. This involves finding out what the user needs the program to do. This will obviously work best if your user is real. You can have an imaginary user, but you will have to think up realistic requirements. It might help if you speak to someone who does a similar job to your imaginary user and ask what they would require from such a program. Having investigated what the user's needs are, you should document these needs in the project specification. This document will describe, in detail, what the program will do. You do not have to go into a great deal of technical detail about how the program will work; this will be covered later in the program design. You should include the following details:

- how the program will be started and exited
- what menu options will be available and what functions the program will provide
- the layout of the program forms or other screen output
- what data is input into the program
- how input will be validated and how invalid input will be dealt with
- what processing will be done on the input data (e.g. calculations)
- what output will be provided
- what reports or other printed output will be provided by the program.

The specification is an important document because not only does it tell the user what to expect from the program, but it should also be used later in the project for two important purposes:

1. When creating your test plan, the specification should tell you what the correct result is for any particular input (e.g. what inputs are valid and invalid and how invalid data should be dealt with).
2. When completing your evaluation, you should refer back to the specification to see whether the program you produced actually does what you said it would.

In the real world, the project specification is usually agreed by the customer and forms a legally binding contract describing what the software developer will provide. You should ask your teacher to review your specification document to ensure that it is sufficiently detailed and that it is achievable within the timescale and with the resources available.

### Assessment activity 29.2

Write the specification for the program you are planning to develop, describing the user facilities and technical aspects of your proposed program.

### Case study: Jessica

Jessica arranges a meeting at Emma's primary school with her teacher. The teacher is very interested in the idea of a computer game to help the children to practise their adding and subtracting. The teacher points out there is only one computer in the classroom so it would be useful if the program recognised each child's name and remembered how well that child had done the previous time. The program should also restrict the time each child can use the program and prevent the same child using the game twice in a row. The program would only need to ask the children to do sums with whole numbers between 1 and 10. As the children receive 'smiley face' stickers for good work, it would be good if the program also awarded smiley faces based on how well they did. At the end of each child's session, the program should print a report showing the sums done and the smiley faces awarded.

**What are the advantages of using a computer game to help the children, compared with other ways maths practice could be provided?**

# Project planning and management

Once you have completed your project specification, you need to start work on your project plan, showing how it is broken down into phases. Your project should have at least five phases and each will require you to use various tools that you have learned about in other units:

- *Initial fact-finding and investigation:* Using techniques such as interviews, observation and questionnaires will help you to develop a clear understanding of the current situation, and what the new system needs to do.
- *Analysis:* Using structured tools such as data flow diagrams, you can describe how the product will work.
- *Design:* Detailed technical descriptions will be needed of how the solution will be implemented. This may involve using process modelling tools such as structure charts and pseudo code.
- *Implementation:* This involves producing the system, using the design as a guide.
- *Testing and documentation:* At this stage, you will be creating a test plan to check that the system works correctly and writing user and technical documentation.

Refer back to Unit 6 for details of the major phases of the software development process. Each phase should then be broken down into individual tasks (such as interview users, draw dataflow diagrams, etc.) You will need to show when you plan to do each task (some tasks will have to be done in a certain order) and how long you estimate each task will take.

One of the problems you may face during this project is completing everything on time. Your plan must show not only how long each task takes but also by which date each individual task will be complete. Then, once the project is underway, you can monitor your actual progress against your plan. Remember that the project must be completed by a certain date, so, if some tasks take longer than expected you will have to make up time later on. Estimating the time each phase will take can be difficult. The design phase of your project should take about a quarter of the time you spend on the whole project.

It is important to produce a good design, as this is the foundation of your product; you cannot produce a good product from a poor design. When estimating the duration of each task you will have to consider how long it took to complete similar tasks in other units, and also seek guidance from your teacher. Your plan should identify timescales, deliverables and milestones:

- **Timescales** specify when you plan to start doing each task and how long you estimate it will take.
- **Deliverables** are things that you will actually provide, such as a working network, user documentation, etc. You will need to identify a date by when you plan to complete each of your project deliverables.
- **Milestones** are important events that occur as your project progresses, such as gaining approval for the software design.

One useful project-planning tool is the **Gantt chart** (Figure 29.1). This displays planned and actual progress against a horizontal timescale. As well as showing when each task is due to begin and end, it shows the dependencies between tasks, and from this a 'critical' path of a project can be deduced.

Some tasks are dependent on each other and one cannot be started until the other is completed. For example, when analysing the system you cannot draw low-level data flow diagrams until you have drawn the high-level ones. Other tasks, however, may be unrelated and can be completed in parallel, i.e. at the same time. Critical path analysis involves identifying tasks that, if delayed, because of their dependent tasks, would cause a delay in the completion date for the whole project. Special attention must be paid to completing these tasks on time because of their critical importance in completing the whole project on time.

When allocating a duration for each task, it is usually easier to work from the deadline backwards. If you then find you seem to have too much to do in the available time, you may need to rethink your project. Are you taking on too much? Do you need to allocate more time to the project?

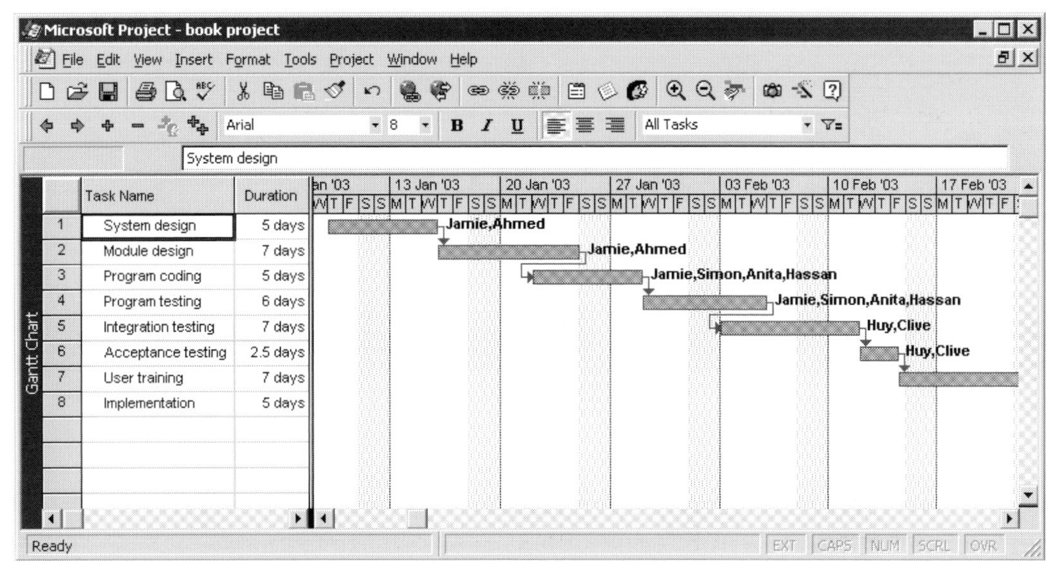

Figure 29.1 A Gantt chart

Once your project proposal is complete, you have to present it to your teacher, and obtain his or her permission to proceed. You will need to convince your teacher about two aspects in particular:

- Is what you are proposing **worthwhile**? In other words, does it meet some genuine user need?
- Is what you are proposing **achievable**? Is it within your capabilities, and can you complete it with the time and resources available?

Your teacher may ask you some searching questions about your project so you must be clear in your own mind what you intend to do. You may have to argue your case, so make sure you have prepared well for the meeting.

### Check your understanding 29.1

You may find it helpful to run through your proposal with a friend beforehand. Another person may see your product from a different point of view and identify problems that you have missed.

Do you have a clear idea of what your real or imaginary users will need from your program? Vague descriptions like 'calculate results' and 'input data' probably need more detail added. Even if your users are imaginary, you should still decide a clear set of well-defined requirements.

### Case study: Jessica

As Jessica's project is based on programming, she needs to produce a program design for her product. She uses the techniques of structure diagrams and pseudo code she learned in Unit 4. She also produces a sketch of the screen design her program will use, and of the report it will print out. She remembers that she will need to find a clip art file of a smiley face. In terms of resources she will need:

- regular access to a computer with Visual Basic installed
- a book or manual on Visual Basic (her college library has several)
- some help and advice from her programming lecturer
- some time with Emma's teacher (an hour or so to have a look at her prototype, and a couple of hours to show the finished product and help her evaluate it).

1 Draw up a list of the project phases and the tasks within those phases for Jessica's project.
2 Estimate how long each task will take and draw a simple Gantt chart.

# 29.2 Develop the project

Once you have permission to proceed, the next stage is to design your project in more detail. The design stage is very important. Producing something from a poor design will never result in a successful project.

## Design structure

Software design is a complex process and a number of different methodologies have been developed during its relatively short history. Methodologies provide a framework in which the design of the system can be modelled, and are intended to improve the efficiency of the software development process and improve the quality of the resulting system. The choice of methodology will depend on the following:

- *The type of project you are attempting:* For example, if the software you are developing will work with a database then techniques of data analysis such as entity relationship modelling may be relevant. If you are planning a control system, you will need to use real-time design techniques.
- *The techniques you are familiar with:* You will probably have used the structured design technique known as SSADM, described in Unit 6, but other techniques exist such as object-orientated development.

Whatever design techniques you use, you will have to produce designs for the various parts of your program:

- The forms or screens used will need to be designed, using simple sketches or, if your program has more sophisticated graphics (such as a game), you may want to use storyboards.
- The processing in your program will need modelling using techniques such as structure charts or pseudo-code. If you are using object-orientated techniques, you will need to complete your object design and use appropriate methods.
- Your data will need analysing and designing using techniques such as entity relationship diagrams.

### Assessment activity 29.3

Compare a number of possible solutions to meet the requirements of your project and select the most appropriate. Select an appropriate design method and create a design for your project.

# Development

One choice you have to make at this stage is the software you will use to develop the program. There are lots of programming languages available. Many, such as Microsoft® *Visual Basic* and Borland *Delphi*, are built into commercial software.

Your choice of development environment will be dictated by what you have available and what you are familiar with. It would be unwise to attempt to develop your project using a language you have not used before. Some development environments are better suited to particular applications. For example, if you are developing a web-based system then you need to consider program languages such as *JavaScript* or *PhP*. If you are going to create a program that interfaces with a database such as Microsoft® *Access*, then Microsoft® *Visual Basic* has built-in tools to allow you to connect the *Access* databases.

### Case study: Winston

Winston considers which web programming language he should use to develop his online assignment marks system. A database he has developed uses Microsoft® *Access*, so the logical choice is the Microsoft product designed to provide web access to Microsoft® databases, *ASP*. Several different programming languages can be used with *ASP*, but as Winston has already used *Visual Basic* he decides to use *VBscript*, which is related to *Visual Basic*.

**What programming languages could you use to write your project? Make a list of the advantages and disadvantages of each.**

## Documentation

You need to carefully document your design and your project plan. You need to take the diagrams you have used in the design stage and produce a written narrative that describes them. The same is true of the project plan you have produced.

Your design and project plan are both dynamic documents in that you will use and update them throughout the implementation of the project. As the program is written, you may well find that the original design is inadequate or incorrect in places. In these circumstances, you need to modify the original design to reflect the changes you found necessary. You should keep track of these changes; they will form part of the evaluation that you need to complete at the end of the project. Also, as the project progresses, you should compare your original project plan with the tasks you actually complete and the time they take. Tracking actual progress against the original plan is important because it helps you to identify whether you are running late. This tracking information will also help you when you come to write your evaluation at the end of the project.

### Case study: Jessica

Jessica's project starts off well, and goes according to plan. However, four weeks into the project she gets the flu and is off for a week, which puts her behind. She also underestimates how difficult the programming is and how many problems she will run into. This puts her another three weeks behind schedule. With the deadline approaching rapidly, she decides she will have to leave out the part of the program that prints a report on each child's progress. Unless she does this, her project will not be complete by the deadline.

**How could you avoid the sort of things that delayed Jessica's project from preventing you from completing your project on time?**

# 29.3 Implement the project

Once the design is complete, you need to begin work on the product. The more detailed the planning and design you have done at earlier stages, the easier this stage will be.

## Implementation

There are various approaches to the implementation of a product to consider; prototyping and incremental development are two possible approaches.

- **Prototyping** involves building a simplified version of the application, perhaps with limited functionality, and then showing it to your user to see how well it meets their needs. If it is not a good match, you can modify your approach at an early stage, rather than finding out you have misunderstood the user's needs when the project is almost complete. An advantage of this approach is that it can help you to produce an application that matches more closely your user's needs, and allows you to include ideas and suggestions in the final product.
- **Incremental development** is similar in some ways to prototyping in that, rather than developing the complete full-featured product from the start, the product is developed in a number of stages, starting with a fairly simple, limited functionality version and then

adding additional functions in a number of stages. The advantage of this approach, particularly in your situation, is that if things take longer to develop than you envisaged then, even if you run out of time, you will have a version of the application completed, albeit with limited functionality.

The design you have previously completed should guide your progress, but you will probably find there are problems or tasks that you did not anticipate at the design stage. You must go back to your time plan regularly, check your progress and amend your plan if things have not gone as you planned. Without this monitoring, you may find yourself bogged down in one small area of the project and, when the deadline arrives, the rest of the project is incomplete.

**Assessment activity 29.4**

Compare the various languages that could be used to implement your program and select the most suitable. Implement your program using the design you created and the software you chose.

# Testing

When testing your product, you need to be sure that it works both when it is being used correctly and when it is being used incorrectly. You should remember that the user of the product might not be an expert in using computers, so it needs to be easy to use and difficult to break – in other words, robust and idiot proof.

Your testing needs to be systematic and thorough. As well as testing the product yourself, it helps to have someone else test it. Because you have been working closely on the project, you may not notice if something is wrong. Someone who understands how the system works and yet is unfamiliar with it may spot something you have missed. The testing process you follow will involve you creating a test plan that defines how you will do both the **data testing** and the **event testing**.

**What does it mean?**

**Data testing** checks that the program can deal correctly with the data that is input by the user and produces the correct output.

**Event testing** involves checking that the program responds correctly to the choices the user makes; for example that when the user clicks a certain button or makes a certain menu choice, the correct menu appears or correct action takes place (e.g. a printout is produced).

For data testing, you need to produce some test data for input into your application, including both valid and invalid data, and to list the expected result that the program should produce when this data is input. (You may need to refer back to your original specification to check what the results should be.) You must then input the test data into the program and record the actual results. Any differences between the expected and actual results will need further investigation as this indicates that the program is not working as it should. Where faults are identified, you must correct your program and then fully re-test it to check that your corrections have been successful and that you have not accidentally introduced any other faults.

Event testing can be done by simply making a list of all the choices that the user can make and then checking that, when each choice is made, the correct event occurs. You will need to make sure that all the different combinations of choices and options that can be made, produce the desired results.

**Assessment activity 29.5**

Carry out testing of your system using a test plan. Complete the test plan and gather evidence of any errors discovered and your corrections.

# Documentation

You also need to produce two sets of documents, **user documentation** and **technical documentation**.

**What does it mean?**

**User documentation** explains to the user how the product is to be used.
**Technical documentation** explains how the product was created.

Depending on the type of software you develop, the user documentation might include the following details:

- how to start and exit the software
- examples of how the software can be used, including screen shots
- explanations of the different types of input that can be made
- explanations of the different types of output than the program can produce
- what error messages mean
- what different menus, toolbars, buttons and icons are for
- a troubleshooting guide and a FAQ (frequently asked questions) section.

Remember to use language that your users will be able to understand. Unless they are computer experts, technical jargon will only confuse them. Remember also that you may have to explain some things to novice users that would be obvious to computer experts.

**Check your understanding 29.2**

The things you include in your user documentation will, to some extent, depend on the type of program you are developing. Make a list of the things you will include.

The content of the technical documentation will depend on the type of product you have created, but may include the following details:

- the document you created at the design stage
- hardware and software requirements
- lists of modules or procedures
- lists of names, locations and contents of files required
- details of testing carried out (test plan)
- designs of database tables.

**Check your understanding 29.3**

What things will you include in the technical documentation for your program?

## Installation

Having designed, written, tested and documented your program, it is now ready to be installed and given to your users. Even if your users are imaginary, you will find it enlightening to install your program on a friend's computer and ask that person to try it out. Having worked on your program for many months, you will know it very well and understand how it should be used. Your users, on the other hand, will not have seen the program before (unless you provided them with a prototype) and you may be surprised at their comments and how they use the program. This is the real test of your project. If your users are happy with it, find it easy to use and effective, you have truly succeeded. However, you should not be surprised or disappointed if they find things which are confusing or do not work the way they expect. Their reactions should provide some good material for your evaluation.

# 29.4 Evaluation

Finally, it is important that you review your work. Producing an evaluation helps you to understand what you have learned and what you might be able to do better next time. Because others may benefit from your experiences, it is a good idea to present your evaluation to your fellow students and teachers.

## Demonstration

Demonstrating a program to a group of people can be a daunting task. Preparation and making sure you are organised beforehand is the key to any demonstration running smoothly. Plan your demonstration well ahead of time, making notes on what you will cover. Make sure that your demonstration has a sensible structure:

- *Introduction:* what the program is for, what you will cover
- *The main demonstration:* show the program carrying out some realistic task
- *Conclusion:* explain what you have shown your audience
- *Any questions?*

Run through the whole demonstration several times before you do it for real, making sure that everything works as you expect.

It is essential to consider your audience when planning the demonstration of your program. Make sure you plan to cover the things they will want to hear and that you explain things in a way they will understand.

## Documentation

Your written evaluation should cover these four points:

1 **Your design and planning**
   - Was it realistic? Did you run out of time? If so, why?
   - Did your project follow your plan closely or did you have to constantly modify the plan?
   - How closely does your finished product match your original design? If there are differences, why?

2 **Your use of time and resources**
- How would you improve your product if you had more time?
- Were you able to use the resources you needed when you needed them?
- How would you improve your product if you had more and better resources?

3 **What did you learn?**
- What worked well and what worked not so well, and why?
- What techniques did you use that you might use again?

4 **What does the user think of the product?**

This is the real test of success; after all, your product should have been designed to meet the needs of a user.
- How did the user react when he or she tried the product? Was the user happy with it? If not, why not?
- Did the user find the product easy to use? Was the user documentation suitable? If not, why not?
- Did your product meet the needs of the user?
- Were there any improvements the user could suggest to your product?

### Assessment activity 29.6

Collate all the documentation you have produced during the project, including the project specification, project plan, design, user and technical documentation to provide full documentation for all the stages of the project.

Write an evaluation of the project comparing the program you developed with the original specification and plan. Demonstrate that all user requirements have been met. Propose recommendations for how the program could be further improved in the future.

### Test your knowledge

1. What are the objectives of a brainstorming session?
2. Explain the rules of brainstorming.
3. Explain what is meant by 'resources'.
4. What is described in the project specification?
5. What are the main phases of a project?
6. What is a Gantt chart?
7. Describe the purpose of critical path analysis.
8. What is prototyping?
9. What is meant by incremental development?
10. What does the term 'robust' mean?
11. Distinguish between data and event testing.
12. Distinguish between user and technical documentation.
13. Give three tips for anyone about to embark on a project.

# UNIT 32: VISUAL PROGRAMMING

The aim of this unit is to enable you to appreciate the programming languages that use a visual and object-oriented environment. More and more programming languages are becoming object-oriented and a visual environment is a perfect way for you to learn this. It aims to take the programming skills that you have already acquired and help you to transfer this knowledge to a visual environment. It uses the jargon from *Visual Basic*, but the principles apply to any visual programming environment. This unit presents opportunities for you to demonstrate Key Skills in communication, information technology, improving own learning and performance and problem solving.

## Learning objectives

- To demonstrate an understanding of the tools and techniques available for programming in a visual environment
- To investigate, review and produce examples of graphical programs
- To create and use graphical objects using suitable programming techniques for a specific purpose
- To evaluate graphical programs produced and suggest improvements

# 32.1 Programming in a visual environment

The languages that you have learned so far have given you general programming skills. Unit 8 covers this in detail. Programmers who built early Windows-targeted systems used these **procedural languages** such as C. The program is in control of what happens next; it performs a series of actions based on the user's expected input. Similarly, programming a server, when there is a well-defined process of input, process and output to the problem or when there is a batch system, uses a procedural or traditional programming language.

However, in the Windows® environment, the user needs to be in control, because, at almost any time, he or she can click the mouse anywhere on the screen, press a key, move the mouse, select from a menu or switch from window to window. A visual programming language is used when what is wanted from the program is event-driven, PC or screen-based. It is also used when graphics or the user interface are an important part of the computer system.

**Check your understanding 32.1**

1 List different types of computer program, for example, payroll system, PC 'arcade' game, word processor.
2 Say whether you would write each in a visual or procedural language or either, giving the reasons for your choice.

## Graphical components

A number of new concepts in visual programming are defined here. Later in this unit, they are explained in more detail and examples given of how they are used.

An **event** is a message that is sent out to alert that something has happened. For example, there could be a screen or form containing a button with a 'click' event defined that alerts when the user clicks the button. To take action on this click, the program needs an **event handler routine**. This runs when the event happens and the code gives instructions to the computer as to what to do.

**Check your understanding 32.2**

1 Write code to create a form with a button.
2 Write a click button event handler which changes the text on the button when clicked, e.g. from sentence case to 'all caps' case.
3 Test that this code works.

In a real visual application, the user clicking an 'OK' button often causes the main body of the program to run. When the user clicks an 'Exit' button, it returns control to either a higher level of the program or to the operating system. A click on the 'Cancel' or 'Undo' button needs code to return the user's environment to the state it was in before the code made its last set of changes.

**Check your understanding 32.3**

For a desktop program you know, list some of the buttons that it has from its menus and icons. List the actions from each of these buttons.

A **class** is the specification that lets the developer create an object. The developer may create a class based on an existing class, and the new class can inherit (include) all the methods and properties of the existing class. This is called **inheritance**. The developer can then override (change) some of these methods and properties to create a class with the exact specification that is wanted. A class library offers the developer already written components that do many of the actions that may be needed in a program. By including them in a program, with appropriate inheritance and overrides, the developer can produce a program with much reduced effort and time.

**Check your understanding 32.4**

1 Find where on your system your class library is.
2 Find where it is documented.
3 How is it included in any program that you write?

# Visual programming languages

Visual programming languages such as Visual BASIC (VB) and Visual C++ are used in creating software with a graphical user interface (GUI). Visual BASIC and Visual C++ are developments of the traditional languages, BASIC and C++. In addition to the procedural capabilities of their predecessors, they have an object-oriented programming (OOP) development environment to create applications that run under Windows®. The example below shows two fragments of code, one in BASIC and one in Visual BASIC, to reveal similarities and differences between the two languages.

Basic

```
Print "Hello World"
```

Visual Basic

```
Private Sub Form_Load
Form1.show
print "Hello World"
End Sub
```

# Programming languages for creating web page applets

Web pages initially brought text, graphics and hyperlinks to open up the world of the Internet. However, these pages were essentially static; any changes to the screen had to be driven from the server. To make web pages more dynamic, the concept of an applet was developed. This is a form of program that is downloaded from a server as part of a web page. It provides local functionality without the browser user having to load a special program. In the mid-1990s, Sun Microsystems developed the language Java (probably the best known of these languages) as a programming language and environment that would run in a web browser. Within security restrictions, users can interact with Java applets as they would with any program resident on their computer. The developer can also write Java applications which run on a server.

*How does a Java applet work?* The developer writes the applet in Java code for a Java virtual machine (JVM). This is then compiled into bytecode, which is a hardware and browser independent language. The developer then codes an HTML web page which includes the bytecode, surrounded by <APPLET> tags. At run-time, the user downloads the web page. The user's Java-aware browser interprets the bytecode into hardware and operating system specific code that then runs on the user's computer. This is usually done to provide dynamic graphics, animation or a very fast response time to expected user actions such as simple games. Java is a development of C++ and has many similar features.

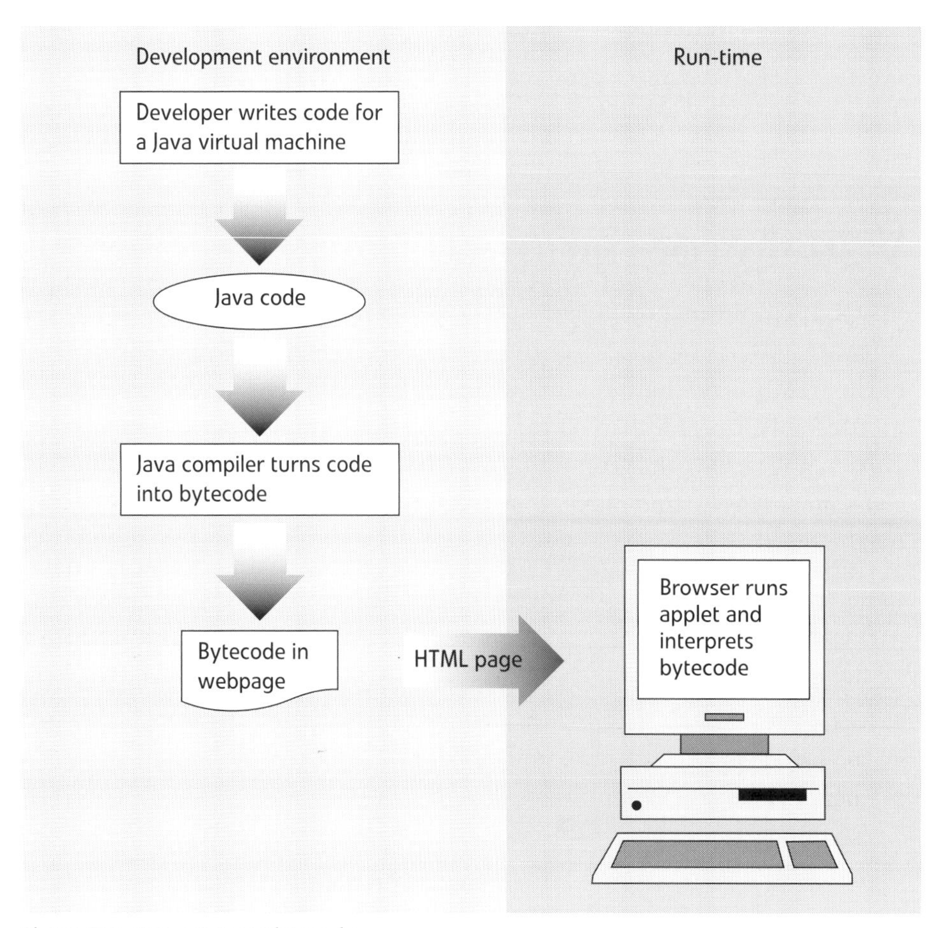


Figure 32.1 How a Java applet works

Here is Hello World written as a Java applet:

```
import java.applet.Applet;
import java.awt.Graphics;
public class HelloWorld extends Applet {
```

```
public void paint(Graphics g) {
g.drawString("Hello world!", 50, 25);
}
}
```

Here it is as a Java application:

```
/**
 * The HelloWorldApp class implements an application that
 * simply displays "Hello World!" to the standard output.
 */
class HelloWorldApp {
public static void main(String[] args) {
System.out.println("Hello World!"); //Display the string.
}
}
```

Source: Sun Microsystems at http://java.sun.com

# Visual environment

The visual environment comes in two forms.

- The **design-time environment** is where the programmer writes code. For more information about this, see page 311.
- The **run-time environment** is where the program performs its business function for the user. This could be as simple as adding two numbers together, or as complex as a word processor, spreadsheet, game, or specialist business application.

The run-time environment can have two states.

- **Running** is when it is actually performing its business function.
- **Stopped** is when the program is not doing anything effective, but waiting for an event to occur such as a user entry from the mouse or keyboard.

It is usually very easy for the designer to switch between run-time and design-time when designing or writing the program. However, the developer will not want to make it too easy for the user to switch from run-time to design-time, for the following reasons:

- It is not the user's function to code programs.
- The user probably does not have a full development environment on the computer.
- There is a performance overhead in maintaining the design-time information for the user.

## ✓ Check your understanding 32.5

In VB, pressing the F5 function key is one way for the developer to switch from design-time to run-time.

List the ways to switch from design-time to run-time in your environment.

# Use of objects

'Objects' is the name for both forms and controls.

- A **form** is what VB calls a window. A title bar appears at the top of each form. Forms may also have a menu bar, a status bar, toolbars, slide bars and other visual elements. A user area or a client area makes up the rest of the form. An application may have just one or many forms.

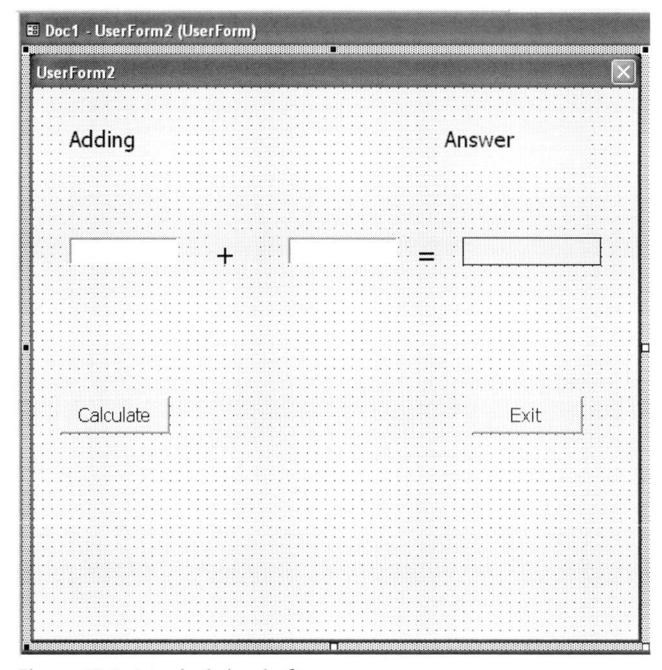


Figure 32.2 A typical simple form

- **Controls** include the icons or screen pictures that the user clicks to make something happen, and what they do. Figure 32.3 shows how they appear to the developer visually as the toolbox. Table 32.1 describes what each does.

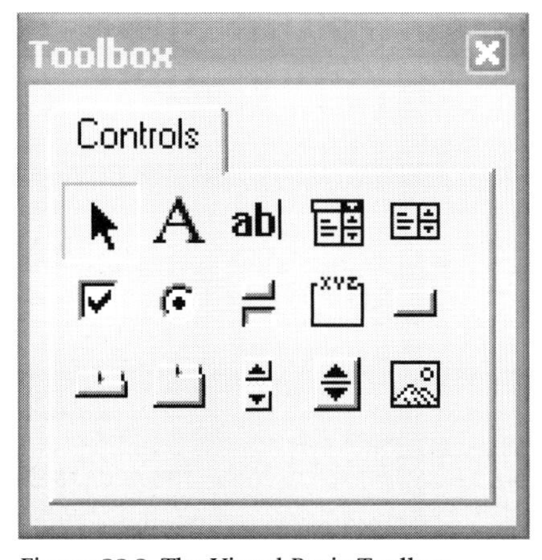


Figure 32.3 The Visual Basic Toolbox

| Control | Description |
|---|---|
| Check box | Lets the user choose a Yes/No response; as a group of check boxes, lets the user choose none, one or many options |
| Combo box | Offers a list of text items to choose from that the user can add to; combines the functions of a list box and text box |
| Command button | Offers the user the option to click on the button to start a program function |
| Data | Displays information from a database |
| Directory list box | Lets the user select from a list of personal folders or directories |
| Drive list box | Lets the user select from a list of drives |
| File list box | Lets the user select from a list of personal files |
| Frame | Groups together other controls; this is often used for a group of option buttons, check boxes or shapes |
| Horizontal scroll bar | Displays a horizontal scroll bar |
| Image box | Displays graphical objects and starts event actions |
| Label | Displays text on a form |
| Line | Draws straight lines in forms |
| List box | Shows a collection of text items; the user may select one text item from the list |
| OLE container | Lets another Windows® application such as *Word* or *Excel* transfer a data object into your application |
| Option button | Offers the user a choice of an option by selecting only one option button within a group |
| Picture box | Displays graphical objects and starts event actions |
| Pointer | Not a control tool, but used in the toolbox to switch in and out of screen design mode |
| Shape | Draws circles, ellipses, squares and rectangles within forms, frames or picture boxes |
| Text box | Displays text and lets the user enter text |
| Timers | Repeats events at specified time intervals |
| Vertical scroll bar | Displays a vertical scroll bar |

Table 32.1 What each control does

Objects have **methods**, **properties** (Figure 32.4) and, usually, **event procedures**.

?

## What does it mean?

A **method** is something that an object does or a predefined action on an object. For example, the method *Show* makes a hidden form visible.

A **property** is something that an object has. Properties define the appearance or behaviour of an object. The properties of an object depend on what sort of an object it is. For example, some of the properties of a command button are name, caption, height, width, background colour, location and font.

An **event procedure** is what the program does when a specific input event occurs.

Properties - Label5

Label5 Label

Alphabetic | Categorized

| (Name) | Label5 |
|---|---|
| Accelerator | |
| AutoSize | False |
| BackColor | &H8000000F& |
| BackStyle | 1 - fmBackStyleOpaque |
| BorderColor | &H80000006& |
| BorderStyle | 1 - fmBorderStyleSingle |
| Caption | |
| ControlTipText | |
| Enabled | True |
| Font | Tahoma |
| ForeColor | &H80000012& |
| Height | 18 |
| HelpContextID | 0 |
| Left | 282 |
| MouseIcon | (None) |
| MousePointer | 0 - fmMousePointerDefault |
| Picture | (None) |
| PicturePosition | 7 - fmPicturePositionAboveCenter |
| SpecialEffect | 0 - fmSpecialEffectFlat |
| TabIndex | 8 |
| TabStop | False |
| Tag | |
| TextAlign | 2 - fmTextAlignCenter |
| Top | 96 |
| Visible | True |
| Width | 90 |
| WordWrap | True |

Figure 32.4 Property box for a label

## Check your understanding 32.6

1 Find out all the different elements of a form or window.
2 List separately those items in Table 32.1 that are visible to the user of the form and those that are only of interest to the developer.

# User interface

Most of what the user knows about a program is what he or she sees on a screen. It is therefore most important that this is as good as the developer can make it. A poor user interface makes the user think that the whole program is poor, even though it might fully meet its specification. These features make for a good user interface:

- pleasing layout
- good use of colour
- appropriate use of other effects
- logical tab order between boxes or fields
- fitting on the screen without scrolling
- appropriate choice of font size and style.

In the visual environment, the developer should first design the forms through which the user enters data into the computer and obtains data from the computer. Then the developer works out the **algorithms** or sets of calculations that the computer needs to perform on the data.

One of the simplest forms you could design is to add two numbers together.

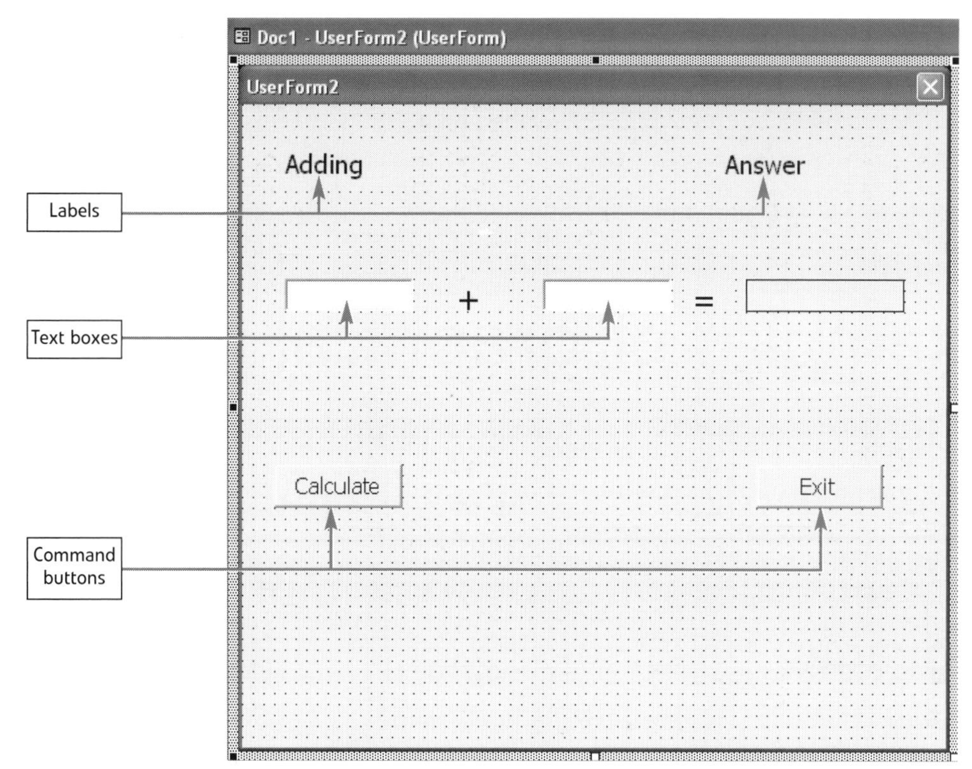


Figure 32.5 A form showing text boxes, labels and command buttons

The parts of a form are as follows:

- A **label** is used for headings, symbols, descriptions or where the developer wants to output data to a screen.
- A **text box** is used when the developer wants the user to input data or parameters, and this can be text, numerics, dates or anything from the keyboard.
- A **command button** is what the user clicks on to run the program and have the program do whatever the developer has programmed it to do.

**Check your understanding 32.7**

1 Compare a program that runs under DOS with an equivalent modern program with a graphical user interface (GUI).
2 In terms of ease of use, what are the advantages of the GUI program?
3 Are there any advantages to the DOS program?

# Design tools

For each programming language, there are usually a number of competing design-time environments, with different features, varying power and varying ease of use. These are sometimes called **development environments** or **software developer kits (SDK)**.

**Check your understanding 32.8**

1 List the sources of documentation for your development environment, for example on-screen Help.
2 List the advantages and disadvantages of each of these sources.

**Further research 32.1**

1 Use the Internet or your library to find out what other development environments exist for your chosen computer language. List the features, system requirements and prices of each of them.
2 Suggest why your location chose the development environment that you use.

# 32.2 Examples of graphical programs

This section looks at programs that generate or manipulate graphics, for example, programs with a graphical user interface (GUI) or Java applets.

## The development of graphical programming languages

One of the strengths of traditional programming languages is that most of them can solve typical problems. However, while these languages may be able to handle output graphics, they are weak at handling graphical input. This input can arrive in an arbitrary sequence and the timing of the input is user- or event-driven rather than under the control of the program that the developer wrote. Non-visual languages also usually assume that there is a constant link between the user and the computer. The much wider use of PCs and the growth of the Internet from the early 1990s led to the development and introduction of new programming languages that made the design and programming to handle graphics much easier.

Almost all of the features of procedural languages are required in a graphical or visual program. There are also features in visual programming that are specific to graphics. The developer learning visual programming therefore first needs to know how a certain graphical language implements these standard program building blocks:

- Variables
- Operators
- Control flow
- Library functions

Only when the person knows how to program these can he or she move on to the more exciting world of visual programming.

### Variables

**What does it mean?**

A **variable** is the name for where a program stores a piece of data.

Variables need to be *declared* before they are used. It is good practice that all variables are declared with the correct **scope** and **data type** before they are first used. This is to make sure that they are set up in the way the developer wants them to be. Sometimes, the default options are not appropriate for that program or situation and so the program works in an unexpected way. There are often language or installation rules on how to give names to variables. This is so that it is easier to know what the program is doing when changes are made later.

**Assignment** involves moving data from one variable to another. This may just be a simple move, where the variables are of the same length and data type. Often it is more complex:

- **Data conversion** converts data from one data type to another.
- **Padding** adds leading zeroes to numeric data or trailing spaces to character data.
- **Truncation** (the opposite of padding) removes the least important part of a data field.

## Operators

Relational operators or comparison operators are used to compare numbers or sets of characters, called **strings**, to form what is called a **logical expression**. The computer program then works out if this is true or false. There are a number of common values:

- equal (=)
- not equal (<> or NOT =)
- less than (<)
- less than or equal to (<=)
- greater than (>)
- greater than or equal to (>=).

Logical operators act on variables to create a result of true or false as shown in Table 32.2.

| Operator | Result is true if |
|---|---|
| AND | Both expressions are true |
| OR | Either expression is true or both expressions are true |
| XOR | Only if one expression is true and one expression is false |
| Not | Expression is false; it reverses the state |
| Equivalent | Both expressions are true or both false |
| Implies | Always true unless first expression is true and the second false |

Table 32.2 Operators and their results

Arithmetic operators act on variables to create a new value:

- addition (+)
- subtraction (−)
- multiplication (×)
- division (/)
- integer division (\)
- integer remainder (Mod)
- negation (-)
- exponentiation (^).

## Control flow

Control flow instructions are needed to effect the standard programming constructs:

- **branching/selection**: If ... Then ... Else and Select Case

- **repetition/looping:** For ... Next and Do Loops.

There will also be some method of stopping program execution.

## Library functions

Languages have many library functions to do common programming tasks. They are already written by the language vendor, the development environment vendor or the developer's installation support staff. They are used in place of variables. The developer calls a library function by stating its function name and any arguments or values a function needs to work on. The function does its work and returns to the calling program the calculated value as if it were a variable. Common functions include:

- mathematical functions: cosine, exponent, logarithm, sine, square root, tangent
- string handling functions: leftmost, middle or rightmost characters, length, uppercase equivalent, lowercase equivalent
- system functions: date, time
- type conversion routines: different types of numerics, numeric to string, string to numeric.

### Check your understanding 32.9

1 Review your programming text and appropriate Internet sites for how to program the standard building blocks described above and for examples of coding.
2 Check out the different types of data and list how you declare them in your language.
3 List the different ways that you can declare a variable which initially holds the value 1, together with possible uses of that type of variable.
4 There is a character variable of length 1 that you need to assign the different variables in Question 3. Write the assignment statements to do this including type conversions.
5 Code and test these program fragments:
   a Declare variables A and B. If the value of A is greater than zero, then set variable B to CREDIT. If A is zero then set B to blank. Otherwise, set B to DEBIT.
   b If the first four characters of variable INP are DATE then set variable OUTP to the current system date.
   c INNUM1, INNUM2 and OUTNUM are each character strings, the first two containing numbers. Add these two together and put the result in OUTNUM by using type conversion routines.
   d Extend your code for (c) by validating that each character of INNUM1 and INNUM2 is numeric. If it is not, then set the variable ERRORFIELD to INNUM1 or INNUM2 as appropriate.
   e Extend your code for (d) by also setting the variable ERRORCHAR to the number of the character in error. Set the variable ERRORMESSAGE to 'Error in input field <ERRORFIELD> at position <ERRORCHAR>'

### Further research 32.2

1 Compare your procedural language with your graphical language.
2 List library functions that are common to both.
3 List library functions that are unique, and give reasons why each type of function is unique.

# Differences between traditional and visual programming languages

## Simple screen output

The most obvious difference between traditional and visual programming is in output to a screen. In its simplest form, this involves writing a text message to a screen.

**Check your understanding 32.10**

On pages 305–7 you saw how VB, Basic, Java and JavaScript write 'Hello World' to the screen. Write a similar code fragment in your language to write 'Hello World'.

## Prompted screen input

Very few program and systems are purely output. Most programs require at least some input from the user, and this is often prompted. The earliest interactive systems expected the user to know what data should be entered in what format and in what order. However, it is more user friendly to give a prompt to the user so that it is clear what the user has to enter next.

**Check your understanding 32.11**

Write a code fragment to output to the user the prompt 'What is your name?'; accept as input from the user his or her <name>; and then output to the user 'Hello <name>'.

## Input events

Input events are described in Unit 8. A major difference between traditional and visual programming is the need for a visual program to be driven by the user and to respond to input events. Many of the inbuilt functions of the visual language take away from the developer the complexities of handling this user input. This allows the developer to focus on writing code to action and reply to these input events.

**Assessment activity 32.1**

Internet websites contain many examples of different programming functions with good and bad programming styles.

1 Search the Internet to find such websites for the languages that you have chosen. Using your chosen language or languages, investigate and review a variety of programs that use a visual environment.
2 Identify a number of programs that generate or manipulate graphics.

The programs seen so far have been of different functions, sizes and complexity. What some of them do and how they do it may have been immediately obvious to you. Others might have been more difficult to understand. Perhaps there were some that, even after study, it was not clear to you what they do. As you learn more about a chosen programming language, you should find that you understand more of the programs you meet. Even where you do not understand the detail of how these programs work, you should understand what they do from the comments and their structure.

**Check your understanding 32.12**

1 For a program that you understand, describe what each bit does.
2 For a program that you don't understand, explain why not, and explore what can you do to find out more.

# How programs generate or handle graphics

How can graphics, such as lines, shapes and images, be used in a program? The visual effect of a program comes from its use of graphics. A developer can easily draw shapes and lines on a form, or include graphic images from files. The detail of how a language implements these features, often known as **controls** and **properties**, should be available in the online Help facility of the development environment.

1 The developer draws lines using the line control. A line can have the following properties:
- colour
- pattern
- start and end position
- width.

2 The most common shapes placed on a form are rectangles, ovals or ellipses and rounded rectangles. Squares and circles are special cases of rectangles and ovals. A shape comprises lines joined in some way and has many more properties, including:
- type of shape, for example rectangle
- height and width
- position
- border pattern
- transparent or opaque background
- interior pattern
- colours, of the border, background and interior pattern.

3 Images can be created using either the Picture box or Image controls. An image has the following properties:
- position on the form
- sizing, where the control will either expand or contract the image, or only display part of the image
- border
- transparency, where background text may show through the image
- source location of the image.

The image to be loaded can be specified at design-time. Alternatively, there is a built-in function for the program to decide which image to load at run-time.

**Check your understanding 32.13**

1 Write the code to display the word DRIVE to the screen. Each letter should appear in a different colour and style.
2 Write the code to display an ellipse on the screen. Change each of the properties and see what effect this has on your shape.
3 Write the code to load an image and display it when the user clicks the command button.

**Further research 32.3**

Develop a program to allow the user to select from list boxes a type of shape, a pattern and a colour, and then to display the requested shape.

# Visual environment benefits

There are several benefits in using a visual environment compared to a non-visual environment. This section covers them in terms of ease of use and understanding general concepts.

The major benefit of a visual environment to the user is that it is much more closely aligned to what the user wants to do. It therefore makes it easier to use, often much easier, than a non-visual environment. There are also many features that are very difficult, if not impossible, to program in a non-visual environment. In general, visual output can be programmed in a traditional way. Visual input, when it is expected, can also be programmed in the traditional way. The benefit of a visual environment, however, comes in handling unexpected and uncontrolled user input.

From a developer's point of view, the benefits of a visual environment come from having an environment where complexities are automatically controlled:

- handling graphics
- managing unexpected interaction with the user
- controlling the graphical run-time environment
- linking input screens and output screens together.

These benefits are gained through the use of objects, classes and inheritance as described on page 305. The designer of the software environment provides a template of how a visual program works and makes that available to the developer. This template handles all of the complexity in managing the visual environment. The benefit of this to the developer is that he or she can concentrate on just the problem in hand or the program he or she is trying to write. The developer only needs to change the way the standard program works if that is necessary to solve the problem.

**Check your understanding 32.14**

1 List the major features of your word processor.
2 Identify which features are visual and which are non-visual.
3 Suggest how some of the visual features are also, or could be made, non-visual.
4 List the drawbacks of making these changes.
5 List any benefits for the non-visual options of those features.

**Further research 32.4**

1 Obtain a DOS-based or other command-line and text-based word processor. Compare this to a modern word processor, listing the features that they both have, and comparing the ease of use of these features.
2 Obtain a DOS-based, non-visual game. What features does it have that today's equivalent has? What sorts of features does it *not* have?
3 What games could you play in a non-visual environment? Design a golf game for a non-visual environment.

# Program production

This section focuses on producing a variety of programs in a visual environment. Many of these programs build on earlier examples, so be sure that each is fully understood before moving on to the next. The program that is developed is a multifunction calculator.

In professional program development, it is always best to understand the overall picture of what the complete program has to do before starting on coding. You should therefore read all of this section before starting coding the first examples.

**Check your understanding 32.15**

1 Design a form for the user to enter two numbers with a third box for an answer and a button to start the calculation.
2 Code a program to add these numbers together and put the answer in the third box.
3 Test that the program works correctly by adding various numbers.
   - What happens if you try to add letters together?
   - What happens if you haven't put any values in the first two boxes and try to add?
4 Redesign the form to have four buttons with +, -, ×, /.
5 Code a program to add, subtract, multiply or divide the two numbers depending on which button is clicked.
6 Test that the program works correctly by doing calculations with various numbers.
   - What happens if you multiply together the two largest numbers that you can?
   - What happens if you try to divide by zero?
7 Were any of your answers to the testing questions unexpected or gave some form of error message? Add validation code and an error message output box to cater for those conditions.
8 Add another two buttons with F→C and C→F on them. Change your program to add Fahrenheit to Centigrade and Centigrade to Fahrenheit conversion routines, with appropriate validation code.
9 Add another button for Square root and use the Square root function in your program to calculate this.

# 32.3 Programming techniques

## Program design

In general, the design concepts and methodologies that are described in Unit 8 also apply to visual programming. The business requirements are identified in the same way. The design of a program is split into input, process and output. This is followed by a coding stage. Then the program or system is tested before going into production. This section discusses the differences for visual program design and should be read together with the appropriate parts of Unit 8.

The differences start at the design for the screens. The visual designer first needs to think about how the user will interact with the program. One useful design tool is the **storyboard**. This is used to paint a picture of what the user could do and how the program reacts to that. The user will be interested mainly in the visual representation, or what appears on the screen, rather than what the computer program does to make that happen. The success of a design depends on how close this can be made to real life. For example, a program to view photographs could be designed using Windows® folders and files. This has been included in recent versions of the Windows® operating system. However, a much more intuitive (easy to understand) concept is that of a photograph album. Many PC software products use this basis.

Once the screen concept has been chosen, the developer and the user need to agree on what each of the screens in the application does. The program may take over the complete environment, but it is more likely to run in a standard Windows® environment. This means the developer can use most of the features provided by both Windows® and the run-time environment of the chosen development language or tool.

- **Input:** The graphical input can be to the screen itself, or to drop-down menus or icons on the screen. There may also be keyboard entry, either of text or of special key combinations such as Ctrl + A. Consistency of design is very important. If the same function, such as program exit, is provided from more than one screen, then there must be the same way of doing it on each screen. If the same function is provided in more than one way on the same screen, then it should work in exactly the same way.
- **Processing:** This is designed in a similar way to a traditional program. The main different design consideration is that, in general, multiple processes may be running at the same time, under the control of the user. This means that the designer may have to be careful about when to make updates and how to handle shared variables.
- **Output:** What the designer has to think about differently here is how to handle multiple processes writing to the same output screen.

**Check your understanding 32.16**

1 For a standard piece of *Office* software, list the multiple inputs for each of five functions such as 'Open a file' or 'Copy' that have more than one way to action them.

2 For any one of those functions, say why the user might want to use each of the different inputs.

# Debugging and testing of programs

There are three forms of error that can occur in a computer program. The first and most serious is that the program does not meet the business need. This may mean changes to the algorithms, to the sizes of some of the data fields, or even to the structure of the programs.

At the programming level, a correct program is one that conforms to the program specification. This would include both the written specification and good practice in terms of validating input, detecting and correcting errors and not crashing under unexpected conditions. There are two types of programming errors: logic errors and syntax errors. All languages, both spoken and computer, have rules of grammar and spelling.

- A **syntax error** is where the developer has broken one of these rules so that the computer is not sure what you want it to do. The computer may detect this when you are writing your program, when you compile your program, or when you are running it, either in testing or in production. In a visual programming environment, the program is usually interpreted (converted into what the computer understands) when you run it.
- A **logic error** is when the program may appear to run successfully, but the results are not what the developer or user expects. It is more difficult for the system to help here.

A successful test plan identifies:

- what the input to the program should look like
- what the output from the program should look like
- what checks the developer should make that the input is valid
- how the program should handle any exceptions.

The final step, when the developer has finished developing the program, is to put it into production. If it is solely for personal use or a friend's use, this might be as simple as copying it from the development to the run-time environment. In a business environment, there is likely to be a program promotion process where this copying from development to production is tightly controlled. If the program is being sold to many third parties, there will be a program release process to put in place.

## Case study: British Logistics

British Logistics expanded from land and air transport into shipping by taking over a shipping line. BL transferred the shipping operations to its existing systems. While almost all of BL's systems continued to operate successfully, there were some failures involving calculations and validations of data such as size, volume, journey time and locations.

1. List what these failures might be.
2. For each, state what programming changes you would need to make.

## ✓ Check your understanding 32.17

Write a visual program that validates a date that has three input boxes for day, month and year, and returns a message saying whether that date is valid or not. It has two command buttons, one for validate and one for exit.

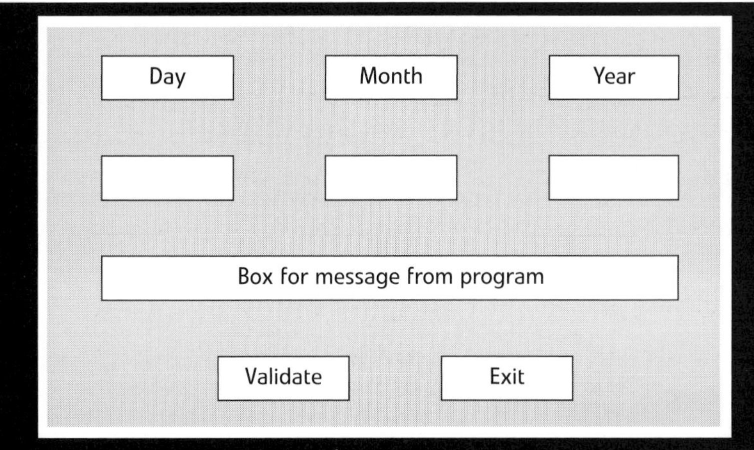

Figure 32.6 Specification of date validation screen

1 Produce a test plan showing the dates you plan to test and if/why they are invalid.
2 List each of your test runs, with what happened overall and what happened to each test case.
3 List each of the changes you make in response to each test run and its effect.
4 How many of your errors were syntax errors? How many were logic errors?
5 How long, on average, did the syntax errors take you to identify and correct? How long did it take to correct the logic errors?
6 Compare your results with those of your colleagues. Do they show a similar pattern?

**Further research 32.5**

Change your date program to produce different validation messages depending on which validation check the date failed.

1 Repeat steps 1–6 above.
2 List any differences in the pattern and number of answers.
3 List your reasons for these differences.
4 Did you find any errors from the first example that only came to light when running this example?

# Documentation

The program specification describes in technical terms both what the program does and how it does it. The 'what' part is written prior to the program. The 'how' part is written as the program is developed. The developer updates both parts for accuracy and completeness when writing and testing the program are completed.

The programmer writes program code comments or remarks within a program to help anyone maintaining that program to understand what it does. At the start of the program, the programmer identifies the author, when it was written, a general description of both what the program does and how it does it, a cross-reference to other documentation about the program, and a blank maintenance history.

At the start of each module, the programmer explains what that module does. Within a module that employs a complex algorithm, the programmer should explain what that algorithm does. There is no need to document the use of straightforward language features.

When a programmer changes a program that is in production, he or she should comment on each of the changes made and provide a reference number. At the start of the program, the programmer should update the maintenance history with the reference number, the date, the programmer who made the changes and why they were made.

When the programmer no longer wants the program to execute a piece of code, he or she should not delete it but comment it out (place the code in comments so it no longer executes). This is so that if there is a need to reinstate that code, or if the program operates wrongly because of that code removal, then it can be put back in whole or in part.

### Case study: British Logistics

British Logistics no longer operate steam trains and want to remove the logic for this from one of their programs. Here are the changes that need to be made to the comments:

*Maintenance history*

- change number 8 made by Jane Coder on 14 March 2002
- remove code referring to operation of steam trains
- system change request number BL/345/AB6 dated 6 March 2002 requested by Ms Customer
- change number 8 – commented out to remove steam train code
- if vehicle = steam_train then ...

1. In your language, list the features there are for documenting code, for example 'Rem'.
2. List the code documentation features in your development environment.
3. When would you use each feature?

### Further research 32.6

1. Look at other languages and list their code documentation features.
2. Compare them with those in your language.

### Assessment activity 32.2

Develop a multifunction calculator for use in a visual environment. You should try to show a good understanding of how programming techniques can be used for this, while going through the full systems lifecycle for developing a program.

1. Plan what functions the calculator will have.
2. Create a well-structured calculator program.
3. Use a variety of tools to build and test the calculator, showing a good understanding of the best use of tools.
4. Produce an explanation of what the program is supposed to do (as part of documenting your program).

# Applet design, creation and testing

When the developer builds a visual program for a web page, there are more things that need to be considered for the design, creation and testing for applets. This is because the applets run in a very controlled environment: a web browser. The applet cannot do the following for security reasons:

- access memory outside the applet
- create, read, rename, copy or write files on the user's PC
- connect to other computers on the user's network
- call the system routines of the user's PC
- remain active on the PC once the user has moved from that web page.

The other major design need for an applet is that it has to download from the web server each time it is run. This can lead to a long delay in starting to run the applet if the user is on a low-speed line or if the applet design does not keep as low as it can the amount of applet code downloaded.

So what are applets best used for, if those are the drawbacks? They are excellent at animating, or adding action to, a web page. Applets can be used to play games, to deliver interactive applications such as maps, and to improve the user interface of web pages. As the user's mouse passes over parts of a web page, for example, the applet could highlight them.

It is sometimes difficult to test that an applet works in the way the developer wants it to. The applet needs to run on different browsers under different operating systems on different hardware. The interpreted nature of an applet means that the program functions should still work on any browser that meets the minimum specification that the applet was written to. However, different browsers may produce different errors when things go wrong, so applet languages in general have good exception handling. The developer tells the program to throw an exception if something unexpected happens. The developer also writes code to catch the exception.

It is also important for the developer to performance test the applet. It should load quickly enough that the user will not want to move on to another web page before the applet starts to run. The applet should also react fast enough to the user's input once it is running. The testing should not be over a high-speed LAN, with a high-powered PC, but over a low-speed dial-up link, with a low-powered machine.

# Games programming

Where a program is developed for the specific purpose of production of a game or animation, there are more design and programming considerations. These are again around the three areas of input, processing and output. For a game or animation, there is always some simulation of reality. At one extreme, the game may be about piloting an imaginary spaceship. Here, reality is very much only in the mind of the program designer. At the other extreme, the game may be a flight, racing car or train simulator. The aim here is to copy as closely as possible the real life characteristics of an aircraft, car or train. For a strategy game, the reality may be in copying how part of the real world works. Examples of this are city or railway simulators. In all these cases, the designer has to work out how to make all this happen on a PC.

- **Input**: The designer should start here either with what the real world is or the imagined world appears to be. From this ideal, the developer needs to make compromises on how to turn this into a usable GUI with a screen, mouse, keyboard and possibly special devices such as a joystick. To control the running of the game, the designer needs to decide whether this can be included in the same style as the main user interface. If that is not possible, game control can still be visual, but it is built in a more traditional 'setting parameters' style. From the user's point of view, this is what he or she sees of the game, so this is the most important part.

- **Processing:** Most games have some form of artificial intelligence (AI) at their heart, which is what simulates the decisions of the real or imagined world. A golf game, for example, can come fairly close to simulating the laws of physics for the travel of the ball. However, the more complex simulation strategy games can only come close to some practical rules based on experience. This is the area of the program that will need the most testing to make sure the rules that the developer writes in the program seem to reflect real life. It is common to design a simpler version of the AI to allow novice users of the game to learn how to play it, before switching into more powerful, more realistic modes. Many games also have cheats designed into the AI to allow the user to gain more resources or to switch on or off various features of the game. These may be intentional for the production version of the game, or they may have just been included to assist in testing and not removed.
- **Output:** This is often the opportunity for the program designer to show off graphics design skills and produce ever more realistic displays of the virtual world in which the game is set. The design and coding trade-off here is to make sure that the program performs fast enough to gain the value of reality.

## Check your understanding 32.18

1. List the features of a PC game that you know well (as you would describe it to a friend).
2. List the features of the same game (as described by the manufacturer on the box or their website).
3. List the features of the same game (from the online help or the user guide).
4. Identify each of those features on your three lists as being input, processing or output.
5. List the reasons why there are different features on your three lists.

## Assessment activity 32.3

This activity gives you an opportunity to demonstrate team working, which is an important part of any commercial computer program development. You are each to develop a computer game, working in pairs or groups. Some group members are to act as the potential users of a game, with the other(s) taking the role of the developer(s). Roles can then be reversed so that everyone works through the full development lifecycle or steps to develop a computer game program for use in a visual environment. Try to show a good understanding of how programming techniques can be used for this.

1. Plan what the game will do and what features it will have, through discussions between the user(s) and the developer(s) in your group.
2. Create a well-structured game.
3. Use a variety of tools to build and test the game, showing a good understanding of the best use of tools. The developer(s) should involve the user(s) in the user testing of the game to make sure that their needs are met.
4. Produce an explanation of what the program is supposed to do as part of documenting your program.

# 32.4 Evaluate graphical programs

## Evaluate against original design and specification

Once the developer has completed testing the program, someone else often evaluates or checks whether the program really does what it is supposed to do. This is usually done both before the program is used and then again when it has been in use for some time and the users have learned how to use it.

The first part of the evaluation is to compare in functional terms what the program was supposed to do with what it actually does. This is done by taking a list of the features of the program and checking whether the delivered program actually does them. This can be either a simple yes or no, or a more complex evaluation of how well the program does this.

The next part of the evaluation is to check how well the program meets the technical specification. The evaluator should identify what hardware, operating systems and other software the program needs to run on. For hardware, the memory, disk storage and screen resolution requirements are the most important. For operating systems, the releases of Windows that it runs under are important, together with any restrictions such as 'this feature does not work under that release'. For other related software, this should specify what run-time environment is needed. For example, if the program has been built using an application builder then how it works under the minimum run-time version of that application should be evaluated.

Robustness is an important attribute of a visual program. It must be able to cope with accepting input when the user wants to give it and not just when the program expects it. However, it is difficult to reproduce this repeatedly in a testing environment. The evaluator should do what they can to make as many mistakes as they can in using the program. They should also test out the limits of the program to make sure that the program behaves properly at these limits. Evaluation should check the following:

- that the mistake was picked up
- that an error message was produced that was meaningful to the user
- that the program did not crash.

The final part of the technical evaluation decides how easy the program will be to maintain. This is evaluated externally for the program documentation and internally for the program code. The documentation should meet these criteria:

- It should be complete; all expected documents should be there.
- It should be accurate; a check should be made on a small part of the program on how well the documentation corresponds to this version of the program.
- It should be readable; the documentation should be easily understood by someone who is not familiar with the detail of that program.

Perhaps the most difficult part of evaluation is to review the program code. Much of this is a matter of individual style. The program should at least conform to whatever programming standards have been laid down by either the compiler vendor, or your computer installation. There should be no compiler errors in the program and the program should produce no unexpected errors on installation or when loaded into and run in the run-time environment. The code should be well-commented and have a clear structure.

**Check your understanding 32.19**

1 You are planning a greatly improved version of your favourite PC game. Produce a list of both new and existing features that you would expect to see in this new version. Evaluate the existing version against the feature list of the improved version.

2 An early operating system produced the cryptic error message 'System error advise supervisor' whenever it hit an unexpected error.
   - List reasons why this is poor development practice.
   - For each reason, list what would be a better approach.

3 List a set of robustness checks for a word processor. How would you evaluate these?

4 List a set of robustness checks for your favourite PC game. How would you evaluate these?

## Evaluate suitability for use

The previous section was about the objective tests that can be used to evaluate a program. Evaluation for suitability for use is much more subjective about how and how well a program does what it is supposed to do.

Developers will often have the latest versions of hardware and system software to use for program development. Evaluation of suitability for use should always be under the minimum recommended hardware and software specification so that the evaluator can experience the worst that the end user will see.

To evaluate suitability for use, the evaluation must be seen from the viewpoint of the person who will use the program, not from the viewpoint of the developer who wrote the program. The evaluation should start from the typical things that the user would want to do with the program. For example, with a word processor, the user would want to write letters, produce documents, record notes or even write a best-selling book. These objectives should be listed and examples developed for each of them. The evaluator should then review the program documentation to find out how the user could use the features of the program to achieve what he or she is trying to do. The evaluator should then list the steps needed to go through to do this. In the 'writing a letter using a word processor' example, there are a few straightforward first steps:

- Load word processor.
- Open new document.
- Right-justify writer's address.
- Insert today's date.

The next evaluation should be on how easy the program is to use. The evaluator should be aware that there is likely to be:

- a wide range of skill levels for the users of the program
- different users holding different views on their preferred usage
- the need to move from a basic level of the program with lots of default values to a more advanced version
- the opportunity to use special equipment to further improve usage or enjoyment of the program; for example, the optional use of a joystick with a flight simulator game.

The evaluator should be looking for an appropriate balance between ease of use and functionality for the power user. The user interface (UI) may not always be visual. To change system parameters or default values and, particularly in some parts of the program designed for the power user, it may be more appropriate to have a non-graphical interface.

The final evaluation should be on how fast the program performs. The standard is that the computer must perform at least as fast as the user works. Thus screen clicks and mouse movements, for example, must be immediately reflected on the screen. Where the program is doing large complex calculations or searching through large volumes of data, then it is acceptable for the computer to be seen to be thinking (with a suitable icon to denote this) as this reflects user behaviour. Where the program is a game and it is repeatedly redrawing graphics, then the motion of the people or objects on the screen must be smooth and reflect reality.

### Case study: Hobby Computing

Hobby Computing produce a family tree program. Their standard user interface is a GUI where boxes are drawn and manipulated to draw a family tree. For complex changes to the family tree, the power user can drop down into a mainly text mode to make these changes.

1 For your favourite game, list the different parts of the UI.
2 List which parts of the UI are mainly for the novice user and which are for the power user.
3 List any improvements you would like to see in that user interface for greater ease of use.

# Suggesting improvements

Most evaluations identify where revisions could be made or improvements should have been made. This will result in an evaluator's list of improvements (Figure 32.7). Initial users of the program will also generate a more functional list of changes that they would like to see. The developer too will have ideas for changes. These separate lists should be put together, reviewed and the improvements put into a priority order.

First, if there is anything that makes the program unusable in any significant way, then this should be fixed before the program is released. This is sometimes called a 'priority one problem'. This fix may not be the final solution, but there should at least be a work-around available as a temporary solution.

The user is then asked to give a relative priority for each of the changes or to identify how important the change is to the user of the program. These are usually direct improvements in terms of adding new features or improving existing features of the program. However, sometimes, an improvement is indirect if it increases the robustness or maintainability of the program or improves the response time. Some indication of the benefits, quantified if possible, is also made. This is so that, by taking a number of these changes together, a business case for the changes can be made. This might be in increased sales of the program in a software selling environment. For an in-house development, this could be the increased value to the business by using the changed program.

Next, the developer reviews the proposed features to assess how to make the changes. There may be opportunities to meet several of the revisions with one major change. The work involved in each of these changes is estimated. There is then a priority-setting process to give the most user benefits, at the least cost. The changes that are most likely to be done first are those that the user values highly but that cost little to do. Big changes with little user benefits are done last, if at all.

When a big change is being done, small changes that would not otherwise be done are often made to that part of the program as the additional cost of making and testing them is small. The documentation is often improved in that area at this time. Finally, the planned changes are grouped into versions. There may be four versions:

- the current production version
- the past production versions that are still maintained for some users
- the version under development whose specification is fixed
- further future versions whose features are being identified and evaluated.

| Evaluation Form | | |
|---|---|---|
| Project | Reference | Build priority |
| Evaluator name | Date | User priority |
| Suggested improvement | | |
| How to do it | | |
| Related changes and comments | | |
| Developer name | Effort needed | |
| Release target | Date implemented | |

Figure 32.7 Evaluation form

## Check your understanding 32.20

1 For your favourite PC game or other graphical program, list a set of features that you would like to see in future releases.
2 Identify at least one user benefit for each of those changes.
3 Suggest how each change might be done and at what cost (large, medium or small).
4 Prioritise the list of changes into three future versions.

## Assessment activity 32.4

Obtain copies of the design specifications and programs for the calculator and game written by your colleagues in Assessment activities 32.2 and 32.3.

1 Evaluate your colleagues' calculator and game programs against their original design specifications.
2 Suggest areas where their calculator and game programs can be improved.
3 Evaluate your own calculator and game programs against their original design specification.
4 Suggest areas where your own calculator and game programs can be improved.

## Test your knowledge

1 What is an event and an event handler?
2 Explain the term 'inheritance'.
3 What is a class library?
4 What is a graphical user interface or GUI?
5 What is an applet?
6 How does an applet work?
7 Explain the terms 'methods' and 'properties'.
8 What are the features of a good user interface?
9 List the relational, arithmetic and logical operators.
10 List the properties of lines, shapes and images.
11 What are the benefits to a developer of a visual environment?
12 What is the difference between a logic error and a syntax error?
13 List what things an applet cannot do that an ordinary program can.
14 Why is an applet restricted in what it can do?
15 What is AI in a games program?

# UNIT 12: HUMAN COMPUTER INTERFACE

The advance in design of highly interactive computer systems continues at an ever-increasing pace, with new developments in hardware and software being announced more frequently than ever before. The pace of change, which is unlikely to diminish, has placed an increasing burden on the design of the way in which users interact with computer systems.

The way in which computers and people interact is known as the human computer interface (HCI).

The aim of this unit is to provide an understanding of the importance of HCI in the development of user-friendly computer software. You will learn about the currently available HCI technologies and designs, and the appropriateness of each for particular applications and user groups. As a prerequisite, you should have completed Unit 4. This unit presents opportunities to demonstrate Key Skills in communication and problem solving.

## Learning objectives

- To describe a range of HCI developments and the applications and user groups to which they are suited
- To describe the relationship between the user and the interface, in terms of human motor, sensory and cognitive abilities
- To give examples of specific HCIs which are designed to solve specific problems and produce HCI designs to specification
- To evaluate the effectiveness of HCI models with particular reference to the chosen designs

# 12.1 HCI developments and their applications

**HCI** is a fascinating field of study. It looks at how people and computers communicate with each other, and how their interaction can be improved.

**What does it mean?**

HCI stands for **human computer interface**, or sometimes human computer **interaction.**

HCI begins with the premise that computers, and the people who use them, must be seen as a complete unit and that the quality of the work done using a computer depends on four factors:

- the hardware devices that the user is in direct contact with
- the user interface displayed on the screen
- the response of the human user to the computer system
- the environment in which the computer and human are placed.

Organisations invest very heavily in ICT, so they want their computer systems to be used as productively as possible. Many are now aware that to achieve this they need to pay attention to all four factors.

Most of the units in this book focus on the use of a network of desktop computers in a place of work, but much of what we know about IT systems also applies in other contexts, such as in the home. At work, computer users usually have access to support staff, whereas the home user is largely on his or her own, so the quality of the HCI is of even greater importance.

HCI is also becoming a significant issue in the development of other related technologies. Digital televisions, mobile phones and personal digital assistants (PDAs) have more and more features in common, and we refer to a *convergence* of the technologies. Soon these products, along with desktop computers, will all offer a very similar range of services. The main difference between them will be their size, which will determine the type of input and output devices that can be used with them.

## Developments in hardware

You will already be familiar with a number of input and output devices. In this unit, you will not be studying technologies themselves but instead you will be considering the impact that some of these devices have on the way in which people interact with computers. The perspective will always be that of the user, not of the technician.

### Input devices

The only way in which a human user can pass information to a computer system is through an input device. The input device carries out two functions: entering information and issuing instructions. Information is in the form of text, numbers, sound and images, all of which have to be transferred from the outside world to the inner workings of the computer system. Instructions tell the computer what to do with the information. Of course, the computer system does not make such a distinction, as all signals from input devices are simply treated as data. The user's perception is important though, and has led to the development of different devices for the two functions.

## Data entry devices

These are used to enter information into the computer system. They include keyboards, readers, image capture and recognition systems.

**Keyboards:** These provide the primary method by which a user enters information into a computer. Various types and layouts are produced.

- The **standard keyboard** uses the QWERTY key layout, which was originally developed for typewriters over a century ago. The arrangement of the keys was designed to prevent the levers from hitting each other and jamming the machine, and to slow down the typist. This layout migrated to the computer keyboard because it was familiar to office workers, even though the original justification was no longer relevant. The standard keyboard includes a calculator-like numeric keypad, which duplicates the keys above the letters, but enables fast entry of numerical data. It also provides a set of control keys and programmable function keys.
- **Ergonomically designed keyboards** (Figure 12.1) use a similar layout to the standard one, but are shaped to make them more comfortable to use.

Figure 12.1 An ergonomic keyboard

- Experiments with alternative layouts of keys have not proved to be commercially successful for business computers. Some keyboards do use the keys arranged in alphabetical order, and these are found on systems designed to enable people with motor control disabilities to communicate, and also on some children's products. Numerical keypads can be used to enter characters, as any mobile phone user knows, and this makes it possible to use a limited keyboard on a handheld device.
- A touch-sensitive keyboard which can be programmed and varied in layout is known as a **concept keyboard**. They can be seen in fast food outlets, (Figure 12.2) where an overlay on

the surface identifies the areas that have been programmed to accept input. A concept keyboard can also be used by children, or by people with disabilities, as the 'keys' can be made as large as necessary.

Figure 12.2 A concept keyboard in a fast food outlet

- A **touch-sensitive** screen can simulate a keyboard, and a stylus or finger can be used to select keys. These can be seen on PDAs and information kiosks. Either QWERTY or alphabetical layouts can be used.

> ✓ **Check your understanding 12.1**
>
> 1 Why is the QWERTY key layout widely used on keyboards, and why have manufacturers enjoyed little success in getting the public to switch to other layouts?
>
> 2 Describe three or four different keyboards, other than the familiar desktop computer keyboard, that can be used within an HCI. Identify a context where each could be used.

**Readers**: Sometimes information has already been produced and the user needs a method to transfer this into the computer system. In these cases, a reader device of some kind is used.

- A **magnetic card reader** inputs the data stored on either a magnetic strip or a chip embedded into a small card. They are widely used by banks (for cash and credit cards), by shops (for loyalty cards), by transport operators (for tickets) and by hotels (for electronic door keys), and are being increasingly used by organisations for ID cards.
- A **smart card reader** inputs data held on a chip on a plastic card. A complete processor with memory is contained on a single integrated circuit. Their use is expected to grow, especially as travel and entertainment tickets, as cash top-up cards, and to store personal data such as medical records.

**Image capture devices**: Images are as important as text in HCIs, so methods for inputting and manipulating images are of some significance.

- A **digital camera** stores a photograph as a bitmap, which can then be uploaded to a computer system.

- An **image scanner** is used to digitise existing documents and photos. The output is a bitmap version of the original. The bitmap may then be subjected to further analysis and interpreted as characters or barcodes. Both flat-bed and handheld scanners can be purchased.

**Recognition systems:** These are complex systems that add sophisticated analytical software to existing hardware technologies.

- **Character recognition systems** use optical character recognition (OCR) software to analyse the patterns in a bitmap and interpret them as characters. This involves careful matching against standard fonts, and is not entirely error free. The system generates a text or word processing file. Character recognition software usually works in conjunction with a scanner. Specialised systems are used by blind users to input text, which can then be output as speech or in Braille.
- **Handwriting recognition systems** are mainly used in PDAs and other hand-held devices with touch-sensitive screens. The user writes characters with a stylus one at a time on to the screen and these are then interpreted by the software. Before the system can be used the system has to be given samples of all the characters written by the user. A person's handwriting does vary so this system is not foolproof, and errors do appear.
- **Speech recognition systems** use a microphone to capture and digitise speech. They then match the phonemes (speech components) against a built-in library of words, and store the text as a text file or word processing document. Just as a handwriting system has to 'learn' the user's style, so a speech recognition system has to record some standard text spoken by the user. Even so, the system is prone to error. Speech may be difficult to recognise if the speaker has a cold or has a strong regional accent, or if there is background noise.

**Further research 12.1**

1. Switch on the teletext subtitles while you are watching a live broadcast, such as a football match. The television companies use speech recognition systems to analyse and present the commentary. Note down the errors that occur.
2. Are the errors simply amusing or would they cause difficulties for a person who could not hear the spoken words?

In addition to devices for entering information, a number of input devices are used primarily for entering user instructions. These include a range of pointing devices and many of the components of games and virtual reality systems.

## Pointing devices

These let the user issue instructions in a natural way and without having to enter words. They can only be used in conjunction with a suitable user interface, which places a pointer icon on the screen that moves in response to inputs from the device.

- A **mouse** fits neatly into the hand, and its movements across a smooth surface are mirrored by the on-screen pointer. A mouse has two standard types of control: the rollers that touch the ball to register movement, and buttons. The standard mouse has two buttons, which can each be clicked or double-clicked. The use of these buttons is determined by the software and, in addition, the user can often configure the buttons to suit his or her speed of movement or handedness.

- A **light pen** is a pen-like device that is connected to an input port and held close to the screen. It detects the individual pixels of light as they are projected onto the screen and this allows the software to detect the position of the pen. The pen can be used to make on-screen selections.
- A **tracker ball** (Figure 12.3) is similar to a mouse but with the ball on the top. The user rotates the ball directly, rather than moving it over a surface. Tracker balls are often built in to portable computers as an alternative to a separate mouse.

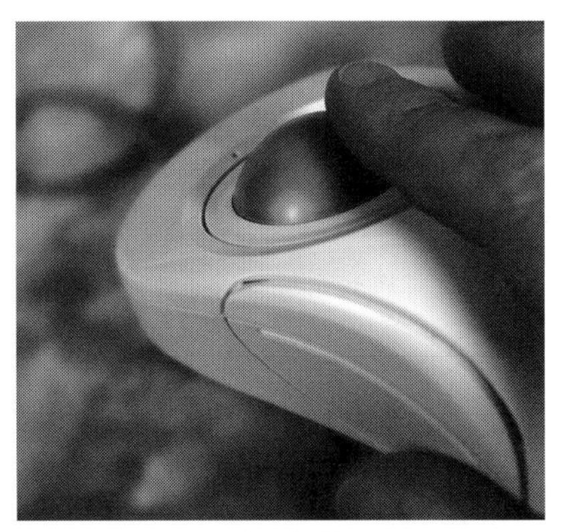

Figure 12.3 A tracker ball

- A **joystick** is familiar to games players, and is another variant on a mouse. The stick itself can be rotated and tilted, corresponding to mouse movements. Buttons are placed on the stick or on the base.
- An **eye gaze system** requires the user to wear a device that positions a small (safe) laser unit in front of the eye. This records the movement of the eye and can be used as a hands-free method of moving an on-screen pointer. These systems have been mainly used by the military, but are also used increasingly to enable people with very limited movement to control communication devices and computers.

**Check your understanding 12.2**

Why are there so many different types of pointing devices when they seem to carry out very similar functions?

## Movement-sensing devices

These are complex devices that allow the user to move around in three-dimensional space and to issue instructions through their position and motion. Virtual reality (VR) systems combine movement-sensing devices with multi-sensory output and these are considered in more detail later.

- **Data gloves** are worn like ordinary gloves. They have optical fibres built in to the fabric and these detect movement of the finger joints when, for example, the hand makes a grasping movement. Additional sensors measure the position of the hand and the way in which the wrist rotates. Data gloves are used in VR systems.

- A **headset** or helmet can track the position and movement of the user's head (Figure 12.4). Sometimes these are combined with eye gaze systems. These can again be used in VR simulations or for hands-free real-life control.

Figure 12.4 A VR head set

- **Whole-body tracking systems** place movement sensors either directly on the body or on the chair in which the user sits. These systems are in their infancy but will, no doubt, become increasingly important in the entertainment industry.

## Output devices

Humans are traditionally described as having five senses, so computer systems could, in theory, produce output that can be seen, heard, touched, smelt or tasted. In practice, the last two have not yet been exploited by the IT world, largely because no one has yet found a satisfactory method for digitising, and then reproducing, smells and tastes.

### Visual output devices

Sight is the dominant sense for humans; so, most research into user interfaces has concentrated on the presentation of visual information.

- Computer **screens** are also referred to as visual display units (VDUs) or monitors. The most common type is the cathode ray tube (CRT) which fires an electron beam at a coated screen. It fires lines of pixels one after another down the screen, taking around one thirtieth of a second to cover a complete screen. An alternative is the liquid crystal display (LCD) screen, which sends signals to the individual crystals that represent each pixel every time they have to change colour. LCD screens are flat, and are lighter in weight than CRT screens, but are more expensive and can sometimes be more difficult to view. They are widely used in portable machines, such as laptop computers, PDAs and mobile phones.
- **Printers** are complex systems in their own right. Their large memory buffers enable them to store and process tasks independently of the rest of the computer system. Inkjet and laser printers offer a range of capabilities and print quality.

### Sound output devices

These play an important, but under-recognised, role in HCIs.

- All desktop computers have a small **speaker** for sound output, and this is often supplemented with a pair of better quality external speakers. Sound is used for playing music and for effects in games, but the HCI also uses sounds to enhance the visual impact on the screen of actions. Many events in both system and application software can be accompanied by a sound, for example, for opening, closing or deleting a file. These sounds catch the user's attention and confirm the action.
- **Speech synthesis** is a specialised use of sound output facilities, and uses software that generates the voice patterns for text. This is of immediate use to those with visual impairment; for them, a computer can read back word-processed documents, or read text that has been scanned in or viewed on the Internet. Speech synthesis systems can also be used by people who are unable to speak themselves for medical reasons.

## Tactile output devices

Touch provides immediate information about the world, but is not as well understood as sight, and is only just beginning to be exploited by computer developers.

- A **Braille printer** outputs text in Braille, which uses raised dots to represent characters. Blind users who have learned Braille can print and take their documents with them, giving this form of output an advantage over speech output.
- Tactile feedback can be provided by a **data glove**. It is produced by creating pressure on parts of the hand to give the impression that an object is being touched.

## Multi-modal systems

The most sophisticated systems combine two or more types of output into an integrated presentation.

- **Multimedia systems** combine visual and sound outputs. Multimedia is commonly used for reference content (such as encyclopaedias) on CD-ROMs, for games, and for business presentations (using presentation packages such as PowerPoint). The major impact of multimedia, though, has been through the new communications channels that have opened up in the last 20 years. The Internet, 3G mobile networks and digital TV have all exploited visual and sound outputs and have developed new interface standards.
- **Virtual reality (VR)** systems integrate visual, sound and touch outputs. A complete virtual reality system can include a headset which may have both eye gaze and movement sensors, together with one or more data gloves. The visual output can then be provided through screens placed in the headset and just in front of each eye. 3D vision is created by having a screen for each eye displaying slightly different images.

### Check your understanding 12.3

You may be familiar with some leisure uses of VR systems. Can you list some, non-leisure applications that currently use VR technologies, or that could use VR in the future?

## Processing

Many of the input and output devices we have mentioned are themselves components in complex input or output systems. For example, a printer is normally viewed as an output device, but it has all the features of any computer system, in that it receives input from the CPU, it stores data in its memory, it stores configuration data in memory, it processes data using an onboard processor, it sends signals to the CPU, and it sends the main output data to the actual printing components.

Similarly, hand and speech recognition systems include hardware and software components. They take input from the interface, interpret that information with software that draws on artificial intelligence (AI) techniques, and then output the interpreted data to the main system.

## Memory and secondary storage

All forms of output and input have data storage requirements, both in main RAM memory and in secondary backing store.

- **Text** takes up relatively little space in either main memory or backing store. ASCII files use 1 byte per character. This unit has around 100,000 characters, including spaces, so the text alone could be stored in a 100 Kb ASCII file. In practice, much text these days is stored in word-processed files which use considerably more storage space to hold formatting commands. A text-only version of this unit, with no illustrations, could be stored in a word-processed file of around 430 Kb.

- **Images** can be very memory hungry. An image that is 200 × 300 pixels has 60,000 pixels. Assuming that the image uses colours, the data about each pixel is stored in either 1, 2 or 3 bytes. One byte per pixel gives 256 different colours so is only useful for simple images like cartoons and icons. Two bytes per pixel (high colour) give over 65,000 colours, but photo-realism can only really be achieved with 3 bytes per pixel (true colour), which provides more colour choices than the human eye can distinguish. So the approximate uncompressed memory requirements for images would be as shown in Table 12.1.

  Images are often compressed, using algorithms that avoid the need to keep repeating identical colour values. Compression can bring the size of an image file from megabytes down to a few kilobytes, without any visible loss of quality.

| Bytes per pixel | Number of colours | 200 × 300 | 800 × 600 | 1024 × 768 |
|---|---|---|---|---|
| 1 | 256 | 60 Kb | 480 Kb | 768 Kb |
| 2 (High colour) | 65,536 | 120 Kb | 960 Kb | 1.54 Mb |
| 3 (True colour) | 16,777,216 | 180 Kb | 1.44 Mb | 2.34 Mb |

Table 12.1 Memory requirements of images

- **Animations** display many images per second, so they use even more memory. Although images that require a substantial amount of memory can usually be stored in today's high capacity hard disks, they can transfer slowly into main memory, and main memory itself may fill up with too many images.

- **Sound input** is digitised by a process that samples successive moments of sounds, and then gives each sample a set of values representing the pitch and intensity. The quality of the recording depends on the sampling rate (i.e. how often the sound is sampled per second) and the sampling resolution (i.e. the number of bytes used to store each sample). Again, popular sound formats used on computer systems compress the sound with minimal loss of quality.

### Check your understanding 12.4

Calculate the amount of memory required to store these uncompressed bitmap images:

1 An icon 15 pixels square, using 256 colours
2 A small decorative graphic, 120 × 20 pixels, using 2 bytes to store each pixel
3 A 400 × 300 true colour photograph.

## Limitations of current and projected developments

There is much imaginative work going on in the HCI field. Future developments will always be constrained by the capabilities of the hardware available at the time, but demands from HCI designers encourage the hardware designers to develop new technologies. The limitations usually revolve around these factors:

- the capacity of and speed of access to internal memory
- the capacity of and speed of access to storage devices
- the speed of processors
- the physical dimensions of devices.

### Further research 12.2

Identify a recent development in HCI. It could be a device which has become widely available in the last year or so, it could be the latest generation of mobile phones, or it could be a new use for virtual reality systems. Why was this innovation not available a few years ago? What technical limitations had to be overcome?

# Styles of interaction and their development

The term 'user interface' usually denotes the screen display generated by a computer system. As sight is the dominant sense, the design of user interfaces has become a major concern of HCI research. **Graphical user interfaces (GUIs)** have largely, but not entirely, replaced non-graphical ones.

### What does it mean?

A **graphical user interface (GUI)** incorporates graphics into the visual display. The graphics are not simply used as decoration but are used to replace text and to convey meaning to the user.

## Non-graphical interfaces

It is sometimes difficult to imagine a computer without its familiar GUI, but you will probably be familiar with, or can remember, teletext on television in its original, non-digital form (Figure 12.5). This used only text characters in a simple and limited display. Block images were created by using the IBM extended character set. Input comes from the remote control, which is a simple keyboard.

Figure 12.5 A teletext screen

Non-graphical interfaces can also be seen on many point-of-sale terminals in shops. The output displays on some machines used by the public, such as ticket machines and some bank ATMs, still use them. Most calculators are non-graphical, as are many of the control displays for devices such as printers. Non-graphical interfaces usually take input from keys and do not use pointing devices, like mice. The user interfaces for many desktop computers in the 1980s were entirely text-based. Although graphical display units were available they were expensive and so they were restricted to specialised users.

Once graphical displays became cheaper and more common, GUIs became the norm. Some of the more useful features of non-graphical user interfaces are still used, especially on small displays.

## Command line environment (CLE)

This is a type of non-graphical interface that was widely used in the past. Before GUIs were introduced, all operating systems were controlled using simple text commands. Systems administrators became very adept at using these commands, and some of them today still find that they can work faster in the command line environment than in a GUI.

### Further research 12.3

If you are using a version of Microsoft® Windows you can switch into the MS-DOS command line environment.

Find the MS-DOS Prompt. Click on this and the window shown in Figure 12.6 will open. As you are still technically in a graphical environment, there are a few icons at the top of the window, but they did not exist on the original DOS-based machines. Once you move into the main black screen you will find yourself in a world in which the mouse does not work, and there are no icons or drop down menus. To make anything happen at all you will have to enter some commands from the keyboard.

Figure 12.6 The MS-DOS window

You will notice that you are in the Windows® directory (folder) on the C drive. Try keying in these commands:

- **DIR** lists all the files in the current directory (Figure 12.7). The screen will scroll rapidly as the details of all the files and subdirectories are displayed. At the end of the list, the system will state how many files and subdirectories there are in the Windows® directory.

Figure 12.7 A directory listing in MS-DOS

- **DIR /P** pauses the display. This allows you to read the information one screen at a time.
- **CD <directory name>** changes the directory.
- **CD HELP** opens a subdirectory called HELP. Use DIR /P to see its contents.
- **CD..** changes the directory to the root directory, which is the main directory for the C drive itself.
- **MD <directory name>** makes a directory. For example, MD MYFILES will create a subdirectory called MYFILES in the current directory.
- **DEL <filename>** deletes a file.
- **EXIT** leaves MS-DOS.

### Menu-driven systems

Menus can be used in a purely text-based system, without a mouse. The simplest menu system is that offered by teletext, in which the viewer keys in the number of the required option on a key pad. A menu-driven system is a more usable non-graphical alternative to a CLE.

Other menu-driven systems use the cursor keys to move between options and the enter key to select. There are many contexts where it would not be convenient to use a mouse, such as at a point-of-sale terminal.

### Form-fill systems

Software applications often require the user to enter data. In a simple user interface the user will be presented with a form to complete. Data will be keyed into small text boxes, known as **response fields**. The user will usually be able to move from one field to another using the tab key, or sometimes the cursor keys. Figure 12.8 shows a form-fill dialogue used in a simple text editor.

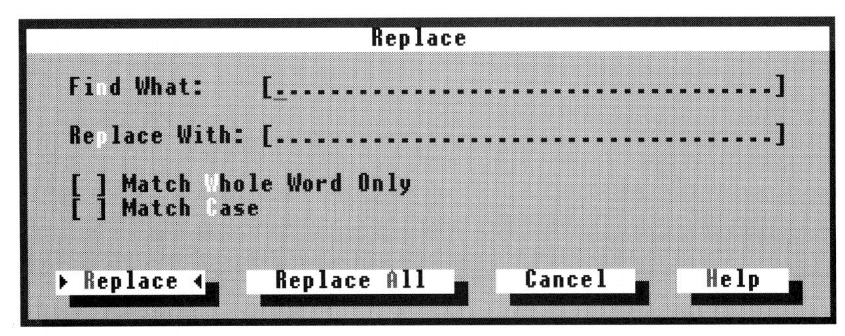


Figure 12.8 A form-fill dialogue

Forms are used in GUIs as well, and they often include extra graphical features such as check boxes and radio buttons.

### Hot keys

Selecting from a menu can be a slow process, whether using the cursor keys to sweep through a menu, or a mouse to activate a drop-down menu and then click on an option. A much more direct method is to hit a hot key which will select the option straightaway. The user soon learns the keys or key combinations that are frequently used.

**What does it mean?**

A **hot key**, or keyboard shortcut, is a key which initiates an action. Sometimes a key combination of two or more keys have to be pressed together.

## Graphical user interfaces

Non-graphical user interfaces served their purpose well while computers were only being used by trained specialists. The rapid expansion of desktop computing forced software and hardware suppliers to consider the needs of ordinary, non-technical users. Software developers started by introducing GUIs for operating systems, so they were able to sell their stand-alone systems to a wider market, including for unsupported home use.

A working model of a GUI was first developed as long ago as 1973 by Xerox, for its research Alto computer. It was designed to help a non-technical user to work effectively with the operating system. By the early 1980s, the GUI (Figure 12.9) had a three-button mouse and a black and white bit-mapped display with a **WIMP** environment. This was quite remarkable at the time as all other visual display units could only present text and used command line interfaces.

> **What does it mean?**
>
> **WIMP** stands for Window, Icon, Menu, Pointer. These are the significant components in a GUI.

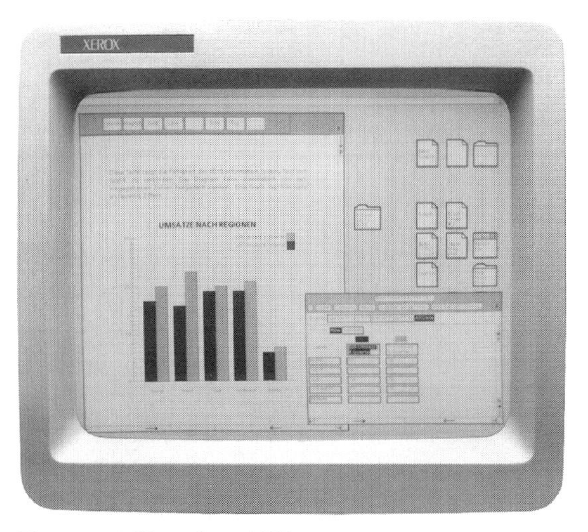


Figure 12.9 Xerox Star, 1981

Apple, and then Microsoft, launched their GUI-based systems in the early 1980s. The first version of Microsoft® Windows had **windows** that could not be overlapped but introduced the task bar at the bottom of the screen (Figure 12.10).

> **What does it mean?**
>
> A **window** is a rectangular area that displays what a program is doing. It allows the user to interact with one process, for example, to edit a picture, save a document, or change preferences.

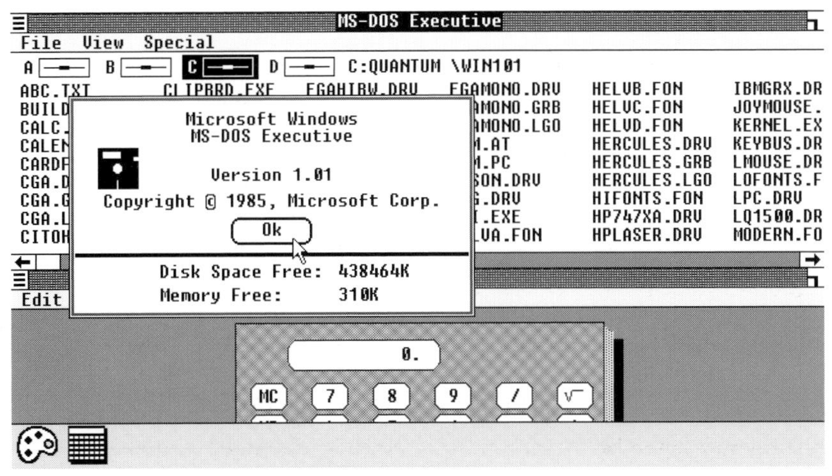


Figure 12.10 Microsoft Windows, 1985

The standards that were developed for operating systems were gradually adopted by applications developers as well. Most GUIs today make use of one or more of the WIMP elements.

## Windows

Windows are widely used in business applications, although they are less commonly used in some multimedia software, especially games. Windows support multi-tasking, as several windows can be open at the same time and the user can often switch between them. At any one time, only one window will be active, that is, ready for the user to input, and this will usually appear to be on top of the other windows. There are two types of window.

- **Standard windows** carry out the core processes of an application, such as viewing, entering and editing data. They can usually be positioned and sized by the user. In some applications, a standard window can be subdivided into separate mini-windows, known as panes (Figure 12.11). The user can select which panes will appear on screen.

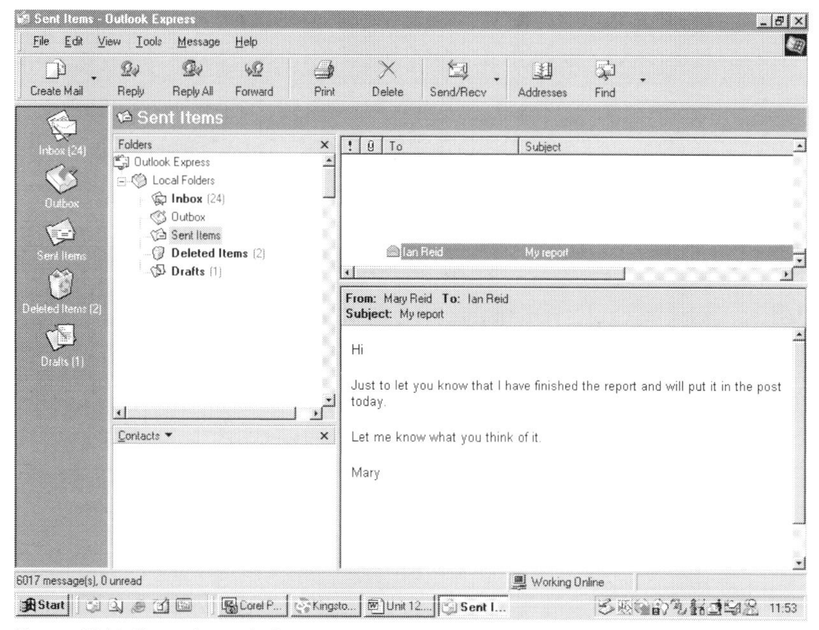


Figure 12.11 Panes in a window

- **Dialogue windows** enable the user to select options to carry out a specific action (Figure 12.12). They usually appear in response to a selection from a menu. The appearance of a dialogue window depends on the selections that the user makes, and buttons or lists will help the user to choose.

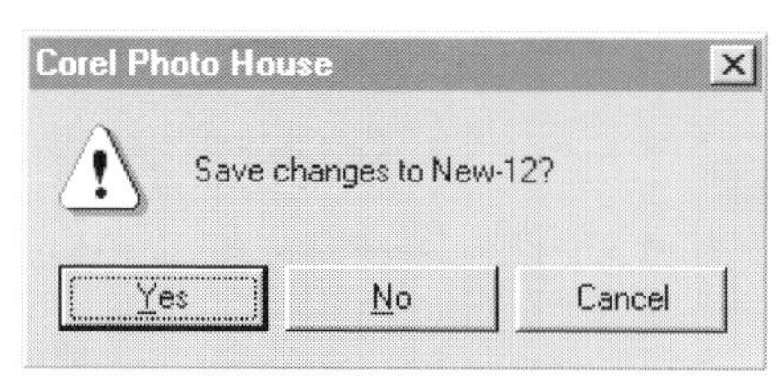


Figure 12.12 A simple dialogue window

## Icons

An icon is a graphic which represents an action that the software can carry out, and which the user can select (Figure 12.13). Icons are used instead of words to reduce the space needed on screen and to enhance the user's understanding.

**What does it mean?**

An **icon** is a small image that represents an action.

Figure 12.13 Some icons

GUI designers try to design icons that convey the same meaning to all users irrespective of the languages they speak, but this can be difficult to achieve. Sometimes words or labels (pop-up screen tips) are added to each icon to explain the meaning.

## Menus

While non-graphical menus have been offered to users ever since the first software applications, they have become much more flexible in GUI environments. The main function of a menu is to allow the user to make a selection from a fixed set of options. It also prevents the user from making an invalid selection.

GUIs offer many types of menu.

- A **static menu** offers a consistent set of choices throughout the application. It is often placed along the top of the screen or down the left-hand side. The main static menus on websites are often referred to as **navigation bars**.
- A **pull-down menu** hides the choices until the user is ready to make a decision. A pull-down menu drops down below the main menu bar when one of the items in the menu bar is selected, and it disappears again when not needed.
- A **pop-up menu** often appears similar to a pull-down menu, except that it can be positioned anywhere on the screen.
- A **context-sensitive menu** (Figure 12.14) is a type of pop-up menu, which provides the user with a list of options that depend on the context.

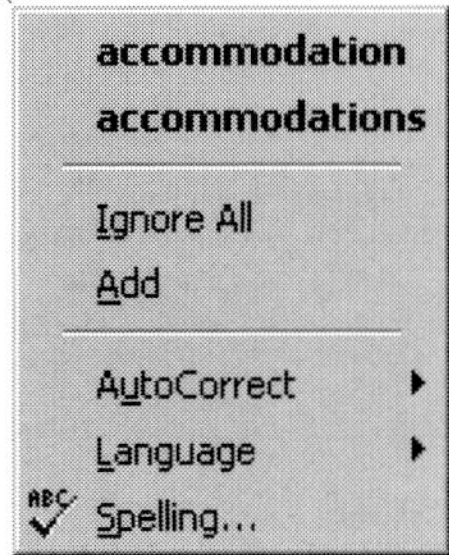


Figure 12.14 A context-sensitive menu

- **Sub-menus** offer extra choices, which would otherwise overcrowd a menu.

## Pointers

The main function of a pointer is to allow the user to make selections on screen, under the control of a pointing device. A pointer is often known as a cursor, especially when editing text.

**What does it mean?**

A **pointer** is an icon that is moved around the screen under the control of the mouse or other device.

Pointers are very important in a GUI as the user feels as though he or she is directly carrying out the actions.

## Object- and event-driven software

Vector graphics can also be described as **object-oriented** graphics. Each object in a drawing can be manipulated independently of the others; for example you can fill one object, such as a rectangle, with a colour or reposition it, without affecting any other objects on the screen. An object, in this technical sense, possesses properties (such as size, position, colour, transparency) and methods, which are operations that can be applied to the object (such as dragging or rotating).

Object-oriented programming languages, such as Java and C++, let the programmer create objects out of all kinds of things, such as documents, sounds, records, files or even a complete database.

A GUI environment is programmed using an **event-driven** language. An event is an occurrence, like a key press or a click of a mouse, which initiates an action by the operating system. For example, when a user clicks on a button which will open a dialogue window, the event is actually instructing the operating system to switch to the program module that controls that window. Some traditional programs simply carry out a series of actions in sequence, but event-driven software waits for an event to happen before doing anything. Most of the event-driven languages used to create GUIs have object-orientated features. Visual Basic and Delphi are both event-driven languages and are used to build interfaces that conform to the Microsoft Windows standards. Each has some object-oriented elements as well.

## Artificial intelligence (AI)

Although the term 'artificial intelligence' is widely used in science fiction, it is important to recognise that it covers a set of advanced software technologies that are already in common use. AI uses rules to analyse problems, much as humans do. As an example, software enables computers to play chess. The simple approach is for the computer system to analyse every single combination of chess moves that could be made from a given position, and then identify those that are more likely to lead to a win. This requires an enormous amount of processing and cannot usually be done in the time allowed. Good chess players do not think in this way. Instead, over time they build up rules for themselves about which moves are likely to be successful; in other words, they learn from their experience. A chess program developed with AI techniques will include the rules that have been developed by a good player. Some chess programs 'learn' by developing further rules from games that they play.

AI is used in HCIs to analyse and interpret inputs. They are able to solve problems in real time that would otherwise take far too long to be useful. An AI application also builds up a database, known as a knowledge base, which contains facts and rules that have been gleaned from experience. Here is a selection of uses of AI in HCIs.

## Interface agents

An interface agent is a software tool, rather like an inbuilt personal assistant, that provides support to the user of an application (Figure 12.15). It learns the user's preferences and habits (by storing them in the knowledge base).

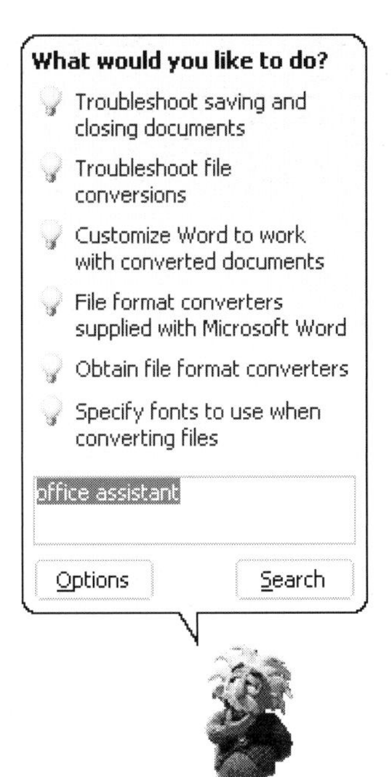


Figure 12.15 An interface agent

## Image analysis

AI techniques are sometimes needed to analyse captured images. For example, in handwriting recognition, the system has to learn the handwriting style of the user and continue to make intelligent guesses about inputs, even though an individual user's handwriting will vary from time to time.

## Natural language analysis

Natural language is the ordinary language (in this case, English) that we all use. One of the main aims of AI research is to develop an interface that will allow the user to write or speak in natural language, which will then be interpreted and a response given, also in natural language. With such a system, users would hold conversations with their computers that would appear to be very much like normal human interactions.

There are three main problems with natural language that the software has to deal with:

- There are many ways of expressing the same thought in language. 'Let's get a bite to eat' means much the same as 'Do you want to go for lunch?'.
- The meaning of a sentence often depends on the context. 'How's Jim?' will be understood by the hearer who will know who Jim is.
- In conversation, we express a lot of meaning through non-verbal body language. This may not be so relevant if the user writes the words, but, as speech systems develop, users will tend to treat their computer more and more like a person.

You will have come across the simple natural language interface used by some search engines such as www.ask.co.uk. This takes natural language input from the keyboard, analyses this and converts it into a request for searches.

### Further research 12.4

Alan Turing laid down all the foundations of the modern electronic computer when he built machines to decipher German military codes during the Second World War. Even back in 1950, Turing was foreseeing computers playing chess and other aspects of what we now call artificial intelligence.

The Turing Test derived from his thinking about how we judge intelligence. Imagine a user confronted by two computers. The user asks both computers questions (the input method is irrelevant, but a keyboard is the most likely). One of the computers generates its own responses using software; the other one relays the questions to another person sitting in another room, who then sends the answers back. The problem is this: Can the user tell which responses come from a human and which come from a computer? If the user cannot distinguish them, then the software can be said to be 'intelligent'.

The Loebner Prize is an annual challenge to produce a software system that is the most human-like in its responses and closest to meeting the conditions of the Turing test. Find out about recent winners of the Loebner Prize, and how convincing their systems were.

### Assessment activity 12.1

For this assessment, you should present your findings either in a written report or as a presentation. Your material should cover all these points:

1. Explain what is meant by the human computer interface.
2. Describe a number of different HCIs and the software applications that they support. In each case, explain how the HCI enhances the use of the application.
3. Select at least three specialist environments and describe the hardware and software that is needed to support each. Try to include different types of HCI. For example, you might select a point-of-sale terminal in a particular shop, a games machine in an arcade, and a system used by someone with a disability.

# Users

Users can be categorised in several ways.

- *Level of expertise:* Users range from beginners, through intermediate to advanced. Advanced users are sometimes known as power users, as they make the most efficient use of all the functions in the software.
- *Familiarity with the system:* A user who is new to a particular system is sometimes referred to as a naïve user.
- *Age:* Children, adults of working age and the elderly respond to systems differently.
- *Usage:* A user of a software package may be using it as a professional, maybe as a business non-specialist, and/or it could be for leisure purposes.

## Needs of users

Users' individual needs vary greatly. It is important that an HCI meets the needs of each individual who uses it, but that does pose a problem for HCI designers. How do they design an HCI to meet the individual needs of a wide cross-section of the public?

One approach would be to try to design an interface that will suit everyone. This may seem like a good aim to have, but it can rarely be achieved, except for the simplest of software. A better solution is to design an interface that can be customised to meet individual needs, and this is the solution adopted by most designers. Users can adapt the HCI to suit individual preferences, by, for example, changing the handedness of a mouse, creating a toolbar with their most commonly used buttons, altering the characteristics of the screen display, changing the default font styles, altering the volume and tone of sounds, or altering the sounds themselves.

Some users have special needs, which cannot be catered for so easily using customisable interfaces. They need specially designed HCIs. These users include those with visual impairment, hearing loss, limited motor (movement) control and learning difficulties.

# Applications developments

An HCI designer can draw from many developments in the field of user interaction when assembling an HCI. We will look at some of the key underlying concepts.

## Direct manipulation

In many HCIs, the users are given the impression that they are directly controlling the objects on the screen. A user may use the mouse to apparently pick up an object and then move it to somewhere else (also known as 'drag and drop'). Direct manipulation like this makes the interface seem natural and familiar to the user. The techniques are made possible through the use of event-driven programming languages coupled with fast processors and high-resolution screens. Interfaces that use direct manipulation well are sometimes described as **intuitive**.

## Metaphors

HCI designers often base their interfaces on real-world situations. Most applications are used in offices, so it does seem sensible to use the familiar language and images of a desktop, such as folder, document and bin. On the other hand, an application created for an artist would be more likely to use terms like palette, canvas, brush and pen.

IT professionals talk of files, directories and programs, but these ideas can be very confusing for a non-technical user. So the GUI designer invents a 'virtual world' that the users understand, employing the images and terms that they use in their work. Icons, often acted on by direct manipulation, give the world an air of realism. This virtual world is known as a *metaphor*. These are the most widely used metaphors:

- office desktop
- control panel
- personal organiser
- book
- artist's easel
- workbench
- landscape.

The desktop metaphor is now used widely for operating systems on personal computers. It has also been extended to most office applications. Unfortunately, the metaphor does not always work very well. Programs are referred to as applications, even though the word 'application' would not be used in an office. In addition, terms from other metaphors are often used, such as control panel, task bar and toolbar.

**Check your understanding 12.5**

1 Find examples of each of the types of metaphor listed above.
2 Which ones use the metaphor effectively?
3 Did you find any examples of metaphors that were inappropriate or unhelpful?

## Hypertext

The concept of hypertext was developed by Vannevar Bush in 1945, although the actual term was not invented until 20 years later. Scientists across the world were having difficulty in keeping up to date with the rapidly growing body of scientific research. Long before multimedia applications and the **WWW** made use of the concept of hypertext, Bush recognised that individual research papers referred to other papers, which in turn referred to others, linking them all together in a vast information network.

Hypertext was not developed successfully as a technology until the 1980s when it appeared in Help systems and some educational software, using **hyperlinks** on a screen to act as links to other pages of information. Strictly speaking, **hypertext** is a system that uses hyperlinks to link one page of text to another, while **multimedia** or **hypermedia** add images, sounds and other electronic media to the purely textual ones. In practice the three terms are used interchangeably.

### What does it mean?

WWW stands for World Wide Web.

A **hyperlink** is a hotspot on a page that links it to other files.

## Multimedia

Once hypertext systems had been developed, the way was open for CD-based encyclopaedias and games to integrate all types of file (sound, image, etc.) into coherent multimedia applications.

Although the Internet was developed in the 1960s, it was not until Tim Berners-Lee invented the WWW in 1990 that Bush's original vision of a global interconnected system became a reality. The WWW consists of text files written in a hypertext code. A software utility called a browser interprets these files as pages of information with hyperlinks embedded in them. The innovative aspect of the WWW was that these links could link to any other page that uses the same protocol, and this was possible because each page on the Web has its own address, known as its **URL**.

### What does it mean?

URL stands for uniform resource locator.

The WWW was always intended to be a multimedia system, and plug-ins can be downloaded today so that any type of file can be shared with any user.

### Assessment activity 12.2

Use the Internet, television programmes, books and magazines to research recent developments in the field of HCI. You can also watch out for news about new technologies that are about to emerge.

Present your findings, and make sure you identify the applications and the intended users for whom the HCIs have been designed.

# 12.2 HCI and the user

An effective HCI integrates the hardware and software with the humans and with the physical environment. To emphasise the significance of the individual humans in all this, they are sometimes referred to as 'livewire'. Human users have specific skills and needs that must be understood by the designer. The term 'livewire' also suggests that, in some respects at least, humans are a bit like computer systems. In this section, we consider human senses (our input devices), human memory (our storage devices) and human cognition (our processing methods).

## Human senses

Human senses are the input methods whereby we capture information about our environment. As mentioned before, humans have five senses, or six if the sense of movement is included. HCI designers work mainly with four of these: vision, hearing, touch and movement. In each case, the sense includes two elements:

- **Physical reception** – this is how the relevant organs (eye, ear, skin and the movement sensors in the inner ear) receive stimuli from the outside world.
- **Perception** – this is how the brain interprets the stimulus, so that we interpret it as an image, a sound, an object or motion.

### Vision

The lens at the front of each eye focuses light on to the retina at the back. The retina has over 100 million photoreceptors (light sensitive cells). There are two types of photoreceptors: rods, which react to light, even when light levels are low; and cones, which give us colour vision. The rods and cones generate electrical impulses, which travel to the brain along the optic nerve.

Our two eyes are not in the same position, so each receives slightly different stimuli. The images projected on to the back of the eyes are upside down, so, to make any sense of them, the information gathered by the photoreceptors has to be processed by the brain. This processing, called visual perception, also helps us to perceive the size of objects and to work out whether an object is near us or far away. Perception also relates the image to our previous understanding of the world, so we sometimes see what we expect to see, rather than what is actually there.

When designing an HCI, certain aspects of vision have to be considered:

- The **brightness** of an object is the amount of light it is giving off. Our eyes do not always perceive brightness consistently. The rods and cones in our eyes do compensate for low light levels, so we can perceive the same image as having greater or less brightness depending on the overall level of light.
- **Contrast** is the comparison of the brightness of two objects.
- We can distinguish between about 7 million different **colours**. The colour of an object has three components – hue, saturation and brightness (also called intensity). The hue is the actual wavelength of the light which determines whether we see it as blue, red, etc. Saturation is the amount of white in the colour.

## Hearing

Sound waves pass through the canal of the external ear and make the eardrum vibrate. Tiny bones on the other side of the eardrum, in the middle ear, pick up the vibrations and pass them to the inner ear. The inner ear is filled with fluid, and also holds a spiral tube called the cochlea. Tiny hairs called cilia are attached to nerve cells inside the cochlea and these are moved by the vibrations in the fluid. These generate the electrical impulses that go to the brain (Figure 12.16).

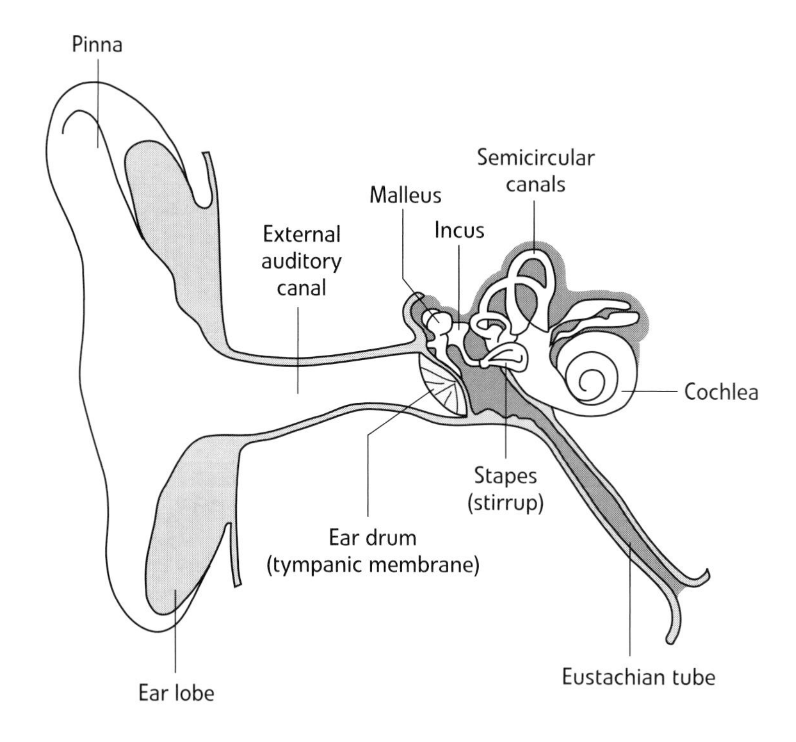


Figure 12.16 The ear

Sound perception processes these signals and interprets them as sounds. We can appreciate a wide variety of sounds, some of which are used with great subtlety in music and speech. Two ears enable us to work out the direction from which a sound originates.

Humans identify the following components of sound:

- **Pitch** is the sound frequency and determines how high or low it sounds. The human ear can hear frequencies in the range 20Hz to 15khz. (One Hz is one cycle, or vibration, per second).
- **Intensity** is the amplitude or loudness of the sound and is measured in decibels. Just as our eyes do not always interpret the brightness of an image consistently, so the way in which we assess the loudness of a sound does depend on the other sounds around it.
- **Quality** (or timbre) depends on how pure the sound is. Most sounds, especially those produced by musical instruments, carry secondary sounds as well, which give them their characteristic tone.

### Touch

Humans have three types of receptors in the skin which respond to heat, pressure and pain. Some parts of the body, such as the fingers, have a greater concentration of receptors than others and are more sensitive. The nerve endings in the skin send signals to the brain, which are then interpreted as sensations of touching.

### Movement

Movement of the body is detected by three semicircular canals, which are also located in the inner ear. The three canals lie in the three perpendicular planes. When the head is moved, the liquid inside the canals moves, and stimulates nerve cells.

## Human memory

Human memory is our method for storing information for future recall. Storing and recalling information are not as straightforward as in a computer, because all the information that we hold in our memory is constantly being re-examined and re-interpreted in the light of our experience. We do also genuinely lose memories.

### Short-term memory

Short-term (or working) memory stores information for immediate use. When you read from a book, short-term memory holds the previous words so that you are able to make sense of a whole sentence.

Information stays in short-term memory for about 20 seconds. It can hold from 5 to 9 pieces of information at any one time.

Some of what we remember in short-term memory is transferred to long-term memory after a few seconds. Information is more likely to be transferred to long-term memory in certain circumstances:

- when it has meaning for the person
- when the person has repeated it out loud (i.e. reframed the information)
- when the person can visualise the information.

### Long-term memory

There appears to be no limit to the amount of information that can be stored in long-term memory. It is where we store everything we know. Long-term memory is of two types.

- The memories of events in our lives are held in **episodic memory**. This links together a number of memories that are all associated with the same event, so that when we remember part of the event we also remember the rest.
- The term 'semantic' refers to meaning, and **semantic memory** is our memory of all the facts, rules, concepts and skills that we know. It is our own knowledge base. The concepts that we have are linked to each other and, indeed, we cannot learn a new fact unless we can relate it to something we know already.

How do we retrieve (remember) the right information in memory when we need it? There are two processes.

- We use **recall** when we bring information back from memory.

- We use **recognition** when some information that we have at present acts as a cue to finding information in long-term memory. The new information is compared with the information that is already known.

Long-term memory is capable of storing memories for a lifetime, so we may wonder how we manage to forget information that we once knew. Sometimes new information seems to interfere with and blot out old information. For example, once you have learned the number of your new mobile phone, you will find it difficult to remember the old one. Sometimes, the emotional content of memories makes them painful and we avoid remembering them. Some researchers believe that we do not forget anything at all, but simply find some information difficult to recall.

# Human cognition

Humans process the information that is input through their senses and is stored in their memories. In academic circles, this processing is known as 'cognition', but most of us just refer to it as 'thinking'. Human cognition includes learning, knowing, understanding, reasoning, problem solving, imagining, using language, and planning. We will look at two of these in more detail and then examine why humans make errors.

## Reasoning

This is the process of drawing conclusions from information. For example, if you look out of the window and notice that people in the street are putting up umbrellas, you could reason that it has started to rain. You would base this conclusion on your visual perceptions of the scene before you, together with your semantic memories of rain and umbrellas. There are two main types of reasoning process.

- **Deductive reasoning** takes the facts and rules that we know and moves forward to a conclusion. In the umbrella case, the fact that 'people have put up their umbrellas' together with the rule 'if people put up umbrellas then it must be raining' leads logically to the conclusion that it must be raining.
- You might wonder where the rule about umbrellas has come from, and this is where **inductive reasoning** comes in. Over time, our semantic memories make links and connections between bits of information. If we see two events happening together often enough, we create a rule for ourselves. So, through our lives we will have noted that umbrellas and rain seem to go together and will formulate a rule about them: 'if people put up umbrellas, then it must be raining'. Inductive reasoning is the process of forming a general rule from a number of experiences. The more experiences we have, the more confident we become about our rules.

### Check your understanding 12.6

In each of the following scenarios, is deductive or inductive reasoning being used?

1. In other software packages that I have used, a picture of a disk represented saving, so if I click on the disk in this package it will save my work.
2. If I go left at this point I will fall into the dungeon, so I had better go right.
3. In my word processor, some words become underlined with a wavy red line. If I right click on any one of them, up pops an alternative spelling. Therefore, it looks as though the wavy line is telling me that I have made a spelling mistake.
4. Does that ping mean that a new e-mail has arrived in my mailbox?

## Problem solving

This is the process of finding a solution to a problem. We all solve problems every day of our lives, for example, how to travel from A to B, how to pass this unit, or how to avoid speaking to someone we do not like. We may not be aware of the methods we use to solve these problems, but we tend to rely on a few strategies for finding the solutions.

- One strategy is to use trial and error, but in the mind only, and, in this context, it is known as **generate-and-test**. This is the simple approach to playing chess mentioned in relation to artificial intelligence on page 346. You try out all the possible solutions in a systematic way and check whether each works.
- Another approach is to break a problem down into sub-problems and try to solve each one independently. This is the standard approach to writing programs, but it can be used for all kinds of problems.
- Another strategy is to work backwards from the goal. Suppose your problem is choosing which course to take next year. You could start by thinking of the kind of job that you would like to be doing in five years' time. You could then work backwards by finding out what qualifications you would need to enter that profession, and hence what you would need to do to be on the right path.
- If you have met a similar problem before then you can use **reasoning by analogy**. You compare the two problems and check that they are similar enough at the critical points. You then see whether the solution to the previous problem helps you to solve the current one. The power of analogy is exploited all the time in HCIs.

## Errors

We are not always successful in finding the solution to a problem, or we arrive at a solution, only to find later that we made a mistake along the way. None of the approaches to reasoning and problem solving is infallible, and any of them can result in errors.

- Some errors arise because we have our facts wrong. This may be due to inaccurate perception. If the 'facts' are then used to make a deduction, then we could find ourselves making an error.
- We may use inductive reasoning to come up with a rule that is simply wrong. This is because each of us only has a limited experience of the world. For example, until you studied this unit you might have believed, based on your own experience, that all HCIs on desktop computers use GUIs.
- The generate-and-test method for solving problems depends on analysing each alternative solution carefully. One simple error at an early stage could mean that no solution is found.
- Breaking a problem down into its sub-problems can lead to error if the sub-problems are not properly defined.
- Reasoning by analogy is fraught with dangers. It assumes that the previous problem and the current one are similar in the respects that matter, but that may not be the case. Analogy is widely used in HCIs, and must be used with care.

# Ergonomics in HCI design

**What does it mean?**

**Ergonomics** is the study of the design of equipment for the workplace. Its aim is to enable workers to be more productive.

Ergonomics experts look at how humans do their work in their physical environment, so they are interested in office furniture, lighting, heating and the layout of rooms. When they consider people who work with IT, they also study the layout of the computer equipment, the quality of the screen display and the effects that these have on the user's health and well being. As we saw before, HCI includes the physical environment where the computer is used, so ergonomic considerations are a component of HCI.

Sometimes, specialist environments are created for users with special needs, but the vast majority of people share similar work environments. HCI designers have to create environments that would suit potential users whatever their gender, age, height or build. They also have to support many different types of work including rapid data entry, intensive on-screen editing of text and images, information retrieval, e-mail and the use of the telephone. They also have to consider all the other non-IT activities that go on around the computer, such as writing documents, reading books, drinking coffee and talking with colleagues.

## Arrangement of controls and displays

**What does it mean?**

**Controls** are the elements of a screen display that the user can interact with. They include buttons, input boxes, menus, list boxes and sliders.

The function of a screen display is to enable the user to do work effectively, and the actual layout and appearance of the screen elements can have a significant effect on this.

- **Controls** can be arranged on screen in the sequence in which they should be used. For example, if the user has to key in personal data from a data collection form, then the order of the input boxes should match the order in which the information appears on the document. Data entry errors are easily made when this is not done.
- Some controls, especially buttons that trigger actions, should be grouped with other controls offering similar functions.
- If the same controls appear on several related screens, then they should appear in the same position on each screen.
- Controls that are used more frequently than others should be easy to find.
- Some controls should not be placed next to each other if they have opposing effects. For example, if a 'save' button is placed next to a 'delete' button, then mistakes will inevitably occur.

Text and images should be a suitable size, so that the user can see them without effort. The actual size will depend on the resolution and dimensions of the screen, but should be customisable by the user. The brightness and contrast of the display should be comfortable on the eye, and should also be customisable.

Colour should be used carefully. HCI designers have to be aware of the needs of users with achromatic vision (colour blindness) who cannot distinguish between hues. Colour should be used on a screen to enhance the information, but should not usually be used to convey information.

**Check your understanding 12.7**

Select an application that you use and list all the controls that appear on the screen.

## Arrangement of equipment

If users cannot reach the computer equipment easily, or are uncomfortable, then they will not be as productive as they could be.

- **Work surfaces** should be large enough for the tasks to be done, should be clear of obstructions and should have a matt surface. Ideally, it should be possible to raise or lower the work surface to suit the user. There should be sufficient space for a mouse mat.
- **Chairs** should be fully adjustable. The best office chairs can be raised and lowered, the tilt of the seat can be altered and the angle that the back makes with the seat can be changed.
- **Screens** should have brightness controls and be capable of tilt and swivel. They should be positioned to avoid glare and reflections by placing them at 90 degrees to a window. A document holder can be attached to a screen to hold documents at eye level.
- **Keyboards** should be movable, and the angle of the slope should be adjustable. A wrist support should be built in to the keyboard or provided separately. The pressure required to depress the keys should be checked; if too much pressure is required then the user's hands will ache, but if too little then the fingers will tend to slip off the keys.
- **Storage** for books, files, manuals, disks, stationery, pens and office equipment should be designed so that items are easy to reach but do not interfere with work.
- **Cabling** should be ducted or fixed in place so that it cannot cause an accident.

## Arrangement of users

The seating and work surface, together with the layout of the IT equipment, should allow the user to adopt a comfortable position whilst working (Figure 12.17). The user's feet should be flat on the ground or placed on an angled footrest. Office chairs should be adjusted to give the best position. The top of the screen should be at about the same level as the user's eyes. The screen can be tilted slightly upwards so that the user looks down on to the screen. Looking up for a long period can cause aches in the neck and shoulders. The screen should be placed about an arm's length from the user. The user should try to keep the forearms horizontal. Armrests on a chair can help, but only if they are at the right height.

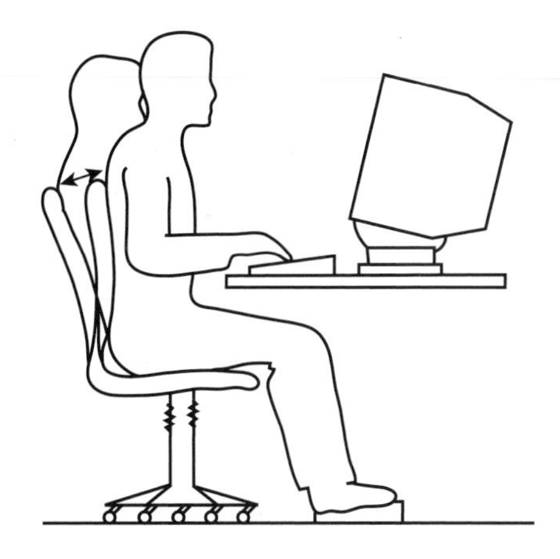

Figure 12.17 The correct position for a someone using a desk top computer

Left-handed users should ensure that their equipment is laid out to suit the way they work. Left-handed and ambidextrous mice are available.

## Environmental issues

Health and safety regulations cover many aspects of the workplace, such as electrical safety, fire precautions, ventilation, exposure to toxins, and these apply to IT workers as much as anyone else. The HCI designers can take these for granted, but there are some environmental matters that are particularly important for IT workers.

The temperature of the work environment should be controlled. People do not work well if they are too hot or too cold. The ideal temperature is around 21°C. People should not sit close to radiators or doors. Heating and air conditioning systems can also control the humidity. Inappropriate temperatures and humidity can affect the equipment as well as the users.

Background noise can be very distracting, so the workplace should be designed with quiet floor coverings. Open plan offices should have screens to muffle sounds. The equipment itself can sometimes be a problem; whining CPU fans, whirring disk drives and grating printers can all add to stress levels.

The overhead lighting should be satisfactory. Low-frequency fluorescent strip lighting must not be used in rooms that have computer screens because they cause flicker and visual disturbances.

Some years ago, there was concern about the level of electromagnetic radiation that was given off by computer monitors. International recommendations were adopted in the UK and many other countries, which forced the manufacturers to produce monitors than came well within the safety limits. It is now impossible to buy a screen that emits radiation above the safe level.

### Further research 12.5

In 1992, health and safety regulations relating to display screen equipment were introduced in the UK. The regulations require employers to:

- assess and reduce risks
- ensure workstations meet minimum requirements
- plan breaks or changes of activity
- provide eye tests on request (and special spectacles, where the test shows these are necessary for the work)
- provide health and safety information and training.

Find out more about these regulations on www.hse.gov.uk.

## Health issues

Computer users can develop physical health problems as a direct result of their work, but these can usually be avoided if care is taken.

**Repetitive strain injury (RSI)** causes pain in the shoulder, neck, arm, wrist or hand. In some cases, the problem can become permanent. Not surprisingly, some enthusiastic games players develop RSI. Users can avoid RSI by using properly adjustable chairs, by changing position from time to time, and by taking frequent breaks, especially from repetitive work at the keyboard. Long periods spent looking at a computer screen can cause eyestrain in the form of headaches and sore eyes. There is no evidence that eyes can actually be damaged by using a computer.

### Assessment activity 12.3

1 Select at least three HCIs with which you are familiar. These could be the ones that you looked at in Assessment activity 12.1. In each case, describe how the HCI design meets the needs of the users and helps them to carry out their tasks.
2 Consider other designs that could have been used. In each case, describe these alternative designs and compare them with the design that was used.

# Commercial considerations in HCI design and selection

Good HCIs help people to work more effectively. It might seem surprising that some well-run companies still use applications with poor quality interfaces. The reason they do so, is that the decision to upgrade software must be taken on business grounds. A business organisation has to weigh up the costs of upgrading against the benefits that it might bring. The costs will be measured in financial terms. The benefits may also be measured in terms of the money they save the organisation or the increase in profit. A business will not normally invest in a new system unless there are clear advantages in doing so.

- **Software upgrades** can be developed in-house or bought as off-the-shelf software applications. If the software already in use carries out all the functions needed by the organisation, then it may be possible to build a new user interface on to the existing system. This is a common approach for upgrading database systems, because the underlying structure of the database (tables and relationships) is developed and stored independently of the user interface (screen forms).

- **Hardware upgrades** may be necessary if the input and output devices are inadequate to support new software. For example, a good GUI should be viewed on a high-resolution screen. Extra memory and backing storage may be needed to support the additional processing.

- **Environmental improvements** can be expensive. New furniture, heating systems, lighting, and flooring may be needed, and complete remodelling of offices may be required.

- **Training** is always necessary when software is changed. An organisation can either send employees to outside training agencies, or provide it in-house. In both cases, the employees will not be doing their normal work while they are being trained, so temporary staff may have to be hired. A good HCI should minimise the amount of training that is needed.

Improved HCIs could bring one or more of the following benefits to an organisation.

- The main reason for investing in new systems is to increase productivity. Employees will be more productive if they can do more work during the day, or if their work is more accurate and requires less correction. These are exactly the aims of HCI designers.

**What does it mean?**

**Productivity** measures the amount of goods or services produced by workers in a given time.

- An effective HCI will give the organisation more control over the quality of output. If users are clear about what they should do when using an application, they are less likely to make mistakes, and more likely to do work that matches the standards laid down.
- Changes happen all the time within organisations; employees are promoted and new staff take on their work, new business develops so the nature of the work may change for some staff, new premises are acquired, and equipment is updated. Through all these changes, it is important that the business systems have resilience to outside pressures, so that the work can carry on uninterrupted. Good HCI designs across an organisation will ensure that old and new employees will continue to use software applications effectively, and will adapt quickly to new ones. This is because the skills learned using an effective HCI can be transferred to other contexts.

**Assessment activity 12.4**

Write a short report in which you assess the importance of HCI design in society.

# 12.3 Examples of HCIs

In this section, you will examine the process of creating an HCI and develop some examples yourself.

## Project development

All projects go through a number of phases:

- analysis, leading to a requirements specification
- design
- implementation
- testing and evaluation.

This approach does not just apply to ICT projects, but can be used for any project that has to be planned and managed from start to finish. HCI development is always part of a larger project, the end result of which will be an IT application. Indeed, any application should have two main facets, functionality and HCI. The functionality of an application is the tasks that it can perform, while the HCI is the means by which the user can interact with the application to perform those tasks. It is a mistake to design functionality first and then to add the HCI as an afterthought; the two facets should be designed and implemented in conjunction with each other.

The stages in a project are given different names and varying degrees of significance depending on the context. When this process is applied to software projects it is known as the **software life cycle**.

Traditionally, software projects were developed in a strict sequence. The complete design had to be approved and checked against the specification, before the programmers were allowed to start on the implementation. No changes to the design were allowed once implementation had begun. This disciplined process, known as the **waterfall approach**, ensured that the final product matched the specification exactly.

# HCI model design

## User-centred design

The traditional waterfall approach to software development is very successful if all the requirements of the system can be established before the design begins. Today, software engineers recognise that this is not usually the case when producing interactive systems, and it is interactive systems that need effective HCIs. The alternative approach to software development for interactive systems is known as user-centred design.

**What does it mean?**

An **interactive system** is one in which the user and the system communicate with each other throughout a process.

User-centred design is user-centred in two senses:

- It involves the users directly at all stages of a project.
- It focuses on the needs of the users.

## User-centred analysis

The analysis stage for user-centred design includes four main elements:

- task analysis
- user analysis
- environment analysis
- usability requirements.

The HCI designer will be fully involved throughout the analysis stage.

### Task analysis

This studies the way people perform tasks. It can include tasks that are done on the computer as well as related tasks that are purely manual. The description of task is known as a **model** of the task. HCI designers need to know what tasks people want to do when using an IT system, and the sequence in which they carry out those tasks. They can investigate this by reading manuals, observing users at work and interviewing users.

Tasks can usually be decomposed (broken down) into subtasks. Below is an example of task decomposition.

*To write a report:*

- carry out research
- write the report using word processing software
- check the report

- edit the report
- distribute the report.

The task of writing a report has been decomposed into five subtasks. Each of these can now be broken down further. We usually number the subtasks to show the hierarchy.

*To write a report:*

1 carry out research
2 write the report using word processing software
  2.1 create a new document
  2.2 write an introduction
  2.3 create the main headings
  2.4 write the text for each section
  2.5 write the conclusion or recommendations
3 check the report
4 edit the report
5 distribute the report.

Subtasks 1, 3, 4 and 5 can also be decomposed (and so could each of the subtasks within subtask 2).

Planning is used to decide the sequence in which the task should be done. So the plan for carrying out the whole task could look like this:

Plan 0: Do 1, 2, 3 in that order.
If the report needs to be amended do 4, then 3. Repeat until satisfied.
Do 5.

Subtask 2 can also be planned. Although the subtasks 2.1–2.5 appear to be in a logical sequence, most people write the introduction last of all. So the plan for this subtask could be:

Plan 2: Do 2.1, 2.3, 2.4, 2.5, 2.2 in that order.

More decomposition can be done on the task of writing a report, and plans can be drawn up for each subtask. The final version of tasks and plans is known as the **task model**. The task model for an HCI includes all the tasks that should be carried out using the HCI. Once a task model is ready, the HCI can be designed to match the way in which users work.

## User analysis

This establishes the needs of the intended user. There is hardly any software that has been designed for the specific needs of a single person, the main exception being systems designed for individuals with complex disabilities. Most software is used by a variety of users, so the problem for the HCI designer is to create, on paper, a user model. This would describe how the typical user would normally be expected to work with the software, but would also cover some variations to allow for human differences.

User analysis identifies all the people who are affected by the application, known as stakeholders. Stakeholders fall into four groups:

- **Primary users** are people who use the application directly.
- **Secondary users** use the application indirectly, by receiving output from it or preparing input for it (e.g. the manager who reads a computer-generated report, or a market surveyor who collects data for input).

- **Tertiary users** do not use the application but are affected by the system (e.g. the directors of a company, or the general public).
- **Facilitators** are the technical specialists who design and maintain the system.

Several questions have to be answered about each stakeholder. The following questions would be asked to the primary and secondary users:

- What role does the person play in the organisation?
- What task (from the task analysis list) does each person do?
- What knowledge and skills does each person have?
- What **work groups** does the person belong to?
- Does the person have to abide by privacy or security procedures?

**What does it mean?**

A **work group** is a group of people who work together on a task.

At the end of this process, the designer should have a clear picture of the typical primary and secondary users of the application.

## Environmental analysis

This investigates the physical environment where the system will be used:

- the physical environment, i.e. location, temperature, etc.
- the technical environment, i.e. existing hardware, software and networking that are relevant to the new design
- the organisational environment, i.e. the structure of the organisation, and who will be using it.

## Usability requirements

The concept of usability is central to HCI design. It assesses the extent to which a system supports interactivity. We commonly refer to the 'user friendliness' of interactive interfaces, but that term is used very loosely. Usability is a much more precise technical term, covering similar ideas. The usability requirements are effectively those HCI requirements that can be measured. Usability is defined by an internationally agreed standard as 'the extent to which a product can be used by specified users to achieve specified goals with effectiveness, efficiency and satisfaction in a specified context of use' (ISO 9241).

User analysis will identify the 'specified users', task analysis will identify the 'specified goals', and environmental analysis will identify the 'specified context'. The usability requirements then lay down some rules about what would count as **effectiveness**, **efficiency** and **user satisfaction**. These can then be checked, along with all the other requirements, at the testing stage.

**What does it mean?**

The **effectiveness** of an HCI (or any other IT development) is the extent to which the user can carry out tasks accurately and completely.

The **efficiency** of an HCI is the amount of resources (especially time) needed to carry out tasks.

**User satisfaction** is the acceptability of the HCI to the users.

Below are some possible ways of measuring the usability of an HCI:

*Effectiveness:*

- percentage of a task completed by a new user
- number of software features used
- ratio of successes to failed attempts to complete a task
- number of times the users seek help.

*Efficiency:*

- time taken to complete a task
- time taken for a new user to learn to do a task
- number of errors made when carrying out a task.

*Satisfaction:*

- number of users who prefer the new system
- ratings (e.g. on a scale of 1 to 5) given to the new system by users.

**Check your understanding 12.8**

1 Describe the components of user-centred analysis.
2 Why is each important in the development of an HCI?

## User-centred design and implementation

At the end of the analysis stage, the usability and other requirements will be written down and agreed, and these will then drive the next stage: the design and implementation of the HCI. The outcomes of the analysis, with the detailed usability specification, enable the designer to produce a design for the HCI. At this stage, it will be a preliminary design and, as we shall see, the design may go through several versions before being finalised.

The designer should answer the following questions:

- What input and output devices should be used in the HCI?
- If non-standard equipment is needed, what should it do and how should it be laid out?
- What style of interaction is needed?
- What should the screen interface look like?
- Are there any environmental design issues?

The aim of all HCI design is to maximise usability. There are a number of techniques that can help the designer to create a good design rather than a mediocre one.

### Standards and guidelines

These are rules that can be followed by the designer, although none is, strictly speaking, obligatory.

- Standards are set by national or international bodies, such as the British Standards Institution (BSI) and the International Organisation for Standardisation (ISO). You have already met ISO 9241 which lays down the standards for developing usability (page 363). It also deals with a number of ergonomic issues for people using computers in the office. Another relevant standard is ISO 13407: *Human-centred design processes for interactive systems,* which describes many of the procedures that are mentioned in this section. This states that user-centred design should involve the user at all the stages in the project, from analysis to testing.

The BSI standards that are relevant to HCI are mainly concerned with general health and safety issues, such as BS 1335-2, which deals with the safety requirements of office chairs. There are also several that relate to broader IT issues such as data protection, security, document management and the physical environment, such as BS 7083: *Guide to the accommodation and operating environment for information technology (IT) equipment.*

- Guidelines are not as widely adopted as standards and are produced by individual suppliers or organisations. Both Apple and Microsoft produce HCI guidelines for developers who want to produce software for their platforms. There are several guidelines for producing user interfaces for people with special needs; for example, the World Wide Web Consortium (W3C) publishes its *Web Content Accessibility Guidelines*, which give advice on making a web-style user interface accessible to people with a variety of disabilities.

## Iterative design

### What does it mean?

**Iterative design** is a method for developing software in which a design is implemented and tested with users. In the light of their reactions, the design may be amended, and checked again. In some cases, the specification may also be changed in response to the testing.

The waterfall approach to software development can be too rigid for projects in which the HCI is important. This is because the developer has to agree the specification with the client before anything is produced, yet it is often difficult to describe the final application so that the client can visualise it in action. HCIs have to be experienced before users can be sure that they meet their needs.

It would clearly be wasteful to develop a full working application first time through and then go back and change the design in response to tests with users. So a cut-down version of the HCI, known as a **prototype**, is developed and checked with users. There are two main methods for developing prototypes, and both can be used at different points in the same project:

- **Storyboards** are created on paper, and are simply drawings of the HCI designs. A series of pictures show how the HCI changes as the result of actions by a user. Storyboards can be produced quickly and cheaply and give the user a good idea of what the final application will look like.
- **Computer-based simulations** are generated using software tools, plus mock-ups of any new hardware devices. The prototype will represent the look and feel of the interface, but will not carry out the functions of the applications. A developer can develop the prototype with any suitable software tool, and is not forced to work with the software that will be used to build the final application.

### Check your understanding 12.9

1 What is a prototype?
2 Why do software developers use prototypes when designing HCIs?

## General design issues

There are a number of design issues that the HCI designer may need to consider.

- Professional users will have different expectations of systems than general users. In the first place, they will be very familiar with their field of work so will need support that relates to their level of knowledge and does not start from the beginning. Second, they will be **power users**, in other words, people who use their systems very efficiently, so prefer to use hot keys instead of mouse-driven menu selections. Third, they will want systems with a high level of functionality, and which match any industry standards.
- **System navigation** refers to how the user moves from one subtask to another. In a GUI, menus and submenus are commonly used, menu bars display the most commonly used options, and hot key alternatives are provided for the power user. Context-sensitive menus will display only those options that are directly relevant to the action being taken. Normal menus can be made more sensitive to context by greying out options that are not accessible at the time.
- **Simulators, virtual reality** and **games** all develop their own virtual worlds, and do not have to match the accepted standards for office software. Indeed, they lie at the cutting edge of developments, so can be as innovative as the designers choose.

## Design issues for special needs

The 'typical user' envisaged for many HCIs is a healthy, normal sized adult, with no disabilities or learning difficulties. They do not always cater for children, for elderly users, for very short people, for people with common conditions, such as achromatic vision, and they may well be frustrating for a typical user who is simply not feeling well. The designer should bear in mind the needs of these groups when designing the HCI for a system aimed at the general public. Some HCIs are designed to meet the specific needs of individuals or groups of users, and particularly for those with special needs.

- HCIs can be designed for users with **visual impairment**, which may vary from partial to complete blindness. Outputs include screen readers, speech synthesis and Braille printing.
- Users with **hearing loss** need interfaces that do not rely on sound clues.
- Speech loss can be overcome with an HCI that incorporates **speech synthesis**.
- Input devices can be adapted or developed for users with **limited motor control**. A concept keyboard can be programmed so that the touch-sensitive areas are large, and easily used variations on the mouse can be produced. Speech input suits some users. Devices can also be attached to the user's foot or head, exploiting whatever movement is possible. Eye gaze systems have been used successfully by users with very limited movement.
- People with learning difficulties often benefit from a well-designed HCI. Users with dyslexia work well with GUIs with a high graphical content, and they can use intelligent correction software (built-in to some word processors) to produce text output.
- Children have needs that are very different from those of adult users, and HCIs for children must take account of these.

# User-centred testing

In any kind of IT project, all designs should be subjected to two processes, known as **validation** and **verification**. These are the testing techniques that are used throughout the iterative design process.

## ? What does it mean?

Confusingly, the same two terms, validation and verification, are used in the context of checking data input, but they mean something completely different here. This famous definition was given by Barry Boehm:

**Validation:** Are we building the right product?
**Verification:** Are we building the product right?

In this unit, we are only thinking about the HCI, not about the functionality of the application but, of course, validation and verification tests have to be carried out on all aspects of the software.

- **Validation** tests check that the application meets the client's expectations. All aspects of an application can be submitted to the user for testing at the validation stage, but it is a particularly important method for assessing the HCI.
- **Verification** tests check that the application matches the full requirements specification. In traditional software development, this covered the functionality only. Formal program testing is carried out to show that the application performs all the functions accurately, and that it handles normal, extreme and erroneous data.

## Case study: Automatic Teller Machine (ATM)

ATMs (or bank cash machines) are terminals that link directly to a bank's main networks.

Figure 12.18 An ATM

The features of the HCI of a typical ATM, like the one in Figure 12.18, include:

- input devices, e.g. card reader, numeric keypad, up to eight additional keys alongside the screen
- output devices, e.g. screen, printer, cash dispenser
- user interface, e.g. a simple GUI (although some non-graphical interfaces can still be found)
- devices laid out so that card, printout and cash are handled on the right
- robust physical design for outdoor public use and to resist theft
- shaped for maximum privacy and readability
- usable by a naïve adult user

- not (usually) accessible to wheelchair users, very short people, or users with visual impairment.

The original developers of the ATMs had to work to a specification provided by the bank. This would have detailed the functionality required, e.g. to check the ID and status of the user, to dispense cash up to a limit specified by the account, to display details of the account and to provide printouts of transactions and information. The HCI designers would have worked closely with the application developers to create an environment that would allow the user to carry out transactions quickly and with as few errors as possible. They would have suggested several alternative HCIs, from which they would have chosen the final one.

Look at the ATMs for various banks and building societies and note the variations in HCI design.

1 What alternative input devices are used?
2 Are there variations in the positioning of the devices?
3 How do the screen interfaces differ?
4 Can you suggest why some of these choices were made by the designers?

**Assessment activity 12.5**

Find three examples of HCIs that meet the needs of different types of user. Imagine that you were the designer who developed each HCI.

1 Can you work out what happened at the analysis stage? What were the usability requirements? You may be able to find some clues in the manuals that accompany the software or in advertising material or reviews. You will probably not be able to state the requirements in any measurable detail, but you should be able to deduce the intentions in general terms.
2 Do the HCIs match up with the usability requirements?

# Development of HCIs

This section explores some of the practical issues around designing an HCI. You will be expected to design your own HCIs for assessment.

An HCI is a window on to an application. For assessment purposes, you are not expected to develop a full application, so you have two options:

1 Design the HCI for an application that you are developing, or have already developed, for another unit. This is the most straightforward option.
2 Design the HCI for a new application. In this case, you should specify the application, but you will not be expected to implement any of the functionality of the application.

In each case, you are expected to go as far as producing a final prototype. You are not expected to implement a fully working HCI.

## Selection of correct interface

Before you design an interface, you should carry out a full analysis (task analysis, user analysis and environmental analysis) and then write the usability specification. On the basis of this, you should then make some initial decisions. See page 364 for advice on the choices you need to make.

## Selection of correct tools

Prototypes can be demonstrated on paper (storyboards) or on a computer (computer-based simulations).

Some designers like to use graphical design software to draw the screens for a storyboard. Vector drawing packages are usually more suitable than bitmap painting packages, because individual objects, such as pictures of buttons, can be repositioned easily.

Computer-based simulations can be generated using any suitable software. They do not have to be created in the same software that will be used to generate the final application. Computer-based simulations should have clickable buttons and menus that appear to work, in the sense that they jump to another screen or produce a message. However, they do not have to carry out the functionality of the application.

You can create prototypes using any of the following:

- form design tools in database management systems such as Microsoft Access
- form design tools in standard office software such as Microsoft Excel or Word
- customisable toolbars, menus and other components in standard office software
- web design editors such as Macromedia Dreamweaver
- event-driven programming languages such as Visual Basic.

There are also some specialist prototyping tools on the market, but you do not need to have access to these to complete your assessments.

## Development of working model

You then need to go through a period of evaluation of your prototype. For more details on how to carry out an evaluation see page 370. You may go back and change the design as the result of the evaluation.

Carry on until you are satisfied with the prototype. For assessment purposes, you are not required to create a working application, but if you are developing the application for another unit, you may like to implement it fully.

### Assessment activity 12.6

1 Design HCIs for one or more applications. Page 361 describes the steps you should take when preparing a design, and page 364 gives you some practical advice for this activity. Note that you do not have to implement the application (although you can design an HCI for an application that you have developed for another unit). You should take the design to the point where an on-screen prototype of screen interactions responds to events, even if it does not process any data. Designs for non-standard input and output devices should be drawn on paper and, if appropriate, simple mock-ups can be built.

   Your designs should, between them, cover at least three different input methods and at least three different output methods. Keep detailed notes of all stages of the projects and provide full evidence of the analysis, design, prototyping and evaluations that you carried out.

2 Write a short report analysing your HCI designs, picking out any unusual or non-standard features. Compare them with other solutions to the same problems.

# 12.4 Evaluate the effectiveness of HCI models

Evaluation is an alternative term for the validation processes that are part of the testing stages. It is not simply an informal assessment of what worked and what did not work. Instead, it is a structured process for comparing the design with the usability requirements. User-centred design involves the user at all stages. It also uses iterative design methods, which means that designs are prototyped then evaluated, and this process is repeated until the final design is agreed.

## Evaluation of an HCI

Usability is 'the extent to which a product can be used by specified users to achieve specified goals with effectiveness, efficiency and satisfaction in a specified context of use', and usability requirements lay down some rules about what counts as effectiveness, efficiency and user satisfaction. Therefore, evaluation of an HCI focuses on effectiveness, efficiency and user satisfaction.

## Evaluating a particular HCI

Some techniques for carrying out evaluation with users are described below.

- **Walkthroughs**. An evaluator presents a user with a prototype of the HCI and asks the user to carry out some tasks. The user has to explore the prototype and learn to use it. There are two ways of managing a walkthrough. In the first, the evaluator observes the user, but does not give any help. In the second, known as co-operative evaluation, the evaluator prompts the user by asking 'what-if?' questions and can help if necessary.
- **Interviews**. Any formal discussion between two people can be described as an interview. For HCI evaluation purposes, the evaluator prepares questions in advance about the tasks that the user has to do.
- **Questionnaires**. Questions can be general, open or closed. General questions ask for simple factual information (e.g. When did you join the company?). Open questions simply leave space for the users to say whatever they like in response (e.g. What improvements could be made to the interface?). Closed questions allow the users to select from a fixed number of options. Closed questions can be posed as multiple-choice questions, where the users can select from several possible options, with tick boxes for the responses.

### Evaluating effectiveness

Effectiveness is best evaluated through walkthroughs, although some useful additional information can be gained from interviews and questionnaires. The evaluator is trying to discover whether the HCI enables the users to do their tasks accurately, using the correct functions and without making mistakes. An evaluation of effectiveness should provide answers to these questions:

- What percentage of each task did each new user manage to complete?
- If several users tried the same task, what was the ratio of success to failure?
- How many options (buttons, menu choices, etc.) did the user try before discovering the 'right' way of carrying out a task?
- How many errors (e.g. incorrect key presses) were made by a user for each task?
- How many software features were used by each user?

## Evaluating efficiency

Efficiency can be measured by carefully analysing walkthroughs. The evaluator needs to know whether the user is carrying out the task in the shortest possible time and with the least effort. An efficient user will be more productive – he or she will be able to do more work for the same amount of effort.

An efficiency evaluation will answer questions like these:

- How long did it take for a user to learn how to do a task?
- How long did it take for a user to complete each task, having learned how to do it?
- What percentage of the time taken to do a task was spent making errors?
- What percentage of the time taken to do each task was spent finding out what to do next?

The users might also provide some ideas in their interviews and questionnaires about how tasks could be simplified.

## Evaluating user satisfaction

User satisfaction is best evaluated through a questionnaire with closed questions. It could ask users to rate various aspects of the HCI on a scale from 1 to 5. For example, they could be asked questions like those shown in Table 12.2.

| | **5 Strongly agree** | **4 Agree** | **3 Neither agree nor disagree** | **2 Disagree** | **1 Strongly disagree** |
|---|---|---|---|---|---|
| I found it easy to carry out the task. | | | | | |
| I was able to find help when I needed it. | | | | | |
| I could find my way around all the screens. | | | | | |
| It was easy to see what each button was for. | | | | | |
| The colours used on the screen did not distract me from the task. | | | | | |
| The messages that the system gave me were easy to understand. | | | | | |
| Overall, I found the system easy to use. | | | | | |

Table 12.2 Example questionnaire to evaluate user satisfaction

The responses to these questions are often known as **satisfaction ratings**, especially to general questions like the last one. The responses can be analysed by comparing the numerical values and calculating the mean for a group of users. The HCI designer should certainly take action if satisfaction ratings are 3 or less.

# Alternative techniques for evaluation

So far, we have been thinking about how to evaluate HCIs that are aimed at the general user, but some HCIs are developed to meet the needs of users with specific disabilities, or even for individual users. In these cases, walkthroughs, interviews and questionnaires should still be used, but they can be augmented by other methods of evaluation.

For such projects, the usability requirements must be developed with great care. The HCI designers will have worked with the user (or a group of typical users) to establish the specific needs, but will also have talked to experts. The usability requirements will themselves be thoroughly discussed with both users and experts. Evaluation will be carried out at all stages of the project. So we can see that systems designed to meet special needs should be subjected to even more rigorous evaluation than systems for the general user. Two alternative evaluation techniques can also be used for general systems but are particularly valuable for systems developed for specific needs.

- **Heuristic evaluation.** Several evaluators work independently with an early prototype. They should all be experts in the type of needs that the HCI addresses. Each evaluator applies the ten usability heuristics developed by Jakob Neilson. These are a set of guidelines that deal with consistency in the user interface, error handling, feedback to the user, etc., and can be used to identify usability problems. The evaluators then compare their findings. In practice, it has been found that five evaluators will between them uncover 75 per cent of usability problems.
- **Review-based evaluation**. There has been a great deal of research into HCIs and also into the needs of users with a variety of special needs. The designer should research all the relevant expertise and academic knowledge, and find out whether similar systems have been built before and how successful they were.

### Further research 12.6

1 Use the Internet or books to find Jakob Neilson's ten usability heuristics.
2 Use the ten heuristics to analyse your own HCI designs.

### Assessment activity 12.7

1 Refer back to one of the HCIs that you designed. Carry out a full evaluation of it.
2 Describe the role of verification and validation in the development of an HCI and explain why it is important that they are done.

## Test your knowledge

1. What are the main factors that must be considered when designing an HCI?
2. What are the advantages of ergonomically designed keyboards over standard ones?
3. What is a smart card? Describe three different uses for a smart card.
4. Where can you find a handwriting recognition system, and why is it used in that context?
5. What are the main features of a data glove?
6. What is the difference between speech recognition and speech synthesis?
7. What is virtual reality?
8. Why do images and sound files take up so much memory? What techniques can be used to reduce their size?
9. Identify at least three non-graphical user interfaces that are still in use today.
10. What is the difference between a pointer and a pointing device?
11. Some programming languages are object-orientated and event-driven. Explain the two terms.
12. Outline some uses for artificial intelligence in HCIs.
13. Outline the hardware and software that would be needed for a system that could hold a conversation in spoken natural language with a user.
14. What are the main components of colour and sound?
15. What is the difference between long-term and short-term memory in humans?
16. Describe how a workstation in an office should be laid out.
17. What are the possible costs and benefits to an organisation of upgrading a system to one with an improved HCI?
18. What is the waterfall approach to software projects, and how does it differ from the user-centred approach?
19. What is usability?
20. Distinguish between verification and validation in the context of testing software.

# UNIT 31: WEBSITE DEVELOPMENT

This unit enables you to create Internet and intranet websites. The focus is on the creation of dynamic web pages and sites, and the unit also deals with the organisation of files on a web server. Although primarily based as a unit covering website design, this unit could be studied with reference to an intranet. You are expected to have a good understanding of the basic terminology of the Internet and related topics, especially e-mail. This unit presents opportunities to demonstrate Key Skills in communication and information technology, and is an internally assessed unit.

## Learning objectives

- To design web pages
- To design and build a website
- To publish website files on a server and review them
- To be aware of security and copyright with regard to websites and their servers

# 31.1 Design web pages

## Planning a website

Like any other software project, the development of a website must be taken through the usual stages of analysis, design, implementation and evaluation (review). User interfaces (as discussed in Unit 12), which are of particular importance in websites, are usually developed using **user-centred design** methods.

> **What does it mean?**
>
> **User-centred design** is an approach to the design and implementation of software, especially the user interface, which involves the user at every stage of the project. At the design stage, a prototype is created which is reviewed by the user and alternative designs developed in response.

The term 'user' is a bit ambiguous in this case. It can refer to both the client who commissions the website, and the end user who visits it. In practice, both are involved, although the client is the main user who is considered. At the final stages of evaluation, typical site visitors can also be asked to assess the site.

The design process usually follows this pattern:

- analysis
- design specification
- prototyping and implementation
- technical testing and publishing
- evaluation against specification.

### Analysis

Through interviews with the client, the designer must establish the purpose of the website and the target audience. Websites can be developed for a variety of purposes, and many sites have more than one purpose:

- *To inform:* All websites provide some information, which is one reason why the Internet became known as the Information Superhighway.
- *To sell:* Websites can be used to promote products and services to visitors.
- *To interact:* Websites can easily offer interactivity, allowing the visitor to send information and ideas back to the organisation and to engage in dialogue.

The intended audience may be the general public, or it may be targeted at specified age bands (children, the elderly), communities of interest (members of a club, people who enjoy a leisure activity, researchers, political or pressure groups), shoppers, travellers, etc.

### Design specification

Based on the analysis, the designer draws up a design specification which is agreed with the client. The design requirements of a website can be broken down into three areas: content, visual design, and technical design.

The **content** of a site covers all the information that it will contain, together with any interactive features. All sites should normally include, as a minimum, this information:

- *How to contact the organisation.* This information should always be provided somewhere on the site. It may be offered through an online form, or an e-mail address may be given.
- *Basic details about the organisation.* Who does it include and what does it do?
- *Privacy policy* (if personal data is collected from the visitor). This is a statement about how the organisation will handle any information given to them by a visitor. This is necessary to comply with the Data Protection Act and to give the visitor the confidence to do business with the organisation.

In addition, the content part of the design specification should describe in outline:

- the information that should be provided – text, visual information (charts, photographs, videos, etc.) and sound (music, etc.)
- the main categories of information so as to identify the headings that will appear in the main **navigation** bar
- the style of language appropriate to the subject matter (business sites will tend to use more formal language than sites devoted to leisure interests).

As a general rule, the visitor should not be overwhelmed with information that they do not want. Links can be given to more in-depth coverage of a topic.

### What does it mean?

**Navigation** refers to the way visitors find their way around a website, using links provided on the pages. Text or images can act as navigation links, and image links are often called buttons. Some of the most important links may be positioned together in a navigation bar.

The **visual design** of the site should specify:

- the overall impression to be given, e.g. businesslike, friendly, busy, formal, casual
- the required components, e.g. company logo or corporate colours
- the colour scheme, e.g. background, text and spot colours
- the appearance of text, e.g. consistent text styles, length of paragraphs
- the use of images, e.g. for information, as decoration, or to create a mood or style
- the use of animation and video, e.g. appropriate use to entertain and inform
- the layout of the home page and of subsequent pages.

In general, a website should use all its visual elements consistently. The main navigation bar should be accessible throughout the site, and should appear in the same position on each page.

The **technical design** concentrates on a number of usability issues:

- Navigation, e.g. links selected for the main navigation bar, establishes the linking structure for all the other pages.
- The use of search tools, e.g. list boxes, keyword search boxes and site maps, can help visitors to find their way around.
- The download times should confirm that a web page will download within an acceptable time. The page itself as well as all the images on it have to be downloaded individually from the server, so altogether they should not usually take longer than one minute to download using the slowest communication link. Larger files can be made available provided the visitor is warned about their size.

- Browser compatibility is essential. A web page can change in appearance when viewed with different browsers. The designer will try to minimise these variations.
- The site should be easy to maintain, that is, to update pages. The frequency of maintenance will depend on the purpose of the site.

## Prototyping and implementation

A prototype is a cut-down version of the site which can be used as the basis for a design review with the client. The first prototype, known as a **storyboard**, is created on paper to match the design specification. The storyboard is usually sketched by hand and should indicate:

- the layout of the home page and other pages
- the links on the main navigation bar
- the use of colour for background and text
- the use of images for information and decoration.

The storyboard should be reviewed with the client. This discussion will often highlight aspects of the design specification that were overlooked or not specified clearly enough. At this stage, the client will often be inspired with new ideas for the site and these can also be incorporated into the design specification.

The designer then creates a computer-based prototype, based on the agreed storyboard, using web design software. The design is then subject to review and amendment, and this is repeated until the client is satisfied. The prototype will normally consist of the home page plus a small number of indicative pages.

Once the client has agreed on the prototype, the remaining pages can then be fully implemented.

## Technical testing and publishing

The website goes live at the moment when it is published, that is, when it is uploaded to a web server and becomes accessible to visitors. Before that happens, the site should be subjected to thorough technical testing.

## Evaluation against specification

The website will have been reviewed with the client throughout its development, but the finished site must be subjected to a final review with the client against the original specification. At this stage, any errors that emerge can be dealt with.

### Assessment activity 31.1

All the assessment activities in this unit should be viewed as one project, broken down into stages. You will be given a client specification for a website. This could be provided by a real client, who runs a small business or other type of organisation. Alternatively, your tutor may provide you with a realistic but simulated specification, and he or she will act as your client for assessment purposes. The client specification will be short, and will describe the purpose of the site, the target audience and any specific requirements.

Draw up a design specification, covering the content, visual design and technical design of the website.

# Creating web pages

This section offers an introduction to creating individual web pages, while pages 390–416 describe some more advanced techniques that you can use to enable you to develop a complete functioning website. If you already have some experience in developing websites, you may prefer to skim through this introductory section fairly quickly, but do not omit it entirely as it may contain some ideas that are new to you.

## Selecting an appropriate web authoring package

Web authoring packages, or web page generating software, provide facilities that are very similar to DTP packages, but are geared to the specific demands of the web environment. As the web designer is constructing a web page, the package generates the HTML source code. This code can be edited directly and can also be enhanced with scripts for dynamic effects.

There are a number of useful web authoring packages available, such as Microsoft *FrontPage* and Macromedia *Dreamweaver*. Another simple web authoring package, Netscape *Composer*, can be downloaded free with the browser, Netscape *Navigator*. These packages provide the designer with an environment which helps to automate the process of linking pages together to form a complete website.

Most of these packages provide useful page templates that can be used to lay out the content. A beginner can use any of these, although to gain a real understanding of how web pages are built it is better to start with a blank page. Web authoring packages often provide wizards that can be used to create complete sites, with built-in themed graphics and page layouts. Although some of the results can be pleasing, they are rather limiting. Websites produced in this way are sometimes difficult to modify and update, and they look very similar to each other.

In this unit, all the examples are based on Microsoft *FrontPage 2000*. Similar features will be found in later versions of *FrontPage*, and also in other web authoring packages.

### Case study: Getting started with *FrontPage*

When you launch Microsoft® *FrontPage*, it usually opens with a blank page. If anything else is displayed instead, then you can click on Page in the Views bar (see Figure 31.1, left-hand side of the window).

You can then type in some text, as you would in a word processor, and save the page, giving it a suitable name. All standard web pages are saved with either .htm or .html as the filename extension.

As in most word processors, pressing the Enter key starts a new paragraph, whereas pressing Shift+Enter starts a new line omitting the paragraph spacing.

When a page is saved, *FrontPage* creates some additional folders, notably one called 'images', and another called '_private' which is used to store files on a website that will be kept hidden from a visitor.

*FrontPage*, like most web authoring packages, will allow you to display the page in three modes:

- Normal (page editor)
- HTML
- Preview

You can create the page in Normal mode, and then check what it will look like when displayed by a browser in the Preview mode. At this stage, they will look very similar, but differences will emerge as you use more advanced features.

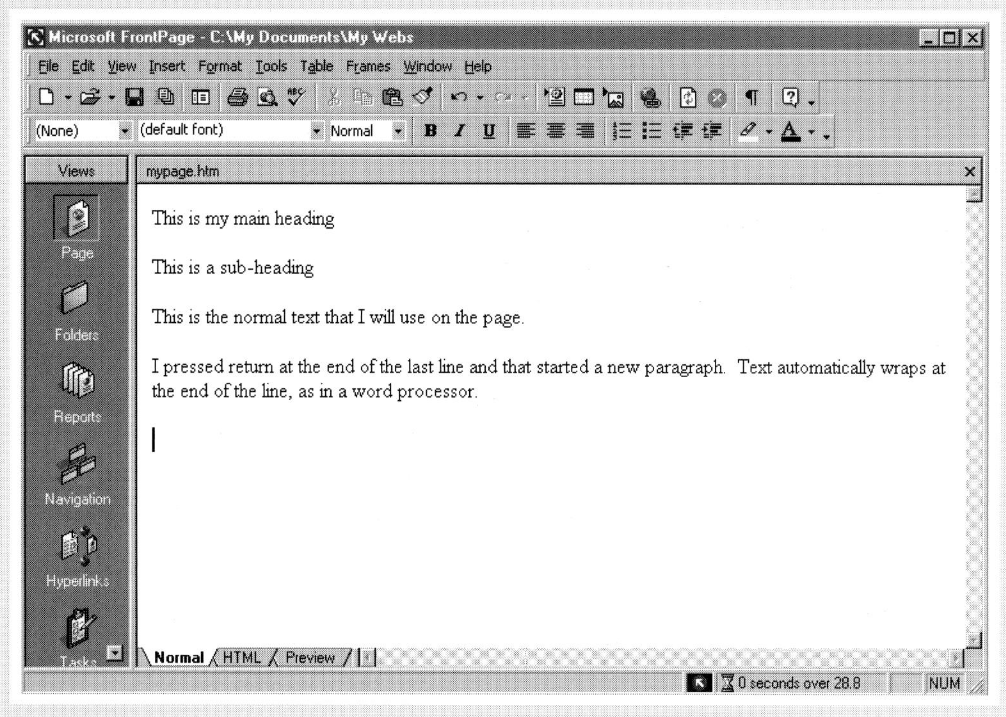


Figure 31.1 Entering text in page editor (Normal) mode in *FrontPage*

**Launch your web authoring package, and create and save one page similar to that shown in Figure 31.1.**

# The web authoring environment

A web authoring environment includes a page editor and an HTML editor. As the page is developed in the page editor, the HTML code is being generated in the background. Web designers can work in either editor and can easily switch between them.

The environment also provides a means of viewing the page in a browser. Some provide a built-in preview mode, which gives an immediate impression of how the page will be displayed. Some web design environments allow you to specify a standard browser that can be used for previewing the pages. However, there are some differences in the way different browsers (and different versions of the same browser) interpret HTML code, so it is important to check web pages in a range of standard browsers before they are published.

## Understanding HTML

The HTML code for the web page displayed in Figure 31.1 would look like that shown below:

```
<html>

<head>
<meta http-equiv="Content-Language" content="en-gb">
<meta http-equiv="Content-Type" content="text/html; charset=windows-1252">
```

```
<meta name="GENERATOR" content="Microsoft FrontPage 4.0">
<meta name="ProgId" content="FrontPage.Editor.Document">
<title>This is my main heading</title>
</head>

<body>

<p>This is my main heading</p>
<p>This is a sub-heading</p>
<p>This is the normal text that I will use on the page.</p>
<p>I pressed return at the end of the last line and that started a new
paragraph.  Text automatically wraps at the end of the line, as in a word
processor.</p>

</body>

</html>
```

The markup codes placed between triangular brackets are called **tags**. Tags are not case sensitive. Most tags come in pairs; the start tag (e.g. <p>) and the end tag (e.g. </p>). Note the overall structure of the HTML code:

```
<html>
<head>
</head>
<body>
</body>
</html>
```

Lines placed between the head tags are hidden from the visitor, but can be used very powerfully, as we will see on page 393.

- **<p>** and **</p>** mark the beginning and end of a paragraph.
- ** ** is an abbreviation for non-breaking space and is the code for a normal space character.
- **<br>** (not shown here) marks a line break.

## Using heading and paragraph styles

The page editor allows the designer to highlight text and to apply a style from a style list. This list is similar to the style list found in word processing packages, but is initially limited to a fixed set of styles. The list will always include Normal (or default), Heading 1 to Heading 6, plus bulleted and numbered list styles.

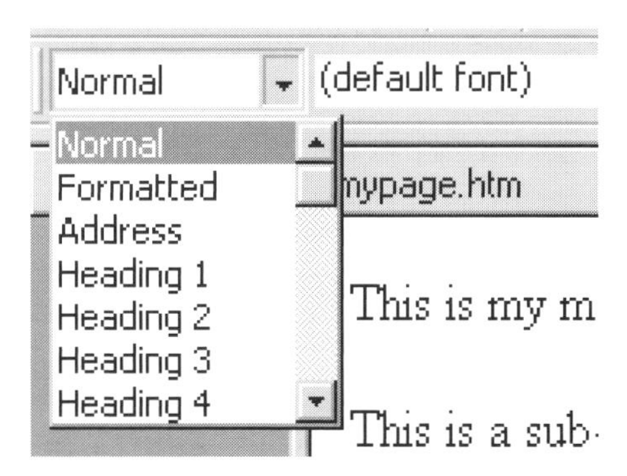


Figure 31.2 The style list in *FrontPage*

## Case study: Headings and paragraph styles in *FrontPage*

In Normal mode, you can use pre-set styles with any of the text. The style list is found at the left end of the formatting toolbar, and the drop-down list displays the styles available (Figure 31.2).

1 Highlight the lines of text in turn and apply the Heading 1, Heading 2 and Bulleted List styles from the style list (Normal is the default style for the page). Check the HTML code to see what effect this has had, and compare this with Figure 31.3.

2 In Normal mode try replacing the bulleted list style with the numbered list style, and then check the HTML code again.

You may be tempted to use the other options in the formatting toolbar, and introduce other fonts, but try to resist this for the moment.

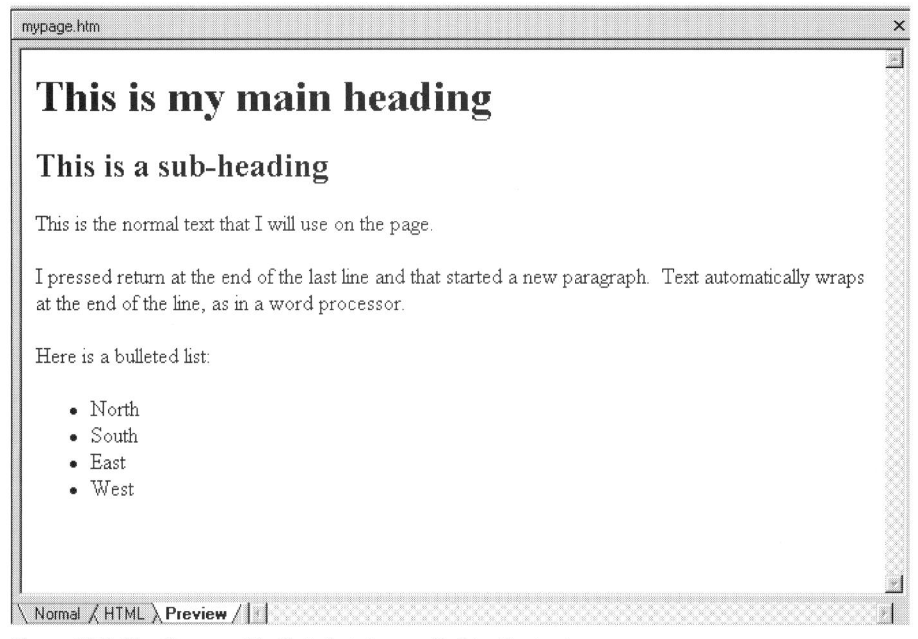


Figure 31.3 Headings and bulleted styles applied to the text

The HTML code for the body of the page uses a different tag for each style, as shown below. The <h1> and <h2> tags represent Heading 1 and 2 styles; <ul> marks the beginning of an unordered (i.e. unnumbered) list, and <li> is a list item.

```
<body>

<h1>This is my main heading</h1>
<h2>This is a sub-heading</h2>
<p>This is the normal text that I will use on the page.</p>
<p>I pressed return at the end of the last line and that started a new
paragraph.  Text automatically wraps at the end of the line, as in a word
processor.</p>
<p>Here is a bulleted list:</p>
<ul>
```

```
    <li>North</li>
    <li>South</li>
    <li>East</li>
    <li>West</li>
</ul>

</body>
```

All tags use the 'Normal' (default) style from the style list, except those that have been specially defined.

A page editor also allows the designer to format text using the font options, which are usually displayed on a formatting toolbar. A visitor's browser will be able to display a font only if it is already resident on the visitor's computer. So, although a web designer may want to use an attractive but obscure font for a heading, the visitor will only be able to see the characters displayed in the font if they already have that font on board. If they do not have the required font then the browser will display the text in the default font for that browser; on a Microsoft Windows system the default font is normally Times New Roman, but the visitor can change the default font to whatever he or she wishes.

## Preparing images for a website

All images should be prepared for web use before they are inserted into a web page. Images are prepared by reducing them to the appropriate size, and by compressing them in one of the standard web formats.

A computer graphic has a 'size' in two senses: the **memory** needed to store the image and the **dimensions** of the image measured in pixels.

- Most computer graphics use a very large amount of memory. For example, a photograph taken with a digital camera will be 2 Mb or more. On a slow connection, a picture this size could take half an hour or more to download from the Internet.
- It is very important that an image created for a web page is exactly the right size for the space it is going to occupy. This ensures that it has no more pixels than it really needs.

Because of the memory problems, all images used on websites are stored in a compressed format. Compression reduces significantly the amount of memory needed to store an image of given dimensions.

Two compressed formats are commonly used on the Web:

- **jpg** is used mainly for photos. Jpgs can use 16-bit or 24-bit colour values and so can provide a photorealistic quality.
- **gif** is used for most other images. Gifs only use 8-bit colour values and so are limited to 256 different colours.

As a general rule, the total size of all the images on a normal web page should be no more than 60 KB, although 30 KB is preferable to ensure that visitors using the slowest modems are not kept waiting too long. Larger images can be displayed on a web page, but only if the visitor is warned about the size before loading the page.

## Case study: Adding an image using *FrontPage*

A word of warning: when you are working in *FrontPage* do not use Windows® *Explorer* to copy images directly into the images folder. You have to find them elsewhere, insert them on your page and then allow *FrontPage* to place them in the images folder.

If you are using another web authoring package, then you should create an images folder alongside all your page files. You will probably be able to place images into the images folder before you insert them into a page.

1 In *FrontPage*, in Normal mode, place the cursor at the point where you want an image to appear, then use Insert / Picture / From File. You will have to click on the folder icon in the dialogue box in order to navigate to the location where the image is stored on your system. The image should appear on the page, as in Figure 31.4.

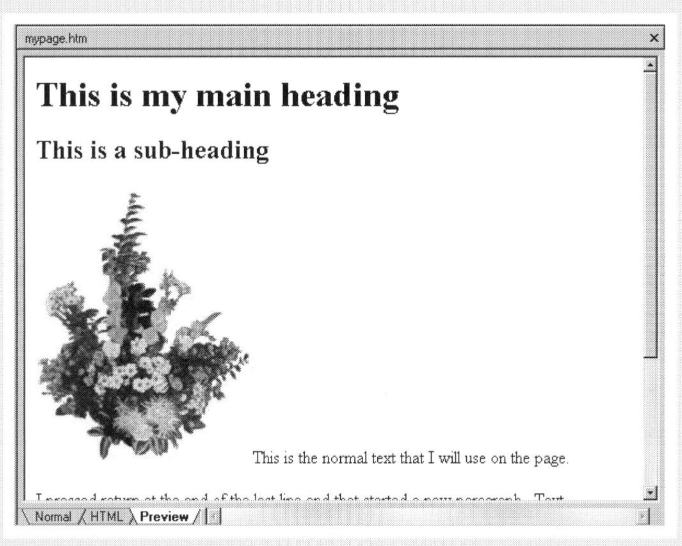


Figure 31.4 An image inserted onto a web page

2 *FrontPage* has already created an image folder for you. When you next save the web page, *FrontPage* prompts you to save the image as well, with the dialogue shown in Figure 31.5. The image should be saved in the images folder, so if 'images/' does not appear in the Folder field, click on Change Folder and open the images folder.

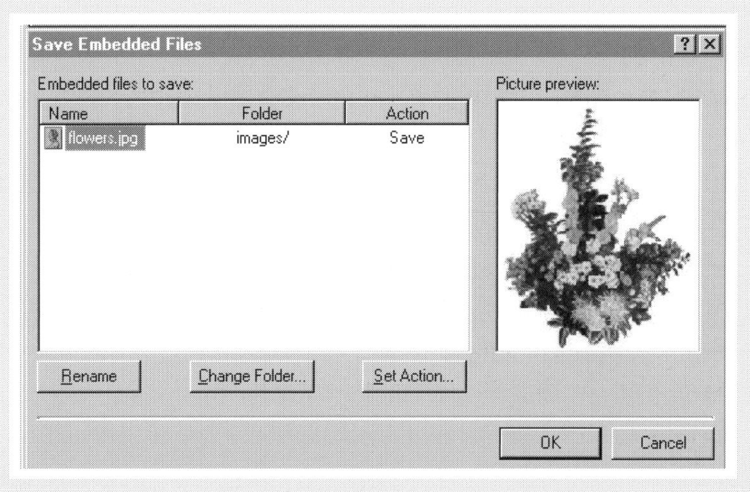


Figure 31.5 Saving an image for a web page

## Adding an image to a page

Once an image has been prepared for web use then it can be inserted on to a page. Images viewed on web pages are stored as independent files. This means that when a page is downloaded into a browser, the browser then has to download each of the image files from the server as well. All the image files that are used on a web page are stored on the server alongside the page files.

It is common practice to store all the images on a website in a folder called 'images'. A web authoring package always provides a means of inserting images on a page, usually from an Insert menu.

Once an image has been placed on a page, the HTML coding includes an <img> tag, such as:

```
<img border="0" src="images/flowers.jpg" width="199" height="251">
```

Border, source (src), width and height are all **attributes** of the <img> tag. Attributes are HTML's way of listing the properties of the image.

- **src** is the filename of the image and its location relative to the page.
- **width** and **height** are the dimensions of the image. Altering these values will distort the image but will not change the memory needed.

Images cannot be manipulated as simply as they can in DTP packages, but further attributes can be added to the <img> tag. Most web authoring packages provide an image properties dialogue, usually accessed by right clicking the image in page edit mode, and this generates more attributes, such as:

```
<img border="2" src="images/flowers.jpg" alt="A flower arrangement" align="right"
hspace="10" vspace="10" width="199" height="251">
```

- **alt** text appears as a screen label in a browser, when the mouse is held over an image (see Figure 31.6). This acts as a marker if an image is slow to download and it also provides a useful description to the visitor. Alt text is essential to make a site accessible to blind visitors, who will use text readers to understand the content.
- **align** positions the image relative to the text next to it; the effect depends entirely on where the cursor was placed when the image was inserted.
- **border** values greater than zero draw a border around the image, with the given thickness measured in pixels.
- **hspace** (horizontal) and **vspace** (vertical) create space around the image.

### Case study: Changing the image properties using *FrontPage*

In this activity, you will experiment with changing image properties, using *FrontPage*.

1. In Normal mode, right-click on the image and select Picture Properties. Any changes that you make to the properties of an image will be listed as <img> attributes in the HTML code.
2. On the first canvas of the dialogue box, enter some descriptive text in the Alternative Representations Text box. This is the 'alt' text for the image.
3. Next, click on the *Appearance* tab. Do not alter the size properties, but experiment with the Layout properties. All the values are in pixels. When you have made your selections view the page in Preview mode and compare it with Figure 31.6.

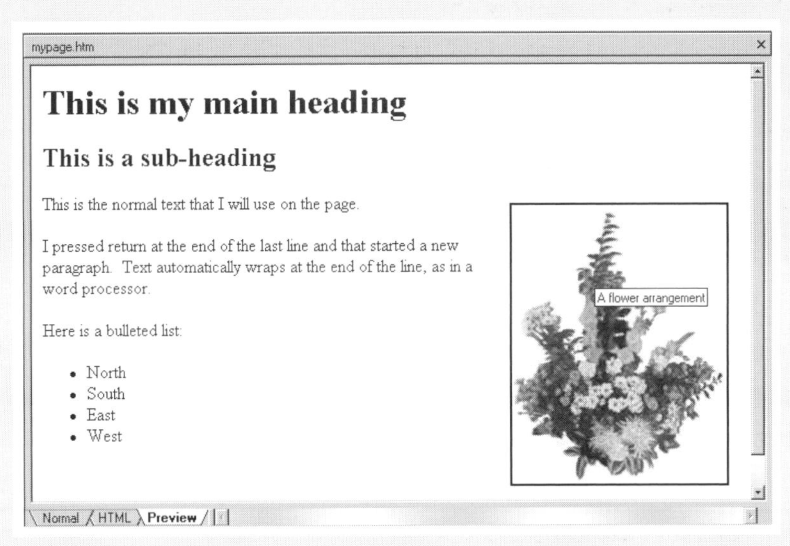


Figure 31.6 The effect of changing the properties of an image

## Using animated gifs

The gif format can be used to create short repeating animated sequences. Many examples of these are displayed on websites, and there are many free sources on the Web. Animated gifs should be used, if at all, with great care. The eye is drawn to an animation, especially if it lies on the periphery of vision, and can distract the visitor from the main content.

As a general rule, animated gifs should only be used to draw attention directly to an item on the page, such as a warning, or to request a visitor to take an action straightaway (e.g. to confirm some information), or for amusement.

### Further research 31.1

Check out some of the most widely visited sites, such as BBCi (www.bbc.co.uk) and see what use they make, if any, of animated gifs.

## Adding other graphic elements

A horizontal line can be added to the page, usually using the Insert menu on the web authoring package. The tag for this is simply <hr>, for horizontal rule, and there is no end tag in this case.

The colour of the background can be changed, usually through a Page Properties dialogue. Most web authoring packages offer a palette of colours. The HTML adds the 'bgcolor' attribute to the <body> tag:

```
<body bgcolor="#FFFF00">
```

**bgcolor** gives the background colour, with the value expressed either as a six digit hexadecimal code, e.g. #FFFF00, or as an RGB code, e.g. rgb(255, 255, 0), or as a standard colour word, e.g. yellow.

A background image can also be applied to a page instead of a background colour, although the image should be chosen carefully as too much detail can distract the visitor from the text.

All backgrounds are automatically tiled, that is, repeated to fill the space, so a small image can be used. Web authoring packages usually provide a selection of background images, which can be inserted through a Page Properties dialogue, and are defined in HTML like this:

```
<body background="images/ripple.gif">
```

Here, **background** gives the location and name of the image that is used for the background.

### Case study: Adding lines and a background using *FrontPage*

1. In *FrontPage*, use Insert / Horizontal Line to add a standard grey line that extends across the page.
2. In Normal mode, right-click anywhere on the page, then select *Page Properties* to view the page properties dialogue. Click on the *Background* tab. Select a colour under *Colors: Background* (note that *Format / Background* gives a shortcut to this dialogue).
3. Experiment with using the same dialogue to insert a background image. This will tile across the whole page.

## Using hyperlinks within the same page

Hyperlinks can be used to link to:

- another position on the same page
- another page on the same website
- another website.

We will look at the first of these now, and the other two on page 394.

In a browser, a hyperlink can jump to an invisible bookmark placed elsewhere on a page. Using a page editor, bookmarks can be set anywhere on a page. In HTML code, a bookmark is denoted with the <a> tag (standing for 'anchor') which has a name attribute to identify it. In the example below, a heading with the title 'First section' has been bookmarked so that a hyperlink somewhere else on the page can link to it:

```
<h2><a name="First section">First section</a></h2>
```

The text that is to become the hyperlink is then highlighted and formatted as a link. The HTML code for the hyperlink itself uses the <a> tag again and looks like this:

```
<p><a href="#First section">Link to first section</a></p>
```

**href** stands for hyperlink reference, and states the location that the hyperlink links to. In this case, '#First section' is the name of the bookmark where it links to, with the # used to identify it as a bookmark.

By default, hyperlinks take on a familiar appearance, with underlined blue text.

Images can also be used as hyperlinks; these are often referred to as buttons. The HTML for a graphical hyperlink looks like this:

```
<p><a href="#First section"><img border="0" src="images/mybutton.gif" width="120"
height="30"></a></p>
```

## Case study: Creating hyperlinks using *FrontPage*

1 Create a new page and enter text similar to that in Figure 31.7, with three distinct sections, each with a subheading. The three lines below the main heading will become hyperlinks to the content further down the page.

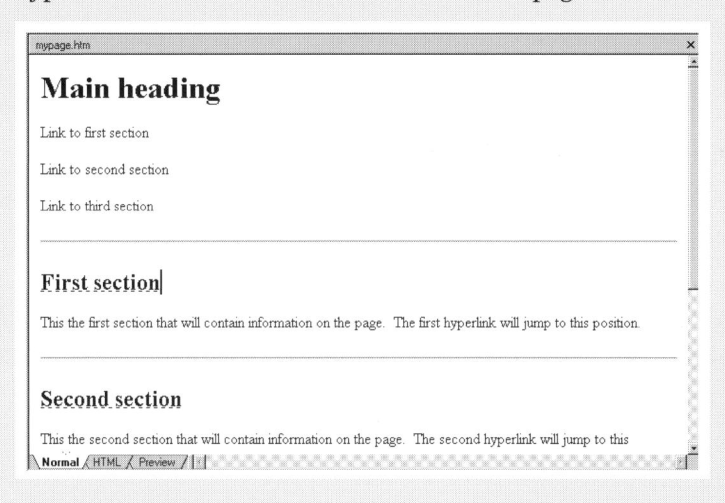


Figure 31.7 The subheading 'First section' has been bookmarked in *FrontPage* page editor mode.

2 To insert a bookmark, highlight the subheading to be bookmarked, then select *Insert / Bookmark*. By default, this gives the bookmark the same name as the subheading. A bookmark is displayed in Normal mode by a dotted underlining (as in Figure 31.7), but is invisible in Preview mode.

The hyperlink to a bookmark is inserted by highlighting the text 'Link to first section' that will act as the hyperlink, then selecting Insert / Hyperlink. In the dialogue box, the relevant bookmark is selected from the Bookmark list, as in Figure 31.8.

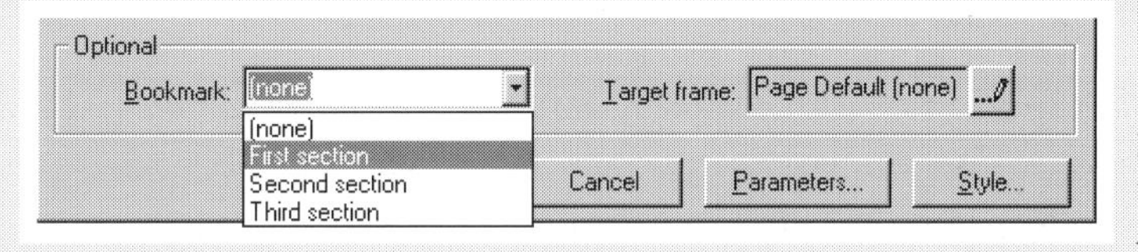


Figure 31.8 Selecting a bookmark that the hyperlink will link to in *FrontPage*

3 Add the remaining hyperlinks and then try them out in Preview mode (Figure 31.9).

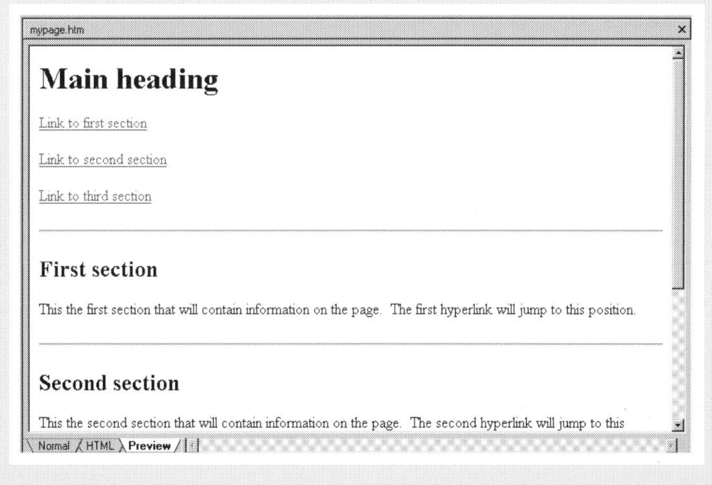


Figure 31.9 Hyperlinks to bookmarks on the same page

4 To make a graphical hyperlink, insert a suitable image and then highlight it and use *Insert / Hyperlink* in exactly the same way as you did with text.

## Using tables

Tables can be created on a web page, just as they can using a word processor. Although a table can be used to display data in boxes in the traditional way, tables are more commonly used on web pages as a way of arranging text and images on screen.

Web authoring packages provide dialogues for creating tables, usually from a Table menu. They also allow the designer to set the properties of tables and of individual cells in a table, often by right-clicking on the table or cell in page edit mode. It is useful to see how HTML handles tables and their properties. The HTML code for a table has the basic structure shown below.

```
<table>
    <tr>
        <td> </td>
        <td> </td>
        <td> </td>
    </tr>
    <tr>
        <td> </td>
        <td> </td>
        <td> </td>
    </tr>
</table>
```

This table consists of two rows each with a <tr> tag (for table row). Each row has three cells each with a <td> tag (for table data).

Text and images can be inserted into any or all of the table cells, to give a layout like the one in Figure 31.10.

| First cell in the top row | Second cell in the top row | Third cell in the top row |
|---|---|---|
| First cell in the second row | | Third cell in the second row. |

Figure 31.10 A table with a border

The HTML code for the table displayed in Figure 31.10 is shown below.

```
<table width="600" border="1">
    <tr>
        <td>First cell in the top row</td>
        <td>Second cell in the top row</td>
        <td>Third cell in the top row</td>
    </tr>
    <tr>
        <td>First cell in the second row</td>
        <td><img border="0" src="images/car.gif" width="83" height="30"></td>
        <td>Third cell in the second row </td>
    </tr>
</table>
```

- **width** is the width of the whole table, in pixels.
- **border** fixes the thickness of the border around the perimeter of the whole table. If the

border is given the value 0, not only does the outside border disappear, but so do the boundaries of the individual cells. This technique can be used to create a page layout in which the text and images are arranged in columns with invisible borders.

Individual cells can be given their own properties, as in:

```
<td align="center" valign="top">
```

- **align** is the horizontal alignment (the default value is "left").
- **valign** is the vertical alignment, in this case placing the contents of the cell at the top (the default value is "middle").

## Case study: Creating a table using *FrontPage*

1 Create a new blank page before you start experimenting with tables. Select *Table / Insert / Table* and then enter values in the dialogue box as in Figure 31.11. Check the HTML code.

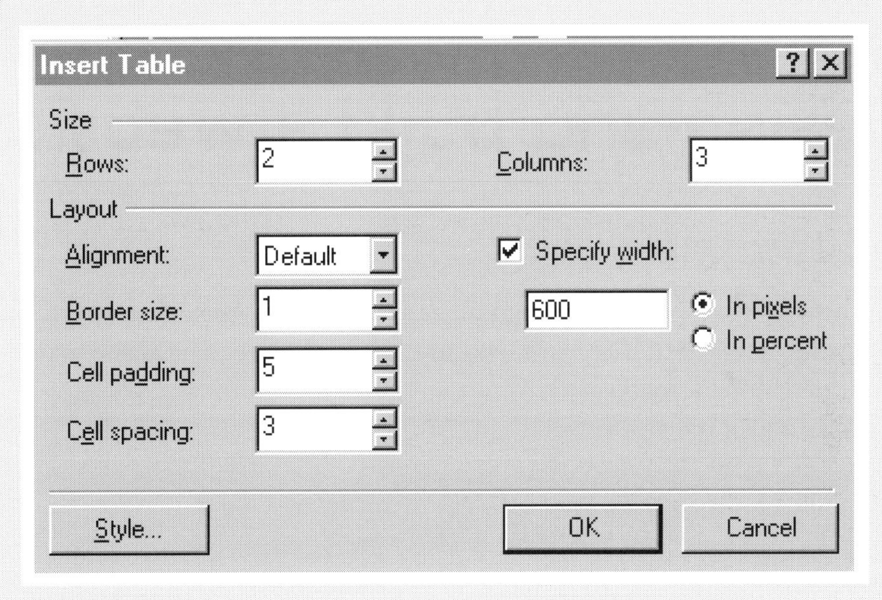


Figure 31.11 Inserting a table in *FrontPage*

2 In Normal mode, enter some text in each of the cells and place an image in one of the cells. Make sure that the image is a suitable width; preferably no more than 150 pixels wide. Then check the HTML code again.

3 Experiment with the table properties in Normal mode by right-clicking anywhere inside the table, then selecting *Table properties*. You can add colour to the borders and change their appearance, and you can give the whole table a background colour.

You will have probably found that the individual columns vary in width as you enter the text. You can fix the width of each cell to prevent this happening. Right click on a cell and select *Cell properties*, then specify the width as a percentage of the total width of the table; make sure that the percentages in a row add up to 100 per cent. You only need to do this across one row of a table, as all the cells in any one column will line up with the one that has a fixed width.

You can also fix the width of a whole column by dragging a column border to a new position. This action automatically adds a width attribute into every cell in the table.

4. Use the *Cell Properties* to set the background colour for a cell in a table, and to align the text vertically (top, middle or bottom) and horizontally (left, centre, right or justified). Check the HTML code to see how these are recorded in the attributes of the cells.
5. To add an extra row or column to a table, click where you want it to go, then select *Table / Insert / Rows* or *Columns* and make your choices. If you have added a column you should check the widths of the cells again.
6. You can merge all the cells in a row, but note that if you merge the cells where you have set width properties, that width data will no longer be valid. For example, you might want to merge all the cells in the top row to give a header that will span all three columns. Highlight the top three cells, right click and select *Merge Cells*.

# 31.2 Design and build a website

## Creating a website

A website consists of a set of web pages that are linked together. A number of single pages can be created in a web authoring package and the hyperlinks can be added manually, or the website management tools that are built in to most web authoring packages can be used to automate some of the processes.

### Site management software

The site management tools in web authoring packages vary, but they often enable the designer to:

- manage the folders and files for a site
- view and modify the navigation structure of a site
- create and maintain navigation bars automatically
- check all the hyperlinks
- create a site map
- create a design theme for a site
- publish the site to a server
- manage a website project.

All websites include one page called index.htm or index.html. This is the first page that any visitor will download. When a URL, such as http://www.yahoo.com, is entered into the address box of a browser, the browser actually searches for the index page, i.e. http://www.yahoo.com/index.htm. On many sites, the index page holds the home page, although it can sometimes hold instructions for downloading other pages.

## Case study: Exploring *FrontPage*'s site management facilities

*FrontPage* provides a number of tools in the Views bar that can help you to construct and manage a site. To see how they work, you will use one of the website templates or wizards to create an instant site. You should not use these whole site templates for assessment work, but they are a quick way of demonstrating the principles.

In *FrontPage* each website that you create is stored on your system in a separate web folder. *FrontPage* refers to these as webs. To close a web folder, select *File / Close Web* or simply exit from *FrontPage*. To open a web folder select *File / Open Web*, and select the folder name.

1 First close any pages or webs that are open. Select *File / New / Web*, then select Personal Web.
2 To the right, you will see a text box in which you can specify the location of a new web (Figure 31.12). The default location for all *FrontPage* webs is in a folder called My Webs. The default name for a web folder is 'mywebnn' but you should change this to a meaningful name, such as 'personal'. *FrontPage* will create the folder for you.

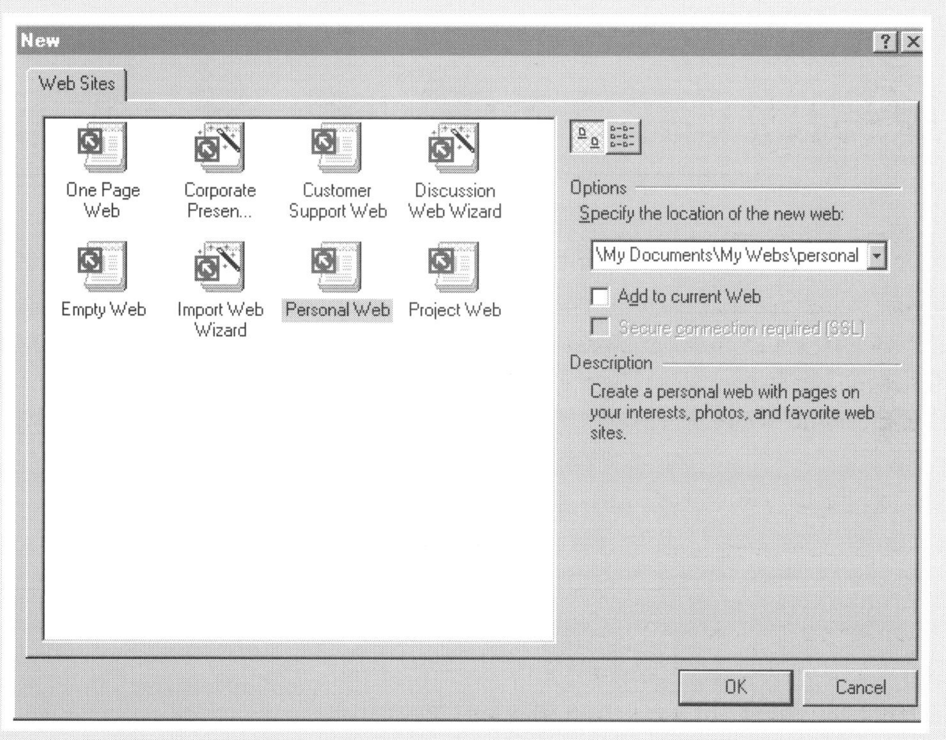


Figure 31.12 Setting up a new web in *FrontPage*

The structure of the site will be created for you.

3 The tools (or views) for developing the site are displayed in the Views bar. Experiment with these tools.
   - *Folders:* Click on the Folders icon in the Views bar. *FrontPage* has created a new web folder and generated five web pages in the Personal website. It has also created _private and images folders specifically for this website.

     Double-click on index.htm, then view the page in Preview mode. You can now explore the website, which is not, of course, finished, but do not edit the pages. Close any open pages before the next steps.

- *Reports:* The Reports view on the Views bar lists some statistics about the site which will become more significant as your site grows.
- *Navigation:* You can see how all the pages are linked together by selecting the Navigation view (Figure 31.13). You can edit any page by clicking on it in Navigation view, and this is usually the most convenient way of accessing pages. The Navigation view can be used to add new pages to your website structure.

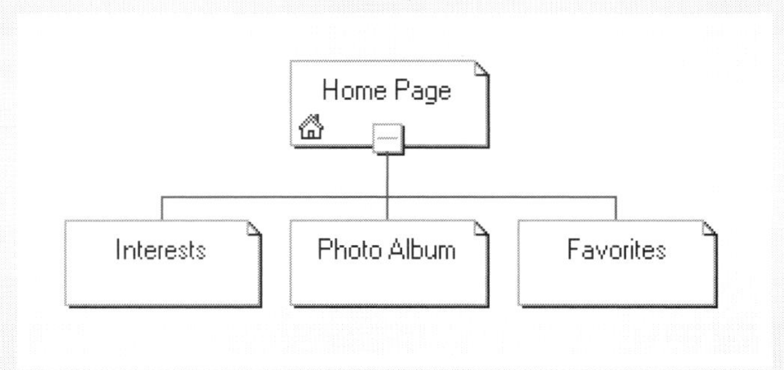


Figure 31.13 The navigation structure of a personal website in *FrontPage*

- *Hyperlinks:* The Hyperlinks view displays links between pages (Figure 31.14). Note the direction of the arrows in the diagram; on the left end of an arrow is the page which carries the hyperlink and on the right end is the page or external website that it links to. Click on the + buttons to expand the diagram.

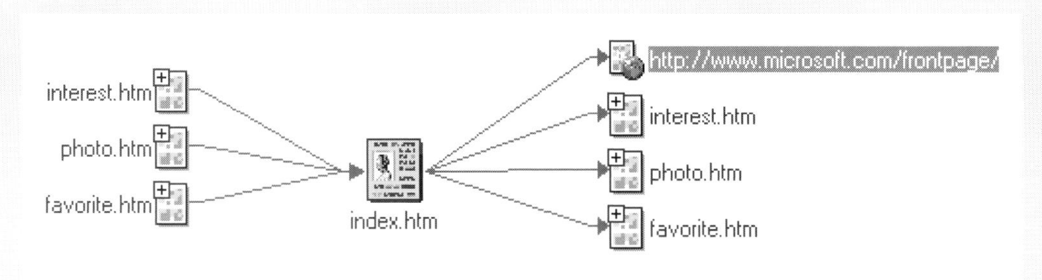


Figure 31.14 Hyperlinks view of a website in *FrontPage*

- *Tasks:* This view allows you to list all the tasks that you have to complete and is a very useful planning tool.

In the next activity, you will create a website for a fast food outlet. The home page will give basic information, such as the name, address and phone number, and details about the delivery service. A second page will contain the fast food menu, and another page will list any job vacancies in the company. Instructions are given for *FrontPage*, but you may use whatever web authoring software is available to you.

## Case study: Using site management tools in *FrontPage*

1. Close any open webs, then select *File / New / Web* and create a new one page web. Click on Folder View, and you will see that the index (home) page has been created for you. Double-click on the index page and it will open in Page view.
2. Enter the name and address and any other text, as in Figure 31.15. Use the styles in the style list but do not use any other formatting options at this stage. You will be developing a complete design theme for the whole site very soon. Save the page.

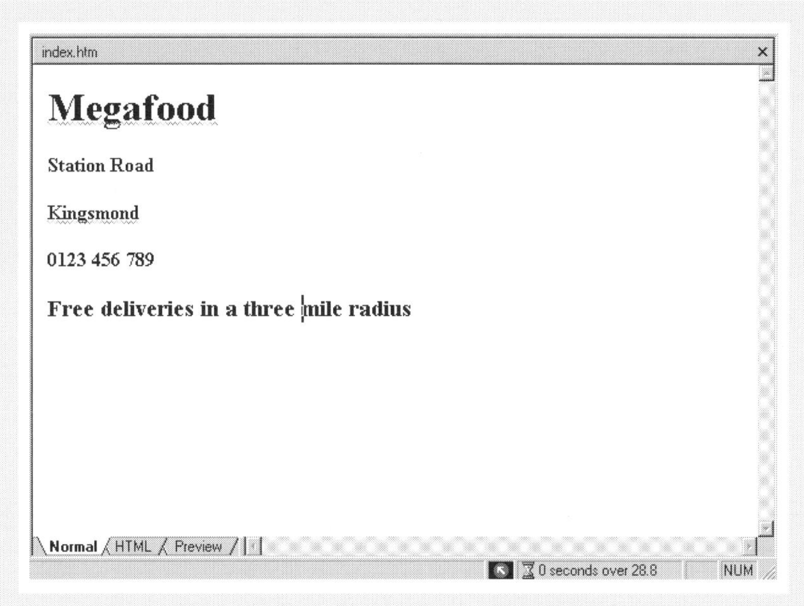


Figure 31.15 An index page for a site for a fast food business

3 Now use *File / New / Page* to create two more pages in Page view, save them as menu.htm and jobs.htm, and add a small amount of suitable text to each. You can use a table to hold the menu. You will find it useful to be able to see the list of pages in the web folder, so select *View / Folder List*. (Figure 31.16).

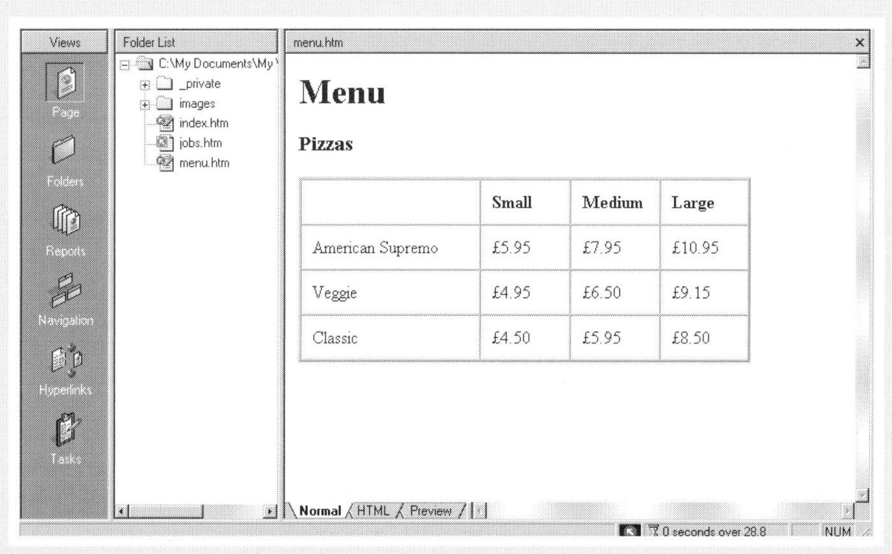


Figure 31.16 The folder list in *FrontPage* and a basic page

## Using metatags and other head tags

The HTML code between the <head> tags of a page, such as that shown below, contains some important information.

```
<head>
<meta http-equiv="Content-Type" content="text/html; charset=windows-1252">
<meta name="GENERATOR" content="Microsoft FrontPage 4.0">
<meta name="ProgId" content="FrontPage.Editor.Document">
<title>Menu</title>
</head>
```

These tags provide information about the page that follows, and a number of them are used by search engines. These can be edited directly in HTML code, or web authoring tools can be used instead.

The **<title>** tag gives the title of the page, and usually appears in the browser title bar. Web authoring packages like *FrontPage* often use the first line of text on the page for the title, but it can be changed to something like:

```
<title>Pizzas, pastas and more to enjoy at Megafood</title>
```

Search engines display the title of a page when they list a site in response to a query, so this is a good reason for making it meaningful.

The remaining tags are known as **metatags**. The default ones created by the web authoring package should not be changed, but a couple of very important ones are omitted in the code above:

- The **keyword metatag** contains a list of keywords that people might use in a search engine:

```
<meta name="keywords" content="Megafood, fast food, pizza, pasta">
```

- The **description metatag** contains a description of the site which may also be quoted by a search engine when it lists a site:

```
<meta name="description" content="Welcome to Megafood – where you can find the
best fast food in Kingsmond. Pizzas, pastas and more.">
```

# Linking web pages

On the Web, the links between pages create one vast global network. An individual site will ensure that the visitor explores what the site has to offer by offering internal links to other pages on the same site, as well as external links to other sites.

## Creating hyperlinks

All web authoring packages allow the designer to convert text or an image into a hyperlink. Usually the Insert or Format menu includes a Hyperlink item which opens up a dialogue. The HTML code for a link to a page called news.htm looks like this:

```
<a href="news.htm">Latest news</a>
```

A hyperlink can also link to a page in another website. In that case the full URL must be given:

```
<a href="http://news.bbc.co.uk/" target="_blank">BBC News</a>
```

- **target** defines the window where the page is opened. The default value is the same page.
- **target="_blank"** opens the page in a new window.

A hyperlink can also be used to send an e-mail:

```
<a href="mailto:myname@mydomain.co.uk" >Email me</a>
```

When this hyperlink is clicked, a new e-mail window opens in the visitor's e-mail client software, with the e-mail address in the recipient field.

An image can be used as a button instead of text for any of these links. The code will look like this:

```
<a href="news.htm"><img border="0" src="images/newsbutton.gif" width="120"
height="30"> Latest news</a>
```

## Using site management tools to create navigation bars

Site management tools usually assume that the site has a tree structure. They can sometimes generate and insert one or more navigation bars on a page on demand. Any additional links must be created individually on the page.

Figure 31.17 shows the Navigation bar dialogue in *FrontPage*, which offers a number of options. The 'Child pages under Home' option creates the main navigation bar and this can be placed on each page, together with a link to the home page. A secondary navigation bar can be inserted using the 'Same level' option.

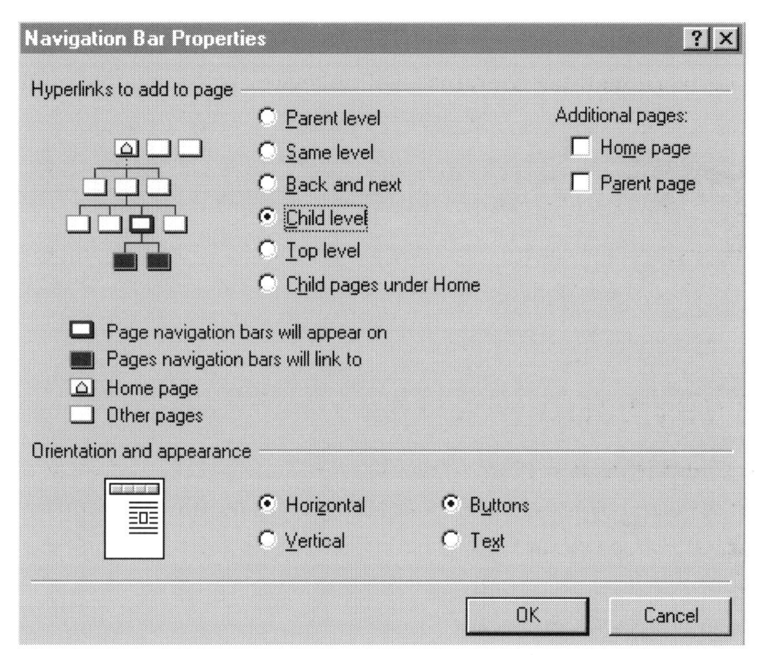


Figure 31.17 Setting the properties of a navigation bar in *FrontPage*

The Navigation bar tool in *FrontPage* generates HTML something like this at the position where the navigation bar is inserted:

```
<!--webbot bot="Navigation" S-Type="children" S-Orientation="horizontal"
S-Rendering="graphics" B-Include-Home B-Include-Up U-Page S-Target -->
```

This is not standard HTML code, but calls on a procedure (a webbot) that is specific to *FrontPage*. The Navigation bar tool can create text or image hyperlinks.

### Case study: Setting up the navigation structure using *FrontPage*

1 Open the fast food site, or if it is already open, close any pages.
2 Click on the Navigation view. An icon representing the index page will be shown, as in Figure 31.18, with the title 'Home Page'
You will also find it useful if you can see the folder list at the same time as the Navigation View, so select *View / Folder List*.

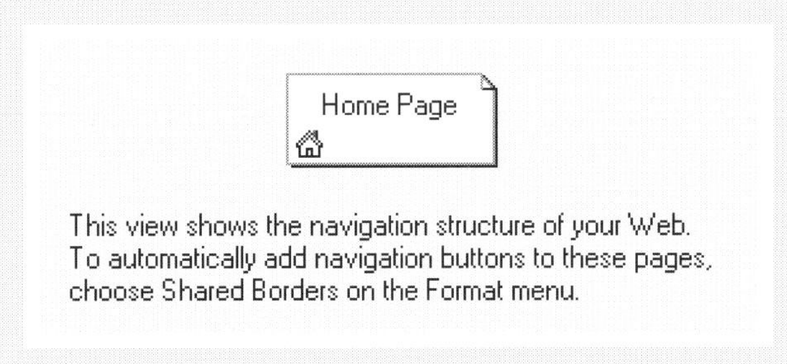


Figure 31.18 The index page for the fast food website displayed in Navigation view in *FrontPage*

3 Drag the menu and jobs pages from the Folders list on to the diagram to give the navigation structure as shown in Figure 31.19. This has defined the relationships between the pages. The index page is the parent to the menu and jobs pages, and the menu page is a child of the index page.

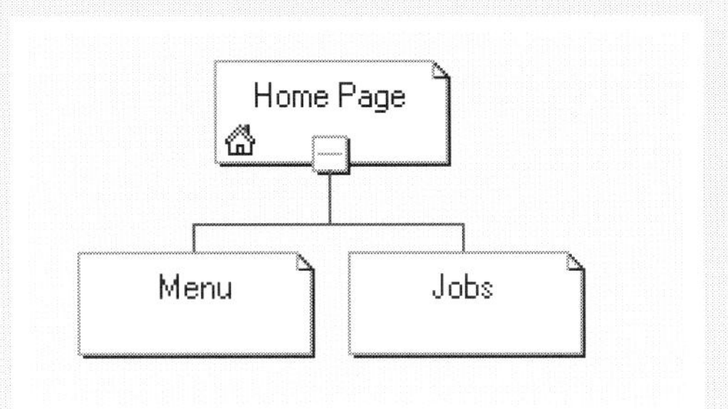


Figure 31.19 The navigation structure in *FrontPage* for the fast food website

The site management tools can now create the navigation bars on the pages.

4 Open the index page by clicking on its name in the Folders list or on the page icon in Navigation view. Place the cursor where you want the navigation bar to appear. Select *Insert / Navigation Bar*. Under *Hyperlinks to add to page* select *Child level*. Then under *Orientation and Appearance* select horizontal and buttons, as in Figure 31.17.

In Preview mode the page should look similar to Figure 31.20. The buttons do not look very impressive yet, but will be transformed in the next activity.

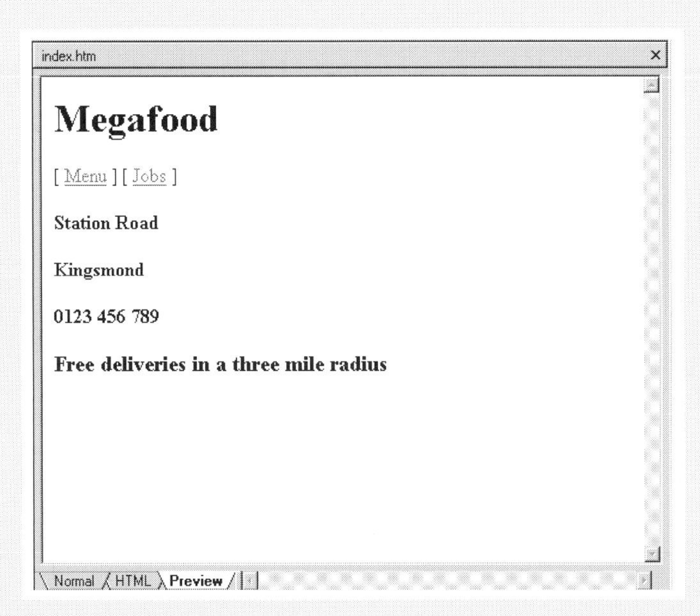


Figure 31.20 A navigation bar created on the index page by *FrontPage*

5 Now add navigation bars to the other two pages. Repeat the process that you used for the home page. This time provide links pages at the same level, and also to the Home page (as an additional page).

When you try out the links in Preview mode you will see that the navigation bar includes a non-functioning button that refers to the page that it is on (see Figure 31.21). This is equivalent to a greyed out item on a drop-down menu in Windows-based software. It is important to include this non-functioning button as it means that the navigation bar items appear in the same positions on different pages. *FrontPage* always places the Home button to the left of the others.

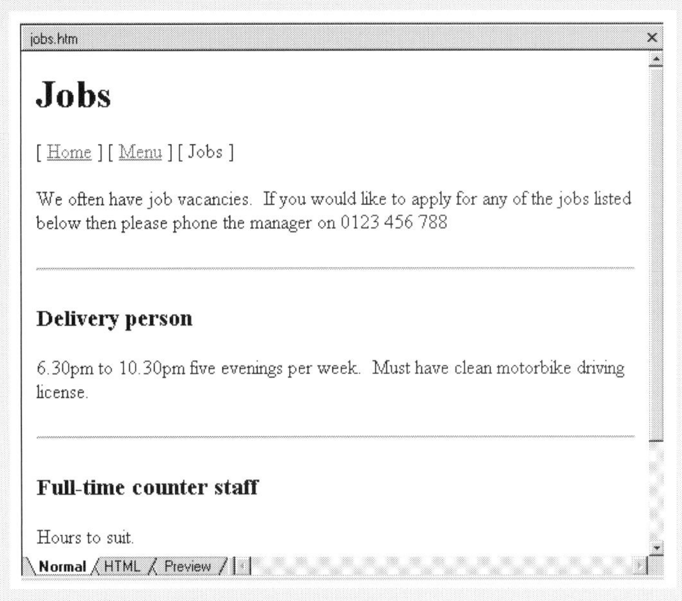

Figure 31.21 The Jobs page with a navigation bar created in *FrontPage*

## External links

Links to other sites can be added to any web page. Some sites provide no external links at all, because they do not want the visitor to leave the site once there. On the other hand, some sites contain many links to other sites; if that is the main purpose they are known as **portal sites**.

### Further research 31.2

1 Look at a number of websites and note the position of:
- the main navigation bar
- secondary navigation bars
- other links to pages on the site.

2 Discuss the usability of the various styles that you find.

### Assessment activity 31.2

1 Use a web authoring package to create a prototype of the website. This should demonstrate your ability to use graphics and to link your pages together using a suitable navigation system.
2 Check the prototype with your client.
3 Keep a detailed log of the development of the project, which should include screen shots of your work and witness testimonies from your client.

# Enhancing web pages

The sites demonstrated so far lack any visual appeal. Well-designed sites have a consistent look, with the same textual and graphical elements repeated across all the pages. In creating a consistent design, these design components should be considered:

- font type, size, style and colour
- background colours and images for pages, tables and cells
- graphic elements such as lines, buttons and images.

The implementation of the visual design can be approached using three distinct methods; text formatting, themes (provided by web authoring packages) and cascading style sheets.

## Using text formatting options

In web authoring packages, it is always possible to highlight some text and use the formatting toolbar to format it, making a selection from fonts, font styles, text alignment and colours. Unfortunately, if this method is used, every single paragraph and heading on every page of a website has to be individually formatted. This is a tedious process and some text can easily be overlooked. Worse still, if the web designer decides at some point to change the formatting, for example, to use a different colour for the main text, then every single instance has to be laboriously changed. Figure 31.22 shows a page that could be created in this way. Each of the buttons had to be designed and hyperlinked individually, and a background inserted. The HTML code for part of the page is shown below.

Figure 31.22 A formatted page

```
<h3><font face="Arial" size="5" color="#800000">Delivery person</font></h3>
<p><font face="Arial" size="3" color="#0000FF"><i>6.30 pm to 10.30 pm five
evenings per week.  Must have clean motorbike driving license.</i></font></p>
```

## Using design themes

*FrontPage* and other web authoring packages provide predesigned themes that can be applied across a website. These themes initially look pleasing, so they are very popular, especially on personal websites. They do appear again and again on the Web, so it is not advisable to use them, unmodified, for serious web development. However, most elements within a theme can be modified, and this technique can be used to give an acceptable and distinctive appearance to a simple site.

When a theme is used, the HTML code may not appear to change much. For example, in *FrontPage* a theme is simply referenced by a tag in the head like this:

```
<meta name="Microsoft Theme" content="citrus 011, default">
```

However, this is a bit misleading as *FrontPage* does insert formatting codes when the page is uploaded to the server.

## Case study: Using a FrontPage theme

1 Open the fast food site.
2 If you have already applied paragraph formatting to a page, then open each page in turn in Normal mode, select *Edit / Select All then Format / Remove Formatting.*
3 In *FrontPage* select *Format / Themes* and then make sure that you check 'All Pages'. Browse through the themes and select one. You will be impressed by the immediate improvement to all your pages (Figure 31.23). You can go back to the Themes dialogue to change a theme at any time.

Figure 31.23 A web page using the Citrus Punch theme in *FrontPage*

4 Experiment with modifying any of the elements of a theme by clicking on Modify in the Themes dialogue.

## Using cascading style sheets (CSS)

For more advanced work, cascading style sheets (CSS) should be used. Style sheets can be used in three ways: inline styles, embedded styles and external style sheets. Of these, we will be looking at **external style sheets** because these generate the most efficient code, and give the best control over the appearance of a site.

A style sheet is a separate page, hidden from the visitor, which is uploaded to the server along with the web pages. It contains a set of definitions for the styles used in the style list. In fact, any tag in the HTML code can have its own style definition. The style definitions in a style sheet can be applied to all the pages on a site. This means that a simple change to the style sheet can have an affect right across a large site, and in this way visual consistency can be maintained. A style sheet can be created in a web authoring package or in any simple text editor, such as *Notepad*. Sample style sheets are often provided as well, and these can be a good starting point.

## Case study: Using CSSs in *FrontPage*

For this activity, you will create a website for a local group. You will use a cascading style sheet to give the page its style and will later add a separate side frame to hold the navigation bar.

It is a good idea to work in 1024 resolution. The pages will be designed to be viewed at 800 resolution, but by using a wider window in *FrontPage* you will also be able to see the Views bar and the Folder List at the same time as the page itself.

1 Create a new empty web. Create a new page and save it as home.htm. Although this will be the home page for the site it will not actually be the first page that is loaded, so it is not saved as index.htm.
2 Set up a table to hold the contents of the page. It should be 600 pixels wide, and aligned to the left. The border value should be zero.
3 Use the Page properties to set the page margins to zero. This ensures that the page takes up no more than 600 pixels.
4 Now add some text and images to the page. Use the styles from the style list, such as Heading 1, but do not use any formatting options yet. Include at least one external hyperlink. An example is given in Figure 31.24.

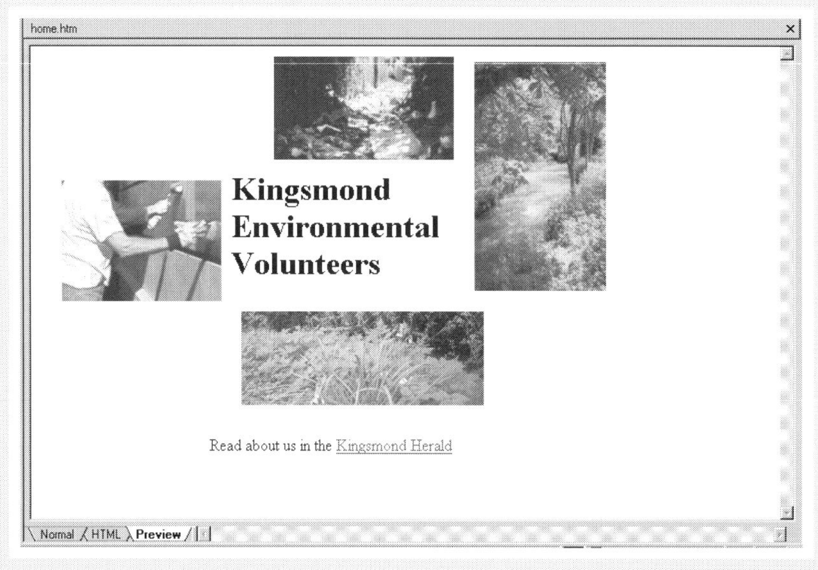


Figure 31.24 A basic web page before a style sheet is used

5 Select *File / New / Page*, then click on the style sheets tab. Select one of the predesigned style sheets, such as 'Street'. When the style sheet code appears, save it as mystyles.css.

6 Click on the Home page in the Folder list, then select *Format / Style sheet links*. Click on Add, then click on mystyles.css in the file list, as in Figure 31.25. The page now takes its font styles and colours from the style sheet, as displayed in Figure 31.26.

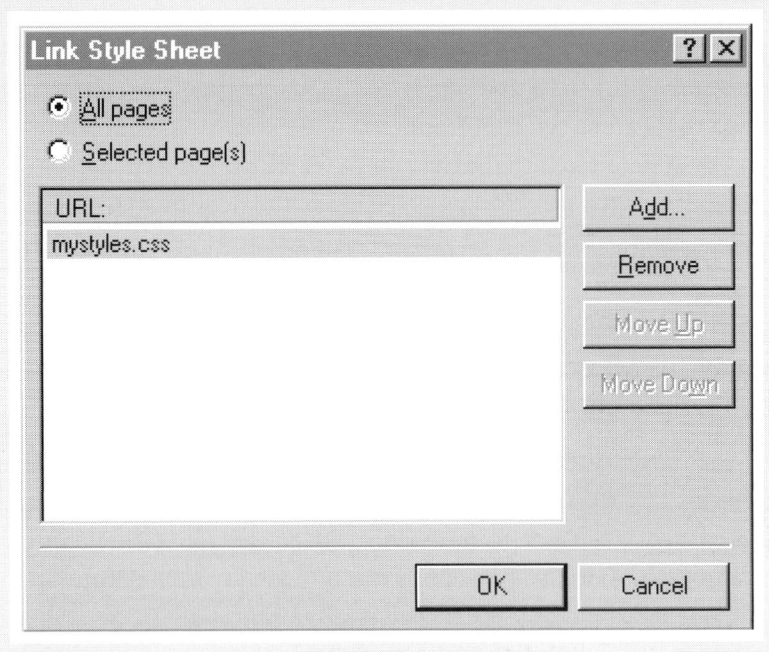


Figure 31.25 Style sheet linking dialogue in *FrontPage*

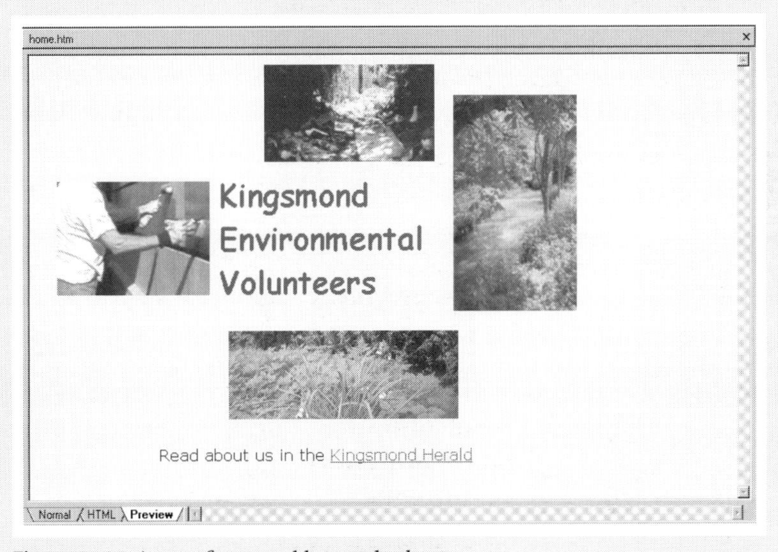


Figure 31.26 A page formatted by a style sheet

The style sheet used in the above example is one of the samples provided with *FrontPage*, although it has been given the filename mystyles.css. This line is added to the head section:

```
<link rel="stylesheet" type="text/css" href="mystyles.css">
```

When a browser interprets the HTML code on this page, it will refer to the style sheet called mystyles.css to find the styles (if any) that have been defined for each of the tags. Each style definition refers to one or more of the HTML tags. This is the body style definition in the style sheet:

```
body
{
    font-family: Verdana, Arial, Helvetica;
    background-color: rgb(204,255,255);
    color: rgb(0,0,102);
}
```

This defines some properties that apply to the whole page between the <body> tags. The Normal style that can be selected from the style list is the default style, and this is initially defined by the system settings for the computer. The body style definition sets up the basic style for the page, and a browser will use this as the default style for the page.

- **background-color** (note the American spelling of colour) applies to the background of the whole page.
- **color** defines the default colour for the text on the page.
- **font-family**, in this case, lists three fonts, although the list can be of any length. The browser works along the list until it finds a font that it can use.

The visitor can only view a font if that font is already resident on his or her own system. So although in this case the designer would prefer the visitor to view the text in Verdana, the other two fonts are listed as fallback options. Only widely used fonts should be included in a style sheet, but as a precaution two basic fonts can be added to each definition, one font for Windows systems and one for Apple systems. If the preferred font is a serif font then Times New Roman and Times should be included; if the preferred font is sans serif then Arial and Helvetica should be added.

Another style definition applies to more than one tag:

```
h1, h2, h3, h4, h5, h6
{
    font-family: Comic Sans MS, Arial, Helvetica;
}
```

The Heading 1 style in the style list generates the <h1> tag in the HTML code and so on. This style rule applies to all six heading tags and sets Comic Sans MS as the font for all the headings, with Arial and Helvetica as the fallback options.

The browser has to deal with the seeming contradiction between the font properties for the body and for the headings. The font defined for the body is the default font and applies throughout the page except where another tag defines it differently. So the Verdana font is used everywhere except in the headings where Comic Sans MS is used.

The next style rule defines the colour of one of the headings, and there are similar rules for all the remaining heading styles:

```
h1
{
    color: rgb(153,0,0);
}
```

The <h1> tag has been used in Figure 31.26 for the central text 'Kingsmond Environmental Volunteers'.

By default, heading styles are always bold, and the sizes decrease from h1 to h6.

### Further research 31.3

Colours in style sheets can be expressed as red-green-blue (RGB) codes, as decimal values or as hexadecimal codes. Alternatively, a limited range of colour names can be used. Find out more about these. Investigate the use of 'safe' colours on the Web.

The next style definitions define three states that the hyperlinks take. The <a> tag is used for both bookmarks and hyperlinks, but these styles only affect the hyperlinks themselves.

```
a:link
{
    color: rgb(0,102,102);
}
a:visited
{
    color: rgb(0,153,153);
}
a:active
{
    color: rgb(255,102,0);
}
```

- **a:link** is the normal style used for the hyperlink.
- **a:visited** is the style used for a hyperlink that has already been followed.
- **a:active** is the style used when the mouse button is held down on a hyperlink.
- **a:hover** (not used in this example) is the style used when the mouse passes over the hyperlink.

The link to the Kingsmond Herald at the bottom of the window in Figure 31.26 uses the <a> tag, and it can take on one of three different colours.

## Editing cascading style sheets

Sample style sheets provided by web authoring packages normally need to be edited. Alternatively, a new style sheet can be written in a text editor such as Notepad and saved with a .css filename extension. If a new style sheet is created then it must be linked to the page.

### Case study: Editing a stylesheet in *FrontPage*

For this activity, although *FrontPage* does offer a Style dialogue, you would be advised to edit a style sheet directly. A style sheet must be saved before any changes can be observed in a page. If you amend a style sheet while a page is open, when you switch back to the page you will have to click on the Refresh button to view the effects of the changes. There are many properties that can be applied to tags in style sheet rules, and you would need to consult a handbook on cascading style sheets to see them all.

1 In Page view, first close any pages that are open, then open mystyles.css.
2 Make changes and save it.

3 Now create another page for the website, in which the content should be set inside a table 600 pixels wide. Use *Format / Style Sheet* links to link mystyles.css to this page. Do not include any navigation links at this stage.

A new style sheet could look like this:

```
a:link
{
   font-weight: bold;
   color: gray;
   text-decoration: none;
}
a:visited
{
   font-weight: bold;
   color: gray;
   text-decoration: none;
}
a:hover
{
   font-weight: bold;
   color: silver;
   text-decoration: none;
}
body
{
   font-family: Verdana, Arial, Helvetica;
   font-size: 12pt;
   background-color: white;
   color: rgb(0,102,51);
}
h1
{
   font-family: Comic Sans MS, Arial, Helvetica;
   font-size: 20pt;
   text-align: center;
   color: white;
   background-color: rgb(0,102,51);
   border-width: 5pt;
   border-style: double;
   border-color: white;
   padding:3pt;
}
```

The effect of this style sheet can be seen in Figure 31.27. The underlining on the 'Kingsmond Herald' hyperlink has been removed, but the use of a different colour and bold face indicates to the visitor that it is a hyperlink. This is confirmed by its hover state; when the mouse is passed over the link it changes from a dark grey to a light grey.

Fast and effective hover links can be created using a style sheet and without the use of images. The background, border and padding properties can be used to give a rectangular box

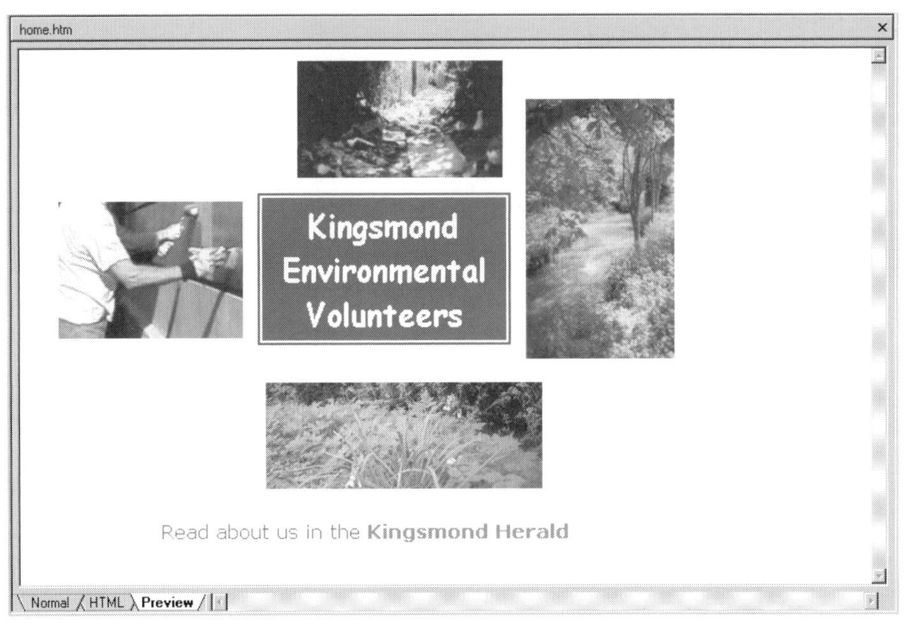


Figure 31.27 A new style sheet applied to the page

around the text, which could change colour in hover mode. A list of all the style sheet properties used in these examples is given in the Teacher's Resource File.

## Using frames

The display in a browser can be split into two or more frames (or panes), each of which holds a separate web page. This technique is often used so that constant information is shown in one frame while the contents of another frame may change. For example, a main navigation bar can be displayed in a narrow frame at the top or side of a page, with the main page contents varying according to which link has been selected.

A frame page is a separate web page which will not be visible to the visitor. Instead it describes the structure of the frames in the window and assigns initial pages to the frames. A frame page with a layout like the middle diagram in Figure 31.28 will have HTML code similar to that shown on page 406.

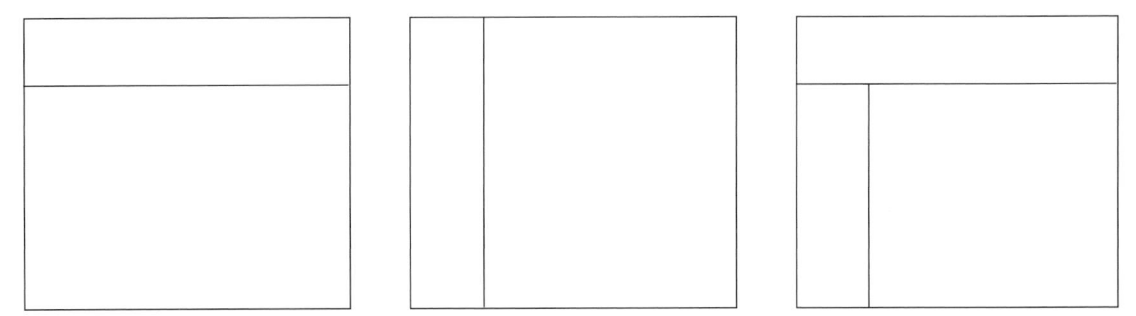

Figure 31.28 Three common frame configurations

```
<html>

<head>
<meta http-equiv="Content-Type" content="text/html; charset=windows-1252">
<title>New Page 1</title>
<meta name="GENERATOR" content="Microsoft FrontPage 4.0">
<meta name="ProgId" content="FrontPage.Editor.Document">
</head>

<frameset cols="180,*" frameborder="0" framespacing="0" border="0">
   <frame name="contents" target="main" marginwidth="0" marginheight="0"
scrolling="no" noresize src="side.htm">
   <frame name="main" src="home.htm">
   <noframes>
   <body>

   <p>This page uses frames, but your browser doesn't support them.</p>

   </body>
   </noframes>
</frameset>

</html>
```

Frame pages introduce some new tags:

- **<frameset>** encloses the set of frames.
- **<frame>** defines an individual frame.
- **<noframes>** gives the text that will appear on a browser that does not support frames.

These frames tags use some specific attributes:

- **cols** gives the width of the frames in the frameset. In this case, the first frame is 180 pixels wide and the second is of indeterminate width, represented by the *. The attribute rows is used for horizontally split frames.
- **name** identifies each of the frames.
- **src** is the page that appears in the frame when it is first opened.
- **target** is the frame where linked pages should open. In this case, any links in the contents frame will open pages in the main frame.
- **scrolling** determines whether a scroll bar can appear on the page.

## Case study: Creating frames with *FrontPage*

In this activity, you will create a vertical navigation bar which will appear in a frame to the left side of the page. The side page will be 180 pixels wide, so that it will sit alongside the 600 pixels wide main pages. The total width of 780 pixels allows for the scroll bar to the right side of a 800 pixel width window.

When using frames, you should not use the Navigation tool in *FrontPage*.

1 First create a new page and save it as side.htm. Use the Page properties to set the page margins to zero.

2 Create a table 180 pixels wide, with one column and one row. The cell padding should be non-zero, so that text is not pushed up against the sides of the frame.
3 Enter an image or some information at the top. Then add links to home.htm and to the other page that you have already created.
4 Use *Format / Style* Sheet links to link mystyles.css to this page. See Figure 31.29 for an example of how the side page might look.

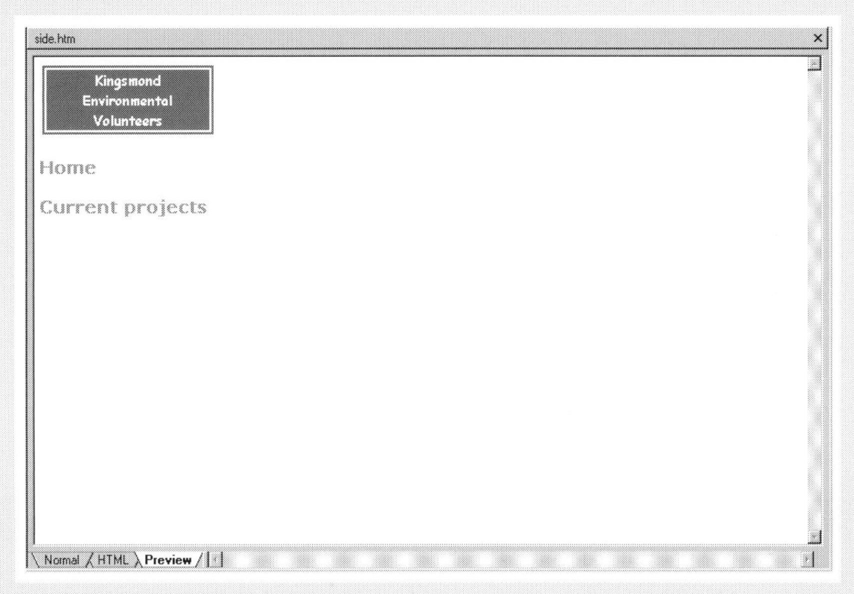


Figure 31.29 A navigation page before it has been integrated into a frame

5 Next, create the frame page itself. Select *File / New / Page,* then click on the *Frames Pages* tab. Select the Contents template. The frame structure will appear as in Figure 31.30. Save the page as index.htm.

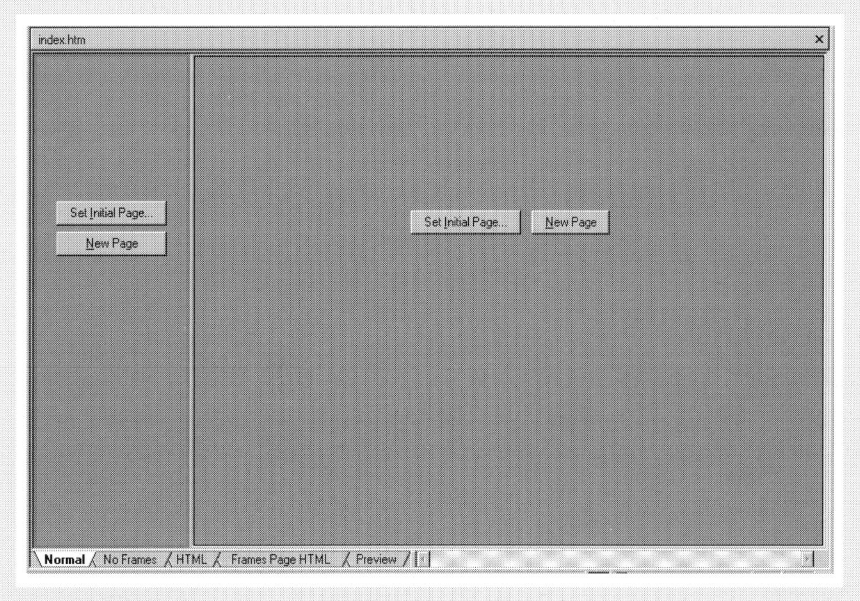


Figure 31.30 The frame structure displayed in *FrontPage*

Right-click anywhere in the left frame, and click on *Frame properties*. Set the width to 180 pixels, and both the margins to zero. Under *Options*, you do not want the frame to be resizable, so remove the tick. You also do not want a scroll bar to appear in this frame, so for *Show Scroll bars* select Never. The dialogue should appear as in Figure 31.31.

Frame Properties
Name: contents
Initial page: Browse...
Frame size
Width 180 Pixels
Row Height 1 Relative
Margins
Width: 0
Height: 0
Options
Resizable in Browser
Frames Page...
Show scrollbars: Never
Style... OK Cancel

Figure 31.31 The frame properties dialogue in *FrontPage*

In the right frame set the margins to zero.

In the left frame, click on *Set Initial Page*, then select side.htm. Similarly, select home.htm for the right frame. Save the frame page again.

View the whole frame page by selecting Preview mode (see Figure 31.32).

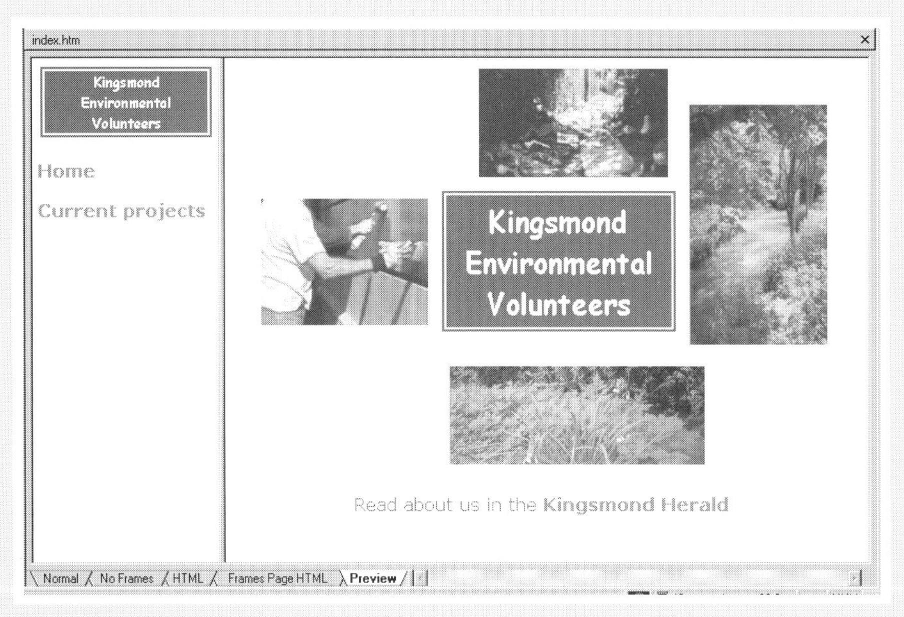


Figure 31.32 A two-frame page

6 The border between the two frames can be removed. Return to Normal mode on the index page, then right-click in the left frame and select *Frame Properties* again. Click on the *Frames Pages* button, and on the *Frames* tab set *Frame spacing* to zero and make sure that the *Show Borders* box is not ticked.
7 Check the page again in Preview mode. Select the other page in the navigation bar and check that it loads into the main frame, as in Figure 31.33.

Figure 31.33 The contents of the main frame can scroll past the fixed left frame

## Adding dynamic elements to a web page

Although HTML is the basic code used for constructing web pages, short programs and modules written in certain programming languages can also be inserted to create interesting effects. We will be looking at three possibilities:

- **javascripts**, written in a scripting language that derives from, but is not the same as, Java
- **dynamic HTML** (DHTML) which assigns javascripts to events
- **Java applets** which are independent Java modules.

Web designers do not have to be proficient Java or javascript programmers to use these. Web authoring packages provide a number of built-in scripts and dynamic effects that can be dropped into a page. There are also many sources of copyright-free and shareware scripts and applets on the Web, and these can be copied and inserted into the HTML code, provided the conditions of use are followed.

### Using javascripts

A simple javascript is shown below. It checks the visitor's system clock, and then greets the visitor with the message 'Good morning', 'Good afternoon' or 'Good evening' depending on the time of day. The complete script can be inserted in the HTML code at the point where the message should appear.

```
<script language="javascript">
<!--
day = new Date()
hr = day.getHours()

if (hr < 12)
document.write("Good morning")
else if (hr > 18)
document.write("Good evening")
else
document.write("Good afternoon")
-->

</script>
```

If a javascript is used on more than one page it can be saved as a separate text file, with the .js filename extension. In our example, the greeting script would be copied into a text editor like Notepad, but without the <script> and comment tags. This could then be saved as greetings.js:

```
day = new Date()
hr = day.getHours()

if (hr < 12)
document.write("Good morning")
else if (hr > 18)
document.write("Good evening")
else
document.write("Good afternoon")
```

The greetings script would then be called by placing this line at the correct point in the HTML code:

```
<script language="javascript" src="greetings.js" type="text/javascript"></script>
```

## Using DHTML

DHTML uses javascripts, but they are activated only when an event occurs. Events on a web page include loading the page, passing the mouse over an object such as an image, clicking on a button, etc.

Normally the javascript itself consists of one or more functions, and these are often placed in the head of the HTML code. The event itself is then identified somewhere in the body.

The javascript below launches a small popup window. The contents of that window would be a small page designed for the purpose, called (in this example) smallpage.htm. This could be an advertisement for a sponsor, or it could contain a snippet of information for the visitor. The properties of the window, such as its size, can be adjusted.

```
<script language="javascript">

<!--
function popupwindow()
{window.open("smallpage.htm", "popup", "width=400, height=320, toolbar=no,
```

```
menubar=no, scrollbars=yes, resizable=yes")}
-->

</script>
```

This javascript should be inserted before the </head> tag. An event handler is needed to trigger this event, and this is placed in the body tag.

```
<body onload="popupwindow()">
```

This code uses the onload event handler. Other useful event handlers include onclick, onmouseover (which can both be used with hyperlinks) and onkeypress.

## Using Java applets

A Java applet is a module written in Java and stored in a separate file with the file extension .class. Values can be passed to the applet as parameters. Web authoring packages offer a number of Java applets. For example, hover buttons in *FrontPage* are generated by a Java applet. The HTML includes a call to an applet called fphover.class, and passes parameters that define the appearance and behaviour of the button:

```
<applet code="fphover.class" codebase="./" width="120" height="24">
   <param name="text" value="Home">
   <param name="color" value="#000080">
   <param name="hovercolor" value="#0000FF">
   <param name="textcolor" value="#FFFFFF">
   <param name="effect" value="glow">
</applet>
```

### Case study: Dynamic elements in *FrontPage*

*FrontPage* provides a number of dynamic elements based on DHTML and Java applets. Here are some to try:

**1 Swapping pictures (DHTML)**

When the mouse passes over an image it will swap it for another image. Ideally the two images should be the same dimensions; if not, then *FrontPage* will stretch the second image to fit the space.

In Normal mode click on the image on the page, then select *Format / Dynamic HTML Effects*. The DHTML dialogue box appears as in Figure 31.34. It looks like a toolbar, but you have to make a selection from each of the list boxes starting from the left. The options offered in each list box depend on the type of object you selected.

Figure 31.34 The DHTML dialogue box

In the *On* list select *Mouse over*; this sets up an onmouseover event.

In the *Apply* list select *Swap Picture*, then in the final list choose the picture for the swap.

Save the page and save the new image to the images folder, then view the effect in Preview mode. In Figure 31.35, when the mouse hovers over the picture of a littered path the words 'Clearing paths...' appear in its place. The words are, in fact, an image created in a graphics package, then saved as a jpg.

Note that *FrontPage* will have saved the javascript in a file called animate.js.

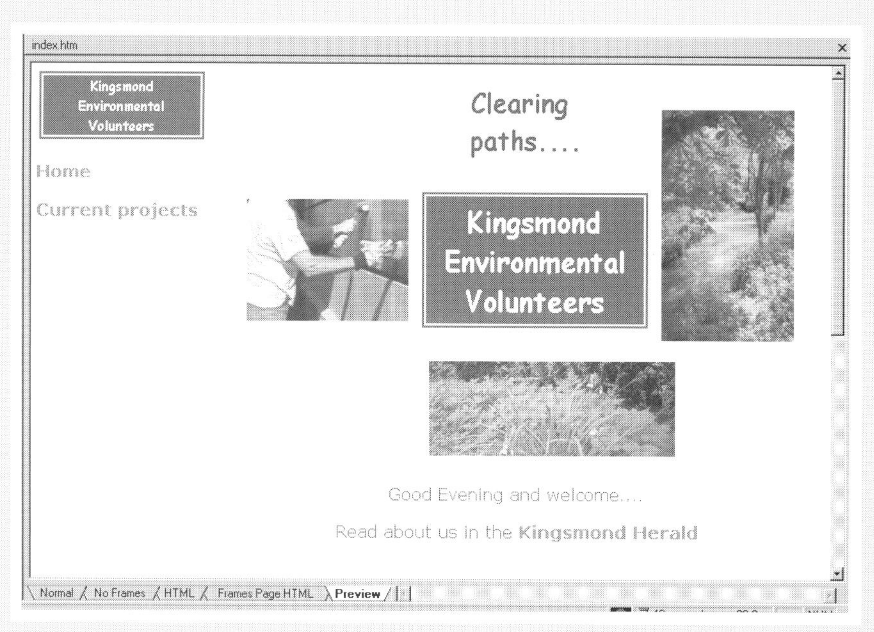


Figure 31.35 Swapping the photo for an image containing text

2 **Page load events (DHTML)**

Highlight some text or an image, and use the same DHTML dialogue to create an onload event. Experiment with the different actions in the *Apply* list.

3 **Hit counters**

Hit counters can be fun on a personal website but should not normally be used on a commercial site. Most organisations would treat data about the number of visitors to a website as commercially sensitive information. Instead, they would arrange to have web statistics forwarded to them from the web server.

In Normal mode, select the position where the hit counter should appear. Then select *Insert / Component / Hit Counter* and select the style you want.

The hit counter becomes operational only when the website is published, and requires *FrontPage* extensions on the server.

## Using forms

An online form can be incorporated into a website to enable visitors to send information to the organisation. The data can be sent as an e-mail, or can be stored in a separate file or database on the server. Web authoring packages provide templates and wizards which simplify the complex process of creating forms.

## Case study: Creating a form in *FrontPage* and storing the results

*FrontPage* offers some very useful tools which will help you to create a feedback form and store the data in a file. In the next activity (steps 1–3) you will create a form that allows a visitor to ask for more information about the organisation with a view to joining.

Once the site has been published, the data collected on a form must be made available to you or to the organisation. There are three options:

- Data can be sent via individual e-mails to a named recipient.
- Data can be collected in a text file (this is the default option).
- Data can be stored in an *Access* database.

In steps 4–7 you will look at the last option. Note that it will work only if *FrontPage* extensions are stored on the web server.

1 Select *File / New / Page*, then click on the *Feedback Form* template (Figure 31.36). Save the page as contact.htm.

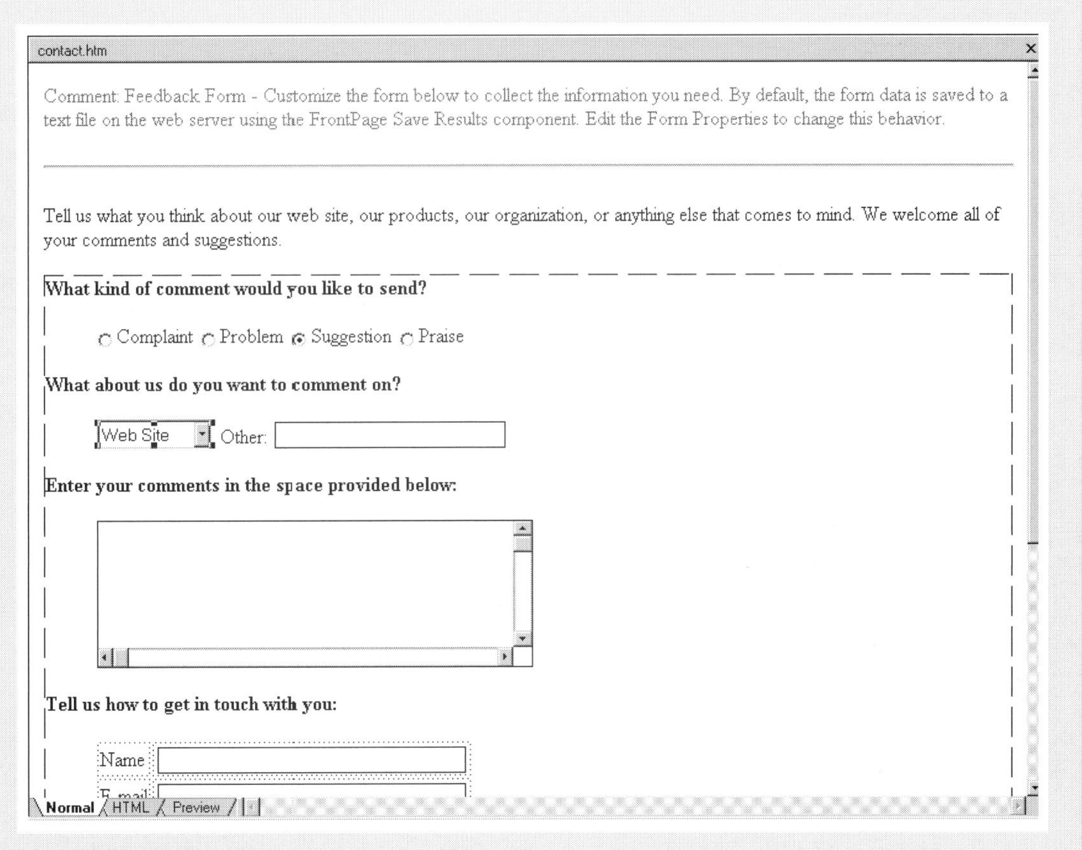


Fig 31.36 The feedback form template in *FrontPage*

The purple text at the top of the page is not visible in Preview mode. The dotted line shows the boundaries of the form itself.

2 Modify the text and the layout of the page. Individual form items can be deleted. New ones can be added from *Insert / Form*.

3 Save the page and add a link to the contact page from the navigation bar in side.htm, as in Figure 31.37.

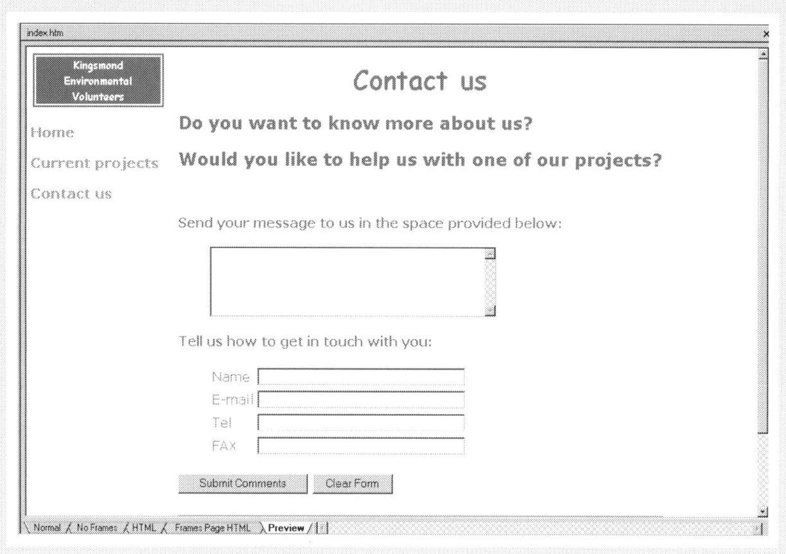


Figure 31.37 A feedback form modified from the *FrontPage* template

4 In Normal mode right click anywhere inside the form, and select *Form Properties*. In the dialogue (Figure 31.38) click on *Send to Database*. Key in 'contact' for the *Form name*. Then click on the *Options* button.

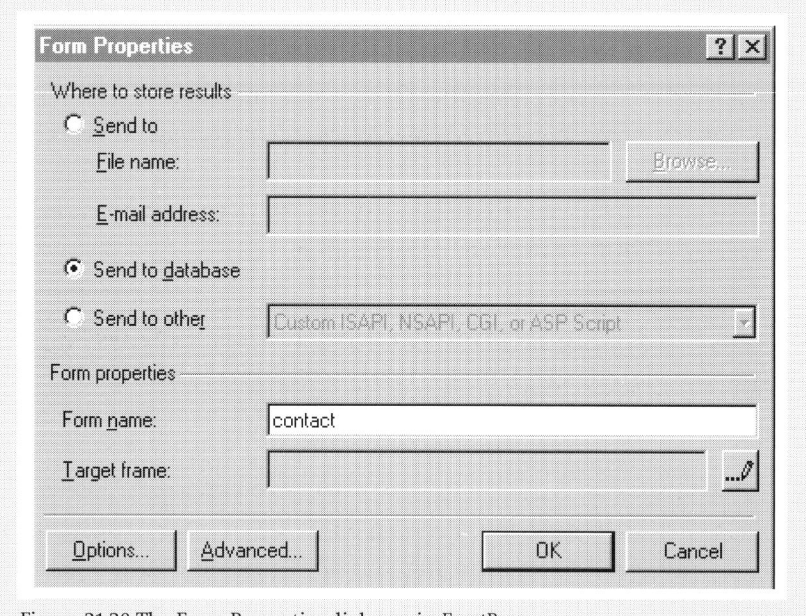


Figure 31.38 The Form Properties dialogue in *FrontPage*

5 In the *Options for Saving Results to Database* dialogue, click on *Create Database*.

6 *FrontPage* will then create a database called contact.mdb. You will then be told that the database can be found at fpdb/contact.htm, and that when you use the Database Results Wizard you should use the data connection 'contact'.
7 *FrontPage* next prompts you to save the contact page with the .asp filename extension as it now functions as an Active Server Page (ASP). Close the page, then right-click on it in the Folders list, and select Rename. Rename it as contact.asp. *FrontPage* will then offer to update the links to that page.

## Including multimedia on a web page

Multimedia components, such as movies, sound, animations and videos can be included on a web page. Most of these must be completely downloaded to the browser before they can be presented. In comparison, a streaming media system continues to download sound or video after the presentation has begun, and is used for real-time broadcasts. Two types of software are associated with multimedia on the Web:

- **Plug-in software** allows the website visitor to view the components as intended.
- **Authoring software** allows the designer to assemble and create the multimedia presentation.

When a browser downloads a page it will search for any plug-ins that are required to display the content. If a plug-in is missing, the visitor will be invited to download it without charge from the Internet. Multimedia components are produced in a variety of formats. For web use, compressed formats must be used so that the files can be downloaded quickly enough. Here are some of the most popular formats at present, as indicated by their filename extensions:

- **wav**, **au**, **aif** and **midi** are all standard audio formats.
- **avi** and **mpeg** are standard video formats.
- **ra** and **ram** are the RealMedia formats for streaming audio and streaming video respectively.
- **swf** is the format used for *Flash* movie files. Macromedia *Flash* is a vector-based graphics package that can create dynamic effects from images, text and sound specifically for web use. There are a number of other packages that can create movies in swf format, such as CoffeeCup Firestarter.
- **mov** is generated by the QuickTime authoring system, which can be used to integrate files in a variety of formats into one presentation.

### Case study: Including multimedia components in *FrontPage*

Experiment with these multimedia options:

1 **Sounds**

You can add a background sound to a page. In *FrontPage*, right-click on the page, select *Page Properties*, then the *General tab*. Under *Background sound Location*: select a sound file that is in an acceptable compressed format. This could be in a standard or streaming sound format, or in one of the multimedia formats.

Under *Loop*: tick *Forever* if you want the sound to repeat itself continuously. Use this feature very sparingly as many visitors are irritated by background sounds. If *Forever* is not ticked you can specify how many times the sound file should loop.

2 **Videos**

*FrontPage* enables you to include any multimedia files that are supported by Windows® Media Player. These are limited to .avi, .asf, RealAudio and RealMedia formats.

The Windows® Media Player plug-in is supported by Internet Explorer and is supplied with recent versions.

If you have a suitable video, then position the cursor in Normal mode and select *Insert / Picture / Video.*

3 **Flash movies**

Before you create a movie you will have to create or find some suitable images.

If you have access to an authoring package that generates Flash movies, experiment with it to create a short sequence. This can be placed on an introductory page before the home page is loaded. You should always offer the visitor a 'Skip intro' option.

The package will generate the HTML code that you should copy on to the web page. This will call a Java applet that will be downloaded from the Macromedia website.

**Assessment activity 31.3**

Enlarge and enhance your website to meet the design specification. Use a range of suitable features which should include:

- a scripting language to create some dynamic web pages
- graphics and multimedia software to create suitable images, animations or sounds.

Keep detailed evidence of the completed site, including annotated printouts of code, screen shots, and witness testimonies.

# 31.3 Publish website files on a server and review

To publish a website on the Web a designer needs:

- access to web space on a web server
- a domain name that points to the website on the server
- the means to transfer the pages and other files to the web space.

## Selecting a web server

All the files and folders that make up a website must be uploaded to a web server before they can be made available on the Internet. A large commercial organisation may own its own web server, but the majority of websites are hosted by web hosts.

**What does it mean?**

A **web server** is a computer linked to the Internet which stores one or more websites.
A **web host** is a company that owns one or more web servers, and rents out space on the web servers to others.

Most Internet service providers (ISPs) also act as web hosts, and many include a certain amount of web space with their accounts. Typically, the space will be 20 Mb to 30 Mb in size, which is more than enough for a substantial site. Larger amounts of web space can usually be acquired at additional cost.

There are also some specialist web hosting companies that offer web space. These companies can be found easily by searching the Web for 'web hosts'. Sometimes free space is offered, but this often carries the condition that the site must display some advertising for the host. It may be acceptable to display advertising of this kind on a personal website, but it is not appropriate on a website for a commercial enterprise.

## Server side scripts

Some sites can function properly only if they are hosted on servers that also store additional support software (or scripts). The designer must ensure that the web server used supports all the needs. Sites developed in *FrontPage* often include special functions that make use of additional software, known as *FrontPage* Server extensions, stored on the web server. These are not made available by all web servers; in particular, a number of the major ISPs that include web space in their low-cost packages do not support *FrontPage* extensions.

## Registering a domain name

A domain name, such as mydomain.co.uk, must be registered with one of the registration organisations. All domain names ending with .uk are registered with Nominet. There are a number of official registries for .com and other domains. A yearly fee is charged for domain name registration.

Domain names are often registered through ISPs who then carry out the formal registration process on behalf of the organisation or individual. Once the domain name has been registered, the ISP will ensure that the domain name points to the correct web space on their web server.

A Whois server can be searched to find out which domain names are currently registered and which are still free. Again, most ISPs provide a Whois search facility. Choosing a domain name can be a challenging task, as many millions of names have already been registered. There have been some legal moves to protect commercial names from being registered by individuals who have no connection with the companies, as in the past so-called cyber-squatters have tried to charge well-known organisations large sums to transfer registered domain names to them.

# Publishing a website

Before a site is published on the Web, it should be subjected to thorough technical testing, and the tests should all be repeated after the site has been published, along with additional tests. These tests should be constructed to check that the final website matches the original design specification, bearing in mind any amendments that may have been made during the prototyping stage. The technical testing of a website concentrates on the following usability issues:

- Navigation should be tested both before and after publishing.
- The use of search tools is best tested after publishing.
- Download times are best tested after publishing.
- Browser compatibility should be tested both before and after publishing.
- Maintenance is best tested with the client after publishing.

All testing should be carried out in a browser, not in the Preview mode of a web authoring package. The site can be opened in a browser, by navigating to the position of the index page on the local drive.

## Testing navigation

Every internal hyperlink should be tested to make sure that it links to the correct page. Where a bookmark is used, the hyperlink should also link to the correct position in the page. The designer should:

- test each of the links from the navigation bar on each page
- test any other internal links on pages.

This testing should be carried out systematically and the results logged.

## Testing browser compatibility

Web pages do not appear in exactly the same format on each browser. These things affect the appearance of a page:

- the screen resolution which is usually 800 or 1024 pixels wide
- the browser used, usually Internet Explorer or Netscape, although there are some other browsers, such as Opera, which are used by smaller numbers of visitors
- the version of the browser that is used – old versions continue to be used around the world, long after much newer versions have been launched.

The site should first be checked in the resident browser at both 800 and 1024 pixel screen resolutions. The full width of each page should be visible at 800 pixels without scrolling sideways. The site should also look reasonable when a full-size window is opened at 1024 pixel width.

The site should then be checked in the alternative browser at both resolutions. If possible, the site should then be checked in the oldest versions of each browser that is available (note that both Internet Explorer and Netscape can be downloaded without charge from their respective websites).

Changes may have to be made to the pages to ensure that the displays in all cases are as compatible as possible and that any minor differences are acceptable. In some extreme cases, it may be necessary to create alternative versions of pages to suit different browsers. The javascript shown below, which should be placed on an otherwise empty index page, detects which browser the visitor is using and immediately jumps to the next page, either ie.htm, netscape.htm or others.htm.

```
<script language="JavaScript">
<!--
if (navigator.appName.indexOf("Microsoft")>=0
   {location.href="ie.htm";}
else if (navigator.appName.indexOf("Netscape")>=0
   {location.href="netscape.htm";}
else {location.href="others.htm";}
// -->
</script>
```

## Uploading a website to a web server

When a website has been tested it can be uploaded (published) to the chosen web server. If the web server is in-house, that is, owned by the organisation, then the system administrators will provide guidance to users about how to transfer their files to the web server.

If an external web server managed by an ISP is used, then all the files and directories will have to be transferred by the designer. This can be done either using the publishing tool built into the web authoring package, or by using file transfer protocol (FTP) software. In both cases the following data is needed:

- the domain name
- the user's name (as registered with the ISP)
- the user's password.

FTP shareware software, free for educational use, can be downloaded from the Internet. To use it, the user must be online. A dialogue asks for the required data, then locates the web space on the remote server. Figure 31.39 shows a typical layout; the left side shows the files and directories on the home computer (local system) and the right side shows the files and directories on the web server (remote system). The user highlights the files and directories to be uploaded from the left side, then clicks on the right-pointing arrow to transfer them across.

All the files that make up the site must be transferred, including page files, style sheets, any script files, the images directory and its contents, plus any folders and files that may have been created by the web authoring package.

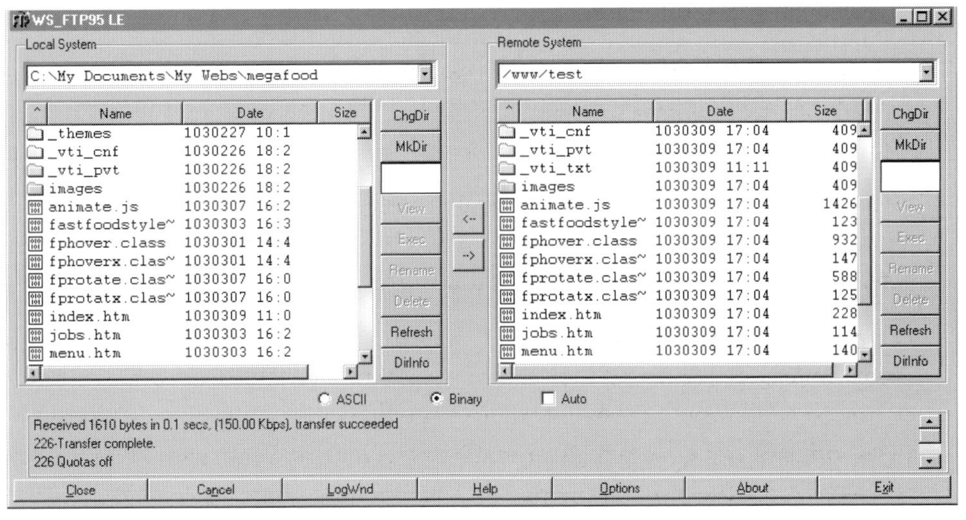


Figure 31.39 FTP software (Ipswitch)

## Case study: Publishing a website in *FrontPage*

1 Select *File / Publish Web.*

2 Enter the URL of the domain, then click on *Publish all pages* (if this is not visible, click on the Options button) (Figure 31.40). Click on *Publish.*

You will then be asked for your user name and password, as used with your ISP.

An animation records the progress, and when the site has been successfully uploaded you will be informed and prompted to view it in your browser.

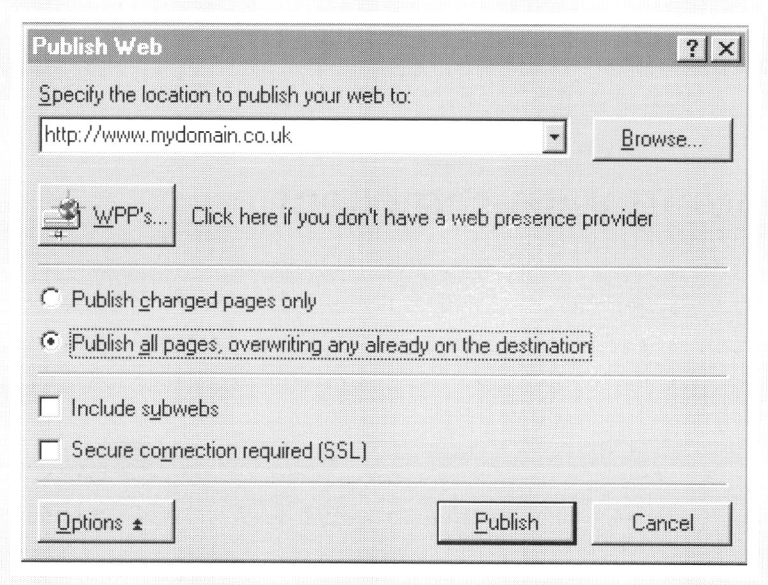


Figure 31.40 The Publish Web dialogue in *FrontPage*

## Testing a website after uploading

Immediately after a site has been uploaded to the web server, it should be tested by entering the URL in a browser. The full set of technical tests should then be repeated. The most common errors found at this stage occur if a file has not been uploaded, or if one has been uploaded to an incorrect remote directory.

The following additional technical testing can be carried out:

- Test each external link to ensure that it loads the correct site.
- Test how long it takes to download each page, including all the images, using the slowest dial-up connections.

## Assessment activity 31.4

1 Test your website before it is uploaded to the web server, and correct any errors.

2 Upload the website to the web server. Test your website after it is uploaded, and correct any errors.

3 Review your website with the client. Check the final site against the design specification, taking into account any changes made during the prototyping stage. Assess the extent to which the site meets the client's needs.

4 Keep detailed records of all the testing, and of the review with the client.

### Registering a website with search engines

Search engines are continually checking the Web by following all the links from one site to another. As they do this, they maintain huge indexing databases about the sites. In particular, they note the keywords and descriptions in the metatags, and they also extract keywords from the text on pages. The indexes are then referred to whenever a user enters text in a search engine.

It can take some time for a search engine to find a new website, but sites can be registered directly with them. Many search engines have UK versions which enable the visitor to restrict the search to UK sites if they wish. The most widely used search engines are Google (www.google.co.uk), AllTheWeb (www.alltheweb.com), Yahoo (uk.yahoo.com) which is powered by Google, MSN Search (search.msn.co.uk) and Ask Jeeves (www.ask.co.uk).

## Reviewing with the client

Once the technical testing has been completed, the site can then be reviewed with the client. The site will have been discussed with the client at every stage of its development, from early prototype to final version, so the review at the end will serve the purpose of signing off the project. In the review, the live site should be given a final check, with the client, against the specification.

Throughout the prototyping stages, the content and the visual design of the site will have been constantly assessed and, where necessary, amended. The final review will check the content and ensure that:

- all the required information has been provided
- the style of language is appropriate to the subject matter.

The visual design of the site will also be assessed, paying attention to:

- the overall impression of the site
- the required graphical and text elements, e.g. logo, colours, images, text styles
- the layout of pages.

Finally, the client will check that the maintenance strategy is achievable. Some sites are maintained, that is, kept up to date, by the web designer; in other cases, the maintenance is carried out in-house. Whichever has been agreed, it is important that the site can be updated easily. The client will want to see some test updates as evidence.

# 31.4 Security and copyright

## Security issues

In order to upload files to a web server the designer needs only three items of data: the domain name, plus the user name and password for the account. If the web server is owned by an organisation and connected to its internal network, then unauthorised access may be possible from within the organisation. Employees who have legitimate access to the server can at times be careless with their user IDs. Even if confidentiality is not breached, user names usually follow a standard pattern within an organisation, and passwords can often be predicted. It can sometimes be easy for an employee who wants to damage the organisation, or who simply wants to play a joke, to gain access to the web space and change the content. Such behaviour would be traceable and would lead to instant dismissal.

Web servers located within organisations can be protected from external interference by firewalls. A web server owned by an ISP is much more vulnerable. Someone who knows the username and password for a domain can gain access to the web space from any computer that is connected to the Internet anywhere in the world.

The Computer Misuse Act (1990) makes any unauthorised access ('hacking') to a computer system illegal. It defines three offences in increasing order of seriousness:

- *Unauthorised access to computer material:* The key issues here are whether someone was *authorised* to access a computer system, and whether the person deliberately did something *with the intention of* gaining unlawful access. If someone accidentally gains access to a system then that person is not guilty of an offence, provided he or she does not continue to explore the system.
- *Unauthorised access with intent to commit or facilitate commission of further offences:* This deals with cases where the person intends to commit another crime, such as theft or blackmail, and is gaining unauthorised access in order to do so.
- *Unauthorised modification of computer material:* The section outlaws the intentional alteration or deletion of data when the person does not have authority to do so.

A web server may hold database files, containing information collected from the website through an online form. Organisations that collect personal data from customers in this way have to be particularly vigilant in protecting their web servers from unauthorised access. They need to do this:

- to comply with the Data Protection Act
- to reassure customers that personal data about them will be secure
- to encourage customers to provide credit card details for online transactions.

A secure server encrypts all the data stored on it, so if anyone does gain illegal access he or she will not be able to understand or use the data. Secure servers are used for all financial transactions over the Internet, and increasingly for the collection of other personal data.

## Copyright issues

Writing, music, films and works of art are described as intellectual property, and the creators (or their employers) normally own the copyright to their work. This means that no one else may copy, print, perform or film work without the copyright owner's permission. In the UK, copyright usually extends for 50 years after the creator's death, and the rights extend to their heirs.

For many years, it was not clear whether copyright laws covered software products. The Copyright, Designs and Patents Act (1988) states that software (including websites) should be treated in the same way as all other intellectual property. The copyright for a website belongs to the organisation that commissions it, not to the web designer.

All content on a website should fall into one of these three categories:

- material created within the organisation
- material used with the permission of the copyright owner
- material that is free of copyright.

Permission must be sought before using text, photographs, images, videos, music and other sounds that have originated elsewhere. This applies whether they are found on a website or in books or recordings. Software used on websites, such as scripts in Java, Visual Basic and other languages, as well as Flash animations, are also covered by copyright. The copyright holder will usually charge for permission to use their materials.

In general, it is wise to assume that any material published in any format, including on the Web, is covered by copyright, unless it explicitly states that it is copyright-free. Copyright-free material is not necessarily cost-free, but on the Web there are many sources of copyright-free materials which can be downloaded and used at no charge.

There are several other terms used for software and other materials in relation to their copyright status:

- **Shareware** is software that has been copyrighted by the originator, but is sold (or given) to users with permission to copy it and to share it with others. Sometimes the conditions of use prevent the shareware from being used for commercial purposes. Shareware may be offered free of charge on an evaluation basis, but with payment required for continuing use. Many scripts are offered as shareware.
- **Open source** software is software that can be distributed without restrictions, so that all users can view and modify the code. Open source software is not necessarily free of charge.
- **Public domain** materials are items that are completely free of copyright and can be used by anyone.

**Further research 31.4**

Find sources of copyright-free, no-cost, materials on the Web that can be used legally on a website. You could look for images, photos, animations, literature, articles and music.

# Legal issues

The Data Protection Act, the Computer Misuse Act and the Copyright, Designs and Patents Act all have implications for the publication of websites. There are a number of other UK laws, regulations and guidelines which apply to any published materials that can be accessed from the UK, and some of these relate to offensive material.

The content of a website could be judged to be offensive if it is libellous, pornographic, racist, blasphemous, sexist, homophobic, over-violent or inciting to hatred, although there is no single definition in law.

The Child Protection Act makes it a criminal offence to possess child pornography, such as indecent pictures of children or pictures of a person under the age of 16 in a sexual act. The publication of such materials, on the Web or elsewhere, is an even more serious offence. The Obscene Publications Act covers the publication of other pornographic and violent material.

The Race Relations Act, Sex Discrimination Act, Disability Discrimination Act and Equal Opportunities Act all identify areas of discrimination which could lead to actions in the criminal or civil courts. In general, material should not be published which encourages discrimination on the grounds of race, ethnic origin, colour, nationality, sex, sexual orientation, disability or religious beliefs.

The Advertising Standards Authority produces a Code of Practice for Advertisers, which requires all advertisements to be legal, decent, truthful and honest. This is self-regulation by the advertising industry, but it is effective. The Office of Fair Trading can take out an injunction in the courts against persistent offenders. On the Web, banners and pop-up advertisements are covered by the Code of Practice, as are any online sales promotions.

Libel is a civil offence, not a criminal offence, which means that someone can take private action in the civil courts if his or her reputation has been damaged.

Most organisations issue internal guidelines to staff identifying unacceptable behaviour that would lead to disciplinary action. Some of these guidelines might relate to material published on a website which could be offensive to visitors. Such guidelines are in addition to legal constraints.

### Assessment activity 31.5

This activity can be carried out as a written task, or as a presentation supported by witness testimonies.

1. Specify the web server and all the other resources that you will need in order to publish your website.
2. Describe the security and copyright issues that are relevant to the publication of a website.
3. Assemble all the evidence for your website project, from client specification to final review. Create a report which explains the choices that were made at each stage, the techniques used and the final outcome. To gain a Distinction grade you should use technical language fluently and correctly in all your written work. You should check your work and eliminate obvious spelling and grammatical errors.
4. Write an evaluation of the whole project. This should answer these questions:
   - Which tasks did you find easy and which ones did you find difficult?
   - How could you have improved your work?
   - How effective was your design specification?

## Test your knowledge

1. The design specification for a website can be arranged under three headings: content, visual design and technical design. List at least three issues that could be considered under each.
2. In the context of web design, what is a prototype?
3. What are the main features of a web authoring package?
4. Why is it advisable to use the style list when formatting the text on a web page?
5. What are the two main compressed image formats used on the Web? Explain the differences between them.
6. What is a bookmark and how can it be used on a web page?
7. How can a table be used to lay out the text and images on a web page?
8. What functions do site management tools offer in a web authoring package?
9. Navigation bars can be placed anywhere on a web page. Using example websites, identify the most common positions for a navigation bar, and in each case explain why the web designer has chosen that position.
10. What are the advantages of using cascading style sheets to control the formatting on a website?
11. Explain the advantages and disadvantages of using frames to lay out a website.
12. Explain these terms:
    - javascript
    - DHTML
    - applet.
13. A small business wants to receive e-mails from visitors to its website. The web designer can choose between providing an e-mail address on the site or creating an online form for site visitors to complete. Why might the designer choose to create a form?
14. What do the following terms mean:
    - Web server
    - Web host
    - ISP
    - Domain name
    - Search engine?
15. List the technical tests that should be carried out on a website before it is published.
16. Outline the copyright issues that are relevant to a website.

# Index